W9-BYG-391

BEST CUSTOMERS

DEMOGRAPHICS OF CONSUMER DEMAND

BEST CUSTOMERS

DEMOGRAPHICS OF CONSUMER DEMAND

BY THE EDITORS OF NEW STRATEGIST PUBLICATIONS

New Strategist Publications, Inc.
Ithaca, New York

Introduction

Welcome to the sixth edition of *Best Customers: Demographics of Consumer Demand*, a unique examination of how changing demographics are reshaping the consumer marketplace. *Best Customers* reveals who the best and biggest customers are for hundreds of individual products and services, alerting marketers to potential booms and busts in the years ahead.

Based on data from the Bureau of Labor Statistics' 2007 Consumer Expenditure Survey, *Best Customers* examines spending patterns by the demographic characteristics of households. For most consumer products and services, demographics drive demand. *Best Customers* analyzes household spending on more than 300 products and services by age of householder, household income, household type, race and Hispanic origin of householder, region of residence, and educational attainment of householder. It identifies which households spend the most on a product or service (the best customers) and which control the largest share of spending (the biggest customers).

Household demographics are not static, but ever changing, influencing the consumer market during good times and bad. Today, the aging of the population is one of the most important factors in determining consumer demand. The rapid growth of Asian, black, and Hispanic populations makes their spending ever more important to business success. Education, living arrangements, and geography also determine who spends what—critical information as the consumer marketplace becomes increasingly competitive. *Best Customers* reveals the demographic trends behind spending, allowing marketers to prepare for what lies ahead.

Demographic trends

Two demographic trends are key to today's consumer markets: the aging of the baby-boom generation and the rise of Asian, black, and Hispanic consumers.

Born between 1946 and 1964, the baby-boom generation spanned the ages of 43 through 61 in 2007. As boomers fill the 55-to-64 age group, the percentage of households headed by empty-nesters is growing each year. Becoming an empty-nester is one of life's major transitions, and spending patterns change accordingly. Empty-nesters spend less on groceries, for example, and more on meals in full-service restaurants. Spending on alcoholic beverages increases after the teetotaler years of child rearing. Empty-nesters are the biggest spenders on travel. And instead of buying children's clothes, they devote more to men's and women's apparel. Although boomers have been severely affected by the economic downturn, their financial problems are going to make them even more important consumers in the years ahead. Millions of two-earner baby-boom couples in their peak-earning years will remain in the labor force much longer than they or the experts had expected. This will boost the incomes and spending power of older Americans, delaying the shift to a reduced standard of living after retirement. An understanding of the spending patterns of these older Americans will be vital to staying afloat in the coming years.

Asians, blacks, Hispanics, and other minorities account for a growing share of the nation's population. In 2007, the 4.2 million Asian, 14.4 million black, and 14.2 million Hispanic households accounted for more than one-quarter of the national total and for more than one in every five dollars spent by American consumers. The average Asian household has a higher income and spends more money than the average non-Hispanic white household. Although the incomes and spending of blacks and Hispanics are below average, both groups spend much more than average on many individual products and services. The distinct spending patterns of Asians, blacks, and Hispanics make them a major force in many consumer markets. As competition for customers becomes ever more heated, effectively wooing Asians, blacks, and Hispanics has never been more important.

How to use this book

Best Customers is divided into 21 chapters, arranged alphabetically, each chapter focusing on a major spending category as defined by the Bureau of Labor Statistics—such as entertainment, groceries (or what the bureau calls "food at home"), transportation, and so on. Within each chapter, individual products and services are arranged alphabetically. Three chapters of *Best Customers*— computers, telephone, and travel—are unique groupings produced by New Strategist to highlight important spending patterns. The Bureau of Labor Statistics includes computer and telephone spending in its housing category, and it groups the travel items into the entertainment, food, housing, and transportation categories.

Most individual products and services included in the Consumer Expenditure Survey are analyzed in *Best Customers*. Two types of items are excluded from the book: "other" categories, such as "other food at home," for which an analysis of spending patterns cannot provide meaningful conclusions; and products and services with spending patterns considered unreliable by New Strategist because of small sample sizes.

Each table in *Best Customers* analyzes household spending on a particular product or service, showing average spending, indexed spending, and market share of spending by age of householder, household income, household type, race and Hispanic origin of householder, region of residence, and educational attainment of householder. New Strategist has calculated the indexes and market shares to reveal the trends. Text accompanies each table that identifies the best and biggest customers, analyzes spending patterns, describes spending trends for the product over the past few years, and predicts future trends based on the nation's changing demographics.

Spending data

Best Customers is based on unpublished, detailed data collected by the Bureau of Labor Statistics' Consumer Expenditure Survey, an ongoing, nationwide survey of household spending. A complete accounting of household expenditures, the Consumer Expenditure Survey includes everything from big-ticket items such as homes and cars, to small purchases like laundry detergent and film. The survey does not include expenditures by government, business, or nonprofit institutions. The lag time between data collection and publication is about two years.

The Consumer Expenditure Survey uses the consumer unit rather than the household as its sampling unit. In this book, the terms "consumer unit" and "household" are used interchangeably. The Bureau of Labor Statistics defines "consumer unit" as "a single person or group of persons in a sample household related by blood, marriage, adoption or other legal arrangement or who share responsibility for at least two out of three major types of expenses—food, housing, and other expenses." For more information about the Consumer Expenditure Survey and consumer units, see Appendix A.

Spending data

• **Average Spending** The average spending figures in *Best Customers* are unpublished data from the Bureau of Labor Statistics' 2007 Consumer Expenditure Survey. The Bureau of Labor Statistics calculates average spending for all households in a segment, not just for those who bought an item. When examining the averages, it is important to remember that by including both purchasers and nonpurchasers in the calculation of the average, the average spending amount is often greatly reduced—especially for infrequently purchased items. For example, the average household spent $268 on day care centers in 2007. Since only a small percentage of households spend money on day care, this figure greatly underestimates the amount spent on day care centers by those who use them. To get a more realistic idea of how much buyers spend on an item, Appendix B shows the percentage of households that purchased individual products and services during the average quarter of 2007, and the amount purchasers spent per quarter. According to Appendix B, only 5 percent of households spent on day care centers during the average quarter of 2007. Purchasers spent an average of $1,241 per quarter, for an estimated annual cost of $4,964—a much more realistic figure than the average of $268 for all households. For frequently purchased items—such as bread—the average spending figures give a fairly accurate account of actual spending. But for most of the products and services examined in *Best Customers*, average spending figures are less revealing than indexes and market shares.

Average spending figures are useful for determining the market potential of a product or service in a local area. By multiplying the average amount married couples spend on children's clothing by the number of married couples in the San Diego metropolitan area, for example, marketers can estimate the size of the market for children's clothing in San Diego. The San Diego media could show those figures to potential advertisers to prove the demand for children's clothing in the area.

(Note: Because of sampling errors, average values can vary—especially for infrequently purchased items. To examine the standard errors for detailed average spending data, contact the Bureau of Labor Statistics Consumer Expenditure Survey statisticians by phone at 202-691-6900 or by email at cexinfo@bls.gov.)

• **Indexed Spending (Best Customers)** Indexed spending figures compare the spending of demographic segments with that of the average household. To compute the indexes, New Strategist's statisticians divide the average amount a household segment spends on a particular item by how much the average household spends on the item, then multiply the resulting figure by 100. An index of 100 is the average for all households. An index of 125 means average spending by households in a segment is 25 percent above average (100 plus 25). An index of 80 means average spending by households in a segment is 20 percent below average (100 minus 20).

Spending indexes can reveal hidden markets—household segments with a high propensity to buy a particular product or service but which are overshadowed by larger household segments that account for a bigger share of the total market. Householders aged 65 to 74, for example, account for 11 percent of the market for full-service breakfasts, less than the 14 percent share accounted for by householders aged 25 to 34. But a look at the indexed spending figures reveals that, in fact, the older householders are the better customers. Householders aged 65 to 74 spend 7 percent *more* than the average household on full-service breakfasts, while householders aged 25 to 34 spend 20 percent *less* than the average household on this item. Using the indexed spending tables, marketers can see that older householders are in fact their better customers and adjust their business strategy accordingly. (Note: Because of sampling errors, small differences in index values are usually insignificant. But the broader patterns revealed by indexes can guide marketers to the best customers.)

• **Market Share (Biggest Customers)** To calculate market share figures, New Strategist first determines the total amount all households spend on an item by multiplying average household spending on that item by the total number of households (121,171,000). New Strategist then calculates total household spending for each demographic segment by multiplying the segment's average spending on an item by the number of households in the segment. To calculate the percentage of total spending on the item controlled by a demographic segment—i.e., its market share—New Strategist divides each segment's spending on the item by total household spending on the item.

In 2007, for example, college graduates accounted for 67 percent of total household spending on ship fares. The cruise industry could reach most of its customers if it targeted only this demographic segment. Of course, by single-mindedly targeting the biggest customers, businesses cannot nurture potential growth markets. An additional danger of focusing only on the biggest customers is that businesses may end up ignoring their best customers. This is especially problematic because market shares are unstable, thanks to baby booms and busts over the past half-century. Right now, for example, householders aged 45 to 54 are one of the biggest customers of housekeeping services, controlling 24 percent of the market—but only because the age group is filled with the large baby-boom generation. In fact, the best customers of housekeeping services are older householders. Those aged 75 or older, for example, spend 86 percent more than the average household on housekeeping services, whereas the 45-to-54 age group spends only 16 percent more than average on this item. Although the older age group controls only 18 percent of the housekeeping services market today, the share will expand greatly as boomers age into their seventies. The best customers of housekeeping services will become the biggest customers as well. Marketers who ignore their best customers in favor of the biggest customers may end up with no customers.

• **Age of Householder** Age is one of the best predictors of spending because lifestage determines most consumer wants and needs. Ongoing changes in the age structure of the population will have a profound effect on consumer spending. This is why *Best Customers* explores spending by age in so much detail, using it as the primary guide to consumer trends in the years ahead.

Changes in the size of age groups will dramatically affect spending in many categories over the next few years. The number of adults under age 35 is expanding as the age group fills with the millennial generation. This will boost average household spending on products and services for infants and young children. The small generation X is filling the 35-to-44 age group, reducing the share of the consumer market controlled by that age group. As the large baby-boom generation completely fills the 55-to-64 age group and enters the empty-nest lifestage, look for more spending on full-service restaurants, alcoholic beverages, women's clothing, and travel. Not only will the size of age groups change, but as younger generations replace older ones attitudes and behavior will also change. Younger generations, for example, devote a larger share of their household budget to computers and other high-tech gadgets. In making predictions of future spending trends, New Strategist takes into account not only the changing numbers, but also changing attitudes and lifestyles.

• **Household Income** It is no surprise that the most-affluent households spend the most. For most of the products and services examined in *Best Customers*, households with the highest incomes appear to be the best and biggest customers. Yet the story behind spending is more complex than income alone. Most spending is driven by lifestage (age) or lifestyle (household type), and secondarily by income. For that reason *Best Customers* identifies high-income households as the best and biggest customers only when income has an extraordinary effect on spending or when an item is a purely discretionary expense—such as spending on wine at restaurants and bars. While most businesses would do well to target the affluent, they will find it difficult to design a product or craft a message if they ignore the lifestage and lifestyle reasons for spending.

• **Household Type** Household type is one of the most important determinants of spending for several reasons. The presence of children, for example, means the household spends on products and services children want and need. Not only that, but households with children tend to include more people than those without children, and household size is an important determinant of spending. Because married couples head most of the nation's households, they account for the majority of spending in most categories. But single parents are important in some markets, and single-person households have growing clout because they are becoming a larger share of households. The most important household change to occur in the next few years is the rapid expansion of the number of married couples without children at home as boomers become empty-nesters.

(Note: Market shares by household type do not sum to 100 percent because not all household types are shown.)

• **Race and Hispanic Origin of Householder** The Bureau of Labor Statistics classifies households by the self-identified race and Hispanic origin of the householder. The bureau classifies households into three racial groups: Asian, black, and "white and other" where "other" includes Alaska Natives, American Indians, Native Hawaiians and other Pacific Islanders, as well as those who report more than one race. Because Hispanics may be of any race, the bureau separately classifies all households into one of two Hispanic origin categories: Hispanic or non-Hispanic. Within the non-Hispanic origin group there are blacks and "whites and all other races," which in this classification include non-Hispanic Alaska Natives, American Indians, Asians, Native Hawaiians and other Pacific Islanders, as well as non-Hispanics reporting more than one race.

To simplify things for *Best Customers*, we narrowed the race and Hispanic origin categories to four: Asians (including Hispanic Asians), blacks (including Hispanic blacks), Hispanics (a group

Chapter 1.

Alcoholic Beverages

Alcoholic Beverages

The average household spent $457 on alcoholic beverages in 2007. Spending on alcoholic beverages increased 2 percent since 2000, after adjusting for inflation. Behind the rise is the aging of the baby-boom generation into the empty-nest lifestage. Empty-nesters spend more on alcohol than parents with children at home.

Alcoholic beverage spending is changing. While the largest share of the alcoholic beverage dollar is still devoted to beer (42 percent), the percentage is lower than the 47 percent of 2000. Wine accounted for 29 percent of the alcoholic beverage budget in 2007, up from 26 percent in 2000. Whiskey and other alcoholic beverages accounted for 19 percent of the budget in 2007, slightly greater than the 18 percent of 2000.

Spending on alcoholic beverages

(average annual spending of households on alcoholic beverages, 2000 and 2007; in 2007 dollars)

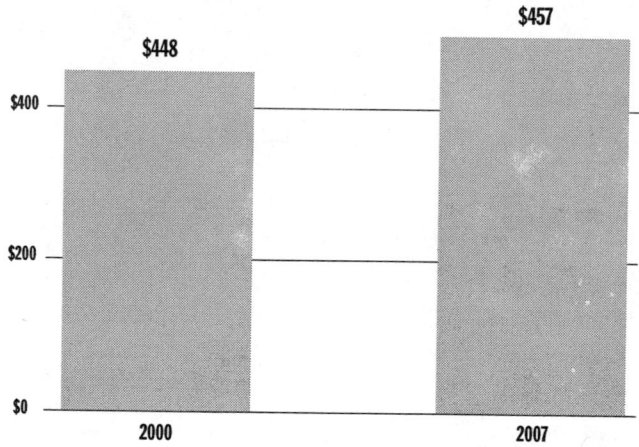

Table 1.1 Alcoholic beverage spending, 2000 to 2007

(average annual household spending on alcoholic beverages, and percent distribution of spending by type, 2000 and 2007; percent change in spending, 2000–07; in 2007 dollars; ranked by amount spent)

	2007		2000		
	average household spending	percent distribution	average household spending (in 2007$)	percent distribution	percent change 2000–07
Average household spending on alcoholic beverages	**$456.59**	**100.0%**	**$447.69**	**100.0%**	**2.0%**
Beer and ale	190.22	41.7	210.08	46.9	–9.5
Beer and ale at home	114.93	25.2	134.87	30.1	–14.8
Beer and ale at restaurants, bars	75.29	16.5	75.21	16.8	0.1
Wine	134.12	29.4	117.79	26.3	13.9
Wine at home	97.21	21.3	96.37	21.5	0.9
Wine at restaurants, bars	36.91	8.1	21.42	4.8	72.3
Whiskey and other alcohol	88.63	19.4	78.59	17.6	12.8
Whiskey and other alcohol at home	27.56	6.0	41.65	9.3	–33.8
Whiskey and other alcohol at restaurants, bars	61.07	13.4	36.94	8.3	65.3
Alcoholic beverages on trips	43.62	9.6	41.23	9.2	5.8

Source: Bureau of Labor Statistics, 2000 and 2007 Consumer Expenditure Surveys; calculations by New Strategist

Beer and Ale at Home

Best customers: Householders under age 25 and aged 45 to 54
Married couples with adult children at home

Customer trends: Average household spending on beer and ale consumed at home is likely to climb in the years ahead as the large millennial generation fills the best-customer age group.

Householders under age 55 spend more than the average household on beer and ale for home consumption, with the index peaking at 39 percent above average among householders under age 25. Married couples with adult children at home spend 44 percent more than average on this item, in part because their households are larger than average.

Average household spending on beer and ale consumed at home fell 15 percent between 2000 and 2007, after adjusting for inflation. Behind the decline is price discounting and household belt tightening in the midst of the economic downturn. Average household spending on beer and ale consumed at home is likely to climb in the years ahead as the large millennial generation fills the best-customer age group.

Table 1.3 Beer and ale at home

Total household spending	$13,811,253,030.00
Average household spends	114.93

AGE OF HOUSEHOLDER	AVERAGE HOUSEHOLD SPENDING	BEST CUSTOMERS (index)	BIGGEST CUSTOMERS (market share)
Average household	**$114.93**	**100**	**100.0%**
Under age 25	159.69	139	9.4
Aged 25 to 34	122.95	107	18.2
Aged 35 to 44	131.72	115	22.3
Aged 45 to 54	154.83	135	28.3
Aged 55 to 64	92.52	81	13.0
Aged 65 to 74	66.87	58	5.8
Aged 75 or older	33.25	29	2.7

	AVERAGE HOUSEHOLD SPENDING	BEST CUSTOMERS (index)	BIGGEST CUSTOMERS (market share)
HOUSEHOLD INCOME			
Average household	**$114.93**	**100**	**100.0%**
Under $20,000	75.07	65	13.4
$20,000 to $39,999	96.89	84	19.6
$40,000 to $49,999	129.17	112	11.1
$50,000 to $69,999	137.60	120	18.3
$70,000 to $79,999	128.66	112	6.5
$80,000 to $99,999	163.85	143	11.6
$100,000 or more	124.54	108	18.6
HOUSEHOLD TYPE			
Average household	**114.93**	**100**	**100.0**
Married couples	123.98	108	54.5
Married couples, no children	106.06	92	19.9
Married couples, with children	137.14	119	29.8
Oldest child under age 6	128.37	112	5.5
Oldest child aged 6 to 17	125.83	109	13.9
Oldest child aged 18 or older	165.99	144	10.6
Single parent with child under age 18	45.24	39	2.3
Single person	102.86	89	26.6
RACE AND HISPANIC ORIGIN			
Average household	**114.93**	**100**	**100.0**
Asian	71.92	63	2.2
Black	80.20	70	8.4
Hispanic	119.38	104	12.3
Non-Hispanic white and other	120.61	105	80.1
REGION			
Average household	**114.93**	**100**	**100.0**
Northeast	94.84	83	15.4
Midwest	122.52	107	24.4
South	117.25	102	36.6
West	120.38	105	23.7
EDUCATION			
Average household	**114.93**	**100**	**100.0**
Less than high school graduate	95.69	83	12.6
High school graduate	123.90	108	27.2
Some college	128.17	112	24.3
Associate's degree	112.74	98	8.7
College graduate	107.11	93	27.0
Bachelor's degree	122.06	106	19.9
Master's, professional, doctoral degree	81.16	71	7.2

Note: Market shares may not sum to 100.0 because of rounding and missing categories by household type. "Asian" and "black" include Hispanics and non-Hispanics who identify themselves as being of the respective race alone. "Hispanic" includes people of any race who identify themselves as Hispanic. "Other" includes people who identify themselves as non-Hispanic and as Alaska Native, American Indian, Asian (who are also included in the "Asian" row), Native Hawaiian or other Pacific Islander, as well as non-Hispanics reporting more than one race. Source: Calculations by New Strategist based on the Bureau of Labor Statistics' 2007 Consumer Expenditure Survey.

Beer and Ale at Restaurants and Bars

Best customers:
    Householders under age 35
    Non-Hispanic whites
    Households in the Midwest

Customer trends:
    Average household spending on beer and ale at restaurants and bars may increase
    as the millennial generation fills the best-customer age groups—but only if
    discretionary income grows.

Householders under age 35 are the best customers of beer and ale from restaurants and bars, spending 40 to 60 percent more than the average household on this item. Non-Hispanic whites spend 20 percent more than average on beer and ale at bars and restaurants. Households in the Midwest spend 49 percent more than the average on this item.

Average household spending on beer and ale consumed at restaurants and bars has been flat since 2000, after adjusting for inflation. Household belt tightening in the midst of the economic downturn is behind the insignificant 0.1 percent rise in spending during those years. Spending on beer and ale at restaurants and bars may rise in the years ahead as the recession loosens its grip—but only if discretionary income grows.

Table 1.4 Beer and ale at restaurants and bars

Total household spending $9,047,674,590.00
Average household spends   75.29

	AVERAGE HOUSEHOLD SPENDING	BEST CUSTOMERS (index)	BIGGEST CUSTOMERS (market share)
AGE OF HOUSEHOLDER			
Average household	**$75.29**	**100**	**100.0%**
Under age 25	105.78	140	9.5
Aged 25 to 34	120.35	160	27.3
Aged 35 to 44	78.98	105	20.4
Aged 45 to 54	72.01	96	20.1
Aged 55 to 64	69.33	92	14.9
Aged 65 to 74	37.62	50	5.0
Aged 75 or older	19.68	26	2.5

	AVERAGE HOUSEHOLD SPENDING	BEST CUSTOMERS (index)	BIGGEST CUSTOMERS (market share)
HOUSEHOLD INCOME			
Average household	**$75.29**	**100**	**100.0%**
Under $20,000	21.74	29	5.9
$20,000 to $39,999	41.89	56	12.9
$40,000 to $49,999	85.49	114	11.2
$50,000 to $69,999	101.49	135	20.6
$70,000 to $79,999	73.66	98	5.7
$80,000 to $99,999	107.04	142	11.6
$100,000 or more	139.38	185	31.7
HOUSEHOLD TYPE			
Average household	**75.29**	**100**	**100.0**
Married couples	71.19	95	47.8
Married couples, no children	76.85	102	22.0
Married couples, with children	69.19	92	22.9
Oldest child under age 6	97.23	129	6.3
Oldest child aged 6 to 17	54.10	72	9.1
Oldest child aged 18 or older	78.48	104	7.7
Single parent with child under age 18	44.98	60	3.5
Single person	79.98	106	31.6
RACE AND HISPANIC ORIGIN			
Average household	**75.29**	**100**	**100.0**
Asian	32.35	43	1.5
Black	15.02	20	2.4
Hispanic	35.75	47	5.6
Non-Hispanic white and other	90.14	120	91.4
REGION			
Average household	**75.29**	**100**	**100.0**
Northeast	86.72	115	21.5
Midwest	112.25	149	34.1
South	52.15	69	24.9
West	64.74	86	19.4
EDUCATION			
Average household	**75.29**	**100**	**100.0**
Less than high school graduate	22.83	30	4.6
High school graduate	53.85	72	18.0
Some college	75.80	101	21.9
Associate's degree	74.06	98	8.7
College graduate	118.18	157	45.4
Bachelor's degree	133.84	178	33.3
Master's, professional, doctoral degree	90.99	121	12.3

Note: Market shares may not sum to 100.0 because of rounding and missing categories by household type. "Asian" and "black" include Hispanics and non-Hispanics who identify themselves as being of the respective race alone. "Hispanic" includes people of any race who identify themselves as Hispanic. "Other" includes people who identify themselves as non-Hispanic and as Alaska Native, American Indian, Asian (who are also included in the "Asian" row), Native Hawaiian or other Pacific Islander, as well as non-Hispanics reporting more than one race. Source: Calculations by New Strategist based on the Bureau of Labor Statistics' 2007 Consumer Expenditure Survey.

Whiskey and Other Alcohol at Restaurants and Bars (except Beer and Wine)

Best customers:	**Householders under age 35** **People who live alone** **Non-Hispanic whites** **Households in the Midwest and Northeast**
Customer trends:	**Average household spending on whiskey and other alcohol at restaurants and bars is likely to continue to increase as the large millennial generation fills the best-customer age group—but only if discretionary income grows.**

Householders under age 35 spend 50 to 62 percent more than the average household on whiskey and other alcohol at restaurants and bars. People who live alone, many of the young adults, spend 19 percent more than average on this item. Non-Hispanic whites also spend19 percent more than average on whiskey and other alcohol at restaurants and bars. Households in the Northeast and Midwest spend 30 and 40 percent more than average on this item.

Average household spending on whiskey and other alcohol at restaurants and bars increased by a substantial 65 percent between 2000 and 2007, after adjusting for inflation. Spending should continue to rise as the large millennial generation fills the best-customer age group—but only if discretionary income grows.

Table 1.6 Whiskey and other alcohol (except beer and wine) at restaurants and bars

Total household spending	$7,338,842,970.00
Average household spends	61.07

	AVERAGE HOUSEHOLD SPENDING	BEST CUSTOMERS (index)	BIGGEST CUSTOMERS (market share)
AGE OF HOUSEHOLDER			
Average household	**$61.07**	**100**	**100.0%**
Under age 25	91.50	150	10.2
Aged 25 to 34	98.65	162	27.6
Aged 35 to 44	57.25	94	18.3
Aged 45 to 54	54.92	90	18.9
Aged 55 to 64	49.35	81	13.1
Aged 65 to 74	43.83	72	7.2
Aged 75 or older	28.96	47	4.5

	AVERAGE HOUSEHOLD SPENDING	BEST CUSTOMERS (index)	BIGGEST CUSTOMERS (market share)
HOUSEHOLD INCOME			
Average household	**$61.07**	**100**	**100.0%**
Under $20,000	22.33	37	7.5
$20,000 to $39,999	37.39	61	14.2
$40,000 to $49,999	68.18	112	11.0
$50,000 to $69,999	71.71	117	18.0
$70,000 to $79,999	56.50	93	5.4
$80,000 to $99,999	74.72	122	10.0
$100,000 or more	121.78	199	34.2
HOUSEHOLD TYPE			
Average household	**61.07**	**100**	**100.0**
Married couples	54.28	89	44.9
Married couples, no children	63.87	105	22.6
Married couples, with children	45.28	74	18.5
Oldest child under age 6	70.67	116	5.6
Oldest child aged 6 to 17	36.52	60	7.6
Oldest child aged 18 or older	44.01	72	5.3
Single parent with child under age 18	40.00	65	3.9
Single person	72.39	119	35.3
RACE AND HISPANIC ORIGIN			
Average household	**61.07**	**100**	**100.0**
Asian	45.26	74	2.6
Black	23.45	38	4.6
Hispanic	21.32	35	4.1
Non-Hispanic white and other	72.46	119	90.6
REGION			
Average household	**61.07**	**100**	**100.0**
Northeast	79.45	130	24.2
Midwest	85.47	140	32.0
South	39.68	65	23.3
West	54.78	90	20.3
EDUCATION			
Average household	**61.07**	**100**	**100.0**
Less than high school graduate	13.57	22	3.4
High school graduate	41.76	68	17.2
Some college	54.48	89	19.4
Associate's degree	76.36	125	11.1
College graduate	100.19	164	47.5
Bachelor's degree	113.20	185	34.7
Master's, professional, doctoral degree	77.59	127	13.0

Note: Market shares may not sum to 100.0 because of rounding and missing categories by household type. "Asian" and "black" include Hispanics and non-Hispanics who identify themselves as being of the respective race alone. "Hispanic" includes people of any race who identify themselves as Hispanic. "Other" includes people who identify themselves as non-Hispanic and as Alaska Native, American Indian, Asian (who are also included in the "Asian" row), Native Hawaiian or other Pacific Islander, as well as non-Hispanics reporting more than one race.
Source: Calculations by New Strategist based on the Bureau of Labor Statistics' 2007 Consumer Expenditure Survey.

Wine at Home

Best customers: Householders aged 55 to 64
Married couples without children at home
Married couples with adult children at home
Non-Hispanic whites
College graduates

Customer trends: Average household spending on wine consumed at home should increase as more boomers become empty-nesters—but only if discretionary income grows.

The best customers of wine consumed at home are married couples without children at home (most of them empty-nesters) and married couples with adult children at home. Couples without children at home spend 51 percent more than average on this item, while those with adult children at home spend 66 percent more. Householders aged 55 to 64, most of them empty-nesters, spend 73 percent more than average on wine consumed at home. College graduates spend twice the average on this item. Non-Hispanic whites spend 18 percent more than average on wine at home and control 90 percent of the market.

Average household spending on wine consumed at home increased 1 percent between 2000 and 2007, after adjusting for inflation. Spending on this item should continue to increase as more boomers become empty-nesters—but only if discretionary income grows.

Table 1.7 Wine at home

Total household spending $11,681,822,910.00
Average household spends   97.21

AGE OF HOUSEHOLDER	AVERAGE HOUSEHOLD SPENDING	BEST CUSTOMERS (index)	BIGGEST CUSTOMERS (market share)
Average household	$97.21	100	100.0%
Under age 25	39.31	40	2.7
Aged 25 to 34	71.23	73	12.5
Aged 35 to 44	95.11	98	19.1
Aged 45 to 54	105.46	108	22.8
Aged 55 to 64	168.44	173	28.1
Aged 65 to 74	106.69	110	11.0
Aged 75 or older	43.62	45	4.3

	AVERAGE HOUSEHOLD SPENDING	BEST CUSTOMERS (index)	BIGGEST CUSTOMERS (market share)
HOUSEHOLD INCOME			
Average household	**$97.21**	**100**	**100.0%**
Under $20,000	17.41	18	3.7
$20,000 to $39,999	47.41	49	11.3
$40,000 to $49,999	66.13	68	6.7
$50,000 to $69,999	80.01	82	12.6
$70,000 to $79,999	106.57	110	6.3
$80,000 to $99,999	115.23	119	9.6
$100,000 or more	289.24	298	51.0
HOUSEHOLD TYPE			
Average household	**97.21**	**100**	**100.0**
Married couples	122.78	126	63.8
Married couples, no children	146.58	151	32.5
Married couples, with children	111.24	114	28.6
Oldest child under age 6	89.25	92	4.5
Oldest child aged 6 to 17	94.14	97	12.3
Oldest child aged 18 or older	161.22	166	12.2
Single parent with child under age 18	43.68	45	2.7
Single person	81.28	84	24.9
RACE AND HISPANIC ORIGIN			
Average household	**97.21**	**100**	**100.0**
Asian	58.39	60	2.1
Black	34.20	35	4.2
Hispanic	41.19	42	5.0
Non-Hispanic white and other	114.80	118	90.1
REGION			
Average household	**97.21**	**100**	**100.0**
Northeast	104.09	107	19.9
Midwest	72.00	74	16.9
South	94.34	97	34.8
West	122.03	126	28.4
EDUCATION			
Average household	**97.21**	**100**	**100.0**
Less than high school graduate	19.38	20	3.0
High school graduate	55.62	57	14.4
Some college	70.47	72	15.8
Associate's degree	61.81	64	5.7
College graduate	198.80	205	59.2
Bachelor's degree	186.87	192	36.0
Master's, professional, doctoral degree	219.51	226	23.0

Note: Market shares may not sum to 100.0 because of rounding and missing categories by household type. "Asian" and "black" include Hispanics and non-Hispanics who identify themselves as being of the respective race alone. "Hispanic" includes people of any race who identify themselves as Hispanic. "Other" includes people who identify themselves as non-Hispanic and as Alaska Native, American Indian, Asian (who are also included in the "Asian" row), Native Hawaiian or other Pacific Islander, as well as non-Hispanics reporting more than one race. Source: Calculations by New Strategist based on the Bureau of Labor Statistics' 2007 Consumer Expenditure Survey.

Wine at Restaurants and Bars

Best customers:	**Householders aged 55 to 64** **High-income households** **Married couples without children at home** **Non-Hispanic whites** **Households in the Northeast** **College graduates**
Customer trends:	**Average household spending on wine at restaurants and bars should continue to increase as more boomers enter the empty-nest lifestage—but only if discretionary income grows.**

The best customers of wine at restaurants and bars are householders with the time and money to relax with a glass of wine, perhaps over a meal. Householders in the highest income group spend well over three times the average on this item, while married couples without children at home (most of them empty-nesters) spend 49 percent more than average. Householders aged 55 to 64 spend 51 percent more than average on wine at restaurants and bars. Non-Hispanic whites spend 17 percent more than average on this item and control 89 percent of the market. Households in the Northeast spend 60 percent more than average on wine at restaurants and bars, while households headed by college graduates spend more than twice the average and control 60 percent of the market.

Average household spending on wine at restaurants and bars grew by a whopping 72 percent between 2000 and 2007, after adjusting for inflation. Behind the increase was the entry of the baby-boom generation into the best-customer lifestage. Spending on this item should continue to increase as more boomers become empty-nesters—but only if discretionary income grows.

Table 1.8 Wine at restaurants and bars

Total household spending	$4,435,511,610.00
Average household spends	36.91

	AVERAGE HOUSEHOLD SPENDING	BEST CUSTOMERS (index)	BIGGEST CUSTOMERS (market share)
AGE OF HOUSEHOLDER			
Average household	**$36.91**	**100**	**100.0%**
Under age 25	9.66	26	1.8
Aged 25 to 34	40.35	109	18.6
Aged 35 to 44	37.71	102	19.9
Aged 45 to 54	33.54	91	19.1
Aged 55 to 64	55.85	151	24.5
Aged 65 to 74	24.58	67	6.7
Aged 75 or older	38.34	104	9.8

	AVERAGE HOUSEHOLD SPENDING	BEST CUSTOMERS (index)	BIGGEST CUSTOMERS (market share)
HOUSEHOLD INCOME			
Average household	**$36.91**	**100**	**100.0%**
Under $20,000	6.15	17	3.4
$20,000 to $39,999	16.01	43	10.1
$40,000 to $49,999	19.79	54	5.3
$50,000 to $69,999	38.27	104	15.9
$70,000 to $79,999	36.36	99	5.7
$80,000 to $99,999	26.95	73	5.9
$100,000 or more	120.28	326	55.8
HOUSEHOLD TYPE			
Average household	**36.91**	**100**	**100.0**
Married couples	45.43	123	62.2
Married couples, no children	54.94	149	32.1
Married couples, with children	35.87	97	24.2
Oldest child under age 6	59.22	160	7.8
Oldest child aged 6 to 17	26.03	71	9.0
Oldest child aged 18 or older	38.20	103	7.6
Single parent with child under age 18	13.22	36	2.1
Single person	28.42	77	22.9
RACE AND HISPANIC ORIGIN			
Average household	**36.91**	**100**	**100.0**
Asian	16.41	44	1.6
Black	12.17	33	4.0
Hispanic	19.94	54	6.4
Non-Hispanic white and other	43.10	117	89.1
REGION			
Average household	**36.91**	**100**	**100.0**
Northeast	58.94	160	29.7
Midwest	34.18	93	21.2
South	28.30	77	27.5
West	34.91	95	21.4
EDUCATION			
Average household	**36.91**	**100**	**100.0**
Less than high school graduate	3.52	10	1.4
High school graduate	16.92	46	11.6
Some college	28.04	76	16.5
Associate's degree	36.06	98	8.7
College graduate	76.36	207	59.9
Bachelor's degree	65.11	176	33.1
Master's, professional, doctoral degree	95.89	260	26.5

Note: Market shares may not sum to 100.0 because of rounding and missing categories by household type. "Asian" and "black" include Hispanics and non-Hispanics who identify themselves as being of the respective race alone. "Hispanic" includes people of any race who identify themselves as Hispanic. "Other" includes people who identify themselves as non-Hispanic and as Alaska Native, American Indian, Asian (who are also included in the "Asian" row), Native Hawaiian or other Pacific Islander, as well as non-Hispanics reporting more than one race. Source: Calculations by New Strategist based on the Bureau of Labor Statistics' 2007 Consumer Expenditure Survey.

Chapter 2.

Apparel

Household Spending on Apparel, 2007

Average household spending on apparel has been falling for years, dropping from $2,235 in 2000, after adjusting for inflation, to just $1,881 in 2007—a 16 percent decline. The apparel category includes men's, women's, and children's clothes as well as shoes, jewelry, watches, dry cleaning, and coin-operated laundry. Falling prices are one factor behind the decline in spending on this category as cheaper imports allow people to buy more for less. Another factor is the shift toward casual dress in the workplace and at social functions.

Average household spending on women's clothes—which account for the largest share of apparel spending (33 percent in 2007)—fell by 14 percent between 2000 and 2007, after adjusting for inflation. Spending on men's clothes fell by a slightly larger 15 percent. Footwear spending decreased between 15 and 28 percent during those years. Spending on children's clothing has fared poorly as well, with a 14 percent decline in average household spending on girls' clothes, and 27 percent on boys' clothes. Spending on infants' clothes held relatively steady (down 5 percent), as did jewelry spending (down 3 percent). Professional laundry and dry cleaning experienced the largest decline, falling by 30 percent.

Average household spending on apparel may continue to slip as boomers approach retirement and no longer need even business casual attire. At some point, however, apparel spending will bottom out and then stabilize.

Spending on apparel

(average annual spending of households on apparel, 2000 and 2007; in 2007 dollars)

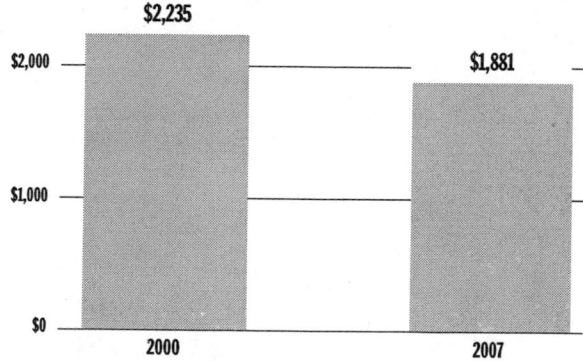

Table 2.1 Apparel Spending, 2000 to 2007

(average annual household spending on apparel, and percent distribution of spending by type, 2000 and 2007; percent change in spending, 2000–07; in 2007 dollars; ranked by amount spent)

	2007		2000		
	average household spending	percent distribution	average household spending (in 2007$)	percent distribution	percent change 2000–07
Average household spending on apparel	**$1,880.72**	**100.0%**	**$2,234.96**	**100.0%**	**−15.8%**
Women's apparel	627.31	33.4	731.01	32.7	−14.2
Men's apparel	351.05	18.7	414.55	18.5	−15.3
Women's shoes	160.33	8.5	187.78	8.4	−14.6
Jewelry	125.79	6.7	129.22	5.8	−2.7
Girls' apparel	121.62	6.5	142.19	6.4	−14.5
Men's shoes	102.60	5.5	141.54	6.3	−27.5
Infants' apparel	93.36	5.0	98.64	4.4	−5.4
Boys' apparel	84.32	4.5	115.30	5.2	−26.9
Children's shoes	64.13	3.4	83.79	3.7	−23.5
Professional apparel laundry and dry cleaning	61.30	3.3	87.18	3.9	−29.7
Coin–operated apparel laundry and dry cleaning	40.75	2.2	45.67	2.0	−10.8
Watches	20.55	1.1	27.25	1.2	−24.6
Sewing material, patterns, and notions	13.42	0.7	11.37	0.5	18.1

Note: Numbers do not add to total because not all categories are shown.
Source: Bureau of Labor Statistics, 2000 and 2007 Consumer Expenditure Surveys; calculations by New Strategist

Boys' Apparel

Best customers:　　　**Married couples with school-aged children**
Single parents
Householders aged 35 to 44
Hispanics and blacks

Customer trends:　　　**Average household spending on children's apparel may increase as the large millennial generation has children.**

Not surprisingly, the best customers of boys' apparel are households with children, driven especially by those with school-aged children. Married couples with children at home spend more than twice the average on this category, while the subgroup with school-aged children spends over three times the average. Single parents spend two-and-one-half times the average on boys' clothes. Householders aged 35 to 44 spend more than double the average on boys' clothes because most are parents. Hispanic and black householders, respectively, spend 34 and 28 percent more than the average household on this category. Behind the higher spending of Hispanics and blacks are their larger families.

Apparel spending fell 16 percent between 2000 and 2007 as less expensive imports drove clothing prices down. Average household spending on boys' clothes fell by an even greater 27 percent during those years. As the large millennial generation has children, average household spending on boys' clothes may increase—especially if the downward spiral in clothing prices comes to an end.

Table 2.2 Boys' apparel

Total household spending $10,132,818,720.00
Average household spends 84.32

AGE OF HOUSEHOLDER	AVERAGE HOUSEHOLD SPENDING	BEST CUSTOMERS (index)	BIGGEST CUSTOMERS (market share)
Average household	$84.32	100	100.0%
Under age 25	33.42	40	2.7
Aged 25 to 34	111.85	133	22.6
Aged 35 to 44	178.26	211	41.2
Aged 45 to 54	86.54	103	21.6
Aged 55 to 64	35.04	42	6.7
Aged 65 to 74	35.67	42	4.2
Aged 75 or older	8.04	10	0.9

	AVERAGE HOUSEHOLD SPENDING	BEST CUSTOMERS (index)	BIGGEST CUSTOMERS (market share)
HOUSEHOLD INCOME			
Average household	$84.32	100	100.0%
Under $20,000	38.18	45	9.3
$20,000 to $39,999	56.44	67	15.6
$40,000 to $49,999	70.71	84	8.3
$50,000 to $69,999	86.02	102	15.6
$70,000 to $79,999	102.92	122	7.1
$80,000 to $99,999	124.48	148	12.0
$100,000 or more	158.65	188	32.2
HOUSEHOLD TYPE			
Average household	84.32	100	100.0
Married couples	117.96	140	70.7
Married couples, no children	23.24	28	5.9
Married couples, with children	193.11	229	57.1
Oldest child under age 6	122.27	145	7.1
Oldest child aged 6 to 17	283.97	337	42.8
Oldest child aged 18 or older	76.41	91	6.7
Single parent with child under age 18	211.53	251	14.9
Single person	13.70	16	4.8
RACE AND HISPANIC ORIGIN			
Average household	84.32	100	100.0
Asian	90.56	107	3.8
Black	108.01	128	15.4
Hispanic	113.27	134	15.9
Non-Hispanic white and other	76.51	91	69.3
REGION			
Average household	84.32	100	100.0
Northeast	96.55	115	21.3
Midwest	86.95	103	23.6
South	78.59	93	33.5
West	80.80	96	21.7
EDUCATION			
Average household	84.32	100	100.0
Less than high school graduate	66.95	79	12.0
High school graduate	63.30	75	18.9
Some college	82.72	98	21.4
Associate's degree	113.16	134	11.9
College graduate	104.02	123	35.7
Bachelor's degree	102.77	122	22.8
Master's, professional, doctoral degree	105.97	126	12.8

Note: Market shares may not sum to 100.0 because of rounding and missing categories by household type. "Asian" and "black" include Hispanics and non-Hispanics who identify themselves as being of the respective race alone. "Hispanic" includes people of any race who identify themselves as Hispanic. "Other" includes people who identify themselves as non-Hispanic and as Alaska Native, American Indian, Asian (who are also included in the "Asian" row), Native Hawaiian or other Pacific Islander, as well as non-Hispanics reporting more than one race. Source: Calculations by New Strategist based on the Bureau of Labor Statistics' 2007 Consumer Expenditure Survey.

Children's Shoes

Best customers:
Married couples with children under age 18
Single parents
Householders aged 25 to 44
Blacks and Hispanics

Customer trends:
Average household spending on shoes for children may increase as the large millennial generation enters parenthood.

Married couples with school-aged children spend more than three times the average on children's shoes and account for 41 percent of the market. Single parents also spend more than three times the average on this item and account for another 19 percent of the market. Married couples with preschoolers spend 44 percent more than average on children's shoes. Black and Hispanic householders are also big spenders on children's shoes. Blacks spend 69 percent more than the average and Hispanics, 68 percent. Because householders aged 25 to 44 are likely to have children at home, their spending on children's shoes is well above average.

Average household spending on children's shoes fell 23 percent between 2000 and 2007, after adjusting for inflation. Less expensive imports are behind the decline, allowing consumers to buy more for less. Spending on children's shoes may rise in the years ahead as the large millennial generation has children and the black and Hispanic populations grow.

Table 2.3 Children's shoes

Total household spending	$7,706,566,230.00
Average household spends	64.13

AGE OF HOUSEHOLDER	AVERAGE HOUSEHOLD SPENDING	BEST CUSTOMERS (index)	BIGGEST CUSTOMERS (market share)
Average household	$64.13	100	100.0%
Under age 25	39.73	62	4.2
Aged 25 to 34	97.13	151	25.8
Aged 35 to 44	120.54	188	36.6
Aged 45 to 54	70.13	109	23.0
Aged 55 to 64	20.29	32	5.1
Aged 65 to 74	29.41	46	4.6
Aged 75 or older	2.87	4	0.4

	AVERAGE HOUSEHOLD SPENDING	BEST CUSTOMERS (index)	BIGGEST CUSTOMERS (market share)
HOUSEHOLD INCOME			
Average household	**$64.13**	**100**	**100.0%**
Under $20,000	35.05	55	11.2
$20,000 to $39,999	59.80	93	21.7
$40,000 to $49,999	65.10	102	10.0
$50,000 to $69,999	72.01	112	17.2
$70,000 to $79,999	99.67	155	9.0
$80,000 to $99,999	61.71	96	7.8
$100,000 or more	86.03	134	23.0
HOUSEHOLD TYPE			
Average household	**64.13**	**100**	**100.0**
Married couples	84.61	132	66.7
Married couples, no children	14.06	22	4.7
Married couples, with children	146.38	228	57.0
Oldest child under age 6	92.17	144	7.0
Oldest child aged 6 to 17	208.97	326	41.4
Oldest child aged 18 or older	62.22	97	7.1
Single parent with child under age 18	201.42	314	18.7
Single person	10.24	16	4.7
RACE AND HISPANIC ORIGIN			
Average household	**64.13**	**100**	**100.0**
Asian	48.16	75	2.6
Black	108.57	169	20.3
Hispanic	107.78	168	19.8
Non-Hispanic white and other	50.96	79	60.7
REGION			
Average household	**64.13**	**100**	**100.0**
Northeast	69.33	108	20.1
Midwest	71.29	111	25.4
South	54.86	86	30.7
West	67.29	105	23.7
EDUCATION			
Average household	**64.13**	**100**	**100.0**
Less than high school graduate	64.47	101	15.2
High school graduate	51.68	81	20.3
Some college	66.32	103	22.5
Associate's degree	68.49	107	9.5
College graduate	71.99	112	32.5
Bachelor's degree	65.05	101	19.0
Master's, professional, doctoral degree	84.05	131	13.4

Note: Market shares may not sum to 100.0 because of rounding and missing categories by household type. "Asian" and "black" include Hispanics and non-Hispanics who identify themselves as being of the respective race alone. "Hispanic" includes people of any race who identify themselves as Hispanic. "Other" includes people who identify themselves as non-Hispanic and as Alaska Native, American Indian, Asian (who are also included in the "Asian" row), Native Hawaiian or other Pacific Islander, as well as non-Hispanics reporting more than one race.
Source: Calculations by New Strategist based on the Bureau of Labor Statistics' 2007 Consumer Expenditure Survey.

Coin-Operated Apparel Laundry and Dry Cleaning

Best customers:
Householders under age 35
Low-income households
Single parents
Asians, blacks, and Hispanics

Customer trends:
Average household spending on coin-operated apparel laundry and dry cleaning
will climb as the large millennial generation fills the young-adult age group
and the Hispanic population grows.

The biggest spenders at coin-operated laundries are householders under age 35, spending 52 to 80 percent more than average. Not surprisingly, low-income households also spend more than average on this category. Many low-income householders are single parents, and the latter spend over twice the average at laundromats. Black householders spend 65 percent more than average at coin-operated laundries, while Hispanic households spend nearly three times the average. Asian households spend 27 percent more. Many Asian, black, and Hispanic householders are renters and do not have a washer or dryer at home.

Average household spending on coin-operated laundry and dry cleaning fell 11 percent between 2000 and 2007, after adjusting for inflation. This decline occurred despite the increase in the young-adult population. As millennials (the oldest of whom turned 30 in 2007) continue to fill the young-adult age group, average household spending on coin-operated laundries should rise. Also boosting spending in this category will be the rapidly growing Hispanic population.

Table 2.4 Coin-operated apparel laundry and dry cleaning

Total household spending $4,896,968,250.00
Average household spends 40.75

	AVERAGE HOUSEHOLD SPENDING	BEST CUSTOMERS (index)	BIGGEST CUSTOMERS (market share)
AGE OF HOUSEHOLDER			
Average household	$40.75	100	100.0%
Under age 25	73.31	180	12.2
Aged 25 to 34	62.11	152	26.0
Aged 35 to 44	47.49	117	22.7
Aged 45 to 54	35.67	88	18.4
Aged 55 to 64	30.32	74	12.1
Aged 65 to 74	20.73	51	5.1
Aged 75 or older	15.39	38	3.6

	AVERAGE HOUSEHOLD SPENDING	BEST CUSTOMERS (index)	BIGGEST CUSTOMERS (market share)
HOUSEHOLD INCOME			
Average household	**$40.75**	**100**	**100.0%**
Under $20,000	58.03	142	29.3
$20,000 to $39,999	54.92	135	31.3
$40,000 to $49,999	49.18	121	11.9
$50,000 to $69,999	35.11	86	13.2
$70,000 to $79,999	26.71	66	3.8
$80,000 to $99,999	20.98	51	4.2
$100,000 or more	15.13	37	6.4
HOUSEHOLD TYPE			
Average household	**40.75**	**100**	**100.0**
Married couples	25.61	63	31.8
Married couples, no children	18.36	45	9.7
Married couples, with children	28.38	70	17.4
Oldest child under age 6	35.87	88	4.3
Oldest child aged 6 to 17	23.02	56	7.2
Oldest child aged 18 or older	32.67	80	5.9
Single parent with child under age 18	92.34	227	13.5
Single person	41.75	102	30.5
RACE AND HISPANIC ORIGIN			
Average household	**40.75**	**100**	**100.0**
Asian	51.81	127	4.5
Black	67.40	165	19.8
Hispanic	113.75	279	32.9
Non-Hispanic white and other	25.39	62	47.6
REGION			
Average household	**40.75**	**100**	**100.0**
Northeast	62.68	154	28.6
Midwest	32.40	80	18.2
South	31.45	77	27.7
West	45.91	113	25.5
EDUCATION			
Average household	**40.75**	**100**	**100.0**
Less than high school graduate	73.84	181	27.5
High school graduate	43.12	106	26.7
Some college	36.38	89	19.4
Associate's degree	32.22	79	7.0
College graduate	27.26	67	19.4
Bachelor's degree	30.07	74	13.8
Master's, professional, doctoral degree	22.12	54	5.5

Note: Market shares may not sum to 100.0 because of rounding and missing categories by household type. "Asian" and "black" include Hispanics and non-Hispanics who identify themselves as being of the respective race alone. "Hispanic" includes people of any race who identify themselves as Hispanic. "Other" includes people who identify themselves as non-Hispanic and as Alaska Native, American Indian, Asian (who are also included in the "Asian" row), Native Hawaiian or other Pacific Islander, as well as non-Hispanics reporting more than one race.
Source: Calculations by New Strategist based on the Bureau of Labor Statistics' 2007 Consumer Expenditure Survey.

Girls' Apparel

Best customers: Married couples with school-aged children
                          Single parents
                          Householders aged 35 to 44
                          Blacks and Asians

Customer trends: Average household spending on children's apparel may increase as the large millennial generation has children.

The average household spends more on clothes for girls than for boys—an average of $122 for girls' clothes versus $84 for boys' clothes in 2007. The big spenders on girls' clothes are, not surprisingly, the same households that spend the most on boys' clothes. Married couples with school-aged children at home spend three-and-one-half times the average on girls' clothes, and single parents spend two-and-one-half times the average. Householders aged 35 to 44 also spend more than twice the average because most are parents. Black and Asian householders spend 30 and 27 percent more than average on girls' clothes, respectively.

Average household spending on girls' clothes fell 14 percent between 2000 and 2007, after adjusting for inflation, as less expensive imports drove clothing prices down. As the large millennial generation has children, spending on girls' clothes may increase—especially if the downward spiral in clothing prices comes to a halt.

Table 2.5 Girls' apparel

Total household spending $14,615,197,020.00
Average household spends 121.62

	AVERAGE HOUSEHOLD SPENDING	BEST CUSTOMERS (index)	BIGGEST CUSTOMERS (market share)
AGE OF HOUSEHOLDER			
Average household	**$121.62**	**100**	**100.0%**
Under age 25	25.01	21	1.4
Aged 25 to 34	158.24	130	22.2
Aged 35 to 44	251.09	206	40.2
Aged 45 to 54	130.24	107	22.5
Aged 55 to 64	69.68	57	9.3
Aged 65 to 74	45.57	37	3.7
Aged 75 or older	8.48	7	0.7

	AVERAGE HOUSEHOLD SPENDING	BEST CUSTOMERS (index)	BIGGEST CUSTOMERS (market share)
HOUSEHOLD INCOME			
Average household	**$121.62**	**100**	**100.0%**
Under $20,000	38.26	31	6.5
$20,000 to $39,999	83.19	68	15.9
$40,000 to $49,999	90.96	75	7.4
$50,000 to $69,999	111.38	92	14.0
$70,000 to $79,999	142.37	117	6.8
$80,000 to $99,999	207.56	171	13.9
$100,000 or more	249.68	205	35.2
HOUSEHOLD TYPE			
Average household	**121.62**	**100**	**100.0**
Married couples	168.35	138	70.0
Married couples, no children	43.76	36	7.8
Married couples, with children	289.15	238	59.3
Oldest child under age 6	165.36	136	6.6
Oldest child aged 6 to 17	433.44	356	45.3
Oldest child aged 18 or older	103.68	85	6.3
Single parent with child under age 18	298.64	246	14.6
Single person	18.06	15	4.4
RACE AND HISPANIC ORIGIN			
Average household	**121.62**	**100**	**100.0**
Asian	154.53	127	4.5
Black	157.63	130	15.6
Hispanic	130.85	108	12.7
Non-Hispanic white and other	114.96	95	72.2
REGION			
Average household	**121.62**	**100**	**100.0**
Northeast	121.45	100	18.6
Midwest	117.18	96	22.0
South	123.71	102	36.5
West	123.04	101	22.9
EDUCATION			
Average household	**121.62**	**100**	**100.0**
Less than high school graduate	64.71	53	8.1
High school graduate	97.11	80	20.1
Some college	115.08	95	20.6
Associate's degree	156.20	128	11.4
College graduate	164.69	135	39.2
Bachelor's degree	153.31	126	23.6
Master's, professional, doctoral degree	184.40	152	15.5

Note: Market shares may not sum to 100.0 because of rounding and missing categories by household type. "Asian" and "black" include Hispanics and non-Hispanics who identify themselves as being of the respective race alone. "Hispanic" includes people of any race who identify themselves as Hispanic. "Other" includes people who identify themselves as non-Hispanic and as Alaska Native, American Indian, Asian (who are also included in the "Asian" row), Native Hawaiian or other Pacific Islander, as well as non-Hispanics reporting more than one race.
Source: Calculations by New Strategist based on the Bureau of Labor Statistics' 2007 Consumer Expenditure Survey.

Infants' Apparel

Best customers:

Married couples with preschoolers
Householders under age 35
Hispanics
Households in the West

Customer trends:

Average household spending on infants' apparel may increase as the large millennial generation has children.

The average household spent $93 on clothes for infants in 2007. By far the biggest spenders on infants' clothes are married couples with preschoolers. This household type spends nearly six times the average on baby clothes. Householders aged 25 to 34 spend over twice the average because many have newborns and toddlers. Those under age 25 spend 55 percent more. Hispanic householders spend 50 percent more than average on infants' clothes because of their larger families. Households in the West, where many Hispanics reside, spend 27 percent more than average on infants' clothes.

Spending on infants' apparel fell 6 percent between 2000 and 2007, a much smaller decline in spending than most other apparel categories. One factor behind the relative stability is the growing Hispanic population. As the large millennial generation has children during the next few years, average household spending on infants' clothes may increase—especially if the downward spiral in clothing prices comes to a halt.

Table 2.6 Infants' apparel

Total household spending $11,219,164,560.00
Average household spends   93.36

AGE OF HOUSEHOLDER	AVERAGE HOUSEHOLD SPENDING	BEST CUSTOMERS (index)	BIGGEST CUSTOMERS (market share)
Average household	$93.36	100	100.0%
Under age 25	144.55	155	10.5
Aged 25 to 34	205.63	220	37.6
Aged 35 to 44	118.64	127	24.8
Aged 45 to 54	53.90	58	12.1
Aged 55 to 64	55.41	59	9.6
Aged 65 to 74	31.99	34	3.4
Aged 75 or older	13.76	15	1.4

	AVERAGE HOUSEHOLD SPENDING	BEST CUSTOMERS (index)	BIGGEST CUSTOMERS (market share)
HOUSEHOLD INCOME			
Average household	**$93.36**	**100**	**100.0%**
Under $20,000	55.84	60	12.3
$20,000 to $39,999	70.31	75	17.5
$40,000 to $49,999	84.17	90	8.9
$50,000 to $69,999	90.43	97	14.8
$70,000 to $79,999	153.78	165	9.5
$80,000 to $99,999	140.61	151	12.3
$100,000 or more	135.26	145	24.8
HOUSEHOLD TYPE			
Average household	**93.36**	**100**	**100.0**
Married couples	129.84	139	70.3
Married couples, no children	53.90	58	12.5
Married couples, with children	189.48	203	50.6
Oldest child under age 6	544.97	584	28.5
Oldest child aged 6 to 17	120.71	129	16.4
Oldest child aged 18 or older	66.04	71	5.2
Single parent with child under age 18	117.80	126	7.5
Single person	19.56	21	6.2
RACE AND HISPANIC ORIGIN			
Average household	**93.36**	**100**	**100.0**
Asian	106.77	114	4.0
Black	103.40	111	13.3
Hispanic	140.34	150	17.7
Non-Hispanic white and other	84.96	91	69.5
REGION			
Average household	**93.36**	**100**	**100.0**
Northeast	82.61	88	16.5
Midwest	88.60	95	21.7
South	86.38	93	33.2
West	118.56	127	28.7
EDUCATION			
Average household	**93.36**	**100**	**100.0**
Less than high school graduate	93.75	100	15.2
High school graduate	81.00	87	21.9
Some college	93.10	100	21.7
Associate's degree	106.00	114	10.1
College graduate	101.07	108	31.3
Bachelor's degree	106.98	115	21.5
Master's, professional, doctoral degree	90.68	97	9.9

Note: Market shares may not sum to 100.0 because of rounding and missing categories by household type. "Asian" and "black" include Hispanics and non-Hispanics who identify themselves as being of the respective race alone. "Hispanic" includes people of any race who identify themselves as Hispanic. "Other" includes people who identify themselves as non-Hispanic and as Alaska Native, American Indian, Asian (who are also included in the "Asian" row), Native Hawaiian or other Pacific Islander, as well as non-Hispanics reporting more than one race.
Source: Calculations by New Strategist based on the Bureau of Labor Statistics' 2007 Consumer Expenditure Survey.

Jewelry

Best customers:

Householders aged 35 to 44
High-income households
Married couples
Households in the Northeast
College graduates

Customer trends:

Average household spending on jewelry may continue to fall in the years ahead as tighter budgets limit discretionary spending.

The best customers of jewelry are the most-affluent households—high-income households, married couples, and college graduates. Households with incomes of $100,000 or more spend three times the average on jewelry, while households headed by college graduates spend twice the average. Married couples spend one-third more than average on jewelry, the figure peaking at more than twice the average among those who have adult children at home. In the Northeast, households spend 49 percent more than average on jewelry.

Average household spending on jewelry barely changed between 2000 and 2007, dropping 3 percent after adjusting for inflation. Spending on jewelry may continue to fall in the years ahead as tighter budgets limit discretionary spending.

Table 2.7 Jewelry

	AVERAGE HOUSEHOLD SPENDING	BEST CUSTOMERS (index)	BIGGEST CUSTOMERS (market share)
Total household spending	$15,116,310,090.00		
Average household spends	125.79		
AGE OF HOUSEHOLDER			
Average household	$125.79	100	100.0%
Under age 25	120.26	96	6.5
Aged 25 to 34	127.15	101	17.2
Aged 35 to 44	204.39	162	31.7
Aged 45 to 54	129.77	103	21.7
Aged 55 to 64	93.10	74	12.0
Aged 65 to 74	72.87	58	5.8
Aged 75 or older	68.58	55	5.2

	AVERAGE HOUSEHOLD SPENDING	BEST CUSTOMERS (index)	BIGGEST CUSTOMERS (market share)
HOUSEHOLD INCOME			
Average household	**$125.79**	**100**	**100.0%**
Under $20,000	18.28	15	3.0
$20,000 to $39,999	40.91	33	7.6
$40,000 to $49,999	95.70	76	7.5
$50,000 to $69,999	101.86	81	12.4
$70,000 to $79,999	113.10	90	5.2
$80,000 to $99,999	180.23	143	11.7
$100,000 or more	387.06	308	52.7
HOUSEHOLD TYPE			
Average household	**125.79**	**100**	**100.0**
Married couples	168.08	134	67.5
Married couples, no children	152.85	122	26.2
Married couples, with children	182.98	145	36.3
Oldest child under age 6	156.17	124	6.1
Oldest child aged 6 to 17	136.54	109	13.8
Oldest child aged 18 or older	280.82	223	16.4
Single parent with child under age 18	43.07	34	2.0
Single person	62.59	50	14.8
RACE AND HISPANIC ORIGIN			
Average household	**125.79**	**100**	**100.0**
Asian	84.05	67	2.4
Black	63.71	51	6.1
Hispanic	77.02	61	7.2
Non-Hispanic white and other	142.87	114	86.7
REGION			
Average household	**125.79**	**100**	**100.0**
Northeast	187.16	149	27.7
Midwest	117.86	94	21.4
South	104.64	83	29.9
West	116.84	93	21.0
EDUCATION			
Average household	**125.79**	**100**	**100.0**
Less than high school graduate	52.90	42	6.4
High school graduate	54.40	43	10.9
Some college	89.57	71	15.5
Associate's degree	126.37	100	8.9
College graduate	253.28	201	58.3
Bachelor's degree	225.83	180	33.6
Master's, professional, doctoral degree	303.71	241	24.6

Note: Market shares may not sum to 100.0 because of rounding and missing categories by household type. "Asian" and "black" include Hispanics and non-Hispanics who identify themselves as being of the respective race alone. "Hispanic" includes people of any race who identify themselves as Hispanic. "Other" includes people who identify themselves as non-Hispanic and as Alaska Native, American Indian, Asian (who are also included in the "Asian" row), Native Hawaiian or other Pacific Islander, as well as non-Hispanics reporting more than one race.
Source: Calculations by New Strategist based on the Bureau of Labor Statistics' 2007 Consumer Expenditure Survey.

Men's Apparel

Best customers: Householders aged 25 to 54
                           Married couples with adult children at home
                           Asians

Customer trends: Average household spending on men's clothes will continue to decline as the large
                           baby-boom generation approaches retirement.

In 2007, the average household spent $351 on men's clothes versus a larger $627 on women's clothes. Both figures are lower than in 2000. Falling prices are one reason for the decline in spending, as cheaper imports allow consumers to buy more for less. Also behind the decline is the trend toward more casual attire in the workplace and at social functions. The biggest spenders on men's clothes are households with working men. This explains why married couples with adult children at home spend 90 percent more than average on this item, since many of these households include more than one working man. Householders ranging in age from 25 to 54 spend 13 to 22 percent more than average on men's clothes.

Average household spending on men's clothes fell 15 percent between 2000 and 2007 as clothing prices fell and more casual attire became the norm in the workplace. Spending on men's clothes will continue to decline as the large baby-boom generation approaches retirement and no longer needs to purchase business attire.

Table 2.8 **Men's apparel**

Total household spending $42,186,029,550.00
Average household spends   351.05

AGE OF HOUSEHOLDER	AVERAGE HOUSEHOLD SPENDING	BEST CUSTOMERS (index)	BIGGEST CUSTOMERS (market share)
Average household	**$351.05**	**100**	**100.0%**
Under age 25	289.98	83	5.6
Aged 25 to 34	396.19	113	19.3
Aged 35 to 44	403.37	115	22.4
Aged 45 to 54	427.59	122	25.6
Aged 55 to 64	366.68	104	16.9
Aged 65 to 74	219.78	63	6.3
Aged 75 or older	151.70	43	4.1

	AVERAGE HOUSEHOLD SPENDING	BEST CUSTOMERS (index)	BIGGEST CUSTOMERS (market share)
HOUSEHOLD INCOME			
Average household	**$351.05**	**100**	**100.0%**
Under $20,000	134.79	38	7.9
$20,000 to $39,999	196.45	56	13.0
$40,000 to $49,999	252.34	72	7.1
$50,000 to $69,999	349.02	99	15.2
$70,000 to $79,999	393.63	112	6.5
$80,000 to $99,999	455.35	130	10.6
$100,000 or more	826.38	235	40.3
HOUSEHOLD TYPE			
Average household	**351.05**	**100**	**100.0**
Married couples	423.78	121	61.0
Married couples, no children	384.57	110	23.6
Married couples, with children	450.80	128	32.0
Oldest child under age 6	347.90	99	4.8
Oldest child aged 6 to 17	379.04	108	13.7
Oldest child aged 18 or older	666.98	190	14.0
Single parent with child under age 18	149.47	43	2.5
Single person	253.42	72	21.5
RACE AND HISPANIC ORIGIN			
Average household	**351.05**	**100**	**100.0**
Asian	511.55	146	5.1
Black	236.18	67	8.1
Hispanic	425.39	121	14.3
Non-Hispanic white and other	358.42	102	77.9
REGION			
Average household	**351.05**	**100**	**100.0**
Northeast	353.84	101	18.8
Midwest	291.94	83	19.0
South	346.23	99	35.4
West	417.31	119	26.9
EDUCATION			
Average household	**351.05**	**100**	**100.0**
Less than high school graduate	228.32	65	9.9
High school graduate	238.47	68	17.1
Some college	291.58	83	18.1
Associate's degree	299.34	85	7.6
College graduate	565.76	161	46.6
Bachelor's degree	529.42	151	28.3
Master's, professional, doctoral degree	629.77	179	18.3

Note: Market shares may not sum to 100.0 because of rounding and missing categories by household type. "Asian" and "black" include Hispanics and non-Hispanics who identify themselves as being of the respective race alone. "Hispanic" includes people of any race who identify themselves as Hispanic. "Other" includes people who identify themselves as non-Hispanic and as Alaska Native, American Indian, Asian (who are also included in the "Asian" row), Native Hawaiian or other Pacific Islander, as well as non-Hispanics reporting more than one race.
Source: Calculations by New Strategist based on the Bureau of Labor Statistics' 2007 Consumer Expenditure Survey.

Men's Shoes

Best customers:

Householders aged 25 to 64
Married couples with children at home
Asians and Hispanics

Customer trends:

Average household spending on men's shoes will decline as the large baby-boom generation approaches retirement.

The best customers of men's shoes are married couples with adult children at home. These households spend 81 percent more than average on men's shoes because there are more men in the household. Married couples with children under age 18 at home spend 22 to 35 percent more than average on men's shoes. Asians and Hispanics spend 46 percent more than average on this item.

In 2007, the average household spent $103 on men's shoes, almost 28 percent less than in 2000 after adjusting for inflation. Low-cost imports are behind the steep decline. Although the growing Asian and Hispanic populations should boost spending on men's shoes, the bigger trend is the aging of the baby-boom generation, which is likely to dampen spending on this item.

Table 2.9 **Men's shoes**

Total household spending $12,329,544,600.00
Average household spends   102.60

	AVERAGE HOUSEHOLD SPENDING	BEST CUSTOMERS (index)	BIGGEST CUSTOMERS (market share)
AGE OF HOUSEHOLDER			
Average household	**$102.60**	**100**	**100.0%**
Under age 25	80.34	78	5.3
Aged 25 to 34	125.76	123	20.9
Aged 35 to 44	113.30	110	21.5
Aged 45 to 54	127.14	124	26.0
Aged 55 to 64	114.46	112	18.1
Aged 65 to 74	31.98	31	3.1
Aged 75 or older	57.44	56	5.3

	AVERAGE HOUSEHOLD SPENDING	BEST CUSTOMERS (index)	BIGGEST CUSTOMERS (market share)
HOUSEHOLD INCOME			
Average household	$102.60	100	100.0%
Under $20,000	48.33	47	9.7
$20,000 to $39,999	66.07	64	15.0
$40,000 to $49,999	101.64	99	9.7
$50,000 to $69,999	120.91	118	18.0
$70,000 to $79,999	98.69	96	5.6
$80,000 to $99,999	141.70	138	11.2
$100,000 or more	184.27	180	30.8
HOUSEHOLD TYPE			
Average household	102.60	100	100.0
Married couples	126.92	124	62.5
Married couples, no children	106.71	104	22.4
Married couples, with children	148.59	145	36.1
Oldest child under age 6	125.52	122	6.0
Oldest child aged 6 to 17	138.51	135	17.1
Oldest child aged 18 or older	185.48	181	13.3
Single parent with child under age 18	86.44	84	5.0
Single person	65.52	64	19.0
RACE AND HISPANIC ORIGIN			
Average household	102.60	100	100.0
Asian	150.19	146	5.2
Black	118.66	116	13.9
Hispanic	149.48	146	17.2
Non-Hispanic white and other	93.31	91	69.4
REGION			
Average household	102.60	100	100.0
Northeast	117.35	114	21.3
Midwest	94.93	93	21.1
South	92.57	90	32.4
West	114.20	111	25.2
EDUCATION			
Average household	102.60	100	100.0
Less than high school graduate	99.79	97	14.8
High school graduate	78.85	77	19.4
Some college	83.73	82	17.8
Associate's degree	100.72	98	8.7
College graduate	138.70	135	39.1
Bachelor's degree	143.32	140	26.2
Master's, professional, doctoral degree	130.70	127	13.0

Note: Market shares may not sum to 100.0 because of rounding and missing categories by household type. "Asian" and "black" include Hispanics and non-Hispanics who identify themselves as being of the respective race alone. "Hispanic" includes people of any race who identify themselves as Hispanic. "Other" includes people who identify themselves as non-Hispanic and as Alaska Native, American Indian, Asian (who are also included in the "Asian" row), Native Hawaiian or other Pacific Islander, as well as non-Hispanics reporting more than one race.
Source: Calculations by New Strategist based on the Bureau of Labor Statistics' 2007 Consumer Expenditure Survey.

Professional Apparel Laundry and Dry Cleaning

Best customers:

Householders aged 35 to 64
High-income households
Married couples
College graduates

Customer trends:

Average household spending on professional apparel laundry and dry cleaning is likely to fall as boomers approach retirement and their need for this service declines.

The biggest spenders on professional laundry and dry cleaning are affluent, educated, middle-aged householders. Households with incomes of $100,000 or more spend three-and-one-half times the average on professional laundry and dry cleaning. College graduates spend more than double the average. Married couples spend 40 percent more than average on this item, the figure peaking at 57 percent among those with adult children at home. Householders ranging in age from 35 to 64 spend 22 to 31 percent more.

Average household spending on professional laundry and dry cleaning declined by a substantial 30 percent between 2000 and 2007, after adjusting for inflation, as casual attire became more common in the workplace. Spending on professional laundry and dry cleaning should continue to decline as boomers retire and fewer dress in business clothes.

Table 2.10 Professional apparel laundry and dry cleaning

Total household spending $7,366,482,300.00
Average household spends   61.30

AGE OF HOUSEHOLDER	AVERAGE HOUSEHOLD SPENDING	BEST CUSTOMERS (index)	BIGGEST CUSTOMERS (market share)
Average household	$61.30	100	100.0%
Under age 25	18.60	30	2.1
Aged 25 to 34	52.11	85	14.5
Aged 35 to 44	77.16	126	24.5
Aged 45 to 54	80.48	131	27.6
Aged 55 to 64	74.48	122	19.7
Aged 65 to 74	47.24	77	7.7
Aged 75 or older	25.59	42	4.0

	AVERAGE HOUSEHOLD SPENDING	BEST CUSTOMERS (index)	BIGGEST CUSTOMERS (market share)
HOUSEHOLD INCOME			
Average household	**$61.30**	**100**	**100.0%**
Under $20,000	9.49	15	3.2
$20,000 to $39,999	18.71	31	7.1
$40,000 to $49,999	34.59	56	5.6
$50,000 to $69,999	39.08	64	9.8
$70,000 to $79,999	51.38	84	4.9
$80,000 to $99,999	77.87	127	10.3
$100,000 or more	211.93	346	59.2
HOUSEHOLD TYPE			
Average household	**61.30**	**100**	**100.0**
Married couples	85.82	140	70.8
Married couples, no children	84.89	138	29.9
Married couples, with children	91.72	150	37.3
Oldest child under age 6	79.37	129	6.3
Oldest child aged 6 to 17	93.73	153	19.4
Oldest child aged 18 or older	96.45	157	11.6
Single parent with child under age 18	31.52	51	3.1
Single person	34.51	56	16.7
RACE AND HISPANIC ORIGIN			
Average household	**61.30**	**100**	**100.0**
Asian	58.83	96	3.4
Black	67.11	109	13.1
Hispanic	36.64	60	7.1
Non-Hispanic white and other	64.23	105	80.0
REGION			
Average household	**61.30**	**100**	**100.0**
Northeast	80.64	132	24.5
Midwest	46.31	76	17.3
South	64.23	105	37.6
West	55.86	91	20.6
EDUCATION			
Average household	**61.30**	**100**	**100.0**
Less than high school graduate	14.84	24	3.7
High school graduate	29.55	48	12.2
Some college	44.61	73	15.8
Associate's degree	51.61	84	7.5
College graduate	128.85	210	60.8
Bachelor's degree	112.15	183	34.3
Master's, professional, doctoral degree	159.52	260	26.5

Note: Market shares may not sum to 100.0 because of rounding and missing categories by household type. "Asian" and "black" include Hispanics and non-Hispanics who identify themselves as being of the respective race alone. "Hispanic" includes people of any race who identify themselves as Hispanic. "Other" includes people who identify themselves as non-Hispanic and as Alaska Native, American Indian, Asian (who are also included in the "Asian" row), Native Hawaiian or other Pacific Islander, as well as non-Hispanics reporting more than one race. Source: Calculations by New Strategist based on the Bureau of Labor Statistics' 2007 Consumer Expenditure Survey.

Sewing Materials

Best customers: **Householders aged 55 to 74**
Married couples without children at home
Households in the West

Customer trends: **Average household spending on sewing materials is likely to fall in the years ahead as younger generations with little sewing experience fill the best-customer age groups.**

The biggest spenders on sewing materials are older householders. Householders aged 55 to 74 spend 64 to 102 percent more than average on sewing materials. Married couples without children at home—most of them empty-nesters—spend almost twice the average on this item. Households in the West spend 39 percent more than the average households on this item.

Average household spending on sewing materials increased by a substantial 18 percent between 2000 and 2007, after adjusting for inflation.

Table 2.11 Sewing materials, patterns, and notions

| Total household spending | $1,612,694,820.00 |
| Average household spends | 13.42 |

	AVERAGE HOUSEHOLD SPENDING	BEST CUSTOMERS (index)	BIGGEST CUSTOMERS (market share)
AGE OF HOUSEHOLDER			
Average household	**$13.42**	**100**	**100.0%**
Under age 25	8.75	65	4.4
Aged 25 to 34	8.48	63	10.8
Aged 35 to 44	10.43	78	15.1
Aged 45 to 54	12.19	91	19.1
Aged 55 to 64	21.97	164	26.5
Aged 65 to 74	27.13	202	20.2
Aged 75 or older	5.51	41	3.9

	AVERAGE HOUSEHOLD SPENDING	BEST CUSTOMERS (index)	BIGGEST CUSTOMERS (market share)
HOUSEHOLD INCOME			
Average household	$13.42	100	100.0%
Under $20,000	5.11	38	7.8
$20,000 to $39,999	5.62	42	9.7
$40,000 to $49,999	10.61	79	7.8
$50,000 to $69,999	16.08	120	18.3
$70,000 to $79,999	15.39	115	6.6
$80,000 to $99,999	27.38	204	16.6
$100,000 or more	25.31	189	32.3
HOUSEHOLD TYPE			
Average household	13.42	100	100.0
Married couples	18.83	140	70.9
Married couples, no children	26.34	196	42.3
Married couples, with children	10.21	76	19.0
Oldest child under age 6	11.02	82	4.0
Oldest child aged 6 to 17	7.48	56	7.1
Oldest child aged 18 or older	15.03	112	8.3
Single parent with child under age 18	2.77	21	1.2
Single person	7.52	56	16.7
RACE AND HISPANIC ORIGIN			
Average household	13.42	100	100.0
Asian	10.09	75	2.7
Black	6.79	51	6.1
Hispanic	9.59	71	8.4
Non-Hispanic white and other	14.99	112	85.3
REGION			
Average household	13.42	100	100.0
Northeast	5.83	43	8.1
Midwest	15.20	113	25.9
South	12.99	97	34.8
West	18.71	139	31.5
EDUCATION			
Average household	13.42	100	100.0
Less than high school graduate	8.22	61	9.3
High school graduate	8.00	60	15.0
Some college	15.23	113	24.7
Associate's degree	20.33	151	13.5
College graduate	17.26	129	37.2
Bachelor's degree	15.28	114	21.3
Master's, professional, doctoral degree	20.70	154	15.7

Note: Market shares may not sum to 100.0 because of rounding and missing categories by household type. "Asian" and "black" include Hispanics and non-Hispanics who identify themselves as being of the respective race alone. "Hispanic" includes people of any race who identify themselves as Hispanic. "Other" includes people who identify themselves as non-Hispanic and as Alaska Native, American Indian, Asian (who are also included in the "Asian" row), Native Hawaiian or other Pacific Islander, as well as non-Hispanics reporting more than one race.
Source: Calculations by New Strategist based on the Bureau of Labor Statistics' 2007 Consumer Expenditure Survey.

Watches

Best customers:
Householders aged 35 to 44 and 55 to 64
Married couples without children at home
Married couples with adult children at home
Asians
College graduates

Customer trends:
Average household spending on watches should continue to decline as imports lower prices.

The biggest spenders on watches are the educated. Households headed by college graduates, which have the highest incomes, spend twice the average on this item and account for 59 percent of the market. Asian householders, the best-educated racial or ethnic group, spend 86 percent more than average on watches. Married couples with adult children at home, who have a larger number of earners than other household types, spend 57 percent more than average on this item.

Average household spending on watches fell 25 percent between 2000 and 2007, after adjusting for inflation. Cheaper imports are one factor for the decline in spending. Another factor is the substitution of cell phones for watches among younger adults. Spending on watches should continue to decline in the years ahead.

Table 2.12 **Watches**

| Total household spending | $2,469,514,050.00 |
| Average household spends | 20.55 |

AGE OF HOUSEHOLDER	AVERAGE HOUSEHOLD SPENDING	BEST CUSTOMERS (index)	BIGGEST CUSTOMERS (market share)
Average household	$20.55	100	100.0%
Under age 25	8.00	39	2.6
Aged 25 to 34	17.72	86	14.7
Aged 35 to 44	29.32	143	27.8
Aged 45 to 54	11.23	55	11.5
Aged 55 to 64	49.00	238	38.6
Aged 65 to 74	7.71	38	3.7
Aged 75 or older	2.92	14	1.3

	AVERAGE HOUSEHOLD SPENDING	BEST CUSTOMERS (index)	BIGGEST CUSTOMERS (market share)
HOUSEHOLD INCOME			
Average household	**$20.55**	**100**	**100.0%**
Under $20,000	7.83	38	7.8
$20,000 to $39,999	8.41	41	9.5
$40,000 to $49,999	25.70	125	12.3
$50,000 to $69,999	23.82	116	17.7
$70,000 to $79,999	22.40	109	6.3
$80,000 to $99,999	18.60	91	7.4
$100,000 or more	47.77	232	39.8
HOUSEHOLD TYPE			
Average household	**20.55**	**100**	**100.0**
Married couples	22.53	110	55.4
Married couples, no children	30.73	150	32.3
Married couples, with children	17.23	84	20.9
Oldest child under age 6	15.73	77	3.7
Oldest child aged 6 to 17	10.20	50	6.3
Oldest child aged 18 or older	32.27	157	11.6
Single parent with child under age 18	11.79	57	3.4
Single person	18.92	92	27.4
RACE AND HISPANIC ORIGIN			
Average household	**20.55**	**100**	**100.0**
Asian	38.23	186	6.6
Black	23.77	116	13.9
Hispanic	25.68	125	14.8
Non-Hispanic white and other	19.29	94	71.7
REGION			
Average household	**20.55**	**100**	**100.0**
Northeast	23.12	113	21.0
Midwest	17.43	85	19.4
South	21.82	106	38.1
West	19.54	95	21.5
EDUCATION			
Average household	**20.55**	**100**	**100.0**
Less than high school graduate	6.96	34	5.1
High school graduate	14.35	70	17.6
Some college	13.54	66	14.3
Associate's degree	5.29	26	2.3
College graduate	41.65	203	58.7
Bachelor's degree	35.26	172	32.2
Master's, professional, doctoral degree	52.76	257	26.2

Note: Market shares may not sum to 100.0 because of rounding and missing categories by household type. "Asian" and "black" include Hispanics and non-Hispanics who identify themselves as being of the respective race alone. "Hispanic" includes people of any race who identify themselves as Hispanic. "Other" includes people who identify themselves as non-Hispanic and as Alaska Native, American Indian, Asian (who are also included in the "Asian" row), Native Hawaiian or other Pacific Islander, as well as non-Hispanics reporting more than one race. Source: Calculations by New Strategist based on the Bureau of Labor Statistics' 2007 Consumer Expenditure Survey.

Women's Apparel

Best customers:

Householders aged 45 to 64
Married couples without children at home
Married couples with adult children at home
Asians

Customer trends:

Average household spending on women's clothes may climb as boomer women become empty-nesters and can spend more freely on themselves.

The average household spends more on women's clothes than on any other apparel category—$627 in 2007, or 33 percent of the apparel dollar. The biggest spenders on women's clothes are householders ranging in age from 45 to 64, who spend 15 to 31 percent more than the average household on this item. Married couples without children at home (most of them older) spend 27 percent more than average on women's clothes. Couples with adult children at home spend 53 percent more than average on this item because there are more women in the household.

Average household spending on women's clothes declined by 14 percent between 2000 and 2007, after adjusting for inflation. Falling prices are one reason for the decline in spending, as cheaper imports allow consumers to buy more for less. Spending on women's clothes may climb as boomer women become empty-nesters and devote more of the apparel dollar to their own rather than their children's clothes.

Table 2.13 Women's apparel

| Total household spending | | | $75,384,470,010.00 |
| Average household spends | | | 627.31 |

	AVERAGE HOUSEHOLD SPENDING	BEST CUSTOMERS (index)	BIGGEST CUSTOMERS (market share)
AGE OF HOUSEHOLDER			
Average household	**$627.31**	**100**	**100.0%**
Under age 25	509.96	81	5.5
Aged 25 to 34	570.27	91	15.5
Aged 35 to 44	604.12	96	18.8
Aged 45 to 54	822.25	131	27.5
Aged 55 to 64	723.32	115	18.7
Aged 65 to 74	590.28	94	9.4
Aged 75 or older	316.13	50	4.8

	AVERAGE HOUSEHOLD SPENDING	BEST CUSTOMERS (index)	BIGGEST CUSTOMERS (market share)
HOUSEHOLD INCOME			
Average household	**$627.31**	**100**	**100.0%**
Under $20,000	255.42	41	8.4
$20,000 to $39,999	363.15	58	13.5
$40,000 to $49,999	494.36	79	7.8
$50,000 to $69,999	669.80	107	16.3
$70,000 to $79,999	804.00	128	7.4
$80,000 to $99,999	784.90	125	10.2
$100,000 or more	1,351.61	215	36.9
HOUSEHOLD TYPE			
Average household	**627.31**	**100**	**100.0**
Married couples	775.79	124	62.5
Married couples, no children	798.09	127	27.4
Married couples, with children	756.03	121	30.1
Oldest child under age 6	530.81	85	4.1
Oldest child aged 6 to 17	735.73	117	14.9
Oldest child aged 18 or older	958.63	153	11.3
Single parent with child under age 18	678.67	108	6.4
Single person	334.17	53	15.8
RACE AND HISPANIC ORIGIN			
Average household	**627.31**	**100**	**100.0**
Asian	1,079.71	172	6.1
Black	512.88	82	9.8
Hispanic	504.98	80	9.5
Non-Hispanic white and other	662.53	106	80.6
REGION			
Average household	**627.31**	**100**	**100.0**
Northeast	690.20	110	20.5
Midwest	703.39	112	25.6
South	514.57	82	29.5
West	677.04	108	24.4
EDUCATION			
Average household	**627.31**	**100**	**100.0**
Less than high school graduate	314.11	50	7.6
High school graduate	421.91	67	17.0
Some college	552.50	88	19.2
Associate's degree	662.42	106	9.4
College graduate	996.09	159	46.0
Bachelor's degree	910.37	145	27.2
Master's, professional, doctoral degree	1,146.37	183	18.6

Note: Market shares may not sum to 100.0 because of rounding and missing categories by household type. "Asian" and "black" include Hispanics and non-Hispanics who identify themselves as being of the respective race alone. "Hispanic" includes people of any race who identify themselves as Hispanic. "Other" includes people who identify themselves as non-Hispanic and as Alaska Native, American Indian, Asian (who are also included in the "Asian" row), Native Hawaiian or other Pacific Islander, as well as non-Hispanics reporting more than one race.
Source: Calculations by New Strategist based on the Bureau of Labor Statistics' 2007 Consumer Expenditure Survey.

Women's Shoes

Best customers: Householders aged 45 to 64
Married couples with adult children at home
Asians

Customer trends: Average household spending on women's shoes may rise as boomer women devote more of their apparel dollar to themselves.

The best customers of women's shoes are married couples with adult children at home. They spend 69 percent more than average on women's shoes. Behind the higher spending are their larger households, many of which include more than one adult female. Householders age 45 to 64 spend 16 to 35 percent more than average on women's shoes. Asian households spend almost double the average on women's shoes.

Average household spending on women's shoes fell 15 percent between 2000 and 2007, after adjusting for inflation. Falling prices are one factor behind the decline in spending on women's shoes as cheaper imports allow consumers to buy more for less. As growing numbers of boomers become empty-nesters, average household spending on women's shoes may increase as women spend more on shoes for themselves.

Table 2.14 Women's shoes

Total household spending $19,267,016,430.00
Average household spends   160.33

	AVERAGE HOUSEHOLD SPENDING	BEST CUSTOMERS (index)	BIGGEST CUSTOMERS (market share)
AGE OF HOUSEHOLDER			
Average household	**$160.33**	**100**	**100.0%**
Under age 25	116.68	73	4.9
Aged 25 to 34	160.17	100	17.0
Aged 35 to 44	164.88	103	20.0
Aged 45 to 54	185.77	116	24.3
Aged 55 to 64	216.66	135	21.9
Aged 65 to 74	148.02	92	9.2
Aged 75 or older	45.48	28	2.7

	AVERAGE HOUSEHOLD SPENDING	BEST CUSTOMERS (index)	BIGGEST CUSTOMERS (market share)
HOUSEHOLD INCOME			
Average household	**$160.33**	**100**	**100.0%**
Under $20,000	66.51	41	8.5
$20,000 to $39,999	107.36	67	15.6
$40,000 to $49,999	129.82	81	8.0
$50,000 to $69,999	124.52	78	11.9
$70,000 to $79,999	150.75	94	5.4
$80,000 to $99,999	209.27	131	10.6
$100,000 or more	382.27	238	40.8
HOUSEHOLD TYPE			
Average household	**160.33**	**100**	**100.0**
Married couples	202.51	126	63.8
Married couples, no children	199.84	125	26.9
Married couples, with children	199.49	124	31.0
Oldest child under age 6	162.00	101	4.9
Oldest child aged 6 to 17	176.97	110	14.0
Oldest child aged 18 or older	271.57	169	12.5
Single parent with child under age 18	146.88	92	5.4
Single person	82.04	51	15.2
RACE AND HISPANIC ORIGIN			
Average household	**160.33**	**100**	**100.0**
Asian	315.58	197	6.9
Black	159.72	100	12.0
Hispanic	150.35	94	11.1
Non-Hispanic white and other	161.64	101	77.0
REGION			
Average household	**160.33**	**100**	**100.0**
Northeast	163.04	102	18.9
Midwest	167.52	104	23.9
South	149.23	93	33.4
West	168.48	105	23.8
EDUCATION			
Average household	**160.33**	**100**	**100.0**
Less than high school graduate	112.18	70	10.6
High school graduate	138.58	86	21.8
Some college	126.00	79	17.1
Associate's degree	105.45	66	5.8
College graduate	241.97	151	43.7
Bachelor's degree	190.73	119	22.3
Master's, professional, doctoral degree	330.94	206	21.1

Note: Market shares may not sum to 100.0 because of rounding and missing categories by household type. "Asian" and "black" include Hispanics and non-Hispanics who identify themselves as being of the respective race alone. "Hispanic" includes people of any race who identify themselves as Hispanic. "Other" includes people who identify themselves as non-Hispanic and as Alaska Native, American Indian, Asian (who are also included in the "Asian" row), Native Hawaiian or other Pacific Islander, as well as non-Hispanics reporting more than one race.
Source: Calculations by New Strategist based on the Bureau of Labor Statistics' 2007 Consumer Expenditure Survey.

Chapter 3.

Computers

Household Spending on Computers, 2007

Thirty years ago the average household spent nothing on computers. Today computers have become a central appliance in most homes and an important expenditure category. Average household spending on computer information services (Internet service) more than doubled since 2000, after adjusting for inflation. The average household spends more on computer information services than on computers themselves. In 2000, computer hardware accounted for 70 percent of the average household's computer budget, while computer information services accounted for just 23 percent. By 2007, computer hardware accounted for a smaller 40 percent of the computer budget, while Internet service accounted for a larger 52 percent.

The average household spent $373 on computer hardware, software, and information services in 2007—15 percent more than in 2000, after adjusting for inflation. Falling prices for computer equipment is one factor behind the relatively small increase in overall spending on computers during the past seven years. In fact, spending on computer hardware fell 35 percent between 2000 and 2007, after adjusting for inflation. Spending on computer software and accessories rose 1 percent, while spending on computer information services surged by 163 percent as online access became a necessity for a growing share of households. Average annual household spending on repair of computer systems more than doubled between 2000 and 2007, after adjusting for inflation.

Spending on computers

(average annual spending of households on computer hardware, software, and information services, 2000 and 2007; in 2007 dollars)

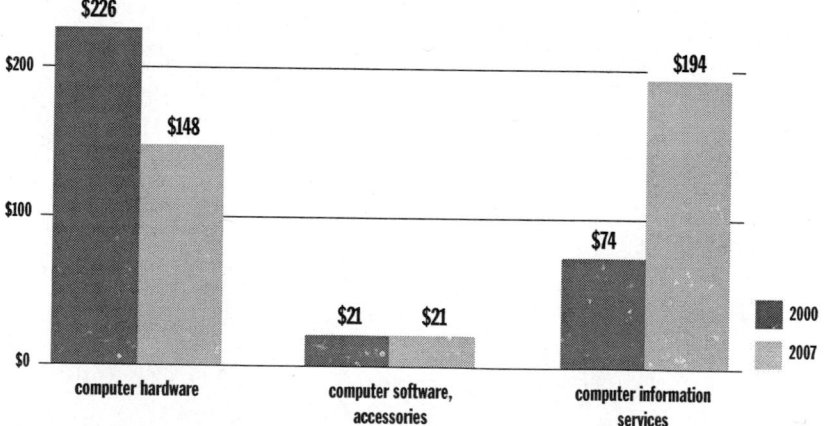

Table 3.1 Computer Spending, 2000 to 2007

(average annual household spending on information products and services, and percent distribution of spending by type, 2000 and 2007; percent change in spending, 2000–07; in 2007 dollars)

	2007		2000		
	average household spending	percent distribution	average household spending (in 2007$)	percent distribution	percent change 2000–07
Average household spending on computer equipment and services for nonbusiness use	**$372.89**	**100.0%**	**$324.41**	**100.0%**	**14.9%**
Computer information services	194.11	52.1	73.88	22.8	162.7
Computers and computer hardware	148.08	39.7	226.16	69.7	−34.5
Computer software and accessories	21.28	5.7	21.06	6.5	1.0
Repair of computer systems	6.99	1.9	3.31	1.0	111.1
Internet services away from home	2.43	0.7	–	–	–

Note: "–" means data are unavailable.
Source: Bureau of Labor Statistics, 2000 and 2007 Consumer Expenditure Surveys; calculations by New Strategist

Computer Information Services

Best customers:

Householders aged 35 to 54
Married couples with children at home
Asians
Households in the West

Customer trends:

Average household spending on computer information services will climb as broadband online access becomes the norm.

The best customers of computer information services (Internet access) are households with children. Householders aged 35 to 54 spend 20 to 21 percent more than the average household on Internet service and control 49 percent of household spending on this item. Married couples with children at home spend 40 percent more than average on Internet service. Asians spend 17 percent more than average on this item, and households in the West, where many Asians reside, 15 percent more.

Average household spending on computer information services increased by 163 percent between 2000 and 2007, after adjusting for inflation. The average household spends four times as much on computer information services as it does on newspaper and magazine subscriptions. Spending for online services will continue to grow as younger generations of wired householders replace older generations with little interest in computers or Internet access.

Table 3.2 Computer information services

Total household spending $23,326,392,810.00
Average household spends 194.11

	AVERAGE HOUSEHOLD SPENDING	BEST CUSTOMERS (index)	BIGGEST CUSTOMERS (market share)
AGE OF HOUSEHOLDER			
Average household	**$194.11**	**100**	**100.0%**
Under age 25	116.08	60	4.1
Aged 25 to 34	201.71	104	17.7
Aged 35 to 44	235.71	121	23.7
Aged 45 to 54	232.90	120	25.2
Aged 55 to 64	213.71	110	17.8
Aged 65 to 74	152.53	79	7.9
Aged 75 or older	75.13	39	3.7

	AVERAGE HOUSEHOLD SPENDING	BEST CUSTOMERS (index)	BIGGEST CUSTOMERS (market share)
HOUSEHOLD INCOME			
Average household	**$194.11**	**100**	**100.0%**
Under $20,000	70.61	36	7.5
$20,000 to $39,999	130.28	67	15.6
$40,000 to $49,999	187.23	96	9.5
$50,000 to $69,999	222.50	115	17.5
$70,000 to $79,999	265.59	137	7.9
$80,000 to $99,999	282.59	146	11.8
$100,000 or more	341.34	176	30.1
HOUSEHOLD TYPE			
Average household	**194.11**	**100**	**100.0**
Married couples	242.96	125	63.3
Married couples, no children	212.12	109	23.6
Married couples, with children	272.27	140	35.0
Oldest child under age 6	257.22	133	6.5
Oldest child aged 6 to 17	278.95	144	18.3
Oldest child aged 18 or older	270.73	139	10.3
Single parent with child under age 18	165.39	85	5.1
Single person	120.97	62	18.5
RACE AND HISPANIC ORIGIN			
Average household	**194.11**	**100**	**100.0**
Asian	226.36	117	4.1
Black	138.49	71	8.6
Hispanic	132.78	68	8.1
Non-Hispanic white and other	212.20	109	83.5
REGION			
Average household	**194.11**	**100**	**100.0**
Northeast	197.65	102	19.0
Midwest	185.72	96	21.9
South	178.72	92	33.1
West	224.12	115	26.1
EDUCATION			
Average household	**194.11**	**100**	**100.0**
Less than high school graduate	74.50	38	5.8
High school graduate	151.79	78	19.7
Some college	202.08	104	22.7
Associate's degree	225.95	116	10.3
College graduate	277.91	143	41.4
Bachelor's degree	265.64	137	25.6
Master's, professional, doctoral degree	300.46	155	15.8

Note: Market shares may not sum to 100.0 because of rounding and missing categories by household type. Asian and black include Hispanics and non-Hispanics who identify themselves as being of the respective race alone. Hispanic includes people of any race who identify themselves as Hispanic. Other includes people who identify themselves as non-Hispanic and as Alaska Native, American Indian, Asian (who are also included in the Asian row), Native Hawaiian or other Pacific Islander, as well as non-Hispanics reporting more than one race.
Source: Calculations by New Strategist based on Bureau of Labor Statistics 2006 Consumer Expenditure Survey

Computer Software and Accessories for Nonbusiness Use

Best customers: Householders aged 55 to 64
Married couples without children at home
Married couples with school-aged or older children at home
Households in the West

Customer trends: Average household spending on computer software and accessories may rebound if new applications can entice buyers.

The best customers of computer software and accessories for nonbusiness use are middle-aged householders. Householders aged 55 to 64 spend 41 percent more than the average household on computer software, many of them upgrading their computers. Married couples without children at home, most of them older empty-nesters, spend 31 percent above average on software. Couples with school-aged or older children at home spend 21 to 48 percent more. Households in the West spend 37 percent more than average on computer software.

Average household spending on computer software and accessories has remained flat since 2000. One factor that explains the lack of growth in spending is software bundling, whereby computer manufacturers include software with their hardware in an attempt to entice buyers. New, must-have software applications may reverse this trend.

Table 3.3 Computer software and accessories for nonbusiness use

Total household spending $2,557,238,880.00
Average household spends 21.28

AGE OF HOUSEHOLDER	AVERAGE HOUSEHOLD SPENDING	BEST CUSTOMERS (index)	BIGGEST CUSTOMERS (market share)
Average household	$21.28	100	100.0%
Under age 25	21.73	102	6.9
Aged 25 to 34	20.92	98	16.8
Aged 35 to 44	20.76	98	19.0
Aged 45 to 54	22.01	103	21.7
Aged 55 to 64	30.11	141	22.9
Aged 65 to 74	18.56	87	8.7
Aged 75 or older	8.82	41	3.9

	AVERAGE HOUSEHOLD SPENDING	BEST CUSTOMERS (index)	BIGGEST CUSTOMERS (market share)
HOUSEHOLD INCOME			
Average household	**$21.28**	**100**	**100.0%**
Under $20,000	8.22	39	7.9
$20,000 to $39,999	11.83	56	12.9
$40,000 to $49,999	11.78	55	5.4
$50,000 to $69,999	24.00	113	17.3
$70,000 to $79,999	23.82	112	6.5
$80,000 to $99,999	34.43	162	13.2
$100,000 or more	45.70	215	36.8
HOUSEHOLD TYPE			
Average household	**21.28**	**100**	**100.0**
Married couples	27.47	129	65.3
Married couples, no children	27.91	131	28.3
Married couples, with children	27.20	128	31.9
Oldest child under age 6	24.35	114	5.6
Oldest child aged 6 to 17	25.81	121	15.4
Oldest child aged 18 or older	31.49	148	10.9
Single parent with child under age 18	18.12	85	5.1
Single person	13.08	61	18.3
RACE AND HISPANIC ORIGIN			
Average household	**21.28**	**100**	**100.0**
Asian	18.62	88	3.1
Black	11.45	54	6.5
Hispanic	14.17	67	7.9
Non-Hispanic white and other	23.88	112	85.7
REGION			
Average household	**21.28**	**100**	**100.0**
Northeast	16.67	78	14.6
Midwest	22.71	107	24.4
South	17.81	84	30.1
West	29.14	137	31.0
EDUCATION			
Average household	**21.28**	**100**	**100.0**
Less than high school graduate	6.14	29	4.4
High school graduate	11.56	54	13.7
Some college	22.70	107	23.2
Associate's degree	31.26	147	13.1
College graduate	33.55	158	45.6
Bachelor's degree	30.32	142	26.7
Master's, professional, doctoral degree	39.49	186	18.9

Note: Market shares may not sum to 100.0 because of rounding and missing categories by household type. Asian and black include Hispanics and non-Hispanics who identify themselves as being of the respective race alone. Hispanic includes people of any race who identify themselves as Hispanic. Other includes people who identify themselves as non-Hispanic and as Alaska Native, American Indian, Asian (who are also included in the Asian row), Native Hawaiian or other Pacific Islander, as well as non-Hispanics reporting more than one race.
Source: Calculations by New Strategist based on Bureau of Labor Statistics 2006 Consumer Expenditure Survey

Computers and Computer Hardware for Nonbusiness Use

Best customers: Householders aged 25 to 54
Married couples with children at home
Asians
Households in the West

Customer trends: Average household spending on computers and computer hardware is likely to decline as prices continue to fall.

The best customers of computers and computer hardware for nonbusiness use are households with children. Householders ranging in age from 25 to 54 spend 14 to 27 percent more than the average household on computers. Married couples with children at home spend 57 percent more than the average household on this item. Asians spend 66 percent more. Households in the West, where many Asians reside, spend 35 percent more than average on computers and computer hardware for nonbusiness use.

Average household spending on computer hardware fell by 35 percent between 2000 and 2007, after adjusting for inflation. Behind the decline are falling prices and market saturation as a growing majority of households has become computer owners. These factors will continue to influence the household market for computer hardware, pointing to a continuing decline in spending on the category.

Table 3.4 **Computers and computer hardware for nonbusiness use**

Total household spending $17,794,921,680.00
Average household spends   148.08

	AVERAGE HOUSEHOLD SPENDING	BEST CUSTOMERS (index)	BIGGEST CUSTOMERS (market share)
AGE OF HOUSEHOLDER			
Average household	$148.08	100	100.0%
Under age 25	155.31	105	7.1
Aged 25 to 34	168.24	114	19.4
Aged 35 to 44	179.16	121	23.6
Aged 45 to 54	187.76	127	26.6
Aged 55 to 64	138.44	93	15.1
Aged 65 to 74	92.24	62	6.2
Aged 75 or older	30.16	20	1.9

	AVERAGE HOUSEHOLD SPENDING	BEST CUSTOMERS (index)	BIGGEST CUSTOMERS (market share)
HOUSEHOLD INCOME			
Average household	**$148.08**	**100**	**100.0%**
Under $20,000	69.30	47	9.6
$20,000 to $39,999	80.89	55	12.7
$40,000 to $49,999	107.16	72	7.1
$50,000 to $69,999	151.28	102	15.6
$70,000 to $79,999	129.93	88	5.1
$80,000 to $99,999	183.40	124	10.1
$100,000 or more	343.79	232	39.8
HOUSEHOLD TYPE			
Average household	**148.08**	**100**	**100.0**
Married couples	183.31	124	62.6
Married couples, no children	133.25	90	19.4
Married couples, with children	232.13	157	39.1
Oldest child under age 6	216.18	146	7.1
Oldest child aged 6 to 17	227.20	153	19.5
Oldest child aged 18 or older	251.19	170	12.5
Single parent with child under age 18	84.50	57	3.4
Single person	102.08	69	20.5
RACE AND HISPANIC ORIGIN			
Average household	**148.08**	**100**	**100.0**
Asian	246.12	166	5.9
Black	86.29	58	7.0
Hispanic	106.75	72	8.5
Non-Hispanic white and other	163.96	111	84.5
REGION			
Average household	**148.08**	**100**	**100.0**
Northeast	144.71	98	18.2
Midwest	147.11	99	22.7
South	117.42	79	28.5
West	200.54	135	30.6
EDUCATION			
Average household	**148.08**	**100**	**100.0**
Less than high school graduate	68.63	46	7.0
High school graduate	89.05	60	15.2
Some college	156.69	106	23.0
Associate's degree	187.73	127	11.3
College graduate	222.53	150	43.5
Bachelor's degree	214.34	145	27.1
Master's, professional, doctoral degree	237.56	160	16.4

Note: Market shares may not sum to 100.0 because of rounding and missing categories by household type. Asian and black include Hispanics and non-Hispanics who identify themselves as being of the respective race alone. Hispanic includes people of any race who identify themselves as Hispanic. Other includes people who identify themselves as non-Hispanic and as Alaska Native, American Indian, Asian (who are also included in the Asian row), Native Hawaiian or other Pacific Islander, as well as non-Hispanics reporting more than one race.
Source: Calculations by New Strategist based on Bureau of Labor Statistics 2006 Consumer Expenditure Survey

Internet Services Away from Home

Best customers: Householders aged 45 to 54
Married couples with adult children at home
Asians
Households in the West

Customer trends: Average household spending on Internet services away from home is likely to be constrained by free wifi connections offered by hotels and coffee shops.

The best customers for Internet services away from home are householders with adult children at home. Married couples with adult children at home spend 43 percent more than average on this item. Householders aged 45 to 54, many with adult children at home, spend 53 percent more than the average household on Internet services away from home. Asians spend 14 percent more than average on this item, while households in the West, where many Asians reside, spend 24 percent more.

Trend data for spending on Internet services away from home are unavailable because it is a category added to the Consumer Expenditure Survey only in 2005. Average household spending on Internet services away from home may not rise much in the years ahead as free wifi reduces the need to buy this item.

Table 3.5 Internet services away from home

Total household spending	$292,015,530.00
Average household spends	2.43

	AVERAGE HOUSEHOLD SPENDING	BEST CUSTOMERS (index)	BIGGEST CUSTOMERS (market share)
AGE OF HOUSEHOLDER			
Average household	**$2.43**	**100**	**100.0%**
Under age 25	2.00	82	5.6
Aged 25 to 34	2.63	108	18.5
Aged 35 to 44	2.57	106	20.6
Aged 45 to 54	3.73	153	32.2
Aged 55 to 64	2.15	88	14.3
Aged 65 to 74	1.60	66	6.6
Aged 75 or older	0.62	26	2.4

	AVERAGE HOUSEHOLD SPENDING	BEST CUSTOMERS (index)	BIGGEST CUSTOMERS (market share)
HOUSEHOLD INCOME			
Average household	$2.43	100	100.0%
Under $20,000	0.92	38	7.8
$20,000 to $39,999	1.99	82	19.0
$40,000 to $49,999	1.86	77	7.5
$50,000 to $69,999	3.23	133	20.3
$70,000 to $79,999	3.56	147	8.5
$80,000 to $99,999	3.35	138	11.2
$100,000 or more	3.65	150	25.7
HOUSEHOLD TYPE			
Average household	2.43	100	100.0
Married couples	2.44	100	50.8
Married couples, no children	2.43	100	21.6
Married couples, with children	2.37	98	24.3
Oldest child under age 6	1.94	80	3.9
Oldest child aged 6 to 17	1.89	78	9.9
Oldest child aged 18 or older	3.48	143	10.6
Single parent with child under age 18	2.16	89	5.3
Single person	1.87	77	22.9
RACE AND HISPANIC ORIGIN			
Average household	2.43	100	100.0
Asian	2.77	114	4.0
Black	1.82	75	9.0
Hispanic	1.97	81	9.6
Non-Hispanic white and other	2.60	107	81.7
REGION			
Average household	2.43	100	100.0
Northeast	2.19	90	16.8
Midwest	2.04	84	19.2
South	2.44	100	36.1
West	3.02	124	28.1
EDUCATION			
Average household	2.43	100	100.0
Less than high school graduate	1.05	43	6.6
High school graduate	2.06	85	21.4
Some college	2.30	95	20.6
Associate's degree	3.14	129	11.5
College graduate	3.37	139	40.1
Bachelor's degree	2.88	119	22.2
Master's, professional, doctoral degree	4.26	175	17.9

Note: Market shares may not sum to 100.0 because of rounding and missing categories by household type. Asian and black include Hispanics and non-Hispanics who identify themselves as being of the respective race alone. Hispanic includes people of any race who identify themselves as Hispanic. Other includes people who identify themselves as non-Hispanic and as Alaska Native, American Indian, Asian (who are also included in the Asian row), Native Hawaiian or other Pacific Islander, as well as non-Hispanics reporting more than one race.
Source: Calculations by New Strategist based on Bureau of Labor Statistics 2006 Consumer Expenditure Survey

Repair of Computer Systems for Nonbusiness Use

Best customers: **Householders aged 45 to 54 and 65 to 74**
Married couples with school-aged or older children at home
People living alone

Customer trends: **Average household spending on computer repair is likely to continue to grow as boomers age and the economic downturn encourages repair rather than replacement.**

The best customers of repair of computer systems for nonbusiness use are older householders and households that include school-aged or older children. Householders aged 45 to 54 spend 37 percent more than the average household on computer repairs, while those aged 65 to 74 spend 29 percent above average. Married couples with school-aged or older children at home spend 16 to 64 percent more than the average household on this item.

Average household spending on repair of computer systems for nonbusiness use grew by an enormous 111 percent between 2000 and 2007, after adjusting for inflation. With computers becoming the norm in most households, many people—particularly older adults—need help setting up and maintaining their systems. Average household spending on computer repair is likely to continue to grow as boomers age and the economic downturn encourages repair rather than replacement.

Table 3.6 Repair of computer systems for nonbusiness use

Total household spending $839,995,290.00
Average household spends   6.99

	AVERAGE HOUSEHOLD SPENDING	BEST CUSTOMERS (index)	BIGGEST CUSTOMERS (market share)
AGE OF HOUSEHOLDER			
Average household	**$6.99**	**100**	**100.0%**
Under age 25	7.92	113	7.7
Aged 25 to 34	4.27	61	10.4
Aged 35 to 44	7.64	109	21.3
Aged 45 to 54	9.59	137	28.8
Aged 55 to 64	4.23	61	9.8
Aged 65 to 74	9.00	129	12.9
Aged 75 or older	6.73	96	9.1

	AVERAGE HOUSEHOLD SPENDING	BEST CUSTOMERS (index)	BIGGEST CUSTOMERS (market share)
HOUSEHOLD INCOME			
Average household	**$6.99**	**100**	**100.0%**
Under $20,000	6.35	91	18.7
$20,000 to $39,999	4.86	70	16.2
$40,000 to $49,999	10.67	153	15.0
$50,000 to $69,999	5.32	76	11.6
$70,000 to $79,999	8.28	118	6.9
$80,000 to $99,999	4.89	70	5.7
$100,000 or more	12.25	175	30.0
HOUSEHOLD TYPE			
Average household	**6.99**	**100**	**100.0**
Married couples	7.33	105	53.0
Married couples, no children	6.24	89	19.3
Married couples, with children	8.89	127	31.7
Oldest child under age 6	6.98	100	4.9
Oldest child aged 6 to 17	8 14	116	14.8
Oldest child aged 18 or older	11.44	164	12.1
Single parent with child under age 18	2.22	32	1.9
Single person	8.84	126	37.6
RACE AND HISPANIC ORIGIN			
Average household	**6.99**	**100**	**100.0**
Asian	2.83	40	1.4
Black	3.19	46	5.5
Hispanic	4.22	60	7.1
Non-Hispanic white and other	8.00	114	87.4
REGION			
Average household	**6.99**	**100**	**100.0**
Northeast	6.26	90	16.7
Midwest	6.09	87	19.9
South	6.98	100	35.9
West	8.52	122	27.6
EDUCATION			
Average household	**6.99**	**100**	**100.0**
Less than high school graduate	1.28	18	2.8
High school graduate	3.05	44	11.0
Some college	7.08	101	22.1
Associate's degree	9.33	133	11.9
College graduate	12.63	181	52.3
Bachelor's degree	11.30	162	30.3
Master's, professional, doctoral degree	15.07	216	22.0

Note: Market shares may not sum to 100.0 because of rounding and missing categories by household type. Asian and black include Hispanics and non-Hispanics who identify themselves as being of the respective race alone. Hispanic includes people of any race who identify themselves as Hispanic. Other includes people who identify themselves as non-Hispanic and as Alaska Native, American Indian, Asian (who are also included in the Asian row), Native Hawaiian or other Pacific Islander, as well as non-Hispanics reporting more than one race.
Source: Calculations by New Strategist based on Bureau of Labor Statistics 2006 Consumer Expenditure Survey

Chapter 4.

Education

Household Spending on Education, 2007

Because few households have educational expenses in a given year, average spending on education is relatively low. In 2007, the average household spent $945 on education, including $585 spent on college tuition. With public colleges costing thousands of dollars a year, and private colleges costing tens of thousands, this figure is artificially low because few households have education expenses. A more realistic spending figure for college tuition can be found in Appendix B, which shows the spending of purchasers only. During the average quarter of 2007, just 5 percent of households spent on college tuition, and those who did spent $2,943.66 per quarter. Between 2000 and 2007, average household spending on college tuition increased by 34 percent, after adjusting for inflation.

More important than average spending figures are the patterns of spending by demographic characteristic. Householders under age 25 and those aged 45 to 54 are the biggest spenders on college tuition. The younger householders are paying for their own college education, while the older ones are paying for their children's education. Because of volatility in the financial markets and tighter lending standards, average household spending on education may stabilize or even decline in the years ahead.

Spending on college tuition

(average household spending on college tuition, 2000 and 2007; in 2007 dollars)

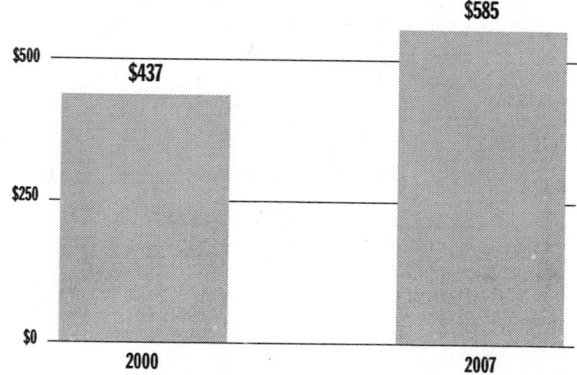

Table 4.1 Education Spending, 2000 to 2007

(average annual household spending on education, and percent distribution of spending by type, 2000 and 2007; percent change in spending, 2000–07; in 2007 dollars; ranked by amount spent)

	2007		2000		
	average household spending	percent distribution	average household spending (in 2007$)	percent distribution	percent change 2000–07
Average annual household spending on education	**$945.29**	**100.0%**	**760.89**	**100.0%**	**24.2%**
Tuition, college	585.20	61.9	437.43	57.5	33.8
Tuition, elementary and high school	153.18	16.2	122.12	16.0	25.4
Books and supplies, college	61.94	6.6	63.41	8.3	-2.3
Miscellaneous school expenses and supplies	47.01	5.0	59.16	7.8	-20.5
Other school expenses incl. rentals	42.83	4.5	28.90	3.8	48.2
Tuition, other schools	20.13	2.1	29.40	3.9	*
Books and supplies, elementary and high school	16.16	1.7	16.76	2.2	-3.6
Tuition, vocational, technical schools	15.42	1.6	–	–	–
Books and supplies, other schools	2.46	0.3	–	–	–
Books and supplies, vocational and technical schools	0.56	0.1	–	–	–
Books and supplies, day care and nursery	0.41	0.0	3.72	0.5	*

* Spending amounts for 2000 and 2007 are not comparable because of changes in methodology.
Note: "–" means data are unavailable.
Source: Bureau of Labor Statistics, 2000 and 2007 Consumer Expenditure Surveys; calculations by New Strategist

Books and Supplies, College

Best customers: Householders under age 25 and aged 45 to 54
Married couples with adult children at home
Asians

Customer trends: Average household spending on college books and supplies will continue to decline
as college students search for less-expensive alternatives such as renting or
downloading texts.

Not surprisingly, college students are the best customers of college books and supplies. Householders under age 25 spend almost four times the average on this item and account for 26 percent of the market. Married couples with children aged 18 or older at home spend over three times the average on college books and supplies. Asian households spend 46 percent more than average on this item.

Average household spending on college books and supplies fell 2 percent between 2000 and 2007, after adjusting for inflation. Behind the small drop in spending on this item is the attempt by students and parents to cut costs as tuition soars. The decline in spending on books and supplies may accelerate in the future as students search for less-expensive books via the Internet.

Table 4.2 Books and supplies, college

Total household spending $7,443,391,740.00
Average household spends   61.94

	AVERAGE HOUSEHOLD SPENDING	BEST CUSTOMERS (index)	BIGGEST CUSTOMERS (market share)
AGE OF HOUSEHOLDER			
Average household	**$61.94**	**100**	**100.0%**
Under age 25	235.58	380	25.8
Aged 25 to 34	48.91	79	13.5
Aged 35 to 44	38.14	62	12.0
Aged 45 to 54	106.20	171	36.0
Aged 55 to 64	38.41	62	10.0
Aged 65 to 74	13.46	22	2.2
Aged 75 or older	3.31	5	0.5

	AVERAGE HOUSEHOLD SPENDING	BEST CUSTOMERS (index)	BIGGEST CUSTOMERS (market share)
HOUSEHOLD INCOME			
Average household	**$61.94**	**100**	**100.0%**
Under $20,000	63.82	103	21.2
$20,000 to $39,999	32.24	52	12.1
$40,000 to $49,999	38.98	63	6.2
$50,000 to $69,999	54.90	89	13.6
$70,000 to $79,999	61.50	99	5.7
$80,000 to $99,999	81.24	131	10.7
$100,000 or more	110.43	178	30.5
HOUSEHOLD TYPE			
Average household	**61.94**	**100**	**100.0**
Married couples	61.69	100	50.3
Married couples, no children	44.15	71	15.4
Married couples, with children	78.80	127	31.7
Oldest child under age 6	33.08	53	2.6
Oldest child aged 6 to 17	30.06	49	6.2
Oldest child aged 18 or older	193.13	312	23.0
Single parent with child under age 18	36.89	60	3.5
Single person	56.50	91	27.1
RACE AND HISPANIC ORIGIN			
Average household	**61.94**	**100**	**100.0**
Asian	90.51	146	5.2
Black	48.24	78	9.3
Hispanic	28.70	46	5.5
Non-Hispanic white and other	69.21	112	85.3
REGION			
Average household	**61.94**	**100**	**100.0**
Northeast	63.49	103	19.1
Midwest	83.99	136	31.0
South	52.05	84	30.2
West	54.09	87	19.7
EDUCATION			
Average household	**61.94**	**100**	**100.0**
Less than high school graduate	10.48	17	2.6
High school graduate	26.89	43	11.0
Some college	103.45	167	36.4
Associate's degree	65.23	105	9.4
College graduate	87.21	141	40.8
Bachelor's degree	97.42	157	29.5
Master's, professional, doctoral degree	68.46	111	11.3

Note: Market shares may not sum to 100.0 because of rounding and missing categories by household type. "Asian" and "black" include Hispanics and non-Hispanics who identify themselves as being of the respective race alone. "Hispanic" includes people of any race who identify themselves as Hispanic. "Other" includes people who identify themselves as non-Hispanic and as Alaska Native, American Indian, Asian (who are also included in the "Asian" row), Native Hawaiian or other Pacific Islander, as well as non-Hispanics reporting more than one race.
Source: Calculations by New Strategist based on the Bureau of Labor Statistics' 2007 Consumer Expenditure Survey.

Books and Supplies, Elementary and High School

Best customers:

Householders aged 35 to 54
Married couples with school-aged or older children at home
Single parents
Asians and Hispanics

Customer trends:

Average household spending on books and supplies for elementary and high schools will continue to decline as alternatives to high-priced textbooks become more widely available.

The best customers of books and supplies for elementary and high school are parents with school-aged children. Married couples with children aged 6 to 17 spend four times the average on this item. Single parents spend two-and-one-half times the average on books and supplies for elementary and high school. Together these groups control almost two-thirds of the market. Householders aged 35 to 44 spend over twice the average on this item because many have school-aged children at home. Those aged 45 to 54 spend 37 percent more than average. Asians and Hispanics spend, respectively, 32 and 29 percent more than average on elementary and high school books and supplies.

Average household spending on books and supplies for elementary and high school declined by 4 percent between 2000 and 2007, after adjusting for inflation. Spending on this item will continue to decline as alternatives to high-priced textbooks become more widely available.

Table 4.3 Books and supplies, elementary and high school

Total household spending: $1,941,963,360.00
Average household spends: 16.16

AGE OF HOUSEHOLDER	AVERAGE HOUSEHOLD SPENDING	BEST CUSTOMERS (index)	BIGGEST CUSTOMERS (market share)
Average household	$16.16	100	100.0%
Under age 25	5.92	37	2.5
Aged 25 to 34	13.19	82	13.9
Aged 35 to 44	38.44	238	46.4
Aged 45 to 54	22.13	137	28.8
Aged 55 to 64	6.38	39	6.4
Aged 65 to 74	2.22	14	1.4
Aged 75 or older	1.15	7	0.7

	AVERAGE HOUSEHOLD SPENDING	BEST CUSTOMERS (index)	BIGGEST CUSTOMERS (market share)
HOUSEHOLD INCOME			
Average household	$16.16	100	100.0%
Under $20,000	5.59	35	7.1
$20,000 to $39,999	10.47	65	15.1
$40,000 to $49,999	13.89	86	8.5
$50,000 to $69,999	15.36	95	14.5
$70,000 to $79,999	16.24	100	5.8
$80,000 to $99,999	29.12	180	14.7
$100,000 or more	32.37	200	34.3
HOUSEHOLD TYPE			
Average household	16.16	100	100.0
Married couples	23.40	145	73.2
Married couples, no children	1.89	12	2.5
Married couples, with children	41.41	256	63.9
Oldest child under age 6	3.96	25	1.2
Oldest child aged 6 to 17	64.78	401	50.9
Oldest child aged 18 or older	25.93	160	11.8
Single parent with child under age 18	40.71	252	15.0
Single person	2.77	17	5.1
RACE AND HISPANIC ORIGIN			
Average household	16.16	100	100.0
Asian	21.39	132	4.7
Black	10.14	63	7.5
Hispanic	20.87	129	15.2
Non-Hispanic white and other	16.36	101	77.3
REGION			
Average household	16.16	100	100.0
Northeast	10.00	62	11.5
Midwest	16.69	103	23.6
South	17.78	110	39.5
West	18.10	112	25.3
EDUCATION			
Average household	16.16	100	100.0
Less than high school graduate	11.15	69	10.5
High school graduate	10.50	65	16.4
Some college	16.17	100	21.8
Associate's degree	23.93	148	13.2
College graduate	21.30	132	38.2
Bachelor's degree	22.28	138	25.8
Master's, professional, doctoral degree	19.51	121	12.3

Note: Market shares may not sum to 100.0 because of rounding and missing categories by household type. "Asian" and "black" include Hispanics and non-Hispanics who identify themselves as being of the respective race alone. "Hispanic" includes people of any race who identify themselves as Hispanic. "Other" includes people who identify themselves as non-Hispanic and as Alaska Native, American Indian, Asian (who are also included in the "Asian" row), Native Hawaiian or other Pacific Islander, as well as non-Hispanics reporting more than one race.
Source: Calculations by New Strategist based on the Bureau of Labor Statistics' 2007 Consumer Expenditure Survey.

Tuition, College

Best customers: Householders under age 25 and aged 45 to 54
                               Married couples with adult children at home
                               Asians

Customer trends: Average household spending on college tuition may stabilize or even decline in the
                               years ahead as the nation's economic problems crimp the college market.

The biggest spenders on college tuition are, not surprisingly, young adults attending college and the parents paying for those expenses. This explains why householders under age 25 spend two-and-one-half times the average on college tuition, while householders aged 45 to 54 spend 74 percent more than average. Married couples with children aged 18 or older at home spend three times the average on college tuition since many have children in school. Asian households spend 74 percent more than average on college tuition.

Average household spending on college tuition rose 34 percent between 2000 and 2007, after adjusting for inflation. Behind the increase was the growing proportion of households with children in college as boomers sent their children to school. Also behind the increase is the rapid rise in the cost of college. Average household spending on college tuition may stabilize or even decline in the years ahead as the nation's economic problems make college unaffordable for a growing share of families.

Table 4.4 **Tuition, college**

Total household spending $70,324,069,200.00
Average household spends   585.20

AGE OF HOUSEHOLDER	AVERAGE HOUSEHOLD SPENDING	BEST CUSTOMERS (index)	BIGGEST CUSTOMERS (market share)
Average household	$585.20	100	100.0%
Under age 25	1,449.61	248	16.8
Aged 25 to 34	423.13	72	12.3
Aged 35 to 44	269.71	46	9.0
Aged 45 to 54	1,020.61	174	36.6
Aged 55 to 64	726.31	124	20.1
Aged 65 to 74	133.60	23	2.3
Aged 75 or older	176.95	30	2.9

	AVERAGE HOUSEHOLD SPENDING	BEST CUSTOMERS (index)	BIGGEST CUSTOMERS (market share)
HOUSEHOLD INCOME			
Average household	**$585.20**	**100**	**100.0%**
Under $20,000	487.82	83	17.1
$20,000 to $39,999	211.63	36	8.4
$40,000 to $49,999	321.03	55	5.4
$50,000 to $69,999	352.19	60	9.2
$70,000 to $79,999	503.90	86	5.0
$80,000 to $99,999	513.80	88	7.1
$100,000 or more	1,630.06	279	47.7
HOUSEHOLD TYPE			
Average household	**585.20**	**100**	**100.0**
Married couples	724.00	124	62.5
Married couples, no children	707.63	121	26.1
Married couples, with children	785.57	134	33.5
Oldest child under age 6	240.69	41	2.0
Oldest child aged 6 to 17	404.83	69	8.8
Oldest child aged 18 or older	1,802.99	308	22.7
Single parent with child under age 18	411.74	70	4.2
Single person	480.09	82	24.4
RACE AND HISPANIC ORIGIN			
Average household	**585.20**	**100**	**100.0**
Asian	1,019.20	174	6.1
Black	433.58	74	8.9
Hispanic	188.20	32	3.8
Non-Hispanic white and other	669.34	114	87.3
REGION			
Average household	**585.20**	**100**	**100.0**
Northeast	696.00	119	22.2
Midwest	842.46	144	32.9
South	441.04	75	27.1
West	462.88	79	17.9
EDUCATION			
Average household	**585.20**	**100**	**100.0**
Less than high school graduate	79.33	14	2.1
High school graduate	223.55	38	9.6
Some college	736.34	126	27.4
Associate's degree	423.84	72	6.4
College graduate	1,101.28	188	54.5
Bachelor's degree	973.80	166	31.2
Master's, professional, doctoral degree	1,335.50	228	23.3

Note: Market shares may not sum to 100.0 because of rounding and missing categories by household type. "Asian" and "black" include Hispanics and non-Hispanics who identify themselves as being of the respective race alone. "Hispanic" includes people of any race who identify themselves as Hispanic. "Other" includes people who identify themselves as non-Hispanic and as Alaska Native, American Indian, Asian (who are also included in the "Asian" row), Native Hawaiian or other Pacific Islander, as well as non-Hispanics reporting more than one race.
Source: Calculations by New Strategist based on the Bureau of Labor Statistics' 2007 Consumer Expenditure Survey.

Tuition, Elementary and High School

Best customers:
Householders aged 35 to 54
High-income households
Married couples with school-aged children
Asians
Households in the Northeast
College graduates

Customer trends:
Average household spending on elementary and high school tuition may stabilize or even decline as the nation's economic problems make private school unaffordable for a growing share of families.

The biggest spenders on elementary and high school tuition are affluent parents with school-aged children. Householders aged 35 to 54 spend just about twice the average on private school tuition because many are parents. Married couples with school-aged children spend five times the average on this item. Households with incomes of $100,000 or more spend more than four times the average on elementary and high school tuition. Asians spend over twice as much as the average household on elementary and high school tuition. College graduates, who rank among the most affluent householders, spend two-and-one-half times the average on this item.

Average household spending on private school tuition rose 25 percent between 2000 and 2007, after adjusting for inflation. Behind the increase was the burgeoning number of parents searching for alternatives to public school. Also behind the increase is the rapid rise in private school tuition. Average household spending on elementary and high school tuition may stabilize or even decline as the nation's economic problems make private school unaffordable for a growing share of families.

Table 4.5 Tuition, elementary and high school

Total household spending $18,407,793,780.00
Average household spends 153.18

AGE OF HOUSEHOLDER	AVERAGE HOUSEHOLD SPENDING	BEST CUSTOMERS (index)	BIGGEST CUSTOMERS (market share)
Average household	$153.18	100	100.0%
Under age 25	10.69	7	0.5
Aged 25 to 34	40.48	26	4.5
Aged 35 to 44	302.43	197	38.5
Aged 45 to 54	296.66	194	40.7
Aged 55 to 64	57.53	38	6.1
Aged 65 to 74	33.71	22	2.2
Aged 75 or older	122.60	80	7.6

	AVERAGE HOUSEHOLD SPENDING	BEST CUSTOMERS (index)	BIGGEST CUSTOMERS (market share)
HOUSEHOLD INCOME			
Average household	**$153.18**	**100**	**100.0%**
Under $20,000	8.68	6	1.2
$20,000 to $39,999	24.26	16	3.7
$40,000 to $49,999	33.37	22	2.1
$50,000 to $69,999	84.58	55	8.4
$70,000 to $79,999	98.85	65	3.7
$80,000 to $99,999	195.51	128	10.4
$100,000 or more	632.13	413	70.7
HOUSEHOLD TYPE			
Average household	**153.18**	**100**	**100.0**
Married couples	265.00	173	87.5
Married couples, no children	10.63	7	1.5
Married couples, with children	477.53	312	77.8
Oldest child under age 6	71.61	47	2.3
Oldest child aged 6 to 17	769.85	503	63.8
Oldest child aged 18 or older	242.42	158	11.7
Single parent with child under age 18	126.45	83	4.9
Single person	16.39	11	3.2
RACE AND HISPANIC ORIGIN			
Average household	**153.18**	**100**	**100.0**
Asian	334.72	219	7.7
Black	129.01	84	10.1
Hispanic	106.25	69	8.2
Non-Hispanic white and other	165.07	108	82.3
REGION			
Average household	**153.18**	**100**	**100.0**
Northeast	262.34	171	31.9
Midwest	113.17	74	16.9
South	113.97	74	26.7
West	165.99	108	24.5
EDUCATION			
Average household	**153.18**	**100**	**100.0**
Less than high school graduate	11.56	8	1.1
High school graduate	46.23	30	7.6
Some college	80.72	53	11.5
Associate's degree	97.60	64	5.7
College graduate	392.19	256	74.1
Bachelor's degree	308.35	201	37.7
Master's, professional, doctoral degree	546.23	357	36.4

Note: Market shares may not sum to 100.0 because of rounding and missing categories by household type. "Asian" and "black" include Hispanics and non-Hispanics who identify themselves as being of the respective race alone. "Hispanic" includes people of any race who identify themselves as Hispanic. "Other" includes people who identify themselves as non-Hispanic and as Alaska Native, American Indian, Asian (who are also included in the "Asian" row), Native Hawaiian or other Pacific Islander, as well as non-Hispanics reporting more than one race.
Source: Calculations by New Strategist based on the Bureau of Labor Statistics' 2007 Consumer Expenditure Survey.

Tuition, Vocational and Technical Schools

Best customers: **Householders under age 25 and aged 45 to 54**
                             High-income households
                             Married couples with adult children at home

Customer trends: **Average household spending on vocational and technical school tuition may rise in the years ahead as parents search for lower-cost alternatives to college.**

The biggest spenders on vocational and technical school tuition are householders under age 25 and affluent parents with adult children at home. Householders under age 25 spend twice the average on vocational and technical school tuition, while those aged 45 to 54 spend over three times the average on tuition because many are parents. Married couples with adult children at home spend more than eight times the average on this item. Households with incomes of $100,000 or more spend three-and-one-half times the average on vocational and technical school tuition.

Spending on vocational and technical schools tuition became part of the Consumer Expenditure Survey only in 2007, and data from earlier years are nonexistent. Average annual household spending on vocational and technical school tuition may rise in the years ahead as a burgeoning number of parents search for lower-cost alternatives to college.

Table 4.6 **Tuition, vocational and technical schools**

Total household spending $1,853,036,820.00
Average household spends   15.42

	AVERAGE HOUSEHOLD SPENDING	BEST CUSTOMERS (index)	BIGGEST CUSTOMERS (market share)
AGE OF HOUSEHOLDER			
Average household	**$15.42**	**100**	**100.0%**
Under age 25	31.22	202	13.7
Aged 25 to 34	3.26	21	3.6
Aged 35 to 44	5.80	38	7.3
Aged 45 to 54	47.66	309	64.9
Aged 55 to 64	6.67	43	7.0
Aged 65 to 74	–	–	–
Aged 75 or older	5.47	35	3.4

	AVERAGE HOUSEHOLD SPENDING	BEST CUSTOMERS (index)	BIGGEST CUSTOMERS (market share)
HOUSEHOLD INCOME			
Average household	**$15.42**	**100**	**100.0%**
Under $20,000	10.02	65	13.4
$20,000 to $39,999	3.22	21	4.9
$40,000 to $49,999	0.63	4	0.4
$50,000 to $69,999	8.82	57	8.8
$70,000 to $79,999	18.98	123	7.1
$80,000 to $99,999	9.17	59	4.8
$100,000 or more	54.58	354	60.6
HOUSEHOLD TYPE			
Average household	**15.42**	**100**	**100.0**
Married couples	19.41	126	63.6
Married couples, no children	0.93	6	1.3
Married couples, with children	37.85	245	61.2
Oldest child under age 6	–	–	–
Oldest child aged 6 to 17	2.67	17	2.2
Oldest child aged 18 or older	123.57	801	59.0
Single parent with child under age 18	18.08	117	7.0
Single person	9.40	61	18.1
RACE AND HISPANIC ORIGIN			
Average household	**15.42**	**100**	**100.0**
Asian	3.61	23	0.8
Black	1.83	12	1.4
Hispanic	3.61	23	2.8
Non-Hispanic white and other	19.35	125	95.8
REGION			
Average household	**15.42**	**100**	**100.0**
Northeast	3.40	22	4.1
Midwest	36.51	237	54.1
South	10.88	71	25.3
West	11.20	73	16.4
EDUCATION			
Average household	**15.42**	**100**	**100.0**
Less than high school graduate	1.38	9	1.4
High school graduate	33.65	218	55.0
Some college	11.18	73	15.8
Associate's degree	15.52	101	8.9
College graduate	10.04	65	18.8
Bachelor's degree	12.27	80	14.9
Master's, professional, doctoral degree	5.94	39	3.9

Note: Market shares may not sum to 100.0 because of rounding and missing categories by household type. "Asian" and "black" include Hispanics and non-Hispanics who identify themselves as being of the respective race alone. "Hispanic" includes people of any race who identify themselves as Hispanic. "Other" includes people who identify themselves as non-Hispanic and as Alaska Native, American Indian, Asian (who are also included in the "Asian" row), Native Hawaiian or other Pacific Islander, as well as non-Hispanics reporting more than one race. Source: Calculations by New Strategist based on the Bureau of Labor Statistics' 2007 Consumer Expenditure Survey.

Chapter 5.

Entertainment

Household Spending on Entertainment, 2007

Average household spending on entertainment climbed 20 percent between 2000 and 2007, rising from $2,244 to $2,698 after adjusting for inflation. The 44 percent increase in spending on cable television and the more than doubling of spending on (high-definition) television sets account for most of the increase in entertainment spending.

While overall entertainment spending rose during the past seven years, many entertainment categories saw declines in spending, some precipitous. Categories with the largest percentage losses in spending were film (down 82 percent); musical instruments and accessories (down 61 percent); photo processing (down 58 percent); video cassette recorders and video disc players (down 48 percent); compact discs, records, and audio tapes (down 42 percent); sound components, equipment, and accessories (down 42 percent); rental of video cassettes, tapes, discs, films (down 38 percent); and toys, games, hobbies, and tricycles (down 18 percent). Household penny pinching is behind some of these declines, but changing technologies are an obvious factor. While, for example, digital cameras have reduced spending on film and photo processing, average household spending on photographic equipment (i.e., said cameras) rose 32 percent between 2000 and 2007.

Average household spending on entertainment has been rising for more than a decade, but behind the increase are big gains in just a few categories. This is a troubling trend for the entertainment industry, which has become such an important part of the U.S. economy.

Spending on entertainment

(average annual spending of households on entertainment 2000 and 2007; in 2007 dollars)

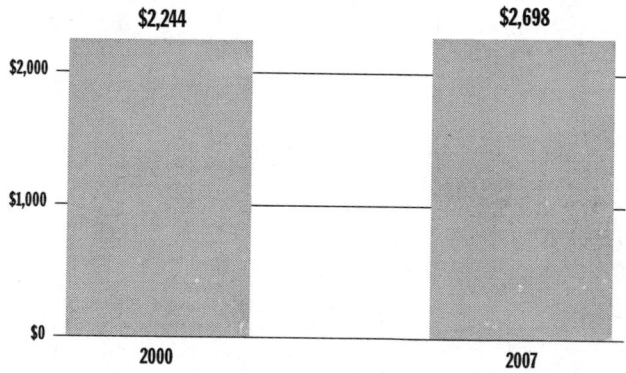

Table 5.1 Entertainment Spending, 2000 to 2007

(average annual household spending on entertainment, and percent distribution of spending by type, 2000 and 2007; percent change in spending, 2000–07; in 2007 dollars; ranked by amount spent)

	2007		2000		
	average household spending	percent distribution	average household spending (in 2007$)	percent distribution	percent change 2000–07
Average household spending on entertainment	**$2,697.99**	**100.0%**	**$2,243.80**	**100.0%**	**20.2%**
Cable and satellite television services	555.13	20.6	386.73	17.2	43.5
Television sets	162.24	6.0	78.64	3.5	106.3
Movie, theater, amusement park, and other admissions (including on trips)	159.35	5.9	161.47	7.2	–1.3
Fees for participant sports (including on trips)	148.90	5.5	128.28	5.7	16.1
Motorized recreational vehicles	147.76	5.5	98.69	4.4	49.7
Pet food	146.88	5.4	103.51	4.6	41.9
Pet purchase, supplies, medicines	139.06	5.2	45.88	2.0	203.1
Club memberships (civic, recreational, and social)	123.48	4.6	118.22	5.3	4.5
Toys, games, hobbies, and tricycles	119.93	4.4	145.65	6.5	–17.7
Veterinary services	113.18	4.2	79.47	3.5	42.4
Fees for recreational lessons	105.56	3.9	89.99	4.0	17.3
Athletic gear, game tables, exercise equipment	65.55	2.4	70.61	3.1	–7.2
Admission to sports events (including on trips)	65.02	2.4	60.58	2.7	7.3
Video game hardware and software	63.10	2.3	22.54	1.0	179.9
Video cassettes, tapes, and discs	38.32	1.4	25.04	1.1	53.0
Photographic equipment	32.24	1.2	24.33	1.1	32.5
Pet services	31.68	1.2	23.31	1.0	35.9
Rental of video cassettes, tapes, discs, films	30.87	1.1	50.04	2.2	–38.3
Sound components, equipment, and accessories	29.54	1.1	51.11	2.3	–42.2
Compact discs, records, audio tapes	27.39	1.0	47.51	2.1	–42.4
Photographer's fees	25.13	0.9	24.29	1.1	3.5
Personal digital audio players	17.39	0.6	–	–	–
Bicycles	16.72	0.6	14.12	0.6	18.4
Photo processing	15.98	0.6	37.84	1.7	–57.8
Musical instruments and accessories	14.99	0.6	38.17	1.7	–60.7
Video cassette recorders and video disc players	14.83	0.5	28.66	1.3	–48.3
Satellite radio service	12.01	0.4	–	–	–
Rental of party supplies for catered affairs	9.36	0.3	–	–	–
Live entertainment for catered affairs	9.18	0.3	–	–	–
Film	4.69	0.2	25.77	1.1	–81.8
Stamp and coin collecting	4.02	0.1	–	–	–
Streamed and downloaded audio	3.68	0.1	–	–	–
Streamed and downloaded video	1.03	0.0	–	–	–
Installation of televisions	0.98	0.0	–	–	–

Note: Numbers do not add to total because not all categories are shown. "–" means data are not available.
Source: Bureau of Labor Statistics, 2000 and 2007 Consumer Expenditure Surveys; calculations by New Strategist

Admission to Sports Events (Including on Trips)

Best customers: **Householders aged 35 to 44**
                             High-income households
                             Married couples with children at home
                             Non-Hispanic whites

Customer trends: **Average household spending on admissions to sports events may slide as house
                             holds tighten their belts and high-definition television substitutes for the real thing.**

The best customers of sports events are affluent married couples with children at home. Households with school-aged children spend 93 percent more than the average on this item, while those with younger children and those with adult children at home spend, respectively, 81 and 54 percent more than average. Householders aged 35 to 44 spend 60 percent more than average on admissions to sports events because many are parents. Households with incomes of $100,000 or more spend more than three times the average on admissions to sports events and account for 60 percent the market. Non-Hispanic whites far outspend other racial and ethnic groups.

Average household spending on admissions to sports events grew 7 percent between 2000 and 2007, after adjusting for inflation. Spending on sports events may fall in the years ahead as households tighten their belts and high-definition television substitutes for the real thing.

Table 5.2 Admission to sports events (including on trips)

| Total household spending | $7,813,518,420.00 |
| Average household spends | 65.02 |

AGE OF HOUSEHOLDER	AVERAGE HOUSEHOLD SPENDING	BEST CUSTOMERS (index)	BIGGEST CUSTOMERS (market share)
Average household	$65.02	100	100.0%
Under age 25	33.69	52	3.5
Aged 25 to 34	57.00	88	15.0
Aged 35 to 44	103.85	160	31.1
Aged 45 to 54	76.43	118	24.7
Aged 55 to 64	58.65	90	14.6
Aged 65 to 74	49.52	76	7.6
Aged 75 or older	23.98	37	3.5

	AVERAGE HOUSEHOLD SPENDING	BEST CUSTOMERS (index)	BIGGEST CUSTOMERS (market share)
HOUSEHOLD INCOME			
Average household	**$65.02**	**100**	**100.0%**
Under $20,000	16.49	25	5.2
$20,000 to $39,999	18.99	29	6.8
$40,000 to $49,999	32.64	50	4.9
$50,000 to $69,999	44.63	69	10.5
$70,000 to $79,999	48.31	74	4.3
$80,000 to $99,999	71.58	110	9.0
$100,000 or more	225.02	346	59.3
HOUSEHOLD TYPE			
Average household	**65.02**	**100**	**100.0**
Married couples	95.02	146	73.9
Married couples, no children	72.26	111	24.0
Married couples, with children	116.65	179	44.8
Oldest child under age 6	117.55	181	8.8
Oldest child aged 6 to 17	125.71	193	24.6
Oldest child aged 18 or older	100.42	154	11.4
Single parent with child under age 18	30.71	47	2.8
Single person	31.61	49	14.5
RACE AND HISPANIC ORIGIN			
Average household	**65.02**	**100**	**100.0**
Asian	48.23	74	2.6
Black	19.88	31	3.7
Hispanic	29.35	45	5.3
Non-Hispanic white and other	77.56	119	91.1
REGION			
Average household	**65.02**	**100**	**100.0**
Northeast	67.52	104	19.3
Midwest	68.21	105	24.0
South	63.08	97	34.8
West	62.83	97	21.9
EDUCATION			
Average household	**65.02**	**100**	**100.0**
Less than high school graduate	13.92	21	3.2
High school graduate	28.41	44	11.0
Some college	56.09	86	18.8
Associate's degree	71.41	110	9.8
College graduate	128.46	198	57.2
Bachelor's degree	117.20	180	33.8
Master's, professional, doctoral degree	149.15	229	23.4

Note: Market shares may not sum to 100.0 because of rounding and missing categories by household type. "Asian" and "black" include Hispanics and non-Hispanics who identify themselves as being of the respective race alone. "Hispanic" includes people of any race who identify themselves as Hispanic. "Other" includes people who identify themselves as non-Hispanic and as Alaska Native, American Indian, Asian (who are also included in the "Asian" row), Native Hawaiian or other Pacific Islander, as well as non-Hispanics reporting more than one race.
Source: Calculations by New Strategist based on the Bureau of Labor Statistics' 2007 Consumer Expenditure Survey.

Athletic Gear, Game Tables, and Exercise Equipment

Best customers: **Householders aged 35 to 54**
                           High-income households
                           Married couples
                           Single parents
                           Asians

Customer trends: **Average household spending on athletic gear is likely to continue to decline as households tighten their belts and the small generation X fills the best-customer age groups.**

The best customers of athletic gear, game tables, and exercise equipment are middle-aged married couples. Married couples with school-aged children at home spend 54 percent more than average on this item, while those without children at home spend 33 percent more than average. Householders aged 35 to 54 spend 50 to 100 percent more than average on athletic equipment because many are parents. Single parents spend 6 percent more. Householders with incomes of $100,000 or more spend over three times as much as the average household on sports gear. Asians—a relative affluent group—spend 39 percent more than average on this item.

Average household spending on athletic gear, game tables, and exercise equipment fell 7 percent between 2000 and 2007, after adjusting for inflation. As households tighten their belts and the small generation X enters the best-customer age groups, average household spending on athletic gear is likely to decline further.

Table 5.3 Athletic gear, game tables, and exercise equipment

Total household spending — $7,877,209,050.00
Average household spends — 65.55

	AVERAGE HOUSEHOLD SPENDING	BEST CUSTOMERS (index)	BIGGEST CUSTOMERS (market share)
AGE OF HOUSEHOLDER			
Average household	**$65.55**	**100**	**100.0%**
Under age 25	40.27	61	4.2
Aged 25 to 34	38.94	59	10.1
Aged 35 to 44	130.81	200	38.9
Aged 45 to 54	98.54	150	31.6
Aged 55 to 64	45.43	69	11.2
Aged 65 to 74	26.30	40	4.0
Aged 75 or older	1.02	2	0.1

	AVERAGE HOUSEHOLD SPENDING	BEST CUSTOMERS (index)	BIGGEST CUSTOMERS (market share)
HOUSEHOLD INCOME			
Average household	**$65.55**	**100**	**100.0%**
Under $20,000	18.73	29	5.9
$20,000 to $39,999	14.14	22	5.0
$40,000 to $49,999	43.50	66	6.5
$50,000 to $69,999	33.17	51	7.7
$70,000 to $79,999	87.98	134	7.8
$80,000 to $99,999	51.86	79	6.4
$100,000 or more	244.04	372	63.8
HOUSEHOLD TYPE			
Average household	**65.55**	**100**	**100.0**
Married couples	88.45	135	68.2
Married couples, no children	87.21	133	28.7
Married couples, with children	88.40	135	33.6
Oldest child under age 6	78.39	120	5.8
Oldest child aged 6 to 17	100.82	154	19.5
Oldest child aged 18 or older	71.15	109	8.0
Single parent with child under age 18	69.42	106	6.3
Single person	22.47	34	10.2
RACE AND HISPANIC ORIGIN			
Average household	**65.55**	**100**	**100.0**
Asian	90.89	139	4.9
Black	11.27	17	2.1
Hispanic	38.83	59	7.0
Non-Hispanic white and other	77.67	118	90.5
REGION			
Average household	**65.55**	**100**	**100.0**
Northeast	75.81	116	21.5
Midwest	70.91	108	24.7
South	47.85	73	26.2
West	79.85	122	27.5
EDUCATION			
Average household	**65.55**	**100**	**100.0**
Less than high school graduate	10.34	16	2.4
High school graduate	28.04	43	10.8
Some college	40.40	62	13.4
Associate's degree	132.01	201	17.9
College graduate	122.75	187	54.2
Bachelor's degree	113.55	173	32.5
Master's, professional, doctoral degree	138.73	212	21.6

Note: Market shares may not sum to 100.0 because of rounding and missing categories by household type. "Asian" and "black" include Hispanics and non-Hispanics who identify themselves as being of the respective race alone. "Hispanic" includes people of any race who identify themselves as Hispanic. "Other" includes people who identify themselves as non-Hispanic and as Alaska Native, American Indian, Asian (who are also included in the "Asian" row), Native Hawaiian or other Pacific Islander, as well as non-Hispanics reporting more than one race.
Source: Calculations by New Strategist based on the Bureau of Labor Statistics' 2007 Consumer Expenditure Survey.

Bicycles

Best customers:
Householders aged 35 to 54
Married couples with school-aged or older children at home
Non-Hispanic whites
College graduates

Customer trends:
Average household spending on bicycles will decline as the small generation X enters the best-customer lifestage unless communities aggressively promote the use of bicycles as an alternative to automobiles.

Parents are the best customers of bicycles, buying them for their children. Married couples with school-aged children spend 57 percent more than average on bicycles, while householders aged 35 to 54—many of them parents— spend 37 to 53 percent more. Married couples with adult children at home, however, trump everyone by spending in excess of three times the average on bicycles. Non-Hispanic whites spend 20 percent more than average on bicycles and control 91 percent of the market. College graduates spend twice the average amount on bicycles and control 58 percent of the market.

Average household spending on bicycles climbed 18 percent between 2000 and 2007, after adjusting for inflation. Spending on bicycles may decline in the years ahead as the small generation X fills the best-customer lifestage unless communities aggressively promote the use of bicycles as an alternative to automobiles.

Table 5.4 Bicycles

Total household spending $2,009,259,120.00
Average household spends   16.72

	AVERAGE HOUSEHOLD SPENDING	BEST CUSTOMERS (index)	BIGGEST CUSTOMERS (market share)
AGE OF HOUSEHOLDER			
Average household	**$16.72**	**100**	**100.0%**
Under age 25	10.42	62	4.2
Aged 25 to 34	14.41	86	14.7
Aged 35 to 44	25.61	153	29.8
Aged 45 to 54	22.86	137	28.7
Aged 55 to 64	18.16	109	17.6
Aged 65 to 74	4.83	29	2.9
Aged 75 or older	3.54	21	2.0

	AVERAGE HOUSEHOLD SPENDING	BEST CUSTOMERS (index)	BIGGEST CUSTOMERS (market share)
HOUSEHOLD INCOME			
Average household	**$16.72**	**100**	**100.0%**
Under $20,000	6.10	36	7.5
$20,000 to $39,999	7.93	47	11.0
$40,000 to $49,999	15.24	91	9.0
$50,000 to $69,999	14.49	87	13.3
$70,000 to $79,999	11.00	66	3.8
$80,000 to $99,999	19.49	117	9.5
$100,000 or more	44.82	268	45.9
HOUSEHOLD TYPE			
Average household	**16.72**	**100**	**100.0**
Married couples	22.83	137	69.0
Married couples, no children	15.41	92	19.9
Married couples, with children	31.26	187	46.6
Oldest child under age 6	11.98	72	3.5
Oldest child aged 6 to 17	26.23	157	19.9
Oldest child aged 18 or older	52.71	315	23.2
Single parent with child under age 18	14.36	86	5.1
Single person	8.82	53	15.7
RACE AND HISPANIC ORIGIN			
Average household	**16.72**	**100**	**100.0**
Asian	7.10	42	1.5
Black	5.74	34	4.1
Hispanic	5.99	36	4.2
Non-Hispanic white and other	20.08	120	91.7
REGION			
Average household	**16.72**	**100**	**100.0**
Northeast	17.09	102	19.0
Midwest	23.80	142	32.5
South	9.72	58	20.9
West	20.36	122	27.5
EDUCATION			
Average household	**16.72**	**100**	**100.0**
Less than high school graduate	4.11	25	3.7
High school graduate	11.53	69	17.4
Some college	10.82	65	14.1
Associate's degree	12.06	72	6.4
College graduate	33.70	202	58.3
Bachelor's degree	30.55	183	34.2
Master's, professional, doctoral degree	39.49	236	24.1

Note: Market shares may not sum to 100.0 because of rounding and missing categories by household type. "Asian" and "black" include Hispanics and non-Hispanics who identify themselves as being of the respective race alone. "Hispanic" includes people of any race who identify themselves as Hispanic. "Other" includes people who identify themselves as non-Hispanic and as Alaska Native, American Indian, Asian (who are also included in the "Asian" row), Native Hawaiian or other Pacific Islander, as well as non-Hispanics reporting more than one race.
Source: Calculations by New Strategist based on the Bureau of Labor Statistics' 2007 Consumer Expenditure Survey.

Cable and Satellite Television Services

Best customers:	**Householders aged 35 to 64** **Married couples**
Customer trends:	**Average household spending on cable and satellite television service will continue to rise if cable and satellite can continue to innovate.**

Cable and satellite television service is the number-one entertainment expenditure of the average household. Because cable service is nearly universal, average household spending on the service does not vary much by demographic characteristic. By age, the best customers are householders aged 35 to 64, who spend 8 to 12 percent more than average on this item and account for 62 percent of household spending on cable and satellite television service. Married couples spend 16 percent more than average on cable television. Their spending peaks at 25 percent above average among couples with adult children at home.

Spending on cable television and satellite television service grew by a substantial 44 percent between 2000 and 2007, after adjusting for inflation. This increase accounted for a large share of the overall rise in entertainment spending during those years. Behind the increased spending on cable service are more cable channels and services. If cable and satellite television can continue to innovate, households will continue to spend—at the expense of other entertainment categories, however.

Table 5.5 Cable and satellite television services

Total household spending	$66,710,527,230.00
Average household spends	555.13

	AVERAGE HOUSEHOLD SPENDING	BEST CUSTOMERS (index)	BIGGEST CUSTOMERS (market share)
AGE OF HOUSEHOLDER			
Average household	**$555.13**	**100**	**100.0%**
Under age 25	305.86	55	3.7
Aged 25 to 34	519.57	94	16.0
Aged 35 to 44	597.82	108	21.0
Aged 45 to 54	620.16	112	23.5
Aged 55 to 64	614.73	111	17.9
Aged 65 to 74	554.00	100	10.0
Aged 75 or older	464.95	84	7.9

	AVERAGE HOUSEHOLD SPENDING	BEST CUSTOMERS (index)	BIGGEST CUSTOMERS (market share)
HOUSEHOLD INCOME			
Average household	**$555.13**	**100**	**100.0%**
Under $20,000	342.99	62	12.7
$20,000 to $39,999	463.26	83	19.4
$40,000 to $49,999	553.96	100	9.8
$50,000 to $69,999	603.88	109	16.6
$70,000 to $79,999	625.80	113	6.5
$80,000 to $99,999	686.88	124	10.1
$100,000 or more	805.04	145	24.8
HOUSEHOLD TYPE			
Average household	**555.13**	**100**	**100.0**
Married couples	641.83	116	58.4
Married couples, no children	629.03	113	24.4
Married couples, with children	654.09	118	29.4
Oldest child under age 6	624.67	113	5.5
Oldest child aged 6 to 17	642.63	116	14.7
Oldest child aged 18 or older	693.34	125	9.2
Single parent with child under age 18	490.96	88	5.3
Single person	416.21	75	22.3
RACE AND HISPANIC ORIGIN			
Average household	**555.13**	**100**	**100.0**
Asian	439.14	79	2.8
Black	534.00	96	11.5
Hispanic	447.25	81	9.5
Non-Hispanic white and other	575.12	104	79.1
REGION			
Average household	**555.13**	**100**	**100.0**
Northeast	612.97	110	20.6
Midwest	510.72	92	21.0
South	572.31	103	37.0
West	525.12	95	21.4
EDUCATION			
Average household	**555.13**	**100**	**100.0**
Less than high school graduate	421.05	76	11.5
High school graduate	546.39	98	24.8
Some college	535.09	96	21.0
Associate's degree	595.14	107	9.5
College graduate	635.81	115	33.2
Bachelor's degree	618.70	111	20.9
Master's, professional, doctoral degree	667.25	120	12.3

Note: Market shares may not sum to 100.0 because of rounding and missing categories by household type. "Asian" and "black" include Hispanics and non-Hispanics who identify themselves as being of the respective race alone. "Hispanic" includes people of any race who identify themselves as Hispanic. "Other" includes people who identify themselves as non-Hispanic and as Alaska Native, American Indian, Asian (who are also included in the "Asian" row), Native Hawaiian or other Pacific Islander, as well as non-Hispanics reporting more than one race.
Source: Calculations by New Strategist based on the Bureau of Labor Statistics' 2007 Consumer Expenditure Survey.

Club Memberships (Civic, Recreational, Social)

Best customers:
Householders aged 45 or older
High-income households
Married couples without children at home
Married couples with school-aged children
College graduates

Customer trends:
Average household spending on club memberships may increase as aging boomers look for ways to belong.

Club memberships are an important entertainment expenditure, ranking sixth among entertainment categories. The best customers of club memberships are affluent, educated, older married couples. These households are the glue of every community, funding and supporting a variety of organizations ranging from civic groups to the YMCA to country clubs. The best customers of clubs, householders aged 45 or older spend more than the average household on club memberships. Married couples without children at home spend 71 percent more than average on this item, while those with school-aged children spend 54 percent more. Households with incomes of $100,000 or more spend more than triple the average on club memberships and account for 55 percent of spending in this category. College graduates spend more than twice the average and account for than 67 percent of the market.

Average household spending on club memberships rose 4 percent between 2000 and 2007, after adjusting for inflation. Spending on clubs may grow further in the years ahead as aging boomers gain more free time and look for ways to plug into their community.

Table 5.6 **Club memberships (civic, recreational, social)**

Total household spending $14,838,715,080.00
Average household spends 123.48

AGE OF HOUSEHOLDER	AVERAGE HOUSEHOLD SPENDING	BEST CUSTOMERS (index)	BIGGEST CUSTOMERS (market share)
Average household	**$123.48**	**100**	**100.0%**
Under age 25	54.76	44	3.0
Aged 25 to 34	91.57	74	12.6
Aged 35 to 44	124.06	100	19.6
Aged 45 to 54	136.63	111	23.2
Aged 55 to 64	150.04	122	19.7
Aged 65 to 74	128.51	104	10.4
Aged 75 or older	149.01	121	11.4

	AVERAGE HOUSEHOLD SPENDING	BEST CUSTOMERS (index)	BIGGEST CUSTOMERS (market share)
HOUSEHOLD INCOME			
Average household	$123.48	100	100.0%
Under $20,000	19.57	16	3.3
$20,000 to $39,999	42.25	34	8.0
$40,000 to $49,999	71.18	58	5.7
$50,000 to $69,999	91.69	74	11.4
$70,000 to $79,999	131.00	106	6.1
$80,000 to $99,999	163.05	132	10.7
$100,000 or more	395.44	320	54.9
HOUSEHOLD TYPE			
Average household	123.48	100	100.0
Married couples	177.67	144	72.7
Married couples, no children	210.85	171	36.8
Married couples, with children	163.23	132	33.0
Oldest child under age 6	122.63	99	4.8
Oldest child aged 6 to 17	190.37	154	19.6
Oldest child aged 18 or older	143.35	116	8.6
Single parent with child under age 18	50.22	41	2.4
Single person	76.34	62	18.4
RACE AND HISPANIC ORIGIN			
Average household	123.48	100	100.0
Asian	113.92	92	3.3
Black	40.51	33	3.9
Hispanic	57.73	47	5.5
Non-Hispanic white and other	146.61	119	90.6
REGION			
Average household	123.48	100	100.0
Northeast	145.62	118	22.0
Midwest	128.95	104	23.9
South	88.91	72	25.9
West	154.61	125	28.3
EDUCATION			
Average household	123.48	100	100.0
Less than high school graduate	16.08	13	2.0
High school graduate	44.58	36	9.1
Some college	73.15	59	12.9
Associate's degree	126.37	102	9.1
College graduate	285.49	231	66.9
Bachelor's degree	253.39	205	38.5
Master's, professional, doctoral degree	344.45	279	28.5

Note: Market shares may not sum to 100.0 because of rounding and missing categories by household type. "Asian" and "black" include Hispanics and non-Hispanics who identify themselves as being of the respective race alone. "Hispanic" includes people of any race who identify themselves as Hispanic. "Other" includes people who identify themselves as non-Hispanic and as Alaska Native, American Indian, Asian (who are also included in the "Asian" row), Native Hawaiian or other Pacific Islander, as well as non-Hispanics reporting more than one race.
Source: Calculations by New Strategist based on the Bureau of Labor Statistics' 2007 Consumer Expenditure Survey.

Compact Disks, Audio Tapes, and Records

Best customers: **Householders aged 35 to 54**
      Married couples with school-aged or older children at home

Customer trends: **Average household spending on compact disks, audio tapes, and records will decline as online downloads become the dominant mode for purchasing music.**

Households with children dominate spending on compact disks, audio tapes, and records. Householders aged 35 to 54, most of them parents, spend 19 to 27 percent more than average on this item and control half the market. Married couples with school-aged or older children at home spend 33 to 37 percent more than average on CDs, audio tapes, and records.

Average household spending on CDs, audiotapes, and records fell 42 percent between 2000 and 2007, after adjusting for inflation. The decline in spending should continue as downloads replace compact disks as the preferred way to purchase music.

Table 5.7 Compact disks, audio tapes, and records

Total household spending $3,291,483,690.00
Average household spends   27.39

AGE OF HOUSEHOLDER	AVERAGE HOUSEHOLD SPENDING	BEST CUSTOMERS (index)	BIGGEST CUSTOMERS (market share)
Average household	**$27.39**	**100**	**100.0%**
Under age 25	30.64	112	7.6
Aged 25 to 34	25.94	95	16.2
Aged 35 to 44	32.69	119	23.3
Aged 45 to 54	34.72	127	26.6
Aged 55 to 64	28.53	104	16.9
Aged 65 to 74	19.26	70	7.0
Aged 75 or older	7.10	26	2.5

	AVERAGE HOUSEHOLD SPENDING	BEST CUSTOMERS (index)	BIGGEST CUSTOMERS (market share)
HOUSEHOLD INCOME			
Average household	**$27.39**	**100**	**100.0%**
Under $20,000	12.37	45	9.3
$20,000 to $39,999	17.19	63	14.6
$40,000 to $49,999	27.89	102	10.0
$50,000 to $69,999	30.83	113	17.2
$70,000 to $79,999	30.89	113	6.5
$80,000 to $99,999	38.27	140	11.4
$100,000 or more	49.52	181	31.0
HOUSEHOLD TYPE			
Average household	**27.39**	**100**	**100.0**
Married couples	30.39	111	56.1
Married couples, no children	24.81	91	19.5
Married couples, with children	34.56	126	31.5
Oldest child under age 6	23.72	87	4.2
Oldest child aged 6 to 17	37.60	137	17.4
Oldest child aged 18 or older	36.49	133	9.8
Single parent with child under age 18	24.62	90	5.3
Single person	20.95	76	22.7
RACE AND HISPANIC ORIGIN			
Average household	**27.39**	**100**	**100.0**
Asian	19.40	71	2.5
Black	23.32	85	10.2
Hispanic	24.49	89	10.6
Non-Hispanic white and other	28.50	104	79.4
REGION			
Average household	**27.39**	**100**	**100.0**
Northeast	30.73	112	20.9
Midwest	24.92	91	20.8
South	24.00	88	31.5
West	32.49	119	26.8
EDUCATION			
Average household	**27.39**	**100**	**100.0**
Less than high school graduate	15.63	57	8.7
High school graduate	19.21	70	17.7
Some college	28.66	105	22.8
Associate's degree	30.74	112	10.0
College graduate	38.68	141	40.9
Bachelor's degree	36.62	134	25.1
Master's, professional, doctoral degree	42.47	155	15.8

Note: Market shares may not sum to 100.0 because of rounding and missing categories by household type. "Asian" and "black" include Hispanics and non-Hispanics who identify themselves as being of the respective race alone. "Hispanic" includes people of any race who identify themselves as Hispanic. "Other" includes people who identify themselves as non-Hispanic and as Alaska Native, American Indian, Asian (who are also included in the "Asian" row), Native Hawaiian or other Pacific Islander, as well as non-Hispanics reporting more than one race.
Source: Calculations by New Strategist based on the Bureau of Labor Statistics' 2007 Consumer Expenditure Survey.

Fees for Participant Sports (Including on Trips)

Best customers:	**Householders aged 35 to 54** **High-income households** **Married couples** **College graduates**
Customer trends:	**Average household spending on fees for participant sports is likely to decline as households tighten their belts and the small generation X enters the best-customer age groups.**

Fees for participant sports include a broad range of recreational charges from greens fees for golfers to fees for children's sports leagues. Those who spend the most on fees for participant sports are affluent, educated, married couples. Householders ranging in age from 35 to 54 spend 22 to 77 percent more than average on fees for participant sports and account for 60 percent of the market. Householders with incomes of $100,000 or more spend more than three times the average on this item. College graduates, a relatively affluent group, spend twice the average. Married couples without children at home (most of them empty-nesters) spend 67 percent more than average on this item, while those with school-aged or older children at home spend 45 to 98 percent more than average on fees for participant sports.

Average household spending on fees for participant sports grew 16 percent between 2000 and 2007 after adjusting for inflation. Spending on this category is likely to fall in the years ahead as households tighten their belts and the small generation X enters the best-customer age groups.

Table 5.8 **Fees for participant sports (including on trips)**

Total household spending $17,893,461,900.00
Average household spends   148.90

AGE OF HOUSEHOLDER	AVERAGE HOUSEHOLD SPENDING	BEST CUSTOMERS (index)	BIGGEST CUSTOMERS (market share)
Average household	**$148.90**	**100**	**100.0%**
Under age 25	44.01	30	2.0
Aged 25 to 34	95.57	64	10.9
Aged 35 to 44	263.45	177	34.5
Aged 45 to 54	182.04	122	25.7
Aged 55 to 64	133.13	89	14.5
Aged 65 to 74	143.25	96	9.6
Aged 75 or older	44.77	30	2.8

	AVERAGE HOUSEHOLD SPENDING	BEST CUSTOMERS (index)	BIGGEST CUSTOMERS (market share)
HOUSEHOLD INCOME			
Average household	**$148.90**	**100**	**100.0%**
Under $20,000	19.69	13	2.7
$20,000 to $39,999	51.18	34	8.0
$40,000 to $49,999	75.90	51	5.0
$50,000 to $69,999	132.16	89	13.6
$70,000 to $79,999	114.93	77	4.5
$80,000 to $99,999	221.56	149	12.1
$100,000 or more	477.97	321	55.0
HOUSEHOLD TYPE			
Average household	**148.90**	**100**	**100.0**
Married couples	237.82	160	80.7
Married couples, no children	249.37	167	36.1
Married couples, with children	249.50	168	41.8
Oldest child under age 6	177.01	119	5.8
Oldest child aged 6 to 17	294.23	198	25.1
Oldest child aged 18 or older	215.59	145	10.7
Single parent with child under age 18	90.37	61	3.6
Single person	49.18	33	9.8
RACE AND HISPANIC ORIGIN			
Average household	**148.90**	**100**	**100.0**
Asian	167.51	112	4.0
Black	24.52	16	2.0
Hispanic	35.08	24	2.8
Non-Hispanic white and other	184.51	124	94.6
REGION			
Average household	**148.90**	**100**	**100.0**
Northeast	201.75	135	25.2
Midwest	129.26	87	19.8
South	86.80	58	20.9
West	224.30	151	34.1
EDUCATION			
Average household	**148.90**	**100**	**100.0**
Less than high school graduate	25.76	17	2.6
High school graduate	62.39	42	10.6
Some college	147.08	99	21.5
Associate's degree	97.35	65	5.8
College graduate	299.37	201	58.2
Bachelor's degree	324.73	218	40.9
Master's, professional, doctoral degree	256.28	172	17.6

Note: Market shares may not sum to 100.0 because of rounding and missing categories by household type. "Asian" and "black" include Hispanics and non-Hispanics who identify themselves as being of the respective race alone. "Hispanic" includes people of any race who identify themselves as Hispanic. "Other" includes people who identify themselves as non-Hispanic and as Alaska Native, American Indian, Asian (who are also included in the "Asian" row), Native Hawaiian or other Pacific Islander, as well as non-Hispanics reporting more than one race.
Source: Calculations by New Strategist based on the Bureau of Labor Statistics' 2007 Consumer Expenditure Survey.

Fees for Recreational Lessons

Best customers:
Householders aged 35 to 54
High-income households
Married couples with school-aged children
Single parents
Asians
College graduates

Customer trends:
Average household spending on fees for recreational lessons may decline as households tighten their belts and the small generation X enters the best-customer age groups.

Married couples with school-aged children spend more than four times the average on fees for recreational lessons and control 52 percent of the market. Single parents spend 22 percent more, despite their low incomes. Householders aged 35 to 54, who are likely to be parents, spend 66 to 114 percent more than average on this category. Households with incomes of $100,000 or more spend more than three times the average on this item and control over half the market. Asians spend more than two-and-one-half times the average on fees for recreational lessons, while college graduates spend more than twice the average on this item.

Average household spending on fees for recreational lessons climbed 17 percent between 2000 and 2007, after adjusting for inflation. Behind the rise is the parental frenzy to ensure that children are well rounded. As households tighten their belts and generation X fills the best-customer age groups, spending on this category may decline in the years ahead.

Table 5.9 Fees for recreational lessons

Total household spending $12,685,250,760.00
Average household spends   105.56

	AVERAGE HOUSEHOLD SPENDING	BEST CUSTOMERS (index)	BIGGEST CUSTOMERS (market share)
AGE OF HOUSEHOLDER			
Average household	**$105.56**	**100**	**100.0%**
Under age 25	17.57	17	1.1
Aged 25 to 34	63.44	60	10.3
Aged 35 to 44	226.09	214	41.7
Aged 45 to 54	175.43	166	34.9
Aged 55 to 64	44.42	42	6.8
Aged 65 to 74	42.80	41	4.1
Aged 75 or older	12.29	12	1.1

	AVERAGE HOUSEHOLD SPENDING	BEST CUSTOMERS (index)	BIGGEST CUSTOMERS (market share)
HOUSEHOLD INCOME			
Average household	**$105.56**	**100**	**100.0%**
Under $20,000	12.50	12	2.4
$20,000 to $39,999	26.31	25	5.8
$40,000 to $49,999	47.15	45	4.4
$50,000 to $69,999	63.96	61	9.3
$70,000 to $79,999	121.40	115	6.7
$80,000 to $99,999	194.28	184	15.0
$100,000 or more	347.94	330	56.5
HOUSEHOLD TYPE			
Average household	**105.56**	**100**	**100.0**
Married couples	164.05	155	78.6
Married couples, no children	40.06	38	8.2
Married couples, with children	277.61	263	65.6
Oldest child under age 6	96.45	91	4.5
Oldest child aged 6 to 17	434.15	411	52.2
Oldest child aged 18 or older	127.71	121	8.9
Single parent with child under age 18	128.30	122	7.2
Single person	30.64	29	8.6
RACE AND HISPANIC ORIGIN			
Average household	**105.56**	**100**	**100.0**
Asian	278.77	264	9.3
Black	24.39	23	2.8
Hispanic	45.24	43	5.1
Non-Hispanic white and other	127.63	121	92.3
REGION			
Average household	**105.56**	**100**	**100.0**
Northeast	147.42	140	26.0
Midwest	106.55	101	23.1
South	66.97	63	22.8
West	131.34	124	28.1
EDUCATION			
Average household	**105.56**	**100**	**100.0**
Less than high school graduate	9.31	9	1.3
High school graduate	31.89	30	7.6
Some college	81.82	78	16.9
Associate's degree	120.97	115	10.2
College graduate	233.33	221	64.0
Bachelor's degree	202.80	192	36.0
Master's, professional, doctoral degree	289.41	274	28.0

Note: Market shares may not sum to 100.0 because of rounding and missing categories by household type. "Asian" and "black" include Hispanics and non-Hispanics who identify themselves as being of the respective race alone. "Hispanic" includes people of any race who identify themselves as Hispanic. "Other" includes people who identify themselves as non-Hispanic and as Alaska Native, American Indian, Asian (who are also included in the "Asian" row), Native Hawaiian or other Pacific Islander, as well as non-Hispanics reporting more than one race.
Source: Calculations by New Strategist based on the Bureau of Labor Statistics' 2007 Consumer Expenditure Survey.

Film

Best customers: Householders aged 45 to 54 and 65 to 74
Married couples with school-aged or older children at home

Customer trends: Average household spending on film will continue to decline as digital cameras make film obsolete.

Married couples with children at home spend 54 percent more than the average household on film as they photograph the milestones in their children's lives, the figure peaking among those with adult children at home, at 89 percent above average. Householders aged 45 to 54 and those 65 to 74, many of them parents and grandparents, spend, respectively, 44 and 45 percent more than average on this item.

Average household spending on film fell by an enormous 82 percent between 2000 and 2007, after adjusting for inflation. Behind the decline was the shift to digital photography, rendering film obsolete. This trend should continue as virtually all households replace their film cameras with digital models.

Table 5.10 Film

Total household spending		$563,601,990.00	
Average household spends		4.69	

	AVERAGE HOUSEHOLD SPENDING	BEST CUSTOMERS (index)	BIGGEST CUSTOMERS (market share)
AGE OF HOUSEHOLDER			
Average household	**$4.69**	**100**	**100.0%**
Under age 25	2.20	47	3.2
Aged 25 to 34	3.75	80	13.6
Aged 35 to 44	4.32	92	17.9
Aged 45 to 54	6.75	144	30.2
Aged 55 to 64	4.75	101	16.4
Aged 65 to 74	6.81	145	14.5
Aged 75 or older	2.03	43	4.1

	AVERAGE HOUSEHOLD SPENDING	BEST CUSTOMERS (index)	BIGGEST CUSTOMERS (market share)
HOUSEHOLD INCOME			
Average household	**$4.69**	**100**	**100.0%**
Under $20,000	2.03	43	8.9
$20,000 to $39,999	3.67	78	18.2
$40,000 to $49,999	4.58	98	9.6
$50,000 to $69,999	5.48	117	17.9
$70,000 to $79,999	5.30	113	6.5
$80,000 to $99,999	5.47	117	9.5
$100,000 or more	8.03	171	29.3
HOUSEHOLD TYPE			
Average household	**4.69**	**100**	**100.0**
Married couples	6.18	132	66.6
Married couples, no children	4.95	106	22.8
Married couples, with children	7.20	154	38.3
Oldest child under age 6	5.16	110	5.4
Oldest child aged 6 to 17	7.01	149	19.0
Oldest child aged 18 or older	8.88	189	14.0
Single parent with child under age 18	4.43	94	5.6
Single person	2.69	57	17.1
RACE AND HISPANIC ORIGIN			
Average household	**4.69**	**100**	**100.0**
Asian	3.45	74	2.6
Black	2.76	59	7.1
Hispanic	3.63	77	9.1
Non-Hispanic white and other	5.15	110	83.8
REGION			
Average household	**4.69**	**100**	**100.0**
Northeast	4.94	105	19.6
Midwest	4.73	101	23.0
South	4.37	93	33.5
West	4.94	105	23.8
EDUCATION			
Average household	**4.69**	**100**	**100.0**
Less than high school graduate	3.03	65	9.8
High school graduate	4.44	95	23.9
Some college	3.82	81	17.7
Associate's degree	4.95	106	9.4
College graduate	6.35	135	39.2
Bachelor's degree	6.65	142	26.6
Master's, professional, doctoral degree	5.80	124	12.6

Note: Market shares may not sum to 100.0 because of rounding and missing categories by household type. "Asian" and "black" include Hispanics and non-Hispanics who identify themselves as being of the respective race alone. "Hispanic" includes people of any race who identify themselves as Hispanic. "Other" includes people who identify themselves as non-Hispanic and as Alaska Native, American Indian, Asian (who are also included in the "Asian" row), Native Hawaiian or other Pacific Islander, as well as non-Hispanics reporting more than one race.
Source: Calculations by New Strategist based on the Bureau of Labor Statistics' 2007 Consumer Expenditure Survey.

Installation of Television Sets

Best customers:
Householders aged 25 to 54
Married couples with school-aged children
Single parents
Asians and blacks
Households in the Northeast

Customer trends:
Average household spending on the installation of television sets could grow as television sets become more complex.

The best customers of installation services for television sets are consumers faced with the task of wiring up their new high-definition TVs. Householders aged 25 to 54 spend 19 to 84 percent more than average on this item and represent 87 percent of the market. Married couples with school-aged children and single parents spend more than average on television installation. Blacks and especially Asians spend well above average on this item, as do households in the Northeast.

Installation of television sets is a relatively new item in the Consumer Expenditure Survey and comparable data from 2000 do not exist. Average household spending on this item is likely to rise in the years to come as television sets become more complex.

Table 5.11 Installation of television sets

Total household spending $117,767,580.00
Average household spends   0.98

	AVERAGE HOUSEHOLD SPENDING	BEST CUSTOMERS (index)	BIGGEST CUSTOMERS (market share)
AGE OF HOUSEHOLDER			
Average household	**$0.98**	**100**	**100.0%**
Under age 25	0.44	45	3.0
Aged 25 to 34	1.43	146	24.9
Aged 35 to 44	1.17	119	23.3
Aged 45 to 54	1.80	184	38.6
Aged 55 to 64	0.04	4	0.7
Aged 65 to 74	0.85	87	8.7
Aged 75 or older	0.07	7	0.7

	AVERAGE HOUSEHOLD SPENDING	BEST CUSTOMERS (index)	BIGGEST CUSTOMERS (market share)
HOUSEHOLD INCOME			
Average household	**$0.98**	**100**	**100.0%**
Under $20,000	0.34	35	7.1
$20,000 to $39,999	0.41	42	9.8
$40,000 to $49,999	1.04	106	10.4
$50,000 to $69,999	0.82	84	12.8
$70,000 to $79,999	0.49	50	2.9
$80,000 to $99,999	1.41	144	11.7
$100,000 or more	2.74	280	47.9
HOUSEHOLD TYPE			
Average household	**0.98**	**100**	**100.0**
Married couples	1.05	107	54.2
Married couples, no children	0.90	92	19.8
Married couples, with children	1.06	108	27.0
Oldest child under age 6	0.25	26	1.2
Oldest child aged 6 to 17	1.70	173	22.0
Oldest child aged 18 or older	0.50	51	3.8
Single parent with child under age 18	2.38	243	14.4
Single person	0.67	68	20.3
RACE AND HISPANIC ORIGIN			
Average household	**0.98**	**100**	**100.0**
Asian	2.52	257	9.1
Black	1.50	153	18.4
Hispanic	0.30	31	3.6
Non-Hispanic white and other	1.00	102	77.9
REGION			
Average household	**0.98**	**100**	**100.0**
Northeast	1.77	181	33.6
Midwest	1.02	104	23.8
South	0.74	76	27.1
West	0.65	66	15.0
EDUCATION			
Average household	**0.98**	**100**	**100.0**
Less than high school graduate	0.53	54	8.2
High school graduate	0.39	40	10.0
Some college	1.11	113	24.7
Associate's degree	1.80	184	16.3
College graduate	1.38	141	40.8
Bachelor's degree	1.10	112	21.0
Master's, professional, doctoral degree	1.90	194	19.8

Note: Market shares may not sum to 100.0 because of rounding and missing categories by household type. "Asian" and "black" include Hispanics and non-Hispanics who identify themselves as being of the respective race alone. "Hispanic" includes people of any race who identify themselves as Hispanic. "Other" includes people who identify themselves as non-Hispanic and as Alaska Native, American Indian, Asian (who are also included in the "Asian" row), Native Hawaiian or other Pacific Islander, as well as non-Hispanics reporting more than one race.
Source: Calculations by New Strategist based on the Bureau of Labor Statistics' 2007 Consumer Expenditure Survey.

Live Entertainment for Catered Affairs

Best customers:
Householders aged 25 to 34 and 45 to 64
Married couples without children at home
Married couples with adult children at home
People living alone

Customer trends:
Average household spending on live entertainment for catered affairs is likely to decline in the years ahead as households tighten their belts.

The best customers of live entertainment for catered affairs are young adults who are getting married and their parents. Householders aged 25 to 34 spend 61 percent more than average on live entertainment for catered affairs. Householders aged 45 to 64 spend 29 to 63 percent more on this item. Married couples without children at home, married couples with adult children home, and people who live alone spend respectively, 29, 21, and 32 percent more than average on live entertainment for catered affairs.

Live entertainment for catered affairs is a new item in the Consumer Expenditure Survey, and comparable data from 2000 do not exist. Average household spending on this item is likely to decline in the years ahead as households tighten their belts.

Table 5.12 Live entertainment for catered affairs

Total household spending $1,103,169,780.00
Average household spends   9.18

	AVERAGE HOUSEHOLD SPENDING	BEST CUSTOMERS (index)	BIGGEST CUSTOMERS (market share)
AGE OF HOUSEHOLDER			
Average household	$9.18	100	100.0%
Under age 25	2.37	26	1.8
Aged 25 to 34	14.75	161	27.4
Aged 35 to 44	5.24	57	11.1
Aged 45 to 54	14.94	163	34.2
Aged 55 to 64	11.81	129	20.8
Aged 65 to 74	2.62	29	2.9
Aged 75 or older	1.74	19	1.8

	AVERAGE HOUSEHOLD SPENDING	BEST CUSTOMERS (index)	BIGGEST CUSTOMERS (market share)
HOUSEHOLD INCOME			
Average household	**$9.18**	**100**	**100.0%**
Under $20,000	1.65	18	3.7
$20,000 to $39,999	5.86	64	14.8
$40,000 to $49,999	1.02	11	1.1
$50,000 to $69,999	4.75	52	7.9
$70,000 to $79,999	5.91	64	3.7
$80,000 to $99,999	37.33	407	33.1
$100,000 or more	19.08	208	35.6
HOUSEHOLD TYPE			
Average household	**9.18**	**100**	**100.0**
Married couples	8.29	90	45.6
Married couples, no children	11.80	129	27.7
Married couples, with children	6.58	72	17.9
Oldest child under age 6	3.70	40	2.0
Oldest child aged 6 to 17	5.07	55	7.0
Oldest child aged 18 or older	11.11	121	8.9
Single parent with child under age 18	2.15	23	1.4
Single person	12.13	132	39.3
RACE AND HISPANIC ORIGIN			
Average household	**9.18**	**100**	**100.0**
Asian	0.97	11	0.4
Black	8.18	89	10.7
Hispanic	2.66	29	3.4
Non-Hispanic white and other	10.32	112	85.8
REGION			
Average household	**9.18**	**100**	**100.0**
Northeast	3.27	36	6.6
Midwest	22.79	248	56.7
South	6.34	69	24.8
West	4.78	52	11.8
EDUCATION			
Average household	**9.18**	**100**	**100.0**
Less than high school graduate	0.97	11	1.6
High school graduate	3.18	35	8.7
Some college	18.14	198	43.0
Associate's degree	15.65	170	15.2
College graduate	9.97	109	31.4
Bachelor's degree	3.95	43	8.1
Master's, professional, doctoral degree	21.02	229	23.4

Note: Market shares may not sum to 100.0 because of rounding and missing categories by household type. "Asian" and "black" include Hispanics and non-Hispanics who identify themselves as being of the respective race alone. "Hispanic" includes people of any race who identify themselves as Hispanic. "Other" includes people who identify themselves as non-Hispanic and as Alaska Native, American Indian, Asian (who are also included in the "Asian" row), Native Hawaiian or other Pacific Islander, as well as non-Hispanics reporting more than one race.
Source: Calculations by New Strategist based on the Bureau of Labor Statistics' 2007 Consumer Expenditure Survey.

Motorized Recreational Vehicles (Including RVs and Boats)

Best customers:
Householders aged 65 to 74
High-income households
Married couples without children at home
Non-Hispanic whites

Customer trends:
Average household spending on motorized recreational vehicles is likely to decline in the years ahead as households tighten their belts, early retirement becomes less common, and higher gasoline prices drive up costs.

Householders aged 65 to 74 are by far the best customers for motorized recreational vehicles such as campers and boats. They spend well more than four times the average on this item and control 42 percent of the market. The most affluent householders, those with incomes above $100,000, spend more than three times the average on RVs and motorboats. Married couples without children at home (most of them empty-nesters) spend 60 percent more than average. Non-Hispanic whites completely dominate the recreational vehicle market and account for 91 percent of spending in this category.

Average household spending on motorized recreational vehicles grew by 50 percent between 2000 and 2007, after adjusting for inflation. Behind the increase were low-interest loans available during the time period, spurring many retirees to buy recreational vehicles. Spending in this category is likely to decline in the years ahead as households tighten their belts, early retirement becomes less common, and higher gasoline prices drive up costs.

Table 5.13 Motorized recreational vehicles (including RVs and boats)

Total household spending $17,756,466,960.00
Average household spends 147.76

AGE OF HOUSEHOLDER	AVERAGE HOUSEHOLD SPENDING	BEST CUSTOMERS (index)	BIGGEST CUSTOMERS (market share)
Average household	$147.76	100	100.0%
Under age 25	38.20	26	1.8
Aged 25 to 34	83.77	57	9.7
Aged 35 to 44	128.93	87	17.0
Aged 45 to 54	132.84	90	18.9
Aged 55 to 64	62.47	42	6.8
Aged 65 to 74	626.53	424	42.4
Aged 75 or older	54.04	37	3.5

	AVERAGE HOUSEHOLD SPENDING	BEST CUSTOMERS (index)	BIGGEST CUSTOMERS (market share)
HOUSEHOLD INCOME			
Average household	**$147.76**	**100**	**100.0%**
Under $20,000	20.94	14	2.9
$20,000 to $39,999	109.80	74	17.3
$40,000 to $49,999	64.31	44	4.3
$50,000 to $69,999	111.07	75	11.5
$70,000 to $79,999	–	–	–
$80,000 to $99,999	169.15	114	9.3
$100,000 or more	476.20	322	55.2
HOUSEHOLD TYPE			
Average household	**147.76**	**100**	**100.0**
Married couples	187.65	127	64.2
Married couples, no children	236.13	160	34.5
Married couples, with children	157.91	107	26.7
Oldest child under age 6	40.68	28	1.3
Oldest child aged 6 to 17	186.28	126	16.0
Oldest child aged 18 or older	186.63	126	9.3
Single parent with child under age 18	99.37	67	4.0
Single person	9.05	6	1.8
RACE AND HISPANIC ORIGIN			
Average household	**147.76**	**100**	**100.0**
Asian	8.19	6	0.2
Black	33.10	22	2.7
Hispanic	82.05	56	6.6
Non-Hispanic white and other	175.68	119	90.8
REGION			
Average household	**147.76**	**100**	**100.0**
Northeast	103.26	70	13.0
Midwest	100.98	68	15.6
South	85.09	58	20.7
West	331.22	224	50.7
EDUCATION			
Average household	**147.76**	**100**	**100.0**
Less than high school graduate	81.69	55	8.4
High school graduate	86.49	59	14.8
Some college	137.20	93	20.2
Associate's degree	17.26	12	1.0
College graduate	283.81	192	55.6
Bachelor's degree	72.64	49	9.2
Master's, professional, doctoral degree	671.76	455	46.4

Note: Market shares may not sum to 100.0 because of rounding and missing categories by household type. "Asian" and "black" include Hispanics and non-Hispanics who identify themselves as being of the respective race alone. "Hispanic" includes people of any race who identify themselves as Hispanic. "Other" includes people who identify themselves as non-Hispanic and as Alaska Native, American Indian, Asian (who are also included in the "Asian" row), Native Hawaiian or other Pacific Islander, as well as non-Hispanics reporting more than one race.
Source: Calculations by New Strategist based on the Bureau of Labor Statistics' 2007 Consumer Expenditure Survey.

Movie, Theater, Amusement Park, and Other Admissions (Including on Trips)

Best customers:	Householders aged 35 to 54 Married couples with school-aged or older children at home
Customer trends:	Average household spending on movie, theater, amusement park, and other admissions may continue to decline as households tighten their belts and boomers become empty-nesters.

Spending on movie tickets dominates this item, which is the third-largest entertainment category. The best customers of movie, theater, amusement park, and other admissions are teenagers, which explains why householders aged 35 to 54 spend 19 to 20 percent more than average on this item—many have teenagers at home. Married couples with school-aged or older children spend 39 to 64 percent more than average on movie, theater, amusement park, and other admissions.

Average household spending on movie, theater, amusement park and other admissions was essentially flat between 2000 and 2007, falling 1 percent after adjusting for inflation. Behind the flat spending was changing technology, as DVDs and pay-per-view streaming allow consumers to see movies at home rather than in a theater. Spending on this category is likely to remain stable or even decline during the next few years as households tighten their belts and the small generation X fills the best-customer lifestage.

Table 5.14 Movie, theater, amusement park, and other admissions (including on trips)

Total household spending $19,149,248,850.00
Average household spends   159.35

AGE OF HOUSEHOLDER	AVERAGE HOUSEHOLD SPENDING	BEST CUSTOMERS (index)	BIGGEST CUSTOMERS (market share)
Average household	$159.35	100	100.0%
Under age 25	110.46	69	4.7
Aged 25 to 34	147.67	93	15.8
Aged 35 to 44	189.41	119	23.2
Aged 45 to 54	190.67	120	25.1
Aged 55 to 64	178.53	112	18.1
Aged 65 to 74	145.06	91	9.1
Aged 75 or older	66.34	42	3.9

	AVERAGE HOUSEHOLD SPENDING	BEST CUSTOMERS (index)	BIGGEST CUSTOMERS (market share)
HOUSEHOLD INCOME			
Average household	**$159.35**	**100**	**100.0%**
Under $20,000	42.59	27	5.5
$20,000 to $39,999	78.08	49	11.4
$40,000 to $49,999	121.41	76	7.5
$50,000 to $69,999	149.83	94	14.4
$70,000 to $79,999	183.65	115	6.7
$80,000 to $99,999	219.56	138	11.2
$100,000 or more	403.15	253	43.3
HOUSEHOLD TYPE			
Average household	**159.35**	**100**	**100.0**
Married couples	207.71	130	65.9
Married couples, no children	194.48	122	26.3
Married couples, with children	226.64	142	35.5
Oldest child under age 6	144.13	90	4.4
Oldest child aged 6 to 17	261.59	164	20.9
Oldest child aged 18 or older	221.05	139	10.2
Single parent with child under age 18	130.04	82	4.8
Single person	100.20	63	18.7
RACE AND HISPANIC ORIGIN			
Average household	**159.35**	**100**	**100.0**
Asian	171.41	108	3.8
Black	81.06	51	6.1
Hispanic	111.95	70	8.3
Non-Hispanic white and other	178.86	112	85.7
REGION			
Average household	**159.35**	**100**	**100.0**
Northeast	177.13	111	20.7
Midwest	152.30	96	21.8
South	124.14	78	28.0
West	207.68	130	29.5
EDUCATION			
Average household	**159.35**	**100**	**100.0**
Less than high school graduate	49.92	31	4.8
High school graduate	90.95	57	14.4
Some college	146.00	92	20.0
Associate's degree	158.02	99	8.8
College graduate	286.73	180	52.1
Bachelor's degree	248.53	156	29.2
Master's, professional, doctoral degree	356.92	224	22.8

Note: Market shares may not sum to 100.0 because of rounding and missing categories by household type. "Asian" and "black" include Hispanics and non-Hispanics who identify themselves as being of the respective race alone. "Hispanic" includes people of any race who identify themselves as Hispanic. "Other" includes people who identify themselves as non-Hispanic and as Alaska Native, American Indian, Asian (who are also included in the "Asian" row), Native Hawaiian or other Pacific Islander, as well as non-Hispanics reporting more than one race.
Source: Calculations by New Strategist based on the Bureau of Labor Statistics' 2007 Consumer Expenditure Survey.

Musical Instruments and Accessories

Best customers:
Householders aged 45 to 54
Married couples with school-aged or older children at home
Single parents
Asians
Households in the West

Customer trends:
Average household spending on musical instruments and accessories will decline as school budget cuts eliminate music programs.

The best customers of musical instruments and accessories are parents with school-aged children. Married couples with school-aged children spend well over twice the average, and single parents spend 56 percent more than average on this item. Together the two groups control 38 percent of the market. Householders aged 45 to 54 spend 79 percent more than the average on this item. Asians spend 82 percent more than average on musical instruments, while households in the West, where many Asians reside, spend 45 percent more than average.

Average household spending on musical instruments and accessories declined between 2000 and 2007, falling by an enormous 61 percent after adjusting for inflation. Behind the decline are school budget woes, which make fewer music programs available to schoolchildren. Spending will continue to decline in the years ahead because of ongoing school budget problems.

Table 5.15 Musical instruments and accessories

Total household spending $1,801,363,290.00
Average household spends   14.99

	AVERAGE HOUSEHOLD SPENDING	BEST CUSTOMERS (index)	BIGGEST CUSTOMERS (market share)
AGE OF HOUSEHOLDER			
Average household	**$14.99**	**100**	**100.0%**
Under age 25	12.11	81	5.5
Aged 25 to 34	15.19	101	17.3
Aged 35 to 44	13.80	92	17.9
Aged 45 to 54	26.90	179	37.7
Aged 55 to 64	10.20	68	11.0
Aged 65 to 74	14.10	94	9.4
Aged 75 or older	1.85	12	1.2

	AVERAGE HOUSEHOLD SPENDING	BEST CUSTOMERS (index)	BIGGEST CUSTOMERS (market share)
HOUSEHOLD INCOME			
Average household	**$14.99**	**100**	**100.0%**
Under $20,000	8.86	59	12.1
$20,000 to $39,999	12.19	81	18.9
$40,000 to $49,999	10.12	68	6.6
$50,000 to $69,999	10.28	69	10.5
$70,000 to $79,999	13.81	92	5.3
$80,000 to $99,999	35.76	239	19.4
$100,000 or more	23.69	158	27.1
HOUSEHOLD TYPE			
Average household	**14.99**	**100**	**100.0**
Married couples	17.28	115	58.3
Married couples, no children	10.79	72	15.5
Married couples, with children	23.22	155	38.7
Oldest child under age 6	6.85	46	2.2
Oldest child aged 6 to 17	33.35	222	28.3
Oldest child aged 18 or older	16.58	111	8.1
Single parent with child under age 18	23.37	156	9.3
Single person	7.57	51	15.0
RACE AND HISPANIC ORIGIN			
Average household	**14.99**	**100**	**100.0**
Asian	27.22	182	6.4
Black	1.44	10	1.2
Hispanic	7.06	47	5.6
Non-Hispanic white and other	18.32	122	93.3
REGION			
Average household	**14.99**	**100**	**100.0**
Northeast	14.80	99	18.4
Midwest	18.24	122	27.8
South	8.72	58	20.9
West	21.81	145	32.9
EDUCATION			
Average household	**14.99**	**100**	**100.0**
Less than high school graduate	4.61	31	4.7
High school graduate	6.91	46	11.6
Some college	19.85	132	28.8
Associate's degree	14.99	100	8.9
College graduate	23.82	159	46.0
Bachelor's degree	20.87	139	26.1
Master's, professional, doctoral degree	29.23	195	19.9

Note: Market shares may not sum to 100.0 because of rounding and missing categories by household type. "Asian" and "black" include Hispanics and non-Hispanics who identify themselves as being of the respective race alone. "Hispanic" includes people of any race who identify themselves as Hispanic. "Other" includes people who identify themselves as non-Hispanic and as Alaska Native, American Indian, Asian (who are also included in the "Asian" row), Native Hawaiian or other Pacific Islander, as well as non-Hispanics reporting more than one race.
Source: Calculations by New Strategist based on the Bureau of Labor Statistics' 2007 Consumer Expenditure Survey.

Personal Digital Audio Players

Best customers: Householders aged 35 to 54
Married couples with children at home

Customer trends: Average household spending on personal digital audio players
is dependent on trends in technology.

Apple's sleek iPods have created such a demand for personal digital audio players that the Bureau of Labor Statistics added them as a new expenditure category in 2005. The best customers of these devices are married couples with children. Married couples with school-aged children spend well more than twice the average on this item, while those with adult children at home spend 96 percent more than average. Householders aged 35 to 54, most with children, spend 45 to 57 percent more than average on personal digital audio players.

Because the Consumer Expenditure Survey did not include personal digital audio players in 2000, there are no spending trends for the category. Average household spending on personal digital audio players could increase in the years ahead as manufacturers release new models with new features. But the category could wither in the competition with smart phones.

Table 5.16 Personal digital audio players

Total household spending $2,089,773,690.00
Average household spends   17.39

	AVERAGE HOUSEHOLD SPENDING	BEST CUSTOMERS (index)	BIGGEST CUSTOMERS (market share)
AGE OF HOUSEHOLDER			
Average household	**$17.39**	**100**	**100.0%**
Under age 25	15.53	89	6.1
Aged 25 to 34	19.14	110	18.8
Aged 35 to 44	27.30	157	30.6
Aged 45 to 54	25.28	145	30.5
Aged 55 to 64	11.94	69	11.1
Aged 65 to 74	3.52	20	2.0
Aged 75 or older	1.62	9	0.9

	AVERAGE HOUSEHOLD SPENDING	BEST CUSTOMERS (index)	BIGGEST CUSTOMERS (market share)
HOUSEHOLD INCOME			
Average household	**$17.39**	**100**	**100.0%**
Under $20,000	5.14	30	6.1
$20,000 to $39,999	6.32	36	8.4
$40,000 to $49,999	13.68	79	7.7
$50,000 to $69,999	16.85	97	14.8
$70,000 to $79,999	15.80	91	5.3
$80,000 to $99,999	26.47	152	12.4
$100,000 or more	45.94	264	45.3
HOUSEHOLD TYPE			
Average household	**17.39**	**100**	**100.0**
Married couples	24.76	142	72.0
Married couples, no children	13.86	80	17.2
Married couples, with children	35.18	202	50.5
Oldest child under age 6	21.64	124	6.1
Oldest child aged 6 to 17	41.04	236	30.0
Oldest child aged 18 or older	34.05	196	14.4
Single parent with child under age 18	15.47	89	5.3
Single person	6.54	38	11.2
RACE AND HISPANIC ORIGIN			
Average household	**17.39**	**100**	**100.0**
Asian	20.47	118	4.2
Black	11.44	66	7.9
Hispanic	14.07	81	9.6
Non-Hispanic white and other	19.04	109	83.6
REGION			
Average household	**17.39**	**100**	**100.0**
Northeast	17.47	100	18.7
Midwest	16.95	97	22.3
South	14.72	85	30.4
West	22.00	127	28.6
EDUCATION			
Average household	**17.39**	**100**	**100.0**
Less than high school graduate	3.45	20	3.0
High school graduate	10.62	61	15.4
Some college	24.11	139	30.2
Associate's degree	12.85	74	6.6
College graduate	26.92	155	44.8
Bachelor's degree	27.28	157	29.4
Master's, professional, doctoral degree	26.26	151	15.4

Note: Market shares may not sum to 100.0 because of rounding and missing categories by household type. "Asian" and "black" include Hispanics and non-Hispanics who identify themselves as being of the respective race alone. "Hispanic" includes people of any race who identify themselves as Hispanic. "Other" includes people who identify themselves as non-Hispanic and as Alaska Native, American Indian, Asian (who are also included in the "Asian" row), Native Hawaiian or other Pacific Islander, as well as non-Hispanics reporting more than one race.
Source: Calculations by New Strategist based on the Bureau of Labor Statistics' 2007 Consumer Expenditure Survey.

Pet Food

Best customers: **Householders aged 45 to 64**
                    Married couples without children at home
                    Married couples with adult children at home

Customer trends: **Average household spending on pet food will continue to rise as boomers become empty-nesters and devote more attention to their pets.**

Middle-aged married couples spend the most on pets. Many acquire pets when their children are young and care for them long after their children have grown and left home. Pet food accounts for the largest share of pet expenses. Householders aged 45 to 64 spend 33 to 39 percent more than the average household on pet food. Married couples with adult children at home spend two-thirds more than average on this item, while couples without children at home (many of them empty-nesters) spend 39 percent more.

Average household spending on pet food rose 42 percent between 2000 and 2007, after adjusting for inflation. Spending on pet food should continue to climb as boomers age and devote more of their attention to their pets.

Table 5.17 Pet food

Total household spending $17,650,716,480.00
Average household spends   146.88

AGE OF HOUSEHOLDER	AVERAGE HOUSEHOLD SPENDING	BEST CUSTOMERS (index)	BIGGEST CUSTOMERS (market share)
Average household	$146.88	100	100.0%
Under age 25	59.84	41	2.8
Aged 25 to 34	109.97	75	12.8
Aged 35 to 44	156.64	107	20.8
Aged 45 to 54	204.80	139	29.3
Aged 55 to 64	195.61	133	21.6
Aged 65 to 74	140.73	96	9.6
Aged 75 or older	56.69	39	3.7

	AVERAGE HOUSEHOLD SPENDING	BEST CUSTOMERS (index)	BIGGEST CUSTOMERS (market share)
HOUSEHOLD INCOME			
Average household	**$146.88**	**100**	**100.0%**
Under $20,000	59.79	41	8.4
$20,000 to $39,999	107.09	73	16.9
$40,000 to $49,999	114.62	78	7.7
$50,000 to $69,999	158.64	108	16.5
$70,000 to $79,999	168.51	115	6.6
$80,000 to $99,999	261.36	178	14.5
$100,000 or more	245.12	167	28.6
HOUSEHOLD TYPE			
Average household	**146.88**	**100**	**100.0**
Married couples	182.79	124	62.9
Married couples, no children	203.94	139	30.0
Married couples, with children	163.36	111	27.8
Oldest child under age 6	88.64	60	2.9
Oldest child aged 6 to 17	149.74	102	13.0
Oldest child aged 18 or older	245.16	167	12.3
Single parent with child under age 18	94.78	65	3.8
Single person	81.80	56	16.6
RACE AND HISPANIC ORIGIN			
Average household	**146.88**	**100**	**100.0**
Asian	60.71	41	1.5
Black	46.87	32	3.8
Hispanic	89.06	61	7.2
Non-Hispanic white and other	171.68	117	89.2
REGION			
Average household	**146.88**	**100**	**100.0**
Northeast	136.22	93	17.3
Midwest	151.57	103	23.6
South	135.14	92	33.0
West	169.98	116	26.2
EDUCATION			
Average household	**146.88**	**100**	**100.0**
Less than high school graduate	92.73	63	9.6
High school graduate	138.75	94	23.8
Some college	133.89	91	19.9
Associate's degree	227.83	155	13.8
College graduate	165.09	112	32.5
Bachelor's degree	159.77	109	20.4
Master's, professional, doctoral degree	174.31	119	12.1

Note: Market shares may not sum to 100.0 because of rounding and missing categories by household type. "Asian" and "black" include Hispanics and non-Hispanics who identify themselves as being of the respective race alone. "Hispanic" includes people of any race who identify themselves as Hispanic. "Other" includes people who identify themselves as non-Hispanic and as Alaska Native, American Indian, Asian (who are also included in the "Asian" row), Native Hawaiian or other Pacific Islander, as well as non-Hispanics reporting more than one race.
Source: Calculations by New Strategist based on the Bureau of Labor Statistics' 2007 Consumer Expenditure Survey.

Pet Purchase, Supplies, and Medicines

Best customers: Householders aged 35 to 64
Married couples

Customer trends: Average household spending on pet purchase, supplies, and medicines is likely to rise as empty-nesters devote more attention to their pets and the pet industry offers a greater variety of supplies and medicines.

Pets are so popular in the United States that spending on pets, pet supplies, and pet medicines does not vary much by demographic characteristic. Householders ranging in age from 35 to 64 spend more than average on pets, pet supplies, and pet medicines. Married couples spend 25 percent more, the figure peaking at 28 percent among couples with school-aged or older children. To understand the market, it is almost more helpful to know who is least likely to spend on pets—single parents, single persons, and householders with the lowest incomes.

Average household spending on pets, pet supplies, and pet medicines doubled between 2000 and 2007, after adjusting for inflation, as pharmaceutical companies offered a growing variety of pricey medications for flea prevention, heart-worm protection, allergy relief, and so on. This category will continue to grow as boomers age and devote more attention to their pets.

Table 5.18 Pet purchase, supplies, and medicines

| | Total household spending | $16,710,979,260.00 |
| | Average household spends | 139.06 |

	AVERAGE HOUSEHOLD SPENDING	BEST CUSTOMERS (index)	BIGGEST CUSTOMERS (market share)
AGE OF HOUSEHOLDER			
Average household	**$139.06**	**100**	**100.0%**
Under age 25	75.31	54	3.7
Aged 25 to 34	127.99	92	15.7
Aged 35 to 44	176.91	127	24.8
Aged 45 to 54	167.14	120	25.2
Aged 55 to 64	154.76	111	18.0
Aged 65 to 74	112.49	81	8.1
Aged 75 or older	65.76	47	4.5

	AVERAGE HOUSEHOLD SPENDING	BEST CUSTOMERS (index)	BIGGEST CUSTOMERS (market share)
HOUSEHOLD INCOME			
Average household	**$139.06**	**100**	**100.0%**
Under $20,000	61.75	44	9.1
$20,000 to $39,999	96.77	70	16.2
$40,000 to $49,999	125.37	90	8.9
$50,000 to $69,999	165.75	119	18.2
$70,000 to $79,999	147.78	106	6.2
$80,000 to $99,999	188.57	136	11.0
$100,000 or more	246.79	177	30.4
HOUSEHOLD TYPE			
Average household	**139.06**	**100**	**100.0**
Married couples	174.08	125	63.3
Married couples, no children	170.22	122	26.4
Married couples, with children	172.30	124	30.9
Oldest child under age 6	147.42	106	5.2
Oldest child aged 6 to 17	178.26	128	16.3
Oldest child aged 18 or older	178.51	128	9.5
Single parent with child under age 18	89.92	65	3.8
Single person	82.95	60	17.7
RACE AND HISPANIC ORIGIN			
Average household	**139.06**	**100**	**100.0**
Asian	70.93	51	1.8
Black	46.19	33	4.0
Hispanic	95.30	69	8.1
Non-Hispanic white and other	160.29	115	88.0
REGION			
Average household	**139.06**	**100**	**100.0**
Northeast	127.37	92	17.1
Midwest	127.85	92	21.0
South	141.93	102	36.6
West	155.47	112	25.3
EDUCATION			
Average household	**139.06**	**100**	**100.0**
Less than high school graduate	98.40	71	10.7
High school graduate	120.99	87	21.9
Some college	134.34	97	21.0
Associate's degree	155.05	111	9.9
College graduate	174.77	126	36.4
Bachelor's degree	162.06	117	21.8
Master's, professional, doctoral degree	198.11	142	14.5

Note: Market shares may not sum to 100.0 because of rounding and missing categories by household type. "Asian" and "black" include Hispanics and non-Hispanics who identify themselves as being of the respective race alone. "Hispanic" includes people of any race who identify themselves as Hispanic. "Other" includes people who identify themselves as non-Hispanic and as Alaska Native, American Indian, Asian (who are also included in the "Asian" row), Native Hawaiian or other Pacific Islander, as well as non-Hispanics reporting more than one race.
Source: Calculations by New Strategist based on the Bureau of Labor Statistics' 2007 Consumer Expenditure Survey.

Pet Services

Householders aged 45 to 64
Married couples without children at home
Married couples with school-aged or older children at home
Households in the West

Customer trends:

Average household spending on pet services is likely to rise as empty-nesters of the baby-boom generation devote more attention to their pets.

The best customers of pet services—such as grooming and dog walking—are older married couples. Householders ranging in age from 45 to 64 spend 30 to 49 percent more than average on this item. Married couples with school-aged or older children at home and those without children at home (most of them empty-nesters) spend 25 to 35 percent more than average on this item. (Note: The high spending by single parents on pet services is a divergence from the pattern in previous years and is most likely an anomaly in this year's spending data.) Households in the West spend 45 percent more than average on pet services.

Average household spending on pet services rose 36 percent between 2000 and 2007, after adjusting for inflation. Spending on pet services will continue to grow as boomers age and devote more attention to their pets.

Table 5.19 Pet services

Total household spending $3,807,017,280.00
Average household spends   31.68

	AVERAGE HOUSEHOLD SPENDING	BEST CUSTOMERS (index)	BIGGEST CUSTOMERS (market share)
AGE OF HOUSEHOLDER			
Average household	**$31.68**	**100**	**100.0%**
Under age 25	3.44	11	0.7
Aged 25 to 34	19.06	60	10.3
Aged 35 to 44	34.03	107	20.9
Aged 45 to 54	47.16	149	31.3
Aged 55 to 64	41.30	130	21.1
Aged 65 to 74	31.58	100	10.0
Aged 75 or older	19.10	60	5.7

	AVERAGE HOUSEHOLD SPENDING	BEST CUSTOMERS (index)	BIGGEST CUSTOMERS (market share)
HOUSEHOLD INCOME			
Average household	**$31.68**	**100**	**100.0%**
Under $20,000	10.85	34	7.0
$20,000 to $39,999	14.42	46	10.6
$40,000 to $49,999	18.27	58	5.7
$50,000 to $69,999	31.76	100	15.3
$70,000 to $79,999	31.38	99	5.7
$80,000 to $99,999	49.24	155	12.6
$100,000 or more	79.47	251	43.0
HOUSEHOLD TYPE			
Average household	**31.68**	**100**	**100.0**
Married couples	39.94	126	63.7
Married couples, no children	39.53	125	26.9
Married couples, with children	40.28	127	31.7
Oldest child under age 6	34.11	108	5.3
Oldest child aged 6 to 17	42.76	135	17.1
Oldest child aged 18 or older	40.10	127	9.3
Single parent with child under age 18	49.06	155	9.2
Single person	20.90	66	19.6
RACE AND HISPANIC ORIGIN			
Average household	**31.68**	**100**	**100.0**
Asian	5.25	17	0.6
Black	6.72	21	2.5
Hispanic	12.78	40	4.8
Non-Hispanic white and other	38.48	121	92.7
REGION			
Average household	**31.68**	**100**	**100.0**
Northeast	25.66	81	15.1
Midwest	32.92	104	23.7
South	25.13	79	28.5
West	45.78	145	32.7
EDUCATION			
Average household	**31.68**	**100**	**100.0**
Less than high school graduate	10.87	34	5.2
High school graduate	21.53	68	17.1
Some college	31.11	98	21.4
Associate's degree	25.54	81	7.2
College graduate	53.74	170	49.1
Bachelor's degree	43.16	136	25.5
Master's, professional, doctoral degree	73.18	231	23.6

Note: Market shares may not sum to 100.0 because of rounding and missing categories by household type. "Asian" and "black" include Hispanics and non-Hispanics who identify themselves as being of the respective race alone. "Hispanic" includes people of any race who identify themselves as Hispanic. "Other" includes people who identify themselves as non-Hispanic and as Alaska Native, American Indian, Asian (who are also included in the "Asian" row), Native Hawaiian or other Pacific Islander, as well as non-Hispanics reporting more than one race.
Source: Calculations by New Strategist based on the Bureau of Labor Statistics' 2007 Consumer Expenditure Survey.

Photo Processing

Best customers: **Householders aged 35 to 54**
                                   Married couples with children at home

Customer trends: **Average household spending on photo processing will slip as home printers reduce processing needs.**

The best customers of photo processing are married couples with children at home. Couples with preschoolers spend three times the average on photo processing as they get digital and film pictures of their children processed into prints. Couples with school-aged or older children at home spend 46 to 66 percent more than average on this item. Householders aged 35 to 54, many of them parents, spend 15 to 44 percent more than average on photo processing.

Average household spending on photo processing fell by an enormous 58 percent between 2000 and 2007, after adjusting for inflation. Behind the decline was the shift to digital photography, which allows families to process pictures on their computers and printers at home. This trend should intensify as more households replace their film cameras with digital models, but the popularity of digital photo processing centers in drugstores and groceries may limit the decline in spending on this category.

Table 5.20 Photo processing

Total household spending		$1,920,332,580.00	
Average household spends		15.98	

	AVERAGE HOUSEHOLD SPENDING	BEST CUSTOMERS (index)	BIGGEST CUSTOMERS (market share)
AGE OF HOUSEHOLDER			
Average household	**$15.98**	**100**	**100.0%**
Under age 25	10.31	65	4.4
Aged 25 to 34	15.79	99	16.9
Aged 35 to 44	23.02	144	28.1
Aged 45 to 54	18.30	115	24.1
Aged 55 to 64	13.69	86	13.9
Aged 65 to 74	14.39	90	9.0
Aged 75 or older	6.41	40	3.8

	AVERAGE HOUSEHOLD SPENDING	BEST CUSTOMERS (index)	BIGGEST CUSTOMERS (market share)
HOUSEHOLD INCOME			
Average household	**$15.98**	**100**	**100.0%**
Under $20,000	5.25	33	6.8
$20,000 to $39,999	8.33	52	12.1
$40,000 to $49,999	14.20	89	8.7
$50,000 to $69,999	15.08	94	14.4
$70,000 to $79,999	18.99	119	6.9
$80,000 to $99,999	25.75	161	13.1
$100,000 or more	35.42	222	38.0
HOUSEHOLD TYPE			
Average household	**15.98**	**100**	**100.0**
Married couples	23.64	148	74.8
Married couples, no children	17.51	110	23.6
Married couples, with children	29.76	186	46.5
Oldest child under age 6	47.74	299	14.6
Oldest child aged 6 to 17	26.55	166	21.1
Oldest child aged 18 or older	23.40	146	10.8
Single parent with child under age 18	9.56	60	3.6
Single person	7.12	45	13.3
RACE AND HISPANIC ORIGIN			
Average household	**15.98**	**100**	**100.0**
Asian	13.12	82	2.9
Black	6.47	40	4.9
Hispanic	5.96	37	4.4
Non-Hispanic white and other	19.00	119	90.8
REGION			
Average household	**15.98**	**100**	**100.0**
Northeast	16.14	101	18.8
Midwest	21.22	133	30.3
South	12.51	78	28.1
West	16.08	101	22.8
EDUCATION			
Average household	**15.98**	**100**	**100.0**
Less than high school graduate	5.43	34	5.2
High school graduate	12.03	75	19.0
Some college	14.01	88	19.1
Associate's degree	17.38	109	9.7
College graduate	26.01	163	47.1
Bachelor's degree	25.08	157	29.4
Master's, professional, doctoral degree	27.72	173	17.7

Note: Market shares may not sum to 100.0 because of rounding and missing categories by household type. "Asian" and "black" include Hispanics and non-Hispanics who identify themselves as being of the respective race alone. "Hispanic" includes people of any race who identify themselves as Hispanic. "Other" includes people who identify themselves as non-Hispanic and as Alaska Native, American Indian, Asian (who are also included in the "Asian" row), Native Hawaiian or other Pacific Islander, as well as non-Hispanics reporting more than one race.
Source: Calculations by New Strategist based on the Bureau of Labor Statistics' 2007 Consumer Expenditure Survey.

Photographer's Fees

Best customers: **Householders aged 25 to 54**
Married couples with children at home
Single parents
Households in the Northeast

Customer trends: **Average household spending on photographer's fees is likely to decline in the years ahead as the small generation X fills the best-customer lifestage.**

Average household spending on photographer's fees is all about children. The best customers of this item are parents. Householders ranging in age from 25 to 54 spend 23 to 123 percent more than average on this item because most are parents. They control 91 percent of the market. Married couples with children at home spend more than twice the average on this item and account for 54 percent of the market. Single parents spend 17 percent more. Households in the Northeast spend 59 percent more than average on photographer's fees.

Average household spending on photographer's fees climbed by 3 percent between 2000 and 2007. Spending on this category is likely to decline in the years ahead as households tighten their belts, the small generation X fills the best-customer lifestage, and professional photographers lose ground in the competition with digital technology.

Table 5.21 **Photographer's fees**

Total household spending $3,019,897,230.00
Average household spends   25.13

	AVERAGE HOUSEHOLD SPENDING	BEST CUSTOMERS (index)	BIGGEST CUSTOMERS (market share)
AGE OF HOUSEHOLDER			
Average household	$25.13	100	100.0%
Under age 25	11.42	45	3.1
Aged 25 to 34	31.52	125	21.4
Aged 35 to 44	56.08	223	43.5
Aged 45 to 54	30.85	123	25.8
Aged 55 to 64	5.25	21	3.4
Aged 65 to 74	5.52	22	2.2
Aged 75 or older	1.50	6	0.6

	AVERAGE HOUSEHOLD SPENDING	BEST CUSTOMERS (index)	BIGGEST CUSTOMERS (market share)
HOUSEHOLD INCOME			
Average household	**$25.13**	**100**	**100.0%**
Under $20,000	8.35	33	6.8
$20,000 to $39,999	6.34	25	5.9
$40,000 to $49,999	19.11	76	7.5
$50,000 to $69,999	48.14	192	29.3
$70,000 to $79,999	30.46	121	7.0
$80,000 to $99,999	17.59	70	5.7
$100,000 or more	59.92	238	40.9
HOUSEHOLD TYPE			
Average household	**25.13**	**100**	**100.0**
Married couples	33.83	135	68.1
Married couples, no children	8.23	33	7.1
Married couples, with children	54.70	218	54.3
Oldest child under age 6	30.98	123	6.0
Oldest child aged 6 to 17	73.07	291	36.9
Oldest child aged 18 or older	35.76	142	10.5
Single parent with child under age 18	29.33	117	6.9
Single person	2.16	9	2.6
RACE AND HISPANIC ORIGIN			
Average household	**25.13**	**100**	**100.0**
Asian	16.96	67	2.4
Black	9.26	37	4.4
Hispanic	29.52	117	13.9
Non-Hispanic white and other	26.94	107	81.8
REGION			
Average household	**25.13**	**100**	**100.0**
Northeast	40.04	159	29.7
Midwest	19.84	79	18.0
South	17.79	71	25.4
West	29.80	119	26.8
EDUCATION			
Average household	**25.13**	**100**	**100.0**
Less than high school graduate	4.15	17	2.5
High school graduate	29.89	119	30.0
Some college	19.41	77	16.8
Associate's degree	24.14	96	8.5
College graduate	35.10	140	40.4
Bachelor's degree	40.57	161	30.3
Master's, professional, doctoral degree	25.59	102	10.4

Note: Market shares may not sum to 100.0 because of rounding and missing categories by household type. "Asian" and "black" include Hispanics and non-Hispanics who identify themselves as being of the respective race alone. "Hispanic" includes people of any race who identify themselves as Hispanic. "Other" includes people who identify themselves as non-Hispanic and as Alaska Native, American Indian, Asian (who are also included in the "Asian" row), Native Hawaiian or other Pacific Islander, as well as non-Hispanics reporting more than one race.
Source: Calculations by New Strategist based on the Bureau of Labor Statistics' 2007 Consumer Expenditure Survey.

Photographic Equipment

Best customers: **Householders aged 25 to 54**
                          Married couples with children under age 18

Customer trends: **Average household spending on photographic equipment will continue to grow as digital cameras replace film cameras in most homes.**

Household spending on digital cameras is the driving force in this category. The best customers of photographic equipment are households that snap a lot of pictures: married couples with children. This explains why householders ranging in age from 25 to 54, many of whom are parents, are the best customers of photographic equipment—spending 11 to 39 percent more than average. Married couples with children under age 18 spend 68 to 99 percent more than average on this item.

Average household spending on photographic equipment grew by a substantial 227 percent between 2000 and 2007 after adjusting for inflation. The replacement of film cameras with digital cameras is behind the increase, a substitution that should continue to drive spending in this category for several more years.

Table 5.22 Photographic equipment

Total household spending $3,874,313,040.00
Average household spends   32.24

	AVERAGE HOUSEHOLD SPENDING	BEST CUSTOMERS (index)	BIGGEST CUSTOMERS (market share)
AGE OF HOUSEHOLDER			
Average household	**$32.24**	**100**	**100.0%**
Under age 25	23.30	72	4.9
Aged 25 to 34	35.84	111	19.0
Aged 35 to 44	44.90	139	27.1
Aged 45 to 54	35.76	111	23.3
Aged 55 to 64	31.17	97	15.7
Aged 65 to 74	23.73	74	7.4
Aged 75 or older	9.10	28	2.7

	AVERAGE HOUSEHOLD SPENDING	BEST CUSTOMERS (index)	BIGGEST CUSTOMERS (market share)
HOUSEHOLD INCOME			
Average household	**$32.24**	**100**	**100.0%**
Under $20,000	9.57	30	6.1
$20,000 to $39,999	17.25	54	12.4
$40,000 to $49,999	21.56	67	6.6
$50,000 to $69,999	34.97	108	16.6
$70,000 to $79,999	58.47	181	10.5
$80,000 to $99,999	30.98	96	7.8
$100,000 or more	75.19	233	40.0
HOUSEHOLD TYPE			
Average household	**32.24**	**100**	**100.0**
Married couples	43.65	135	68.4
Married couples, no children	36.62	114	24.5
Married couples, with children	54.22	168	42.0
Oldest child under age 6	54.31	168	8.2
Oldest child aged 6 to 17	64.12	199	25.3
Oldest child aged 18 or older	37.09	115	8.5
Single parent with child under age 18	16.29	51	3.0
Single person	18.28	57	16.9
RACE AND HISPANIC ORIGIN			
Average household	**32.24**	**100**	**100.0**
Asian	34.57	107	3.8
Black	12.05	37	4.5
Hispanic	21.01	65	7.7
Non-Hispanic white and other	37.09	115	87.8
REGION			
Average household	**32.24**	**100**	**100.0**
Northeast	27.57	86	15.9
Midwest	39.83	124	28.2
South	25.56	79	28.5
West	39.01	121	27.4
EDUCATION			
Average household	**32.24**	**100**	**100.0**
Less than high school graduate	11.26	35	5.3
High school graduate	17.04	53	13.3
Some college	34.46	107	23.3
Associate's degree	30.86	96	8.5
College graduate	55.23	171	49.6
Bachelor's degree	54.09	168	31.4
Master's, professional, doctoral degree	57.31	178	18.1

Note: Market shares may not sum to 100.0 because of rounding and missing categories by household type. "Asian" and "black" include Hispanics and non-Hispanics who identify themselves as being of the respective race alone. "Hispanic" includes people of any race who identify themselves as Hispanic. "Other" includes people who identify themselves as non-Hispanic and as Alaska Native, American Indian, Asian (who are also included in the "Asian" row), Native Hawaiian or other Pacific Islander, as well as non-Hispanics reporting more than one race.
Source: Calculations by New Strategist based on the Bureau of Labor Statistics' 2007 Consumer Expenditure Survey.

Rental of Party Supplies for Catered Affairs

Best customers:	**Householders aged 25 to 34 and 45 to 64** **High-income households** **Married couples without children at home** **Married couples with adult children at home**
Customer trends:	**Average household spending on the rental of party supplies for catered affairs is likely to decline in the years ahead as households tighten their belts.**

The best customers of rented party supplies for catered affairs are young adults who are getting married and their parents. Householders aged 25 to 34 spend 75 percent more than average on rented party supplies for catered affairs. Householders aged 45 to 64 spend 17 to 32 percent more on this item. Married couples without children at home spend 50 percent more than average on rented party supplies for catered affair. Couples with adult children at home spend more than twice the average.

Rental of party supplies for catered affairs is a new item in the Consumer Expenditure Survey, and comparable data from 2000 do not exist. Average household spending on this item is likely to decline in the years ahead as households tighten their belts.

Table 5.23 Rental of party supplies for catered affairs

Total household spending	$1,124,800,560.00
Average household spends	9.36

AGE OF HOUSEHOLDER	AVERAGE HOUSEHOLD SPENDING	BEST CUSTOMERS (index)	BIGGEST CUSTOMERS (market share)
Average household	$9.36	100	100.0%
Under age 25	1.41	15	1.0
Aged 25 to 34	16.37	175	29.8
Aged 35 to 44	7.89	84	16.4
Aged 45 to 54	12.32	132	27.7
Aged 55 to 64	10.92	117	18.9
Aged 65 to 74	4.65	50	5.0
Aged 75 or older	1.18	13	1.2

	AVERAGE HOUSEHOLD SPENDING	BEST CUSTOMERS (index)	BIGGEST CUSTOMERS (market share)
HOUSEHOLD INCOME			
Average household	**$9.36**	**100**	**100.0%**
Under $20,000	2.24	24	4.9
$20,000 to $39,999	5.42	58	13.5
$40,000 to $49,999	2.18	23	2.3
$50,000 to $69,999	6.81	73	11.1
$70,000 to $79,999	3.61	39	2.2
$80,000 to $99,999	15.11	161	13.1
$100,000 or more	28.86	308	52.8
HOUSEHOLD TYPE			
Average household	**9.36**	**100**	**100.0**
Married couples	12.61	135	68.1
Married couples, no children	14.03	150	32.3
Married couples, with children	12.62	135	33.6
Oldest child under age 6	8.95	96	4.7
Oldest child aged 6 to 17	9.91	106	13.4
Oldest child aged 18 or older	19.73	211	15.5
Single parent with child under age 18	2.00	21	1.3
Single person	4.42	47	14.0
RACE AND HISPANIC ORIGIN			
Average household	**9.36**	**100**	**100.0**
Asian	1.67	18	0.6
Black	9.31	99	11.9
Hispanic	7.78	83	9.8
Non-Hispanic white and other	9.59	102	78.2
REGION			
Average household	**9.36**	**100**	**100.0**
Northeast	10.90	116	21.7
Midwest	11.45	122	28.0
South	7.93	85	30.4
West	8.25	88	19.9
EDUCATION			
Average household	**9.36**	**100**	**100.0**
Less than high school graduate	1.15	12	1.9
High school graduate	4.89	52	13.2
Some college	9.82	105	22.8
Associate's degree	16.15	173	15.3
College graduate	15.13	162	46.8
Bachelor's degree	13.46	144	27.0
Master's, professional, doctoral degree	18.20	194	19.8

Note: Market shares may not sum to 100.0 because of rounding and missing categories by household type. "Asian" and "black" include Hispanics and non-Hispanics who identify themselves as being of the respective race alone. "Hispanic" includes people of any race who identify themselves as Hispanic. "Other" includes people who identify themselves as non-Hispanic and as Alaska Native, American Indian, Asian (who are also included in the "Asian" row), Native Hawaiian or other Pacific Islander, as well as non-Hispanics reporting more than one race.
Source: Calculations by New Strategist based on the Bureau of Labor Statistics' 2007 Consumer Expenditure Survey.

Satellite Radio Service

Best customers:	**Householders aged 25 to 44 and 55 to 64**
	Married couples without children at home
	Married couples with children under age 18
Customer trends:	**Average household spending on satellite radio service will depend more on trends in technology than on demographic change in the years ahead.**

Householders aged 25 to 44 and 55 to 64 spend 11 to 24 percent more than average on satellite radio service. Married couples without children at home, most of them empty-nesters, spend 36 percent more than average on this item. Couples with children under age 18 at home spend 41 to 50 percent more than average on satellite radio service.

Satellite radio service is a new item in the Consumer Expenditure Survey, and comparable data from 2000 do not exist. Average household spending on satellite radio service in the years ahead will depend more on trends in technology than on demographic change

Table 5.24 **Satellite radio service**

Total household spending $1,443,253,710.00
Average household spends 12.01

AGE OF HOUSEHOLDER	AVERAGE HOUSEHOLD SPENDING	BEST CUSTOMERS (index)	BIGGEST CUSTOMERS (market share)
Average household	$12.01	100	100.0%
Under age 25	7.06	59	4.0
Aged 25 to 34	13.37	111	19.0
Aged 35 to 44	14.81	123	24.0
Aged 45 to 54	10.78	90	18.9
Aged 55 to 64	14.87	124	20.1
Aged 65 to 74	11.93	99	9.9
Aged 75 or older	5.26	44	4.2

	AVERAGE HOUSEHOLD SPENDING	BEST CUSTOMERS (index)	BIGGEST CUSTOMERS (market share)
HOUSEHOLD INCOME			
Average household	**$12.01**	**100**	**100.0%**
Under $20,000	5.21	43	8.9
$20,000 to $39,999	7.31	61	14.2
$40,000 to $49,999	9.19	77	7.5
$50,000 to $69,999	13.71	114	17.5
$70,000 to $79,999	21.51	179	10.4
$80,000 to $99,999	15.27	127	10.3
$100,000 or more	21.88	182	31.2
HOUSEHOLD TYPE			
Average household	**12.01**	**100**	**100.0**
Married couples	15.86	132	66.8
Married couples, no children	16.35	136	29.4
Married couples, with children	15.35	128	31.9
Oldest child under age 6	17.98	150	7.3
Oldest child aged 6 to 17	16.92	141	17.9
Oldest child aged 18 or older	10.90	91	6.7
Single parent with child under age 18	7.83	65	3.9
Single person	6.49	54	16.1
RACE AND HISPANIC ORIGIN			
Average household	**12.01**	**100**	**100.0**
Asian	7.55	63	2.2
Black	7.38	61	7.4
Hispanic	10.27	86	10.1
Non-Hispanic white and other	12.98	108	82.5
REGION			
Average household	**12.01**	**100**	**100.0**
Northeast	10.43	87	16.2
Midwest	11.74	98	22.3
South	13.27	110	39.7
West	11.58	96	21.8
EDUCATION			
Average household	**12.01**	**100**	**100.0**
Less than high school graduate	6.22	52	7.9
High school graduate	9.60	80	20.2
Some college	15.00	125	27.2
Associate's degree	10.78	90	8.0
College graduate	15.27	127	36.8
Bachelor's degree	14.41	120	22.5
Master's, professional, doctoral degree	16.84	140	14.3

Note: Market shares may not sum to 100.0 because of rounding and missing categories by household type. "Asian" and "black" include Hispanics and non-Hispanics who identify themselves as being of the respective race alone. "Hispanic" includes people of any race who identify themselves as Hispanic. "Other" includes people who identify themselves as non-Hispanic and as Alaska Native, American Indian, Asian (who are also included in the "Asian" row), Native Hawaiian or other Pacific Islander, as well as non-Hispanics reporting more than one race.
Source: Calculations by New Strategist based on the Bureau of Labor Statistics' 2007 Consumer Expenditure Survey.

Sound Components, Equipment, and Accessories (Including Radios and Tape Recorders)

Best customers: Householders aged 25 to 34 and 45 to 54
Married couples
Households in the West

Customer trends: Average household spending on sound equipment is unlikely to rise in the years ahead because of continued price discounting and product substitution.

The best customers of sound components, equipment, and accessories are households with preschoolers (who are outfitting their first home with sound equipment) or adult children at home (who are buying their first sound systems). This explains why householders aged 25 to 34 and those aged 45 to 54 spend 35 to 39 percent more than average on this item. Married couples with preschoolers and those with adult children at home spend 89 percent more than average on sound components, equipment, and accessories. Households in the West spend 55 percent more than the average household on sound equipment.

Average household spending on sound components, equipment, and accessories fell 30 percent between 2000 and 2007. Behind the decline is the substitution of personal digital audio equipment (such as iPods) for larger systems. Average household spending on this category is unlikely to rise in the years ahead because of continued price discounting and product substitution.

Table 5.25 Sound components, equipment, and accessories (including radios and tape recorders)

Total household spending $4,285,297,860.00
Average household spends 35.66

AGE OF HOUSEHOLDER	AVERAGE HOUSEHOLD SPENDING	BEST CUSTOMERS (index)	BIGGEST CUSTOMERS (market share)
Average household	$35.66	100	100.0%
Under age 25	30.37	85	5.8
Aged 25 to 34	49.56	139	23.7
Aged 35 to 44	32.79	92	17.9
Aged 45 to 54	48.24	135	28.4
Aged 55 to 64	36.94	104	16.8
Aged 65 to 74	18.90	53	5.3
Aged 75 or older	8.60	24	2.3

	AVERAGE HOUSEHOLD SPENDING	BEST CUSTOMERS (index)	BIGGEST CUSTOMERS (market share)
HOUSEHOLD INCOME			
Average household	$35.66	100	100.0%
Under $20,000	12.59	35	7.3
$20,000 to $39,999	15.16	43	9.9
$40,000 to $49,999	17.38	49	4.8
$50,000 to $69,999	35.27	99	15.1
$70,000 to $79,999	44.93	126	7.3
$80,000 to $99,999	49.60	139	11.3
$100,000 or more	93.03	261	44.7
HOUSEHOLD TYPE			
Average household	35.66	100	100.0
Married couples	49.94	140	70.8
Married couples, no children	45.62	128	27.6
Married couples, with children	54.01	151	37.8
Oldest child under age 6	67.46	189	9.2
Oldest child aged 6 to 17	42.89	120	15.3
Oldest child aged 18 or older	67.34	189	13.9
Single parent with child under age 18	9.08	25	1.5
Single person	17.81	50	14.9
RACE AND HISPANIC ORIGIN			
Average household	35.66	100	100.0
Asian	19.44	55	1.9
Black	13.56	38	4.6
Hispanic	37.77	106	12.5
Non-Hispanic white and other	38.77	109	83.0
REGION			
Average household	35.66	100	100.0
Northeast	29.26	82	15.3
Midwest	32.62	91	20.9
South	28.71	81	28.9
West	55.15	155	35.0
EDUCATION			
Average household	35.66	100	100.0
Less than high school graduate	16.70	47	7.1
High school graduate	24.89	70	17.6
Some college	29.78	84	18.2
Associate's degree	37.98	107	9.5
College graduate	57.74	162	46.9
Bachelor's degree	58.45	164	30.7
Master's, professional, doctoral degree	56.23	158	16.1

Note: Market shares may not sum to 100.0 because of rounding and missing categories by household type. "Asian" and "black" include Hispanics and non-Hispanics who identify themselves as being of the respective race alone. "Hispanic" includes people of any race who identify themselves as Hispanic. "Other" includes people who identify themselves as non-Hispanic and as Alaska Native, American Indian, Asian (who are also included in the "Asian" row), Native Hawaiian or other Pacific Islander, as well as non-Hispanics reporting more than one race.
Source: Calculations by New Strategist based on the Bureau of Labor Statistics' 2007 Consumer Expenditure Survey.

Stamp and Coin Collecting

Best customers:	**Householders aged 55 or older** **Married couples without children at home** **Married couples with adult children at home** **People who live alone** **Non-Hispanic whites** **Households in the Midwest and West**
Customer trends:	**Average household spending on stamp and coin collecting may decline as younger cohorts move into the best-customer age groups.**

The best customers for stamp and coin collecting are older householders. Householders aged 55 or older spend substantially more than average on this item, with those in the 65-to-74 age group spending more than double the average. Married couples without children at home (most of them empty-nesters) spend 31 percent more than average on this hobby, while those with adult children at home spend almost twice the average on stamp and coin collecting. People who live alone spend 40 percent more than average on this item. Households in the Midwest spend 72 percent more than average, those in the West, 53 percent more than average.

Average household spending on stamp and coin collecting may decline in the years ahead as younger cohorts with no history of collecting move into the best-customer age groups.

Table 5.26 Stamp and coin collecting

Total household spending	$483,087,420.00
Average household spends	4.02

	AVERAGE HOUSEHOLD SPENDING	BEST CUSTOMERS (index)	BIGGEST CUSTOMERS (market share)
AGE OF HOUSEHOLDER			
Average household	**$4.02**	**100**	**100.0%**
Under age 25	1.84	46	3.1
Aged 25 to 34	3.08	77	13.1
Aged 35 to 44	1.45	36	7.0
Aged 45 to 54	3.92	98	20.5
Aged 55 to 64	5.00	124	20.1
Aged 65 to 74	8.66	215	21.5
Aged 75 or older	6.26	156	14.8

	AVERAGE HOUSEHOLD SPENDING	BEST CUSTOMERS (index)	BIGGEST CUSTOMERS (market share)
HOUSEHOLD INCOME			
Average household	**$4.02**	**100**	**100.0%**
Under $20,000	0.95	24	4.9
$20,000 to $39,999	5.00	124	28.9
$40,000 to $49,999	2.18	54	5.3
$50,000 to $69,999	3.56	89	13.6
$70,000 to $79,999	0.86	21	1.2
$80,000 to $99,999	6.68	166	13.5
$100,000 or more	7.67	191	32.7
HOUSEHOLD TYPE			
Average household	**4.02**	**100**	**100.0**
Married couples	4.01	100	50.4
Married couples, no children	5.25	131	28.2
Married couples, with children	3.45	86	21.4
Oldest child under age 6	0.63	16	0.8
Oldest child aged 6 to 17	2.04	51	6.4
Oldest child aged 18 or older	7.76	193	14.2
Single parent with child under age 18	0.90	22	1.3
Single person	5.63	140	41.7
RACE AND HISPANIC ORIGIN			
Average household	**4.02**	**100**	**100.0**
Asian	–	–	–
Black	0.65	16	1.9
Hispanic	0.22	5	0.6
Non-Hispanic white and other	5.14	128	97.6
REGION			
Average household	**4.02**	**100**	**100.0**
Northeast	1.75	44	8.1
Midwest	6.92	172	39.3
South	2.03	50	18.1
West	6.15	153	34.6
EDUCATION			
Average household	**4.02**	**100**	**100.0**
Less than high school graduate	1.00	25	3.8
High school graduate	4.51	112	28.3
Some college	2.29	57	12.4
Associate's degree	5.93	148	13.1
College graduate	5.91	147	42.6
Bachelor's degree	4.64	115	21.6
Master's, professional, doctoral degree	8.23	205	20.9

Note: Market shares may not sum to 100.0 because of rounding and missing categories by household type. "Asian" and "black" include Hispanics and non-Hispanics who identify themselves as being of the respective race alone. "Hispanic" includes people of any race who identify themselves as Hispanic. "Other" includes people who identify themselves as non-Hispanic and as Alaska Native, American Indian, Asian (who are also included in the "Asian" row), Native Hawaiian or other Pacific Islander, as well as non-Hispanics reporting more than one race.
Source: Calculations by New Strategist based on the Bureau of Labor Statistics' 2007 Consumer Expenditure Survey.

Streamed and Downloaded Audio

Best customers: **Householders aged 25 to 54**
                          Married couples with children under age 18
                          Households in the West

Customer trends: **Average household spending on streamed and downloaded audio should rise in the**
                          years ahead as downloads become the norm for buying music.

Streamed and downloaded audio is a spending category newly added to the Consumer Expenditure Survey in 2005. It captures spending on music downloads from sites such as iTunes and pay-per-listen programming. The best customers of audio downloads are households with school-aged children, which spend more than twice the average on this item. Householders ranging in age from 25 to 54, many with children, spend 20 to 46 percent more than average on streamed and downloaded audio and cumulatively account for 79 percent of the market. Households in the West spend 45 percent more than average on audio downloads.

Streamed and downloaded audio is a relatively new item in the Consumer Expenditure Survey and comparable data from 2000 do not exist. In light of soaring sales of personal digital audio players, and with this capability being built into a growing number of cell phones, average household spending on music downloads should increase greatly in the years ahead.

Table 5.27 Streamed and downloaded audio

Total household spending $442,229,280.00
Average household spends   3.68

	AVERAGE HOUSEHOLD SPENDING	BEST CUSTOMERS (index)	BIGGEST CUSTOMERS (market share)
AGE OF HOUSEHOLDER			
Average household	**$3.68**	**100**	**100.0%**
Under age 25	3.93	107	7.2
Aged 25 to 34	5.38	146	24.9
Aged 35 to 44	5.38	146	28.5
Aged 45 to 54	4.41	120	25.2
Aged 55 to 64	1.96	53	8.6
Aged 65 to 74	1.64	45	4.5
Aged 75 or older	0.38	10	1.0

	AVERAGE HOUSEHOLD SPENDING	BEST CUSTOMERS (index)	BIGGEST CUSTOMERS (market share)
HOUSEHOLD INCOME			
Average household	**$3.68**	**100**	**100.0%**
Under $20,000	1.23	33	6.9
$20,000 to $39,999	1.57	43	9.9
$40,000 to $49,999	2.88	78	7.7
$50,000 to $69,999	3.73	101	15.5
$70,000 to $79,999	4.06	110	6.4
$80,000 to $99,999	5.15	140	11.4
$100,000 or more	9.06	246	42.2
HOUSEHOLD TYPE			
Average household	**3.68**	**100**	**100.0**
Married couples	4.62	126	63.5
Married couples, no children	2.64	72	15.5
Married couples, with children	6.49	176	44.0
Oldest child under age 6	6.55	178	8.7
Oldest child aged 6 to 17	7.76	211	26.8
Oldest child aged 18 or older	4.26	116	8.5
Single parent with child under age 18	2.93	80	4.7
Single person	2.30	63	18.6
RACE AND HISPANIC ORIGIN			
Average household	**3.68**	**100**	**100.0**
Asian	2.91	79	2.8
Black	1.90	52	6.2
Hispanic	1.40	38	4.5
Non-Hispanic white and other	4.30	117	89.2
REGION			
Average household	**3.68**	**100**	**100.0**
Northeast	3.91	106	19.8
Midwest	3.00	82	18.6
South	2.93	80	28.6
West	5.35	145	32.9
EDUCATION			
Average household	**3.68**	**100**	**100.0**
Less than high school graduate	0.69	19	2.8
High school graduate	2.51	68	17.2
Some college	3.65	99	21.6
Associate's degree	3.52	96	8.5
College graduate	6.33	172	49.8
Bachelor's degree	6.20	168	31.6
Master's, professional, doctoral degree	6.57	179	18.2

Note: Market shares may not sum to 100.0 because of rounding and missing categories by household type. "Asian" and "black" include Hispanics and non-Hispanics who identify themselves as being of the respective race alone. "Hispanic" includes people of any race who identify themselves as Hispanic. "Other" includes people who identify themselves as non-Hispanic and as Alaska Native, American Indian, Asian (who are also included in the "Asian" row), Native Hawaiian or other Pacific Islander, as well as non-Hispanics reporting more than one race.
Source: Calculations by New Strategist based on the Bureau of Labor Statistics' 2007 Consumer Expenditure Survey.

Television Sets

Best customers:
    Householders aged 25 to 54
    Married couples with school-aged children
    Asians

Customer trends:
    Average household spending on television sets is likely to decline once most households have replaced their old sets with HD versions.

The best customers of television sets are married couples with school-aged children. Married couples spend 36 percent more than average on television sets, with the figure peaking at 65 percent among couples with children aged 6 to 17. Householders aged 25 to 54, many with children, spend 14 to 22 percent more than average on this item and account for 68 percent of the market. Asian householders spend 34 percent more than average on this item.

Average household spending on television sets more than doubled between 2000 and 2007, after adjusting for inflation, making it the second-fastest-growing entertainment category and catapulting it into second place in the entertainment spending hierarchy. Behind the increase is the replacement of older televisions with new high-definition sets. Average household spending on television sets is likely to decline once most households have replaced their old sets with HD versions.

Table 5.28 Television sets

| Total household spending | $19,496,543,040.00 |
| Average household spends | 162.24 |

AGE OF HOUSEHOLDER	AVERAGE HOUSEHOLD SPENDING	BEST CUSTOMERS (index)	BIGGEST CUSTOMERS (market share)
Average household	**$162.24**	**100**	**100.0%**
Under age 25	125.33	77	5.2
Aged 25 to 34	185.68	114	19.5
Aged 35 to 44	189.62	117	22.8
Aged 45 to 54	197.33	122	25.6
Aged 55 to 64	154.72	95	15.4
Aged 65 to 74	128.22	79	7.9
Aged 75 or older	61.14	38	3.6

	AVERAGE HOUSEHOLD SPENDING	BEST CUSTOMERS (index)	BIGGEST CUSTOMERS (market share)
HOUSEHOLD INCOME			
Average household	**$162.24**	**100**	**100.0%**
Under $20,000	45.89	28	5.8
$20,000 to $39,999	98.94	61	14.2
$40,000 to $49,999	117.49	72	7.1
$50,000 to $69,999	139.77	86	13.2
$70,000 to $79,999	130.03	80	4.6
$80,000 to $99,999	215.51	133	10.8
$100,000 or more	419.10	258	44.3
HOUSEHOLD TYPE			
Average household	**162.24**	**100**	**100.0**
Married couples	220.59	136	68.7
Married couples, no children	208.76	129	27.8
Married couples, with children	230.87	142	35.5
Oldest child under age 6	189.30	117	5.7
Oldest child aged 6 to 17	267.71	165	21.0
Oldest child aged 18 or older	194.89	120	8.9
Single parent with child under age 18	87.72	54	3.2
Single person	85.74	53	15.7
RACE AND HISPANIC ORIGIN			
Average household	**162.24**	**100**	**100.0**
Asian	216.66	134	4.7
Black	92.65	57	6.9
Hispanic	140.11	86	10.2
Non-Hispanic white and other	176.70	109	83.1
REGION			
Average household	**162.24**	**100**	**100.0**
Northeast	146.57	90	16.8
Midwest	149.93	92	21.1
South	163.08	101	36.1
West	186.26	115	26.0
EDUCATION			
Average household	**162.24**	**100**	**100.0**
Less than high school graduate	90.32	56	8.4
High school graduate	115.26	71	17.9
Some college	146.99	91	19.7
Associate's degree	131.25	81	7.2
College graduate	261.86	161	46.7
Bachelor's degree	265.98	164	30.7
Master's, professional, doctoral degree	254.30	157	16.0

Note: Market shares may not sum to 100.0 because of rounding and missing categories by household type. "Asian" and "black" include Hispanics and non-Hispanics who identify themselves as being of the respective race alone. "Hispanic" includes people of any race who identify themselves as Hispanic. "Other" includes people who identify themselves as non-Hispanic and as Alaska Native, American Indian, Asian (who are also included in the "Asian" row), Native Hawaiian or other Pacific Islander, as well as non-Hispanics reporting more than one race.
Source: Calculations by New Strategist based on the Bureau of Labor Statistics' 2007 Consumer Expenditure Survey.

Toys, Games, Hobbies, and Tricycles

Best customers:

Householders aged 25 to 44
Married couples with children under age 18
Single parents

Customer trends:

Average household spending on toys, games, hobbies, and tricycles will continue to
fall as the small generation X fills the best-customer lifestage.

The best customers of toys, games, hobbies, and tricycles are parents with children under age 18. This explains why householders aged 25 to 44, many of them parents, spend 43 to 44 percent more than average on this item and account for 52 percent of the market. Married couples with preschoolers spend three times the average on toys, and those with school-aged children spend a still substantial 78 percent more than average. Even single parents, who spend considerably less than average on the vast majority of spending categories, spend 2 percent more than the average household on toys, games, hobbies, and tricycles.

Average household spending on toys, games, hobbies, and tricycles fell 18 percent between 2000 and 2007, after adjusting for inflation. Behind the decline are falling prices for toys due to cheaper imports. Also behind the decline is the entry of the small generation X into the best-customer lifestage. Belt tightening during the recession probably means spending on this category will continue to decline.

Table 5.29 Toys, games, hobbies, and tricycles

Total household spending $14,412,108,030.00
Average household spends 119.93

AGE OF HOUSEHOLDER	AVERAGE HOUSEHOLD SPENDING	BEST CUSTOMERS (index)	BIGGEST CUSTOMERS (market share)
Average household	$119.93	100	100.0%
Under age 25	67.71	56	3.8
Aged 25 to 34	171.32	143	24.4
Aged 35 to 44	172.24	144	28.0
Aged 45 to 54	108.88	91	19.1
Aged 55 to 64	101.55	85	13.7
Aged 65 to 74	102.24	85	8.5
Aged 75 or older	30.25	25	2.4

	AVERAGE HOUSEHOLD SPENDING	BEST CUSTOMERS (index)	BIGGEST CUSTOMERS (market share)
HOUSEHOLD INCOME			
Average household	$119.93	100	100.0%
Under $20,000	30.95	26	5.3
$20,000 to $39,999	63.88	53	12.4
$40,000 to $49,999	97.06	81	8.0
$50,000 to $69,999	144.68	121	18.5
$70,000 to $79,999	152.71	127	7.4
$80,000 to $99,999	206.12	172	14.0
$100,000 or more	238.73	199	34.1
HOUSEHOLD TYPE			
Average household	119.93	100	100.0
Married couples	168.26	140	70.9
Married couples, no children	111.08	93	20.0
Married couples, with children	219.97	183	45.8
Oldest child under age 6	352.14	294	14.3
Oldest child aged 6 to 17	213.85	178	22.7
Oldest child aged 18 or older	135.06	113	8.3
Single parent with child under age 18	122.55	102	6.1
Single person	49.55	41	12.3
RACE AND HISPANIC ORIGIN			
Average household	119.93	100	100.0
Asian	124.28	104	3.7
Black	55.00	46	5.5
Hispanic	86.40	72	8.5
Non-Hispanic white and other	134.60	112	85.7
REGION			
Average household	119.93	100	100.0
Northeast	124.65	104	19.4
Midwest	110.08	92	21.0
South	109.22	91	32.7
West	143.37	120	27.0
EDUCATION			
Average household	119.93	100	100.0
Less than high school graduate	53.97	45	6.8
High school graduate	89.92	75	18.9
Some college	127.57	106	23.2
Associate's degree	141.78	118	10.5
College graduate	164.78	137	39.8
Bachelor's degree	171.54	143	26.8
Master's, professional, doctoral degree	153.05	128	13.0

Note: Market shares may not sum to 100.0 because of rounding and missing categories by household type. "Asian" and "black" include Hispanics and non-Hispanics who identify themselves as being of the respective race alone. "Hispanic" includes people of any race who identify themselves as Hispanic. "Other" includes people who identify themselves as non-Hispanic and as Alaska Native, American Indian, Asian (who are also included in the "Asian" row), Native Hawaiian or other Pacific Islander, as well as non-Hispanics reporting more than one race.
Source: Calculations by New Strategist based on the Bureau of Labor Statistics' 2007 Consumer Expenditure Survey.

Veterinary Services

Best customers:
Householders aged 35 to 64
Married couples without children at home
Married couples with school-aged or older children at home

Customer trends:
Average household spending on veterinary services will continue to rise as boomers age and devote a larger share of their discretionary income to their pets.

The best customers of veterinary services are middle-aged and older married couples, many of whom have older pets that require extensive veterinary care. Householders aged 45 to 54 spend 57 percent more than average on this item. Married couples without children at home (most of them empty-nesters) spend 58 percent more than average on this item and control 34 percent of the market. Couples with adult children at home spend 48 percent more.

Average household spending on veterinary services rose 42 percent between 2000 and 2007, after adjusting for inflation. Spending on this category will continue to grow as more boomers age and devote a larger share of their discretionary income to their pets.

Table 5.30 **Veterinary services**

Total household spending $13,600,953,780.00
Average household spends 113.18

AGE OF HOUSEHOLDER	AVERAGE HOUSEHOLD SPENDING	BEST CUSTOMERS (index)	BIGGEST CUSTOMERS (market share)
Average household	$113.18	100	100.0%
Under age 25	32.99	29	2.0
Aged 25 to 34	43.30	38	6.5
Aged 35 to 44	174.62	154	30.1
Aged 45 to 54	177.13	157	32.9
Aged 55 to 64	148.53	131	21.3
Aged 65 to 74	32.37	29	2.9
Aged 75 or older	61.06	54	5.1

	AVERAGE HOUSEHOLD SPENDING	BEST CUSTOMERS (index)	BIGGEST CUSTOMERS (market share)
HOUSEHOLD INCOME			
Average household	**$113.18**	**100**	**100.0%**
Under $20,000	7.00	6	1.3
$20,000 to $39,999	62.91	56	12.9
$40,000 to $49,999	65.97	58	5.7
$50,000 to $69,999	76.25	67	10.3
$70,000 to $79,999	260.30	230	13.3
$80,000 to $99,999	129.78	115	9.3
$100,000 or more	319.53	282	48.4
HOUSEHOLD TYPE			
Average household	**113.18**	**100**	**100.0**
Married couples	152.31	135	68.0
Married couples, no children	179.16	158	34.1
Married couples, with children	142.05	126	31.3
Oldest child under age 6	41.52	37	1.8
Oldest child aged 6 to 17	166.52	147	18.7
Oldest child aged 18 or older	167.39	148	10.9
Single parent with child under age 18	126.32	112	6.6
Single person	49.54	44	13.0
RACE AND HISPANIC ORIGIN			
Average household	**113.18**	**100**	**100.0**
Asian	37.18	33	1.2
Black	17.04	15	1.8
Hispanic	28.60	25	3.0
Non-Hispanic white and other	139.94	124	94.4
REGION			
Average household	**113.18**	**100**	**100.0**
Northeast	154.17	136	25.4
Midwest	91.32	81	18.4
South	99.39	88	31.5
West	123.25	109	24.6
EDUCATION			
Average household	**113.18**	**100**	**100.0**
Less than high school graduate	14.79	13	2.0
High school graduate	104.16	92	23.2
Some college	102.90	91	19.8
Associate's degree	125.98	111	9.9
College graduate	170.24	150	43.5
Bachelor's degree	152.74	135	25.3
Master's, professional, doctoral degree	200.62	177	18.1

Note: Market shares may not sum to 100.0 because of rounding and missing categories by household type. "Asian" and "black" include Hispanics and non-Hispanics who identify themselves as being of the respective race alone. "Hispanic" includes people of any race who identify themselves as Hispanic. "Other" includes people who identify themselves as non-Hispanic and as Alaska Native, American Indian, Asian (who are also included in the "Asian" row), Native Hawaiian or other Pacific Islander, as well as non-Hispanics reporting more than one race.
Source: Calculations by New Strategist based on the Bureau of Labor Statistics' 2007 Consumer Expenditure Survey.

Video Cassette Recorders and Video Disc Players

Best customers: Householders aged 25 to 44
                            Married couples with children at home

Customer trends: Average household spending on video cassette recorders and video disc players will
                            continue to decline because of technological change.

The best customers of video cassette recorders and video disk players are young and middle-aged householders buying equipment for their family's enjoyment. Householders aged 25 to 44 spend 32 to 34 percent more than average on VCRs and DVD players. Married couples with children at home spend 43 percent more than average on VCRs and DVD players, the figure peaking at more than double the average among parents of preschoolers.

Average household spending on video cassette recorders and video disc players fell by 48 percent between 2000 and 2007, after adjusting for inflation. Changing technology and falling prices were behind the decline as VCRs became obsolete, cheaper imports reduced costs, and high-definition television sets allowed users to download movies. Technological change, coupled with the fact that the small generation X is in the best-customer lifestage, suggest that average household spending on this category will continue to decline.

Table 5.31 Video cassette recorders and video disc players

Total household spending $1,782,135,930.00
Average household spends   14.83

	AVERAGE HOUSEHOLD SPENDING	BEST CUSTOMERS (index)	BIGGEST CUSTOMERS (market share)
AGE OF HOUSEHOLDER			
Average household	**$14.83**	**100**	**100.0%**
Under age 25	8.99	61	4.1
Aged 25 to 34	19.64	132	22.6
Aged 35 to 44	19.88	134	26.1
Aged 45 to 54	16.45	111	23.3
Aged 55 to 64	12.85	87	14.0
Aged 65 to 74	11.31	76	7.6
Aged 75 or older	3.41	23	2.2

	AVERAGE HOUSEHOLD SPENDING	BEST CUSTOMERS (index)	BIGGEST CUSTOMERS (market share)
HOUSEHOLD INCOME			
Average household	**$14.83**	**100**	**100.0%**
Under $20,000	4.75	32	6.6
$20,000 to $39,999	11.21	76	17.6
$40,000 to $49,999	11.78	79	7.8
$50,000 to $69,999	11.45	77	11.8
$70,000 to $79,999	13.03	88	5.1
$80,000 to $99,999	23.87	161	13.1
$100,000 or more	32.91	222	38.0
HOUSEHOLD TYPE			
Average household	**14.83**	**100**	**100.0**
Married couples	18.18	123	62.0
Married couples, no children	14.74	99	21.4
Married couples, with children	21.28	143	35.8
Oldest child under age 6	30.54	206	10.1
Oldest child aged 6 to 17	19.77	133	16.9
Oldest child aged 18 or older	17.77	120	8.8
Single parent with child under age 18	7.45	50	3.0
Single person	12.19	82	24.4
RACE AND HISPANIC ORIGIN			
Average household	**14.83**	**100**	**100.0**
Asian	14.19	96	3.4
Black	7.67	52	6.2
Hispanic	15.66	106	12.5
Non-Hispanic white and other	15.81	107	81.4
REGION			
Average household	**14.83**	**100**	**100.0**
Northeast	12.25	83	15.4
Midwest	16.52	111	25.5
South	12.68	86	30.7
West	18.64	126	28.4
EDUCATION			
Average household	**14.83**	**100**	**100.0**
Less than high school graduate	7.43	50	7.6
High school graduate	9.76	66	16.6
Some college	12.96	87	19.0
Associate's degree	18.83	127	11.3
College graduate	23.29	157	45.5
Bachelor's degree	23.78	160	30.1
Master's, professional, doctoral degree	22.39	151	15.4

Note: Market shares may not sum to 100.0 because of rounding and missing categories by household type. "Asian" and "black" include Hispanics and non-Hispanics who identify themselves as being of the respective race alone. "Hispanic" includes people of any race who identify themselves as Hispanic. "Other" includes people who identify themselves as non-Hispanic and as Alaska Native, American Indian, Asian (who are also included in the "Asian" row), Native Hawaiian or other Pacific Islander, as well as non-Hispanics reporting more than one race.
Source: Calculations by New Strategist based on the Bureau of Labor Statistics' 2007 Consumer Expenditure Survey.

Video Cassettes, Tapes, and Discs

Best customers: **Householders under age 45**
                                 Married couples with children under age 18

Customer trends: **Average household spending on video cassettes, tapes, and discs may continue to increase as households buy high-definition versions of their favorite movies.**

The best customers of video cassettes, tapes, and discs are young to middle-aged married couples with children, many of them buying children's programming to keep the kids entertained. Householders under age 45 spend 29 to 34 percent more than average on videos and DVDs and account for 56 percent of the market. Couples with children under age 18 spend 35 to 54 percent more than average on this item.

Average household spending on video cassettes, tapes, and discs rose by a hefty 53 percent between 2000 and 2007, after adjusting for inflation. Behind the increase was the substitution of DVDs for videos as DVD players replaced VCRs. Now that the high-definition format battle has played out, consumers are likely to replace their DVDs with HD versions of their favorite movies. This may push average household spending on the category even higher in the years ahead.

Table 5.32 Video cassettes, tapes, and discs

Total household spending $4,604,952,720.00
Average household spends   38.32

	AVERAGE HOUSEHOLD SPENDING	BEST CUSTOMERS (index)	BIGGEST CUSTOMERS (market share)
AGE OF HOUSEHOLDER			
Average household	**$38.32**	**100**	**100.0%**
Under age 25	51.48	134	9.1
Aged 25 to 34	47.88	125	21.3
Aged 35 to 44	49.59	129	25.2
Aged 45 to 54	43.33	113	23.8
Aged 55 to 64	32.04	84	13.5
Aged 65 to 74	19.81	52	5.2
Aged 75 or older	7.64	20	1.9

	AVERAGE HOUSEHOLD SPENDING	BEST CUSTOMERS (index)	BIGGEST CUSTOMERS (market share)
HOUSEHOLD INCOME			
Average household	$38.32	100	100.0%
Under $20,000	18.52	48	9.9
$20,000 to $39,999	25.58	67	15.5
$40,000 to $49,999	43.66	114	11.2
$50,000 to $69,999	41.15	107	16.4
$70,000 to $79,999	56.73	148	8.6
$80,000 to $99,999	58.36	152	12.4
$100,000 or more	58.00	151	25.9
HOUSEHOLD TYPE			
Average household	38.32	100	100.0
Married couples	44.61	116	58.8
Married couples, no children	34.19	89	19.2
Married couples, with children	52.96	138	34.5
Oldest child under age 6	51.89	135	6.6
Oldest child aged 6 to 17	58.88	154	19.5
Oldest child aged 18 or older	43.45	113	8.4
Single parent with child under age 18	36.12	94	5.6
Single person	24.52	64	19.0
RACE AND HISPANIC ORIGIN			
Average household	38.32	100	100.0
Asian	26.16	68	2.4
Black	27.24	71	8.5
Hispanic	31.40	82	9.7
Non-Hispanic white and other	41.14	107	82.0
REGION			
Average household	38.32	100	100.0
Northeast	33.40	87	16.2
Midwest	36.46	95	21.7
South	35.58	93	33.3
West	48.58	127	28.7
EDUCATION			
Average household	38.32	100	100.0
Less than high school graduate	22.67	59	9.0
High school graduate	31.44	82	20.7
Some college	44.00	115	25.0
Associate's degree	44.24	115	10.3
College graduate	46.40	121	35.0
Bachelor's degree	46.52	121	22.8
Master's, professional, doctoral degree	46.18	121	12.3

Note: Market shares may not sum to 100.0 because of rounding and missing categories by household type. "Asian" and "black" include Hispanics and non-Hispanics who identify themselves as being of the respective race alone. "Hispanic" includes people of any race who identify themselves as Hispanic. "Other" includes people who identify themselves as non-Hispanic and as Alaska Native, American Indian, Asian (who are also included in the "Asian" row), Native Hawaiian or other Pacific Islander, as well as non-Hispanics reporting more than one race.
Source: Calculations by New Strategist based on the Bureau of Labor Statistics' 2007 Consumer Expenditure Survey.

Video Game Hardware and Software

Best customers: Householders under age 45
Married couples with school-aged or older children at home
Single parents
Asians
Households in the West

Customer trends: Average household spending on video games will continue to rise as younger
generations, raised on video games, become a larger share of the overall population.

Children and teenagers are the best customers of video game hardware and software. That explains why householders under age 45—most having children at home—spend more than others on this item. Together the under-45 age groups control 77 percent of household spending in this market. Married couples with school-aged children spend two-and-one-half times the average on video game hardware and software, and those with adult children at home spend over three times the average. Even single parents are some of the best customers of video game hardware and software, spending 18 percent more than the average household on this item. Households in the West spend one-third more than average on video games.

Average household spending on video game hardware and software soared 180 percent between 2000 and 2007, after adjusting for inflation. Behind the increase are powerful new game players and a host of exciting new games. Average household spending on video game hardware and software should continue to increase as younger generations, raised on video games, become a larger share of the overall population.

Table 5.33 Video game hardware and software

| Total household spending | $7,582,790,100.00 |
| Average household spends | 63.10 |

	AVERAGE HOUSEHOLD SPENDING	BEST CUSTOMERS (index)	BIGGEST CUSTOMERS (market share)
AGE OF HOUSEHOLDER			
Average household	**$63.10**	**100**	**100.0%**
Under age 25	93.86	149	10.1
Aged 25 to 34	76.60	121	20.7
Aged 35 to 44	150.85	239	46.6
Aged 45 to 54	49.98	79	16.6
Aged 55 to 64	14.47	23	3.7
Aged 65 to 74	9.61	15	1.5
Aged 75 or older	0.23	0	0.0

	AVERAGE HOUSEHOLD SPENDING	BEST CUSTOMERS (index)	BIGGEST CUSTOMERS (market share)
HOUSEHOLD INCOME			
Average household	**$63.10**	**100**	**100.0%**
Under $20,000	33.89	54	11.0
$20,000 to $39,999	35.73	57	13.2
$40,000 to $49,999	35.48	56	5.5
$50,000 to $69,999	105.75	168	25.6
$70,000 to $79,999	31.91	51	2.9
$80,000 to $99,999	133.01	211	17.1
$100,000 or more	87.95	139	23.9
HOUSEHOLD TYPE			
Average household	**63.10**	**100**	**100.0**
Married couples	86.07	136	69.0
Married couples, no children	32.66	52	11.2
Married couples, with children	139.48	221	55.2
Oldest child under age 6	26.37	42	2.0
Oldest child aged 6 to 17	151.95	241	30.6
Oldest child aged 18 or older	197.79	313	23.1
Single parent with child under age 18	74.16	118	7.0
Single person	20.76	33	9.8
RACE AND HISPANIC ORIGIN			
Average household	**63.10**	**100**	**100.0**
Asian	137.02	217	7.7
Black	7.29	12	1.4
Hispanic	53.70	85	10.0
Non-Hispanic white and other	72.99	116	88.3
REGION			
Average household	**63.10**	**100**	**100.0**
Northeast	62.87	100	18.6
Midwest	48.56	77	17.6
South	59.79	95	34.0
West	83.62	133	30.0
EDUCATION			
Average household	**63.10**	**100**	**100.0**
Less than high school graduate	30.97	49	7.4
High school graduate	46.22	73	18.5
Some college	66.43	105	22.9
Associate's degree	133.92	212	18.9
College graduate	69.91	111	32.1
Bachelor's degree	70.83	112	21.0
Master's, professional, doctoral degree	68.32	108	11.0

Note: Market shares may not sum to 100.0 because of rounding and missing categories by household type. "Asian" and "black" include Hispanics and non-Hispanics who identify themselves as being of the respective race alone. "Hispanic" includes people of any race who identify themselves as Hispanic. "Other" includes people who identify themselves as non-Hispanic and as Alaska Native, American Indian, Asian (who are also included in the "Asian" row), Native Hawaiian or other Pacific Islander, as well as non-Hispanics reporting more than one race.
Source: Calculations by New Strategist based on the Bureau of Labor Statistics' 2007 Consumer Expenditure Survey.

Video Tape, Disc, and Film Rental

Best customers: Householders 25 to 44
Married couples with children at home
Single parents
Households in the West

Customer trends: Average household spending on video rentals will continue to decline as
video-on-demand becomes more popular.

Parents are the best customers of video rentals. This explains why householders aged 25 to 44—many of whom are parents—spend 38 to 51 percent more than the average household on this item and control more than half the market. Married couples with children at home spend 69 percent more than average on video rentals. Even single parents spend 22 percent more than the average household on this category.

Average household spending on video and DVD rentals fell 38 percent between 2000 and 2007, after adjusting for inflation. Falling prices and changing technology are behind the decline as competition in the rental market reduced fees and more households opted for downloads or streaming video. Also behind the decline is entry of the small generation X into the best-customer lifestage. Average household spending is likely to continue to decline as video-on-demand becomes more popular.

Table 5.34 Video tape, disc, and film rental

Total household spending	$3,709,678,770.00		
Average household spends	30.87		

	AVERAGE HOUSEHOLD SPENDING	BEST CUSTOMERS (index)	BIGGEST CUSTOMERS (market share)
AGE OF HOUSEHOLDER			
Average household	**$30.87**	**100**	**100.0%**
Under age 25	34.14	111	7.5
Aged 25 to 34	42.61	138	23.5
Aged 35 to 44	46.69	151	29.5
Aged 45 to 54	35.08	114	23.9
Aged 55 to 64	21.07	68	11.1
Aged 65 to 74	10.41	34	3.4
Aged 75 or older	3.88	13	1.2

	AVERAGE HOUSEHOLD SPENDING	BEST CUSTOMERS (index)	BIGGEST CUSTOMERS (market share)
HOUSEHOLD INCOME			
Average household	**$30.87**	**100**	**100.0%**
Under $20,000	11.50	37	7.7
$20,000 to $39,999	21.47	70	16.2
$40,000 to $49,999	29.46	95	9.4
$50,000 to $69,999	37.13	120	18.4
$70,000 to $79,999	45.11	146	8.5
$80,000 to $99,999	42.50	138	11.2
$100,000 or more	51.76	168	28.7
HOUSEHOLD TYPE			
Average household	**30.87**	**100**	**100.0**
Married couples	38.35	124	62.8
Married couples, no children	24.76	80	17.3
Married couples, with children	52.04	169	42.1
Oldest child under age 6	38.25	124	6.0
Oldest child aged 6 to 17	60.36	196	24.8
Oldest child aged 18 or older	46.84	152	11.2
Single parent with child under age 18	37.79	122	7.3
Single person	15.20	49	14.6
RACE AND HISPANIC ORIGIN			
Average household	**30.87**	**100**	**100.0**
Asian	26.19	85	3.0
Black	17.38	56	6.8
Hispanic	25.36	82	9.7
Non-Hispanic white and other	33.80	109	83.6
REGION			
Average household	**30.87**	**100**	**100.0**
Northeast	24.01	78	14.5
Midwest	34.08	110	25.2
South	25.97	84	30.2
West	41.06	133	30.1
EDUCATION			
Average household	**30.87**	**100**	**100.0**
Less than high school graduate	12.27	40	6.0
High school graduate	24.85	80	20.3
Some college	36.36	118	25.6
Associate's degree	39.27	127	11.3
College graduate	39.16	127	36.7
Bachelor's degree	37.12	120	22.5
Master's, professional, doctoral degree	42.90	139	14.2

Note: Market shares may not sum to 100.0 because of rounding and missing categories by household type. "Asian" and "black" include Hispanics and non-Hispanics who identify themselves as being of the respective race alone. "Hispanic" includes people of any race who identify themselves as Hispanic. "Other" includes people who identify themselves as non-Hispanic and as Alaska Native, American Indian, Asian (who are also included in the "Asian" row), Native Hawaiian or other Pacific Islander, as well as non-Hispanics reporting more than one race.
Source: Calculations by New Strategist based on the Bureau of Labor Statistics' 2007 Consumer Expenditure Survey.

Chapter 6.

Financial Products and Services

Household Spending on Financial Services, 2007

Average household spending on financial services and miscellaneous items rose 7 percent between 2000 and 2007, after adjusting for inflation. Mixed trends were behind the growth in spending, including less spending on taxes and more spending on charitable contributions.

Average household spending on federal taxes declined by a substantial 46 percent between 2000 and 2007 because of tax cuts. Spending on state and local taxes fell 31 percent. Other losing categories were life and other personal insurance (down 36 percent), finance charges except for mortgage and vehicle (down 45 percent), funeral expenses (down 32 percent), occupational expenses (down 58 percent), and bank service charges (down 13 percent).

Cash contributions increased strongly between 2000 and 2007. The average household's cash contribution to educational institutions more than doubled between 2000 and 2007. Contributions to charitable organizations rose 64 percent during those years, after adjusting for inflation. Cash contributions to political organizations rose 31 percent, and those to religious organizations, 28 percent.

Cash contributions to religious organizations

(average annual spending of households on cash contributions to religious organizations, 2000 and 2007; in 2007 dollars)

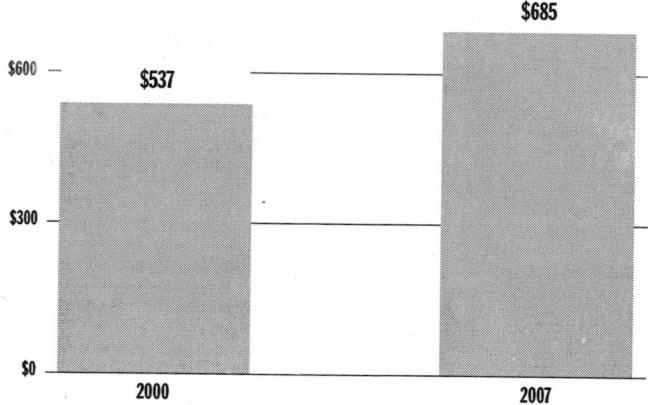

Table 6.1 Financial Spending, 2000 to 2007

(average annual household spending on financial products and services and cash contributions, and percent distribution of spending by type, 2000 and 2007; percent change in spending, 2000–07; in 2007 dollars; ranked by amount spent)

	2007		2000		
	average household spending	percent distribution	average household spending (in 2007$)	percent distribution	percent change 2000–07
Average household spending on financial products and services	**$9,829.46**	**100.0%**	**$9,161.29**	**100.0%**	**7.3%**
Deductions for Social Security	3,907.94	39.8	2,577.22	28.1	51.6
Tax, federal income (net, after refund)	1,569.13	16.0	2,901.02	31.7	–45.9
Cash contributions to religious organizations	684.76	7.0	536.57	5.9	27.6
Deductions for private pensions (payroll deductions)	558.59	5.7	436.65	4.8	27.9
Contributions to retirement accounts (nonpayroll deposits)	482.66	4.9	469.17	5.1	2.9
Tax, state and local income (net, after refund)	468.06	4.8	676.45	7.4	–30.8
Cash gifts	409.71	4.2	–	–	–
Insurance, life and other personal except health	309.47	3.1	479.96	5.2	–35.5
Cash contributions to charitable organizations	275.94	2.8	168.41	1.8	63.8
Child support	198.01	2.0	–	–	–
Finance charges, except mortgage and vehicle	167.63	1.7	305.08	3.3	–45.1
Legal fees	156.59	1.6	125.18	1.4	25.1
Support for college students	99.06	1.0	–	–	–
Accounting fees	77.08	0.8	66.44	0.7	16.0
Deductions for government retirement	74.57	0.8	84.67	0.9	–11.9
Lottery and gambling losses	72.53	0.7	50.09	0.5	44.8
Gifts to members of other households of stocks, bonds, and mutual funds	62.25	0.6	–	–	–
Funeral expenses	58.28	0.6	85.12	0.9	–31.5
Cash contributions to educational institutions	51.10	0.5	24.03	0.3	112.6
Occupational expenses	48.95	0.5	115.88	1.3	–57.8
Alimony expenses	30.19	0.3	–	–	–
Bank service charges	20.77	0.2	23.95	0.3	–13.3
Cemetery lots, vaults, maintenance fees	15.39	0.2	16.22	0.2	–5.1
Cash contributions to political organizations	10.47	0.1	8.01	0.1	30.8
Vacation clubs	8.16	0.1	–	–	–
Shopping club membership fees	7.09	0.1	–	–	–
Safe deposit box rental	3.42	0.0	5.51	0.1	–38.0
Credit card membership fees	1.66	0.0	5.67	0.1	–70.7

Note: "–" means data are unavailable.
Source: Bureau of Labor Statistics, 2000 and 2007 Consumer Expenditure Surveys; calculations by New Strategist

Accounting Fees

Best customers:	**Householders aged 55 to 64** **High-income households** **Married couples without children at home** **Households in the West** **College graduates**
Customer trends:	**Average household spending on accounting fees may continue to rise as aging boomers settle their parents' estates and attempt to simplify their own.**

The best customers of accountants are households with the most complex financial matters. High-income households spend three times the average amount on accounting fees. Householders aged 55 to 64 spend well more than twice the average on accounting fees. Married couples without children at home (most of them older empty-nesters) also spend double the average. Not only are these households less likely to be computer savvy, but they often have complex financial matters as they settle their parents' estates and attempt to simplify their own. Households in the West spend twice the national average on accounting fees, as do households headed by college graduates.

Average household spending on accounting fees increased 16 percent between 2000 and 2007, after adjusting for inflation. Since the tax system is becoming increasingly complex, spending on accounting fees may continue to climb in the years ahead, especially as aging boomers settle their parents' estates and attempt to simplify their own.

Table 6.2 Accounting fees

Total household spending $9,262,780,680.00
Average household spends 77.08

	AVERAGE HOUSEHOLD SPENDING	BEST CUSTOMERS (index)	BIGGEST CUSTOMERS (market share)
AGE OF HOUSEHOLDER			
Average household	**$77.08**	**100**	**100.0%**
Under age 25	16.04	21	1.4
Aged 25 to 34	39.88	52	8.8
Aged 35 to 44	47.91	62	12.1
Aged 45 to 54	71.14	92	19.4
Aged 55 to 64	177.80	231	37.4
Aged 65 to 74	88.67	115	11.5
Aged 75 or older	76.52	99	9.4

	AVERAGE HOUSEHOLD SPENDING	BEST CUSTOMERS (index)	BIGGEST CUSTOMERS (market share)
HOUSEHOLD INCOME			
Average household	**$77.08**	**100**	**100.0%**
Under $20,000	15.06	20	4.0
$20,000 to $39,999	24.92	32	7.5
$40,000 to $49,999	52.75	68	6.7
$50,000 to $69,999	62.95	82	12.5
$70,000 to $79,999	69.89	91	5.2
$80,000 to $99,999	82.77	107	8.7
$100,000 or more	248.59	323	55.3
HOUSEHOLD TYPE			
Average household	**77.08**	**100**	**100.0**
Married couples	109.32	142	71.7
Married couples, no children	160.74	209	45.0
Married couples, with children	73.02	95	23.6
Oldest child under age 6	65.63	85	4.2
Oldest child aged 6 to 17	66.20	86	10.9
Oldest child aged 18 or older	89.68	116	8.6
Single parent with child under age 18	29.34	38	2.3
Single person	49.26	64	19.0
RACE AND HISPANIC ORIGIN			
Average household	**77.08**	**100**	**100.0**
Asian	69.22	90	3.2
Black	25.08	33	3.9
Hispanic	38.96	51	6.0
Non-Hispanic white and other	91.09	118	90.2
REGION			
Average household	**77.08**	**100**	**100.0**
Northeast	71.68	93	17.3
Midwest	56.60	73	16.8
South	41.66	54	19.4
West	158.47	206	46.5
EDUCATION			
Average household	**77.08**	**100**	**100.0**
Less than high school graduate	24.11	31	4.7
High school graduate	40.66	53	13.3
Some college	52.39	68	14.8
Associate's degree	53.02	69	6.1
College graduate	162.55	211	61.0
Bachelor's degree	96.47	125	23.5
Master's, professional, doctoral degree	283.95	368	37.6

Note: Market shares may not sum to 100.0 because of rounding and missing categories by household type. "Asian" and "black" include Hispanics and non-Hispanics who identify themselves as being of the respective race alone. "Hispanic" includes people of any race who identify themselves as Hispanic. "Other" includes people who identify themselves as non-Hispanic and as Alaska Native, American Indian, Asian (who are also included in the "Asian" row), Native Hawaiian or other Pacific Islander, as well as non-Hispanics reporting more than one race.
Source: Calculations by New Strategist based on the Bureau of Labor Statistics' 2007 Consumer Expenditure Survey.

Bank Service Charges

Best customers:　　　　**Householders aged 35 to 54**
Married couples with children at home
Households in the West

Customer trends:　　　　**Average household spending on bank service charges may rise as new regulations**
tighten standards in the financial services industry and as millennials age into their
thirties.

The biggest spenders on bank service charges are middle-aged householders who cannot maintain the larger bank balances necessary to receive free checking and other services. Householders aged 35 to 54 spend 24 to 31 percent more than the average household on bank service charges and account for over half the market. Married couples with children at home, many of them struggling to make ends meet, spend 33 percent more than average on this item. Households in the West spend 30 percent more than average on bank fees.

Average household spending on bank service charges fell 13 percent between 2000 and 2007, after adjusting for inflation. Behind the decline was the elimination of fees as banks competed for customers. Expect average household spending on bank service charges to rise in the years ahead as new regulations tighten standards in the financial services industry.

Table 6.3 Bank service charges

Total household spending　　　　　　　　$2,495,951,670.00
Average household spends　　　　　　　　　　20.77

	AVERAGE HOUSEHOLD SPENDING	BEST CUSTOMERS (index)	BIGGEST CUSTOMERS (market share)
AGE OF HOUSEHOLDER			
Average household	**$20.77**	**100**	**100.0%**
Under age 25	20.95	101	6.8
Aged 25 to 34	23.13	111	19.0
Aged 35 to 44	27.16	131	25.5
Aged 45 to 54	25.69	124	26.0
Aged 55 to 64	20.18	97	15.7
Aged 65 to 74	10.12	49	4.9
Aged 75 or older	4.56	22	2.1

	AVERAGE HOUSEHOLD SPENDING	BEST CUSTOMERS (index)	BIGGEST CUSTOMERS (market share)
HOUSEHOLD INCOME			
Average household	**$20.77**	**100**	**100.0%**
Under $20,000	11.04	53	10.9
$20,000 to $39,999	14.27	69	16.0
$40,000 to $49,999	18.82	91	8.9
$50,000 to $69,999	24.19	116	17.8
$70,000 to $79,999	27.59	133	7.7
$80,000 to $99,999	26.88	129	10.5
$100,000 or more	34.09	164	28.1
HOUSEHOLD TYPE			
Average household	**20.77**	**100**	**100.0**
Married couples	22.65	109	55.1
Married couples, no children	15.93	77	16.5
Married couples, with children	27.58	133	33.1
Oldest child under age 6	28.81	139	6.8
Oldest child aged 6 to 17	27.20	131	16.6
Oldest child aged 18 or older	27.42	132	9.7
Single parent with child under age 18	21.44	103	6.1
Single person	17.13	82	24.5
RACE AND HISPANIC ORIGIN			
Average household	**20.77**	**100**	**100.0**
Asian	13.63	66	2.3
Black	20.56	99	11.9
Hispanic	16.28	78	9.3
Non-Hispanic white and other	21.47	103	78.9
REGION			
Average household	**20.77**	**100**	**100.0**
Northeast	18.01	87	16.2
Midwest	21.19	102	23.3
South	18.02	87	31.2
West	26.96	130	29.4
EDUCATION			
Average household	**20.77**	**100**	**100.0**
Less than high school graduate	10.26	49	7.5
High school graduate	14.67	71	17.8
Some college	23.20	112	24.3
Associate's degree	26.21	126	11.2
College graduate	28.08	135	39.1
Bachelor's degree	25.96	125	23.4
Master's, professional, doctoral degree	31.96	154	15.7

Note: Market shares may not sum to 100.0 because of rounding and missing categories by household type. "Asian" and "black" include Hispanics and non-Hispanics who identify themselves as being of the respective race alone. "Hispanic" includes people of any race who identify themselves as Hispanic. "Other" includes people who identify themselves as non-Hispanic and as Alaska Native, American Indian, Asian (who are also included in the "Asian" row), Native Hawaiian or other Pacific Islander, as well as non-Hispanics reporting more than one race.
Source: Calculations by New Strategist based on the Bureau of Labor Statistics' 2007 Consumer Expenditure Survey.

Cash Contributions to Charitable Organizations

Best customers:	**Householders aged 55 to 64 and 75 or older** **High-income households** **Married couples without children at home** **Married couples with school-aged children** **Households in the West** **College graduates**
Customer trends:	**The average household will cut back on cash gifts to charities until discretionary income rebounds.**

The biggest cash donors to charitable organizations are households with the greatest amount of discretionary income—older, affluent, educated, married couples. Householders aged 55 to 64 spend more than twice the average on this item, while those aged 75 or older spend one-and-one-half times the average on charitable donations. The two age groups account for 53 percent of all household giving to charities. Married couples without children at home (most of them empty-nesters) spend well more than twice the average on cash gifts to charities, and those with school-aged children spend 57 percent more than average on this item. Households with incomes of $100,000 or more spend more than four times the average on this item, while college graduates (who dominate the affluent) spend more than two-and-one-half times the average. Households in the West contribute more than twice the average to charitable organizations.

Average household giving to charitable organizations rose by a substantial 64 percent between 2000 and 2007, after adjusting for inflation. Behind the increase is the entry of the baby-boom generation into the best-customer age groups. Expect to see spending on cash gifts to charities stabilize or even decline in the coming years unless discretionary income rises.

Table 6.4 Cash contributions to charitable organizations

Total household spending	$33,159,985,740.00
Average household spends	275.94

	AVERAGE HOUSEHOLD SPENDING	BEST CUSTOMERS (index)	BIGGEST CUSTOMERS (market share)
AGE OF HOUSEHOLDER			
Average household	**$275.94**	**100**	**100.0%**
Under age 25	16.35	6	0.4
Aged 25 to 34	59.30	21	3.7
Aged 35 to 44	192.42	70	13.6
Aged 45 to 54	283.51	103	21.6
Aged 55 to 64	652.47	236	38.3
Aged 65 to 74	217.05	79	7.9
Aged 75 or older	425.26	154	14.6

	AVERAGE HOUSEHOLD SPENDING	BEST CUSTOMERS (index)	BIGGEST CUSTOMERS (market share)
HOUSEHOLD INCOME			
Average household	**$275.94**	**100**	**100.0%**
Under $20,000	52.93	19	3.9
$20,000 to $39,999	65.72	24	5.5
$40,000 to $49,999	87.44	32	3.1
$50,000 to $69,999	109.25	40	6.1
$70,000 to $79,999	294.49	107	6.2
$80,000 to $99,999	173.44	63	5.1
$100,000 or more	1,128.31	409	70.1
HOUSEHOLD TYPE			
Average household	**275.94**	**100**	**100.0**
Married couples	442.54	160	81.1
Married couples, no children	657.34	238	51.4
Married couples, with children	287.29	104	26.0
Oldest child under age 6	100.45	36	1.8
Oldest child aged 6 to 17	433.95	157	20.0
Oldest child aged 18 or older	158.21	57	4.2
Single parent with child under age 18	71.95	26	1.5
Single person	121.79	44	13.1
RACE AND HISPANIC ORIGIN			
Average household	**275.94**	**100**	**100.0**
Asian	229.45	83	2.9
Black	41.28	15	1.8
Hispanic	39.45	14	1.7
Non-Hispanic white and other	348.90	126	96.5
REGION			
Average household	**275.94**	**100**	**100.0**
Northeast	223.93	81	15.1
Midwest	173.10	63	14.3
South	161.23	58	21.0
West	604.84	219	49.6
EDUCATION			
Average household	**275.94**	**100**	**100.0**
Less than high school graduate	36.11	13	2.0
High school graduate	68.78	25	6.3
Some college	130.82	47	10.3
Associate's degree	130.06	47	4.2
College graduate	736.13	267	77.2
Bachelor's degree	414.77	150	28.2
Master's, professional, doctoral degree	1,326.56	481	49.0

Note: Market shares may not sum to 100.0 because of rounding and missing categories by household type. "Asian" and "black" include Hispanics and non-Hispanics who identify themselves as being of the respective race alone. "Hispanic" includes people of any race who identify themselves as Hispanic. "Other" includes people who identify themselves as non-Hispanic and as Alaska Native, American Indian, Asian (who are also included in the "Asian" row), Native Hawaiian or other Pacific Islander, as well as non-Hispanics reporting more than one race.
Source: Calculations by New Strategist based on the Bureau of Labor Statistics' 2007 Consumer Expenditure Survey.

Cash Contributions to Educational Organizations

Best customers:

Householders aged 45 to 64
High-income households
Married couples without children at home
Married couples with school-aged children
Asians
Households in the West
College graduates

Customer trends:

Average household spending on contributions to educational organizations is likely to decline in the years ahead as the economic downturn limits discretionary spending.

The biggest spenders on educational contributions are older, affluent, and educated. These are the households with the discretionary income to spend on their alma mater. Householders aged 45 to 64 spend 67 to 121 percent more than the average household on contributions to educational organizations, while those with incomes of $100,000 or more give almost five times the average. Married couples without children at home (most of them empty-nesters) give 79 percent more than average to educational organizations, while couples with school-aged children give three times the average. Asians, the highest-educated racial or ethnic group, give double the average to educational organizations, and households in the West, where many Asians reside, donate nearly twice the average amount to schools and universities. College graduates, who dominate the affluent, spend three times the average on this item.

Average household spending on donations to educational organizations soared between 2000 and 2007, more than doubling after adjusting for inflation. Behind the increase was the entry of the baby-boom generation into the best-customer age groups. Spending on contributions to educational organizations is likely to decline in the years ahead as the economic downturn limits discretionary spending.

Table 6.5 Cash contributions to educational institutions

Total household spending	$6,140,738,100.00
Average household spends	51.10

	AVERAGE HOUSEHOLD SPENDING	BEST CUSTOMERS (index)	BIGGEST CUSTOMERS (market share)
AGE OF HOUSEHOLDER			
Average household	**$51.10**	**100**	**100.0%**
Under age 25	1.38	3	0.2
Aged 25 to 34	11.52	23	3.8
Aged 35 to 44	24.32	48	9.3
Aged 45 to 54	85.28	167	35.1
Aged 55 to 64	113.04	221	35.8
Aged 65 to 74	24.40	48	4.8
Aged 75 or older	59.54	117	11.0

	AVERAGE HOUSEHOLD SPENDING	BEST CUSTOMERS (index)	BIGGEST CUSTOMERS (market share)
HOUSEHOLD INCOME			
Average household	**$51.10**	**100**	**100.0%**
Under $20,000	2.33	5	0.9
$20,000 to $39,999	8.58	17	3.9
$40,000 to $49,999	11.30	22	2.2
$50,000 to $69,999	18.06	35	5.4
$70,000 to $79,999	30.88	60	3.5
$80,000 to $99,999	27.03	53	4.3
$100,000 or more	237.97	466	79.8
HOUSEHOLD TYPE			
Average household	**51.10**	**100**	**100.0**
Married couples	85.35	167	84.4
Married couples, no children	91.52	179	38.6
Married couples, with children	91.64	179	44.7
Oldest child under age 6	40.18	79	3.8
Oldest child aged 6 to 17	152.12	298	37.8
Oldest child aged 18 or older	21.45	42	3.1
Single parent with child under age 18	4.74	9	0.6
Single person	22.57	44	13.1
RACE AND HISPANIC ORIGIN			
Average household	**51.10**	**100**	**100.0**
Asian	100.73	197	7.0
Black	4.51	9	1.1
Hispanic	2.48	5	0.6
Non-Hispanic white and other	65.88	129	98.4
REGION			
Average household	**51.10**	**100**	**100.0**
Northeast	34.59	68	12.6
Midwest	41.05	80	18.4
South	38.59	76	27.1
West	94.74	185	41.9
EDUCATION			
Average household	**51.10**	**100**	**100.0**
Less than high school graduate	3.30	6	1.0
High school graduate	15.03	29	7.4
Some college	10.27	20	4.4
Associate's degree	9.45	18	1.6
College graduate	151.10	296	85.6
Bachelor's degree	68.19	133	25.0
Master's, professional, doctoral degree	303.44	594	60.6

Note: Market shares may not sum to 100.0 because of rounding and missing categories by household type. "Asian" and "black" include Hispanics and non-Hispanics who identify themselves as being of the respective race alone. "Hispanic" includes people of any race who identify themselves as Hispanic. "Other" includes people who identify themselves as non-Hispanic and as Alaska Native, American Indian, Asian (who are also included in the "Asian" row), Native Hawaiian or other Pacific Islander, as well as non-Hispanics reporting more than one race.
Source: Calculations by New Strategist based on the Bureau of Labor Statistics' 2007 Consumer Expenditure Survey.

Cash Contributions to Political Organizations

Best customers:

Householders aged 45 to 74
High-income households
Married couples without children at home
Married couples with school-aged children
Non-Hispanic whites
Households in the Northeast
College graduates

Customer trends:

Average household spending on contributions to political organizations depend largely on the degree of political divisiveness among voters.

The biggest spenders on political contributions are older, affluent, and educated. These are the households with the discretionary income to devote to political causes. Householders aged 45 to 74 spend 37 to 119 percent more than the average on contributions to political organizations, while those with incomes of $100,000 or more give more than three times the average. Married couples without children at home (most of them empty-nesters) give 63 percent more than average to political contributions, while those with school-aged children give 49 percent more. Non-Hispanic whites give 21 percent more than average to political organizations. College graduates, who dominate the affluent, spend two-and-one-half times the average on this item. The contributions of households in the Northeast are more than twice as high as the average and account for 43 percent of all political giving.

Average household spending on donations to political organizations rose 31 percent between 2000 and 2007, after adjusting for inflation. Behind the increase is political polarization, driving both right and left to give money to organizations promoting their causes. Expect to see a continuing climb in average household spending on political donations in the 2008 spending data.

Table 6.6 Cash contributions to political organizations

Total household spending $1,258,190,370.00
Average household spends   10.47

	AVERAGE HOUSEHOLD SPENDING	BEST CUSTOMERS (index)	BIGGEST CUSTOMERS (market share)
AGE OF HOUSEHOLDER			
Average household	$10.47	100	100.0%
Under age 25	1.07	10	0.7
Aged 25 to 34	1.71	16	2.8
Aged 35 to 44	7.55	72	14.1
Aged 45 to 54	14.36	137	28.8
Aged 55 to 64	14.85	142	23.0
Aged 65 to 74	22.91	219	21.9
Aged 75 or older	9.80	94	8.9

	AVERAGE HOUSEHOLD SPENDING	BEST CUSTOMERS (index)	BIGGEST CUSTOMERS (market share)
HOUSEHOLD INCOME			
Average household	**$10.47**	**100**	**100.0%**
Under $20,000	1.80	17	3.5
$20,000 to $39,999	3.19	30	7.1
$40,000 to $49,999	2.79	27	2.6
$50,000 to $69,999	4.05	39	5.9
$70,000 to $79,999	15.42	147	8.5
$80,000 to $99,999	12.46	119	9.7
$100,000 or more	38.30	366	62.7
HOUSEHOLD TYPE			
Average household	**10.47**	**100**	**100.0**
Married couples	13.58	130	65.6
Married couples, no children	17.04	163	35.1
Married couples, with children	12.23	117	29.1
Oldest child under age 6	12.37	118	5.8
Oldest child aged 6 to 17	15.59	149	18.9
Oldest child aged 18 or older	6.35	61	4.5
Single parent with child under age 18	1.47	14	0.8
Single person	10.76	103	30.6
RACE AND HISPANIC ORIGIN			
Average household	**10.47**	**100**	**100.0**
Asian	3.16	30	1.1
Black	5.18	49	5.9
Hispanic	1.50	14	1.7
Non-Hispanic white and other	12.68	121	92.4
REGION			
Average household	**10.47**	**100**	**100.0**
Northeast	24.05	230	42.8
Midwest	6.21	59	13.6
South	7.31	70	25.1
West	8.63	82	18.6
EDUCATION			
Average household	**10.47**	**100**	**100.0**
Less than high school graduate	1.73	17	2.5
High school graduate	1.45	14	3.5
Some college	8.70	83	18.1
Associate's degree	3.55	34	3.0
College graduate	26.38	252	72.9
Bachelor's degree	13.63	130	24.4
Master's, professional, doctoral degree	49.82	476	48.5

Note: Market shares may not sum to 100.0 because of rounding and missing categories by household type. "Asian" and "black" include Hispanics and non-Hispanics who identify themselves as being of the respective race alone. "Hispanic" includes people of any race who identify themselves as Hispanic. "Other" includes people who identify themselves as non-Hispanic and as Alaska Native, American Indian, Asian (who are also included in the "Asian" row), Native Hawaiian or other Pacific Islander, as well as non-Hispanics reporting more than one race.
Source: Calculations by New Strategist based on the Bureau of Labor Statistics' 2007 Consumer Expenditure Survey.

Cash Contributions to Religious Organizations

Best customers:
Householders aged 45 or older
Married couples without children at home
Married couples with school-aged or older children at home

Customer trends:
Average household spending on contributions to religious organizations may climb as boomers enter the lifestage of increased giving.

Contributions to religious organizations are one of the most important items in the household budget, ranking 16th among the items on which households spend the most. Those donating the most to religious organizations are middle-aged and older married couples. Householders aged 45 or older spend 18 to 53 percent more than the average household on cash contributions to churches and religious organizations and account for 72 percent of total giving. Married couples without children at home (most of them empty-nesters) spend 86 percent more than the average, while couples with school-aged or older children at home spend 26 to 54 percent more.

Average household giving to religious organizations rose 28 percent between 2000 and 2007, after adjusting for inflation. The aging of the population into the lifestage when giving is greatest suggests continued growth in this category.

Table 6.7 Cash contributions to religious organizations

Total household spending $82,288,293,960.00
Average household spends   684.76

AGE OF HOUSEHOLDER	AVERAGE HOUSEHOLD SPENDING	BEST CUSTOMERS (index)	BIGGEST CUSTOMERS (market share)
Average household	$684.76	100	100.0%
Under age 25	210.16	31	2.1
Aged 25 to 34	393.74	58	9.8
Aged 35 to 44	567.33	83	16.1
Aged 45 to 54	807.50	118	24.8
Aged 55 to 64	863.94	126	20.4
Aged 65 to 74	839.29	123	12.3
Aged 75 or older	1,048.34	153	14.5

	AVERAGE HOUSEHOLD SPENDING	BEST CUSTOMERS (index)	BIGGEST CUSTOMERS (market share)
HOUSEHOLD INCOME			
Average household	**$684.76**	**100**	**100.0%**
Under $20,000	243.03	35	7.3
$20,000 to $39,999	385.47	56	13.1
$40,000 to $49,999	769.83	112	11.1
$50,000 to $69,999	597.95	87	13.4
$70,000 to $79,999	874.73	128	7.4
$80,000 to $99,999	877.35	128	10.4
$100,000 or more	1,493.87	218	37.4
HOUSEHOLD TYPE			
Average household	**684.76**	**100**	**100.0**
Married couples	1,041.36	152	76.9
Married couples, no children	1,272.48	186	40.1
Married couples, with children	886.83	130	32.3
Oldest child under age 6	699.44	102	5.0
Oldest child aged 6 to 17	861.97	126	16.0
Oldest child aged 18 or older	1,053.84	154	11.3
Single parent with child under age 18	288.94	42	2.5
Single person	334.34	49	14.5
RACE AND HISPANIC ORIGIN			
Average household	**684.76**	**100**	**100.0**
Asian	742.48	108	3.8
Black	674.85	99	11.8
Hispanic	205.71	30	3.5
Non-Hispanic white and other	759.76	111	84.7
REGION			
Average household	**684.76**	**100**	**100.0**
Northeast	426.42	62	11.6
Midwest	707.42	103	23.6
South	738.49	108	38.7
West	789.30	115	26.1
EDUCATION			
Average household	**684.76**	**100**	**100.0**
Less than high school graduate	276.92	40	6.1
High school graduate	599.24	88	22.1
Some college	561.01	82	17.8
Associate's degree	602.14	88	7.8
College graduate	1,091.46	159	46.1
Bachelor's degree	982.90	144	26.9
Master's, professional, doctoral degree	1,290.93	189	19.2

Note: Market shares may not sum to 100.0 because of rounding and missing categories by household type. "Asian" and "black" include Hispanics and non-Hispanics who identify themselves as being of the respective race alone. "Hispanic" includes people of any race who identify themselves as Hispanic. "Other" includes people who identify themselves as non-Hispanic and as Alaska Native, American Indian, Asian (who are also included in the "Asian" row), Native Hawaiian or other Pacific Islander, as well as non-Hispanics reporting more than one race.
Source: Calculations by New Strategist based on the Bureau of Labor Statistics' 2007 Consumer Expenditure Survey.

Cash Gifts, Other than Charitable, Educational, Political, or Religious

Best customers:	**Householders aged 55 or older**
	Married couples without children at home
	Hispanics
Customer trends:	**Average household spending in this category is likely to grow as aging boomers attempt to help their struggling adult children.**

Many older parents give money to their adult children to help them make a down payment on a home, to defray a grandchild's college expenses, or to cover necessities like health insurance and day care. Householders aged 75 or older spend more than twice the average on such cash gifts. Householders aged 65 to 74 give 64 percent more than the average household in cash gifts, and those aged 55 to 64 give 33 percent more. Those three age groups account for 59 percent of all such giving. Married couples without children at home (most of them empty-nesters) give 68 percent more than average in cash gifts. Hispanics, many remitting a part of their income to relatives in Latin America, give 23 percent more than average in cash gifts other than to charitable, educational, political, or religious organizations.

With the cost of necessities rising and wages barely keeping pace, many adult children find themselves struggling to make ends meet. Parents are heeding the call. As millions more boomers become empty-nesters, average household spending on cash gifts is likely to grow.

Table 6.8 Cash gifts, other than charitable, educational, political, or religious

Total household spending		$49,235,260,410.00	
Average household spends		409.71	

	AVERAGE HOUSEHOLD SPENDING	BEST CUSTOMERS (index)	BIGGEST CUSTOMERS (market share)
AGE OF HOUSEHOLDER			
Average household	**$409.71**	**100**	**100.0%**
Under age 25	220.31	54	3.6
Aged 25 to 34	201.68	49	8.4
Aged 35 to 44	280.19	68	13.3
Aged 45 to 54	296.01	72	15.2
Aged 55 to 64	546.70	133	21.6
Aged 65 to 74	673.12	164	16.4
Aged 75 or older	926.05	226	21.4

	AVERAGE HOUSEHOLD SPENDING	BEST CUSTOMERS (index)	BIGGEST CUSTOMERS (market share)
HOUSEHOLD INCOME			
Average household	**$409.71**	**100**	**100.0%**
Under $20,000	164.16	40	8.2
$20,000 to $39,999	265.48	65	15.1
$40,000 to $49,999	435.92	106	10.5
$50,000 to $69,999	393.50	96	14.7
$70,000 to $79,999	455.76	111	6.4
$80,000 to $99,999	901.46	220	17.9
$100,000 or more	650.34	159	27.2
HOUSEHOLD TYPE			
Average household	**409.71**	**100**	**100.0**
Married couples	448.17	109	55.3
Married couples, no children	687.15	168	36.2
Married couples, with children	252.90	62	15.4
Oldest child under age 6	140.81	34	1.7
Oldest child aged 6 to 17	211.49	52	6.6
Oldest child aged 18 or older	398.57	97	7.2
Single parent with child under age 18	96.39	24	1.4
Single person	418.36	102	30.4
RACE AND HISPANIC ORIGIN			
Average household	**409.71**	**100**	**100.0**
Asian	307.54	75	2.6
Black	145.16	35	4.3
Hispanic	504.65	123	14.5
Non-Hispanic white and other	435.93	106	81.2
REGION			
Average household	**409.71**	**100**	**100.0**
Northeast	423.74	103	19.3
Midwest	414.48	101	23.1
South	409.68	100	35.9
West	393.37	96	21.7
EDUCATION			
Average household	**409.71**	**100**	**100.0**
Less than high school graduate	303.08	74	11.2
High school graduate	382.09	93	23.5
Some college	299.36	73	15.9
Associate's degree	315.01	77	6.8
College graduate	601.75	147	42.5
Bachelor's degree	560.15	137	25.6
Master's, professional, doctoral degree	678.16	166	16.9

Note: Market shares may not sum to 100.0 because of rounding and missing categories by household type. "Asian" and "black" include Hispanics and non-Hispanics who identify themselves as being of the respective race alone. "Hispanic" includes people of any race who identify themselves as Hispanic. "Other" includes people who identify themselves as non-Hispanic and as Alaska Native, American Indian, Asian (who are also included in the "Asian" row), Native Hawaiian or other Pacific Islander, as well as non-Hispanics reporting more than one race.
Source: Calculations by New Strategist based on the Bureau of Labor Statistics' 2007 Consumer Expenditure Survey.

Cemetery Lots, Vaults, Maintenance Fees

Best customers: Householders aged 55 or older
                                       Married couples without children at home

Customer trends: Average household spending on cemetery lots should rise as the population ages unless more choose cremation or other less expensive options.

Not surprisingly, the biggest spenders on cemetery lots, vaults, and maintenance fees are older Americans. Householders aged 55 or older spend between two and three-and-one-half times the average on cemetery lots as they bury their parents and spouses. Married couples without children at home (most of them older) spend twice the average on this item.

Average household spending on cemetery lots, vaults, and maintenance fees fell 5 percent between 2000 and 2007, after adjusting for inflation. Spending on cemetery lots, vaults, and maintenance fees should rise with the aging of the population, unless more choose cremation.

Table 6.9 Cemetery lots, vaults, maintenance fees

Total household spending $1,849,431,690.00
Average household spends   15.39

	AVERAGE HOUSEHOLD SPENDING	BEST CUSTOMERS (index)	BIGGEST CUSTOMERS (market share)
AGE OF HOUSEHOLDER			
Average household	**$15.39**	**100**	**100.0%**
Under age 25	0.67	4	0.3
Aged 25 to 34	0.19	1	0.2
Aged 35 to 44	3.40	22	4.3
Aged 45 to 54	6.70	44	9.1
Aged 55 to 64	30.47	198	32.1
Aged 65 to 74	52.73	343	34.2
Aged 75 or older	32.06	208	19.7

	AVERAGE HOUSEHOLD SPENDING	BEST CUSTOMERS (index)	BIGGEST CUSTOMERS (market share)
HOUSEHOLD INCOME			
Average household	**$15.39**	**100**	**100.0%**
Under $20,000	7.57	49	10.1
$20,000 to $39,999	20.67	134	31.2
$40,000 to $49,999	16.59	108	10.6
$50,000 to $69,999	10.67	69	10.6
$70,000 to $79,999	38.82	252	14.6
$80,000 to $99,999	4.95	32	2.6
$100,000 or more	18.17	118	20.2
HOUSEHOLD TYPE			
Average household	**15.39**	**100**	**100.0**
Married couples	18.82	122	61.8
Married couples, no children	32.25	210	45.2
Married couples, with children	8.68	56	14.1
Oldest child under age 6	1.22	8	0.4
Oldest child aged 6 to 17	4.27	28	3.5
Oldest child aged 18 or older	21.22	138	10.2
Single parent with child under age 18	0.67	4	0.3
Single person	13.19	86	25.5
RACE AND HISPANIC ORIGIN			
Average household	**15.39**	**100**	**100.0**
Asian	10.05	65	2.3
Black	12.26	80	9.6
Hispanic	8.70	57	6.7
Non-Hispanic white and other	16.89	110	83.8
REGION			
Average household	**15.39**	**100**	**100.0**
Northeast	20.69	134	25.0
Midwest	11.84	77	17.6
South	16.48	107	38.5
West	12.88	84	18.9
EDUCATION			
Average household	**15.39**	**100**	**100.0**
Less than high school graduate	16.09	105	15.9
High school graduate	18.47	120	30.3
Some college	18.39	119	26.0
Associate's degree	24.19	157	14.0
College graduate	7.38	48	13.9
Bachelor's degree	5.85	38	7.1
Master's, professional, doctoral degree	10.20	66	6.8

Note: Market shares may not sum to 100.0 because of rounding and missing categories by household type. "Asian" and "black" include Hispanics and non-Hispanics who identify themselves as being of the respective race alone. "Hispanic" includes people of any race who identify themselves as Hispanic. "Other" includes people who identify themselves as non-Hispanic and as Alaska Native, American Indian, Asian (who are also included in the "Asian" row), Native Hawaiian or other Pacific Islander, as well as non-Hispanics reporting more than one race.
Source: Calculations by New Strategist based on the Bureau of Labor Statistics' 2007 Consumer Expenditure Survey.

Child Support

Best customers:	Householders aged 25 to 44
	Married couples with preschoolers
	Hispanics
Customer trends:	Average household spending on child support is likely to decline as the small generation X fills the most-divorce-prone age group.

The biggest spenders on child support are householders aged 35 to 44, who spend more than twice the average on this item. Householders aged 25 to 34 spend 60 percent more than average on this item. Married couples with preschoolers—many of them step-families with children living elsewhere—spend over twice the average on child support. Hispanics, who tend to have more children, spend 44 percent more than average on child support.

Average household spending on child support has been growing as laws regarding child support become more widely enforced. With the much smaller generation X now filling the most-divorce-prone 35-to-44 age group, average household spending on child support may decline.

Table 6.10 **Child support**

| Total household spending | $23,795,059,710.00 |
| Average household spends | 198.01 |

	AVERAGE HOUSEHOLD SPENDING	BEST CUSTOMERS (index)	BIGGEST CUSTOMERS (market share)
AGE OF HOUSEHOLDER			
Average household	**$198.01**	**100**	**100.0%**
Under age 25	80.84	41	2.8
Aged 25 to 34	317.57	160	27.4
Aged 35 to 44	412.11	208	40.6
Aged 45 to 54	216.08	109	22.9
Aged 55 to 64	61.60	31	5.0
Aged 65 to 74	25.48	13	1.3
Aged 75 or older	1.48	1	0.1

	AVERAGE HOUSEHOLD SPENDING	BEST CUSTOMERS (index)	BIGGEST CUSTOMERS (market share)
HOUSEHOLD INCOME			
Average household	**$198.01**	**100**	**100.0%**
Under $20,000	69.16	35	7.2
$20,000 to $39,999	137.13	69	16.1
$40,000 to $49,999	204.96	104	10.2
$50,000 to $69,999	246.34	124	19.0
$70,000 to $79,999	288.27	146	8.4
$80,000 to $99,999	301.80	152	12.4
$100,000 or more	308.28	156	26.7
HOUSEHOLD TYPE			
Average household	**198.01**	**100**	**100.0**
Married couples	159.20	80	40.6
Married couples, no children	94.82	48	10.3
Married couples, with children	212.53	107	26.8
Oldest child under age 6	407.03	206	10.0
Oldest child aged 6 to 17	203.88	103	13.1
Oldest child aged 18 or older	98.59	50	3.7
Single parent with child under age 18	173.75	88	5.2
Single person	211.37	107	31.7
RACE AND HISPANIC ORIGIN			
Average household	**198.01**	**100**	**100.0**
Asian	88.89	45	1.6
Black	227.75	115	13.8
Hispanic	285.24	144	17.0
Non-Hispanic white and other	179.78	91	69.3
REGION			
Average household	**198.01**	**100**	**100.0**
Northeast	170.10	86	16.0
Midwest	181.33	92	20.9
South	215.05	109	39.0
West	210.81	106	24.1
EDUCATION			
Average household	**198.01**	**100**	**100.0**
Less than high school graduate	118.44	60	9.1
High school graduate	192.13	97	24.5
Some college	243.34	123	26.8
Associate's degree	273.88	138	12.3
College graduate	187.44	95	27.4
Bachelor's degree	183.21	93	17.3
Master's, professional, doctoral degree	195.22	99	10.1

Note: Market shares may not sum to 100.0 because of rounding and missing categories by household type. "Asian" and "black" include Hispanics and non-Hispanics who identify themselves as being of the respective race alone. "Hispanic" includes people of any race who identify themselves as Hispanic. "Other" includes people who identify themselves as non-Hispanic and as Alaska Native, American Indian, Asian (who are also included in the "Asian" row), Native Hawaiian or other Pacific Islander, as well as non-Hispanics reporting more than one race.
Source: Calculations by New Strategist based on the Bureau of Labor Statistics' 2007 Consumer Expenditure Survey.

Contributions to Retirement Accounts (Nonpayroll Deposits)

Best customers:

Householders aged 35 to 64
High-income households
Married couples without children at home
Married couples with school-aged or older children at home
Non-Hispanic whites
College graduates

Customer trends:

Average household spending on contributions to retirement accounts should grow as aging boomers attempt to recoup the losses in their retirement accounts—but only if households can afford to save.

Affluent householders approaching retirement make the largest nonpayroll deposits to retirement accounts. Householders aged 35 to 64 spent 24 to 44 percent more than average on such accounts in 2007 and account for three-quarters of all such contributions. Households with incomes of $100,000 or more squirrel away more than three-and-one-half times the average and account for 62 percent of the market. Married couples spend 47 percent more than average on contributions to retirement accounts, and non-Hispanic whites spend 24 percent more. College graduates, who dominate the affluent, contribute more than twice the average to their retirement portfolios.

Average household spending on contributions to retirement accounts grew 3 percent between 2000 and 2007, after adjusting for inflation. The current economic downturn has reduced the retirement accounts of many households. This fact could boost contributions to retirement accounts in the years ahead as aging boomers attempt to recoup their losses—but only if households can afford to save.

Table 6.11 Contributions to retirement accounts (nonpayroll deposits)

Total household spending $58,001,734,860.00
Average household spends 482.66

	AVERAGE HOUSEHOLD SPENDING	BEST CUSTOMERS (index)	BIGGEST CUSTOMERS (market share)
AGE OF HOUSEHOLDER			
Average household	**$482.66**	**100**	**100.0%**
Under age 25	73.72	15	1.0
Aged 25 to 34	283.13	59	10.0
Aged 35 to 44	596.64	124	24.1
Aged 45 to 54	623.16	129	27.1
Aged 55 to 64	696.42	144	23.4
Aged 65 to 74	531.65	110	11.0
Aged 75 or older	171.78	36	3.4

	AVERAGE HOUSEHOLD SPENDING	BEST CUSTOMERS (index)	BIGGEST CUSTOMERS (market share)
HOUSEHOLD INCOME			
Average household	$482.66	100	100.0%
Under $20,000	65.69	14	2.8
$20,000 to $39,999	185.71	38	8.9
$40,000 to $49,999	142.02	29	2.9
$50,000 to $69,999	290.45	60	9.2
$70,000 to $79,999	311.00	64	3.7
$80,000 to $99,999	640.29	133	10.8
$100,000 or more	1,736.36	360	61.6
HOUSEHOLD TYPE			
Average household	482.66	100	100.0
Married couples	708.73	147	74.2
Married couples, no children	925.60	192	41.4
Married couples, with children	593.53	123	30.7
Oldest child under age 6	531.18	110	5.4
Oldest child aged 6 to 17	588.99	122	15.5
Oldest child aged 18 or older	642.66	133	9.8
Single parent with child under age 18	458.38	95	5.6
Single person	221.97	46	13.7
RACE AND HISPANIC ORIGIN			
Average household	482.66	100	100.0
Asian	485.80	101	3.6
Black	126.98	26	3.2
Hispanic	80.27	17	2.0
Non-Hispanic white and other	599.91	124	94.9
REGION			
Average household	482.66	100	100.0
Northeast	426.40	88	16.5
Midwest	467.69	97	22.1
South	421.45	87	31.4
West	641.33	133	30.0
EDUCATION			
Average household	482.66	100	100.0
Less than high school graduate	194.76	40	6.1
High school graduate	262.17	54	13.7
Some college	245.83	51	11.1
Associate's degree	345.74	72	6.4
College graduate	1,045.92	217	62.7
Bachelor's degree	841.00	174	32.7
Master's, professional, doctoral degree	1,422.39	295	30.1

Note: Market shares may not sum to 100.0 because of rounding and missing categories by household type. "Asian" and "black" include Hispanics and non-Hispanics who identify themselves as being of the respective race alone. "Hispanic" includes people of any race who identify themselves as Hispanic. "Other" includes people who identify themselves as non-Hispanic and as Alaska Native, American Indian, Asian (who are also included in the "Asian" row), Native Hawaiian or other Pacific Islander, as well as non-Hispanics reporting more than one race.
Source: Calculations by New Strategist based on the Bureau of Labor Statistics' 2007 Consumer Expenditure Survey.

Credit Card Membership Fees

Best customers:

Householders aged 55 to 74
Married couples without children at home
Married couples with preschoolers
Asians
Households in the West
College graduates

Customer trends:

Average household spending on credit card membership fees may rise as new financial regulations tighten lending standards.

The biggest spenders on credit card memberships are households that carry the largest number of cards—older married couples. Householders aged 55 to 74 spend 27 to 45 percent more than the average household on credit card membership fees. Married couples without children at home, most of them older empty-nesters, spend 52 percent more than average, while those with preschoolers spend 43 percent more. Asians, who are relatively affluent, spend two-thirds more than average on credit card fees, and households in the West, where many Asians reside, spend 78 percent more than average. College graduates spend twice the average on credit card memberships.

As competition among credit cards has grown, fees have fallen or disappeared entirely. Consequently, average household spending on credit card memberships has plummeted—down 71 percent between 2000 and 2007, after adjusting for inflation. Spending on this item may increase as new financial regulations tighten lending standards.

Table 6.12 Credit card membership fees

Total household spending $199,483,860.00
Average household spends 1.66

	AVERAGE HOUSEHOLD SPENDING	BEST CUSTOMERS (index)	BIGGEST CUSTOMERS (market share)
AGE OF HOUSEHOLDER			
Average household	**$1.66**	**100**	**100.0%**
Under age 25	1.40	84	5.7
Aged 25 to 34	1.38	83	14.2
Aged 35 to 44	1.61	97	18.9
Aged 45 to 54	1.72	104	21.8
Aged 55 to 64	2.41	145	23.5
Aged 65 to 74	2.11	127	12.7
Aged 75 or older	0.60	36	3.4

	AVERAGE HOUSEHOLD SPENDING	BEST CUSTOMERS (index)	BIGGEST CUSTOMERS (market share)
HOUSEHOLD INCOME			
Average household	$1.66	100	100.0%
Under $20,000	0.34	21	4.3
$20,000 to $39,999	1.41	85	19.7
$40,000 to $49,999	1.02	61	6.0
$50,000 to $69,999	0.90	54	8.3
$70,000 to $79,999	2.08	125	7.3
$80,000 to $99,999	1.97	119	9.7
$100,000 or more	4.35	262	44.9
HOUSEHOLD TYPE			
Average household	1.66	100	100.0
Married couples	1.90	114	57.9
Married couples, no children	2.52	152	32.7
Married couples, with children	1.38	83	20.7
Oldest child under age 6	2.38	143	7.0
Oldest child aged 6 to 17	1.09	66	8.3
Oldest child aged 18 or older	1.22	73	5.4
Single parent with child under age 18	0.64	39	2.3
Single person	1.27	77	22.8
RACE AND HISPANIC ORIGIN			
Average household	1.66	100	100.0
Asian	2.74	165	5.8
Black	0.68	41	4.9
Hispanic	0.80	48	5.7
Non-Hispanic white and other	1.95	117	89.7
REGION			
Average household	1.66	100	100.0
Northeast	1.62	98	18.2
Midwest	0.99	60	13.6
South	1.30	78	28.1
West	2.95	178	40.2
EDUCATION			
Average household	1.66	100	100.0
Less than high school graduate	0.74	45	6.8
High school graduate	0.93	56	14.1
Some college	1.19	72	15.6
Associate's degree	1.23	74	6.6
College graduate	3.28	198	57.2
Bachelor's degree	2.76	166	31.2
Master's, professional, doctoral degree	4.22	254	25.9

Note: Market shares may not sum to 100.0 because of rounding and missing categories by household type. "Asian" and "black" include Hispanics and non-Hispanics who identify themselves as being of the respective race alone. "Hispanic" includes people of any race who identify themselves as Hispanic. "Other" includes people who identify themselves as non-Hispanic and as Alaska Native, American Indian, Asian (who are also included in the "Asian" row), Native Hawaiian or other Pacific Islander, as well as non-Hispanics reporting more than one race.
Source: Calculations by New Strategist based on the Bureau of Labor Statistics' 2007 Consumer Expenditure Survey.

Deductions for Government Retirement

Best customers:

Householders aged 35 to 64
High-income households
Married couples with school-aged or older children at home
Asians
College graduates

Customer trends:

Average household spending on deductions for government retirement may decline in the years ahead if federal, state, and local governments reduce their workforce.

Affluent middle-aged married couples spend the most on government retirement plans. Householders aged 35 to 64 spend 23 to 87 percent more than average on deductions for government retirement. High-income householders devote triple the average amount to this item. Married couples with school-aged or older children at home spend 61 to 93 percent more than average on this item. Asians, a relatively affluent demographic, spend 40 percent more than average on deductions to government retirement. College graduates, another affluent demographic, spend more than twice the average.

Average household spending on deductions for government retirement fell 12 percent between 2000 and 2007, after adjusting for inflation. Spending on this item may continue to decline in the years ahead if job cuts in federal, state, and local government eliminate workers.

Table 6.13 **Deductions for government retirement**

Total household spending $8,961,151,470.00
Average household spends 74.57

AGE OF HOUSEHOLDER	AVERAGE HOUSEHOLD SPENDING	BEST CUSTOMERS (index)	BIGGEST CUSTOMERS (market share)
Average household	$74.57	100	100.0%
Under age 25	13.41	18	1.2
Aged 25 to 34	39.62	53	9.1
Aged 35 to 44	91.58	123	23.9
Aged 45 to 54	139.21	187	39.2
Aged 55 to 64	105.31	141	22.9
Aged 65 to 74	25.42	34	3.4
Aged 75 or older	2.26	3	0.3

	AVERAGE HOUSEHOLD SPENDING	BEST CUSTOMERS (index)	BIGGEST CUSTOMERS (market share)
HOUSEHOLD INCOME			
Average household	**$74.57**	**100**	**100.0%**
Under $20,000	3.00	4	0.8
$20,000 to $39,999	12.11	16	3.8
$40,000 to $49,999	47.51	64	6.3
$50,000 to $69,999	50.35	68	10.3
$70,000 to $79,999	102.63	138	8.0
$80,000 to $99,999	150.51	202	16.4
$100,000 or more	236.80	318	54.4
HOUSEHOLD TYPE			
Average household	**74.57**	**100**	**100.0**
Married couples	106.79	143	72.4
Married couples, no children	89.51	120	25.9
Married couples, with children	117.83	158	39.4
Oldest child under age 6	72.23	97	4.7
Oldest child aged 6 to 17	120.43	161	20.5
Oldest child aged 18 or older	143.56	193	14.2
Single parent with child under age 18	26.63	36	2.1
Single person	43.05	58	17.2
RACE AND HISPANIC ORIGIN			
Average household	**74.57**	**100**	**100.0**
Asian	104.44	140	4.9
Black	45.11	60	7.3
Hispanic	38.82	52	6.1
Non-Hispanic white and other	84.59	113	86.6
REGION			
Average household	**74.57**	**100**	**100.0**
Northeast	53.77	72	13.4
Midwest	63.21	85	19.4
South	88.34	118	42.5
West	81.31	109	24.7
EDUCATION			
Average household	**74.57**	**100**	**100.0**
Less than high school graduate	8.32	11	1.7
High school graduate	30.99	42	10.5
Some college	57.78	77	16.9
Associate's degree	94.56	127	11.3
College graduate	153.75	206	59.7
Bachelor's degree	110.15	148	27.7
Master's, professional, doctoral degree	233.85	314	32.0

Note: Market shares may not sum to 100.0 because of rounding and missing categories by household type. "Asian" and "black" include Hispanics and non-Hispanics who identify themselves as being of the respective race alone. "Hispanic" includes people of any race who identify themselves as Hispanic. "Other" includes people who identify themselves as non-Hispanic and as Alaska Native, American Indian, Asian (who are also included in the "Asian" row), Native Hawaiian or other Pacific Islander, as well as non-Hispanics reporting more than one race.
Source: Calculations by New Strategist based on the Bureau of Labor Statistics' 2007 Consumer Expenditure Survey.

Deductions for Private Pensions (Payroll Deductions)

Best customers:

Householders aged 35 to 64
High-income households
Married couples
College graduates

Customer trends:

Average household spending on deductions for private pensions may grow as aging boomers attempt to recoup the losses in their retirement accounts, but only if households can afford to save.

Affluent, middle-aged married couples are the biggest spenders on deductions for private pensions. Households with incomes of $100,000 or more spend three-and-one-half times the average on this item and control 62 percent of the market. Householders aged 35 to 64, who have the highest incomes, spend 25 to 76 percent more than average. Married couples—most of them two-earner—spend 44 percent more than average on this item, the figure peaking at 62 percent above average for households with the most earners, married couples with adult children at home.

Average household spending on deductions for private pensions may grow as aging boomers attempt to recoup the losses in their retirement accounts, but only if households can afford to save.

Table 6.14 Deductions for private pensions (payroll deductions)

	AVERAGE HOUSEHOLD SPENDING	BEST CUSTOMERS (index)	BIGGEST CUSTOMERS (market share)
Total household spending	$67,126,318,890.00		
Average household spends	558.59		
AGE OF HOUSEHOLDER			
Average household	$558.59	100	100.0%
Under age 25	139.34	25	1.7
Aged 25 to 34	447.91	80	13.7
Aged 35 to 44	735.07	132	25.6
Aged 45 to 54	980.58	176	36.9
Aged 55 to 64	699.45	125	20.3
Aged 65 to 74	87.40	16	1.6
Aged 75 or older	15.75	3	0.3

	AVERAGE HOUSEHOLD SPENDING	BEST CUSTOMERS (index)	BIGGEST CUSTOMERS (market share)
HOUSEHOLD INCOME			
Average household	**$558.59**	**100**	**100.0%**
Under $20,000	6.30	1	0.2
$20,000 to $39,999	85.62	15	3.6
$40,000 to $49,999	235.72	42	4.2
$50,000 to $69,999	439.04	79	12.0
$70,000 to $79,999	605.82	108	6.3
$80,000 to $99,999	804.04	144	11.7
$100,000 or more	2,022.67	362	62.0
HOUSEHOLD TYPE			
Average household	**558.59**	**100**	**100.0**
Married couples	805.55	144	72.9
Married couples, no children	769.94	138	29.7
Married couples, with children	879.21	157	39.3
Oldest child under age 6	836.62	150	7.3
Oldest child aged 6 to 17	879.79	158	20.0
Oldest child aged 18 or older	906.40	162	12.0
Single parent with child under age 18	347.20	62	3.7
Single person	285.59	51	15.2
RACE AND HISPANIC ORIGIN			
Average household	**558.59**	**100**	**100.0**
Asian	661.08	118	4.2
Black	226.56	41	4.9
Hispanic	162.01	29	3.4
Non-Hispanic white and other	671.08	120	91.7
REGION			
Average household	**558.59**	**100**	**100.0**
Northeast	511.53	92	17.1
Midwest	640.55	115	26.2
South	535.92	96	34.5
West	550.52	99	22.3
EDUCATION			
Average household	**558.59**	**100**	**100.0**
Less than high school graduate	60.50	11	1.6
High school graduate	259.58	46	11.7
Some college	450.57	81	17.6
Associate's degree	651.59	117	10.4
College graduate	1,132.90	203	58.7
Bachelor's degree	1,015.77	182	34.1
Master's, professional, doctoral degree	1,348.10	241	24.6

Note: Market shares may not sum to 100.0 because of rounding and missing categories by household type. "Asian" and "black" include Hispanics and non-Hispanics who identify themselves as being of the respective race alone. "Hispanic" includes people of any race who identify themselves as Hispanic. "Other" includes people who identify themselves as non-Hispanic and as Alaska Native, American Indian, Asian (who are also included in the "Asian" row), Native Hawaiian or other Pacific Islander, as well as non-Hispanics reporting more than one race.
Source: Calculations by New Strategist based on the Bureau of Labor Statistics' 2007 Consumer Expenditure Survey.

Deductions for Social Security

Best customers:
Householders aged 35 to 54
Married couples with children at home
Asians

Customer trends:
Average household spending on deductions for Social Security should grow until boomers begin to retire.

Since Social Security deductions are a percentage of earnings, households with workers in their peak earning years are the ones that have the most deducted from their paychecks for Social Security. Householders aged 35 to 54, who are in their peak earning years, spend 35 to 37 percent more than the average household on Social Security deductions. Married couples with children at home, many of them at the height of their career, spend 62 percent more than the average on this item. Asians, who have the highest average income among racial and ethnic groups, spend 35 percent more than the average on Social Security deductions.

The average household spends nearly twice as much on Social Security deductions as on federal, state, and local income taxes combined—an average of $3,908 in 2007. Spending on this item should continue to grow until large numbers of boomers retire.

Table 6.15 Deductions for Social Security

Total household spending — $469,621,057,740.00
Average household spends — 3,907.94

	AVERAGE HOUSEHOLD SPENDING	BEST CUSTOMERS (index)	BIGGEST CUSTOMERS (market share)
AGE OF HOUSEHOLDER			
Average household	**$3,907.94**	**100**	**100.0%**
Under age 25	2,174.26	56	3.8
Aged 25 to 34	4,222.25	108	18.4
Aged 35 to 44	5,267.31	135	26.3
Aged 45 to 54	5,341.94	137	28.7
Aged 55 to 64	4,222.23	108	17.5
Aged 65 to 74	1,580.69	40	4.0
Aged 75 or older	526.59	13	1.3

	AVERAGE HOUSEHOLD SPENDING	BEST CUSTOMERS (index)	BIGGEST CUSTOMERS (market share)
HOUSEHOLD INCOME			
Average household	**$3,907.94**	**100**	**100.0%**
Under $20,000	385.19	10	2.0
$20,000 to $39,999	1,618.27	41	9.6
$40,000 to $49,999	2,826.17	72	7.1
$50,000 to $69,999	4,082.83	104	16.0
$70,000 to $79,999	5,301.57	136	7.9
$80,000 to $99,999	6,325.39	162	13.2
$100,000 or more	10,087.50	258	44.2
HOUSEHOLD TYPE			
Average household	**3,907.94**	**100**	**100.0**
Married couples	5,363.83	137	69.4
Married couples, no children	4,231.81	108	23.4
Married couples, with children	6,326.10	162	40.4
Oldest child under age 6	5,861.15	150	7.3
Oldest child aged 6 to 17	6,319.98	162	20.5
Oldest child aged 18 or older	6,644.66	170	12.5
Single parent with child under age 18	2,219.57	57	3.4
Single person	1,789.56	46	13.6
RACE AND HISPANIC ORIGIN			
Average household	**3,907.94**	**100**	**100.0**
Asian	5,264.13	135	4.8
Black	2,871.59	73	8.8
Hispanic	3,447.72	88	10.4
Non-Hispanic white and other	4,141.22	106	80.9
REGION			
Average household	**3,907.94**	**100**	**100.0**
Northeast	4,224.19	108	20.1
Midwest	3,792.95	97	22.2
South	3,602.35	92	33.1
West	4,248.91	109	24.6
EDUCATION			
Average household	**3,907.94**	**100**	**100.0**
Less than high school graduate	2,014.75	52	7.8
High school graduate	2,939.23	75	19.0
Some college	3,616.38	93	20.2
Associate's degree	4,342.69	111	9.9
College graduate	5,830.11	149	43.2
Bachelor's degree	5,482.97	140	26.3
Master's, professional, doctoral degree	6,467.89	166	16.9

Note: Market shares may not sum to 100.0 because of rounding and missing categories by household type. "Asian" and "black" include Hispanics and non-Hispanics who identify themselves as being of the respective race alone. "Hispanic" includes people of any race who identify themselves as Hispanic. "Other" includes people who identify themselves as non-Hispanic and as Alaska Native, American Indian, Asian (who are also included in the "Asian" row), Native Hawaiian or other Pacific Islander, as well as non-Hispanics reporting more than one race.
Source: Calculations by New Strategist based on the Bureau of Labor Statistics' 2007 Consumer Expenditure Survey.

Finance Charges, except Mortgage and Vehicle

Best customers: .   **Householders aged 25 to 54**
                                  Married couples with children at home

Customer trends: **Average household spending on finance charges could rise along with interest rates.**

The biggest spenders on finance charges (except mortgage and vehicle) are the households most likely to carry credit card debt. These are middle-aged families with children—many of them outfitting their homes for expanding families. Householders ranging in age from 25 to 54 spend 22 to 28 percent more than average on finance charges and account for two-thirds of the market. Married couples with children at home spend 43 percent more, the figure peaking at 61 percent above average among couples with adult children at home.

Average household spending on finance charges fell 45 percent between 2000 and 2007, after adjusting for inflation. Falling interest rates were behind the decline. If interest rates creep back up, average household spending on finance charges could rise.

Table 6.16 Finance charges, except mortgage and vehicle

Total household spending $20,144,264,730.00
Average household spends   167.63

	AVERAGE HOUSEHOLD SPENDING	BEST CUSTOMERS (index)	BIGGEST CUSTOMERS (market share)
AGE OF HOUSEHOLDER			
Average household	**$167.63**	**100**	**100.0%**
Under age 25	72.40	43	2.9
Aged 25 to 34	214.95	128	21.9
Aged 35 to 44	206.38	123	24.0
Aged 45 to 54	204.81	122	25.7
Aged 55 to 64	167.22	100	16.2
Aged 65 to 74	117.25	70	7.0
Aged 75 or older	42.31	25	2.4

	AVERAGE HOUSEHOLD SPENDING	BEST CUSTOMERS (index)	BIGGEST CUSTOMERS (market share)
HOUSEHOLD INCOME			
Average household	**$167.63**	**100**	**100.0%**
Under $20,000	48.97	29	6.0
$20,000 to $39,999	123.13	73	17.1
$40,000 to $49,999	140.26	84	8.2
$50,000 to $69,999	197.23	118	18.0
$70,000 to $79,999	294.84	176	10.2
$80,000 to $99,999	246.70	147	12.0
$100,000 or more	279.11	167	28.5
HOUSEHOLD TYPE			
Average household	**167.63**	**100**	**100.0**
Married couples	208.82	125	63.0
Married couples, no children	174.87	104	22.5
Married couples, with children	239.08	143	35.6
Oldest child under age 6	228.65	136	6.7
Oldest child aged 6 to 17	225.52	135	17.1
Oldest child aged 18 or older	269.37	161	11.8
Single parent with child under age 18	106.89	64	3.8
Single person	106.28	63	18.9
RACE AND HISPANIC ORIGIN			
Average household	**167.63**	**100**	**100.0**
Asian	119.20	71	2.5
Black	126.45	75	9.1
Hispanic	138.83	83	9.8
Non-Hispanic white and other	178.90	107	81.5
REGION			
Average household	**167.63**	**100**	**100.0**
Northeast	180.02	107	20.0
Midwest	177.17	106	24.2
South	151.69	90	32.5
West	173.08	103	23.3
EDUCATION			
Average household	**167.63**	**100**	**100.0**
Less than high school graduate	64.55	39	5.8
High school graduate	122.87	73	18.5
Some college	159.60	95	20.7
Associate's degree	249.39	149	13.2
College graduate	241.58	144	41.7
Bachelor's degree	246.71	147	27.6
Master's, professional, doctoral degree	232.17	139	14.1

Note: Market shares may not sum to 100.0 because of rounding and missing categories by household type. "Asian" and "black" include Hispanics and non-Hispanics who identify themselves as being of the respective race alone. "Hispanic" includes people of any race who identify themselves as Hispanic. "Other" includes people who identify themselves as non-Hispanic and as Alaska Native, American Indian, Asian (who are also included in the "Asian" row), Native Hawaiian or other Pacific Islander, as well as non-Hispanics reporting more than one race.
Source: Calculations by New Strategist based on the Bureau of Labor Statistics' 2007 Consumer Expenditure Survey.

Funeral Expenses

Best customers: **Householders aged 65 or older**
Married couples without children at home
Households in the Northeast

Customer trends: **Average household spending on funerals should rise as the population ages unless more choose cremation or other less expensive options.**

Not surprisingly, the biggest spenders on funeral expenses are older Americans. Householders aged 65 or older spend between two and three times the average on funeral costs as they bury their spouses. Married couples without children at home (most of them older) spend 72 percent more than average on funeral costs. Households in the Northeast spend 57 percent more than average on funerals.

Average household spending on funeral expenses fell 32 percent between 2000 and 2007, after adjusting for inflation. This decline occurred despite the aging of the population and could be due to price discounting on caskets and other funeral expenses. Spending on funeral expenses should rise with the aging of the population, unless more choose cremation or other less expensive options when disposing of their loved one's remains.

Table 6.17 Funeral expenses

Total household spending $7,003,565,880.00
Average household spends   58.28

AGE OF HOUSEHOLDER	AVERAGE HOUSEHOLD SPENDING	BEST CUSTOMERS (index)	BIGGEST CUSTOMERS (market share)
Average household	**$58.28**	**100**	**100.0%**
Under age 25	2.37	4	0.3
Aged 25 to 34	16.46	28	4.8
Aged 35 to 44	33.29	57	11.1
Aged 45 to 54	33.66	58	12.1
Aged 55 to 64	62.83	108	17.5
Aged 65 to 74	187.71	322	32.2
Aged 75 or older	135.27	232	22.0

	AVERAGE HOUSEHOLD SPENDING	BEST CUSTOMERS (index)	BIGGEST CUSTOMERS (market share)
HOUSEHOLD INCOME			
Average household	**$58.28**	**100**	**100.0%**
Under $20,000	33.39	57	11.8
$20,000 to $39,999	63.43	109	25.3
$40,000 to $49,999	66.80	115	11.3
$50,000 to $69,999	76.98	132	20.2
$70,000 to $79,999	74.79	128	7.4
$80,000 to $99,999	63.33	109	8.8
$100,000 or more	51.60	89	15.2
HOUSEHOLD TYPE			
Average household	**58.28**	**100**	**100.0**
Married couples	58.46	100	50.7
Married couples, no children	100.15	172	37.1
Married couples, with children	21.68	37	9.3
Oldest child under age 6	1.91	3	0.2
Oldest child aged 6 to 17	17.03	29	3.7
Oldest child aged 18 or older	42.79	73	5.4
Single parent with child under age 18	16.80	29	1.7
Single person	47.72	82	24.4
RACE AND HISPANIC ORIGIN			
Average household	**58.28**	**100**	**100.0**
Asian	36.01	62	2.2
Black	53.91	93	11.1
Hispanic	35.16	60	7.1
Non-Hispanic white and other	62.44	107	81.8
REGION			
Average household	**58.28**	**100**	**100.0**
Northeast	91.28	157	29.2
Midwest	68.36	117	26.8
South	45.73	78	28.2
West	40.85	70	15.9
EDUCATION			
Average household	**58.28**	**100**	**100.0**
Less than high school graduate	55.11	95	14.3
High school graduate	94.08	161	40.7
Some college	44.93	77	16.8
Associate's degree	43.48	75	6.6
College graduate	43.34	74	21.5
Bachelor's degree	30.69	53	9.9
Master's, professional, doctoral degree	66.58	114	11.7

Note: Market shares may not sum to 100.0 because of rounding and missing categories by household type. "Asian" and "black" include Hispanics and non-Hispanics who identify themselves as being of the respective race alone. "Hispanic" includes people of any race who identify themselves as Hispanic. "Other" includes people who identify themselves as non-Hispanic and as Alaska Native, American Indian, Asian (who are also included in the "Asian" row), Native Hawaiian or other Pacific Islander, as well as non-Hispanics reporting more than one race.
Source: Calculations by New Strategist based on the Bureau of Labor Statistics' 2007 Consumer Expenditure Survey.

Insurance, Life and Other Personal except Health

Best customers: Householders aged 45 to 74
                        Married couples without children at home
                        Married couples with school-aged or older children at home

Customer trends: Average household spending on life and other personal insurance will continue to
                        decline as boomers become empty-nesters.

The biggest spenders on life and other personal insurance are middle-aged and older married couples with children and assets to protect. Householders aged 45 to 74 spend 21 to 49 percent more than the average household on life and other personal insurance. Married couples without children at home, most of them empty-nesters, spend 43 percent more than average on insurance. Those with school-aged or older children at home spend 63 to 89 percent more. Together, these three household types account for 65 percent of the market.

Average household spending on life and other personal insurance fell 36 percent between 2000 and 2007, after adjusting for inflation. The declining popularity of life insurance as an investment vehicle is one factor behind the decline. As more boomers become empty-nesters and their children no longer need financial protection, spending on life and other personal insurance will continue to decline.

Table 6.18 **Insurance, life and other personal except health**

Total household spending $37,189,319,370.00
Average household spends   309.47

AGE OF HOUSEHOLDER	AVERAGE HOUSEHOLD SPENDING	BEST CUSTOMERS (index)	BIGGEST CUSTOMERS (market share)
Average household	$309.47	100	100.0%
Under age 25	39.45	13	0.9
Aged 25 to 34	164.02	53	9.0
Aged 35 to 44	285.64	92	18.0
Aged 45 to 54	401.96	130	27.3
Aged 55 to 64	461.43	149	24.1
Aged 65 to 74	375.23	121	12.1
Aged 75 or older	279.40	90	8.6

	AVERAGE HOUSEHOLD SPENDING	BEST CUSTOMERS (index)	BIGGEST CUSTOMERS (market share)
HOUSEHOLD INCOME			
Average household	**$309.47**	**100**	**100.0%**
Under $20,000	95.92	31	6.4
$20,000 to $39,999	192.30	62	14.4
$40,000 to $49,999	183.88	59	5.8
$50,000 to $69,999	254.23	82	12.6
$70,000 to $79,999	333.50	108	6.2
$80,000 to $99,999	482.20	156	12.7
$100,000 or more	755.99	244	41.9
HOUSEHOLD TYPE			
Average household	**309.47**	**100**	**100.0**
Married couples	464.61	150	75.9
Married couples, no children	441.05	143	30.7
Married couples, with children	489.14	158	39.4
Oldest child under age 6	305.98	99	4.8
Oldest child aged 6 to 17	504.13	163	20.7
Oldest child aged 18 or older	584.64	189	13.9
Single parent with child under age 18	145.11	47	2.8
Single person	145.97	47	14.0
RACE AND HISPANIC ORIGIN			
Average household	**309.47**	**100**	**100.0**
Asian	352.82	114	4.0
Black	244.68	79	9.5
Hispanic	108.66	35	4.1
Non-Hispanic white and other	350.47	113	86.4
REGION			
Average household	**309.47**	**100**	**100.0**
Northeast	342.30	111	20.6
Midwest	347.35	112	25.6
South	298.22	96	34.6
West	262.01	85	19.1
EDUCATION			
Average household	**309.47**	**100**	**100.0**
Less than high school graduate	136.19	44	6.7
High school graduate	257.38	83	21.0
Some college	268.78	87	18.9
Associate's degree	327.55	106	9.4
College graduate	470.72	152	44.0
Bachelor's degree	434.21	140	26.3
Master's, professional, doctoral degree	537.80	174	17.7

Note: Market shares may not sum to 100.0 because of rounding and missing categories by household type. "Asian" and "black" include Hispanics and non-Hispanics who identify themselves as being of the respective race alone. "Hispanic" includes people of any race who identify themselves as Hispanic. "Other" includes people who identify themselves as non-Hispanic and as Alaska Native, American Indian, Asian (who are also included in the "Asian" row), Native Hawaiian or other Pacific Islander, as well as non-Hispanics reporting more than one race.
Source: Calculations by New Strategist based on the Bureau of Labor Statistics' 2007 Consumer Expenditure Survey.

Legal Fees

Best customers: **Householders aged 45 to 54**
          Single parents
          Households in the West

Customer trends: **Average household spending on legal fees should fall as the small generation X moves into the divorce-prone age group.**

Single parents are the big spenders on legal fees. This household type spends well more than twice the average amount on this item as separated spouses hire attorneys to negotiate divorces and child custody arrangements. Householders aged 45 to 54, many of them in the process of getting a divorce or spending on legal fees as they buy and sell houses and settle estates, spend 56 percent more than average on legal fees. Householders in the West spend 51 percent more than average on legal fees.

Average household spending on legal fees grew by 25 percent between 2000 and 2007, after adjusting for inflation. The increased number of real estate transactions during the housing boom is one factor behind the substantial rise in spending on this item. Average household spending on legal fees should stabilize or even decline in the years ahead because of the slump in the housing market and because the small generation X is filling the divorce-prone age group.

Table 6.19 **Legal fees**

Total household spending $18,817,576,890.00
Average household spends   156.59

AGE OF HOUSEHOLDER	AVERAGE HOUSEHOLD SPENDING	BEST CUSTOMERS (index)	BIGGEST CUSTOMERS (market share)
Average household	**$156.59**	**100**	**100.0%**
Under age 25	114.11	73	4.9
Aged 25 to 34	116.14	74	12.7
Aged 35 to 44	138.45	88	17.2
Aged 45 to 54	244.10	156	32.7
Aged 55 to 64	184.88	118	19.1
Aged 65 to 74	123.44	79	7.9
Aged 75 or older	89.77	57	5.4

	AVERAGE HOUSEHOLD SPENDING	BEST CUSTOMERS (index)	BIGGEST CUSTOMERS (market share)
HOUSEHOLD INCOME			
Average household	**$156.59**	**100**	**100.0%**
Under $20,000	98.20	63	12.9
$20,000 to $39,999	80.40	51	11.9
$40,000 to $49,999	157.28	100	9.9
$50,000 to $69,999	167.41	107	16.4
$70,000 to $79,999	143.14	91	5.3
$80,000 to $99,999	204.89	131	10.6
$100,000 or more	301.59	193	33.0
HOUSEHOLD TYPE			
Average household	**156.59**	**100**	**100.0**
Married couples	150.28	96	48.5
Married couples, no children	138.88	89	19.1
Married couples, with children	151.14	97	24.1
Oldest child under age 6	172.82	110	5.4
Oldest child aged 6 to 17	184.25	118	14.9
Oldest child aged 18 or older	79.69	51	3.7
Single parent with child under age 18	362.27	231	13.7
Single person	116.03	74	22.0
RACE AND HISPANIC ORIGIN			
Average household	**156.59**	**100**	**100.0**
Asian	169.54	108	3.8
Black	72.60	46	5.6
Hispanic	68.61	44	5.2
Non-Hispanic white and other	183.11	117	89.3
REGION			
Average household	**156.59**	**100**	**100.0**
Northeast	129.00	82	15.3
Midwest	171.83	110	25.1
South	110.97	71	25.4
West	236.36	151	34.1
EDUCATION			
Average household	**156.59**	**100**	**100.0**
Less than high school graduate	46.22	30	4.5
High school graduate	111.99	72	18.0
Some college	174.25	111	24.2
Associate's degree	158.19	101	9.0
College graduate	239.53	153	44.3
Bachelor's degree	222.62	142	26.6
Master's, professional, doctoral degree	270.59	173	17.6

Note: Market shares may not sum to 100.0 because of rounding and missing categories by household type. "Asian" and "black" include Hispanics and non-Hispanics who identify themselves as being of the respective race alone. "Hispanic" includes people of any race who identify themselves as Hispanic. "Other" includes people who identify themselves as non-Hispanic and as Alaska Native, American Indian, Asian (who are also included in the "Asian" row), Native Hawaiian or other Pacific Islander, as well as non-Hispanics reporting more than one race.
Source: Calculations by New Strategist based on the Bureau of Labor Statistics' 2007 Consumer Expenditure Survey.

Lottery and Gambling Losses

Best customers: **Householders aged 45 to 54**
                            Married couples without children at home
                            Married couples with adult children at home
                            Households in the West

Customer trends: **Average household spending on lotteries and gambling will rise as more boomers become empty-nesters and casinos become more widespread.**

The biggest spenders (losers) on lotteries and gambling are households with discretionary time and income. Hoping to strike it rich they buy lottery tickets, travel to Las Vegas, or visit Indian reservations to try their luck. Householders aged 45 to 54 lose 92 percent more than average. Married couples without children at home lose more than twice the average to lotteries and casinos, as do those with adult children at home. Householders in the West lose nearly twice the average to gambling.

Average household losses on lotteries and gambling rose by an enormous 45 percent between 2000 and 2007, after adjusting or inflation. Spending on this item will continue to rise in the years ahead as casinos become more widespread and more boomers become empty-nesters.

Table 6.20 Lottery and gambling losses

Total household spending $8,716,002,630.00
Average household spends   72.53

AGE OF HOUSEHOLDER	AVERAGE HOUSEHOLD SPENDING	BEST CUSTOMERS (index)	BIGGEST CUSTOMERS (market share)
Average household	$72.53	100	100.0%
Under age 25	12.83	18	1.2
Aged 25 to 34	18.82	26	4.4
Aged 35 to 44	77.41	107	20.8
Aged 45 to 54	139.51	192	40.4
Aged 55 to 64	84.62	117	18.9
Aged 65 to 74	68.12	94	9.4
Aged 75 or older	43.38	60	5.7

	AVERAGE HOUSEHOLD SPENDING	BEST CUSTOMERS (index)	BIGGEST CUSTOMERS (market share)
HOUSEHOLD INCOME			
Average household	**$72.53**	**100**	**100.0%**
Under $20,000	29.70	41	8.4
$20,000 to $39,999	103.41	143	33.1
$40,000 to $49,999	35.92	50	4.9
$50,000 to $69,999	98.19	135	20.7
$70,000 to $79,999	62.24	86	5.0
$80,000 to $99,999	117.13	161	13.1
$100,000 or more	54.39	75	12.8
HOUSEHOLD TYPE			
Average household	**72.53**	**100**	**100.0**
Married couples	103.54	143	72.2
Married couples, no children	149.42	206	44.4
Married couples, with children	68.33	94	23.5
Oldest child under age 6	18.38	25	1.2
Oldest child aged 6 to 17	47.51	66	8.3
Oldest child aged 18 or older	146.23	202	14.9
Single parent with child under age 18	19.18	26	1.6
Single person	39.17	54	16.1
RACE AND HISPANIC ORIGIN			
Average household	**72.53**	**100**	**100.0**
Asian	60.64	84	2.9
Black	37.24	51	6.2
Hispanic	43.12	59	7.0
Non-Hispanic white and other	82.07	113	86.4
REGION			
Average household	**72.53**	**100**	**100.0**
Northeast	93.79	129	24.1
Midwest	51.27	71	16.2
South	32.93	45	16.3
West	140.25	193	43.7
EDUCATION			
Average household	**72.53**	**100**	**100.0**
Less than high school graduate	54.16	75	11.3
High school graduate	50.68	70	17.6
Some college	120.74	166	36.3
Associate's degree	144.33	199	17.7
College graduate	44.72	62	17.8
Bachelor's degree	44.09	61	11.4
Master's, professional, doctoral degree	45.82	63	6.4

Note: Market shares may not sum to 100.0 because of rounding and missing categories by household type. "Asian" and "black" include Hispanics and non-Hispanics who identify themselves as being of the respective race alone. "Hispanic" includes people of any race who identify themselves as Hispanic. "Other" includes people who identify themselves as non-Hispanic and as Alaska Native, American Indian, Asian (who are also included in the "Asian" row), Native Hawaiian or other Pacific Islander, as well as non-Hispanics reporting more than one race.
Source: Calculations by New Strategist based on the Bureau of Labor Statistics' 2007 Consumer Expenditure Survey.

Occupational Expenses

Best customers: Householders aged 35 to 54
Married couples with children at home

Customer trends: Average household spending on occupational expenses may continue to decline
along with manufacturing employment.

The biggest spenders on occupational expenses are households with workers, particularly union members. Householders aged 35 to 54 spent 42 to 65 percent more than average on this item. Married couples with children at home, most of them having two or more earners, spend 81 percent more than average on occupational expenses.

Average household spending on occupational expenses fell steeply between 2000 and 2007, down 58 percent after adjusting for inflation. Behind the decline is the loss of union jobs as manufacturing employment fell over the past few years. Spending on this item may continue to decline along with manufacturing employment.

Table 6.21 Occupational expenses

Total household spending $5,882,370,450.00
Average household spends   48.95

AGE OF HOUSEHOLDER	AVERAGE HOUSEHOLD SPENDING	BEST CUSTOMERS (index)	BIGGEST CUSTOMERS (market share)
Average household	$48.95	100	100.0%
Under age 25	14.56	30	2.0
Aged 25 to 34	39.16	80	13.6
Aged 35 to 44	80.74	165	32.1
Aged 45 to 54	69.30	142	29.7
Aged 55 to 64	56.70	116	18.8
Aged 65 to 74	13.50	28	2.8
Aged 75 or older	4.87	10	0.9

	AVERAGE HOUSEHOLD SPENDING	BEST CUSTOMERS (index)	BIGGEST CUSTOMERS (market share)
HOUSEHOLD INCOME			
Average household	**$48.95**	**100**	**100.0%**
Under $20,000	8.04	16	3.4
$20,000 to $39,999	18.79	38	8.9
$40,000 to $49,999	39.75	81	8.0
$50,000 to $69,999	44.00	90	13.8
$70,000 to $79,999	77.84	159	9.2
$80,000 to $99,999	98.41	201	16.4
$100,000 or more	115.41	236	40.4
HOUSEHOLD TYPE			
Average household	**48.95**	**100**	**100.0**
Married couples	65.07	133	67.2
Married couples, no children	55.91	114	24.6
Married couples, with children	71.63	146	36.5
Oldest child under age 6	55.40	113	5.5
Oldest child aged 6 to 17	67.99	139	17.6
Oldest child aged 18 or older	88.64	181	13.3
Single parent with child under age 18	23.79	49	2.9
Single person	28.30	58	17.2
RACE AND HISPANIC ORIGIN			
Average household	**48.95**	**100**	**100.0**
Asian	36.52	75	2.6
Black	31.75	65	7.8
Hispanic	34.69	71	8.4
Non-Hispanic white and other	53.91	110	84.1
REGION			
Average household	**48.95**	**100**	**100.0**
Northeast	49.77	102	18.9
Midwest	58.16	119	27.2
South	36.16	74	26.5
West	59.29	121	27.4
EDUCATION			
Average household	**48.95**	**100**	**100.0**
Less than high school graduate	19.04	39	5.9
High school graduate	36.30	74	18.7
Some college	53.95	110	24.0
Associate's degree	47.43	97	8.6
College graduate	72.35	148	42.8
Bachelor's degree	61.06	125	23.4
Master's, professional, doctoral degree	93.10	190	19.4

Note: Market shares may not sum to 100.0 because of rounding and missing categories by household type. "Asian" and "black" include Hispanics and non-Hispanics who identify themselves as being of the respective race alone. "Hispanic" includes people of any race who identify themselves as Hispanic. "Other" includes people who identify themselves as non-Hispanic and as Alaska Native, American Indian, Asian (who are also included in the "Asian" row), Native Hawaiian or other Pacific Islander, as well as non-Hispanics reporting more than one race.
Source: Calculations by New Strategist based on the Bureau of Labor Statistics' 2007 Consumer Expenditure Survey.

Safe Deposit Box Rental

Best customers:

Householders aged 55 or older
Married couples without children at home
Married couples with adult children at home
Asians

Customer trends:

Average household spending on safe deposit boxes will continue to decline as paper records give way to electronic and as more households purchase high-tech home security systems.

Older Americans are the best customers of safe deposit box rentals because they grew up in an era when only a single paper copy of many important documents existed. Householders aged 55 to 74 spend 60 to 92 percent more than average on safe deposit boxes, and householders aged 75 or older spend more than twice the average. Together, householders aged 55 or older control 65 percent of the market for safe deposit boxes. Married couples without children at home, many of them empty-nesters, spend 93 percent more than average on this item. Those with adult children at home spend 34 percent more. Asians spend more than twice the average on safe deposit box rentals.

Average household spending on safe deposit boxes plummeted between 2000 and 2007, falling by 38 percent after adjusting for inflation. Electronic record keeping and high-tech home security systems are reducing the need for safe deposit boxes, which should limit spending on this item in the future.

Table 6.22 Safe deposit box rental

| Total household spending | $410,984,820.00 |
| Average household spends | 3.42 |

AGE OF HOUSEHOLDER	AVERAGE HOUSEHOLD SPENDING	BEST CUSTOMERS (index)	BIGGEST CUSTOMERS (market share)
Average household	$3.42	100	100.0%
Under age 25	0.12	4	0.2
Aged 25 to 34	0.54	16	2.7
Aged 35 to 44	1.79	52	10.2
Aged 45 to 54	3.50	102	21.5
Aged 55 to 64	5.47	160	25.9
Aged 65 to 74	6.58	192	19.2
Aged 75 or older	7.33	214	20.3

	AVERAGE HOUSEHOLD SPENDING	BEST CUSTOMERS (index)	BIGGEST CUSTOMERS (market share)
HOUSEHOLD INCOME			
Average household	**$3.42**	**100**	**100.0%**
Under $20,000	1.33	39	8.0
$20,000 to $39,999	2.41	70	16.3
$40,000 to $49,999	3.20	94	9.2
$50,000 to $69,999	2.74	80	12.3
$70,000 to $79,999	3.81	111	6.4
$80,000 to $99,999	3.98	116	9.5
$100,000 or more	7.65	224	38.3
HOUSEHOLD TYPE			
Average household	**3.42**	**100**	**100.0**
Married couples	4.52	132	66.8
Married couples, no children	6.61	193	41.7
Married couples, with children	3.07	90	22.4
Oldest child under age 6	1.20	35	1.7
Oldest child aged 6 to 17	2.90	85	10.8
Oldest child aged 18 or older	4.59	134	9.9
Single parent with child under age 18	0.49	14	0.9
Single person	2.66	78	23.1
RACE AND HISPANIC ORIGIN			
Average household	**3.42**	**100**	**100.0**
Asian	7.06	206	7.3
Black	0.78	23	2.7
Hispanic	0.72	21	2.5
Non-Hispanic white and other	4.25	124	94.9
REGION			
Average household	**3.42**	**100**	**100.0**
Northeast	3.35	98	18.2
Midwest	4.14	121	27.7
South	3.31	97	34.8
West	2.94	86	19.4
EDUCATION			
Average household	**3.42**	**100**	**100.0**
Less than high school graduate	1.72	50	7.6
High school graduate	2.20	64	16.2
Some college	2.51	73	16.0
Associate's degree	3.15	92	8.2
College graduate	6.15	180	52.0
Bachelor's degree	4.72	138	25.9
Master's, professional, doctoral degree	8.78	257	26.2

Note: Market shares may not sum to 100.0 because of rounding and missing categories by household type. "Asian" and "black" include Hispanics and non-Hispanics who identify themselves as being of the respective race alone. "Hispanic" includes people of any race who identify themselves as Hispanic. "Other" includes people who identify themselves as non-Hispanic and as Alaska Native, American Indian, Asian (who are also included in the "Asian" row), Native Hawaiian or other Pacific Islander, as well as non-Hispanics reporting more than one race.
Source: Calculations by New Strategist based on the Bureau of Labor Statistics' 2007 Consumer Expenditure Survey.

Shopping Club Membership Fees

Best customers:

Householders aged 45 to 74
Married couples without children at home
Married couples with school-aged or older children at home
Asians
Households in the West

Customer trends:

Average household spending on shopping club memberships may decline as competition among discounters heats up.

Older married couples are the best customers of shopping club memberships. Householders in the 45-to-74 age range spend 16 to 37 percent more than average on this item. Married couples without children at home spend 51 percent more, while those with school-aged or older children at home spend 48 to 55 percent more than average on shopping club memberships. Households in the West spend close to twice the average on this item. Asians, many of whom live in the West, spend 52 percent more than average on shopping club memberships.

Average household spending on shopping club memberships is minimal and may fall in the years ahead as competition among discounters reduces the need to join the club for savings.

Table 6.23 Shopping club membership fees

Total household spending $852,012,390.00
Average household spends   7.09

	AVERAGE HOUSEHOLD SPENDING	BEST CUSTOMERS (index)	BIGGEST CUSTOMERS (market share)
AGE OF HOUSEHOLDER			
Average household	**$7.09**	**100**	**100.0%**
Under age 25	1.19	17	1.1
Aged 25 to 34	5.70	80	13.7
Aged 35 to 44	7.14	101	19.6
Aged 45 to 54	8.22	116	24.4
Aged 55 to 64	9.71	137	22.2
Aged 65 to 74	9.38	132	13.2
Aged 75 or older	4.35	61	5.8

	AVERAGE HOUSEHOLD SPENDING	BEST CUSTOMERS (index)	BIGGEST CUSTOMERS (market share)
HOUSEHOLD INCOME			
Average household	**$7.09**	**100**	**100.0%**
Under $20,000	2.13	30	6.2
$20,000 to $39,999	4.38	62	14.4
$40,000 to $49,999	6.59	93	9.1
$50,000 to $69,999	6.33	89	13.7
$70,000 to $79,999	9.42	133	7.7
$80,000 to $99,999	9.75	138	11.2
$100,000 or more	15.65	221	37.8
HOUSEHOLD TYPE			
Average household	**7.09**	**100**	**100.0**
Married couples	10.25	145	73.1
Married couples, no children	10.68	151	32.5
Married couples, with children	9.80	138	34.5
Oldest child under age 6	6.27	88	4.3
Oldest child aged 6 to 17	10.47	148	18.8
Oldest child aged 18 or older	10.97	155	11.4
Single parent with child under age 18	3.42	48	2.9
Single person	3.00	42	12.6
RACE AND HISPANIC ORIGIN			
Average household	**7.09**	**100**	**100.0**
Asian	10.80	152	5.4
Black	3.56	50	6.0
Hispanic	7.62	107	12.7
Non-Hispanic white and other	7.55	106	81.3
REGION			
Average household	**7.09**	**100**	**100.0**
Northeast	4.40	62	11.6
Midwest	6.10	86	19.7
South	5.34	75	27.0
West	13.09	185	41.8
EDUCATION			
Average household	**7.09**	**100**	**100.0**
Less than high school graduate	3.45	49	7.4
High school graduate	5.15	73	18.3
Some college	7.70	109	23.7
Associate's degree	8.46	119	10.6
College graduate	9.82	139	40.1
Bachelor's degree	9.18	129	24.3
Master's, professional, doctoral degree	11.00	155	15.8

Note: Market shares may not sum to 100.0 because of rounding and missing categories by household type. "Asian" and "black" include Hispanics and non-Hispanics who identify themselves as being of the respective race alone. "Hispanic" includes people of any race who identify themselves as Hispanic. "Other" includes people who identify themselves as non-Hispanic and as Alaska Native, American Indian, Asian (who are also included in the "Asian" row), Native Hawaiian or other Pacific Islander, as well as non-Hispanics reporting more than one race.
Source: Calculations by New Strategist based on the Bureau of Labor Statistics' 2007 Consumer Expenditure Survey.

Support for College Students

Best customers:
> Householders aged 45 to 64
> High-income households
> Married couples without children at home
> Married couples with adult children at home
> Asians
> College graduates

Customer trends:
> Average household spending on support for college students is likely to grow as boomers help their children through college.

Many parents give money to their college-bound children for living expenses and other items. Householders aged 45 to 64 spend about twice the average amount on such support. Householders with incomes of $100,000 or more spend more than three times the average on this item. Married couples without children at home (most of them empty-nesters) and those with adult children at home spend more than twice the average on support for college students. Asians spend 31 percent more than average on support, and college graduates spend more than twice the average on this item.

Average household spending on support for college students is likely to grow as boomers help their children through college.

Table 6.24 Support for college students

Total household spending	$11,904,139,260.00
Average household spends	99.06

	AVERAGE HOUSEHOLD SPENDING	BEST CUSTOMERS (index)	BIGGEST CUSTOMERS (market share)
AGE OF HOUSEHOLDER			
Average household	**$99.06**	**100**	**100.0%**
Under age 25	17.89	18	1.2
Aged 25 to 34	18.02	18	3.1
Aged 35 to 44	57.27	58	11.3
Aged 45 to 54	216.93	219	46.0
Aged 55 to 64	182.10	184	29.8
Aged 65 to 74	61.34	62	6.2
Aged 75 or older	25.49	26	2.4

	AVERAGE HOUSEHOLD SPENDING	BEST CUSTOMERS (index)	BIGGEST CUSTOMERS (market share)
HOUSEHOLD INCOME			
Average household	**$99.06**	**100**	**100.0%**
Under $20,000	17.83	18	3.7
$20,000 to $39,999	37.26	38	8.7
$40,000 to $49,999	62.48	63	6.2
$50,000 to $69,999	69.34	70	10.7
$70,000 to $79,999	60.25	61	3.5
$80,000 to $99,999	111.26	112	9.1
$100,000 or more	335.22	338	58.0
HOUSEHOLD TYPE			
Average household	**99.06**	**100**	**100.0**
Married couples	150.63	152	76.9
Married couples, no children	205.03	207	44.6
Married couples, with children	119.70	121	30.1
Oldest child under age 6	6.25	6	0.3
Oldest child aged 6 to 17	80.12	81	10.3
Oldest child aged 18 or older	263.10	266	19.6
Single parent with child under age 18	60.59	61	3.6
Single person	45.10	46	13.5
RACE AND HISPANIC ORIGIN			
Average household	**99.06**	**100**	**100.0**
Asian	130.13	131	4.6
Black	70.63	71	8.6
Hispanic	26.01	26	3.1
Non-Hispanic white and other	114.68	116	88.4
REGION			
Average household	**99.06**	**100**	**100.0**
Northeast	74.36	75	14.0
Midwest	104.18	105	24.0
South	100.92	102	36.6
West	111.25	112	25.4
EDUCATION			
Average household	**99.06**	**100**	**100.0**
Less than high school graduate	12.64	13	1.9
High school graduate	37.30	38	9.5
Some college	75.23	76	16.5
Associate's degree	53.61	54	4.8
College graduate	230.04	232	67.2
Bachelor's degree	157.65	159	29.8
Master's, professional, doctoral degree	363.05	366	37.4

Note: Market shares may not sum to 100.0 because of rounding and missing categories by household type. "Asian" and "black" include Hispanics and non-Hispanics who identify themselves as being of the respective race alone. "Hispanic" includes people of any race who identify themselves as Hispanic. "Other" includes people who identify themselves as non-Hispanic and as Alaska Native, American Indian, Asian (who are also included in the "Asian" row), Native Hawaiian or other Pacific Islander, as well as non-Hispanics reporting more than one race.
Source: Calculations by New Strategist based on the Bureau of Labor Statistics' 2007 Consumer Expenditure Survey.

Tax, Federal Income (Net, after Refund)

Best customers: Householders aged 45 to 64
High-income households
Married couples
College graduates

Customer trends: Average household spending on federal income taxes is likely to climb as tax rates increase to pay for services demanded by the middle class.

Households with the highest incomes pay the most in federal income tax. Sixty-eight percent of federal income taxes are paid by households with incomes of $100,000 or more. Householders aged 45 to 64, who have the highest incomes, pay 42 to 59 percent more than average in federal taxes. Married couples, the most affluent household type, pay 38 percent more than average in federal income taxes, the figure peaking at 69 percent above average among couples without children at home. Households headed by college graduates, who dominate the nation's affluent, spend more than twice the average on federal income taxes.

The average household paid $1,569 in federal income taxes in 2007—a substantial amount, but considerably less than half of what the average household devotes to Social Security contributions. Average household federal income taxes fell by a significant 46 percent between 2000 and 2007, after adjusting for inflation. In the years ahead, spending on this item is likely to rise as the aging middle class demands more services.

Table 6.25 Tax, federal income (net, after refund)

Total household spending	$188,563,921,230.00		
Average household spends	1,569.13		

	AVERAGE HOUSEHOLD SPENDING	BEST CUSTOMERS (index)	BIGGEST CUSTOMERS (market share)
AGE OF HOUSEHOLDER			
Average household	$1,569.13	100	100.0%
Under age 25	432.91	28	1.9
Aged 25 to 34	982.22	63	10.7
Aged 35 to 44	1,740.62	111	21.6
Aged 45 to 54	2,490.07	159	33.3
Aged 55 to 64	2,234.48	142	23.1
Aged 65 to 74	1,003.04	64	6.4
Aged 75 or older	504.68	32	3.0

	AVERAGE HOUSEHOLD SPENDING	BEST CUSTOMERS (index)	BIGGEST CUSTOMERS (market share)
HOUSEHOLD INCOME			
Average household	**$1,569.13**	**100**	**100.0%**
Under $20,000	-64.56	-4	-0.8
$20,000 to $39,999	98.06	6	1.5
$40,000 to $49,999	499.50	32	3.1
$50,000 to $69,999	1,092.78	70	10.7
$70,000 to $79,999	1,664.77	106	6.1
$80,000 to $99,999	2,293.89	146	11.9
$100,000 or more	6,188.58	394	67.6
HOUSEHOLD TYPE			
Average household	**1,569.13**	**100**	**100.0**
Married couples	2,160.82	138	69.6
Married couples, no children	2,655.93	169	36.5
Married couples, with children	1,905.97	121	30.3
Oldest child under age 6	1,805.53	115	5.6
Oldest child aged 6 to 17	1,811.61	115	14.7
Oldest child aged 18 or older	2,135.21	136	10.0
Single parent with child under age 18	143.09	9	0.5
Single person	1,033.04	66	19.6
RACE AND HISPANIC ORIGIN			
Average household	**1,569.13**	**100**	**100.0**
Asian	1,488.53	95	3.3
Black	511.44	33	3.9
Hispanic	462.85	29	3.5
Non-Hispanic white and other	1,904.73	121	92.7
REGION			
Average household	**1,569.13**	**100**	**100.0**
Northeast	1,596.43	102	18.9
Midwest	1,163.68	74	16.9
South	1,582.50	101	36.2
West	1,935.14	123	27.9
EDUCATION			
Average household	**1,569.13**	**100**	**100.0**
Less than high school graduate	274.11	17	2.6
High school graduate	650.08	41	10.5
Some college	1,198.82	76	16.6
Associate's degree	1,432.09	91	8.1
College graduate	3,369.39	215	62.2
Bachelor's degree	2,867.08	183	34.2
Master's, professional, doctoral degree	4,292.26	274	27.9

Note: Market shares may not sum to 100.0 because of rounding and missing categories by household type. "Asian" and "black" include Hispanics and non-Hispanics who identify themselves as being of the respective race alone. "Hispanic" includes people of any race who identify themselves as Hispanic. "Other" includes people who identify themselves as non-Hispanic and as Alaska Native, American Indian, Asian (who are also included in the "Asian" row), Native Hawaiian or other Pacific Islander, as well as non-Hispanics reporting more than one race.
Source: Calculations by New Strategist based on the Bureau of Labor Statistics' 2007 Consumer Expenditure Survey.

Tax, State and Local Income (Net, after Refund)

Best customers:
　　Householders aged 35 to 64
　　High-income households
　　Married couples
　　Asians

Customer trends:
　　Average household spending on state and local income taxes will rise as states and localities, squeezed for cash, raise taxes to pay for necessary services.

Households with the highest incomes pay the most in state and local income taxes. More than half of state and local income taxes are paid by households with incomes of $100,000 or more. Householders aged 35 to 64, who have the highest incomes, spend 18 to 61 percent more than average on this item. Married couples, the most affluent household type, pay 37 percent more than average in state and local income taxes. Asians, who as a group are relatively affluent, pay 34 percent more than average in state and local income taxes.

Average household spending on state and local income taxes fell by a significant 31 percent between 2000 and 2007, after adjusting for inflation. Now states and localities are squeezed for cash, and the pendulum is likely to swing the other way. Look for average household spending on state and local income taxes to rise.

Table 6.26 Tax, state and local income (net, after refund)

Total household spending	$56,247,238,260.00
Average household spends	468.06

AGE OF HOUSEHOLDER	AVERAGE HOUSEHOLD SPENDING	BEST CUSTOMERS (index)	BIGGEST CUSTOMERS (market share)
Average household	$468.06	100	100.0%
Under age 25	190.82	41	2.8
Aged 25 to 34	413.05	88	15.1
Aged 35 to 44	560.92	120	23.4
Aged 45 to 54	753.60	161	33.8
Aged 55 to 64	550.96	118	19.1
Aged 65 to 74	138.53	30	3.0
Aged 75 or older	147.50	32	3.0

	AVERAGE HOUSEHOLD SPENDING	BEST CUSTOMERS (index)	BIGGEST CUSTOMERS (market share)
HOUSEHOLD INCOME			
Average household	**$468.06**	**100**	**100.0%**
Under $20,000	11.21	2	0.5
$20,000 to $39,999	99.90	21	5.0
$40,000 to $49,999	257.12	55	5.4
$50,000 to $69,999	397.18	85	13.0
$70,000 to $79,999	647.87	138	8.0
$80,000 to $99,999	667.05	143	11.6
$100,000 or more	1,544.97	330	56.6
HOUSEHOLD TYPE			
Average household	**468.06**	**100**	**100.0**
Married couples	642.15	137	69.4
Married couples, no children	675.69	144	31.1
Married couples, with children	657.66	141	35.1
Oldest child under age 6	666.62	142	7.0
Oldest child aged 6 to 17	654.41	140	17.8
Oldest child aged 18 or older	657.32	140	10.3
Single parent with child under age 18	179.06	38	2.3
Single person	268.58	57	17.1
RACE AND HISPANIC ORIGIN			
Average household	**468.06**	**100**	**100.0**
Asian	627.56	134	4.7
Black	174.66	37	4.5
Hispanic	172.23	37	4.3
Non-Hispanic white and other	558.59	119	91.1
REGION			
Average household	**468.06**	**100**	**100.0**
Northeast	599.40	128	23.9
Midwest	466.56	100	22.8
South	324.87	69	24.9
West	588.79	126	28.4
EDUCATION			
Average household	**468.06**	**100**	**100.0**
Less than high school graduate	165.71	35	5.4
High school graduate	264.51	57	14.3
Some college	409.86	88	19.1
Associate's degree	481.98	103	9.2
College graduate	843.42	180	52.2
Bachelor's degree	750.69	160	30.1
Master's, professional, doctoral degree	1,013.78	217	22.1

Note: Market shares may not sum to 100.0 because of rounding and missing categories by household type. "Asian" and "black" include Hispanics and non-Hispanics who identify themselves as being of the respective race alone. "Hispanic" includes people of any race who identify themselves as Hispanic. "Other" includes people who identify themselves as non-Hispanic and as Alaska Native, American Indian, Asian (who are also included in the "Asian" row), Native Hawaiian or other Pacific Islander, as well as non-Hispanics reporting more than one race.
Source: Calculations by New Strategist based on the Bureau of Labor Statistics' 2007 Consumer Expenditure Survey.

Chapter 7.

Furnishings and Equipment

Household Spending on Furnishings and Equipment, 2007

Average household spending on home furnishings and equipment grew by 1 percent from 2000 to 2007, a minute increase, especially in light of the surge in home buying during those years. The average household spent $1,422 on everything from major appliances to indoor plants and outdoor furniture. This was just above the inflation-adjusted $1,402 spent in 2000. Behind this essentially level performance was the increased spending on housing itself, which left little discretionary income for furnishings.

The largest home furnishings category, major appliances (such as refrigerators and washing machines) accounts for 16 percent of the dollars spent on home furnishings and equipment. Average household spending on major appliances increased by 2 percent between 2000 and 2007, after adjusting for inflation. Some categories experienced much larger increases. Average household spending on lamps and lighting fixtures nearly tripled, and spending on closet and storage items and on lawn and garden equipment doubled. Spending on outdoor equipment jumped 80 percent, on laundry and cleaning equipment 53 percent, and on outdoor furniture 43 percent.

The second largest spending category among home furnishings, decorative items for the home, was one of the biggest losers, as average household spending on such items dropped 27 percent from 2000 to 2007, after adjusting for inflation. Other losing categories included mattresses and springs (down 13 percent), living room chairs (down 13 percent), kitchen and dining room furniture (down 16 percent), indoor plants and fresh flowers (down 17 percent), wall-to-wall carpeting (down 24 percent), living room tables (down 24 percent), curtains and draperies (down 25 percent), and kitchen and dining room linens (down 41 percent).

Average household spending on home furnishings may increase in the years ahead as millions of boomers become empty-nesters and redecorate their homes, but only if discretionary income grows.

Spending on furnishings and equipment

(average annual spending of households on furnishings and equipment, 2000 and 2007; in 2007 dollars)

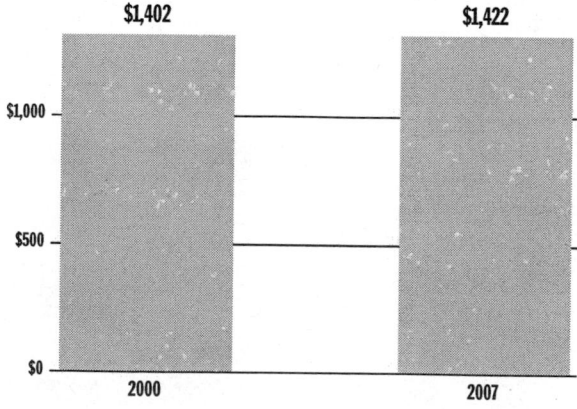

Table 7.1 Household Furnishings Spending, 2000 to 2007

(average annual spending of households on household furnishings, and percent distribution of spending by type, 2000 and 2007; percent change, 2000–07; in 2007 dollars)

	2007		2000		
	average household spending	percent distribution	average household spending (in 2007$)	percent distribution	percent change 2000–07
Average household spending on furnishings and equipment	**$1,422.03**	**100.0%**	**$1,402.20**	**100.0%**	**1.4%**
Appliances, major	231.32	16.3	227.52	16.2	1.7
Decorative items for the home	154.92	10.9	213.48	15.2	−27.4
Lawn and garden equipment	114.63	8.1	56.37	4.0	103.3
Sofas	112.62	7.9	107.34	7.7	4.9
Bedroom furniture, except mattresses and springs	76.91	5.4	83.21	5.9	−7.6
Housewares	70.44	5.0	78.11	5.6	−9.8
Bedroom linens	67.07	4.7	53.61	3.8	25.1
Wall units, cabinets, other furniture	56.79	4.0	60.94	4.3	−6.8
Plants and fresh flowers, indoor	56.78	4.0	68.64	4.9	−17.3
Mattresses and springs	55.53	3.9	63.79	4.5	−13.0
Kitchen and dining room furniture	47.05	3.3	55.94	4.0	−15.9
Living room chairs	45.85	3.2	52.79	3.8	−13.1
Outdoor equipment	39.82	2.8	22.14	1.6	79.8
Lamps and lighting fixtures	36.69	2.6	13.00	0.9	182.1
Outdoor furniture	26.06	1.8	18.25	1.3	42.8
Floor coverings, wall-to-wall	25.51	1.8	33.45	2.4	−23.7
Bathroom linens	24.80	1.7	21.13	1.5	17.4
Power tools	24.41	1.7	25.67	1.8	−4.9
Infants' equipment and furniture	23.16	1.6	17.13	1.2	35.2
Floor coverings, nonpermanent	20.96	1.5	18.33	1.3	14.4
Closet and storage items	20.32	1.4	9.67	0.7	110.2
Kitchen appliances, small electric	19.17	1.3	20.52	1.5	−6.6
Curtains and draperies	18.98	1.3	25.36	1.8	−25.2
Laundry and cleaning equipment	18.62	1.3	12.14	0.9	53.4
Living room tables	15.78	1.1	20.70	1.5	−23.8
Sewing materials for household items	11.21	0.8	11.74	0.8	−4.5
Kitchen and dining room linens	6.63	0.5	11.21	0.8	−40.9

Source: Bureau of Labor Statistics, 2000 and 2007 Consumer Expenditure Surveys; calculations by New Strategist

Appliances, Kitchen, Small Electric

Best customers:	**Householders aged 45 to 64** **Married couples without children at home** **Married couples with preschoolers**
Customer trends:	**Average household spending on small electric kitchen appliances should stabilize now that boomers are solidly in the best-customer age groups, but the economic downturn may take a toll on this category.**

The category small electric kitchen appliances includes coffee makers, food processors, bread makers, and so on. The best customers of small electric kitchen appliances are older married couples. Householders ranging in age from 45 to 64 spend 21 to 27 percent more than average on this item. Married couples without children at home (most of them older) spend 44 percent more than average on small electric kitchen appliances, some helping grown children outfit their first homes. Couples with preschoolers spend 25 percent more than average on this item.

Average household spending on small electric kitchen appliances fell 7 percent between 2000 and 2007, after adjusting for inflation. Spending on this item should have grown as boomers filled the best-customer age groups, but lower prices offered by discounters erased the potential increase. Spending on small electric kitchen appliances should stabilize now that boomers are solidly in the best-customer age groups, but the economic downturn may take a toll on this category.

Table 7.2 Appliances, kitchen, small electric

Total household spending	$2,303,678,070.00
Average household spends	19.17

	AVERAGE HOUSEHOLD SPENDING	BEST CUSTOMERS (index)	BIGGEST CUSTOMERS (market share)
AGE OF HOUSEHOLDER			
Average household	**$19.17**	**100**	**100.0%**
Under age 25	12.21	64	4.3
Aged 25 to 34	16.08	84	14.3
Aged 35 to 44	18.18	95	18.5
Aged 45 to 54	24.43	127	26.8
Aged 55 to 64	23.10	121	19.5
Aged 65 to 74	17.68	92	9.2
Aged 75 or older	14.91	78	7.4

	AVERAGE HOUSEHOLD SPENDING	BEST CUSTOMERS (index)	BIGGEST CUSTOMERS (market share)
HOUSEHOLD INCOME			
Average household	**$19.17**	**100**	**100.0%**
Under $20,000	10.10	53	10.8
$20,000 to $39,999	11.34	59	13.7
$40,000 to $49,999	15.75	82	8.1
$50,000 to $69,999	16.95	88	13.5
$70,000 to $79,999	25.43	133	7.7
$80,000 to $99,999	27.52	144	11.7
$100,000 or more	38.55	201	34.5
HOUSEHOLD TYPE			
Average household	**19.17**	**100**	**100.0**
Married couples	24.54	128	64.7
Married couples, no children	27.60	144	31.1
Married couples, with children	21.91	114	28.5
Oldest child under age 6	23.91	125	6.1
Oldest child aged 6 to 17	21.15	110	14.0
Oldest child aged 18 or older	21.88	114	8.4
Single parent with child under age 18	11.49	60	3.6
Single person	12.64	66	19.6
RACE AND HISPANIC ORIGIN			
Average household	**19.17**	**100**	**100.0**
Asian	14.19	74	2.6
Black	10.98	57	6.9
Hispanic	15.82	83	9.7
Non-Hispanic white and other	21.00	110	83.6
REGION			
Average household	**19.17**	**100**	**100.0**
Northeast	19.78	103	19.2
Midwest	20.46	107	24.4
South	17.73	92	33.2
West	19.65	103	23.2
EDUCATION			
Average household	**19.17**	**100**	**100.0**
Less than high school graduate	11.82	62	9.4
High school graduate	14.17	74	18.6
Some college	18.60	97	21.1
Associate's degree	23.29	121	10.8
College graduate	26.53	138	40.1
Bachelor's degree	26.00	136	25.4
Master's, professional, doctoral degree	27.50	143	14.6

Note: Market shares may not sum to 100.0 because of rounding and missing categories by household type. "Asian" and "black" include Hispanics and non-Hispanics who identify themselves as being of the respective race alone. "Hispanic" includes people of any race who identify themselves as Hispanic. "Other" includes people who identify themselves as non-Hispanic and as Alaska Native, American Indian, Asian (who are also included in the "Asian" row), Native Hawaiian or other Pacific Islander, as well as non-Hispanics reporting more than one race.
Source: Calculations by New Strategist based on the Bureau of Labor Statistics' 2007 Consumer Expenditure Survey.

Appliances, Major

Best customers:
      Householders aged 35 to 64
      Married couples

Customer trends:
      Average household spending on major appliances may fall as growth in homeownership slows and the small generation X moves into the peak-spending age group.

The biggest spenders on major appliances are married couples who are outfitting their home for expanding families or upgrading appliances after their children leave home. This explains why householders ranging in age from 35 to 64 spend 8 to 23 percent more than average on this item and account for two-thirds of the market. Married couples spend 38 percent more than average on major appliances, and those without children at home spend 49 percent above average.

Average household spending on major appliances rose 2 percent between 2000 and 2007, after adjusting for inflation. Behind the increase was the baby-boom generation's solid presence in the best-customer lifestage. Average household spending on major appliances is likely to fall in the years ahead as growth in homeownership slows and the small generation X enters the best-customer age group.

Table 7.3 Appliances, major

Total household spending $27,797,955,720.00
Average household spends   231.32

AGE OF HOUSEHOLDER	AVERAGE HOUSEHOLD SPENDING	BEST CUSTOMERS (index)	BIGGEST CUSTOMERS (market share)
Average household	$231.32	100	100.0%
Under age 25	121.60	53	3.6
Aged 25 to 34	212.54	92	15.7
Aged 35 to 44	250.97	108	21.1
Aged 45 to 54	285.07	123	25.9
Aged 55 to 64	265.98	115	18.6
Aged 65 to 74	205.42	89	8.9
Aged 75 or older	152.50	66	6.2

	AVERAGE HOUSEHOLD SPENDING	BEST CUSTOMERS (index)	BIGGEST CUSTOMERS (market share)
HOUSEHOLD INCOME			
Average household	**$231.32**	**100**	**100.0%**
Under $20,000	99.40	43	8.8
$20,000 to $39,999	142.72	62	14.3
$40,000 to $49,999	139.70	60	5.9
$50,000 to $69,999	222.38	96	14.7
$70,000 to $79,999	283.62	123	7.1
$80,000 to $99,999	324.32	140	11.4
$100,000 or more	508.29	220	37.6
HOUSEHOLD TYPE			
Average household	**231.32**	**100**	**100.0**
Married couples	319.46	138	69.8
Married couples, no children	344.80	149	32.2
Married couples, with children	299.92	130	32.4
Oldest child under age 6	296.24	128	6.3
Oldest child aged 6 to 17	298.74	129	16.4
Oldest child aged 18 or older	305.20	132	9.7
Single parent with child under age 18	153.40	66	3.9
Single person	112.44	49	14.5
RACE AND HISPANIC ORIGIN			
Average household	**231.32**	**100**	**100.0**
Asian	195.64	85	3.0
Black	119.23	52	6.2
Hispanic	136.17	59	6.9
Non-Hispanic white and other	263.35	114	86.9
REGION			
Average household	**231.32**	**100**	**100.0**
Northeast	239.61	104	19.3
Midwest	233.19	101	23.0
South	222.33	96	34.5
West	236.74	102	23.1
EDUCATION			
Average household	**231.32**	**100**	**100.0**
Less than high school graduate	134.84	58	8.8
High school graduate	177.26	77	19.3
Some college	234.46	101	22.1
Associate's degree	278.41	120	10.7
College graduate	312.07	135	39.0
Bachelor's degree	303.10	131	24.6
Master's, professional, doctoral degree	328.31	142	14.5

Note: Market shares may not sum to 100.0 because of rounding and missing categories by household type. "Asian" and "black" include Hispanics and non-Hispanics who identify themselves as being of the respective race alone. "Hispanic" includes people of any race who identify themselves as Hispanic. "Other" includes people who identify themselves as non-Hispanic and as Alaska Native, American Indian, Asian (who are also included in the "Asian" row), Native Hawaiian or other Pacific Islander, as well as non-Hispanics reporting more than one race.
Source: Calculations by New Strategist based on the Bureau of Labor Statistics' 2007 Consumer Expenditure Survey.

Bathroom Linens

Best customers:

Householders aged 45 to 64
Married couples without children at home
Married couples with adult children at home
Hispanics

Customer trends:

Average household spending on bathroom linens is likely to stabilize or even decline now that boomers have filled the best customer age groups and the economic downturn limits discretionary spending.

The biggest spenders on bathroom linens are the largest households and older householders. Married couples with adult children at home spend 48 percent more than the average household on this item. Married couples without children at home (most of them older) spend 33 percent more than average on bathroom linens, some of them buying for adult children living elsewhere. Householders aged 45 to 64 spend 13 to 18 percent more than average on this item.

Average household spending on bathroom linens rose 17 percent between 2000 and 2007, after adjusting for inflation. Behind the increase was the baby-boom generation's entry into the best-customer age groups. Average household spending on bathroom linens is likely to stabilize or even decline now that boomers have filled the best customer age groups and the economic downturn limits discretionary spending.

Table 7.4 **Bathroom linens**

Total household spending $2,980,240,800.00
Average household spends 24.80

AGE OF HOUSEHOLDER	AVERAGE HOUSEHOLD SPENDING	BEST CUSTOMERS (index)	BIGGEST CUSTOMERS (market share)
Average household	$24.80	100	100.0%
Under age 25	11.60	47	3.2
Aged 25 to 34	22.17	89	15.2
Aged 35 to 44	25.77	104	20.2
Aged 45 to 54	28.14	113	23.8
Aged 55 to 64	29.19	118	19.1
Aged 65 to 74	26.11	105	10.5
Aged 75 or older	21.49	87	8.2

	AVERAGE HOUSEHOLD SPENDING	BEST CUSTOMERS (index)	BIGGEST CUSTOMERS (market share)
HOUSEHOLD INCOME			
Average household	**$24.80**	**100**	**100.0%**
Under $20,000	13.12	53	10.9
$20,000 to $39,999	17.93	72	16.8
$40,000 to $49,999	21.84	88	8.7
$50,000 to $69,999	21.64	87	13.4
$70,000 to $79,999	23.96	97	5.6
$80,000 to $99,999	38.37	155	12.6
$100,000 or more	46.28	187	32.0
HOUSEHOLD TYPE			
Average household	**24.80**	**100**	**100.0**
Married couples	32.45	131	66.1
Married couples, no children	33.03	133	28.7
Married couples, with children	31.12	125	31.3
Oldest child under age 6	27.89	112	5.5
Oldest child aged 6 to 17	29.47	119	15.1
Oldest child aged 18 or older	36.75	148	10.9
Single parent with child under age 18	12.16	49	2.9
Single person	18.26	74	21.9
RACE AND HISPANIC ORIGIN			
Average household	**24.80**	**100**	**100.0**
Asian	22.63	91	3.2
Black	10.77	43	5.2
Hispanic	37.27	150	17.7
Non-Hispanic white and other	25.21	102	77.6
REGION			
Average household	**24.80**	**100**	**100.0**
Northeast	24.77	100	18.6
Midwest	18.44	74	17.0
South	27.44	111	39.7
West	27.15	109	24.8
EDUCATION			
Average household	**24.80**	**100**	**100.0**
Less than high school graduate	10.84	44	6.6
High school graduate	15.37	62	15.6
Some college	28.97	117	25.4
Associate's degree	35.68	144	12.8
College graduate	33.35	134	38.9
Bachelor's degree	23.85	96	18.0
Master's, professional, doctoral degree	49.83	201	20.5

Note: Market shares may not sum to 100.0 because of rounding and missing categories by household type. "Asian" and "black" include Hispanics and non-Hispanics who identify themselves as being of the respective race alone. "Hispanic" includes people of any race who identify themselves as Hispanic. "Other" includes people who identify themselves as non-Hispanic and as Alaska Native, American Indian, Asian (who are also included in the "Asian" row), Native Hawaiian or other Pacific Islander, as well as non-Hispanics reporting more than one race.
Source: Calculations by New Strategist based on the Bureau of Labor Statistics' 2007 Consumer Expenditure Survey.

Bedroom Furniture, Except Mattresses and Springs

Best customers:	**Householders aged 35 to 44** **Married couples with children under age 18** **Single parents**
Customer trends:	**Average household spending on bedroom furniture could rise in the years ahead as the large millennial generation enters the best-customer lifestage, but the economic downturn may limit any gains in this category.**

The best customers of bedroom furniture except mattresses and springs are households with children under age 18, outfitting their homes for their expanding families. Married couples with preschoolers spend 80 percent more than average on this item, while couples with school-aged children spend 69 percent more. Householders aged 35 to 44, many with children at home, spend 51 percent more than average on this item and account for 29 percent of the market.

Average household spending on bedroom furniture except mattresses and springs fell 7 percent between 2000 and 2007, after adjusting for inflation. Behind the decline was the small generation X in the best-customer lifestage. Average household spending on bedroom furniture could rise in the years ahead as the large millennial generation enters the best-customer lifestage, but the economic downturn may limit any gains in this category.

Table 7.5 Bedroom furniture, except mattresses and springs

Total household spending $9,242,351,610.00
Average household spends   76.91

	AVERAGE HOUSEHOLD SPENDING	BEST CUSTOMERS (index)	BIGGEST CUSTOMERS (market share)
AGE OF HOUSEHOLDER			
Average household	**$76.91**	**100**	**100.0%**
Under age 25	62.40	81	5.5
Aged 25 to 34	88.28	115	19.6
Aged 35 to 44	116.09	151	29.4
Aged 45 to 54	89.66	117	24.5
Aged 55 to 64	47.95	62	10.1
Aged 65 to 74	56.97	74	7.4
Aged 75 or older	28.57	37	3.5

	AVERAGE HOUSEHOLD SPENDING	BEST CUSTOMERS (index)	BIGGEST CUSTOMERS (market share)
HOUSEHOLD INCOME			
Average household	**$76.91**	**100**	**100.0%**
Under $20,000	26.87	35	7.2
$20,000 to $39,999	40.73	53	12.3
$40,000 to $49,999	55.53	72	7.1
$50,000 to $69,999	84.29	110	16.8
$70,000 to $79,999	70.70	92	5.3
$80,000 to $99,999	119.23	155	12.6
$100,000 or more	173.74	226	38.7
HOUSEHOLD TYPE			
Average household	**76.91**	**100**	**100.0**
Married couples	104.15	135	68.5
Married couples, no children	89.83	117	25.2
Married couples, with children	120.04	156	38.9
Oldest child under age 6	138.59	180	8.8
Oldest child aged 6 to 17	130.06	169	21.5
Oldest child aged 18 or older	90.47	118	8.7
Single parent with child under age 18	92.98	121	7.2
Single person	40.41	53	15.6
RACE AND HISPANIC ORIGIN			
Average household	**76.91**	**100**	**100.0**
Asian	104.29	136	4.8
Black	71.95	94	11.2
Hispanic	78.08	102	12.0
Non-Hispanic white and other	77.38	101	76.8
REGION			
Average household	**76.91**	**100**	**100.0**
Northeast	66.02	86	16.0
Midwest	60.12	78	17.9
South	93.16	121	43.5
West	77.05	100	22.7
EDUCATION			
Average household	**76.91**	**100**	**100.0**
Less than high school graduate	39.25	51	7.7
High school graduate	54.74	71	18.0
Some college	85.66	111	24.3
Associate's degree	105.98	138	12.2
College graduate	100.47	131	37.8
Bachelor's degree	100.26	130	24.4
Master's, professional, doctoral degree	100.85	131	13.4

Note: Market shares may not sum to 100.0 because of rounding and missing categories by household type. "Asian" and "black" include Hispanics and non-Hispanics who identify themselves as being of the respective race alone. "Hispanic" includes people of any race who identify themselves as Hispanic. "Other" includes people who identify themselves as non-Hispanic and as Alaska Native, American Indian, Asian (who are also included in the "Asian" row), Native Hawaiian or other Pacific Islander, as well as non-Hispanics reporting more than one race.
Source: Calculations by New Strategist based on the Bureau of Labor Statistics' 2007 Consumer Expenditure Survey.

Bedroom Linens

Best customers: Householders aged 35 to 44 and 55 to 64
Married couples with children at home

Customer trends: Average household spending on bedroom linens is likely to stabilize or even decline now that boomers have filled one of the best customer age groups and the economic downturn limits discretionary spending.

The biggest spenders on bedroom linens are married couples with children at home, who spend 46 percent more than average on bedroom linens. The figure peaks at over twice the average among couples with preschoolers. Householders aged 35 to 44, with expanding families, spend 32 percent more than average on this item. Householders aged 55 to 64, many of whom are redecorating as their children grow up and leave home, spend 27 more.

Average household spending on bedroom linens rose by a substantial 25 percent between 2000 and 2007, after adjusting for inflation. Behind the increase was the baby-boom generation's entry into one of the best-customer age groups. Average household spending on bedroom linens is likely to stabilize or even decline now that boomers have filled one of the best customer age groups and the economic downturn limits discretionary spending.

Table 7.6 Bedroom linens

Total household spending $8,059,868,970.00
Average household spends   67.07

AGE OF HOUSEHOLDER	AVERAGE HOUSEHOLD SPENDING	BEST CUSTOMERS (index)	BIGGEST CUSTOMERS (market share)
Average household	$67.07	100	100.0%
Under age 25	40.03	60	4.0
Aged 25 to 34	66.08	99	16.8
Aged 35 to 44	88.63	132	25.7
Aged 45 to 54	58.37	87	18.3
Aged 55 to 64	85.27	127	20.6
Aged 65 to 74	66.31	99	9.9
Aged 75 or older	33.10	49	4.7

	AVERAGE HOUSEHOLD SPENDING	BEST CUSTOMERS (index)	BIGGEST CUSTOMERS (market share)
HOUSEHOLD INCOME			
Average household	**$67.07**	**100**	**100.0%**
Under $20,000	18.57	28	5.7
$20,000 to $39,999	35.97	54	12.5
$40,000 to $49,999	55.12	82	8.1
$50,000 to $69,999	91.41	136	20.9
$70,000 to $79,999	53.19	79	4.6
$80,000 to $99,999	124.59	186	15.1
$100,000 or more	126.39	188	32.3
HOUSEHOLD TYPE			
Average household	**67.07**	**100**	**100.0**
Married couples	87.87	131	66.2
Married couples, no children	75.65	113	24.3
Married couples, with children	98.03	146	36.5
Oldest child under age 6	144.85	216	10.5
Oldest child aged 6 to 17	87.85	131	16.6
Oldest child aged 18 or older	83.82	125	9.2
Single parent with child under age 18	43.56	65	3.9
Single person	47.78	71	21.2
RACE AND HISPANIC ORIGIN			
Average household	**67.07**	**100**	**100.0**
Asian	47.12	70	2.5
Black	26.13	39	4.7
Hispanic	55.05	82	9.7
Non-Hispanic white and other	75.02	112	85.4
REGION			
Average household	**67.07**	**100**	**100.0**
Northeast	80.85	121	22.5
Midwest	49.19	73	16.8
South	69.50	104	37.2
West	69.92	104	23.6
EDUCATION			
Average household	**67.07**	**100**	**100.0**
Less than high school graduate	25.26	38	5.7
High school graduate	45.45	68	17.1
Some college	60.53	90	19.7
Associate's degree	100.79	150	13.4
College graduate	100.24	149	43.3
Bachelor's degree	96.75	144	27.0
Master's, professional, doctoral degree	106.30	158	16.2

Note: Market shares may not sum to 100.0 because of rounding and missing categories by household type. "Asian" and "black" include Hispanics and non-Hispanics who identify themselves as being of the respective race alone. "Hispanic" includes people of any race who identify themselves as Hispanic. "Other" includes people who identify themselves as non-Hispanic and as Alaska Native, American Indian, Asian (who are also included in the "Asian" row), Native Hawaiian or other Pacific Islander, as well as non-Hispanics reporting more than one race.
Source: Calculations by New Strategist based on the Bureau of Labor Statistics' 2007 Consumer Expenditure Survey.

Closet and Storage Items

Best customers:	Householders aged 45 to 54 and 65 to 74 Married couples
Customer trends:	Average household spending on closet and storage items should increase as more boomers become empty-nesters, but only if discretionary income grows.

Households with children and older householders are the best customers for closet and storage items, which give them the opportunity to stash away their accumulating belongings and organize their lives. Married couples with preschoolers spend more than twice the average on this item. Couples with adult children at home spend 50 percent more than average, while those without children at home (most of them older) spend 55 percent more. Householders aged 45 to 54 spend 28 percent more than average on this category, while those aged 65 to 74 spend 41 percent more.

Average household spending on closet and storage items more than doubled from 2000 to 2007, after adjusting for inflation. Behind the increase was the growing variety of closet and storage items available, as well as the baby-boom generation's aging into the empty-nest lifestage with more time to organize. Average household spending on closet and storage items should continue to increase as more boomers become empty-nesters, but only if discretionary income grows.

Table 7.7 Closet and storage items

Total household spending	$2,441,874,720.00
Average household spends	20.32

	AVERAGE HOUSEHOLD SPENDING	BEST CUSTOMERS (index)	BIGGEST CUSTOMERS (market share)
AGE OF HOUSEHOLDER			
Average household	**$20.32**	**100**	**100.0%**
Under age 25	8.89	44	3.0
Aged 25 to 34	22.96	113	19.3
Aged 35 to 44	21.49	106	20.6
Aged 45 to 54	25.94	128	26.8
Aged 55 to 64	17.69	87	14.1
Aged 65 to 74	28.64	141	14.1
Aged 75 or older	4.69	23	2.2

	AVERAGE HOUSEHOLD SPENDING	BEST CUSTOMERS (index)	BIGGEST CUSTOMERS (market share)
HOUSEHOLD INCOME			
Average household	**$20.32**	**100**	**100.0%**
Under $20,000	5.78	28	5.9
$20,000 to $39,999	11.51	57	13.2
$40,000 to $49,999	14.56	72	7.1
$50,000 to $69,999	17.26	85	13.0
$70,000 to $79,999	21.93	108	6.2
$80,000 to $99,999	52.69	259	21.1
$100,000 or more	38.11	188	32.1
HOUSEHOLD TYPE			
Average household	**20.32**	**100**	**100.0**
Married couples	30.21	149	75.2
Married couples, no children	31.43	155	33.4
Married couples, with children	31.32	154	38.5
Oldest child under age 6	46.27	228	11.1
Oldest child aged 6 to 17	26.16	129	16.4
Oldest child aged 18 or older	30.57	150	11.1
Single parent with child under age 18	13.33	66	3.9
Single person	6.87	34	10.1
RACE AND HISPANIC ORIGIN			
Average household	**20.32**	**100**	**100.0**
Asian	13.95	69	2.4
Black	9.36	46	5.5
Hispanic	9.84	48	5.7
Non-Hispanic white and other	23.47	116	88.2
REGION			
Average household	**20.32**	**100**	**100.0**
Northeast	12.03	59	11.0
Midwest	25.08	123	28.2
South	19.04	94	33.6
West	24.48	120	27.2
EDUCATION			
Average household	**20.32**	**100**	**100.0**
Less than high school graduate	7.21	35	5.4
High school graduate	13.84	68	17.2
Some college	11.58	57	12.4
Associate's degree	55.80	275	24.4
College graduate	28.11	138	40.0
Bachelor's degree	27.43	135	25.3
Master's, professional, doctoral degree	29.28	144	14.7

Note: Market shares may not sum to 100.0 because of rounding and missing categories by household type. "Asian" and "black" include Hispanics and non-Hispanics who identify themselves as being of the respective race alone. "Hispanic" includes people of any race who identify themselves as Hispanic. "Other" includes people who identify themselves as non-Hispanic and as Alaska Native, American Indian, Asian (who are also included in the "Asian" row), Native Hawaiian or other Pacific Islander, as well as non-Hispanics reporting more than one race.
Source: Calculations by New Strategist based on the Bureau of Labor Statistics' 2007 Consumer Expenditure Survey.

Curtains and Draperies

Best customers:
Householders aged 35 to 44
Married couples with children under age 18
Asians
College graduates

Customer trends:
Average household spending on curtains and draperies is likely to continue to fall as the economic downturn limits discretionary spending.

The best customers of curtains and draperies are married couples with children under age 18 at home, spending 79 percent more than average on this item. Householders aged 35 to 44, most with children, spend 85 percent more than average on curtains and draperies. Asians spend more than twice the average, as do college graduates.

Average household spending on curtains and draperies fell 25 percent between 2000 and 2007, after adjusting for inflation. Behind the decline was the entry of the small generation X into the best-customer lifestage. Average household spending on curtains and draperies is likely to continue to fall as the economic downturn limits discretionary spending.

Table 7.8 Curtains and draperies

Total household spending $2,280,845,580.00
Average household spends   18.98

	AVERAGE HOUSEHOLD SPENDING	BEST CUSTOMERS (index)	BIGGEST CUSTOMERS (market share)
AGE OF HOUSEHOLDER			
Average household	**$18.98**	**100**	**100.0%**
Under age 25	6.67	35	2.4
Aged 25 to 34	13.34	70	12.0
Aged 35 to 44	35.11	185	36.0
Aged 45 to 54	11.94	63	13.2
Aged 55 to 64	23.48	124	20.0
Aged 65 to 74	16.86	89	8.9
Aged 75 or older	14.93	79	7.5

	AVERAGE HOUSEHOLD SPENDING	BEST CUSTOMERS (index)	BIGGEST CUSTOMERS (market share)
HOUSEHOLD INCOME			
Average household	**$18.98**	**100**	**100.0%**
Under $20,000	5.08	27	5.5
$20,000 to $39,999	11.56	61	14.2
$40,000 to $49,999	12.68	67	6.6
$50,000 to $69,999	12.20	64	9.8
$70,000 to $79,999	24.48	129	7.5
$80,000 to $99,999	17.33	91	7.4
$100,000 or more	54.34	286	49.0
HOUSEHOLD TYPE			
Average household	**18.98**	**100**	**100.0**
Married couples	26.70	141	71.1
Married couples, no children	21.21	112	24.1
Married couples, with children	33.98	179	44.7
Oldest child under age 6	43.54	229	11.2
Oldest child aged 6 to 17	40.03	211	26.8
Oldest child aged 18 or older	17.22	91	6.7
Single parent with child under age 18	4.49	24	1.4
Single person	11.01	58	17.3
RACE AND HISPANIC ORIGIN			
Average household	**18.98**	**100**	**100.0**
Asian	43.25	228	8.0
Black	6.50	34	4.1
Hispanic	6.62	35	4.1
Non-Hispanic white and other	22.83	120	91.8
REGION			
Average household	**18.98**	**100**	**100.0**
Northeast	22.33	118	21.9
Midwest	15.83	83	19.1
South	15.53	82	29.4
West	24.89	131	29.7
EDUCATION			
Average household	**18.98**	**100**	**100.0**
Less than high school graduate	5.49	29	4.4
High school graduate	8.09	43	10.8
Some college	16.45	87	18.9
Associate's degree	16.12	85	7.5
College graduate	38.32	202	58.4
Bachelor's degree	21.88	115	21.6
Master's, professional, doctoral degree	68.53	361	36.8

Note: Market shares may not sum to 100.0 because of rounding and missing categories by household type. "Asian" and "black" include Hispanics and non-Hispanics who identify themselves as being of the respective race alone. "Hispanic" includes people of any race who identify themselves as Hispanic. "Other" includes people who identify themselves as non-Hispanic and as Alaska Native, American Indian, Asian (who are also included in the "Asian" row), Native Hawaiian or other Pacific Islander, as well as non-Hispanics reporting more than one race.
Source: Calculations by New Strategist based on the Bureau of Labor Statistics' 2007 Consumer Expenditure Survey.

Decorative Items for the Home

Best customers:
Householders aged 55 to 64
Married couples without children at home
Married couples with adult children at home

Customer trends:
Average household spending on decorative items should rise as empty-nest boomers redecorate their homes, but only if discretionary income grows.

Decorative items for the home—a category that includes the many whimsical items of home decor—are the second-largest expense within the home furnishings and equipment category, behind only major appliances. The biggest spenders on decorative items for the home are householders nearing retirement age. Householders aged 55 to 64 spend 42 percent more than the average household on this item. Married couples without children at home, most of them empty-nesters, spend 56 percent more than average on decorative items, while couples with adult children at home spend 58 percent more.

Average household spending on decorative items for the home fell 27 percent between 2000 and 2007, after adjusting for inflation. Behind the spending decline was a reduction in discretionary spending as the economic downturn commenced. Average household spending on decorative items should rise in the years ahead as empty nest boomers redecorate their homes, but only if discretionary income grows.

Table 7.9 Decorative items for the home

Total household spending $18,616,891,320.00
Average household spends 154.92

AGE OF HOUSEHOLDER	AVERAGE HOUSEHOLD SPENDING	BEST CUSTOMERS (index)	BIGGEST CUSTOMERS (market share)
Average household	$154.92	100	100.0%
Under age 25	56.02	36	2.5
Aged 25 to 34	177.68	115	19.6
Aged 35 to 44	153.14	99	19.3
Aged 45 to 54	177.88	115	24.1
Aged 55 to 64	220.43	142	23.0
Aged 65 to 74	130.68	84	8.4
Aged 75 or older	56.49	36	3.5

	AVERAGE HOUSEHOLD SPENDING	BEST CUSTOMERS (index)	BIGGEST CUSTOMERS (market share)
HOUSEHOLD INCOME			
Average household	**$154.92**	**100**	**100.0%**
Under $20,000	32.36	21	4.3
$20,000 to $39,999	80.59	52	12.1
$40,000 to $49,999	87.07	56	5.5
$50,000 to $69,999	134.44	87	13.3
$70,000 to $79,999	210.42	136	7.9
$80,000 to $99,999	158.31	102	8.3
$100,000 or more	453.04	292	50.1
HOUSEHOLD TYPE			
Average household	**154.92**	**100**	**100.0**
Married couples	210.35	136	68.6
Married couples, no children	241.69	156	33.7
Married couples, with children	198.93	128	32.0
Oldest child under age 6	182.87	118	5.8
Oldest child aged 6 to 17	181.56	117	14.9
Oldest child aged 18 or older	245.12	158	11.7
Single parent with child under age 18	53.51	35	2.1
Single person	70.02	45	13.4
RACE AND HISPANIC ORIGIN			
Average household	**154.92**	**100**	**100.0**
Asian	87.82	57	2.0
Black	40.47	26	3.1
Hispanic	105.09	68	8.0
Non-Hispanic white and other	179.57	116	88.5
REGION			
Average household	**154.92**	**100**	**100.0**
Northeast	142.57	92	17.1
Midwest	134.05	87	19.8
South	158.42	102	36.7
West	181.27	117	26.5
EDUCATION			
Average household	**154.92**	**100**	**100.0**
Less than high school graduate	55.71	36	5.5
High school graduate	91.82	59	15.0
Some college	112.29	72	15.8
Associate's degree	154.01	99	8.8
College graduate	286.63	185	53.6
Bachelor's degree	275.08	178	33.3
Master's, professional, doctoral degree	306.69	198	20.2

Note: Market shares may not sum to 100.0 because of rounding and missing categories by household type. "Asian" and "black" include Hispanics and non-Hispanics who identify themselves as being of the respective race alone. "Hispanic" includes people of any race who identify themselves as Hispanic. "Other" includes people who identify themselves as non-Hispanic and as Alaska Native, American Indian, Asian (who are also included in the "Asian" row), Native Hawaiian or other Pacific Islander, as well as non-Hispanics reporting more than one race.
Source: Calculations by New Strategist based on the Bureau of Labor Statistics' 2007 Consumer Expenditure Survey.

Floor Coverings, Nonpermanent

Best customers: **High-income households**
Married couples with children at home
College graduates

Customer trends: **Average household spending on rugs may decline in the years ahead as the economic downturn lowers incomes and discretionary spending.**

The biggest spenders on rugs are affluent married couples with children at home. Householders with incomes of $100,000 or more spend more than three times the average as they outfit their oversized homes with rugs. This income group controls 56 percent of the rug market. Married couples with children at home spend 70 percent more than average on this item.

Average household spending on rugs rose by 14 percent between 2000 and 2007, after adjusting for inflation. Behind the increase was the growing discretionary income of high-income households during those years. Average household spending on rugs may decline in the years ahead as the economic downturn lowers incomes and discretionary spending.

Table 7.10 Floor coverings, nonpermanent

Total household spending $2,518,784,160.00
Average household spends   20.96

AGE OF HOUSEHOLDER	AVERAGE HOUSEHOLD SPENDING	BEST CUSTOMERS (index)	BIGGEST CUSTOMERS (market share)
Average household	$20.96	100	100.0%
Under age 25	3.75	18	1.2
Aged 25 to 34	24.14	115	19.6
Aged 35 to 44	22.30	106	20.7
Aged 45 to 54	23.76	113	23.8
Aged 55 to 64	22.61	108	17.5
Aged 65 to 74	25.78	123	12.3
Aged 75 or older	10.71	51	4.8

	AVERAGE HOUSEHOLD SPENDING	BEST CUSTOMERS (index)	BIGGEST CUSTOMERS (market share)
HOUSEHOLD INCOME			
Average household	**$20.96**	**100**	**100.0%**
Under $20,000	7.32	35	7.2
$20,000 to $39,999	8.48	40	9.4
$40,000 to $49,999	10.14	48	4.8
$50,000 to $69,999	14.07	67	10.3
$70,000 to $79,999	19.81	95	5.5
$80,000 to $99,999	16.92	81	6.6
$100,000 or more	68.94	329	56.4
HOUSEHOLD TYPE			
Average household	**20.96**	**100**	**100.0**
Married couples	28.03	134	67.6
Married couples, no children	19.59	93	20.2
Married couples, with children	35.65	170	42.4
Oldest child under age 6	35.76	171	8.3
Oldest child aged 6 to 17	40.45	193	24.5
Oldest child aged 18 or older	27.29	130	9.6
Single parent with child under age 18	11.06	53	3.1
Single person	11.67	56	16.6
RACE AND HISPANIC ORIGIN			
Average household	**20.96**	**100**	**100.0**
Asian	11.34	54	1.9
Black	13.74	66	7.9
Hispanic	9.96	48	5.6
Non-Hispanic white and other	23.86	114	86.9
REGION			
Average household	**20.96**	**100**	**100.0**
Northeast	28.00	134	24.9
Midwest	18.21	87	19.9
South	15.67	75	26.8
West	26.35	126	28.4
EDUCATION			
Average household	**20.96**	**100**	**100.0**
Less than high school graduate	9.54	46	6.9
High school graduate	8.24	39	9.9
Some college	13.70	65	14.2
Associate's degree	21.31	102	9.0
College graduate	43.39	207	59.9
Bachelor's degree	41.76	199	37.3
Master's, professional, doctoral degree	46.39	221	22.6

Note: Market shares may not sum to 100.0 because of rounding and missing categories by household type. "Asian" and "black" include Hispanics and non-Hispanics who identify themselves as being of the respective race alone. "Hispanic" includes people of any race who identify themselves as Hispanic. "Other" includes people who identify themselves as non-Hispanic and as Alaska Native, American Indian, Asian (who are also included in the "Asian" row), Native Hawaiian or other Pacific Islander, as well as non-Hispanics reporting more than one race.
Source: Calculations by New Strategist based on the Bureau of Labor Statistics' 2007 Consumer Expenditure Survey.

Floor Coverings, Wall-to-Wall

Best customers: **Married couples without children at home**
                                        Married couples with children under age 18

Customer trends: **Average household spending on wall-to-wall carpeting should rise as growing numbers of empty-nest boomers redecorate their homes, but the economic downturn is likely to limit spending on this category.**

The best customers of wall-to-wall floor coverings are married couples with children under age 18—who are outfitting their homes for expanding families—and older married couples who are redecorating after their children leave home. Married couples with school-aged children spend 88 percent more than average on wall-to-wall floor coverings, and those with preschoolers spend twice the average. Couples without children at home, most of them empty-nesters, spend 42 percent more than average on this item.

Average household spending on wall-to-wall floor coverings fell 27 percent between 2000 and 2007, after adjusting for inflation. Behind the spending decline was the pullback in household spending as the economic downturn commenced. Average household spending on wall-to-wall carpeting should rise in the years ahead as more boomers become empty-nesters, but the economic downturn is likely to limit spending in this category.

Table 7.11 Floor coverings, wall-to-wall

Total household spending	$3,065,562,210.00
Average household spends	25.51

AGE OF HOUSEHOLDER	AVERAGE HOUSEHOLD SPENDING	BEST CUSTOMERS (index)	BIGGEST CUSTOMERS (market share)
Average household	$25.51	100	100.0%
Under age 25	0.28	1	0.1
Aged 25 to 34	23.51	92	15.7
Aged 35 to 44	27.67	108	21.1
Aged 45 to 54	30.13	118	24.8
Aged 55 to 64	25.25	99	16.0
Aged 65 to 74	31.91	125	12.5
Aged 75 or older	26.20	103	9.7

	AVERAGE HOUSEHOLD SPENDING	BEST CUSTOMERS (index)	BIGGEST CUSTOMERS (market share)
HOUSEHOLD INCOME			
Average household	**$25.51**	**100**	**100.0%**
Under $20,000	7.14	28	5.8
$20,000 to $39,999	19.47	76	17.7
$40,000 to $49,999	9.74	38	3.8
$50,000 to $69,999	22.60	89	13.6
$70,000 to $79,999	22.57	88	5.1
$80,000 to $99,999	27.05	106	8.6
$100,000 or more	67.68	265	45.5
HOUSEHOLD TYPE			
Average household	**25.51**	**100**	**100.0**
Married couples	36.50	143	72.3
Married couples, no children	36.19	142	30.6
Married couples, with children	39.33	154	38.5
Oldest child under age 6	50.95	200	9.7
Oldest child aged 6 to 17	47.99	188	23.9
Oldest child aged 18 or older	16.71	66	4.8
Single parent with child under age 18	14.47	57	3.4
Single person	12.53	49	14.6
RACE AND HISPANIC ORIGIN			
Average household	**25.51**	**100**	**100.0**
Asian	23.67	93	3.3
Black	18.41	72	8.7
Hispanic	5.45	21	2.5
Non-Hispanic white and other	29.69	116	88.8
REGION			
Average household	**25.51**	**100**	**100.0**
Northeast	41.47	163	30.3
Midwest	25.69	101	23.0
South	20.42	80	28.7
West	20.28	79	18.0
EDUCATION			
Average household	**25.51**	**100**	**100.0**
Less than high school graduate	11.79	46	7.0
High school graduate	19.76	77	19.5
Some college	20.98	82	17.9
Associate's degree	30.85	121	10.7
College graduate	39.49	155	44.8
Bachelor's degree	34.58	136	25.4
Master's, professional, doctoral degree	48.51	190	19.4

Note: Market shares may not sum to 100.0 because of rounding and missing categories by household type. "Asian" and "black" include Hispanics and non-Hispanics who identify themselves as being of the respective race alone. "Hispanic" includes people of any race who identify themselves as Hispanic. "Other" includes people who identify themselves as non-Hispanic and as Alaska Native, American Indian, Asian (who are also included in the "Asian" row), Native Hawaiian or other Pacific Islander, as well as non-Hispanics reporting more than one race.
Source: Calculations by New Strategist based on the Bureau of Labor Statistics' 2007 Consumer Expenditure Survey.

Housewares

Best customers:

Married couples with preschoolers
Married couples with adult children at home
Married couples without children at home

Customer trends:

Average household spending on housewares should rise as boomers help their adult children outfit their homes, but only if discretionary income grows.

Housewares is a category that includes dishes, glassware, flatware, and nonelectric cookware—all the things that fill our kitchen cupboards. The best customers of housewares are young married couples outfitting their first home and older couples who are redecorating or helping grown children outfit their homes. Married couples with preschoolers spend 49 percent more than average on housewares. Couples without children at home (most of them empty-nesters) spend 21 percent more than average on this item. Couples with adult children at home spend 58 percent more.

Average household spending on housewares fell 10 percent between 2000 and 2007, after adjusting for inflation. One factor behind the decline was price discounting, as well as the beginning of the economic downturn, which limited discretionary spending on some categories. Average household spending on housewares should rise as boomers help their adult children outfit their homes, but only if discretionary income grows.

Table 7.12 Housewares

Total household spending $8,464,845,240.00
Average household spends 70.44

AGE OF HOUSEHOLDER	AVERAGE HOUSEHOLD SPENDING	BEST CUSTOMERS (index)	BIGGEST CUSTOMERS (market share)
Average household	$70.44	100	100.0%
Under age 25	42.14	60	4.1
Aged 25 to 34	77.15	110	18.7
Aged 35 to 44	70.10	100	19.4
Aged 45 to 54	78.44	111	23.4
Aged 55 to 64	62.95	89	14.5
Aged 65 to 74	81.77	116	11.6
Aged 75 or older	63.26	90	8.5

	AVERAGE HOUSEHOLD SPENDING	BEST CUSTOMERS (index)	BIGGEST CUSTOMERS (market share)
HOUSEHOLD INCOME			
Average household	**$70.44**	**100**	**100.0%**
Under $20,000	28.70	41	8.4
$20,000 to $39,999	49.72	71	16.4
$40,000 to $49,999	53.48	76	7.5
$50,000 to $69,999	77.76	110	16.9
$70,000 to $79,999	116.56	165	9.6
$80,000 to $99,999	86.38	123	10.0
$100,000 or more	128.35	182	31.2
HOUSEHOLD TYPE			
Average household	**70.44**	**100**	**100.0**
Married couples	86.40	123	62.0
Married couples, no children	84.94	121	26.0
Married couples, with children	92.80	132	32.9
Oldest child under age 6	104.72	149	7.3
Oldest child aged 6 to 17	79.38	113	14.3
Oldest child aged 18 or older	111.41	158	11.7
Single parent with child under age 18	37.98	54	3.2
Single person	55.84	79	23.6
RACE AND HISPANIC ORIGIN			
Average household	**70.44**	**100**	**100.0**
Asian	82.14	117	4.1
Black	40.41	57	6.9
Hispanic	60.66	86	10.2
Non-Hispanic white and other	76.44	109	82.8
REGION			
Average household	**70.44**	**100**	**100.0**
Northeast	68.11	97	18.0
Midwest	61.13	87	19.8
South	59.95	85	30.6
West	98.92	140	31.8
EDUCATION			
Average household	**70.44**	**100**	**100.0**
Less than high school graduate	49.45	70	10.6
High school graduate	36.31	52	13.0
Some college	80.35	114	24.8
Associate's degree	80.64	114	10.2
College graduate	99.90	142	41.1
Bachelor's degree	83.25	118	22.2
Master's, professional, doctoral degree	128.99	183	18.7

Note: Market shares may not sum to 100.0 because of rounding and missing categories by household type. "Asian" and "black" include Hispanics and non-Hispanics who identify themselves as being of the respective race alone. "Hispanic" includes people of any race who identify themselves as Hispanic. "Other" includes people who identify themselves as non-Hispanic and as Alaska Native, American Indian, Asian (who are also included in the "Asian" row), Native Hawaiian or other Pacific Islander, as well as non-Hispanics reporting more than one race.
Source: Calculations by New Strategist based on the Bureau of Labor Statistics' 2007 Consumer Expenditure Survey.

Infants' Equipment and Furniture

Best customers:	**Householders aged 25 to 44** **Married couples with preschoolers** **Hispanics** **Households in the West**
Customer trends:	**Average household spending on infants' equipment and furniture should continue to increase as the large millennial generation has children.**

The best customers of infants' equipment and furniture are young married couples with preschoolers. Married couples with preschoolers spend nearly seven times the average on this item. Householders aged 25 to 44 spend more than twice the average on infants' equipment and furniture. Hispanics, who have relatively large families, spend 30 percent more than average on infants' equipment and furniture. Households in the West, where many Hispanics reside, spend 40 percent more.

Average household spending on infants' equipment and furniture increased by a hefty 35 percent between 2000 and 2007, after adjusting for inflation. Behind the increase was the large millennial generation entering the family formation lifestage. Spending on infants' equipment and furniture is likely to continue to increase as the millennial generation has children.

Table 7.13 Infants' equipment and furniture

Total household spending	$2,783,160,360.00
Average household spends	23.16

	AVERAGE HOUSEHOLD SPENDING	BEST CUSTOMERS (index)	BIGGEST CUSTOMERS (market share)
AGE OF HOUSEHOLDER			
Average household	**$23.16**	**100**	**100.0%**
Under age 25	8.23	36	2.4
Aged 25 to 34	48.50	209	35.7
Aged 35 to 44	48.05	207	40.4
Aged 45 to 54	10.25	44	9.3
Aged 55 to 64	10.85	47	7.6
Aged 65 to 74	7.32	32	3.2
Aged 75 or older	2.89	12	1.2

	AVERAGE HOUSEHOLD SPENDING	BEST CUSTOMERS (index)	BIGGEST CUSTOMERS (market share)
HOUSEHOLD INCOME			
Average household	**$23.16**	**100**	**100.0%**
Under $20,000	4.25	18	3.8
$20,000 to $39,999	15.48	67	15.5
$40,000 to $49,999	16.22	70	6.9
$50,000 to $69,999	18.83	81	12.4
$70,000 to $79,999	26.74	115	6.7
$80,000 to $99,999	31.76	137	11.2
$100,000 or more	59.64	258	44.1
HOUSEHOLD TYPE			
Average household	**23.16**	**100**	**100.0**
Married couples	35.51	153	77.5
Married couples, no children	20.05	87	18.7
Married couples, with children	48.26	208	52.0
Oldest child under age 6	161.64	698	34.1
Oldest child aged 6 to 17	19.94	86	10.9
Oldest child aged 18 or older	22.08	95	7.0
Single parent with child under age 18	17.06	74	4.4
Single person	5.91	26	7.6
RACE AND HISPANIC ORIGIN			
Average household	**23.16**	**100**	**100.0**
Asian	27.19	117	4.1
Black	8.89	38	4.6
Hispanic	30.04	130	15.3
Non-Hispanic white and other	24.28	105	80.0
REGION			
Average household	**23.16**	**100**	**100.0**
Northeast	27.17	117	21.8
Midwest	26.13	113	25.8
South	13.36	58	20.7
West	32.48	140	31.7
EDUCATION			
Average household	**23.16**	**100**	**100.0**
Less than high school graduate	20.47	88	13.4
High school graduate	8.48	37	9.2
Some college	17.40	75	16.4
Associate's degree	30.57	132	11.7
College graduate	39.37	170	49.2
Bachelor's degree	42.38	183	34.3
Master's, professional, doctoral degree	34.29	148	15.1

Note: Market shares may not sum to 100.0 because of rounding and missing categories by household type. "Asian" and "black" include Hispanics and non-Hispanics who identify themselves as being of the respective race alone. "Hispanic" includes people of any race who identify themselves as Hispanic. "Other" includes people who identify themselves as non-Hispanic and as Alaska Native, American Indian, Asian (who are also included in the "Asian" row), Native Hawaiian or other Pacific Islander, as well as non-Hispanics reporting more than one race.
Source: Calculations by New Strategist based on the Bureau of Labor Statistics' 2007 Consumer Expenditure Survey.

Kitchen and Dining Room Furniture

Best customers:

Householders aged 25 to 44
High-income households
Married couples without children at home
Married couples with children under age 18
College graduates

Customer trends:

Average household spending on kitchen and dining room furniture should stabilize as the large millennial generation has children—but only if discretionary income grows.

The best customers of kitchen and dining room furniture are affluent married couples who are outfitting their homes for expanding families. Householders aged 25 to 44 spend 55 to 61 percent more than average on this item and control 58 percent of the market. Married couples with preschoolers spend more than two times the average on kitchen and dining room furniture, while those with school-aged children spend twice the average. High-income households spend three-and-one-half times the average on kitchen and dining room furniture. Married couples without children at home (most of them empty-nesters) spend 44 percent more than average on this item as they redecorate after their children leave home. College graduates, who have higher-than-average incomes, spend over twice the average on kitchen and dining room furniture.

Average household spending on kitchen and dining room furniture fell 16 percent between 2000 and 2007, after adjusting for inflation. Behind the decline was the baby-boom's exit from the best-customer lifestage. Average household spending on kitchen and dining room furniture should stabilize as the large millennial generation has children—but only if discretionary income grows.

Table 7.14 **Kitchen and dining room furniture**

Total household spending $5,654,045,550.00
Average household spends 47.05

AGE OF HOUSEHOLDER	AVERAGE HOUSEHOLD SPENDING	BEST CUSTOMERS (index)	BIGGEST CUSTOMERS (market share)
Average household	$47.05	100	100.0%
Under age 25	22.81	48	3.3
Aged 25 to 34	73.14	155	26.5
Aged 35 to 44	75.76	161	31.4
Aged 45 to 54	41.39	88	18.5
Aged 55 to 64	33.81	72	11.6
Aged 65 to 74	27.62	59	5.9
Aged 75 or older	14.07	30	2.8

	AVERAGE HOUSEHOLD SPENDING	BEST CUSTOMERS (index)	BIGGEST CUSTOMERS (market share)
HOUSEHOLD INCOME			
Average household	**$47.05**	**100**	**100.0%**
Under $20,000	17.53	37	7.7
$20,000 to $39,999	15.20	32	7.5
$40,000 to $49,999	16.30	35	3.4
$50,000 to $69,999	36.19	77	11.8
$70,000 to $79,999	26.17	56	3.2
$80,000 to $99,999	34.25	73	5.9
$100,000 or more	166.17	353	60.5
HOUSEHOLD TYPE			
Average household	**47.05**	**100**	**100.0**
Married couples	71.26	151	76.6
Married couples, no children	67.82	144	31.1
Married couples, with children	77.53	165	41.1
Oldest child under age 6	109.89	234	11.4
Oldest child aged 6 to 17	93.36	198	25.2
Oldest child aged 18 or older	28.82	61	4.5
Single parent with child under age 18	23.03	49	2.9
Single person	22.65	48	14.3
RACE AND HISPANIC ORIGIN			
Average household	**47.05**	**100**	**100.0**
Asian	–	–	–
Black	19.42	41	5.0
Hispanic	26.91	57	6.8
Non-Hispanic white and other	54.49	116	88.4
REGION			
Average household	**47.05**	**100**	**100.0**
Northeast	84.36	179	33.4
Midwest	27.26	58	13.2
South	40.32	86	30.8
West	47.00	100	22.6
EDUCATION			
Average household	**47.05**	**100**	**100.0**
Less than high school graduate	14.07	30	4.5
High school graduate	13.48	29	7.2
Some college	36.08	77	16.7
Associate's degree	44.48	95	8.4
College graduate	102.62	218	63.1
Bachelor's degree	89.49	190	35.6
Master's, professional, doctoral degree	126.75	269	27.5

Note: Market shares may not sum to 100.0 because of rounding and missing categories by household type. "Asian" and "black" include Hispanics and non-Hispanics who identify themselves as being of the respective race alone. "Hispanic" includes people of any race who identify themselves as Hispanic. "Other" includes people who identify themselves as non-Hispanic and as Alaska Native, American Indian, Asian (who are also included in the "Asian" row), Native Hawaiian or other Pacific Islander, as well as non-Hispanics reporting more than one race.
Source: Calculations by New Strategist based on the Bureau of Labor Statistics' 2007 Consumer Expenditure Survey.

Kitchen and Dining Room Linens

Best customers:
Householders aged 25 to 34
Married couples without children at home
Married couples with children under age 18
Single parents

Customer trends:
Average household spending on kitchen and dining room linens should stabilize or even rise as the large millennial generation fills the best-customer lifestage, but only if discretionary income grows.

The best customers of kitchen and dining room linens are younger married couples who are outfitting their first homes. Householders aged 25 to 34 spend 47 percent more than average on kitchen and dining room linens. Married couples with children under age 18 spend 37 to 41 percent more than average on this item, and single parents spend 22 percent more. Married couples without children at home, some of them newly married young adults, spend 88 percent more than average on kitchen and dining room linens.

Average household spending on kitchen and dining room linens fell 41 percent between 2000 and 2007, after adjusting for inflation. Behind the decline was price discounting as cheaper imports lowered costs. Average household spending on kitchen and dining room linens should stabilize or even rise as the large millennial generation fills the best-customer lifestage, but only if discretionary income grows.

Table 7.15 Kitchen and dining room linens

Total household spending $796,733,730.00
Average household spends 6.63

AGE OF HOUSEHOLDER	AVERAGE HOUSEHOLD SPENDING	BEST CUSTOMERS (index)	BIGGEST CUSTOMERS (market share)
Average household	**$6.63**	**100**	**100.0%**
Under age 25	2.00	30	2.0
Aged 25 to 34	9.73	147	25.0
Aged 35 to 44	6.70	101	19.7
Aged 45 to 54	5.85	88	18.5
Aged 55 to 64	7.69	116	18.8
Aged 65 to 74	6.24	94	9.4
Aged 75 or older	4.64	70	6.6

	AVERAGE HOUSEHOLD SPENDING	BEST CUSTOMERS (index)	BIGGEST CUSTOMERS (market share)
HOUSEHOLD INCOME			
Average household	**$6.63**	**100**	**100.0%**
Under $20,000	2.19	33	6.8
$20,000 to $39,999	3.01	45	10.5
$40,000 to $49,999	5.56	84	8.3
$50,000 to $69,999	6.66	100	15.4
$70,000 to $79,999	12.06	182	10.5
$80,000 to $99,999	9.36	141	11.5
$100,000 or more	14.25	215	36.8
HOUSEHOLD TYPE			
Average household	**6.63**	**100**	**100.0**
Married couples	10.22	154	77.9
Married couples, no children	12.47	188	40.6
Married couples, with children	8.21	124	30.9
Oldest child under age 6	9.32	141	6.9
Oldest child aged 6 to 17	9.06	137	17.4
Oldest child aged 18 or older	5.70	86	6.3
Single parent with child under age 18	8.12	122	7.3
Single person	2.35	35	10.5
RACE AND HISPANIC ORIGIN			
Average household	**6.63**	**100**	**100.0**
Asian	2.95	44	1.6
Black	2.08	31	3.8
Hispanic	5.35	81	9.5
Non-Hispanic white and other	7.50	113	86.4
REGION			
Average household	**6.63**	**100**	**100.0**
Northeast	9.11	137	25.6
Midwest	5.29	80	18.2
South	5.28	80	28.6
West	8.06	122	27.5
EDUCATION			
Average household	**6.63**	**100**	**100.0**
Less than high school graduate	2.27	34	5.2
High school graduate	3.77	57	14.3
Some college	6.23	94	20.5
Associate's degree	7.83	118	10.5
College graduate	11.07	167	48.3
Bachelor's degree	13.07	197	36.9
Master's, professional, doctoral degree	7.60	115	11.7

Note: Market shares may not sum to 100.0 because of rounding and missing categories by household type. "Asian" and "black" include Hispanics and non-Hispanics who identify themselves as being of the respective race alone. "Hispanic" includes people of any race who identify themselves as Hispanic. "Other" includes people who identify themselves as non-Hispanic and as Alaska Native, American Indian, Asian (who are also included in the "Asian" row), Native Hawaiian or other Pacific Islander, as well as non-Hispanics reporting more than one race.
Source: Calculations by New Strategist based on the Bureau of Labor Statistics' 2007 Consumer Expenditure Survey.

Lamps and Lighting Fixtures

Best customers:

Householders aged 45 to 64
High-income households
Married couples without children at home
Married couples with school-aged children

Customer trends:

Average household spending on lamps and lighting fixtures could continue to rise as millions of empty-nest boomers redecorate their homes, but only if discretionary income grows.

The best customers of lamps and lighting fixtures are older married couples. Householders aged 45 to 64 spend 28 to 81 percent more than the average on lamps and lighting fixtures and account for 56 percent of the market. Married couples without children at home (most of them older) spend almost twice the average on lamps, while those with school-aged children at home spend two-thirds more than average. High-income households spend over three times the average on lamps and lighting fixtures.

Average household spending on lamps and lighting fixtures more than doubled between 2000 and 2007, after adjusting for inflation. One factor behind the hefty increase was the baby-boom generation's entry into the best-customer lifestage. Average household spending on lamps and lighting fixtures could continue to rise in the years ahead as millions of empty-nest boomers redecorate their homes, but only if discretionary income grows.

Table 7.16 Lamps and lighting fixtures

Total household spending $4,409,073,990.00
Average household spends 36.69

AGE OF HOUSEHOLDER	AVERAGE HOUSEHOLD SPENDING	BEST CUSTOMERS (index)	BIGGEST CUSTOMERS (market share)
Average household	$36.69	100	100.0%
Under age 25	12.15	33	2.2
Aged 25 to 34	25.02	68	11.6
Aged 35 to 44	32.50	89	17.3
Aged 45 to 54	46.80	128	26.8
Aged 55 to 64	66.35	181	29.3
Aged 65 to 74	40.72	111	11.1
Aged 75 or older	8.47	23	2.2

	AVERAGE HOUSEHOLD SPENDING	BEST CUSTOMERS (index)	BIGGEST CUSTOMERS (market share)
HOUSEHOLD INCOME			
Average household	**$36.69**	**100**	**100.0%**
Under $20,000	9.62	26	5.4
$20,000 to $39,999	16.86	46	10.7
$40,000 to $49,999	20.52	56	5.5
$50,000 to $69,999	38.24	104	15.9
$70,000 to $79,999	18.70	51	3.0
$80,000 to $99,999	40.05	109	8.9
$100,000 or more	113.38	309	52.9
HOUSEHOLD TYPE			
Average household	**36.69**	**100**	**100.0**
Married couples	57.04	155	78.6
Married couples, no children	71.06	194	41.8
Married couples, with children	48.52	132	33.0
Oldest child under age 6	22.56	61	3.0
Oldest child aged 6 to 17	60.80	166	21.1
Oldest child aged 18 or older	43.27	118	8.7
Single parent with child under age 18	9.25	25	1.5
Single person	14.62	40	11.9
RACE AND HISPANIC ORIGIN			
Average household	**36.69**	**100**	**100.0**
Asian	21.45	58	2.1
Black	10.10	28	3.3
Hispanic	22.37	61	7.2
Non-Hispanic white and other	42.80	117	89.0
REGION			
Average household	**36.69**	**100**	**100.0**
Northeast	40.89	111	20.8
Midwest	38.25	104	23.8
South	24.93	68	24.4
West	50.49	138	31.1
EDUCATION			
Average household	**36.69**	**100**	**100.0**
Less than high school graduate	13.79	38	5.7
High school graduate	18.91	52	13.0
Some college	32.62	89	19.4
Associate's degree	49.60	135	12.0
College graduate	61.99	169	48.9
Bachelor's degree	38.23	104	19.5
Master's, professional, doctoral degree	103.25	281	28.7

Note: Market shares may not sum to 100.0 because of rounding and missing categories by household type. "Asian" and "black" include Hispanics and non-Hispanics who identify themselves as being of the respective race alone. "Hispanic" includes people of any race who identify themselves as Hispanic. "Other" includes people who identify themselves as non-Hispanic and as Alaska Native, American Indian, Asian (who are also included in the "Asian" row), Native Hawaiian or other Pacific Islander, as well as non-Hispanics reporting more than one race.
Source: Calculations by New Strategist based on the Bureau of Labor Statistics' 2007 Consumer Expenditure Survey.

Laundry and Cleaning Equipment

Best customers: **Householders aged 35 to 54**
                           Married couples
                           Single parents

Customer trends: **Average household spending on laundry and cleaning equipment is likely to stabilize or even decline in the years ahead as the small generation X enters the best-customer lifestage.**

The best customers of laundry and cleaning equipment are households with children. Householders ranging in age from 35 to 54, most with children, spend 17 to 45 percent more than average on this item and control 53 percent of the market. Married couples with adult children at home—the largest households—spend 94 percent more than average on this item. Single parents, despite their low incomes, spend 16 percent more.

Average household spending on laundry and cleaning equipment grew by 54 percent between 2000 and 2007, after adjusting for inflation. Spending on this item is likely to stabilize or even decline in the years ahead as the small generation X enters the best-customer lifestage.

Table 7.17 Laundry and cleaning equipment

Total household spending $2,237,584,020.00
Average household spends   18.62

	AVERAGE HOUSEHOLD SPENDING	BEST CUSTOMERS (index)	BIGGEST CUSTOMERS (market share)
AGE OF HOUSEHOLDER			
Average household	**$18.62**	**100**	**100.0%**
Under age 25	14.64	79	5.3
Aged 25 to 34	14.56	78	13.3
Aged 35 to 44	21.76	117	22.8
Aged 45 to 54	26.99	145	30.5
Aged 55 to 64	16.49	89	14.3
Aged 65 to 74	15.61	84	8.4
Aged 75 or older	10.97	59	5.6

	AVERAGE HOUSEHOLD SPENDING	BEST CUSTOMERS (index)	BIGGEST CUSTOMERS (market share)
HOUSEHOLD INCOME			
Average household	**$18.62**	**100**	**100.0%**
Under $20,000	7.54	41	8.3
$20,000 to $39,999	13.92	75	17.4
$40,000 to $49,999	12.45	67	6.6
$50,000 to $69,999	24.23	130	19.9
$70,000 to $79,999	24.77	133	7.7
$80,000 to $99,999	22.08	119	9.6
$100,000 or more	33.16	178	30.5
HOUSEHOLD TYPE			
Average household	**18.62**	**100**	**100.0**
Married couples	25.45	137	69.1
Married couples, no children	24.52	132	28.4
Married couples, with children	26.26	141	35.2
Oldest child under age 6	24.23	130	6.4
Oldest child aged 6 to 17	22.04	118	15.0
Oldest child aged 18 or older	36.08	194	14.3
Single parent with child under age 18	21.68	116	6.9
Single person	7.83	42	12.5
RACE AND HISPANIC ORIGIN			
Average household	**18.62**	**100**	**100.0**
Asian	18.30	98	3.5
Black	14.38	77	9.3
Hispanic	17.94	96	11.4
Non-Hispanic white and other	19.36	104	79.4
REGION			
Average household	**18.62**	**100**	**100.0**
Northeast	17.01	91	17.0
Midwest	18.27	98	22.4
South	18.29	98	35.3
West	20.87	112	25.3
EDUCATION			
Average household	**18.62**	**100**	**100.0**
Less than high school graduate	12.93	69	10.5
High school graduate	18.57	100	25.2
Some college	14.13	76	16.5
Associate's degree	24.28	130	11.6
College graduate	22.89	123	35.6
Bachelor's degree	23.83	128	24.0
Master's, professional, doctoral degree	21.24	114	11.6

Note: Market shares may not sum to 100.0 because of rounding and missing categories by household type. "Asian" and "black" include Hispanics and non-Hispanics who identify themselves as being of the respective race alone. "Hispanic" includes people of any race who identify themselves as Hispanic. "Other" includes people who identify themselves as non-Hispanic and as Alaska Native, American Indian, Asian (who are also included in the "Asian" row), Native Hawaiian or other Pacific Islander, as well as non-Hispanics reporting more than one race.
Source: Calculations by New Strategist based on the Bureau of Labor Statistics' 2007 Consumer Expenditure Survey.

Living Room Chairs

Best customers:	Householders aged 35 to 44 and 55 to 74
	Married couples without children at home
	Married couples with children under age 18
	Asians
	Households in the Northeast
Customer trends:	Average household spending on living room chairs should rise as empty-nest boomers redecorate their homes, but only if discretionary income grows.

The best customers of living room chairs are married couples redecorating after the children have left home. Householders ranging in age from 55 to 74 spend 14 to 18 percent more than average on living room chairs. Married couples without children at home (most of them older) spend 69 percent more than average on living room chairs. Couples with children under age 18 spend 15 to 25 percent more than average on this item. Asians spend 34 percent above average on living room chairs. Households in the Northeast spend 35 percent more than average on this item.

Average household spending on living room chairs fell 13 percent between 2000 and 2007, after adjusting for inflation. Behind the spending decline was a reduction in discretionary spending on some items, as well as price discounting in the furniture market. Average household spending on living room chairs should rise in the years ahead as more boomers become empty-nesters and redecorate their homes, but only if discretionary income rises.

Table 7.18 Living room chairs

Total household spending $5,509,840,350.00
Average household spends 45.85

	AVERAGE HOUSEHOLD SPENDING	BEST CUSTOMERS (index)	BIGGEST CUSTOMERS (market share)
AGE OF HOUSEHOLDER			
Average household	**$45.85**	**100**	**100.0%**
Under age 25	23.21	51	3.4
Aged 25 to 34	43.76	95	16.3
Aged 35 to 44	57.09	125	24.3
Aged 45 to 54	43.62	95	20.0
Aged 55 to 64	54.22	118	19.2
Aged 65 to 74	52.12	114	11.4
Aged 75 or older	26.75	58	5.5

	AVERAGE HOUSEHOLD SPENDING	BEST CUSTOMERS (index)	BIGGEST CUSTOMERS (market share)
HOUSEHOLD INCOME			
Average household	$45.85	100	100.0%
Under $20,000	19.36	42	8.7
$20,000 to $39,999	15.74	34	8.0
$40,000 to $49,999	31.57	69	6.8
$50,000 to $69,999	45.05	98	15.0
$70,000 to $79,999	50.56	110	6.4
$80,000 to $99,999	49.21	107	8.7
$100,000 or more	124.21	271	46.4
HOUSEHOLD TYPE			
Average household	45.85	100	100.0
Married couples	61.79	135	68.1
Married couples, no children	77.40	169	36.4
Married couples, with children	53.83	117	29.3
Oldest child under age 6	52.68	115	5.6
Oldest child aged 6 to 17	57.21	125	15.9
Oldest child aged 18 or older	48.77	106	7.8
Single parent with child under age 18	27.70	60	3.6
Single person	29.09	63	18.9
RACE AND HISPANIC ORIGIN			
Average household	45.85	100	100.0
Asian	61.39	134	4.7
Black	25.09	55	6.6
Hispanic	18.87	41	4.9
Non-Hispanic white and other	53.20	116	88.6
REGION			
Average household	45.85	100	100.0
Northeast	62.10	135	25.2
Midwest	48.96	107	24.4
South	39.14	85	30.7
West	40.00	87	19.7
EDUCATION			
Average household	45.85	100	100.0
Less than high school graduate	15.99	35	5.3
High school graduate	36.31	79	20.0
Some college	37.95	83	18.0
Associate's degree	42.48	93	8.2
College graduate	76.80	168	48.5
Bachelor's degree	66.69	145	27.3
Master's, professional, doctoral degree	95.36	208	21.2

Note: Market shares may not sum to 100.0 because of rounding and missing categories by household type. "Asian" and "black" include Hispanics and non-Hispanics who identify themselves as being of the respective race alone. "Hispanic" includes people of any race who identify themselves as Hispanic. "Other" includes people who identify themselves as non-Hispanic and as Alaska Native, American Indian, Asian (who are also included in the "Asian" row), Native Hawaiian or other Pacific Islander, as well as non-Hispanics reporting more than one race.
Source: Calculations by New Strategist based on the Bureau of Labor Statistics' 2007 Consumer Expenditure Survey.

Living Room Tables

Best customers: **Householders aged 35 to 44**
Married couples with children at home

Customer trends: **Average household spending on living room tables will continue to decline because the small generation X is in the best-customer lifestage.**

The best customers of living room tables are married couples with children, outfitting their homes for expanding families. Married couples with children at home spend two-thirds more than the average household on this item. Householders aged 35 to 44, most with children, spend 83 percent more than average on living room tables.

Average household spending on living room tables fell 24 percent between 2000 and 2007, after adjusting for inflation. Average household spending on living room tables is likely to continue to decline in the years ahead because the small generation X is in the best-customer lifestage.

Table 7.19 Living room tables

Total household spending		$1,896,298,380.00	
Average household spends		15.78	

	AVERAGE HOUSEHOLD SPENDING	BEST CUSTOMERS (index)	BIGGEST CUSTOMERS (market share)
AGE OF HOUSEHOLDER			
Average household	**$15.78**	**100**	**100.0%**
Under age 25	8.24	52	3.5
Aged 25 to 34	11.24	71	12.2
Aged 35 to 44	28.95	183	35.7
Aged 45 to 54	14.30	91	19.0
Aged 55 to 64	16.84	107	17.3
Aged 65 to 74	13.63	86	8.6
Aged 75 or older	5.94	38	3.6

	AVERAGE HOUSEHOLD SPENDING	BEST CUSTOMERS (index)	BIGGEST CUSTOMERS (market share)
HOUSEHOLD INCOME			
Average household	**$15.78**	**100**	**100.0%**
Under $20,000	3.97	25	5.2
$20,000 to $39,999	5.89	37	8.7
$40,000 to $49,999	12.06	76	7.5
$50,000 to $69,999	19.04	121	18.5
$70,000 to $79,999	21.46	136	7.9
$80,000 to $99,999	15.21	96	7.8
$100,000 or more	40.92	259	44.4
HOUSEHOLD TYPE			
Average household	**15.78**	**100**	**100.0**
Married couples	21.58	137	69.1
Married couples, no children	16.01	101	21.9
Married couples, with children	26.22	166	41.5
Oldest child under age 6	22.26	141	6.9
Oldest child aged 6 to 17	27.84	176	22.4
Oldest child aged 18 or older	26.08	165	12.2
Single parent with child under age 18	9.32	59	3.5
Single person	9.64	61	18.2
RACE AND HISPANIC ORIGIN			
Average household	**15.78**	**100**	**100.0**
Asian	–	–	–
Black	12.71	81	9.7
Hispanic	11.80	75	8.8
Non-Hispanic white and other	16.85	107	81.5
REGION			
Average household	**15.78**	**100**	**100.0**
Northeast	20.66	131	24.4
Midwest	10.36	66	15.0
South	14.59	92	33.2
West	19.12	121	27.4
EDUCATION			
Average household	**15.78**	**100**	**100.0**
Less than high school graduate	7.95	50	7.6
High school graduate	10.42	66	16.7
Some college	19.34	123	26.7
Associate's degree	14.46	92	8.1
College graduate	22.27	141	40.8
Bachelor's degree	20.38	129	24.2
Master's, professional, doctoral degree	25.74	163	16.6

Note: Market shares may not sum to 100.0 because of rounding and missing categories by household type. "Asian" and "black" include Hispanics and non-Hispanics who identify themselves as being of the respective race alone. "Hispanic" includes people of any race who identify themselves as Hispanic. "Other" includes people who identify themselves as non-Hispanic and as Alaska Native, American Indian, Asian (who are also included in the "Asian" row), Native Hawaiian or other Pacific Islander, as well as non-Hispanics reporting more than one race.
Source: Calculations by New Strategist based on the Bureau of Labor Statistics' 2007 Consumer Expenditure Survey.

Mattresses and Springs

Best customers: **Householders aged 25 to 54**
Married couples
Asians and Hispanics

Customer trends: **Average household spending on mattresses and springs should continue to decline in the years ahead as the small generation X fills the best-customer lifestage.**

The best customers of mattresses and springs are married couples, many of them purchasing mattresses for expanding families. Householders ranging in age from 25 to 54 spend 12 to 25 percent more than average on mattresses and springs. Married couples with children at home spend 51 percent more than average, the figure peaking at 78 percent above average among couples with school-aged children. Asians spend 48 percent more than average on this item, and Hispanics, who have the largest families, spend 24 percent more.

Average household spending on mattresses and springs fell 13 percent between 2000 and 2007, after adjusting for inflation. Average household spending on mattresses and springs should continue to decline in the years ahead as the small generation X fills the best-customer lifestage.

Table 7.20 **Mattresses and springs**

Total household spending $6,673,095,630.00
Average household spends   55.53

	AVERAGE HOUSEHOLD SPENDING	BEST CUSTOMERS (index)	BIGGEST CUSTOMERS (market share)
AGE OF HOUSEHOLDER			
Average household	**$55.53**	**100**	**100.0%**
Under age 25	47.69	86	5.8
Aged 25 to 34	64.78	117	19.9
Aged 35 to 44	69.46	125	24.4
Aged 45 to 54	62.35	112	23.6
Aged 55 to 64	55.54	100	16.2
Aged 65 to 74	28.79	52	5.2
Aged 75 or older	28.94	52	4.9

	AVERAGE HOUSEHOLD SPENDING	BEST CUSTOMERS (index)	BIGGEST CUSTOMERS (market share)
HOUSEHOLD INCOME			
Average household	**$55.53**	**100**	**100.0%**
Under $20,000	15.40	28	5.7
$20,000 to $39,999	26.62	48	11.1
$40,000 to $49,999	40.80	73	7.2
$50,000 to $69,999	61.56	111	17.0
$70,000 to $79,999	42.47	76	4.4
$80,000 to $99,999	86.62	156	12.7
$100,000 or more	135.63	244	41.8
HOUSEHOLD TYPE			
Average household	**55.53**	**100**	**100.0**
Married couples	78.68	142	71.6
Married couples, no children	77.12	139	30.0
Married couples, with children	84.04	151	37.8
Oldest child under age 6	69.57	125	6.1
Oldest child aged 6 to 17	98.59	178	22.6
Oldest child aged 18 or older	68.53	123	9.1
Single parent with child under age 18	42.46	76	4.5
Single person	26.44	48	14.2
RACE AND HISPANIC ORIGIN			
Average household	**55.53**	**100**	**100.0**
Asian	82.31	148	5.2
Black	27.12	49	5.9
Hispanic	68.88	124	14.6
Non-Hispanic white and other	57.83	104	79.5
REGION			
Average household	**55.53**	**100**	**100.0**
Northeast	66.83	120	22.4
Midwest	46.68	84	19.2
South	42.80	77	27.7
West	75.39	136	30.7
EDUCATION			
Average household	**55.53**	**100**	**100.0**
Less than high school graduate	24.21	44	6.6
High school graduate	42.26	76	19.2
Some college	50.54	91	19.8
Associate's degree	77.46	139	12.4
College graduate	80.52	145	42.0
Bachelor's degree	83.34	150	28.1
Master's, professional, doctoral degree	75.35	136	13.8

Note: Market shares may not sum to 100.0 because of rounding and missing categories by household type. "Asian" and "black" include Hispanics and non-Hispanics who identify themselves as being of the respective race alone. "Hispanic" includes people of any race who identify themselves as Hispanic. "Other" includes people who identify themselves as non-Hispanic and as Alaska Native, American Indian, Asian (who are also included in the "Asian" row), Native Hawaiian or other Pacific Islander, as well as non-Hispanics reporting more than one race.
Source: Calculations by New Strategist based on the Bureau of Labor Statistics' 2007 Consumer Expenditure Survey.

Outdoor Equipment

Best customers: Householders aged 25 to 34
                             Married couples with school-aged children
                             Non-Hispanic whites
                             College graduates

Customer trends: Average household spending on outdoor equipment is likely to decline in the next
                             few years for two reasons: the small generation X is in the best customer lifestage,
                             and the economic downturn has slashed discretionary spending.

The best customers of outdoor equipment (such as grills) are young married couples. Householders aged 25 to 34 spend 48 percent more than the average household on outdoor equipment. Married couples with school-aged children spend 58 percent more than average on this item. Non-Hispanic whites account for fully 96 percent of the market. College graduates spend over twice the average on outdoor equipment.

Average household spending on outdoor equipment increased by 80 percent between 2000 and 2007, after adjusting for inflation. The increase in homeownership during those years is one factor behind the spending increase, as is the popularity of grilling and the introduction of high-end grills. Average household spending on outdoor equipment is likely to decline in the next few years for two reasons: the small generation X is in the best customer lifestage, and the economic downturn has slashed discretionary spending.

Table 7.21 Outdoor equipment

Total household spending $4,785,209,220.00
Average household spends   39.82

	AVERAGE HOUSEHOLD SPENDING	BEST CUSTOMERS (index)	BIGGEST CUSTOMERS (market share)
AGE OF HOUSEHOLDER			
Average household	**$39.82**	**100**	**100.0%**
Under age 25	12.06	30	2.1
Aged 25 to 34	58.88	148	25.2
Aged 35 to 44	40.73	102	19.9
Aged 45 to 54	36.88	93	19.5
Aged 55 to 64	39.75	100	16.2
Aged 65 to 74	62.30	156	15.6
Aged 75 or older	6.10	15	1.5

	AVERAGE HOUSEHOLD SPENDING	BEST CUSTOMERS (index)	BIGGEST CUSTOMERS (market share)
HOUSEHOLD INCOME			
Average household	**$39.82**	**100**	**100.0%**
Under $20,000	3.60	9	1.9
$20,000 to $39,999	33.12	83	19.3
$40,000 to $49,999	88.01	221	21.7
$50,000 to $69,999	38.18	96	14.7
$70,000 to $79,999	9.88	25	1.4
$80,000 to $99,999	17.44	44	3.6
$100,000 or more	88.92	223	38.3
HOUSEHOLD TYPE			
Average household	**39.82**	**100**	**100.0**
Married couples	44.69	112	56.7
Married couples, no children	47.38	119	25.7
Married couples, with children	46.40	117	29.1
Oldest child under age 6	47.55	119	5.8
Oldest child aged 6 to 17	62.94	158	20.1
Oldest child aged 18 or older	12.80	32	2.4
Single parent with child under age 18	5.87	15	0.9
Single person	30.73	77	23.0
RACE AND HISPANIC ORIGIN			
Average household	**39.82**	**100**	**100.0**
Asian	17.76	45	1.6
Black	3.36	8	1.0
Hispanic	8.82	22	2.6
Non-Hispanic white and other	49.84	125	95.5
REGION			
Average household	**39.82**	**100**	**100.0**
Northeast	59.32	149	27.7
Midwest	50.40	127	28.9
South	15.43	39	13.9
West	51.69	130	29.4
EDUCATION			
Average household	**39.82**	**100**	**100.0**
Less than high school graduate	18.42	46	7.0
High school graduate	18.43	46	11.7
Some college	23.38	59	12.8
Associate's degree	22.98	58	5.1
College graduate	85.02	214	61.8
Bachelor's degree	70.89	178	33.4
Master's, professional, doctoral degree	109.54	275	28.1

Note: Market shares may not sum to 100.0 because of rounding and missing categories by household type. "Asian" and "black" include Hispanics and non-Hispanics who identify themselves as being of the respective race alone. "Hispanic" includes people of any race who identify themselves as Hispanic. "Other" includes people who identify themselves as non-Hispanic and as Alaska Native, American Indian, Asian (who are also included in the "Asian" row), Native Hawaiian or other Pacific Islander, as well as non-Hispanics reporting more than one race.
Source: Calculations by New Strategist based on the Bureau of Labor Statistics' 2007 Consumer Expenditure Survey.

Outdoor Furniture

Best customers:

Householders aged 55 to 64
High-income households
Married couples with school-aged or older children at home
Households in the Northeast and Midwest

Customer trends:

Average household spending on outdoor furniture is likely to fall now that boomers have almost entirely filled the best-customer age group and the economic downturn slashes discretionary income.

The best customers of outdoor furniture are affluent, middle-aged and older married couples. Householders aged 55 to 64 spend well over twice the average on this item and control 36 percent of the market—much greater than their 16 percent share of consumer units. Households with incomes of $100,000 or more spend three-and-one-half times the average and account for 60 percent of the market. Married couples with school-aged children spend 35 percent more than average on outdoor furniture, while those with adult children at home spend more than twice the average. Households in the Northeast and Midwest spend, respectively, 76 and 63 percent more than average on outdoor furniture.

Average household spending on outdoor furniture increased by 43 percent between 2000 and 2007, after adjusting for inflation. Behind the increase was the baby-boom generation's entry into the best-customer age group. Average household spending on outdoor furniture is likely to fall now that boomers have almost entirely filled the best-customer age group and the economic downturn slashes discretionary income.

Table 7.22 Outdoor furniture

| Total household spending | $3,131,656,260.00 | | |
| Average household spends | 26.06 | | |

	AVERAGE HOUSEHOLD SPENDING	BEST CUSTOMERS (index)	BIGGEST CUSTOMERS (market share)
AGE OF HOUSEHOLDER			
Average household	**$26.06**	**100**	**100.0%**
Under age 25	10.59	41	2.8
Aged 25 to 34	31.85	122	20.8
Aged 35 to 44	22.49	86	16.8
Aged 45 to 54	27.27	105	22.0
Aged 55 to 64	57.31	220	35.6
Aged 65 to 74	3.80	15	1.5
Aged 75 or older	3.10	12	1.1

	AVERAGE HOUSEHOLD SPENDING	BEST CUSTOMERS (index)	BIGGEST CUSTOMERS (market share)
HOUSEHOLD INCOME			
Average household	**$26.06**	**100**	**100.0%**
Under $20,000	5.83	22	4.6
$20,000 to $39,999	10.45	40	9.3
$40,000 to $49,999	34.82	134	13.1
$50,000 to $69,999	10.32	40	6.1
$70,000 to $79,999	8.02	31	1.8
$80,000 to $99,999	25.23	97	7.9
$100,000 or more	90.74	348	59.7
HOUSEHOLD TYPE			
Average household	**26.06**	**100**	**100.0**
Married couples	28.02	108	54.4
Married couples, no children	13.25	51	11.0
Married couples, with children	36.46	140	34.9
Oldest child under age 6	13.67	52	2.6
Oldest child aged 6 to 17	35.25	135	17.2
Oldest child aged 18 or older	55.58	213	15.7
Single parent with child under age 18	–	–	–
Single person	13.13	50	15.0
RACE AND HISPANIC ORIGIN			
Average household	**26.06**	**100**	**100.0**
Asian	–	–	–
Black	–	–	–
Hispanic	–	–	–
Non-Hispanic white and other	26.48	102	77.6
REGION			
Average household	**26.06**	**100**	**100.0**
Northeast	45.83	176	32.8
Midwest	42.38	163	37.2
South	13.35	51	18.4
West	12.93	50	11.2
EDUCATION			
Average household	**26.06**	**100**	**100.0**
Less than high school graduate	4.00	15	2.3
High school graduate	11.61	45	11.2
Some college	19.42	75	16.2
Associate's degree	47.21	181	16.1
College graduate	47.54	182	52.8
Bachelor's degree	45.18	173	32.5
Master's, professional, doctoral degree	51.65	198	20.2

Note: Market shares may not sum to 100.0 because of rounding and missing categories by household type. "Asian" and "black" include Hispanics and non-Hispanics who identify themselves as being of the respective race alone. "Hispanic" includes people of any race who identify themselves as Hispanic. "Other" includes people who identify themselves as non-Hispanic and as Alaska Native, American Indian, Asian (who are also included in the "Asian" row), Native Hawaiian or other Pacific Islander, as well as non-Hispanics reporting more than one race.
Source: Calculations by New Strategist based on the Bureau of Labor Statistics' 2007 Consumer Expenditure Survey.

Plants and Fresh Flowers, Indoor

Best customers:	**Householders aged 45 to 64** **Married couples without children at home** **Married couples with adult children at home**
Customer trends:	**Average household spending on indoor plants and fresh flowers should stabilize or even increase as more boomers enter the best-customer lifestage, but only if discretionary income grows.**

The best customers of indoor plants and fresh flowers are older married couples. Many are buying flowers for anniversaries or for ailing friends and relatives. Householders aged 45 to 64 spend 24 to 78 percent more than average on this item. Married couples without children at home (most of them empty-nesters) spend 81 percent more than average on indoor plants and fresh flowers, while those with adult children at home spend 48 percent more.

Average household spending on indoor plants and fresh flowers fell 17 percent between 2000 and 2007, after adjusting for inflation. The lower prices offered by grocery stores and discounters such as Wal-Mart are behind the decline. Average household spending on indoor plants and fresh flowers should stabilize or even increase as more boomers enter the best-customer lifestage, but only if discretionary income grows.

Table 7.23 Plants and fresh flowers, indoor

Total household spending	$6,823,309,380.00
Average household spends	56.78

	AVERAGE HOUSEHOLD SPENDING	BEST CUSTOMERS (index)	BIGGEST CUSTOMERS (market share)
AGE OF HOUSEHOLDER			
Average household	**$56.78**	**100**	**100.0%**
Under age 25	10.33	18	1.2
Aged 25 to 34	36.73	65	11.0
Aged 35 to 44	43.79	77	15.0
Aged 45 to 54	101.33	178	37.5
Aged 55 to 64	70.59	124	20.1
Aged 65 to 74	55.51	98	9.8
Aged 75 or older	36.20	64	6.0

	AVERAGE HOUSEHOLD SPENDING	BEST CUSTOMERS (index)	BIGGEST CUSTOMERS (market share)
HOUSEHOLD INCOME			
Average household	**$56.78**	**100**	**100.0%**
Under $20,000	12.56	22	4.5
$20,000 to $39,999	25.71	45	10.5
$40,000 to $49,999	29.94	53	5.2
$50,000 to $69,999	54.45	96	14.7
$70,000 to $79,999	70.50	124	7.2
$80,000 to $99,999	76.94	136	11.0
$100,000 or more	158.71	280	47.9
HOUSEHOLD TYPE			
Average household	**56.78**	**100**	**100.0**
Married couples	78.00	137	69.4
Married couples, no children	102.49	181	38.9
Married couples, with children	57.19	101	25.1
Oldest child under age 6	45.45	80	3.9
Oldest child aged 6 to 17	47.87	84	10.7
Oldest child aged 18 or older	84.26	148	10.9
Single parent with child under age 18	26.22	46	2.7
Single person	36.15	64	18.9
RACE AND HISPANIC ORIGIN			
Average household	**56.78**	**100**	**100.0**
Asian	25.50	45	1.6
Black	24.96	44	5.3
Hispanic	17.68	31	3.7
Non-Hispanic white and other	67.32	119	90.5
REGION			
Average household	**56.78**	**100**	**100.0**
Northeast	48.96	86	16.1
Midwest	70.27	124	28.3
South	54.56	96	34.5
West	53.04	93	21.1
EDUCATION			
Average household	**56.78**	**100**	**100.0**
Less than high school graduate	18.01	32	4.8
High school graduate	37.79	67	16.8
Some college	41.70	73	16.0
Associate's degree	58.19	102	9.1
College graduate	101.67	179	51.8
Bachelor's degree	107.69	190	35.5
Master's, professional, doctoral degree	91.21	161	16.4

Note: Market shares may not sum to 100.0 because of rounding and missing categories by household type. "Asian" and "black" include Hispanics and non-Hispanics who identify themselves as being of the respective race alone. "Hispanic" includes people of any race who identify themselves as Hispanic. "Other" includes people who identify themselves as non-Hispanic and as Alaska Native, American Indian, Asian (who are also included in the "Asian" row), Native Hawaiian or other Pacific Islander, as well as non-Hispanics reporting more than one race.
Source: Calculations by New Strategist based on the Bureau of Labor Statistics' 2007 Consumer Expenditure Survey.

Power Tools

Best customers:	**Householders aged 25 to 34** **Married couples with children under age 18** **Hispanics**
Customer trends:	**Average household spending on power tools may increase in the years ahead as the large millennial generation enters the do-it-yourself lifestage.**

The best customers of power tools are new homeowners tackling do-it-yourself projects. This explains why householders aged 25 to 34 spend twice the average on power tools. Many are recent homeowners who are taking on remodeling projects. Married couples with preschoolers, many of them new homeowners, spend nearly three times the average on power tools, and those with school-aged children spend nearly twice the average on this item. Hispanics spend over twice the average on power tools and account for a sizeable 27 percent of the market, although their share of consumer units is a mere 12 percent.

Average household spending on power tools fell 5 percent between 2000 and 2007, after adjusting for inflation. One reason for the decline was the small generation X in the best-customer age group. Spending on power tools may increase in the years ahead as the large millennial generation enters the do-it-yourself lifestage.

Table 7.24 Power tools

Total household spending		$2,933,374,110.00	
Average household spends		24.41	

	AVERAGE HOUSEHOLD SPENDING	BEST CUSTOMERS (index)	BIGGEST CUSTOMERS (market share)
AGE OF HOUSEHOLDER			
Average household	**$24.41**	**100**	**100.0%**
Under age 25	7.52	31	2.1
Aged 25 to 34	48.97	201	34.2
Aged 35 to 44	25.70	105	20.5
Aged 45 to 54	17.69	72	15.2
Aged 55 to 64	25.33	104	16.8
Aged 65 to 74	18.31	75	7.5
Aged 75 or older	9.35	38	3.6

	AVERAGE HOUSEHOLD SPENDING	BEST CUSTOMERS (index)	BIGGEST CUSTOMERS (market share)
HOUSEHOLD INCOME			
Average household	**$24.41**	**100**	**100.0%**
Under $20,000	5.92	24	5.0
$20,000 to $39,999	16.36	67	15.6
$40,000 to $49,999	13.76	56	5.5
$50,000 to $69,999	44.62	183	28.0
$70,000 to $79,999	13.87	57	3.3
$80,000 to $99,999	33.88	139	11.3
$100,000 or more	45.40	186	31.9
HOUSEHOLD TYPE			
Average household	**24.41**	**100**	**100.0**
Married couples	33.50	137	69.4
Married couples, no children	23.02	94	20.3
Married couples, with children	45.89	188	46.9
Oldest child under age 6	71.12	291	14.2
Oldest child aged 6 to 17	48.04	197	25.0
Oldest child aged 18 or older	23.12	95	7.0
Single parent with child under age 18	12.14	50	3.0
Single person	12.02	49	14.6
RACE AND HISPANIC ORIGIN			
Average household	**24.41**	**100**	**100.0**
Asian	26.54	109	3.8
Black	3.65	15	1.8
Hispanic	55.35	227	26.8
Non-Hispanic white and other	23.20	95	72.6
REGION			
Average household	**24.41**	**100**	**100.0**
Northeast	12.40	51	9.5
Midwest	24.41	100	22.9
South	30.53	125	44.9
West	24.73	101	22.9
EDUCATION			
Average household	**24.41**	**100**	**100.0**
Less than high school graduate	41.71	171	25.9
High school graduate	14.02	57	14.5
Some college	25.18	103	22.5
Associate's degree	25.69	105	9.4
College graduate	24.54	101	29.1
Bachelor's degree	22.67	93	17.4
Master's, professional, doctoral degree	27.79	114	11.6

Note: Market shares may not sum to 100.0 because of rounding and missing categories by household type. "Asian" and "black" include Hispanics and non-Hispanics who identify themselves as being of the respective race alone. "Hispanic" includes people of any race who identify themselves as Hispanic. "Other" includes people who identify themselves as non-Hispanic and as Alaska Native, American Indian, Asian (who are also included in the "Asian" row), Native Hawaiian or other Pacific Islander, as well as non-Hispanics reporting more than one race.
Source: Calculations by New Strategist based on the Bureau of Labor Statistics' 2007 Consumer Expenditure Survey.

Sewing Materials for Household Items

Best customers:	Householders aged 55 to 74 Married couples without children at home Non-Hispanic whites
Customer trends:	Average household spending on sewing materials for household items may fall in the years ahead as the baby-boom generation, with fewer sewing skills, fills the best-customer age groups.

Sewing is becoming a lost art, and younger generations of women are much less knowledgeable about sewing than older women. The best customers of sewing materials for household items—such as slipcovers and curtains—are householders aged 55 to 74. This age group spends 82 to 128 percent more than average on sewing materials for household items and controls 52 percent of the market. Married couples without children at home (most of them older) spend almost twice the average on sewing materials. Non-Hispanic whites outspend minorities by a 4:1 margin on this item and account for 94 percent of the market.

Average household spending on sewing materials for household items dropped 5 percent between 2000 and 2007, after adjusting for inflation. Average household spending on sewing materials for household items may continued to fall in the years ahead as the baby-boom generation, with fewer sewing skills, continues to fill the best-customer age groups.

Table 7.25 Sewing materials for household items

Total household spending $1,347,116,910.00
Average household spends 11.21

	AVERAGE HOUSEHOLD SPENDING	BEST CUSTOMERS (index)	BIGGEST CUSTOMERS (market share)
AGE OF HOUSEHOLDER			
Average household	**$11.21**	**100**	**100.0%**
Under age 25	1.86	17	1.1
Aged 25 to 34	4.86	43	7.4
Aged 35 to 44	6.58	59	11.4
Aged 45 to 54	10.86	97	20.4
Aged 55 to 64	20.42	182	29.5
Aged 65 to 74	25.60	228	22.8
Aged 75 or older	8.70	78	7.4

	AVERAGE HOUSEHOLD SPENDING	BEST CUSTOMERS (index)	BIGGEST CUSTOMERS (market share)
HOUSEHOLD INCOME			
Average household	**$11.21**	**100**	**100.0%**
Under $20,000	3.67	33	6.7
$20,000 to $39,999	8.04	72	16.7
$40,000 to $49,999	8.55	76	7.5
$50,000 to $69,999	10.04	90	13.7
$70,000 to $79,999	13.65	122	7.0
$80,000 to $99,999	20.87	186	15.1
$100,000 or more	21.69	193	33.1
HOUSEHOLD TYPE			
Average household	**11.21**	**100**	**100.0**
Married couples	15.52	138	70.0
Married couples, no children	21.72	194	41.8
Married couples, with children	10.29	92	22.9
Oldest child under age 6	8.11	72	3.5
Oldest child aged 6 to 17	9.93	89	11.3
Oldest child aged 18 or older	12.37	110	8.1
Single parent with child under age 18	3.30	29	1.7
Single person	5.00	45	13.3
RACE AND HISPANIC ORIGIN			
Average household	**11.21**	**100**	**100.0**
Asian	3.79	34	1.2
Black	2.91	26	3.1
Hispanic	3.10	28	3.3
Non-Hispanic white and other	13.77	123	93.8
REGION			
Average household	**11.21**	**100**	**100.0**
Northeast	6.07	54	10.1
Midwest	13.48	120	27.5
South	6.99	62	22.4
West	19.85	177	40.0
EDUCATION			
Average household	**11.21**	**100**	**100.0**
Less than high school graduate	3.62	32	4.9
High school graduate	7.86	70	17.7
Some college	7.90	70	15.3
Associate's degree	18.62	166	14.8
College graduate	18.31	163	47.3
Bachelor's degree	16.31	145	27.3
Master's, professional, doctoral degree	21.97	196	20.0

Note: Market shares may not sum to 100.0 because of rounding and missing categories by household type. "Asian" and "black" include Hispanics and non-Hispanics who identify themselves as being of the respective race alone. "Hispanic" includes people of any race who identify themselves as Hispanic. "Other" includes people who identify themselves as non-Hispanic and as Alaska Native, American Indian, Asian (who are also included in the "Asian" row), Native Hawaiian or other Pacific Islander, as well as non-Hispanics reporting more than one race.
Source: Calculations by New Strategist based on the Bureau of Labor Statistics' 2007 Consumer Expenditure Survey.

Sofas

Best customers:

Householders aged 25 to 44
Married couples without children at home
Married couples with school-aged children
Asians

Customer trends:

Average household spending on sofas is likely to fall in the years ahead because the small generation X is in the best-customer lifestage and the economic downturn has slashed discretionary spending.

Sofas are the sixth-largest home furnishing expense for the average household, following only major appliances, decorative items, laundry and cleaning supplies, and lawn and garden supplies and equipment. Householders aged 25 to 44 spend 40 percent more than average on sofas. Married couples with school-aged children spend 79 percent more than the average on sofas, and those without children at home, many of them young couples, spend 54 percent more. Asians spend 79 percent more on sofas than the average.

Average household spending on sofas climbed 5 percent between 2000 and 2007, after adjusting for inflation. Behind the increase was the surge in homeownership and the need to outfit new homes. Average household spending on sofas is likely to fall in the years ahead because the small generation X is in the best-customer lifestage and the economic downturn has slashed discretionary spending.

Table 7.26 Sofas

Total household spending $13,533,658,020.00
Average household spends   112.62

	AVERAGE HOUSEHOLD SPENDING	BEST CUSTOMERS (index)	BIGGEST CUSTOMERS (market share)
AGE OF HOUSEHOLDER			
Average household	$112.62	100	100.0%
Under age 25	71.42	63	4.3
Aged 25 to 34	157.41	140	23.8
Aged 35 to 44	157.50	140	27.3
Aged 45 to 54	108.29	96	20.2
Aged 55 to 64	101.16	90	14.5
Aged 65 to 74	77.43	69	6.9
Aged 75 or older	35.54	32	3.0

	AVERAGE HOUSEHOLD SPENDING	BEST CUSTOMERS (index)	BIGGEST CUSTOMERS (market share)
HOUSEHOLD INCOME			
Average household	**$112.62**	**100**	**100.0%**
Under $20,000	34.67	31	6.3
$20,000 to $39,999	54.95	49	11.3
$40,000 to $49,999	70.07	62	6.1
$50,000 to $69,999	105.60	94	14.3
$70,000 to $79,999	103.13	92	5.3
$80,000 to $99,999	107.31	95	7.8
$100,000 or more	320.86	285	48.8
HOUSEHOLD TYPE			
Average household	**112.62**	**100**	**100.0**
Married couples	153.95	137	69.1
Married couples, no children	173.36	154	33.2
Married couples, with children	153.20	136	33.9
Oldest child under age 6	110.67	98	4.8
Oldest child aged 6 to 17	201.59	179	22.7
Oldest child aged 18 or older	97.95	87	6.4
Single parent with child under age 18	72.78	65	3.8
Single person	61.19	54	16.2
RACE AND HISPANIC ORIGIN			
Average household	**112.62**	**100**	**100.0**
Asian	201.97	179	6.3
Black	56.88	51	6.1
Hispanic	113.41	101	11.9
Non-Hispanic white and other	121.06	107	82.1
REGION			
Average household	**112.62**	**100**	**100.0**
Northeast	177.13	157	29.3
Midwest	105.88	94	21.5
South	74.47	66	23.7
West	126.89	113	25.5
EDUCATION			
Average household	**112.62**	**100**	**100.0**
Less than high school graduate	64.95	58	8.7
High school graduate	74.43	66	16.7
Some college	105.01	93	20.3
Associate's degree	96.08	85	7.6
College graduate	181.70	161	46.7
Bachelor's degree	182.53	162	30.4
Master's, professional, doctoral degree	180.17	160	16.3

Note: Market shares may not sum to 100.0 because of rounding and missing categories by household type. "Asian" and "black" include Hispanics and non-Hispanics who identify themselves as being of the respective race alone. "Hispanic" includes people of any race who identify themselves as Hispanic. "Other" includes people who identify themselves as non-Hispanic and as Alaska Native, American Indian, Asian (who are also included in the "Asian" row), Native Hawaiian or other Pacific Islander, as well as non-Hispanics reporting more than one race.
Source: Calculations by New Strategist based on the Bureau of Labor Statistics' 2007 Consumer Expenditure Survey.

Wall Units, Cabinets, and Other Furniture

Best customers:	**Householders aged 35 to 54** **High-income households** **Married couples without children at home** **Married couples with children under age 18** **Asians**
Customer trends:	**Average household spending on wall units could continue to decline in the years ahead as boomers exit the best-customer age groups and the economic downturn cuts discretionary spending.**

The biggest spenders on wall units, cabinets, and other furniture are middle-aged married couples. Householders ranging in age from 35 to 54 spend 24 to 48 percent more than the average household on this item and control 55 percent of the market. Married couples without children at home spend 63 percent more. Those with school-aged children spend almost twice the average on wall units, while those with preschoolers spend 42 percent more than average. Asian spending on wall units is over two times the average.

Average household spending on wall units, cabinets, and other furniture fell 7 percent between 2000 and 2007, after adjusting for inflation. Average household spending on wall units could continue to decline in the years ahead as boomers exit the best-customer age groups and the economic downturn cuts discretionary spending.

Table 7.27 Wall units, cabinets, and other furniture

Total household spending	$6,824,511,090.00
Average household spends	56.79

	AVERAGE HOUSEHOLD SPENDING	BEST CUSTOMERS (index)	BIGGEST CUSTOMERS (market share)
AGE OF HOUSEHOLDER			
Average household	**$56.79**	**100**	**100.0%**
Under age 25	29.59	52	3.5
Aged 25 to 34	44.16	78	13.3
Aged 35 to 44	84.26	148	28.9
Aged 45 to 54	70.65	124	26.1
Aged 55 to 64	63.21	111	18.0
Aged 65 to 74	43.27	76	7.6
Aged 75 or older	15.08	27	2.5

	AVERAGE HOUSEHOLD SPENDING	BEST CUSTOMERS (index)	BIGGEST CUSTOMERS (market share)
HOUSEHOLD INCOME			
Average household	**$56.79**	**100**	**100.0%**
Under $20,000	19.25	34	7.0
$20,000 to $39,999	24.01	42	9.8
$40,000 to $49,999	27.90	49	4.8
$50,000 to $69,999	50.68	89	13.7
$70,000 to $79,999	59.09	104	6.0
$80,000 to $99,999	50.76	89	7.3
$100,000 or more	170.46	300	51.4
HOUSEHOLD TYPE			
Average household	**56.79**	**100**	**100.0**
Married couples	88.69	156	78.9
Married couples, no children	92.78	163	35.2
Married couples, with children	89.73	158	39.4
Oldest child under age 6	80.75	142	6.9
Oldest child aged 6 to 17	111.05	196	24.8
Oldest child aged 18 or older	58.90	104	7.6
Single parent with child under age 18	21.71	38	2.3
Single person	23.74	42	12.4
RACE AND HISPANIC ORIGIN			
Average household	**56.79**	**100**	**100.0**
Asian	120.37	212	7.5
Black	46.02	81	9.7
Hispanic	28.65	50	6.0
Non-Hispanic white and other	62.75	110	84.3
REGION			
Average household	**56.79**	**100**	**100.0**
Northeast	58.65	103	19.2
Midwest	48.33	85	19.4
South	57.99	102	36.7
West	61.91	109	24.7
EDUCATION			
Average household	**56.79**	**100**	**100.0**
Less than high school graduate	22.30	39	6.0
High school graduate	26.89	47	11.9
Some college	45.26	80	17.4
Associate's degree	57.61	101	9.0
College graduate	109.34	193	55.7
Bachelor's degree	93.63	165	30.9
Master's, professional, doctoral degree	138.22	243	24.8

Note: Market shares may not sum to 100.0 because of rounding and missing categories by household type. "Asian" and "black" include Hispanics and non-Hispanics who identify themselves as being of the respective race alone. "Hispanic" includes people of any race who identify themselves as Hispanic. "Other" includes people who identify themselves as non-Hispanic and as Alaska Native, American Indian, Asian (who are also included in the "Asian" row), Native Hawaiian or other Pacific Islander, as well as non-Hispanics reporting more than one race.
Source: Calculations by New Strategist based on the Bureau of Labor Statistics' 2007 Consumer Expenditure Survey.

Chapter 8.

Gifts for People in Other Households

Household Spending on Gifts for People in Other Households, 2007

Average household spending on gifts for people in other households declined by 8 percent between 2000 and 2007, after adjusting for inflation. Gifts of education expenses, which grew by an enormous 56 percent between 2000 and 2007, after adjusting for inflation, account for the largest share (24 percent) of gift giving to people in other households. Many gift-givers are middle-aged and older Americans helping their children and grandchildren pay for college.

The second-biggest gift category, gifts of transportation, accounts for 9 percent of total gift giving. Spending on this category climbed by a substantial 29 percent between 2000 and 2007, after adjusting for inflation. Entertainment, which accounts for slightly less than 9 percent of the total, ranks third among gifts, but spending on gifts of entertainment fell 9 percent between 2000 and 2007. Gifts of food, ranked fourth and constituting 8 percent of gift giving, grew by 10 percent in those years. Most other gift categories experienced double-digit declines in spending during those years, the steepest decreases occurring for gifts of health care expenses (down 50 percent) and of appliances and housewares (down 39 percent).

Spending on gifts for people in other households

(average annual spending of households on gifts for people in other households, 2000 and 2007; in 2007 dollars)

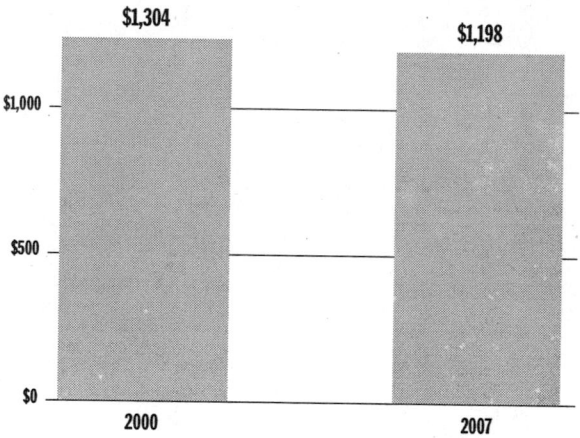

Table 8.1 Spending on Gifts for People in Other Households, 2000 to 2007

(average annual household spending on gifts for people in other households, and percent distribution of spending by type, 2000 and 2007; percent change in spending, 2000–07; in 2007 dollars; ranked by amount spent)

	2007		2000		
	average household spending	percent distribution	average household spending (in 2007$)	percent distribution	percent change 2000–07
Average household spending on gifts for people in other households	**$1,198.19**	**100.0%**	**$1,304.18**	**100.0%**	**–8.1%**
Education expenses	282.92	23.6	181.82	13.9	55.6
Transportation	108.83	9.1	84.61	6.5	28.6
Entertainment	102.71	8.6	112.89	8.7	–9.0
Food	92.80	7.7	84.39	6.5	10.0
Women's and girls' apparel	87.01	7.3	102.68	7.9	–15.3
Men's and boys' apparel	57.15	4.8	81.34	6.2	–29.7
Household equipment	55.13	4.6	84.66	6.5	–34.9
Infants' apparel	45.02	3.8	49.02	3.8	–8.2
Housekeeping supplies	29.97	2.5	47.08	3.6	–36.3
Health care expenses	22.98	1.9	45.85	3.5	–49.9
Appliances and housewares	20.54	1.7	33.88	2.6	–39.4
Jewelry	17.20	1.4	20.29	1.6	–15.2
Household textiles	12.96	1.1	15.89	1.2	–18.5

Note: Numbers do not add to total because not all categories are shown.
Source: Bureau of Labor Statistics, 2000 and 2007 Consumer Expenditure Surveys; calculations by New Strategist

Gifts of Appliances and Housewares

Best customers: **Householders aged 75 or older**
Married couples without children at home
Married couples with preschoolers
Married couples with adult children at home

Customer trends: **Average household spending on gifts of appliances and housewares will increase as more boomers become empty-nesters and help adult children outfit their homes.**

The biggest spenders on gifts of appliances and housewares for people in other households are older married couples, many of them empty-nesters. These householders are buying appliances and housewares for grown children and grandchildren who live elsewhere. Householders aged 75 or older spend 47 percent more than average on this item and account for 14 percent of the market. Married couples without children at home spend 35 percent more than average on appliances and housewares for people in other households. Couples with preschoolers spend more than twice the average on gifts of appliance and housewares, many buying housewarming gifts and baby shower items for friends and relatives. Couples with adult children at home spend 57 percent more than average on this item.

Average household spending on gifts of appliances and housewares for people in other households fell 39 percent between 2000 and 2007, after adjusting for inflation. One reason for the decline is price discounting as cheaper imports lower costs. Average household spending on this item could expand in the years ahead as millions more boomers become empty-nesters and help their children outfit their homes.

Table 8.2 Gifts of appliances and housewares

Total household spending $1,575,441,810.00
Average household spends   13.11

	AVERAGE HOUSEHOLD SPENDING	BEST CUSTOMERS (index)	BIGGEST CUSTOMERS (market share)
AGE OF HOUSEHOLDER			
Average household	**$13.11**	**100**	**100.0%**
Under age 25	3.35	26	1.7
Aged 25 to 34	14.61	111	19.0
Aged 35 to 44	11.53	88	17.1
Aged 45 to 54	12.70	97	20.4
Aged 55 to 64	13.79	105	17.0
Aged 65 to 74	14.52	111	11.1
Aged 75 or older	19.28	147	13.9

	AVERAGE HOUSEHOLD SPENDING	BEST CUSTOMERS (index)	BIGGEST CUSTOMERS (market share)
HOUSEHOLD INCOME			
Average household	**$13.11**	**100**	**100.0%**
Under $20,000	4.81	37	7.5
$20,000 to $39,999	6.23	48	11.0
$40,000 to $49,999	7.26	55	5.4
$50,000 to $69,999	15.73	120	18.4
$70,000 to $79,999	20.60	157	9.1
$80,000 to $99,999	21.92	167	13.6
$100,000 or more	26.46	202	34.6
HOUSEHOLD TYPE			
Average household	**13.11**	**100**	**100.0**
Married couples	15.62	119	60.2
Married couples, no children	17.64	135	29.0
Married couples, with children	15.87	121	30.2
Oldest child under age 6	28.04	214	10.4
Oldest child aged 6 to 17	8.95	68	8.7
Oldest child aged 18 or older	20.56	157	11.6
Single parent with child under age 18	13.42	102	6.1
Single person	12.43	95	28.2
RACE AND HISPANIC ORIGIN			
Average household	**13.11**	**100**	**100.0**
Asian	10.85	83	2.9
Black	7.75	59	7.1
Hispanic	3.44	26	3.1
Non-Hispanic white and other	15.33	117	89.3
REGION			
Average household	**13.11**	**100**	**100.0**
Northeast	13.17	100	18.7
Midwest	12.08	92	21.1
South	13.47	103	36.9
West	13.58	104	23.4
EDUCATION			
Average household	**13.11**	**100**	**100.0**
Less than high school graduate	1.93	15	2.2
High school graduate	4.62	35	8.9
Some college	16.36	125	27.2
Associate's degree	26.11	199	17.7
College graduate	19.74	151	43.6
Bachelor's degree	14.81	113	21.2
Master's, professional, doctoral degree	28.31	216	22.0

Note: Market shares may not sum to 100.0 because of rounding and missing categories by household type. "Asian" and "black" include Hispanics and non-Hispanics who identify themselves as being of the respective race alone. "Hispanic" includes people of any race who identify themselves as Hispanic. "Other" includes people who identify themselves as non-Hispanic and as Alaska Native, American Indian, Asian (who are also included in the "Asian" row), Native Hawaiian or other Pacific Islander, as well as non-Hispanics reporting more than one race.
Source: Calculations by New Strategist based on the Bureau of Labor Statistics' 2007 Consumer Expenditure Survey.

Gifts of Education Expenses

Best customers:
Householders aged 45 to 64
High-income households
Married couples without children at home
Married couples with adult children at home
Households in the Northeast and Midwest
College graduates

Customer trends:
Average household spending on gifts of college tuition should continue to rise in the years ahead as grandparents help their grandchildren pay college bills.

The biggest spenders on gifts of education expenses for people in other households are affluent, educated, middle-aged married couples likely to have children in college. Households with incomes of $100,000 or more spend almost four times the average on gifts of education expenses. Householders aged 45 to 64, married couples without children at home, and college graduates all spend at least twice the average on this item. Households in the Northeast and Midwest spend, respectively, 30 and 36 percent more than average on this item.

Average household spending on gifts of education expenses for people in other households rose by a huge 56 percent between 2000 and 2007, after adjusting for inflation, as the children of boomers went to college. This increase is in contrast to the 8 percent decline in overall gift spending during those years. Average household spending on gifts of college tuition should continue to rise in the years ahead as growing numbers of grandparents help their grandchildren pay college bills.

Table 8.3 **Gifts of education expenses**

Total household spending $33,998,779,320.00
Average household spends 282.92

AGE OF HOUSEHOLDER	AVERAGE HOUSEHOLD SPENDING	BEST CUSTOMERS (index)	BIGGEST CUSTOMERS (market share)
Average household	**$282.92**	**100**	**100.0%**
Under age 25	6.96	2	0.2
Aged 25 to 34	7.12	3	0.4
Aged 35 to 44	78.94	28	5.4
Aged 45 to 54	630.47	223	46.8
Aged 55 to 64	554.34	196	31.7
Aged 65 to 74	154.99	55	5.5
Aged 75 or older	297.03	105	10.0

	AVERAGE HOUSEHOLD SPENDING	BEST CUSTOMERS (index)	BIGGEST CUSTOMERS (market share)
HOUSEHOLD INCOME			
Average household	**$282.92**	**100**	**100.0%**
Under $20,000	30.73	11	2.2
$20,000 to $39,999	70.59	25	5.8
$40,000 to $49,999	142.39	50	5.0
$50,000 to $69,999	157.70	56	8.5
$70,000 to $79,999	271.30	96	5.6
$80,000 to $99,999	241.51	85	6.9
$100,000 or more	1,089.52	385	66.0
HOUSEHOLD TYPE			
Average household	**282.92**	**100**	**100.0**
Married couples	450.52	159	80.5
Married couples, no children	663.71	235	50.6
Married couples, with children	288.06	102	25.4
Oldest child under age 6	11.06	4	0.2
Oldest child aged 6 to 17	310.31	110	13.9
Oldest child aged 18 or older	432.81	153	11.3
Single parent with child under age 18	178.28	63	3.7
Single person	136.38	48	14.3
RACE AND HISPANIC ORIGIN			
Average household	**282.92**	**100**	**100.0**
Asian	334.98	118	4.2
Black	213.17	75	9.0
Hispanic	63.86	23	2.7
Non-Hispanic white and other	327.25	116	88.3
REGION			
Average household	**282.92**	**100**	**100.0**
Northeast	367.49	130	24.2
Midwest	385.89	136	31.2
South	218.02	77	27.7
West	212.26	75	17.0
EDUCATION			
Average household	**282.92**	**100**	**100.0**
Less than high school graduate	39.73	14	2.1
High school graduate	96.80	34	8.6
Some college	200.70	71	15.4
Associate's degree	183.08	65	5.8
College graduate	664.87	235	68.0
Bachelor's degree	513.23	181	34.0
Master's, professional, doctoral degree	943.47	333	34.0

Note: Market shares may not sum to 100.0 because of rounding and missing categories by household type. "Asian" and "black" include Hispanics and non-Hispanics who identify themselves as being of the respective race alone. "Hispanic" includes people of any race who identify themselves as Hispanic. "Other" includes people who identify themselves as non-Hispanic and as Alaska Native, American Indian, Asian (who are also included in the "Asian" row), Native Hawaiian or other Pacific Islander, as well as non-Hispanics reporting more than one race.
Source: Calculations by New Strategist based on the Bureau of Labor Statistics' 2007 Consumer Expenditure Survey.

Gifts of Entertainment

Best customers: **Householders aged 45 to 74**
Married couples without children at home
Asians

Customer trends: **Average household spending on gifts of entertainment will continue to decline if discretionary income does not rise.**

The biggest spenders on gifts of entertainment (which includes items ranging from dance lessons to movie tickets, from iPods to video games) for people in other households are older married couples—most of them buying gifts for their children and grandchildren living elsewhere. Householders aged 45 to 74 spend 22 to 35 percent more than average on this item and account for 60 percent of the market. Married couples without children at home (most of them empty-nesters) spend 62 percent more than average on this item. Asians spend two-thirds more than average on gifts of entertainment.

Average household spending on gifts of entertainment for people in other households fell 9 percent between 2000 and 2007, after adjusting for inflation. Average household spending on gifts of entertainment for people in other households may continue to decline if discretionary incomes are squeezed by the economic downturn and the growing cost of necessities.

Table 8.4 Gifts of entertainment

Total household spending $12,342,763,410.00
Average household spends   102.71

AGE OF HOUSEHOLDER	AVERAGE HOUSEHOLD SPENDING	BEST CUSTOMERS (index)	BIGGEST CUSTOMERS (market share)
Average household	**$102.71**	**100**	**100.0%**
Under age 25	73.58	72	4.9
Aged 25 to 34	88.90	87	14.8
Aged 35 to 44	89.08	87	16.9
Aged 45 to 54	125.10	122	25.6
Aged 55 to 64	138.68	135	21.9
Aged 65 to 74	129.55	126	12.6
Aged 75 or older	36.24	35	3.3

	AVERAGE HOUSEHOLD SPENDING	BEST CUSTOMERS (index)	BIGGEST CUSTOMERS (market share)
HOUSEHOLD INCOME			
Average household	**$102.71**	**100**	**100.0%**
Under $20,000	29.81	29	6.0
$20,000 to $39,999	47.54	46	10.8
$40,000 to $49,999	58.57	57	5.6
$50,000 to $69,999	105.75	103	15.8
$70,000 to $79,999	196.75	192	11.1
$80,000 to $99,999	170.59	166	13.5
$100,000 or more	222.89	217	37.2
HOUSEHOLD TYPE			
Average household	**102.71**	**100**	**100.0**
Married couples	131.13	128	64.5
Married couples, no children	166.22	162	34.9
Married couples, with children	109.79	107	26.7
Oldest child under age 6	82.07	80	3.9
Oldest child aged 6 to 17	123.16	120	15.2
Oldest child aged 18 or older	104.30	102	7.5
Single parent with child under age 18	53.62	52	3.1
Single person	68.41	67	19.8
RACE AND HISPANIC ORIGIN			
Average household	**102.71**	**100**	**100.0**
Asian	169.14	165	5.8
Black	24.30	24	2.8
Hispanic	36.78	36	4.2
Non-Hispanic white and other	124.47	121	92.5
REGION			
Average household	**102.71**	**100**	**100.0**
Northeast	95.77	93	17.4
Midwest	104.61	102	23.3
South	90.97	89	31.8
West	125.23	122	27.6
EDUCATION			
Average household	**102.71**	**100**	**100.0**
Less than high school graduate	17.74	17	2.6
High school graduate	69.79	68	17.1
Some college	111.58	109	23.7
Associate's degree	170.67	166	14.8
College graduate	145.95	142	41.1
Bachelor's degree	147.97	144	27.0
Master's, professional, doctoral degree	143.07	139	14.2

Note: Market shares may not sum to 100.0 because of rounding and missing categories by household type. "Asian" and "black" include Hispanics and non-Hispanics who identify themselves as being of the respective race alone. "Hispanic" includes people of any race who identify themselves as Hispanic. "Other" includes people who identify themselves as non-Hispanic and as Alaska Native, American Indian, Asian (who are also included in the "Asian" row), Native Hawaiian or other Pacific Islander, as well as non-Hispanics reporting more than one race.
Source: Calculations by New Strategist based on the Bureau of Labor Statistics' 2007 Consumer Expenditure Survey.

Gifts of Food

Best customers: **Householders aged 45 to 64**
                        Married couples without children at home

Customer trends: **Average household spending on gifts of food should continue to rise as more boomers become empty-nesters.**

The biggest spenders on gifts of food for people in other households are older empty-nesters. Many gift givers are buying food for grown children and grandchildren who live elsewhere. Householders aged 45 to 64 spend 51 to 112 percent more than average on gifts of food and control two-thirds of the market for this item. Married couples without children at home (most of them empty-nesters) spend over twice the average on gifts of food for people in other households.

Average household spending on gifts of food for people in other households grew 10 percent between 2000 and 2007, after adjusting for inflation. Behind the growth is the entry of the baby-boom generation into the empty-nest lifestage. Average household spending on gifts of food should continue to rise as more boomers become empty-nesters.

Table 8.5 **Gifts of food**

Total household spending $11,151,868,800.00
Average household spends   92.80

AGE OF HOUSEHOLDER	AVERAGE HOUSEHOLD SPENDING	BEST CUSTOMERS (index)	BIGGEST CUSTOMERS (market share)
Average household	$92.80	100	100.0%
Under age 25	39.79	43	2.9
Aged 25 to 34	45.03	49	8.3
Aged 35 to 44	51.14	55	10.7
Aged 45 to 54	140.51	151	31.8
Aged 55 to 64	196.38	212	34.3
Aged 65 to 74	74.49	80	8.0
Aged 75 or older	41.89	45	4.3

	AVERAGE HOUSEHOLD SPENDING	BEST CUSTOMERS (index)	BIGGEST CUSTOMERS (market share)
HOUSEHOLD INCOME			
Average household	**$92.80**	**100**	**100.0%**
Under $20,000	21.44	23	4.7
$20,000 to $39,999	30.25	33	7.6
$40,000 to $49,999	51.89	56	5.5
$50,000 to $69,999	82.77	89	13.6
$70,000 to $79,999	99.76	108	6.2
$80,000 to $99,999	158.21	170	13.9
$100,000 or more	261.72	282	48.3
HOUSEHOLD TYPE			
Average household	**92.80**	**100**	**100.0**
Married couples	124.16	134	67.6
Married couples, no children	196.06	211	45.6
Married couples, with children	75.73	82	20.4
Oldest child under age 6	59.18	64	3.1
Oldest child aged 6 to 17	82.23	89	11.3
Oldest child aged 18 or older	75.49	81	6.0
Single parent with child under age 18	28.84	31	1.8
Single person	60.48	65	19.4
RACE AND HISPANIC ORIGIN			
Average household	**92.80**	**100**	**100.0**
Asian	89.85	97	3.4
Black	27.47	30	3.6
Hispanic	36.04	39	4.6
Non-Hispanic white and other	111.66	120	91.9
REGION			
Average household	**92.80**	**100**	**100.0**
Northeast	91.75	99	18.4
Midwest	100.61	108	24.8
South	93.90	101	36.3
West	83.95	90	20.5
EDUCATION			
Average household	**92.80**	**100**	**100.0**
Less than high school graduate	24.70	27	4.0
High school graduate	50.45	54	13.7
Some college	85.49	92	20.1
Associate's degree	116.58	126	11.2
College graduate	162.03	175	50.5
Bachelor's degree	120.89	130	24.4
Master's, professional, doctoral degree	236.96	255	26.0

Note: Market shares may not sum to 100.0 because of rounding and missing categories by household type. "Asian" and "black" include Hispanics and non-Hispanics who identify themselves as being of the respective race alone. "Hispanic" includes people of any race who identify themselves as Hispanic. "Other" includes people who identify themselves as non-Hispanic and as Alaska Native, American Indian, Asian (who are also included in the "Asian" row), Native Hawaiian or other Pacific Islander, as well as non-Hispanics reporting more than one race.
Source: Calculations by New Strategist based on the Bureau of Labor Statistics' 2007 Consumer Expenditure Survey.

Gifts of Health Care Expenses

Best customers:

Householders aged 45 to 64
Householders aged 75 or older
Married couples without children at home
People living alone
Asians
Households in the West
College graduates

Customer trends:

Average household spending on gifts of health care expenses will continue to decline in the years ahead if a universal health insurance system is put into place in the United States.

The biggest spenders on gifts of health care expenses for people in other households are the oldest householders—many of them paying for a spouse's nursing home care. This explains why householders aged 75 or older spend over two times the average on this item. Householders aged 45 to 64 spend 30 to 53 percent more than average and control over half the market for this item. Married couples without children at home, many of them older empty-nesters, spend 34 percent more than average on gifts of health care expenses, while people living alone, many of them elderly, spend 53 percent more than average on this item. Asians spend 87 percent more than average on this item, and households in the West, where many Asians reside, 54 percent. College graduates spend over twice the average on gifts of health care expenses.

Average household spending on gifts of health care expenses for people in other households was halved between 2000 and 2007, after adjusting for inflation. Spending on gifts of health care expenses for people in other households will continue to decline in the years ahead if a universal health insurance system is put into place in the United States.

Table 8.6 Gifts of health care expenses

Total household spending $2,761,529,580.00
Average household spends   22.98

	AVERAGE HOUSEHOLD SPENDING	BEST CUSTOMERS (index)	BIGGEST CUSTOMERS (market share)
AGE OF HOUSEHOLDER			
Average household	**$22.98**	**100**	**100.0%**
Under age 25	0.79	3	0.2
Aged 25 to 34	4.76	21	3.5
Aged 35 to 44	15.75	69	13.4
Aged 45 to 54	29.94	130	27.4
Aged 55 to 64	35.26	153	24.8
Aged 65 to 74	20.65	90	9.0
Aged 75 or older	52.65	229	21.7

	AVERAGE HOUSEHOLD SPENDING	BEST CUSTOMERS (index)	BIGGEST CUSTOMERS (market share)
HOUSEHOLD INCOME			
Average household	**$22.98**	**100**	**100.0%**
Under $20,000	7.80	34	7.0
$20,000 to $39,999	10.41	45	10.5
$40,000 to $49,999	8.04	35	3.4
$50,000 to $69,999	36.15	157	24.1
$70,000 to $79,999	15.36	67	3.9
$80,000 to $99,999	17.71	77	6.3
$100,000 or more	59.89	261	44.6
HOUSEHOLD TYPE			
Average household	**22.98**	**100**	**100.0**
Married couples	21.35	93	47.0
Married couples, no children	30.81	134	28.9
Married couples, with children	9.16	40	9.9
Oldest child under age 6	9.68	42	2.1
Oldest child aged 6 to 17	6.51	28	3.6
Oldest child aged 18 or older	13.55	59	4.3
Single parent with child under age 18	0.88	4	0.2
Single person	35.06	153	45.4
RACE AND HISPANIC ORIGIN			
Average household	**22.98**	**100**	**100.0**
Asian	42.97	187	6.6
Black	5.83	25	3.0
Hispanic	18.79	82	9.7
Non-Hispanic white and other	26.27	114	87.3
REGION			
Average household	**22.98**	**100**	**100.0**
Northeast	25.86	113	21.0
Midwest	23.58	103	23.4
South	13.36	58	20.9
West	35.30	154	34.7
EDUCATION			
Average household	**22.98**	**100**	**100.0**
Less than high school graduate	5.56	24	3.7
High school graduate	13.05	57	14.3
Some college	16.85	73	16.0
Associate's degree	9.74	42	3.8
College graduate	49.39	215	62.2
Bachelor's degree	41.06	179	33.5
Master's, professional, doctoral degree	64.60	281	28.7

Note: Market shares may not sum to 100.0 because of rounding and missing categories by household type. "Asian" and "black" include Hispanics and non-Hispanics who identify themselves as being of the respective race alone. "Hispanic" includes people of any race who identify themselves as Hispanic. "Other" includes people who identify themselves as non-Hispanic and as Alaska Native, American Indian, Asian (who are also included in the "Asian" row), Native Hawaiian or other Pacific Islander, as well as non-Hispanics reporting more than one race.
Source: Calculations by New Strategist based on the Bureau of Labor Statistics' 2007 Consumer Expenditure Survey.

Gifts of Household Equipment

Best customers:

Householders aged 45 to 54
High-income households
Married couples without children at home
Married couples with school-aged children
Households in the Midwest

Customer trends:

Average household spending on gifts of household equipment for people in other households should rise as the children of boomers set up their own households.

The household equipment category includes many traditional gifts, such as infants' equipment, indoor plants and fresh flowers, and decorative household items. The biggest spenders on gifts of household equipment for people in other households are middle-aged married couples, many with grown children living elsewhere. Householders aged 45 to 54 spend twice the average amount on this item. Married couples without children at home (many of them empty-nesters) spend 67 percent more than average on this item, while those with school-aged children spend 44 percent more than average. Households with incomes of $100,000 or more spend over three times the average on gifts of household equipment. Households in the Midwest spend 47 percent more than average on this item.

Average household spending on gifts of household equipment fell by an enormous 35 percent between 2000 and 2007, after adjusting for inflation. Spending on gifts of household equipment should rise as the children of boomers establish their own households.

Table 8.7 Gifts of household equipment

Total household spending $6,625,027,230.00
Average household spends 55.13

AGE OF HOUSEHOLDER	AVERAGE HOUSEHOLD SPENDING	BEST CUSTOMERS (index)	BIGGEST CUSTOMERS (market share)
Average household	$55.13	100	100.0%
Under age 25	16.39	30	2.0
Aged 25 to 34	42.37	77	13.1
Aged 35 to 44	60.18	109	21.3
Aged 45 to 54	110.44	200	42.1
Aged 55 to 64	41.51	75	12.2
Aged 65 to 74	35.30	64	6.4
Aged 75 or older	20.02	36	3.4

	AVERAGE HOUSEHOLD SPENDING	BEST CUSTOMERS (index)	BIGGEST CUSTOMERS (market share)
HOUSEHOLD INCOME			
Average household	**$55.13**	**100**	**100.0%**
Under $20,000	14.49	26	5.4
$20,000 to $39,999	24.95	45	10.5
$40,000 to $49,999	26.17	47	4.7
$50,000 to $69,999	34.97	63	9.7
$70,000 to $79,999	58.10	105	6.1
$80,000 to $99,999	58.77	107	8.7
$100,000 or more	181.37	329	56.4
HOUSEHOLD TYPE			
Average household	**55.13**	**100**	**100.0**
Married couples	78.00	141	71.5
Married couples, no children	92.32	167	36.1
Married couples, with children	70.84	128	32.1
Oldest child under age 6	54.13	98	4.8
Oldest child aged 6 to 17	79.44	144	18.3
Oldest child aged 18 or older	65.52	119	8.8
Single parent with child under age 18	51.10	93	5.5
Single person	31.34	57	16.9
RACE AND HISPANIC ORIGIN			
Average household	**55.13**	**100**	**100.0**
Asian	42.33	77	2.7
Black	14.71	27	3.2
Hispanic	32.17	58	6.9
Non-Hispanic white and other	64.66	117	89.5
REGION			
Average household	**55.13**	**100**	**100.0**
Northeast	52.73	96	17.8
Midwest	81.13	147	33.6
South	39.35	71	25.6
West	55.69	101	22.8
EDUCATION			
Average household	**55.13**	**100**	**100.0**
Less than high school graduate	15.33	28	4.2
High school graduate	26.73	48	12.2
Some college	51.14	93	20.2
Associate's degree	52.33	95	8.4
College graduate	102.49	186	53.8
Bachelor's degree	111.06	201	37.8
Master's, professional, doctoral degree	88.23	160	16.3

Note: Market shares may not sum to 100.0 because of rounding and missing categories by household type. "Asian" and "black" include Hispanics and non-Hispanics who identify themselves as being of the respective race alone. "Hispanic" includes people of any race who identify themselves as Hispanic. "Other" includes people who identify themselves as non-Hispanic and as Alaska Native, American Indian, Asian (who are also included in the "Asian" row), Native Hawaiian or other Pacific Islander, as well as non-Hispanics reporting more than one race.
Source: Calculations by New Strategist based on the Bureau of Labor Statistics' 2007 Consumer Expenditure Survey.

Gifts of Household Textiles

Best customers:	**Householders aged 55 to 64**
	Married couples without children at home
	Non-Hispanic whites
	Households in the Northeast
Customer trends:	**Average household spending on gifts of household textiles for people in other households should rise as boomers help their adult children outfit their homes.**

The biggest spenders on gifts of household textiles (such as towels and bed linens) for people in other households are older married couples, many of them empty-nesters giving this traditional gift to adult children who live elsewhere. Householders aged 55 to 64 spend nearly twice the average on this item, while married couples without children at home (most of them empty-nesters) spend 71 percent more than average and control 37 percent of the market. Non-Hispanic whites constitute 93 percent of the market for gifts of household textiles. Northeastern householders far outspend householders of other regions on this item.

Already the smallest gift-giving category, average household spending on gifts of household textiles for people in other households dropped by a substantial 18 percent between 2000 and 2007, after adjusting for inflation. Spending on gifts of household textiles should grow in the years ahead as millions of boomers help their adult children outfit their homes.

Table 8.8 **Gifts of household textiles**

Total household spending $1,557,416,160.00
Average household spends 12.96

	AVERAGE HOUSEHOLD SPENDING	BEST CUSTOMERS (index)	BIGGEST CUSTOMERS (market share)
AGE OF HOUSEHOLDER			
Average household	**$12.96**	**100**	**100.0%**
Under age 25	3.43	26	1.8
Aged 25 to 34	12.74	98	16.8
Aged 35 to 44	12.71	98	19.1
Aged 45 to 54	12.07	93	19.6
Aged 55 to 64	25.20	194	31.5
Aged 65 to 74	9.43	73	7.3
Aged 75 or older	6.02	46	4.4

	AVERAGE HOUSEHOLD SPENDING	BEST CUSTOMERS (index)	BIGGEST CUSTOMERS (market share)
HOUSEHOLD INCOME			
Average household	**$12.96**	**100**	**100.0%**
Under $20,000	2.95	23	4.7
$20,000 to $39,999	10.16	78	18.2
$40,000 to $49,999	3.79	29	2.9
$50,000 to $69,999	25.90	200	30.6
$70,000 to $79,999	13.60	105	6.1
$80,000 to $99,999	19.56	151	12.3
$100,000 or more	19.14	148	25.3
HOUSEHOLD TYPE			
Average household	**12.96**	**100**	**100.0**
Married couples	16.78	129	65.5
Married couples, no children	22.11	171	36.8
Married couples, with children	13.33	103	25.7
Oldest child under age 6	5.08	39	1.9
Oldest child aged 6 to 17	15.98	123	15.7
Oldest child aged 18 or older	14.03	108	8.0
Single parent with child under age 18	7.11	55	3.3
Single person	9.41	73	21.6
RACE AND HISPANIC ORIGIN			
Average household	**12.96**	**100**	**100.0**
Asian	0.90	7	0.2
Black	0.88	7	0.8
Hispanic	6.04	47	5.5
Non-Hispanic white and other	15.85	122	93.4
REGION			
Average household	**12.96**	**100**	**100.0**
Northeast	22.73	175	32.7
Midwest	11.23	87	19.8
South	11.49	89	31.8
West	8.81	68	15.4
EDUCATION			
Average household	**12.96**	**100**	**100.0**
Less than high school graduate	2.16	17	2.5
High school graduate	7.31	56	14.2
Some college	12.73	98	21.4
Associate's degree	32.27	249	22.1
College graduate	17.52	135	39.1
Bachelor's degree	15.96	123	23.1
Master's, professional, doctoral degree	20.21	156	15.9

Note: Market shares may not sum to 100.0 because of rounding and missing categories by household type. "Asian" and "black" include Hispanics and non-Hispanics who identify themselves as being of the respective race alone. "Hispanic" includes people of any race who identify themselves as Hispanic. "Other" includes people who identify themselves as non-Hispanic and as Alaska Native, American Indian, Asian (who are also included in the "Asian" row), Native Hawaiian or other Pacific Islander, as well as non-Hispanics reporting more than one race.
Source: Calculations by New Strategist based on the Bureau of Labor Statistics' 2007 Consumer Expenditure Survey.

Gifts of Housekeeping Supplies

Best customers: Householders aged 45 to 64
Married couples without children at home

Customer trends: Average household spending on gifts of housekeeping supplies for people in other households should rise as boomers help their adult children outfit their homes.

The biggest spenders on gifts of housekeeping supplies (such as laundry and cleaning supplies, lawn and garden supplies, postage, and stationery) for people in other households are older married couples. These couples are often giving housekeeping supplies to adult children who live elsewhere. Householders aged 45 to 64 spend 23 to 33 percent more than average on this item and control 47 percent of the market. Married couples without children at home (most of them empty-nesters) spend 43 percent more than average on this item.

Average household spending on gifts of housekeeping supplies for people in other households fell by an enormous 36 percent between 2000 and 2007, after adjusting for inflation. Spending on gifts of housekeeping supplies should increase in the years ahead as millions of boomers help their adult children outfit their homes.

Table 8.9 **Gifts of housekeeping supplies**

Total household spending $3,601,524,870.00
Average household spends 29.97

AGE OF HOUSEHOLDER	AVERAGE HOUSEHOLD SPENDING	BEST CUSTOMERS (index)	BIGGEST CUSTOMERS (market share)
Average household	$29.97	100	100.0%
Under age 25	18.52	62	4.2
Aged 25 to 34	26.94	90	15.3
Aged 35 to 44	25.02	83	16.3
Aged 45 to 54	36.80	123	25.8
Aged 55 to 64	39.77	133	21.5
Aged 65 to 74	30.64	102	10.2
Aged 75 or older	22.26	74	7.0

	AVERAGE HOUSEHOLD SPENDING	BEST CUSTOMERS (index)	BIGGEST CUSTOMERS (market share)
HOUSEHOLD INCOME			
Average household	**$29.97**	**100**	**100.0%**
Under $20,000	10.52	35	7.2
$20,000 to $39,999	21.50	72	16.7
$40,000 to $49,999	15.95	53	5.2
$50,000 to $69,999	40.84	136	20.9
$70,000 to $79,999	38.22	128	7.4
$80,000 to $99,999	49.31	165	13.4
$100,000 or more	50.57	169	28.9
HOUSEHOLD TYPE			
Average household	**29.97**	**100**	**100.0**
Married couples	35.88	120	60.5
Married couples, no children	42.82	143	30.8
Married couples, with children	31.40	105	26.1
Oldest child under age 6	34.26	114	5.6
Oldest child aged 6 to 17	33.99	113	14.4
Oldest child aged 18 or older	24.16	81	5.9
Single parent with child under age 18	30.54	102	6.1
Single person	23.57	79	23.4
RACE AND HISPANIC ORIGIN			
Average household	**29.97**	**100**	**100.0**
Asian	11.80	39	1.4
Black	11.37	38	4.6
Hispanic	23.60	79	9.3
Non-Hispanic white and other	33.82	113	86.1
REGION			
Average household	**29.97**	**100**	**100.0**
Northeast	27.24	91	16.9
Midwest	37.54	125	28.6
South	26.14	87	31.3
West	30.65	102	23.1
EDUCATION			
Average household	**29.97**	**100**	**100.0**
Less than high school graduate	7.98	27	4.0
High school graduate	21.73	73	18.3
Some college	34.65	116	25.2
Associate's degree	32.29	108	9.6
College graduate	43.28	144	41.8
Bachelor's degree	37.27	124	23.3
Master's, professional, doctoral degree	53.71	179	18.3

Note: Market shares may not sum to 100.0 because of rounding and missing categories by household type. "Asian" and "black" include Hispanics and non-Hispanics who identify themselves as being of the respective race alone. "Hispanic" includes people of any race who identify themselves as Hispanic. "Other" includes people who identify themselves as non-Hispanic and as Alaska Native, American Indian, Asian (who are also included in the "Asian" row), Native Hawaiian or other Pacific Islander, as well as non-Hispanics reporting more than one race.
Source: Calculations by New Strategist based on the Bureau of Labor Statistics' 2007 Consumer Expenditure Survey.

Gifts of Infants' Apparel

Best customers:

Householders aged 25 to 44
Married couples
Asians
Households in the West

Customer trends:

Average household spending on gifts of infants' apparel for people in other households should rise as the large millennial generation has children.

The biggest spenders on gifts of infants' apparel for people in other households are young married couples with preschoolers. Many are buying gifts for friends and relatives who have recently had children. Householders ranging in age from 25 to 44 spend 23 to 24 percent more than average on this item. Married couples with children at home spend 52 percent more than average on gifts of infant apparel, the figure peaking among couples with preschoolers at well over twice the average. Asians spend 33 percent more than average on this item, as do householders in the West.

Average household spending on gifts of infants' apparel for people in other households declined by 8 percent between 2000 and 2007, after adjusting for inflation. Spending on gifts of infants' apparel should increase as the millennial generation fills the 25-to-34 age group and has children.

Table 8.10 Gifts of infants' apparel

Total household spending $5,410,098,420.00
Average household spends   45.02

	AVERAGE HOUSEHOLD SPENDING	BEST CUSTOMERS (index)	BIGGEST CUSTOMERS (market share)
AGE OF HOUSEHOLDER			
Average household	**$45.02**	**100**	**100.0%**
Under age 25	42.08	93	6.3
Aged 25 to 34	55.73	124	21.1
Aged 35 to 44	55.37	123	24.0
Aged 45 to 54	44.64	99	20.8
Aged 55 to 64	49.02	109	17.6
Aged 65 to 74	31.58	70	7.0
Aged 75 or older	13.74	31	2.9

	AVERAGE HOUSEHOLD SPENDING	BEST CUSTOMERS (index)	BIGGEST CUSTOMERS (market share)
HOUSEHOLD INCOME			
Average household	**$45.02**	**100**	**100.0%**
Under $20,000	22.91	51	10.5
$20,000 to $39,999	36.11	80	18.6
$40,000 to $49,999	31.83	71	7.0
$50,000 to $69,999	48.04	107	16.3
$70,000 to $79,999	79.46	176	10.2
$80,000 to $99,999	69.10	153	12.5
$100,000 or more	66.74	148	25.4
HOUSEHOLD TYPE			
Average household	**45.02**	**100**	**100.0**
Married couples	61.74	137	69.3
Married couples, no children	53.12	118	25.5
Married couples, with children	68.35	152	37.9
Oldest child under age 6	102.85	228	11.1
Oldest child aged 6 to 17	62.26	138	17.6
Oldest child aged 18 or older	54.04	120	8.8
Single parent with child under age 18	47.13	105	6.2
Single person	19.50	43	12.9
RACE AND HISPANIC ORIGIN			
Average household	**45.02**	**100**	**100.0**
Asian	59.66	133	4.7
Black	36.69	81	9.8
Hispanic	52.58	117	13.8
Non-Hispanic white and other	45.22	100	76.7
REGION			
Average household	**45.02**	**100**	**100.0**
Northeast	36.17	80	15.0
Midwest	41.04	91	20.8
South	42.97	95	34.3
West	59.98	133	30.1
EDUCATION			
Average household	**45.02**	**100**	**100.0**
Less than high school graduate	40.36	90	13.6
High school graduate	40.06	89	22.4
Some college	44.30	98	21.4
Associate's degree	47.81	106	9.4
College graduate	51.67	115	33.2
Bachelor's degree	58.04	129	24.2
Master's, professional, doctoral degree	40.53	90	9.2

Note: Market shares may not sum to 100.0 because of rounding and missing categories by household type. "Asian" and "black" include Hispanics and non-Hispanics who identify themselves as being of the respective race alone. "Hispanic" includes people of any race who identify themselves as Hispanic. "Other" includes people who identify themselves as non-Hispanic and as Alaska Native, American Indian, Asian (who are also included in the "Asian" row), Native Hawaiian or other Pacific Islander, as well as non-Hispanics reporting more than one race.
Source: Calculations by New Strategist based on the Bureau of Labor Statistics' 2007 Consumer Expenditure Survey.

Gifts of Jewelry

Best customers:
Householders aged 35 to 54
People living alone

Customer trends:
Average household spending on gifts of jewelry should continue to decline because of the economic downturn and the loss of discretionary income.

The biggest spenders on gifts of jewelry for people in other households are middle-aged adults, many buying jewelry for children living elsewhere. Householders aged 35 to 54 spend about one-third more than average on this item and account for over half the market. Single-person households—many headed by young adults—spend nearly twice the average on this item and account for 54 percent of the market for gifts of jewelry.

Average household spending on gifts of jewelry for people in other households dropped by 15 percent between 2000 and 2007, after adjusting for inflation. Spending on gifts of jewelry should continue to decline because of the economic downturn and the loss of discretionary income.

Table 8.11 Gifts of jewelry

Total household spending $2,066,941,200.00
Average household spends 17.20

AGE OF HOUSEHOLDER	AVERAGE HOUSEHOLD SPENDING	BEST CUSTOMERS (index)	BIGGEST CUSTOMERS (market share)
Average household	$17.20	100	100.0%
Under age 25	10.08	59	4.0
Aged 25 to 34	13.35	78	13.2
Aged 35 to 44	23.46	136	26.6
Aged 45 to 54	22.72	132	27.7
Aged 55 to 64	9.31	54	8.8
Aged 65 to 74	20.63	120	12.0
Aged 75 or older	14.03	82	7.7

	AVERAGE HOUSEHOLD SPENDING	BEST CUSTOMERS (index)	BIGGEST CUSTOMERS (market share)
HOUSEHOLD INCOME			
Average household	**$17.20**	**100**	**100.0%**
Under $20,000	6.04	35	7.2
$20,000 to $39,999	13.29	77	18.0
$40,000 to $49,999	22.79	133	13.0
$50,000 to $69,999	19.23	112	17.1
$70,000 to $79,999	11.12	65	3.7
$80,000 to $99,999	21.50	125	10.2
$100,000 or more	30.90	180	30.8
HOUSEHOLD TYPE			
Average household	**17.20**	**100**	**100.0**
Married couples	11.06	64	32.5
Married couples, no children	15.34	89	19.2
Married couples, with children	8.52	50	12.4
Oldest child under age 6	10.36	60	2.9
Oldest child aged 6 to 17	8.60	50	6.4
Oldest child aged 18 or older	7.17	42	3.1
Single parent with child under age 18	12.30	72	4.2
Single person	31.22	182	54.0
RACE AND HISPANIC ORIGIN			
Average household	**17.20**	**100**	**100.0**
Asian	15.30	89	3.1
Black	4.94	29	3.4
Hispanic	12.02	70	8.2
Non-Hispanic white and other	19.90	116	88.3
REGION			
Average household	**17.20**	**100**	**100.0**
Northeast	22.33	130	24.2
Midwest	16.35	95	21.7
South	14.02	82	29.3
West	18.90	110	24.8
EDUCATION			
Average household	**17.20**	**100**	**100.0**
Less than high school graduate	6.68	39	5.9
High school graduate	8.58	50	12.6
Some college	16.06	93	20.3
Associate's degree	10.64	62	5.5
College graduate	33.11	193	55.7
Bachelor's degree	42.06	245	45.8
Master's, professional, doctoral degree	16.66	97	9.9

Note: Market shares may not sum to 100.0 because of rounding and missing categories by household type. "Asian" and "black" include Hispanics and non-Hispanics who identify themselves as being of the respective race alone. "Hispanic" includes people of any race who identify themselves as Hispanic. "Other" includes people who identify themselves as non-Hispanic and as Alaska Native, American Indian, Asian (who are also included in the "Asian" row), Native Hawaiian or other Pacific Islander, as well as non-Hispanics reporting more than one race.
Source: Calculations by New Strategist based on the Bureau of Labor Statistics' 2007 Consumer Expenditure Survey.

Gifts of Men's and Boys' Apparel

Best customers:	Householders aged 45 to 64
	Married couples without children at home
	Married couples with adult children at home
	Blacks and Hispanics

Customer trends:	Average household spending on gifts of men's and boys' apparel for people in other households will continue to decline as electronics trump apparel in gift giving to men and boys.

Apparel is the second-biggest gift-giving category. In 2007, the average household spent $144 on gifts of women's, men's, and children's apparel for people in other households. Older married couples dominate gifts of men's and boys' apparel, many of them buying clothes for adult children and grandchildren living elsewhere. Householders aged 45 to 64 spend 25 to 53 percent more than average on gifts of men's and boys' apparel and account for just over half the market. Married couples without children at home (most of them empty-nesters) spend 39 percent more than average, and those with adult children at home spend 37 percent more than average. Hispanics and blacks spend, respectively 16 and 10 percent more than average on gifts of clothes for males.

Average household spending on gifts of men's and boys' apparel for people in other households fell by a substantial 30 percent between 2000 and 2007, after adjusting for inflation. Spending in this category will continue to decline as older Americans are replaced by more technologically sophisticated boomers, who will be more likely to give men and boys gifts of electronics rather than apparel.

Table 8.12 Gifts of men's and boys' apparel

Total household spending	$6,867,772,650.00
Average household spends	57.15

	AVERAGE HOUSEHOLD SPENDING	BEST CUSTOMERS (index)	BIGGEST CUSTOMERS (market share)
AGE OF HOUSEHOLDER			
Average household	**$57.15**	**100**	**100.0%**
Under age 25	46.71	82	5.5
Aged 25 to 34	38.88	68	11.6
Aged 35 to 44	53.87	94	18.4
Aged 45 to 54	71.42	125	26.3
Aged 55 to 64	87.62	153	24.8
Aged 65 to 74	53.29	93	9.3
Aged 75 or older	26.21	46	4.3

	AVERAGE HOUSEHOLD SPENDING	BEST CUSTOMERS (index)	BIGGEST CUSTOMERS (market share)
HOUSEHOLD INCOME			
Average household	**$57.15**	**100**	**100.0%**
Under $20,000	45.76	80	16.5
$20,000 to $39,999	36.34	64	14.8
$40,000 to $49,999	39.31	69	6.8
$50,000 to $69,999	53.17	93	14.2
$70,000 to $79,999	65.69	115	6.7
$80,000 to $99,999	72.81	127	10.4
$100,000 or more	105.33	184	31.6
HOUSEHOLD TYPE			
Average household	**57.15**	**100**	**100.0**
Married couples	59.48	104	52.6
Married couples, no children	79.50	139	30.0
Married couples, with children	47.09	82	20.6
Oldest child under age 6	26.49	46	2.3
Oldest child aged 6 to 17	38.92	68	8.7
Oldest child aged 18 or older	78.12	137	10.1
Single parent with child under age 18	51.01	89	5.3
Single person	63.60	111	33.1
RACE AND HISPANIC ORIGIN			
Average household	**57.15**	**100**	**100.0**
Asian	50.02	88	3.1
Black	62.89	110	13.2
Hispanic	66.19	116	13.7
Non-Hispanic white and other	55.17	97	73.7
REGION			
Average household	**57.15**	**100**	**100.0**
Northeast	57.65	101	18.8
Midwest	51.03	89	20.4
South	66.24	116	41.6
West	48.49	85	19.2
EDUCATION			
Average household	**57.15**	**100**	**100.0**
Less than high school graduate	34.35	60	9.1
High school graduate	40.55	71	17.9
Some college	41.65	73	15.9
Associate's degree	71.81	126	11.2
College graduate	89.42	156	45.3
Bachelor's degree	67.44	118	22.1
Master's, professional, doctoral degree	127.74	224	22.8

Note: Market shares may not sum to 100.0 because of rounding and missing categories by household type. "Asian" and "black" include Hispanics and non-Hispanics who identify themselves as being of the respective race alone. "Hispanic" includes people of any race who identify themselves as Hispanic. "Other" includes people who identify themselves as non-Hispanic and as Alaska Native, American Indian, Asian (who are also included in the "Asian" row), Native Hawaiian or other Pacific Islander, as well as non-Hispanics reporting more than one race.
Source: Calculations by New Strategist based on the Bureau of Labor Statistics' 2007 Consumer Expenditure Survey.

Gifts of Transportation

Best customers:	**Householders aged 55 to 74** **Married couples without children at home** **Married couples with adult children at home** **Asians** **Households in the West and South**
Customer trends:	**Average household spending on gifts of transportation should rise as growing numbers of empty-nest boomers help their adult children come home for a visit.**

The biggest spenders on gifts of transportation for people in other households are older people buying bus or airline tickets for children away at college, or even helping grown children buy a car. Householders aged 55 to 74, many with adult children who live elsewhere, spend 64 to 127 percent more than average on this item and account for just under half the market. Married couples without children at home, most of them empty-nesters, spend well over twice the average amount on gifts of transportation for people in other households, while those with adult children at home spend 37 percent more than average. Asians spend over twice the average amount on this item. Households in the West and South spend, respectively, 39 and 15 percent more than average on gifts of transportation for people in other households.

Average household spending on gifts of transportation for people in other households rose by a strong 29 percent between 2000 and 2007, after adjusting for inflation. Average household spending on gifts of transportation may continue to rise as growing numbers of empty-nest boomers help their adult children come home for a visit.

Table 8.13 Gifts of transportation

Total household spending	$13,078,209,930.00
Average household spends	108.83

	AVERAGE HOUSEHOLD SPENDING	BEST CUSTOMERS (index)	BIGGEST CUSTOMERS (market share)
AGE OF HOUSEHOLDER			
Average household	**$108.83**	**100**	**100.0%**
Under age 25	54.37	50	3.4
Aged 25 to 34	22.87	21	3.6
Aged 35 to 44	70.94	65	12.7
Aged 45 to 54	123.75	114	23.9
Aged 55 to 64	177.99	164	26.5
Aged 65 to 74	247.49	227	22.7
Aged 75 or older	82.02	75	7.1

	AVERAGE HOUSEHOLD SPENDING	BEST CUSTOMERS (index)	BIGGEST CUSTOMERS (market share)
HOUSEHOLD INCOME			
Average household	**$108.83**	**100**	**100.0%**
Under $20,000	21.83	20	4.1
$20,000 to $39,999	47.78	44	10.2
$40,000 to $49,999	32.80	30	3.0
$50,000 to $69,999	130.80	120	18.4
$70,000 to $79,999	251.97	232	13.4
$80,000 to $99,999	121.05	111	9.0
$100,000 or more	264.17	243	41.6
HOUSEHOLD TYPE			
Average household	**108.83**	**100**	**100.0**
Married couples	145.42	134	67.5
Married couples, no children	239.32	220	47.4
Married couples, with children	82.51	76	18.9
Oldest child under age 6	23.50	22	1.1
Oldest child aged 6 to 17	66.49	61	7.8
Oldest child aged 18 or older	149.21	137	10.1
Single parent with child under age 18	22.73	21	1.2
Single person	62.46	57	17.1
RACE AND HISPANIC ORIGIN			
Average household	**108.83**	**100**	**100.0**
Asian	230.48	212	7.5
Black	59.63	55	6.6
Hispanic	66.54	61	7.2
Non-Hispanic white and other	123.22	113	86.4
REGION			
Average household	**108.83**	**100**	**100.0**
Northeast	75.18	69	12.9
Midwest	69.33	64	14.6
South	125.03	115	41.3
West	150.88	139	31.4
EDUCATION			
Average household	**108.83**	**100**	**100.0**
Less than high school graduate	47.71	44	6.6
High school graduate	94.00	86	21.8
Some college	99.28	91	19.9
Associate's degree	118.08	108	9.6
College graduate	157.52	145	41.9
Bachelor's degree	135.99	125	23.4
Master's, professional, doctoral degree	197.09	181	18.5

Note: Market shares may not sum to 100.0 because of rounding and missing categories by household type. "Asian" and "black" include Hispanics and non-Hispanics who identify themselves as being of the respective race alone. "Hispanic" includes people of any race who identify themselves as Hispanic. "Other" includes people who identify themselves as non-Hispanic and as Alaska Native, American Indian, Asian (who are also included in the "Asian" row), Native Hawaiian or other Pacific Islander, as well as non-Hispanics reporting more than one race.
Source: Calculations by New Strategist based on the Bureau of Labor Statistics' 2007 Consumer Expenditure Survey.

Gifts of Women's and Girls' Apparel

Best customers:
Householders aged 45 to 64
Married couples without children at home
Asians

Customer trends:
Average household spending on gifts of women's and girls' apparel should rise as boomers fill the best-customer lifestage.

Older empty-nest couples dominate spending on gifts of women's and girls' apparel, many of them buying clothes for adult children and grandchildren. Householders aged 45 to 64 spend 47 to 53 percent more than average on this item and account for 56 percent of the market. Married couples without children at home, many of them empty-nesters, spend 84 percent more than average on gifts of women's and girls' apparel. Asians spend 31 percent more than average on gifts of apparel for females living elsewhere.

Average household spending on gifts of women's and girls' apparel for people in other households fell by 15 percent between 2000 and 2007, after adjusting for inflation. Price discounting is one factor behind the decline. Average household spending on gifts of women's and girls' apparel could rise in the years ahead as more boomers become empty-nesters and enter the best-customer lifestage.

Table 8.14 Gifts of women's and girls' apparel

Total household spending $10,456,078,710.00
Average household spends   87.01

AGE OF HOUSEHOLDER	AVERAGE HOUSEHOLD SPENDING	BEST CUSTOMERS (index)	BIGGEST CUSTOMERS (market share)
Average household	$87.01	100	100.0%
Under age 25	35.06	40	2.7
Aged 25 to 34	60.50	70	11.9
Aged 35 to 44	56.06	64	12.6
Aged 45 to 54	133.09	153	32.1
Aged 55 to 64	127.94	147	23.8
Aged 65 to 74	102.00	117	11.7
Aged 75 or older	52.49	60	5.7

	AVERAGE HOUSEHOLD SPENDING	BEST CUSTOMERS (index)	BIGGEST CUSTOMERS (market share)
HOUSEHOLD INCOME			
Average household	**$87.01**	**100**	**100.0%**
Under $20,000	30.17	35	7.1
$20,000 to $39,999	43.40	50	11.6
$40,000 to $49,999	74.59	86	8.4
$50,000 to $69,999	109.81	126	19.3
$70,000 to $79,999	91.53	105	6.1
$80,000 to $99,999	119.75	138	11.2
$100,000 or more	185.12	213	36.5
HOUSEHOLD TYPE			
Average household	**87.01**	**100**	**100.0**
Married couples	106.66	123	62.0
Married couples, no children	159.72	184	39.6
Married couples, with children	62.40	72	17.9
Oldest child under age 6	45.17	52	2.5
Oldest child aged 6 to 17	60.34	69	8.8
Oldest child aged 18 or older	78.96	91	6.7
Single parent with child under age 18	43.44	50	3.0
Single person	49.97	57	17.1
RACE AND HISPANIC ORIGIN			
Average household	**87.01**	**100**	**100.0**
Asian	113.77	131	4.6
Black	48.06	55	6.6
Hispanic	66.02	76	9.0
Non-Hispanic white and other	96.09	110	84.3
REGION			
Average household	**87.01**	**100**	**100.0**
Northeast	91.46	105	19.6
Midwest	105.30	121	27.7
South	72.70	84	30.0
West	87.48	101	22.7
EDUCATION			
Average household	**87.01**	**100**	**100.0**
Less than high school graduate	42.27	49	7.4
High school graduate	54.67	63	15.8
Some college	53.05	61	13.3
Associate's degree	113.48	130	11.6
College graduate	152.76	176	50.8
Bachelor's degree	156.20	180	33.6
Master's, professional, doctoral degree	146.81	169	17.2

Note: Market shares may not sum to 100.0 because of rounding and missing categories by household type. "Asian" and "black" include Hispanics and non-Hispanics who identify themselves as being of the respective race alone. "Hispanic" includes people of any race who identify themselves as Hispanic. "Other" includes people who identify themselves as non-Hispanic and as Alaska Native, American Indian, Asian (who are also included in the "Asian" row), Native Hawaiian or other Pacific Islander, as well as non-Hispanics reporting more than one race.
Source: Calculations by New Strategist based on the Bureau of Labor Statistics' 2007 Consumer Expenditure Survey.

Chapter 9.

Groceries

Household Spending on Groceries, 2007

Not surprisingly, groceries are one of the largest household expenses. In 2007, the average household spent $3,465 on groceries (or what the Consumer Expenditure Survey calls food at home). This figure was 5 percent below the $3,638 the average household spent on groceries in 2000, after adjusting for inflation. Falling prices for some grocery items were behind the trend. But another important reason was Americans' growing propensity for eating out rather than cooking at home.

In another sign that cooking is on the way out, prepared foods (except salads, desserts, and frozen meals) have supplanted fresh milk as the grocery category on which households spend the most. In 2007, the average household devoted $148 to prepared foods, up 66 percent from $89 in 2000. They devoted $138 to fresh milk, down 4 percent from the $144 spent in 2000 as milk consumption declined. After prepared foods and milk, households spend the most on cheese, chicken, vegetables, fruits, and potato chips and other snacks.

Average household spending on groceries is determined by household size, larger households spending more than smaller ones on most items. Average household spending on groceries may decline in the years ahead as boomers become empty-nesters and household size drifts downward. But household demographic characteristics and nutritional claims will continue to affect spending patterns—patterns that will determine the future success of grocery retailers and food manufacturers.

Spending on groceries

(average annual spending of households on groceries, 2000 to 2007; in 2007 dollars)

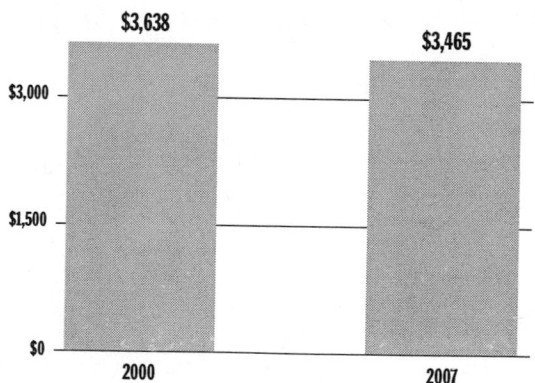

Table 9.1 Spending on Groceries, 2000 to 2007

(average annual and percent distribution of household spending on groceries, 2000 to 2007; percent change in spending, 2000–07; in 2007 dollars; ranked by amount spent)

	2007		2000		
	average household spending	percent distribution	average household spending (in 2007$)	percent distribution	percent change 2000–07
Average household spending on groceries	**$3,465.01**	**100.0%**	**$3,637.52**	**100.0%**	**–4.7%**
Prepared food (except salads, desserts, and frozen meals)	148.07	4.3	88.99	2.4	66.4
Milk, fresh	138.15	4.0	144.02	4.0	–4.1
Cheese	117.15	3.4	115.54	3.2	1.4
Chicken, fresh and frozen	113.50	3.3	137.78	3.8	–17.6
Vegetables, fresh (except potatoes, lettuce, and tomatoes)	100.26	2.9	96.78	2.7	3.6
Fruit, fresh (except apples, bananas, and citrus)	98.51	2.8	82.77	2.3	19.0
Potato chips and other snacks	95.81	2.8	86.30	2.4	11.0
Ground beef	89.11	2.6	105.67	2.9	–15.7
Carbonated drinks, colas	84.96	2.5	104.74	2.9	–18.9
Cereal, ready-to-eat and cooked	84.57	2.4	104.61	2.9	–19.2
Candy and chewing gum	80.35	2.3	91.87	2.5	–12.5
Steak	76.31	2.2	113.81	3.1	–32.9
Lunch meats (cold cuts)	76.14	2.2	81.87	2.3	–7.0
Prepared meals, frozen	71.36	2.1	34.32	0.9	107.9
Prepared food, frozen (except meals)	65.38	1.9	74.29	2.0	–12.0
Fish and shellfish, fresh	63.81	1.8	80.46	2.2	–20.7
Water, bottled	60.72	1.8	–	–	–
Ice cream and related products	57.37	1.7	68.10	1.9	–15.8
Fruit juice, canned and bottled	56.46	1.6	67.68	1.9	–16.6
Bread, other than white	55.32	1.6	57.10	1.6	–3.1
Carbonated drinks, noncolas	46.79	1.4	57.06	1.6	–18.0
Sauces and gravies	46.54	1.3	44.83	1.2	3.8
Cookies	44.89	1.3	57.45	1.6	–21.9
Biscuits and rolls	44.32	1.3	46.39	1.3	–4.5
Eggs	42.71	1.2	41.49	1.1	2.9
Baby food	42.34	1.2	38.84	1.1	9.0
Fish and shellfish, frozen	41.77	1.2	33.29	0.9	25.5
Cakes and cupcakes	40.26	1.2	46.26	1.3	–13.0
Soup, canned and packaged	40.05	1.2	42.79	1.2	–6.4
Dairy products (except butter, eggs, cheese, ice cream, and milk)	39.07	1.1	28.77	0.8	35.8
Other nonalcoholic beverages and ice	36.47	1.1	45.74	1.3	*
Pork (except bacon, frankfurters, ham, chops, and sausage)	35.50	1.0	46.74	1.3	–24.1
Tomatoes, fresh	35.05	1.0	35.56	1.0	–1.4
Apples	34.95	1.0	35.51	1.0	–1.6
Roast beef	34.38	1.0	47.97	1.3	–28.3
Bread, white	33.86	1.0	44.09	1.2	–23.2
Salads, prepared	32.63	0.9	22.34	0.6	46.1
Nuts	32.12	0.9	25.08	0.7	28.1
Coffee, roasted	32.00	0.9	33.11	0.9	–3.4
Ham	31.85	0.9	43.66	1.2	–27.0
Crackers	31.70	0.9	28.08	0.8	12.9

	2007		2000		
	average household spending	percent distribution	average household spending (in 2007$)	percent distribution	percent change 2000–07
Vegetables, frozen	$31.34	0.9%	$31.81	0.9%	−1.5%
Potatoes, fresh	31.19	0.9	33.80	0.9	−7.7
Fats and oils	30.63	0.9	28.12	0.8	8.9
Pork chops	28.87	0.8	48.85	1.3	−40.9
Tea	28.63	0.8	18.88	0.5	51.6
Poultry (except chicken)	28.35	0.8	37.00	1.0	−23.4
Bananas	28.32	0.8	38.17	1.0	−25.8
Bacon	27.84	0.8	31.37	0.9	−11.2
Salad dressings	27.15	0.8	32.73	0.9	−17.0
Bakery products, frozen and refrigerated	26.27	0.8	29.54	0.8	−11.1
Sausage	25.58	0.7	30.39	0.8	−15.8
Pasta, cornmeal, other cereal products	24.77	0.7	34.48	0.9	−28.2
Baking needs and miscellaneous products	24.60	0.7	20.42	0.6	20.5
Salt, spices, and other seasonings	24.07	0.7	24.86	0.7	−3.2
Fruit–flavored drinks, noncarbonated	23.96	0.7	23.38	0.6	2.5
Lettuce	23.79	0.7	24.98	0.7	−4.8
Oranges	22.19	0.6	22.79	0.6	−2.6
Jams, preserves, other sweets	21.81	0.6	23.91	0.7	−8.8
Sweetrolls, coffee cakes, and doughnuts	21.18	0.6	27.31	0.8	−22.4
Butter	20.11	0.6	20.47	0.6	−1.8
Fruit, canned	19.47	0.6	18.64	0.5	4.5
Coffee, instant and freeze-dried	19.07	0.6	17.28	0.5	10.4
Frankfurters	18.73	0.5	24.90	0.7	−24.8
Vegetables, canned (except beans, corn)	18.53	0.5	21.61	0.6	−14.3
Citrus fruit, fresh (other than oranges)	17.77	0.5	17.23	0.5	3.1
Fruit juice, fresh	17.21	0.5	28.22	0.8	−39.0
Rice	16.60	0.5	23.54	0.6	−29.5
Sugar	16.49	0.5	20.23	0.6	−18.5
Fish and seafood, canned	16.35	0.5	18.87	0.5	−13.3
Vegetable juice, fresh and canned	15.56	0.4	11.20	0.3	39.0
Cream	15.53	0.4	13.98	0.4	11.1
Pies, tarts, and turnovers	14.96	0.4	15.99	0.4	−6.4
Nondairy cream and imitation milk	13.56	0.4	11.02	0.3	23.1
Peanut butter	12.87	0.4	14.22	0.4	−9.5
Vegetables, canned beans	12.82	0.4	15.26	0.4	−16.0
Olives, pickles, and relishes	12.80	0.4	11.76	0.3	8.8
Desserts, prepared	12.30	0.4	11.21	0.3	9.7
Flour, prepared mixes	11.60	0.3	16.07	0.4	−27.8
Vegetables, dried (except beans)	8.21	0.2	9.10	0.3	−9.8
Margarine	7.04	0.2	13.98	0.4	−49.6
Fruit juice, frozen	6.13	0.2	12.93	0.4	−52.6
Artificial sweeteners	5.83	0.2	5.05	0.1	15.6
Vegetables, canned corn	5.37	0.2	8.19	0.2	−34.4
Flour	5.14	0.1	9.61	0.3	−46.5
Fruit, frozen	4.97	0.1	4.36	0.1	14.0
Bread and cracker products	4.10	0.1	5.31	0.1	−22.8
Vegetables, dried beans	2.73	0.1	3.05	0.1	−10.4

* Data for 2007 and 2000 are not comparable because of change in methodology.
Note: Numbers do not add to total because not all categories are shown. "–" means data are unavailable.
Source: Bureau of Labor Statistics, 2000 and 2007 Consumer Expenditure Surveys; calculations by New Strategist

Apples

Best customers:

Householders aged 35 to 54
Married couples with children at home
Asians

Customer trends:

Average household spending on apples may fall as more boomers become empty-nesters and household size shrinks.

The largest households spend the most on apples. Married couples with children at home spend 54 percent more than the average household on apples. Householders aged 35 to 54, most with children at home, spend 18 percent more than average on apples. Asians spend 51 percent more.

Average household spending on apples declined 2 percent between 2000 and 2007, after adjusting for inflation. Behind the decline was the large baby-boom generation moving out of the lifestage when household size peaks. Average household spending on apples may fall as more boomers become empty-nesters and household size shrinks.

Table 9.2 Apples

Total household spending $4,199,976,450.00
Average household spends   34.95

	AVERAGE HOUSEHOLD SPENDING	BEST CUSTOMERS (index)	BIGGEST CUSTOMERS (market share)
AGE OF HOUSEHOLDER			
Average household	**$34.95**	**100**	**100.0%**
Under age 25	19.79	57	3.8
Aged 25 to 34	30.12	86	14.7
Aged 35 to 44	41.25	118	23.0
Aged 45 to 54	41.21	118	24.8
Aged 55 to 64	36.39	104	16.9
Aged 65 to 74	33.53	96	9.6
Aged 75 or older	27.49	79	7.5

	AVERAGE HOUSEHOLD SPENDING	BEST CUSTOMERS (index)	BIGGEST CUSTOMERS (market share)
HOUSEHOLD INCOME			
Average household	**$34.95**	**100**	**100.0%**
Under $20,000	19.60	56	11.5
$20,000 to $39,999	24.99	72	16.6
$40,000 to $49,999	33.76	97	9.5
$50,000 to $69,999	37.10	106	16.2
$70,000 to $79,999	41.02	117	6.8
$80,000 to $99,999	43.57	125	10.1
$100,000 or more	59.09	169	29.0
HOUSEHOLD TYPE			
Average household	**34.95**	**100**	**100.0**
Married couples	46.00	132	66.5
Married couples, no children	37.63	108	23.2
Married couples, with children	53.94	154	38.5
Oldest child under age 6	43.25	124	6.0
Oldest child aged 6 to 17	58.30	167	21.2
Oldest child aged 18 or older	53.14	152	11.2
Single parent with child under age 18	29.10	83	4.9
Single person	19.46	56	16.6
RACE AND HISPANIC ORIGIN			
Average household	**34.95**	**100**	**100.0**
Asian	52.77	151	5.3
Black	24.39	70	8.4
Hispanic	34.06	97	11.5
Non-Hispanic white and other	36.70	105	80.2
REGION			
Average household	**34.95**	**100**	**100.0**
Northeast	35.86	103	19.1
Midwest	33.03	95	21.6
South	32.33	93	33.2
West	40.38	116	26.1
EDUCATION			
Average household	**34.95**	**100**	**100.0**
Less than high school graduate	28.21	81	12.2
High school graduate	27.30	78	19.7
Some college	33.39	96	20.8
Associate's degree	32.53	93	8.3
College graduate	46.53	133	38.5
Bachelor's degree	40.23	115	21.6
Master's, professional, doctoral degree	57.47	164	16.8

Note: Market shares may not sum to 100.0 because of rounding and missing categories by household type. "Asian" and "black" include Hispanics and non-Hispanics who identify themselves as being of the respective race alone. "Hispanic" includes people of any race who identify themselves as Hispanic. "Other" includes people who identify themselves as non-Hispanic and as Alaska Native, American Indian, Asian (who are also included in the "Asian" row), Native Hawaiian or other Pacific Islander, as well as non-Hispanics reporting more than one race.
Source: Calculations by New Strategist based on the Bureau of Labor Statistics' 2007 Consumer Expenditure Survey.

Artificial Sweeteners

Best customers:

Householders aged 55 or older
Married couples without children at home
Married couples with school-aged or older children at home
Non-Hispanic whites
Households in the South

Customer trends:

Average household spending on artificial sweeteners may rise as boomers fill the oldest age groups.

Older householders spend the most on artificial sweeteners. Householders aged 55 or older spend 27 to 40 percent more on artificial sweeteners than the average household and control 47 percent of the market. Married couples without children at home (most of them empty-nesters) spend 53 percent more than the average household on this item, while married couples with school-aged or older children at home spend 17 to 28 percent more. Households in the South spend 19 percent more. Non-Hispanic whites spend 13 percent more than the average household on artificial sweeteners.

Average household spending on artificial sweeteners increased by 16 percent between 2000 and 2007, after adjusting for inflation. One factor behind the increase was the growing popularity of Splenda as a substitute for sugar. Spending on artificial sweeteners is likely to continue to rise as boomers fill the oldest age groups and increasingly overweight Americans try to cut calories.

Table 9.3 Artificial sweeteners

Total household spending $700,596,930.00
Average household spends 5.83

AGE OF HOUSEHOLDER	AVERAGE HOUSEHOLD SPENDING	BEST CUSTOMERS (index)	BIGGEST CUSTOMERS (market share)
Average household	$5.83	100	100.0%
Under age 25	2.20	38	2.6
Aged 25 to 34	3.71	64	10.9
Aged 35 to 44	6.74	116	22.5
Aged 45 to 54	4.84	83	17.4
Aged 55 to 64	7.40	127	20.6
Aged 65 to 74	8.19	140	14.0
Aged 75 or older	7.56	130	12.3

	AVERAGE HOUSEHOLD SPENDING	BEST CUSTOMERS (index)	BIGGEST CUSTOMERS (market share)
HOUSEHOLD INCOME			
Average household	$5.83	100	100.0%
Under $20,000	3.13	54	11.0
$20,000 to $39,999	4.60	79	18.3
$40,000 to $49,999	5.02	86	8.5
$50,000 to $69,999	6.93	119	18.2
$70,000 to $79,999	3.86	66	3.8
$80,000 to $99,999	8.91	153	12.4
$100,000 or more	9.35	160	27.5
HOUSEHOLD TYPE			
Average household	5.83	100	100.0
Married couples	7.90	136	68.5
Married couples, no children	8.92	153	33.0
Married couples, with children	6.80	117	29.1
Oldest child under age 6	4.95	85	4.1
Oldest child aged 6 to 17	7.46	128	16.3
Oldest child aged 18 or older	6.84	117	8.6
Single parent with child under age 18	3.32	57	3.4
Single person	2.53	43	12.9
RACE AND HISPANIC ORIGIN			
Average household	5.83	100	100.0
Asian	2.93	50	1.8
Black	3.97	68	8.2
Hispanic	2.66	46	5.4
Non-Hispanic white and other	6.57	113	86.0
REGION			
Average household	5.83	100	100.0
Northeast	5.51	95	17.6
Midwest	3.70	63	14.5
South	6.92	119	42.6
West	6.56	113	25.4
EDUCATION			
Average household	5.83	100	100.0
Less than high school graduate	4.26	73	11.1
High school graduate	6.47	111	28.0
Some college	5.26	90	19.6
Associate's degree	5.36	92	8.2
College graduate	6.57	113	32.6
Bachelor's degree	5.80	99	18.6
Master's, professional, doctoral degree	7.89	135	13.8

Note: Market shares may not sum to 100.0 because of rounding and missing categories by household type. "Asian" and "black" include Hispanics and non-Hispanics who identify themselves as being of the respective race alone. "Hispanic" includes people of any race who identify themselves as Hispanic. "Other" includes people who identify themselves as non-Hispanic and as Alaska Native, American Indian, Asian (who are also included in the "Asian" row), Native Hawaiian or other Pacific Islander, as well as non-Hispanics reporting more than one race.
Source: Calculations by New Strategist based on the Bureau of Labor Statistics' 2007 Consumer Expenditure Survey.

Baby Food

Best customers:
Householders under age 35
Married couples with preschoolers
Single parents
Hispanics

Customer trends:
Average household spending on baby food is likely to rise as the large millennial generation fills the family formation lifestage, but low incomes may limit the increase.

Not surprisingly, married couples with preschoolers spend more on baby food than any other household type—almost seven times the amount the average household spends. Householders under age 35, many with infants, spend two to two-and-one-half times the average on baby food and control 56 percent of the market. Hispanics, who have larger-than-average families, spend 42 percent more than average on baby food.

Average household spending on baby food grew 9 percent between 2000 and 2007, after adjusting for inflation. As the millennial generation fills the family formation lifestage, average household spending on baby food should continue to rise, but low incomes may limit the increase.

Table 9.4 Baby food

Total household spending $5,088,040,140.00
Average household spends 42.34

AGE OF HOUSEHOLDER	AVERAGE HOUSEHOLD SPENDING	BEST CUSTOMERS (index)	BIGGEST CUSTOMERS (market share)
Average household	$42.34	100	100.0%
Under age 25	105.68	250	16.9
Aged 25 to 34	97.18	230	39.2
Aged 35 to 44	47.87	113	22.0
Aged 45 to 54	19.32	46	9.6
Aged 55 to 64	18.27	43	7.0
Aged 65 to 74	8.33	20	2.0
Aged 75 or older	10.10	24	2.3

	AVERAGE HOUSEHOLD SPENDING	BEST CUSTOMERS (index)	BIGGEST CUSTOMERS (market share)
HOUSEHOLD INCOME			
Average household	**$42.34**	**100**	**100.0%**
Under $20,000	15.99	38	7.8
$20,000 to $39,999	49.40	117	27.1
$40,000 to $49,999	48.04	113	11.2
$50,000 to $69,999	34.01	80	12.3
$70,000 to $79,999	37.66	89	5.1
$80,000 to $99,999	74.95	177	14.4
$100,000 or more	51.58	122	20.9
HOUSEHOLD TYPE			
Average household	**42.34**	**100**	**100.0**
Married couples	58.15	137	69.4
Married couples, no children	16.86	40	8.6
Married couples, with children	93.98	222	55.4
Oldest child under age 6	282.59	667	32.6
Oldest child aged 6 to 17	55.17	130	16.6
Oldest child aged 18 or older	32.39	76	5.6
Single parent with child under age 18	83.65	198	11.7
Single person	6.32	15	4.4
RACE AND HISPANIC ORIGIN			
Average household	**42.34**	**100**	**100.0**
Asian	33.69	80	2.8
Black	41.47	98	11.8
Hispanic	60.10	142	16.8
Non-Hispanic white and other	39.91	94	72.0
REGION			
Average household	**42.34**	**100**	**100.0**
Northeast	39.66	94	17.4
Midwest	33.03	78	17.8
South	44.79	106	38.0
West	50.25	119	26.8
EDUCATION			
Average household	**42.34**	**100**	**100.0**
Less than high school graduate	47.21	112	16.9
High school graduate	41.93	99	25.0
Some college	32.98	78	17.0
Associate's degree	80.48	190	16.9
College graduate	36.22	86	24.8
Bachelor's degree	36.40	86	16.1
Master's, professional, doctoral degree	35.91	85	8.7

Note: Market shares may not sum to 100.0 because of rounding and missing categories by household type. "Asian" and "black" include Hispanics and non-Hispanics who identify themselves as being of the respective race alone. "Hispanic" includes people of any race who identify themselves as Hispanic. "Other" includes people who identify themselves as non-Hispanic and as Alaska Native, American Indian, Asian (who are also included in the "Asian" row), Native Hawaiian or other Pacific Islander, as well as non-Hispanics reporting more than one race.
Source: Calculations by New Strategist based on the Bureau of Labor Statistics' 2007 Consumer Expenditure Survey.

Bacon

Best customers:	Married couples with school-aged or older children at home
	Single parents
	Blacks

Customer trends:	Average household spending on bacon could fall as more boomers become empty-nesters and household size shrinks.

Households with children spend the most on bacon. Married couples with school-aged children spend 30 percent more than average on bacon, while those with adult children at home spend 96 percent more. Blacks spend 8 percent more than the average household on this item, and single parents spend 7 percent more.

Average household spending on bacon fell 11 percent between 2000 and 2007, after adjusting for inflation. One factor behind the spending decline is the growing propensity for households to eat fast-food breakfasts or no breakfast at all. Average household spending on bacon could continue to fall as more boomers become empty-nesters and household size shrinks.

Table 9.5 Bacon

Total household spending	$3,345,560,640.00
Average household spends	27.84

	AVERAGE HOUSEHOLD SPENDING	BEST CUSTOMERS (index)	BIGGEST CUSTOMERS (market share)
AGE OF HOUSEHOLDER			
Average household	**$27.84**	**100**	**100.0%**
Under age 25	17.29	62	4.2
Aged 25 to 34	24.79	89	15.2
Aged 35 to 44	31.44	113	22.0
Aged 45 to 54	31.19	112	23.5
Aged 55 to 64	30.20	108	17.6
Aged 65 to 74	32.26	116	11.6
Aged 75 or older	17.67	63	6.0

	AVERAGE HOUSEHOLD SPENDING	BEST CUSTOMERS (index)	BIGGEST CUSTOMERS (market share)
HOUSEHOLD INCOME			
Average household	$27.84	100	100.0%
Under $20,000	16.82	60	12.4
$20,000 to $39,999	24.89	89	20.8
$40,000 to $49,999	25.35	91	9.0
$50,000 to $69,999	30.20	108	16.6
$70,000 to $79,999	36.80	132	7.7
$80,000 to $99,999	38.75	139	11.3
$100,000 or more	35.31	127	21.7
HOUSEHOLD TYPE			
Average household	27.84	100	100.0
Married couples	34.78	125	63.2
Married couples, no children	28.97	104	22.4
Married couples, with children	39.29	141	35.2
Oldest child under age 6	26.53	95	4.7
Oldest child aged 6 to 17	36.33	130	16.6
Oldest child aged 18 or older	54.50	196	14.4
Single parent with child under age 18	29.81	107	6.4
Single person	15.22	55	16.3
RACE AND HISPANIC ORIGIN			
Average household	27.84	100	100.0
Asian	24.60	88	3.1
Black	30.00	108	12.9
Hispanic	22.54	81	9.6
Non-Hispanic white and other	28.27	102	77.5
REGION			
Average household	27.84	100	100.0
Northeast	26.99	97	18.1
Midwest	25.42	91	20.9
South	29.61	106	38.2
West	28.17	101	22.9
EDUCATION			
Average household	27.84	100	100.0
Less than high school graduate	29.18	105	15.9
High school graduate	30.42	109	27.6
Some college	26.86	96	21.0
Associate's degree	26.85	96	8.6
College graduate	25.96	93	27.0
Bachelor's degree	23.89	86	16.1
Master's, professional, doctoral degree	29.55	106	10.8

Note: Market shares may not sum to 100.0 because of rounding and missing categories by household type. "Asian" and "black" include Hispanics and non-Hispanics who identify themselves as being of the respective race alone. "Hispanic" includes people of any race who identify themselves as Hispanic. "Other" includes people who identify themselves as non-Hispanic and as Alaska Native, American Indian, Asian (who are also included in the "Asian" row), Native Hawaiian or other Pacific Islander, as well as non-Hispanics reporting more than one race.
Source: Calculations by New Strategist based on the Bureau of Labor Statistics' 2007 Consumer Expenditure Survey.

Bakery Products, Frozen and Refrigerated

Best customers: Householders aged 35 to 54
Married couples with school-aged or older children at home
Single parents

Customer trends: Average household spending on frozen and refrigerated bakery products should continue to fall as the small generation X fills the best-customer age group.

Households with children spend the most on frozen and refrigerated bakery products. Married couples with school-aged or older children at home spend 70 to 92 percent more than the average household on this item. Many are busy two-earner couples trying to save time by buying heat-and-serve foods. Householders aged 35 to 54, most with children at home, spend 22 to 27 percent more than average on this item. Single parents spend 10 percent more.

Average household spending on frozen and refrigerated bakery products fell 11 percent between 2000 and 2007, after adjusting for inflation. Behind the decline is the ongoing shift away from meal preparation and toward fast-food meals and snacking. Average household spending on frozen and refrigerated bakery products may continue to decline as the small generation X fills the best-customer age group.

Table 9.6 Bakery products, frozen and refrigerated

Total household spending $3,156,892,170.00
Average household spends   26.27

AGE OF HOUSEHOLDER	AVERAGE HOUSEHOLD SPENDING	BEST CUSTOMERS (index)	BIGGEST CUSTOMERS (market share)
Average household	$26.27	100	100.0%
Under age 25	12.05	46	3.1
Aged 25 to 34	24.49	93	15.9
Aged 35 to 44	32.00	122	23.7
Aged 45 to 54	33.29	127	26.6
Aged 55 to 64	23.85	91	14.7
Aged 65 to 74	21.97	84	8.4
Aged 75 or older	21.77	83	7.9

	AVERAGE HOUSEHOLD SPENDING	BEST CUSTOMERS (index)	BIGGEST CUSTOMERS (market share)
HOUSEHOLD INCOME			
Average household	**$26.27**	**100**	**100.0%**
Under $20,000	15.29	58	12.0
$20,000 to $39,999	19.50	74	17.2
$40,000 to $49,999	22.08	84	8.3
$50,000 to $69,999	28.52	109	16.6
$70,000 to $79,999	31.10	118	6.9
$80,000 to $99,999	37.64	143	11.7
$100,000 or more	41.54	158	27.1
HOUSEHOLD TYPE			
Average household	**26.27**	**100**	**100.0**
Married couples	35.40	135	68.1
Married couples, no children	26.67	102	21.9
Married couples, with children	42.79	163	40.6
Oldest child under age 6	27.63	105	5.1
Oldest child aged 6 to 17	44.55	170	21.5
Oldest child aged 18 or older	50.45	192	14.1
Single parent with child under age 18	28.81	110	6.5
Single person	12.95	49	14.7
RACE AND HISPANIC ORIGIN			
Average household	**26.27**	**100**	**100.0**
Asian	21.64	82	2.9
Black	22.46	85	10.3
Hispanic	19.29	73	8.7
Non-Hispanic white and other	27.82	106	80.8
REGION			
Average household	**26.27**	**100**	**100.0**
Northeast	24.51	93	17.4
Midwest	26.29	100	22.9
South	27.95	106	38.2
West	25.04	95	21.6
EDUCATION			
Average household	**26.27**	**100**	**100.0**
Less than high school graduate	19.70	75	11.4
High school graduate	24.35	93	23.4
Some college	26.08	99	21.6
Associate's degree	30.08	115	10.2
College graduate	30.03	114	33.1
Bachelor's degree	29.97	114	21.4
Master's, professional, doctoral degree	30.13	115	11.7

Note: Market shares may not sum to 100.0 because of rounding and missing categories by household type. "Asian" and "black" include Hispanics and non-Hispanics who identify themselves as being of the respective race alone. "Hispanic" includes people of any race who identify themselves as Hispanic. "Other" includes people who identify themselves as non-Hispanic and as Alaska Native, American Indian, Asian (who are also included in the "Asian" row), Native Hawaiian or other Pacific Islander, as well as non-Hispanics reporting more than one race.
Source: Calculations by New Strategist based on the Bureau of Labor Statistics' 2007 Consumer Expenditure Survey.

Baking Needs and Miscellaneous Products

Best customers: Householders aged 35 to 54
Married couples with school-aged or older children at home

Customer trends: Average household spending on products for baking is likely to fall as
cooking-challenged younger generations marry and have children.

Although cooking from scratch has become a lot less common than it once was, many people enjoy whipping up a home-cooked meal or dessert every now and then. Most are married couples, often with children at home. Married couples with school-aged or older children at home spend 57 to 62 percent more than the average household on products for baking and account for 32 percent of the market. Householders ranging in age from 35 to 54 spend 16 to 20 percent more than average on baking needs.

Average household spending on products for baking rose 20 percent between 2000 and 2007, after adjusting for inflation. The popularity of televised cooking programs may account for some of the increase. In the long-term, however, average household spending on products for baking is likely to decline as cooking-challenged younger generations marry and have children.

Table 9.7 Baking needs and miscellaneous products

Total household spending $2,956,206,600.00
Average household spends   24.60

	AVERAGE HOUSEHOLD SPENDING	BEST CUSTOMERS (index)	BIGGEST CUSTOMERS (market share)
AGE OF HOUSEHOLDER			
Average household	**$24.60**	**100**	**100.0%**
Under age 25	12.75	52	3.5
Aged 25 to 34	22.18	90	15.4
Aged 35 to 44	28.58	116	22.6
Aged 45 to 54	29.48	120	25.2
Aged 55 to 64	24.75	101	16.3
Aged 65 to 74	26.64	108	10.8
Aged 75 or older	16.46	67	6.3

	AVERAGE HOUSEHOLD SPENDING	BEST CUSTOMERS (index)	BIGGEST CUSTOMERS (market share)
HOUSEHOLD INCOME			
Average household	**$24.60**	**100**	**100.0%**
Under $20,000	11.59	47	9.7
$20,000 to $39,999	18.49	75	17.5
$40,000 to $49,999	19.08	78	7.6
$50,000 to $69,999	28.20	115	17.5
$70,000 to $79,999	32.25	131	7.6
$80,000 to $99,999	36.35	148	12.0
$100,000 or more	39.81	162	27.7
HOUSEHOLD TYPE			
Average household	**24.60**	**100**	**100.0**
Married couples	33.23	135	68.3
Married couples, no children	28.77	117	25.2
Married couples, with children	36.66	149	37.2
Oldest child under age 6	25.10	102	5.0
Oldest child aged 6 to 17	39.97	162	20.6
Oldest child aged 18 or older	38.60	157	11.6
Single parent with child under age 18	14.39	58	3.5
Single person	11.05	45	13.4
RACE AND HISPANIC ORIGIN			
Average household	**24.60**	**100**	**100.0**
Asian	22.05	90	3.2
Black	13.74	56	6.7
Hispanic	10.72	44	5.1
Non-Hispanic white and other	28.22	115	87.6
REGION			
Average household	**24.60**	**100**	**100.0**
Northeast	26.25	107	19.9
Midwest	27.72	113	25.8
South	21.82	89	31.9
West	24.45	99	22.5
EDUCATION			
Average household	**24.60**	**100**	**100.0**
Less than high school graduate	15.05	61	9.3
High school graduate	21.96	89	22.5
Some college	22.02	90	19.5
Associate's degree	29.47	120	10.6
College graduate	31.76	129	37.4
Bachelor's degree	28.85	117	22.0
Master's, professional, doctoral degree	36.81	150	15.3

Note: Market shares may not sum to 100.0 because of rounding and missing categories by household type. "Asian" and "black" include Hispanics and non-Hispanics who identify themselves as being of the respective race alone. "Hispanic" includes people of any race who identify themselves as Hispanic. "Other" includes people who identify themselves as non-Hispanic and as Alaska Native, American Indian, Asian (who are also included in the "Asian" row), Native Hawaiian or other Pacific Islander, as well as non-Hispanics reporting more than one race.
Source: Calculations by New Strategist based on the Bureau of Labor Statistics' 2007 Consumer Expenditure Survey.

Bananas

Best customers:	**Householders aged 35 to 54**
	Married couples
	Asians and Hispanics
Customer trends:	**Average household spending on bananas may continue to decline as more boomers become empty-nesters and household size shrinks.**

The largest households spend the most on bananas. Married couples with children at home spend 35 percent more than the average household on bananas. Householders aged 35 to 54, most with children at home, spend 8 to 13 percent more on bananas than the average household. Asians and Hispanics, who tend to have large families, spend, respectively, 42 and 28 percent more than average on bananas.

Average household spending on bananas fell 26 percent between 2000 and 2007, after adjusting for inflation. One factor behind the spending decline was the baby-boom generation's exit from the best-customer lifestage. Average household spending on bananas may continue to fall as more boomers become empty-nesters and household size shrinks.

Table 9.8 Bananas

Total household spending	$3,403,242,720.00
Average household spends	28.32

	AVERAGE HOUSEHOLD SPENDING	BEST CUSTOMERS (index)	BIGGEST CUSTOMERS (market share)
AGE OF HOUSEHOLDER			
Average household	**$28.32**	**100**	**100.0%**
Under age 25	15.38	54	3.7
Aged 25 to 34	24.93	88	15.0
Aged 35 to 44	30.49	108	21.0
Aged 45 to 54	31.97	113	23.7
Aged 55 to 64	29.34	104	16.8
Aged 65 to 74	30.02	106	10.6
Aged 75 or older	28.28	100	9.5

	AVERAGE HOUSEHOLD SPENDING	BEST CUSTOMERS (index)	BIGGEST CUSTOMERS (market share)
HOUSEHOLD INCOME			
Average household	**$28.32**	**100**	**100.0%**
Under $20,000	17.51	62	12.7
$20,000 to $39,999	25.11	89	20.6
$40,000 to $49,999	30.30	107	10.5
$50,000 to $69,999	30.18	107	16.3
$70,000 to $79,999	27.81	98	5.7
$80,000 to $99,999	29.17	103	8.4
$100,000 or more	42.49	150	25.7
HOUSEHOLD TYPE			
Average household	**28.32**	**100**	**100.0**
Married couples	35.78	126	63.9
Married couples, no children	31.84	112	24.3
Married couples, with children	38.12	135	33.6
Oldest child under age 6	33.09	117	5.7
Oldest child aged 6 to 17	38.32	135	17.2
Oldest child aged 18 or older	41.39	146	10.8
Single parent with child under age 18	24.39	86	5.1
Single person	17.31	61	18.2
RACE AND HISPANIC ORIGIN			
Average household	**28.32**	**100**	**100.0**
Asian	40.32	142	5.0
Black	22.99	81	9.7
Hispanic	36.36	128	15.2
Non-Hispanic white and other	28.01	99	75.5
REGION			
Average household	**28.32**	**100**	**100.0**
Northeast	31.80	112	20.9
Midwest	26.01	92	21.0
South	25.56	90	32.4
West	32.20	114	25.7
EDUCATION			
Average household	**28.32**	**100**	**100.0**
Less than high school graduate	26.52	94	14.2
High school graduate	25.31	89	22.5
Some college	25.02	88	19.2
Associate's degree	28.69	101	9.0
College graduate	34.04	120	34.8
Bachelor's degree	32.26	114	21.3
Master's, professional, doctoral degree	37.14	131	13.4

Note: Market shares may not sum to 100.0 because of rounding and missing categories by household type. "Asian" and "black" include Hispanics and non-Hispanics who identify themselves as being of the respective race alone. "Hispanic" includes people of any race who identify themselves as Hispanic. "Other" includes people who identify themselves as non-Hispanic and as Alaska Native, American Indian, Asian (who are also included in the "Asian" row), Native Hawaiian or other Pacific Islander, as well as non-Hispanics reporting more than one race.
Source: Calculations by New Strategist based on the Bureau of Labor Statistics' 2007 Consumer Expenditure Survey.

Biscuits and Rolls

Best customers:
Householders aged 35 to 54
Married couples with school-aged or older children at home
Households in the Northeast

Customer trends:
Average household spending on biscuits and rolls may continue to decline as more boomers become empty-nesters and household size shrinks.

The largest households spend the most on biscuits and rolls. Married couples with school-aged children spend 55 percent more than the average household on this item, while those with adult children at home spend 70 percent more. Householders aged 35 to 54, many with children at home, spend 17 to 24 percent more than average on biscuits and rolls and control 49 percent of the market. Households in the Northeast spend 30 more than average on this item.

Average household spending on biscuits and rolls fell 4 percent between 2000 and 2007, after adjusting for inflation. Average household spending on biscuits and rolls may continue to decline as more boomers become empty-nesters and household size shrinks.

Table 9.9 **Biscuits and rolls**

Total household spending $5,325,978,720.00
Average household spends 44.32

	AVERAGE HOUSEHOLD SPENDING	BEST CUSTOMERS (index)	BIGGEST CUSTOMERS (market share)
AGE OF HOUSEHOLDER			
Average household	**$44.32**	**100**	**100.0%**
Under age 25	26.59	60	4.1
Aged 25 to 34	35.35	80	13.6
Aged 35 to 44	52.02	117	22.9
Aged 45 to 54	54.75	124	26.0
Aged 55 to 64	47.75	108	17.4
Aged 65 to 74	42.41	96	9.6
Aged 75 or older	31.47	71	6.7

	AVERAGE HOUSEHOLD SPENDING	BEST CUSTOMERS (index)	BIGGEST CUSTOMERS (market share)
HOUSEHOLD INCOME			
Average household	**$44.32**	**100**	**100.0%**
Under $20,000	21.43	48	9.9
$20,000 to $39,999	32.04	72	16.8
$40,000 to $49,999	41.33	93	9.2
$50,000 to $69,999	49.75	112	17.2
$70,000 to $79,999	52.49	118	6.9
$80,000 to $99,999	60.80	137	11.2
$100,000 or more	74.18	167	28.7
HOUSEHOLD TYPE			
Average household	**44.32**	**100**	**100.0**
Married couples	58.21	131	66.4
Married couples, no children	49.51	112	24.1
Married couples, with children	65.90	149	37.1
Oldest child under age 6	45.73	103	5.0
Oldest child aged 6 to 17	68.63	155	19.7
Oldest child aged 18 or older	75.31	170	12.5
Single parent with child under age 18	39.30	89	5.3
Single person	21.85	49	14.7
RACE AND HISPANIC ORIGIN			
Average household	**44.32**	**100**	**100.0**
Asian	50.45	114	4.0
Black	26.78	60	7.3
Hispanic	32.60	74	8.7
Non-Hispanic white and other	48.66	110	83.8
REGION			
Average household	**44.32**	**100**	**100.0**
Northeast	57.43	130	24.1
Midwest	42.49	96	21.9
South	39.19	88	31.8
West	43.37	98	22.1
EDUCATION			
Average household	**44.32**	**100**	**100.0**
Less than high school graduate	34.66	78	11.9
High school graduate	42.21	95	24.0
Some college	40.32	91	19.8
Associate's degree	49.80	112	10.0
College graduate	51.94	117	33.9
Bachelor's degree	49.66	112	21.0
Master's, professional, doctoral degree	55.91	126	12.9

Note: Market shares may not sum to 100.0 because of rounding and missing categories by household type. "Asian" and "black" include Hispanics and non-Hispanics who identify themselves as being of the respective race alone. "Hispanic" includes people of any race who identify themselves as Hispanic. "Other" includes people who identify themselves as non-Hispanic and as Alaska Native, American Indian, Asian (who are also included in the "Asian" row), Native Hawaiian or other Pacific Islander, as well as non-Hispanics reporting more than one race.
Source: Calculations by New Strategist based on the Bureau of Labor Statistics' 2007 Consumer Expenditure Survey.

Bread and Cracker Products

Best customers: Married couples with school-aged or older children at home
Non-Hispanic whites
Households in the Northeast

Customer trends: Average household spending on bread and cracker products will continue to decline as restaurant and carry-out meals replace home cooking among the younger generations.

Cooking from scratch has become a lot less common than it once was, and households cut their spending on many basic ingredients such as bread and cracker products. The biggest spenders on bread and cracker products are married couples with school-aged or older children at home. These households spend 68 to 105 percent more than average on this item. Non-Hispanic whites outspend minority householders by a large margin and account for 90 percent of the market. Households in the Northeast spend 35 percent more than average on bread and cracker products.

Average household spending on bread and cracker products fell 23 percent between 2000 and 2007, after adjusting for inflation. Behind the decline was the baby-boom generation's exit from the best customer lifestage. Average household spending on bread and cracker products is likely to continue to decline as restaurant and carry-out meals replace home cooking among the younger generations.

Table 9.10 Bread and cracker products

Total household spending $492,701,100.00
Average household spends   4.10

	AVERAGE HOUSEHOLD SPENDING	BEST CUSTOMERS (index)	BIGGEST CUSTOMERS (market share)
AGE OF HOUSEHOLDER			
Average household	**$4.10**	**100**	**100.0%**
Under age 25	2.95	72	4.9
Aged 25 to 34	3.08	75	12.8
Aged 35 to 44	5.12	125	24.3
Aged 45 to 54	4.67	114	23.9
Aged 55 to 64	3.98	97	15.7
Aged 65 to 74	4.91	120	12.0
Aged 75 or older	2.82	69	6.5

	AVERAGE HOUSEHOLD SPENDING	BEST CUSTOMERS (index)	BIGGEST CUSTOMERS (market share)
HOUSEHOLD INCOME			
Average household	**$4.10**	**100**	**100.0%**
Under $20,000	1.48	36	7.4
$20,000 to $39,999	3.01	74	17.1
$40,000 to $49,999	3.71	90	8.9
$50,000 to $69,999	4.87	119	18.2
$70,000 to $79,999	4.93	120	7.0
$80,000 to $99,999	5.28	129	10.5
$100,000 or more	7.39	180	30.9
HOUSEHOLD TYPE			
Average household	**4.10**	**100**	**100.0**
Married couples	5.66	138	69.8
Married couples, no children	4.78	117	25.1
Married couples, with children	6.78	165	41.3
Oldest child under age 6	4.29	105	5.1
Oldest child aged 6 to 17	6.87	168	21.3
Oldest child aged 18 or older	8.42	205	15.1
Single parent with child under age 18	2.83	69	4.1
Single person	1.74	42	12.6
RACE AND HISPANIC ORIGIN			
Average household	**4.10**	**100**	**100.0**
Asian	1.35	33	1.2
Black	1.60	39	4.7
Hispanic	1.98	48	5.7
Non-Hispanic white and other	4.79	117	89.2
REGION			
Average household	**4.10**	**100**	**100.0**
Northeast	5.54	135	25.2
Midwest	3.63	89	20.2
South	3.42	83	30.0
West	4.48	109	24.7
EDUCATION			
Average household	**4.10**	**100**	**100.0**
Less than high school graduate	2.37	58	8.8
High school graduate	3.02	74	18.6
Some college	4.36	106	23.2
Associate's degree	4.70	115	10.2
College graduate	5.49	134	38.8
Bachelor's degree	5.54	135	25.3
Master's, professional, doctoral degree	5.40	132	13.4

Note: Market shares may not sum to 100.0 because of rounding and missing categories by household type. "Asian" and "black" include Hispanics and non-Hispanics who identify themselves as being of the respective race alone. "Hispanic" includes people of any race who identify themselves as Hispanic. "Other" includes people who identify themselves as non-Hispanic and as Alaska Native, American Indian, Asian (who are also included in the "Asian" row), Native Hawaiian or other Pacific Islander, as well as non-Hispanics reporting more than one race.
Source: Calculations by New Strategist based on the Bureau of Labor Statistics' 2007 Consumer Expenditure Survey.

Bread, Other than White

Best customers: Householders aged 45 to 74
Married couples with school-aged or older children at home

Customer trends: Average household spending on nonwhite bread should remain stable as households switch from white to other types of bread, but shrinking household size may limit any gains.

Bread took a beating in the past few years as low-carb diets waxed and waned in popularity. Nonwhite bread held its own, however. In 2000, nonwhite bread accounted for 56 percent of total household spending on bread. By 2007, the figure had grown to 62 percent of the total. The best customers of nonwhite bread are the largest households. Married couples with school-aged or older children at home spend 45 to 62 percent more than the average household on this item. Householders ranging in age from 45 to 74 spend 12 to 21 percent more than average on nonwhite bread.

Spending on nonwhite bread fell slightly between 2000 and 2007, down by 3 percent after adjusting for inflation. During those years, spending on white bread fell by a much larger 23 percent as buyers switched to more nutritional whole-grain breads. Average household spending on nonwhite bread should remain stable as households shift away from white, but shrinking household size could take a toll on bread buying in the years ahead.

Table 9.11 Bread, other than white

Total household spending $6,647,859,720.00
Average household spends 55.32

	AVERAGE HOUSEHOLD SPENDING	BEST CUSTOMERS (index)	BIGGEST CUSTOMERS (market share)
AGE OF HOUSEHOLDER			
Average household	$55.32	100	100.0%
Under age 25	26.89	49	3.3
Aged 25 to 34	45.42	82	14.0
Aged 35 to 44	58.87	106	20.7
Aged 45 to 54	66.94	121	25.4
Aged 55 to 64	62.17	112	18.2
Aged 65 to 74	62.07	112	11.2
Aged 75 or older	43.19	78	7.4

	AVERAGE HOUSEHOLD SPENDING	BEST CUSTOMERS (index)	BIGGEST CUSTOMERS (market share)
HOUSEHOLD INCOME			
Average household	**$55.32**	**100**	**100.0%**
Under $20,000	33.55	61	12.5
$20,000 to $39,999	45.41	82	19.1
$40,000 to $49,999	52.04	94	9.3
$50,000 to $69,999	57.11	103	15.8
$70,000 to $79,999	65.78	119	6.9
$80,000 to $99,999	72.66	131	10.7
$100,000 or more	82.50	149	25.5
HOUSEHOLD TYPE			
Average household	**55.32**	**100**	**100.0**
Married couples	71.62	129	65.4
Married couples, no children	62.13	112	24.2
Married couples, with children	78.78	142	35.5
Oldest child under age 6	59.37	107	5.2
Oldest child aged 6 to 17	80.48	145	18.5
Oldest child aged 18 or older	89.67	162	11.9
Single parent with child under age 18	45.93	83	4.9
Single person	32.22	58	17.3
RACE AND HISPANIC ORIGIN			
Average household	**55.32**	**100**	**100.0**
Asian	52.51	95	3.3
Black	40.48	73	8.8
Hispanic	48.03	87	10.2
Non-Hispanic white and other	58.62	106	80.9
REGION			
Average household	**55.32**	**100**	**100.0**
Northeast	58.03	105	19.5
Midwest	55.56	100	23.0
South	50.84	92	33.0
West	60.01	108	24.5
EDUCATION			
Average household	**55.32**	**100**	**100.0**
Less than high school graduate	41.89	76	11.5
High school graduate	53.04	96	24.2
Some college	50.26	91	19.8
Associate's degree	56.11	101	9.0
College graduate	66.94	121	35.0
Bachelor's degree	64.74	117	21.9
Master's, professional, doctoral degree	70.75	128	13.0

Note: Market shares may not sum to 100.0 because of rounding and missing categories by household type. "Asian" and "black" include Hispanics and non-Hispanics who identify themselves as being of the respective race alone. "Hispanic" includes people of any race who identify themselves as Hispanic. "Other" includes people who identify themselves as non-Hispanic and as Alaska Native, American Indian, Asian (who are also included in the "Asian" row), Native Hawaiian or other Pacific Islander, as well as non-Hispanics reporting more than one race.
Source: Calculations by New Strategist based on the Bureau of Labor Statistics' 2007 Consumer Expenditure Survey.

Bread, White

Best customers: **Householders aged 35 to 54**
Married couples with school-aged or older children at home
Hispanics

Customer trends: **Average household spending on white bread will continue to fall as the small generation X moves into the best-customer age group and consumers switch to nonwhite bread.**

White bread accounts for only 38 percent of the average household's bread spending, down from 44 percent in 2000. The best customers of white bread are the largest households. Married couples with school-aged or older children at home spend 44 to 62 percent more than the average household on this item. Householders aged 35 to 54, many with children at home, spend 15 percent more than average on white bread. Hispanics, whose households tend to be larger than average, spend 14 percent more than the average household on white bread.

Average household spending on white bread declined by a large 23 percent between 2000 and 2007, while spending on nonwhite bread fell by just 3 percent, after adjusting for inflation. Average household spending on white bread should continue to fall as the small generation X fills the best-customer age group and consumers continue to switch to more nutritional, whole-grain bread.

Table 9.12 **Bread, white**

Total household spending $4,068,990,060.00
Average household spends   33.86

	AVERAGE HOUSEHOLD SPENDING	BEST CUSTOMERS (index)	BIGGEST CUSTOMERS (market share)
AGE OF HOUSEHOLDER			
Average household	**$33.86**	**100**	**100.0%**
Under age 25	23.13	68	4.6
Aged 25 to 34	31.68	94	16.0
Aged 35 to 44	38.99	115	22.4
Aged 45 to 54	38.88	115	24.1
Aged 55 to 64	34.61	102	16.6
Aged 65 to 74	33.04	98	9.8
Aged 75 or older	23.83	70	6.7

	AVERAGE HOUSEHOLD SPENDING	BEST CUSTOMERS (index)	BIGGEST CUSTOMERS (market share)
HOUSEHOLD INCOME			
Average household	**$33.86**	**100**	**100.0%**
Under $20,000	26.97	80	16.4
$20,000 to $39,999	28.55	84	19.6
$40,000 to $49,999	33.86	100	9.8
$50,000 to $69,999	35.51	105	16.0
$70,000 to $79,999	39.00	115	6.7
$80,000 to $99,999	37.85	112	9.1
$100,000 or more	43.96	130	22.2
HOUSEHOLD TYPE			
Average household	**33.86**	**100**	**100.0**
Married couples	41.84	124	62.5
Married couples, no children	31.44	93	20.0
Married couples, with children	48.58	143	35.8
Oldest child under age 6	39.14	116	5.6
Oldest child aged 6 to 17	48.87	144	18.3
Oldest child aged 18 or older	54.93	162	12.0
Single parent with child under age 18	31.54	93	5.5
Single person	18.97	56	16.7
RACE AND HISPANIC ORIGIN			
Average household	**33.86**	**100**	**100.0**
Asian	32.48	96	3.4
Black	31.68	94	11.2
Hispanic	38.75	114	13.5
Non-Hispanic white and other	33.48	99	75.5
REGION			
Average household	**33.86**	**100**	**100.0**
Northeast	34.83	103	19.2
Midwest	30.80	91	20.8
South	33.26	98	35.3
West	37.16	110	24.8
EDUCATION			
Average household	**33.86**	**100**	**100.0**
Less than high school graduate	34.71	103	15.5
High school graduate	33.42	99	24.9
Some college	31.90	94	20.5
Associate's degree	35.00	103	9.2
College graduate	34.93	103	29.9
Bachelor's degree	34.18	101	18.9
Master's, professional, doctoral degree	36.22	107	10.9

Note: Market shares may not sum to 100.0 because of rounding and missing categories by household type. "Asian" and "black" include Hispanics and non-Hispanics who identify themselves as being of the respective race alone. "Hispanic" includes people of any race who identify themselves as Hispanic. "Other" includes people who identify themselves as non-Hispanic and as Alaska Native, American Indian, Asian (who are also included in the "Asian" row), Native Hawaiian or other Pacific Islander, as well as non-Hispanics reporting more than one race.
Source: Calculations by New Strategist based on the Bureau of Labor Statistics' 2007 Consumer Expenditure Survey.

Butter

Best customers: **Householders aged 35 to 64**
Married couples without children at home
Married couples with school-aged or older children at home

Customer trends: **Average household spending on butter may stabilize since boomers are in one of the best-customer lifestages and as butter's reputation improves.**

The best customers of butter are the largest households. Married couples with school-aged or older children at home spend 36 to 72 percent more than the average household on butter. Married couples without children at home (most of them empty-nesters) spend 25 percent more than average on this item. Householders ranging in age from aged 35 to 64 spend 9 to 12 percent more than average on butter.

Average household spending on butter fell 2 percent between 2000 and 2007, after adjusting for inflation. Average household spending on butter may stabilize because boomers are in one of the best-customer lifestages and as butter's reputation improves.

Table 9.13 **Butter**

Total household spending $2,416,638,810.00
Average household spends   20.11

AGE OF HOUSEHOLDER	AVERAGE HOUSEHOLD SPENDING	BEST CUSTOMERS (index)	BIGGEST CUSTOMERS (market share)
Average household	**$20.11**	**100**	**100.0%**
Under age 25	11.32	56	3.8
Aged 25 to 34	17.06	85	14.5
Aged 35 to 44	22.50	112	21.8
Aged 45 to 54	21.83	109	22.8
Aged 55 to 64	22.05	110	17.8
Aged 65 to 74	20.88	104	10.4
Aged 75 or older	19.45	97	9.2

	AVERAGE HOUSEHOLD SPENDING	BEST CUSTOMERS (index)	BIGGEST CUSTOMERS (market share)
HOUSEHOLD INCOME			
Average household	**$20.11**	**100**	**100.0%**
Under $20,000	9.57	48	9.8
$20,000 to $39,999	15.21	76	17.6
$40,000 to $49,999	21.09	105	10.3
$50,000 to $69,999	20.84	104	15.9
$70,000 to $79,999	25.42	126	7.3
$80,000 to $99,999	25.58	127	10.3
$100,000 or more	33.60	167	28.6
HOUSEHOLD TYPE			
Average household	**20.11**	**100**	**100.0**
Married couples	28.03	139	70.5
Married couples, no children	25.13	125	27.0
Married couples, with children	30.19	150	37.5
Oldest child under age 6	22.21	110	5.4
Oldest child aged 6 to 17	34.63	172	21.9
Oldest child aged 18 or older	27.25	136	10.0
Single parent with child under age 18	15.40	77	4.5
Single person	9.09	45	13.4
RACE AND HISPANIC ORIGIN			
Average household	**20.11**	**100**	**100.0**
Asian	17.07	85	3.0
Black	12.66	63	7.6
Hispanic	11.36	56	6.7
Non-Hispanic white and other	22.51	112	85.4
REGION			
Average household	**20.11**	**100**	**100.0**
Northeast	22.82	113	21.1
Midwest	21.01	104	23.9
South	17.93	89	32.0
West	20.38	101	22.9
EDUCATION			
Average household	**20.11**	**100**	**100.0**
Less than high school graduate	15.06	75	11.4
High school graduate	19.28	96	24.2
Some college	18.94	94	20.5
Associate's degree	20.95	104	9.3
College graduate	23.77	118	34.2
Bachelor's degree	24.76	123	23.1
Master's, professional, doctoral degree	22.04	110	11.2

Note: Market shares may not sum to 100.0 because of rounding and missing categories by household type. "Asian" and "black" include Hispanics and non-Hispanics who identify themselves as being of the respective race alone. "Hispanic" includes people of any race who identify themselves as Hispanic. "Other" includes people who identify themselves as non-Hispanic and as Alaska Native, American Indian, Asian (who are also included in the "Asian" row), Native Hawaiian or other Pacific Islander, as well as non-Hispanics reporting more than one race.
Source: Calculations by New Strategist based on the Bureau of Labor Statistics' 2007 Consumer Expenditure Survey.

Cakes and Cupcakes

Best customers:	**Householders aged 35 to 44**
	Married couples with school-aged or older children at home
	Single parents
Customer trends:	**Average household spending on cakes and cupcakes should continue to decline as more boomers become empty-nesters and household size shrinks.**

The largest households—those with children—spend the most on cakes and cupcakes. Married couples with school-aged or older children at home spend 45 to 58 percent more than the average household on this item. Householders aged 35 to 44, most with children, spend 14 percent more than average on cakes and cupcakes. Single parents outspend the average on this item by 12 percent.

Average household spending on cakes and cupcakes fell 13 percent between 2000 and 2007, after adjusting for inflation. The baby-boom generation's exit from the best-customer lifestage is one factor behind the decline. Average household spending on cakes and cupcakes should continue to decline as more boomers become empty-nesters and household size shrinks.

Table 9.14 Cakes and cupcakes

Total household spending $4,838,084,460.00
Average household spends 40.26

AGE OF HOUSEHOLDER	AVERAGE HOUSEHOLD SPENDING	BEST CUSTOMERS (index)	BIGGEST CUSTOMERS (market share)
Average household	$40.26	100	100.0%
Under age 25	29.80	74	5.0
Aged 25 to 34	43.27	107	18.3
Aged 35 to 44	45.79	114	22.2
Aged 45 to 54	39.36	98	20.5
Aged 55 to 64	41.34	103	16.6
Aged 65 to 74	39.54	98	9.8
Aged 75 or older	32.05	80	7.5

	AVERAGE HOUSEHOLD SPENDING	BEST CUSTOMERS (index)	BIGGEST CUSTOMERS (market share)
HOUSEHOLD INCOME			
Average household	**$40.26**	**100**	**100.0%**
Under $20,000	19.50	48	10.0
$20,000 to $39,999	29.66	74	17.1
$40,000 to $49,999	39.43	98	9.6
$50,000 to $69,999	50.62	126	19.2
$70,000 to $79,999	41.44	103	6.0
$80,000 to $99,999	55.62	138	11.2
$100,000 or more	62.02	154	26.4
HOUSEHOLD TYPE			
Average household	**40.26**	**100**	**100.0**
Married couples	50.44	125	63.3
Married couples, no children	41.57	103	22.3
Married couples, with children	57.49	143	35.6
Oldest child under age 6	46.60	116	5.6
Oldest child aged 6 to 17	58.51	145	18.5
Oldest child aged 18 or older	63.46	158	11.6
Single parent with child under age 18	44.99	112	6.6
Single person	23.91	59	17.7
RACE AND HISPANIC ORIGIN			
Average household	**40.26**	**100**	**100.0**
Asian	34.15	85	3.0
Black	32.86	82	9.8
Hispanic	28.53	71	8.4
Non-Hispanic white and other	43.05	107	81.6
REGION			
Average household	**40.26**	**100**	**100.0**
Northeast	40.96	102	18.9
Midwest	44.40	110	25.2
South	40.32	100	36.0
West	35.32	88	19.8
EDUCATION			
Average household	**40.26**	**100**	**100.0**
Less than high school graduate	39.72	99	15.0
High school graduate	36.83	91	23.1
Some college	35.45	88	19.2
Associate's degree	32.35	80	7.1
College graduate	49.24	122	35.4
Bachelor's degree	50.83	126	23.7
Master's, professional, doctoral degree	46.48	115	11.8

Note: Market shares may not sum to 100.0 because of rounding and missing categories by household type. "Asian" and "black" include Hispanics and non-Hispanics who identify themselves as being of the respective race alone. "Hispanic" includes people of any race who identify themselves as Hispanic. "Other" includes people who identify themselves as non-Hispanic and as Alaska Native, American Indian, Asian (who are also included in the "Asian" row), Native Hawaiian or other Pacific Islander, as well as non-Hispanics reporting more than one race.
Source: Calculations by New Strategist based on the Bureau of Labor Statistics' 2007 Consumer Expenditure Survey.

Candy and Chewing Gum

Best customers:
Householders aged 35 to 54
Married couples with school-aged or older children at home

Customer trends:
Average household spending on candy and chewing gum will continue to fall as more boomers become empty-nesters and household size shrinks.

Households with children spend the most on candy and chewing gum. Married couples with school-aged children at home spend 50 percent more than the average household on this item, while those with adult children at home spend 71 percent more. Householders aged 35 to 54, most with children, spend 20 to 27 percent more than average on candy and chewing gum.

Average household spending on candy and chewing gum fell 13 percent between 2000 and 2007, after adjusting for inflation. Behind the decline was the large baby-boom generation's exit from the best-customer lifestage. Average household spending on candy and chewing gum could continue to fall as more boomers become empty-nesters and household size shrinks.

Table 9.15 Candy and chewing gum

Total household spending $9,655,739,850.00
Average household spends 80.35

	AVERAGE HOUSEHOLD SPENDING	BEST CUSTOMERS (index)	BIGGEST CUSTOMERS (market share)
AGE OF HOUSEHOLDER			
Average household	**$80.35**	**100**	**100.0%**
Under age 25	44.71	56	3.8
Aged 25 to 34	60.59	75	12.9
Aged 35 to 44	96.10	120	23.3
Aged 45 to 54	102.03	127	26.7
Aged 55 to 64	75.73	94	15.3
Aged 65 to 74	87.80	109	10.9
Aged 75 or older	62.83	78	7.4

	AVERAGE HOUSEHOLD SPENDING	BEST CUSTOMERS (index)	BIGGEST CUSTOMERS (market share)
HOUSEHOLD INCOME			
Average household	**$80.35**	**100**	**100.0%**
Under $20,000	42.37	53	10.8
$20,000 to $39,999	59.77	74	17.3
$40,000 to $49,999	75.57	94	9.3
$50,000 to $69,999	83.29	104	15.9
$70,000 to $79,999	97.70	122	7.0
$80,000 to $99,999	110.44	137	11.2
$100,000 or more	132.38	165	28.2
HOUSEHOLD TYPE			
Average household	**80.35**	**100**	**100.0**
Married couples	101.27	126	63.7
Married couples, no children	85.55	106	23.0
Married couples, with children	115.52	144	35.9
Oldest child under age 6	72.95	91	4.4
Oldest child aged 6 to 17	120.23	150	19.0
Oldest child aged 18 or older	137.44	171	12.6
Single parent with child under age 18	72.91	91	5.4
Single person	45.50	57	16.8
RACE AND HISPANIC ORIGIN			
Average household	**80.35**	**100**	**100.0**
Asian	91.37	114	4.0
Black	48.88	61	7.3
Hispanic	53.71	67	7.9
Non-Hispanic white and other	88.96	111	84.5
REGION			
Average household	**80.35**	**100**	**100.0**
Northeast	79.97	100	18.5
Midwest	85.06	106	24.2
South	72.20	90	32.3
West	88.93	111	25.0
EDUCATION			
Average household	**80.35**	**100**	**100.0**
Less than high school graduate	59.47	74	11.2
High school graduate	71.42	89	22.4
Some college	74.06	92	20.1
Associate's degree	91.72	114	10.1
College graduate	99.03	123	35.7
Bachelor's degree	92.03	115	21.5
Master's, professional, doctoral degree	111.18	138	14.1

Note: Market shares may not sum to 100.0 because of rounding and missing categories by household type. "Asian" and "black" include Hispanics and non-Hispanics who identify themselves as being of the respective race alone. "Hispanic" includes people of any race who identify themselves as Hispanic. "Other" includes people who identify themselves as non-Hispanic and as Alaska Native, American Indian, Asian (who are also included in the "Asian" row), Native Hawaiian or other Pacific Islander, as well as non-Hispanics reporting more than one race.
Source: Calculations by New Strategist based on the Bureau of Labor Statistics' 2007 Consumer Expenditure Survey.

Carbonated Drinks, Colas

Best customers:
Householders aged 35 to 54
Married couples with children at home
Hispanics

Customer trends:
Average household spending on colas will continue to fall as boomers move out of the crowded-nest lifestage, but the substitution of colas for coffee among younger generations may limit the decline.

The best customers of cola-flavored carbonated drinks are the largest households. Married couples with children at home spend 44 percent more than average on this item, the number peaking at 87 percent above average among couples with adult children at home. Householders ranging in age from 35 to 54, many with children at home, spend 16 to 17 percent more than average on colas and control 47 percent of the market. Hispanics, who have relatively large families, spend more than any other racial or ethnic groups on cola-flavored drinks, with an index of 117.

Average household spending on colas purchased at grocery or convenience stores fell 19 percent between 2000 and 2007, after adjusting for inflation. Lower-priced private brands and discounters are behind the decline. Average household spending on colas could continue to fall as more boomers become empty-nesters and household size shrinks. But younger generations, drinking cola rather than coffee, may limit the decline.

Table 9.16 Carbonated drinks, colas

Total household spending $10,209,728,160.00
Average household spends   84.96

	AVERAGE HOUSEHOLD SPENDING	BEST CUSTOMERS (index)	BIGGEST CUSTOMERS (market share)
AGE OF HOUSEHOLDER			
Average household	**$84.96**	**100**	**100.0%**
Under age 25	75.43	89	6.0
Aged 25 to 34	81.64	96	16.4
Aged 35 to 44	98.31	116	22.5
Aged 45 to 54	99.52	117	24.6
Aged 55 to 64	91.80	108	17.5
Aged 65 to 74	73.55	87	8.7
Aged 75 or older	38.88	46	4.3

	AVERAGE HOUSEHOLD SPENDING	BEST CUSTOMERS (index)	BIGGEST CUSTOMERS (market share)
HOUSEHOLD INCOME			
Average household	**$84.96**	**100**	**100.0%**
Under $20,000	59.95	71	14.5
$20,000 to $39,999	73.49	87	20.1
$40,000 to $49,999	87.74	103	10.2
$50,000 to $69,999	91.89	108	16.6
$70,000 to $79,999	119.28	140	8.1
$80,000 to $99,999	94.99	112	9.1
$100,000 or more	104.63	123	21.1
HOUSEHOLD TYPE			
Average household	**84.96**	**100**	**100.0**
Married couples	104.68	123	62.3
Married couples, no children	79.89	94	20.3
Married couples, with children	121.95	144	35.8
Oldest child under age 6	104.58	123	6.0
Oldest child aged 6 to 17	109.67	129	16.4
Oldest child aged 18 or older	159.00	187	13.8
Single parent with child under age 18	79.26	93	5.5
Single person	45.53	54	15.9
RACE AND HISPANIC ORIGIN			
Average household	**84.96**	**100**	**100.0**
Asian	60.60	71	2.5
Black	62.77	74	8.9
Hispanic	99.04	117	13.8
Non-Hispanic white and other	86.42	102	77.6
REGION			
Average household	**84.96**	**100**	**100.0**
Northeast	69.14	81	15.2
Midwest	90.16	106	24.3
South	91.21	107	38.6
West	82.92	98	22.1
EDUCATION			
Average household	**84.96**	**100**	**100.0**
Less than high school graduate	94.94	112	16.9
High school graduate	96.74	114	28.7
Some college	77.15	91	19.8
Associate's degree	80.25	94	8.4
College graduate	77.06	91	26.3
Bachelor's degree	77.88	92	17.2
Master's, professional, doctoral degree	75.63	89	9.1

Note: Market shares may not sum to 100.0 because of rounding and missing categories by household type. "Asian" and "black" include Hispanics and non-Hispanics who identify themselves as being of the respective race alone. "Hispanic" includes people of any race who identify themselves as Hispanic. "Other" includes people who identify themselves as non-Hispanic and as Alaska Native, American Indian, Asian (who are also included in the "Asian" row), Native Hawaiian or other Pacific Islander, as well as non-Hispanics reporting more than one race.
Source: Calculations by New Strategist based on the Bureau of Labor Statistics' 2007 Consumer Expenditure Survey.

Carbonated Drinks, Noncolas

Best customers:

Householders aged 35 to 54
Married couples with school-aged or older children at home
Hispanics

Customer trends:

Average household spending on noncola sodas will continue to fall as the small generation X fills the best customer lifestage.

The average household spends much less on noncola carbonated beverages than on colas. But the best customers of noncola sodas are the same as the best customers of colas—the largest households. Married couples with school-aged or older children at home spend 48 to 70 percent more than the average household on this item. Householders aged 35 to 54, most with children at home, spend 15 to 22 percent more than average on noncola carbonated beverages and account for 48 percent of the market. Hispanics, who have relatively large families, spend 18 percent more than average on this item.

Average household spending on noncola carbonated beverages purchased at grocery or convenience stores fell 18 percent between 2000 and 2007, after adjusting for inflation. One factor behind the decline was price discounting by private-label manufacturers. Average household spending on noncolas will continue to fall as the small generation X fills the best customer lifestage.

Table 9.17 Carbonated drinks, noncolas

Total household spending $5,622,801,090.00
Average household spends 46.79

	AVERAGE HOUSEHOLD SPENDING	BEST CUSTOMERS (index)	BIGGEST CUSTOMERS (market share)
AGE OF HOUSEHOLDER			
Average household	**$46.79**	**100**	**100.0%**
Under age 25	43.99	94	6.4
Aged 25 to 34	50.44	108	18.4
Aged 35 to 44	53.90	115	22.4
Aged 45 to 54	57.30	122	25.7
Aged 55 to 64	43.97	94	15.2
Aged 65 to 74	33.71	72	7.2
Aged 75 or older	23.22	50	4.7

	AVERAGE HOUSEHOLD SPENDING	BEST CUSTOMERS (index)	BIGGEST CUSTOMERS (market share)
HOUSEHOLD INCOME			
Average household	**$46.79**	**100**	**100.0%**
Under $20,000	28.85	62	12.7
$20,000 to $39,999	43.13	92	21.4
$40,000 to $49,999	46.34	99	9.7
$50,000 to $69,999	50.85	109	16.6
$70,000 to $79,999	54.41	116	6.7
$80,000 to $99,999	54.30	116	9.4
$100,000 or more	63.15	135	23.1
HOUSEHOLD TYPE			
Average household	**46.79**	**100**	**100.0**
Married couples	57.65	123	62.3
Married couples, no children	42.60	91	19.6
Married couples, with children	69.10	148	36.8
Oldest child under age 6	54.78	117	5.7
Oldest child aged 6 to 17	69.08	148	18.8
Oldest child aged 18 or older	79.65	170	12.5
Single parent with child under age 18	45.45	97	5.8
Single person	23.30	50	14.8
RACE AND HISPANIC ORIGIN			
Average household	**46.79**	**100**	**100.0**
Asian	27.15	58	2.0
Black	34.86	75	8.9
Hispanic	55.33	118	14.0
Non-Hispanic white and other	47.46	101	77.4
REGION			
Average household	**46.79**	**100**	**100.0**
Northeast	43.48	93	17.3
Midwest	47.43	101	23.2
South	45.60	97	35.0
West	50.87	109	24.6
EDUCATION			
Average household	**46.79**	**100**	**100.0**
Less than high school graduate	44.85	96	14.5
High school graduate	49.26	105	26.6
Some college	44.94	96	20.9
Associate's degree	52.76	113	10.0
College graduate	45.17	97	27.9
Bachelor's degree	45.52	97	18.2
Master's, professional, doctoral degree	44.56	95	9.7

Note: Market shares may not sum to 100.0 because of rounding and missing categories by household type. "Asian" and "black" include Hispanics and non-Hispanics who identify themselves as being of the respective race alone. "Hispanic" includes people of any race who identify themselves as Hispanic. "Other" includes people who identify themselves as non-Hispanic and as Alaska Native, American Indian, Asian (who are also included in the "Asian" row), Native Hawaiian or other Pacific Islander, as well as non-Hispanics reporting more than one race.
Source: Calculations by New Strategist based on the Bureau of Labor Statistics' 2007 Consumer Expenditure Survey.

Cereal, Ready-to-Eat and Cooked

Best customers: **Householders aged 35 to 54**
                       Married couples with children at home
                       Single parents

Customer trends: **Average household spending on cereal should continue to fall as more boomers become empty-nesters.**

The biggest spenders on cereal are households with children. Married couples with children at home spend 57 percent more than the average household on cereal. Householders aged 35 to 54, many of them parents, spend 12 to 24 percent more than average on cereal. Single parents spend 7 percent more than average on this item.

Average household spending on cereal fell 19 percent between 2000 and 2007, after adjusting for inflation. Price discounting is one factor that may have contributed to the spending decline, as well as baby-boomers' exit from the best-customer lifestage. Average household spending on cereal is likely to continue to fall as more boomers become empty-nesters and household size shrinks.

Table 9.18 **Cereal, ready-to-eat and cooked**

Total household spending $10,162,861,470.00
Average household spends 84.57

	AVERAGE HOUSEHOLD SPENDING	BEST CUSTOMERS (index)	BIGGEST CUSTOMERS (market share)
AGE OF HOUSEHOLDER			
Average household	**$84.57**	**100**	**100.0%**
Under age 25	56.93	67	4.6
Aged 25 to 34	85.81	101	17.3
Aged 35 to 44	104.88	124	24.2
Aged 45 to 54	95.09	112	23.6
Aged 55 to 64	77.33	91	14.8
Aged 65 to 74	76.56	91	9.0
Aged 75 or older	58.57	69	6.6

	AVERAGE HOUSEHOLD SPENDING	BEST CUSTOMERS (index)	BIGGEST CUSTOMERS (market share)
HOUSEHOLD INCOME			
Average household	**$84.57**	**100**	**100.0%**
Under $20,000	55.08	65	13.4
$20,000 to $39,999	68.19	81	18.7
$40,000 to $49,999	81.99	97	9.5
$50,000 to $69,999	89.84	106	16.3
$70,000 to $79,999	103.19	122	7.1
$80,000 to $99,999	107.81	127	10.4
$100,000 or more	120.21	142	24.4
HOUSEHOLD TYPE			
Average household	**84.57**	**100**	**100.0**
Married couples	107.13	127	64.0
Married couples, no children	79.25	94	20.2
Married couples, with children	132.82	157	39.2
Oldest child under age 6	100.40	119	5.8
Oldest child aged 6 to 17	143.78	170	21.6
Oldest child aged 18 or older	134.94	160	11.8
Single parent with child under age 18	90.35	107	6.3
Single person	45.10	53	15.9
RACE AND HISPANIC ORIGIN			
Average household	**84.57**	**100**	**100.0**
Asian	71.32	84	3.0
Black	78.79	93	11.2
Hispanic	83.42	99	11.6
Non-Hispanic white and other	85.61	101	77.3
REGION			
Average household	**84.57**	**100**	**100.0**
Northeast	87.79	104	19.3
Midwest	82.38	97	22.3
South	80.01	95	34.0
West	91.43	108	24.4
EDUCATION			
Average household	**84.57**	**100**	**100.0**
Less than high school graduate	70.89	84	12.7
High school graduate	76.48	90	22.8
Some college	79.69	94	20.5
Associate's degree	91.11	108	9.6
College graduate	99.55	118	34.1
Bachelor's degree	92.64	110	20.5
Master's, professional, doctoral degree	111.56	132	13.5

Note: Market shares may not sum to 100.0 because of rounding and missing categories by household type. "Asian" and "black" include Hispanics and non-Hispanics who identify themselves as being of the respective race alone. "Hispanic" includes people of any race who identify themselves as Hispanic. "Other" includes people who identify themselves as non-Hispanic and as Alaska Native, American Indian, Asian (who are also included in the "Asian" row), Native Hawaiian or other Pacific Islander, as well as non-Hispanics reporting more than one race.
Source: Calculations by New Strategist based on the Bureau of Labor Statistics' 2007 Consumer Expenditure Survey.

Cheese

Best customers: **Householders aged 35 to 64**
Married couples with children at home
Households in the West

Customer trends: **Average household spending on cheese should remain stable because boomers are in one of the best-customer lifestages.**

Among grocery items on which households spend the most, cheese ranks third, behind only prepared foods and fresh milk. The largest households spend the most on cheese. Married couples with children at home spend 45 percent more than the average household on this item. Householders aged 35 to 54, most with children at home, spend 13 to 21 percent more than average on cheese. Households in the West spend 15 percent more.

Average household spending on cheese grew by 1 percent between 2000 and 2007, after adjusting for inflation. Behind the stability of spending on cheese is the growing variety of cheeses available in grocery stores and the product's touted nutritional benefits. Average household spending on cheese should remain stable for the next few years because the large baby-boom generation is in one of the best-customer lifestages.

Table 9.19 Cheese

Total household spending	$14,078,032,650.00
Average household spends	117.15

	AVERAGE HOUSEHOLD SPENDING	BEST CUSTOMERS (index)	BIGGEST CUSTOMERS (market share)
AGE OF HOUSEHOLDER			
Average household	**$117.15**	**100**	**100.0%**
Under age 25	67.57	58	3.9
Aged 25 to 34	107.17	91	15.6
Aged 35 to 44	132.05	113	22.0
Aged 45 to 54	141.74	121	25.4
Aged 55 to 64	123.87	106	17.1
Aged 65 to 74	117.07	100	10.0
Aged 75 or older	76.56	65	6.2

	AVERAGE HOUSEHOLD SPENDING	BEST CUSTOMERS (index)	BIGGEST CUSTOMERS (market share)
HOUSEHOLD INCOME			
Average household	**$117.15**	**100**	**100.0%**
Under $20,000	58.93	50	10.3
$20,000 to $39,999	86.48	74	17.2
$40,000 to $49,999	112.35	96	9.4
$50,000 to $69,999	125.89	107	16.4
$70,000 to $79,999	131.35	112	6.5
$80,000 to $99,999	153.47	131	10.7
$100,000 or more	200.31	171	29.3
HOUSEHOLD TYPE			
Average household	**117.15**	**100**	**100.0**
Married couples	154.80	132	66.8
Married couples, no children	135.42	116	24.9
Married couples, with children	170.31	145	36.3
Oldest child under age 6	142.27	121	5.9
Oldest child aged 6 to 17	169.08	144	18.3
Oldest child aged 18 or older	193.32	165	12.2
Single parent with child under age 18	97.37	83	4.9
Single person	63.38	54	16.1
RACE AND HISPANIC ORIGIN			
Average household	**117.15**	**100**	**100.0**
Asian	70.57	60	2.1
Black	68.19	58	7.0
Hispanic	106.02	90	10.7
Non-Hispanic white and other	126.38	108	82.4
REGION			
Average household	**117.15**	**100**	**100.0**
Northeast	121.71	104	19.4
Midwest	115.58	99	22.5
South	104.95	90	32.2
West	134.57	115	26.0
EDUCATION			
Average household	**117.15**	**100**	**100.0**
Less than high school graduate	79.94	68	10.3
High school graduate	97.20	83	20.9
Some college	112.11	96	20.8
Associate's degree	118.90	101	9.0
College graduate	154.85	132	38.3
Bachelor's degree	144.34	123	23.1
Master's, professional, doctoral degree	173.10	148	15.1

Note: Market shares may not sum to 100.0 because of rounding and missing categories by household type. "Asian" and "black" include Hispanics and non-Hispanics who identify themselves as being of the respective race alone. "Hispanic" includes people of any race who identify themselves as Hispanic. "Other" includes people who identify themselves as non-Hispanic and as Alaska Native, American Indian, Asian (who are also included in the "Asian" row), Native Hawaiian or other Pacific Islander, as well as non-Hispanics reporting more than one race.
Source: Calculations by New Strategist based on the Bureau of Labor Statistics' 2007 Consumer Expenditure Survey.

Chicken, Fresh and Frozen

Best customers:

Householders aged 35 to 54
Married couples with school-aged or older children at home
Single parents
Hispanics, blacks, and Asians

Customer trends:

Average household spending on chicken may rise as minority populations grow, but gains will be limited as more boomers become empty-nesters.

The average household spends more on chicken than on any other grocery items except prepared foods, fresh milk, and cheese. The largest households spend the most on chicken. Married couples with school-aged or older children at home are the best customers of chicken. They spend 53 to 89 percent more than the average household on this item. Single parents spend 9 percent more. Householders aged 35 to 54, most with children at home, spend 22 to 30 percent more than average on chicken. Hispanics and blacks, who have relatively large families, spend, respectively, 55 and 32 percent more than average on chicken. Asians spend 15 percent more. Together, the three minorities, which represent 27 percent of households, account for 38 percent of household spending on this item.

Average household spending on chicken fell 18 percent between 2000 and 2007, after adjusting for inflation. One factor behind the decline is the growing propensity of Americans to eat out rather than prepare meals at home. The baby-boom's exit from the best-customer lifestage is another factor in the spending decline. Average household spending on chicken could rise as the black and Hispanic populations grow, but gains will be limited as more boomers become empty-nesters.

Table 9.20 Chicken, fresh and frozen

| Total household spending | $13,639,408,500.00 |
| Average household spends | 113.50 |

AGE OF HOUSEHOLDER	AVERAGE HOUSEHOLD SPENDING	BEST CUSTOMERS (index)	BIGGEST CUSTOMERS (market share)
Average household	**$113.50**	**100**	**100.0%**
Under age 25	76.10	67	4.5
Aged 25 to 34	116.38	103	17.5
Aged 35 to 44	147.17	130	25.3
Aged 45 to 54	138.01	122	25.5
Aged 55 to 64	97.42	86	13.9
Aged 65 to 74	98.16	86	8.6
Aged 75 or older	56.11	49	4.7

	AVERAGE HOUSEHOLD SPENDING	BEST CUSTOMERS (index)	BIGGEST CUSTOMERS (market share)
HOUSEHOLD INCOME			
Average household	**$113.50**	**100**	**100.0%**
Under $20,000	69.29	61	12.5
$20,000 to $39,999	97.66	86	20.0
$40,000 to $49,999	114.86	101	10.0
$50,000 to $69,999	113.28	100	15.3
$70,000 to $79,999	114.41	101	5.8
$80,000 to $99,999	139.22	123	10.0
$100,000 or more	173.56	153	26.2
HOUSEHOLD TYPE			
Average household	**113.50**	**100**	**100.0**
Married couples	143.50	126	63.9
Married couples, no children	97.48	86	18.5
Married couples, with children	173.00	152	38.0
Oldest child under age 6	115.87	102	5.0
Oldest child aged 6 to 17	173.49	153	19.4
Oldest child aged 18 or older	213.95	189	13.9
Single parent with child under age 18	124.05	109	6.5
Single person	55.90	49	14.6
RACE AND HISPANIC ORIGIN			
Average household	**113.50**	**100**	**100.0**
Asian	130.36	115	4.1
Black	149.80	132	15.8
Hispanic	175.63	155	18.3
Non-Hispanic white and other	99.14	87	66.7
REGION			
Average household	**113.50**	**100**	**100.0**
Northeast	123.41	109	20.3
Midwest	87.25	77	17.6
South	115.82	102	36.6
West	128.46	113	25.6
EDUCATION			
Average household	**113.50**	**100**	**100.0**
Less than high school graduate	122.28	108	16.3
High school graduate	108.87	96	24.2
Some college	103.26	91	19.8
Associate's degree	134.10	118	10.5
College graduate	114.92	101	29.3
Bachelor's degree	113.18	100	18.7
Master's, professional, doctoral degree	117.95	104	10.6

Note: Market shares may not sum to 100.0 because of rounding and missing categories by household type. "Asian" and "black" include Hispanics and non-Hispanics who identify themselves as being of the respective race alone. "Hispanic" includes people of any race who identify themselves as Hispanic. "Other" includes people who identify themselves as non-Hispanic and as Alaska Native, American Indian, Asian (who are also included in the "Asian" row), Native Hawaiian or other Pacific Islander, as well as non-Hispanics reporting more than one race.
Source: Calculations by New Strategist based on the Bureau of Labor Statistics' 2007 Consumer Expenditure Survey.

Citrus Fruit Other than Oranges

Best customers:
Householders aged 35 to 64
Married couples
Hispanics and Asians
Households in the West

Customer trends:
Average household spending on fresh citrus fruit other than oranges should rise as the population ages and the Asian and Hispanic populations grow

Older householders and the largest households are the best customers of fresh citrus fruit other than oranges. Married couples with children at home spend 36 percent more than average on fresh citrus fruit (not including oranges), with spending peaking at 59 percent above average among couples with adult children at home. Couples without children at home (most of them empty-nesters) spend 13 percent more than average on this item. Householders ranging in age from 35 to 64 spend 8 to 20 percent more than average on this item. Hispanics spend 61 percent more than average on fresh citrus fruit, and Asians spend an even larger 80 percent more. Together the two minority groups account for a sizeable one-quarter of the market. Households in the West, where fresh citrus fruit is widely available and where many Hispanics and Asians reside, spend 27 percent more than average on this item.

Average household spending on fresh citrus fruit other than oranges increased 3 percent between 2000 and 2007, after adjusting for inflation. Average household spending on fresh citrus may continue to rise as the population ages and the Asian and Hispanic populations grow.

Table 9.21 Citrus fruit other than oranges

Total household spending — $2,135,438,670.00
Average household spends — 17.77

AGE OF HOUSEHOLDER	AVERAGE HOUSEHOLD SPENDING	BEST CUSTOMERS (index)	BIGGEST CUSTOMERS (market share)
Average household	$17.77	100	100.0%
Under age 25	9.17	52	3.5
Aged 25 to 34	16.30	92	15.6
Aged 35 to 44	19.20	108	21.1
Aged 45 to 54	21.34	120	25.2
Aged 55 to 64	20.13	113	18.3
Aged 65 to 74	15.54	87	8.7
Aged 75 or older	14.53	82	7.8

	AVERAGE HOUSEHOLD SPENDING	BEST CUSTOMERS (index)	BIGGEST CUSTOMERS (market share)
HOUSEHOLD INCOME			
Average household	**$17.77**	**100**	**100.0%**
Under $20,000	9.78	55	11.3
$20,000 to $39,999	12.18	69	15.9
$40,000 to $49,999	17.80	100	9.9
$50,000 to $69,999	17.58	99	15.1
$70,000 to $79,999	20.56	116	6.7
$80,000 to $99,999	21.33	120	9.8
$100,000 or more	32.58	183	31.4
HOUSEHOLD TYPE			
Average household	**17.77**	**100**	**100.0**
Married couples	23.01	129	65.5
Married couples, no children	20.03	113	24.3
Married couples, with children	24.21	136	34.0
Oldest child under age 6	23.52	132	6.5
Oldest child aged 6 to 17	22.39	126	16.0
Oldest child aged 18 or older	28.32	159	11.7
Single parent with child under age 18	13.72	77	4.6
Single person	9.02	51	15.1
RACE AND HISPANIC ORIGIN			
Average household	**17.77**	**100**	**100.0**
Asian	32.04	180	6.4
Black	9.74	55	6.6
Hispanic	28.67	161	19.0
Non-Hispanic white and other	17.45	98	75.0
REGION			
Average household	**17.77**	**100**	**100.0**
Northeast	18.67	105	19.6
Midwest	15.32	86	19.7
South	15.88	89	32.1
West	22.57	127	28.7
EDUCATION			
Average household	**17.77**	**100**	**100.0**
Less than high school graduate	15.62	88	13.3
High school graduate	12.92	73	18.3
Some college	13.45	76	16.5
Associate's degree	16.81	95	8.4
College graduate	26.35	148	42.9
Bachelor's degree	21.90	123	23.1
Master's, professional, doctoral degree	34.09	192	19.6

Note: Market shares may not sum to 100.0 because of rounding and missing categories by household type. "Asian" and "black" include Hispanics and non-Hispanics who identify themselves as being of the respective race alone. "Hispanic" includes people of any race who identify themselves as Hispanic. "Other" includes people who identify themselves as non-Hispanic and as Alaska Native, American Indian, Asian (who are also included in the "Asian" row), Native Hawaiian or other Pacific Islander, as well as non-Hispanics reporting more than one race.
Source: Calculations by New Strategist based on the Bureau of Labor Statistics' 2007 Consumer Expenditure Survey.

Coffee, Instant and Freeze-Dried

Best customers:

Householders aged 45 to 74
Married couples without children at home
Married couples with adult children at home
Asians

Customer trends:

Average household spending on instant coffee could continue to grow as boomers fill the best-customer age groups.

Older householders are the biggest spenders on instant coffee. Householders ranging in age from 45 to 74 spend 16 to 55 percent more than the average household on this item and account for 60 percent of the market. Married couples without children at home (most of them older) spend 36 percent more than average on instant coffee, whereas those with adult children at home spend 51 percent more than average. Asians lead all other ethnic and racial groups with an index of 183.

Average household spending on instant coffee climbed 10 percent between 2000 and 2007, after adjusting for inflation. Behind the increase is the entry of the baby-boom generation into the best-customer age groups. Average household spending on instant coffee could continue to grow as boomers fill the best-customer age groups, but coffee faces stiff competition from colas.

Table 9.22 Coffee, instant and freeze-dried

Total household spending $2,291,660,970.00
Average household spends   19.07

	AVERAGE HOUSEHOLD SPENDING	BEST CUSTOMERS (index)	BIGGEST CUSTOMERS (market share)
AGE OF HOUSEHOLDER			
Average household	**$19.07**	**100**	**100.0%**
Under age 25	7.26	38	2.6
Aged 25 to 34	9.03	47	8.1
Aged 35 to 44	19.23	101	19.6
Aged 45 to 54	22.04	116	24.3
Aged 55 to 64	23.73	124	20.2
Aged 65 to 74	29.60	155	15.5
Aged 75 or older	20.27	106	10.1

	AVERAGE HOUSEHOLD SPENDING	BEST CUSTOMERS (index)	BIGGEST CUSTOMERS (market share)
HOUSEHOLD INCOME			
Average household	**$19.07**	**100**	**100.0%**
Under $20,000	15.88	83	17.1
$20,000 to $39,999	14.75	77	18.0
$40,000 to $49,999	11.97	63	6.2
$50,000 to $69,999	20.52	108	16.5
$70,000 to $79,999	23.18	122	7.0
$80,000 to $99,999	23.12	121	9.9
$100,000 or more	28.98	152	26.0
HOUSEHOLD TYPE			
Average household	**19.07**	**100**	**100.0**
Married couples	23.90	125	63.4
Married couples, no children	25.92	136	29.3
Married couples, with children	21.25	111	27.8
Oldest child under age 6	14.98	79	3.8
Oldest child aged 6 to 17	19.76	104	13.2
Oldest child aged 18 or older	28.80	151	11.1
Single parent with child under age 18	10.08	53	3.1
Single person	13.16	69	20.5
RACE AND HISPANIC ORIGIN			
Average household	**19.07**	**100**	**100.0**
Asian	34.97	183	6.5
Black	10.08	53	6.3
Hispanic	14.72	77	9.1
Non-Hispanic white and other	21.07	110	84.3
REGION			
Average household	**19.07**	**100**	**100.0**
Northeast	16.25	85	15.9
Midwest	16.71	88	20.0
South	19.23	101	36.2
West	23.65	124	28.0
EDUCATION			
Average household	**19.07**	**100**	**100.0**
Less than high school graduate	17.82	93	14.2
High school graduate	17.26	91	22.8
Some college	16.38	86	18.7
Associate's degree	20.35	107	9.5
College graduate	22.81	120	34.6
Bachelor's degree	21.69	114	21.3
Master's, professional, doctoral degree	24.75	130	13.2

Note: Market shares may not sum to 100.0 because of rounding and missing categories by household type. "Asian" and "black" include Hispanics and non-Hispanics who identify themselves as being of the respective race alone. "Hispanic" includes people of any race who identify themselves as Hispanic. "Other" includes people who identify themselves as non-Hispanic and as Alaska Native, American Indian, Asian (who are also included in the "Asian" row), Native Hawaiian or other Pacific Islander, as well as non-Hispanics reporting more than one race.
Source: Calculations by New Strategist based on the Bureau of Labor Statistics' 2007 Consumer Expenditure Survey.

Coffee, Roasted

Best customers:

Householders aged 45 to 74
Married couples without children at home
Married couples with adult children at home
Households in the West

Customer trends:

Average household spending on roasted coffee could increase during the next few years as boomers fill the best-customer age groups.

Although Starbucks has been successful in promoting coffee to the masses, it may not be able to reverse the shift away from coffee. Younger generations increasingly get their caffeine jolt from colas rather than coffee. The biggest spenders on roasted coffee purchased in grocery stores are past middle age. Householders aged 45 to 74 spend 16 to 29 percent more than the average household on roasted coffee and control 57 percent of the market. Married couples without children at home (most of them older) spend 33 percent more than average on this item, while those with adult children at home spend 58 percent more. Households in the West spend 19 percent more than the average household on roasted coffee.

Average household spending on roasted coffee purchased at grocery or convenience stores declined by 3 percent between 2000 and 2007, after adjusting for inflation. Behind the decline in spending on roasted coffee are price discounts offered by private store brands. Average household spending on roasted coffee could increase during the next few years as boomers fill the best-customer age groups, but coffee faces stiff competition from colas.

Table 9.23 Coffee, roasted

| Total household spending | $3,845,472,000.00 |
| Average household spends | 32.00 |

AGE OF HOUSEHOLDER	AVERAGE HOUSEHOLD SPENDING	BEST CUSTOMERS (index)	BIGGEST CUSTOMERS (market share)
Average household	$32.00	100	100.0%
Under age 25	9.75	30	2.1
Aged 25 to 34	20.11	63	10.7
Aged 35 to 44	34.15	107	20.8
Aged 45 to 54	37.47	117	24.6
Aged 55 to 64	41.32	129	20.9
Aged 65 to 74	37.02	116	11.6
Aged 75 or older	32.95	103	9.8

	AVERAGE HOUSEHOLD SPENDING	BEST CUSTOMERS (index)	BIGGEST CUSTOMERS (market share)
HOUSEHOLD INCOME			
Average household	**$32.00**	**100**	**100.0%**
Under $20,000	19.79	62	12.7
$20,000 to $39,999	23.86	75	17.3
$40,000 to $49,999	24.28	76	7.5
$50,000 to $69,999	30.44	95	14.6
$70,000 to $79,999	38.78	121	7.0
$80,000 to $99,999	42.26	132	10.7
$100,000 or more	56.50	177	30.2
HOUSEHOLD TYPE			
Average household	**32.00**	**100**	**100.0**
Married couples	41.63	130	65.8
Married couples, no children	42.48	133	28.6
Married couples, with children	39.02	122	30.4
Oldest child under age 6	25.63	80	3.9
Oldest child aged 6 to 17	38.10	119	15.1
Oldest child aged 18 or older	50.67	158	11.7
Single parent with child under age 18	21.24	66	3.9
Single person	18.87	59	17.5
RACE AND HISPANIC ORIGIN			
Average household	**32.00**	**100**	**100.0**
Asian	32.46	101	3.6
Black	16.04	50	6.0
Hispanic	26.30	82	9.7
Non-Hispanic white and other	35.25	110	84.1
REGION			
Average household	**32.00**	**100**	**100.0**
Northeast	32.32	101	18.8
Midwest	31.16	97	22.3
South	28.54	89	32.0
West	38.15	119	27.0
EDUCATION			
Average household	**32.00**	**100**	**100.0**
Less than high school graduate	26.77	84	12.7
High school graduate	26.03	81	20.5
Some college	30.18	94	20.5
Associate's degree	31.72	99	8.8
College graduate	41.00	128	37.1
Bachelor's degree	38.34	120	22.5
Master's, professional, doctoral degree	45.63	143	14.5

Note: Market shares may not sum to 100.0 because of rounding and missing categories by household type. "Asian" and "black" include Hispanics and non-Hispanics who identify themselves as being of the respective race alone. "Hispanic" includes people of any race who identify themselves as Hispanic. "Other" includes people who identify themselves as non-Hispanic and as Alaska Native, American Indian, Asian (who are also included in the "Asian" row), Native Hawaiian or other Pacific Islander, as well as non-Hispanics reporting more than one race.
Source: Calculations by New Strategist based on the Bureau of Labor Statistics' 2007 Consumer Expenditure Survey.

Cookies

Best customers:	**Householders aged 35 to 44** **Married couples with school-aged or older children at home**
Customer trends:	**Average household spending on cookies will continue to fall as the small generation X fills the best-customer lifestage.**

The biggest spenders on cookies are households with children. Married couples with school-aged or older children at home spend 60 to 66 percent more than the average household on this item. Householders aged 35 to 44, most with children at home, spend 26 percent more than average on cookies.

Average household spending on cookies fell 22 percent between 2000 and 2007, after adjusting for inflation. Behind the decline was the baby-boom generation's exit from the best-customer lifestage. Average household spending on cookies will continue to decline as the small generation X fills the best-customer lifestage.

Table 9.24 Cookies

Total household spending $5,394,476,190.00
Average household spends   44.89

	AVERAGE HOUSEHOLD SPENDING	BEST CUSTOMERS (index)	BIGGEST CUSTOMERS (market share)
AGE OF HOUSEHOLDER			
Average household	**$44.89**	**100**	**100.0%**
Under age 25	23.30	52	3.5
Aged 25 to 34	38.49	86	14.6
Aged 35 to 44	56.64	126	24.6
Aged 45 to 54	46.05	103	21.6
Aged 55 to 64	47.27	105	17.1
Aged 65 to 74	48.59	108	10.8
Aged 75 or older	37.85	84	8.0

	AVERAGE HOUSEHOLD SPENDING	BEST CUSTOMERS (index)	BIGGEST CUSTOMERS (market share)
HOUSEHOLD INCOME			
Average household	$44.89	100	100.0%
Under $20,000	23.86	53	10.9
$20,000 to $39,999	34.99	78	18.1
$40,000 to $49,999	42.94	96	9.4
$50,000 to $69,999	47.45	106	16.2
$70,000 to $79,999	58.40	130	7.5
$80,000 to $99,999	59.95	134	10.9
$100,000 or more	69.81	156	26.6
HOUSEHOLD TYPE			
Average household	44.89	100	100.0
Married couples	59.65	133	67.2
Married couples, no children	48.64	108	23.4
Married couples, with children	67.41	150	37.5
Oldest child under age 6	45.33	101	4.9
Oldest child aged 6 to 17	71.92	160	20.4
Oldest child aged 18 or older	74.68	166	12.3
Single parent with child under age 18	43.60	97	5.8
Single person	21.82	49	14.5
RACE AND HISPANIC ORIGIN			
Average household	44.89	100	100.0
Asian	33.92	76	2.7
Black	36.29	81	9.7
Hispanic	33.66	75	8.9
Non-Hispanic white and other	47.77	106	81.2
REGION			
Average household	44.89	100	100.0
Northeast	47.26	105	19.6
Midwest	41.24	92	21.0
South	44.16	98	35.3
West	47.84	107	24.1
EDUCATION			
Average household	44.89	100	100.0
Less than high school graduate	33.81	75	11.4
High school graduate	41.60	93	23.4
Some college	46.58	104	22.6
Associate's degree	40.55	90	8.0
College graduate	52.92	118	34.1
Bachelor's degree	48.02	107	20.0
Master's, professional, doctoral degree	61.42	137	14.0

Note: Market shares may not sum to 100.0 because of rounding and missing categories by household type. "Asian" and "black" include Hispanics and non-Hispanics who identify themselves as being of the respective race alone. "Hispanic" includes people of any race who identify themselves as Hispanic. "Other" includes people who identify themselves as non-Hispanic and as Alaska Native, American Indian, Asian (who are also included in the "Asian" row), Native Hawaiian or other Pacific Islander, as well as non-Hispanics reporting more than one race.
Source: Calculations by New Strategist based on the Bureau of Labor Statistics' 2007 Consumer Expenditure Survey.

Crackers

Best customers:	Householders aged 35 to 54 Married couples with children at home
Customer trends:	Average household spending on crackers should stabilize as more boomers become empty-nesters.

Married couples with children at home are the biggest spenders on crackers. Couples with children at home spend 59 percent more than the average household on crackers. Even single parents spend above average on this item. Householders aged 35 to 54, many with children, spend 13 to 18 percent more than average on this item and account for almost half the market (47 percent).

Average household spending on crackers increased by 13 percent between 2000 and 2007, after adjusting for inflation. Several factors could account for this increase, such as the greater variety of crackers available and the substitution of crackers for cookies in an attempt to cut calories. Average household spending on crackers should stabilize as more boomers become empty-nesters.

Table 9.25 Crackers

Total household spending $3,809,420,700.00
Average household spends   31.70

AGE OF HOUSEHOLDER	AVERAGE HOUSEHOLD SPENDING	BEST CUSTOMERS (index)	BIGGEST CUSTOMERS (market share)
Average household	$31.70	100	100.0%
Under age 25	16.99	54	3.6
Aged 25 to 34	29.85	94	16.1
Aged 35 to 44	35.76	113	22.0
Aged 45 to 54	37.52	118	24.9
Aged 55 to 64	31.07	98	15.9
Aged 65 to 74	33.94	107	10.7
Aged 75 or older	23.59	74	7.1

	AVERAGE HOUSEHOLD SPENDING	BEST CUSTOMERS (index)	BIGGEST CUSTOMERS (market share)
HOUSEHOLD INCOME			
Average household	**$31.70**	**100**	**100.0%**
Under $20,000	16.11	51	10.4
$20,000 to $39,999	23.28	73	17.1
$40,000 to $49,999	32.20	102	10.0
$50,000 to $69,999	34.00	107	16.4
$70,000 to $79,999	35.65	112	6.5
$80,000 to $99,999	40.86	129	10.5
$100,000 or more	53.34	168	28.8
HOUSEHOLD TYPE			
Average household	**31.70**	**100**	**100.0**
Married couples	42.71	135	68.1
Married couples, no children	34.26	108	23.3
Married couples, with children	50.37	159	39.6
Oldest child under age 6	44.83	141	6.9
Oldest child aged 6 to 17	48.37	153	19.4
Oldest child aged 18 or older	58.38	184	13.6
Single parent with child under age 18	32.38	102	6.1
Single person	15.55	49	14.6
RACE AND HISPANIC ORIGIN			
Average household	**31.70**	**100**	**100.0**
Asian	17.48	55	1.9
Black	20.93	66	7.9
Hispanic	18.83	59	7.0
Non-Hispanic white and other	35.16	111	84.7
REGION			
Average household	**31.70**	**100**	**100.0**
Northeast	31.26	99	18.4
Midwest	32.01	101	23.1
South	32.55	103	36.9
West	30.37	96	21.7
EDUCATION			
Average household	**31.70**	**100**	**100.0**
Less than high school graduate	20.67	65	9.9
High school graduate	27.99	88	22.3
Some college	27.60	87	19.0
Associate's degree	35.86	113	10.1
College graduate	41.77	132	38.1
Bachelor's degree	39.77	125	23.5
Master's, professional, doctoral degree	45.25	143	14.6

Note: Market shares may not sum to 100.0 because of rounding and missing categories by household type. "Asian" and "black" include Hispanics and non-Hispanics who identify themselves as being of the respective race alone. "Hispanic" includes people of any race who identify themselves as Hispanic. "Other" includes people who identify themselves as non-Hispanic and as Alaska Native, American Indian, Asian (who are also included in the "Asian" row), Native Hawaiian or other Pacific Islander, as well as non-Hispanics reporting more than one race.
Source: Calculations by New Strategist based on the Bureau of Labor Statistics' 2007 Consumer Expenditure Survey.

Cream

Best customers:	Householders aged 35 to 54 Married couples without children at home Married couples with school-aged or older children at home Households in the West
Customer trends:	Average household spending on cream should increase during the next few years as boomers continue to fill the best-customer lifestage.

Like butter, cream made a comeback when lower-carb diets became popular, especially among baby boomers. The biggest spenders on cream are the largest households—middle-aged married couples with children. Householders aged 35 to 54 spend 10 to 19 percent more than the average household on cream. Married couples with school-aged or older children at home spend 39 to 59 percent more than average on this item. But couples without children at home—many of them boomers—spend a substantial 33 percent more than average on this item. Households in the West spend 23 percent more than average on cream.

Average household spending on cream rose by 11 percent between 2000 and 2007, after adjusting for inflation. Behind the increase is the baby-boom generation's presence in one of the best-customer lifestages. Average household spending on cream should increase during the next few years as boomers continue to fill the best-customer lifestage.

Table 9.26 Cream

Total household spending		$1,866,255,630.00	
Average household spends		15.53	
	AVERAGE HOUSEHOLD SPENDING	BEST CUSTOMERS (index)	BIGGEST CUSTOMERS (market share)
AGE OF HOUSEHOLDER			
Average household	$15.53	100	100.0%
Under age 25	7.86	51	3.4
Aged 25 to 34	13.48	87	14.8
Aged 35 to 44	17.12	110	21.5
Aged 45 to 54	18.52	119	25.1
Aged 55 to 64	15.99	103	16.7
Aged 65 to 74	15.75	101	10.1
Aged 75 or older	14.23	92	8.7

	AVERAGE HOUSEHOLD SPENDING	BEST CUSTOMERS (index)	BIGGEST CUSTOMERS (market share)
HOUSEHOLD INCOME			
Average household	**$15.53**	**100**	**100.0%**
Under $20,000	6.58	42	8.7
$20,000 to $39,999	12.13	78	18.2
$40,000 to $49,999	15.28	98	9.7
$50,000 to $69,999	16.44	106	16.2
$70,000 to $79,999	15.87	102	5.9
$80,000 to $99,999	19.60	126	10.3
$100,000 or more	28.15	181	31.1
HOUSEHOLD TYPE			
Average household	**15.53**	**100**	**100.0**
Married couples	21.35	137	69.5
Married couples, no children	20.60	133	28.6
Married couples, with children	22.14	143	35.6
Oldest child under age 6	16.18	104	5.1
Oldest child aged 6 to 17	24.67	159	20.2
Oldest child aged 18 or older	21.51	139	10.2
Single parent with child under age 18	12.78	82	4.9
Single person	7.26	47	13.9
RACE AND HISPANIC ORIGIN			
Average household	**15.53**	**100**	**100.0**
Asian	8.46	54	1.9
Black	6.91	44	5.3
Hispanic	12.96	83	9.9
Non-Hispanic white and other	17.21	111	84.6
REGION			
Average household	**15.53**	**100**	**100.0**
Northeast	15.72	101	18.9
Midwest	16.05	103	23.6
South	12.94	83	29.9
West	19.03	123	27.7
EDUCATION			
Average household	**15.53**	**100**	**100.0**
Less than high school graduate	11.20	72	10.9
High school graduate	13.90	90	22.6
Some college	16.10	104	22.6
Associate's degree	15.30	99	8.8
College graduate	18.62	120	34.7
Bachelor's degree	18.33	118	22.1
Master's, professional, doctoral degree	19.12	123	12.6

Note: Market shares may not sum to 100.0 because of rounding and missing categories by household type. "Asian" and "black" include Hispanics and non-Hispanics who identify themselves as being of the respective race alone. "Hispanic" includes people of any race who identify themselves as Hispanic. "Other" includes people who identify themselves as non-Hispanic and as Alaska Native, American Indian, Asian (who are also included in the "Asian" row), Native Hawaiian or other Pacific Islander, as well as non-Hispanics reporting more than one race.
Source: Calculations by New Strategist based on the Bureau of Labor Statistics' 2007 Consumer Expenditure Survey.

Dairy Products Other than Butter, Cheese, Cream, Ice Cream, and Milk

Best customers:
Householders aged 35 to 54
Married couples with children at home

Customer trends:
Average household spending on other dairy products should continue to grow as more seek the health benefits of yogurt.

Dairy products have taken a beating in recent years as milk consumption has declined. But some dairy products, such as yogurt, are growing in popularity. The biggest spenders on other dairy products, a category that includes yogurt, are the largest households. Married couples with children at home spend 52 percent more than the average household on other dairy products. Householders aged 35 to 54, many with children, spend 17 to 20 percent more than average on this item and account for 48 percent of the market.

Average household spending on other dairy products rose by a substantial 36 percent between 2000 and 2007, after adjusting for inflation. Behind the increase is the growing popularity of yogurt and yogurt-based drinks. Average household spending on other dairy products may continue to rise as more consumers seek the health benefits of yogurt.

Table 9.27 Dairy products other than butter, cheese, cream, ice cream, and milk

Total household spending $4,695,080,970.00
Average household spends   39.07

	AVERAGE HOUSEHOLD SPENDING	BEST CUSTOMERS (index)	BIGGEST CUSTOMERS (market share)
AGE OF HOUSEHOLDER			
Average household	**$39.07**	**100**	**100.0%**
Under age 25	24.61	63	4.3
Aged 25 to 34	36.83	94	16.1
Aged 35 to 44	46.97	120	23.4
Aged 45 to 54	45.79	117	24.6
Aged 55 to 64	39.60	101	16.4
Aged 65 to 74	37.43	96	9.6
Aged 75 or older	23.72	61	5.8

	AVERAGE HOUSEHOLD SPENDING	BEST CUSTOMERS (index)	BIGGEST CUSTOMERS (market share)
HOUSEHOLD INCOME			
Average household	**$39.07**	**100**	**100.0%**
Under $20,000	19.83	51	10.4
$20,000 to $39,999	26.93	69	16.0
$40,000 to $49,999	39.81	102	10.0
$50,000 to $69,999	38.82	99	15.2
$70,000 to $79,999	51.60	132	7.6
$80,000 to $99,999	47.14	121	9.8
$100,000 or more	70.53	181	30.9
HOUSEHOLD TYPE			
Average household	**39.07**	**100**	**100.0**
Married couples	54.28	139	70.2
Married couples, no children	46.65	119	25.8
Married couples, with children	59.48	152	38.0
Oldest child under age 6	53.87	138	6.7
Oldest child aged 6 to 17	64.09	164	20.8
Oldest child aged 18 or older	54.47	139	10.3
Single parent with child under age 18	34.14	87	5.2
Single person	17.64	45	13.4
RACE AND HISPANIC ORIGIN			
Average household	**39.07**	**100**	**100.0**
Asian	39.33	101	3.6
Black	28.18	72	8.7
Hispanic	39.46	101	11.9
Non-Hispanic white and other	40.74	104	79.6
REGION			
Average household	**39.07**	**100**	**100.0**
Northeast	39.97	102	19.1
Midwest	41.33	106	24.2
South	34.15	87	31.4
West	43.91	112	25.4
EDUCATION			
Average household	**39.07**	**100**	**100.0**
Less than high school graduate	27.88	71	10.8
High school graduate	30.44	78	19.7
Some college	33.41	86	18.6
Associate's degree	41.30	106	9.4
College graduate	55.20	141	40.9
Bachelor's degree	49.29	126	23.6
Master's, professional, doctoral degree	65.46	168	17.1

Note: Market shares may not sum to 100.0 because of rounding and missing categories by household type. "Asian" and "black" include Hispanics and non-Hispanics who identify themselves as being of the respective race alone. "Hispanic" includes people of any race who identify themselves as Hispanic. "Other" includes people who identify themselves as non-Hispanic and as Alaska Native, American Indian, Asian (who are also included in the "Asian" row), Native Hawaiian or other Pacific Islander, as well as non-Hispanics reporting more than one race.
Source: Calculations by New Strategist based on the Bureau of Labor Statistics' 2007 Consumer Expenditure Survey.

Desserts, Prepared

Best customers:	**Married couples with children**
	Households in the Northeast
Customer trends:	**Average household spending on prepared desserts should stabilize in the years ahead as boomers become empty-nesters and the small generation X raises children.**

The best customers of prepared desserts are married couples with children at home. To save time, they are buying prepared desserts rather than cooking from scratch. Couples with children at home spend 42 percent more than the average household on this item, with the figure peaking among couples with preschoolers at 48 percent.

Average household spending on prepared desserts climbed 10 percent between 2000 and 2006, after adjusting for inflation. Behind the increase is consumer preference for the convenience of prepared food. Average household spending on prepared desserts should stabilize in the years ahead as boomers become empty-nesters and the small generation X raises children.

Table 9.28 Desserts, prepared

Total household spending	$1,478,103,300.00
Average household spends	12.30

	AVERAGE HOUSEHOLD SPENDING	BEST CUSTOMERS (index)	BIGGEST CUSTOMERS (market share)
AGE OF HOUSEHOLDER			
Average household	**$12.30**	**100**	**100.0%**
Under age 25	6.03	49	3.3
Aged 25 to 34	11.78	96	16.3
Aged 35 to 44	12.50	102	19.8
Aged 45 to 54	13.32	108	22.7
Aged 55 to 64	12.83	104	16.9
Aged 65 to 74	15.18	123	12.3
Aged 75 or older	11.33	92	8.7

	AVERAGE HOUSEHOLD SPENDING	BEST CUSTOMERS (index)	BIGGEST CUSTOMERS (market share)
HOUSEHOLD INCOME			
Average household	**$12.30**	**100**	**100.0%**
Under $20,000	8.10	66	13.5
$20,000 to $39,999	9.71	79	18.3
$40,000 to $49,999	10.54	86	8.4
$50,000 to $69,999	13.08	106	16.3
$70,000 to $79,999	13.32	108	6.3
$80,000 to $99,999	16.35	133	10.8
$100,000 or more	18.70	152	26.0
HOUSEHOLD TYPE			
Average household	**12.30**	**100**	**100.0**
Married couples	16.20	132	66.6
Married couples, no children	14.51	118	25.4
Married couples, with children	17.51	142	35.5
Oldest child under age 6	18.15	148	7.2
Oldest child aged 6 to 17	17.52	142	18.1
Oldest child aged 18 or older	17.03	138	10.2
Single parent with child under age 18	11.38	93	5.5
Single person	6.56	53	15.9
RACE AND HISPANIC ORIGIN			
Average household	**12.30**	**100**	**100.0**
Asian	7.25	59	2.1
Black	7.59	62	7.4
Hispanic	10.22	83	9.8
Non-Hispanic white and other	13.31	108	82.6
REGION			
Average household	**12.30**	**100**	**100.0**
Northeast	14.66	119	22.2
Midwest	12.82	104	23.8
South	10.24	83	29.9
West	13.08	106	24.0
EDUCATION			
Average household	**12.30**	**100**	**100.0**
Less than high school graduate	10.85	88	13.4
High school graduate	12.54	102	25.7
Some college	9.47	77	16.8
Associate's degree	14.09	115	10.2
College graduate	14.28	116	33.6
Bachelor's degree	14.38	117	21.9
Master's, professional, doctoral degree	14.11	115	11.7

Note: Market shares may not sum to 100.0 because of rounding and missing categories by household type. "Asian" and "black" include Hispanics and non-Hispanics who identify themselves as being of the respective race alone. "Hispanic" includes people of any race who identify themselves as Hispanic. "Other" includes people who identify themselves as non-Hispanic and as Alaska Native, American Indian, Asian (who are also included in the "Asian" row), Native Hawaiian or other Pacific Islander, as well as non-Hispanics reporting more than one race.
Source: Calculations by New Strategist based on the Bureau of Labor Statistics' 2007 Consumer Expenditure Survey.

Eggs

Best customers:
Householders aged 35 to 54
Married couples with school-aged or older children at home
Hispanics and Asians
Households in the West

Customer trends:
Average household spending on eggs may decline as more boomers become empty-nesters and household size shrinks.

Household size is the most important factor in determining spending on eggs, with the largest households spending the most. Married couples with school-aged or older children at home spend 48 to 53 percent more than the average household on eggs. Householders aged 35 to 54, most having children at home, spend 10 to 14 percent more than average on eggs. Asians and Hispanics, whose families are larger than average, spend 40 to 41 percent more than average on this item. Households in the West, where many Asians and Hispanics reside, spend 20 percent above average on eggs.

Average household spending on eggs grew by 3 percent between 2000 and 2007, after adjusting for inflation. Average household spending on eggs is likely to decline as more boomers become empty-nesters and household size shrinks.

Table 9.29 Eggs

Total household spending $5,132,503,410.00
Average household spends 42.71

	AVERAGE HOUSEHOLD SPENDING	BEST CUSTOMERS (index)	BIGGEST CUSTOMERS (market share)
AGE OF HOUSEHOLDER			
Average household	**$42.71**	**100**	**100.0%**
Under age 25	27.04	63	4.3
Aged 25 to 34	41.22	97	16.5
Aged 35 to 44	48.54	114	22.1
Aged 45 to 54	46.82	110	23.0
Aged 55 to 64	43.51	102	16.5
Aged 65 to 74	41.68	98	9.8
Aged 75 or older	35.93	84	8.0

	AVERAGE HOUSEHOLD SPENDING	BEST CUSTOMERS (index)	BIGGEST CUSTOMERS (market share)
HOUSEHOLD INCOME			
Average household	**$42.71**	**100**	**100.0%**
Under $20,000	31.66	74	15.2
$20,000 to $39,999	39.74	93	21.6
$40,000 to $49,999	42.05	98	9.7
$50,000 to $69,999	43.46	102	15.6
$70,000 to $79,999	48.77	114	6.6
$80,000 to $99,999	45.54	107	8.7
$100,000 or more	56.13	131	22.5
HOUSEHOLD TYPE			
Average household	**42.71**	**100**	**100.0**
Married couples	53.43	125	63.2
Married couples, no children	44.19	103	22.3
Married couples, with children	60.27	141	35.2
Oldest child under age 6	44.99	105	5.1
Oldest child aged 6 to 17	63.28	148	18.8
Oldest child aged 18 or older	65.53	153	11.3
Single parent with child under age 18	42.47	99	5.9
Single person	24.43	57	17.0
RACE AND HISPANIC ORIGIN			
Average household	**42.71**	**100**	**100.0**
Asian	59.98	140	5.0
Black	41.18	96	11.6
Hispanic	60.14	141	16.6
Non-Hispanic white and other	40.47	95	72.3
REGION			
Average household	**42.71**	**100**	**100.0**
Northeast	45.21	106	19.7
Midwest	33.43	78	17.9
South	42.09	99	35.4
West	51.18	120	27.1
EDUCATION			
Average household	**42.71**	**100**	**100.0**
Less than high school graduate	44.76	105	15.9
High school graduate	41.99	98	24.8
Some college	41.93	98	21.4
Associate's degree	39.57	93	8.2
College graduate	43.86	103	29.7
Bachelor's degree	43.40	102	19.0
Master's, professional, doctoral degree	44.64	105	10.7

Note: Market shares may not sum to 100.0 because of rounding and missing categories by household type. "Asian" and "black" include Hispanics and non-Hispanics who identify themselves as being of the respective race alone. "Hispanic" includes people of any race who identify themselves as Hispanic. "Other" includes people who identify themselves as non-Hispanic and as Alaska Native, American Indian, Asian (who are also included in the "Asian" row), Native Hawaiian or other Pacific Islander, as well as non-Hispanics reporting more than one race.
Source: Calculations by New Strategist based on the Bureau of Labor Statistics' 2007 Consumer Expenditure Survey.

Fats and Oils

Best customers:

Married couples with school-aged or older children at home
Asians, Hispanics, and blacks

Customer trends:

Average household spending on fats and oils may decline in the years ahead
as cooking from scratch becomes less common and more boomers become
empty-nesters.

The biggest spenders on fats and oils are households with children, who are more likely to cook meals from scratch. Married couples with school-aged or older children at home spend 28 to 65 percent more than average on fats and oils. Households headed by Asians and Hispanics are more likely to include children than the average household. They spend 73 and 54 percent more than average on fats and oils, respectively. Black householders spend 20 percent above average on this item. Together, the three minorities (27 percent of the population) account for 39 percent of the market for fats and oils.

Average household spending on fats and oils rose 9 percent between 2000 and 2007, after adjusting for inflation. Behind the increase was the growth of the Hispanic, black, and Asian populations. Average household spending on fats and oils may decline in the years ahead as more boomers become empty-nesters and eating out absorbs an ever-growing share of the food dollar.

Table 9.30 Fats and oils

Total household spending $3,680,837,730.00

Average household spends 30.63

	AVERAGE HOUSEHOLD SPENDING	BEST CUSTOMERS (index)	BIGGEST CUSTOMERS (market share)
AGE OF HOUSEHOLDER			
Average household	**$30.63**	**100**	**100.0%**
Under age 25	18.92	62	4.2
Aged 25 to 34	26.30	86	14.6
Aged 35 to 44	31.93	104	20.3
Aged 45 to 54	34.70	113	23.8
Aged 55 to 64	30.66	100	16.2
Aged 65 to 74	33.53	109	10.9
Aged 75 or older	32.70	107	10.1

	AVERAGE HOUSEHOLD SPENDING	BEST CUSTOMERS (index)	BIGGEST CUSTOMERS (market share)
HOUSEHOLD INCOME			
Average household	**$30.63**	**100**	**100.0%**
Under $20,000	25.36	83	17.0
$20,000 to $39,999	26.89	88	20.4
$40,000 to $49,999	31.35	102	10.1
$50,000 to $69,999	31.57	103	15.8
$70,000 to $79,999	28.13	92	5.3
$80,000 to $99,999	33.62	110	8.9
$100,000 or more	39.97	130	22.4
HOUSEHOLD TYPE			
Average household	**30.63**	**100**	**100.0**
Married couples	39.88	130	65.8
Married couples, no children	36.39	119	25.6
Married couples, with children	39.37	129	32.1
Oldest child under age 6	24.29	79	3.9
Oldest child aged 6 to 17	39.33	128	16.3
Oldest child aged 18 or older	50.51	165	12.1
Single parent with child under age 18	31.26	102	6.1
Single person	14.89	49	14.5
RACE AND HISPANIC ORIGIN			
Average household	**30.63**	**100**	**100.0**
Asian	52.90	173	6.1
Black	36.87	120	14.4
Hispanic	47.26	154	18.2
Non-Hispanic white and other	27.28	89	68.0
REGION			
Average household	**30.63**	**100**	**100.0**
Northeast	36.97	121	22.5
Midwest	24.17	79	18.0
South	30.64	100	35.9
West	31.93	104	23.6
EDUCATION			
Average household	**30.63**	**100**	**100.0**
Less than high school graduate	34.12	111	16.9
High school graduate	27.13	89	22.3
Some college	25.65	84	18.2
Associate's degree	33.69	110	9.8
College graduate	34.78	114	32.9
Bachelor's degree	34.19	112	20.9
Master's, professional, doctoral degree	35.81	117	11.9

Note: Market shares may not sum to 100.0 because of rounding and missing categories by household type. "Asian" and "black" include Hispanics and non-Hispanics who identify themselves as being of the respective race alone. "Hispanic" includes people of any race who identify themselves as Hispanic. "Other" includes people who identify themselves as non-Hispanic and as Alaska Native, American Indian, Asian (who are also included in the "Asian" row), Native Hawaiian or other Pacific Islander, as well as non-Hispanics reporting more than one race.
Source: Calculations by New Strategist based on the Bureau of Labor Statistics' 2007 Consumer Expenditure Survey.

Fish and Seafood, Canned

Best customers:

Householders aged 35 to 64
Married couples with school-aged or older children at home
Single parents
Households in the Northeast

Customer trends:

Average household spending on canned fish and seafood may continue to fall in the years ahead as the small generation X fills the best-customer lifestage.

The biggest spenders on canned fish and seafood are middle-aged householders with children at home. Householders aged 35 to 64 spend 12 to 22 percent more than the average household on this item and account for two-thirds of the market. Couples with school-aged or older children at home spend 41 to 43 percent more than average on canned fish and seafood, while single parents spend 11 percent more. Households in the Northeast spend 38 percent more than average on canned fish and seafood.

Average household spending on canned fish and seafood fell 13 percent between 2000 and 2007, after adjusting for inflation. One factor behind the decline was the shift from canned to frozen fish, as well as the growing preference for eating out rather than preparing meals from scratch. Average household spending on canned fish and seafood may continue to fall in the years ahead as the small generation X fills the best-customer lifestage.

Table 9.31 Fish and seafood, canned

Total household spending $1,964,795,850.00
Average household spends   16.35

	AVERAGE HOUSEHOLD SPENDING	BEST CUSTOMERS (index)	BIGGEST CUSTOMERS (market share)
AGE OF HOUSEHOLDER			
Average household	$16.35	100	100.0%
Under age 25	11.47	70	4.8
Aged 25 to 34	11.52	70	12.0
Aged 35 to 44	19.95	122	23.8
Aged 45 to 54	18.35	112	23.6
Aged 55 to 64	18.76	115	18.6
Aged 65 to 74	17.20	105	10.5
Aged 75 or older	11.92	73	6.9

	AVERAGE HOUSEHOLD SPENDING	BEST CUSTOMERS (index)	BIGGEST CUSTOMERS (market share)
HOUSEHOLD INCOME			
Average household	**$16.35**	**100**	**100.0%**
Under $20,000	11.28	69	14.2
$20,000 to $39,999	15.44	94	21.9
$40,000 to $49,999	15.96	98	9.6
$50,000 to $69,999	19.95	122	18.7
$70,000 to $79,999	16.65	102	5.9
$80,000 to $99,999	13.89	85	6.9
$100,000 or more	21.78	133	22.8
HOUSEHOLD TYPE			
Average household	**16.35**	**100**	**100.0**
Married couples	19.41	119	60.0
Married couples, no children	17.82	109	23.5
Married couples, with children	20.55	126	31.4
Oldest child under age 6	9.75	60	2.9
Oldest child aged 6 to 17	23.10	141	17.9
Oldest child aged 18 or older	23.41	143	10.5
Single parent with child under age 18	18.16	111	6.6
Single person	11.56	71	21.0
RACE AND HISPANIC ORIGIN			
Average household	**16.35**	**100**	**100.0**
Asian	13.99	86	3.0
Black	14.63	89	10.7
Hispanic	13.47	82	9.7
Non-Hispanic white and other	17.01	104	79.4
REGION			
Average household	**16.35**	**100**	**100.0**
Northeast	22.60	138	25.7
Midwest	13.29	81	18.6
South	14.04	86	30.8
West	17.91	110	24.8
EDUCATION			
Average household	**16.35**	**100**	**100.0**
Less than high school graduate	13.41	82	12.4
High school graduate	15.81	97	24.4
Some college	15.79	97	21.0
Associate's degree	18.27	112	9.9
College graduate	18.02	110	31.9
Bachelor's degree	17.19	105	19.7
Master's, professional, doctoral degree	19.46	119	12.1

Note: Market shares may not sum to 100.0 because of rounding and missing categories by household type. "Asian" and "black" include Hispanics and non-Hispanics who identify themselves as being of the respective race alone. "Hispanic" includes people of any race who identify themselves as Hispanic. "Other" includes people who identify themselves as non-Hispanic and as Alaska Native, American Indian, Asian (who are also included in the "Asian" row), Native Hawaiian or other Pacific Islander, as well as non-Hispanics reporting more than one race.
Source: Calculations by New Strategist based on the Bureau of Labor Statistics' 2007 Consumer Expenditure Survey.

Fish and Shellfish, Fresh

Best customers:	Householders aged 35 to 54
	Married couples with school-aged or older children at home
	Asians and blacks
	Households in the Northeast and West
Customer trends:	Average household spending on fresh fish could rise as aging boomers attempt to improve their diet—but only if discretionary income grows.

The best customers of fresh fish and shellfish are middle-aged householders, the largest households, and minority households. Householders ranging in age from 35 to 54 spend 23 to 26 percent more than average on fresh fish and account for 50 percent of the market. Married couples with school-aged or older children at home spend 28 to 91 percent more than average on this item. Asians spend more three-and-one-half times the average on fresh fish, while blacks spend 22 percent more than average. Together the two minority groups, which represent less than 16 percent of households, account for 27 percent of the market. Households in the Northeast and West spend, respectively, 44 and 31 percent more than average on fresh fish.

Average household spending on fresh fish fell by 21 percent between 2000 and 2007, after adjusting for inflation. Behind the decline was the shift from fresh to frozen fish, as well as the growing propensity of Americans to eat out rather than prepare a meal from scratch. Average household spending on fresh fish could rise in the years ahead as aging boomers attempt to eat more healthfully, but only if discretionary income grows.

Table 9.32 Fish and shellfish, fresh

Total household spending: $7,668,111,510.00
Average household spends: 63.81

	AVERAGE HOUSEHOLD SPENDING	BEST CUSTOMERS (index)	BIGGEST CUSTOMERS (market share)
AGE OF HOUSEHOLDER			
Average household	$63.81	100	100.0%
Under age 25	25.85	41	2.7
Aged 25 to 34	53.89	84	14.4
Aged 35 to 44	78.29	123	23.9
Aged 45 to 54	80.24	126	26.4
Aged 55 to 64	66.01	103	16.8
Aged 65 to 74	64.68	101	10.1
Aged 75 or older	39.71	62	5.9

	AVERAGE HOUSEHOLD SPENDING	BEST CUSTOMERS (index)	BIGGEST CUSTOMERS (market share)
HOUSEHOLD INCOME			
Average household	**$63.81**	**100**	**100.0%**
Under $20,000	28.86	45	9.3
$20,000 to $39,999	42.59	67	15.5
$40,000 to $49,999	71.22	112	11.0
$50,000 to $69,999	62.49	98	15.0
$70,000 to $79,999	75.98	119	6.9
$80,000 to $99,999	69.48	109	8.9
$100,000 or more	125.77	197	33.8
HOUSEHOLD TYPE			
Average household	**63.81**	**100**	**100.0**
Married couples	81.18	127	64.3
Married couples, no children	71.42	112	24.1
Married couples, with children	83.94	132	32.8
Oldest child under age 6	38.47	60	2.9
Oldest child aged 6 to 17	81.50	128	16.2
Oldest child aged 18 or older	122.15	191	14.1
Single parent with child under age 18	59.95	94	5.6
Single person	33.44	52	15.6
RACE AND HISPANIC ORIGIN			
Average household	**63.81**	**100**	**100.0**
Asian	220.50	346	12.2
Black	77.87	122	14.6
Hispanic	66.59	104	12.3
Non-Hispanic white and other	61.28	96	73.3
REGION			
Average household	**63.81**	**100**	**100.0**
Northeast	91.69	144	26.8
Midwest	40.67	64	14.6
South	51.66	81	29.1
West	83.63	131	29.6
EDUCATION			
Average household	**63.81**	**100**	**100.0**
Less than high school graduate	56.67	89	13.5
High school graduate	48.91	77	19.3
Some college	48.41	76	16.5
Associate's degree	67.23	105	9.4
College graduate	90.18	141	40.9
Bachelor's degree	76.25	119	22.4
Master's, professional, doctoral degree	114.36	179	18.3

Note: Market shares may not sum to 100.0 because of rounding and missing categories by household type. "Asian" and "black" include Hispanics and non-Hispanics who identify themselves as being of the respective race alone. "Hispanic" includes people of any race who identify themselves as Hispanic. "Other" includes people who identify themselves as non-Hispanic and as Alaska Native, American Indian, Asian (who are also included in the "Asian" row), Native Hawaiian or other Pacific Islander, as well as non-Hispanics reporting more than one race.
Source: Calculations by New Strategist based on the Bureau of Labor Statistics' 2007 Consumer Expenditure Survey.

Fish and Shellfish, Frozen

Best customers:
Householders aged 35 to 54
Married couples with school-aged or older children at home
Single parents
Asians

Customer trends:
Average household spending on frozen fish may stabilize as more boomers become empty-nesters and household size shrinks.

Households with children are the best customers of frozen fish. Married couples with school-aged or older children at home spend 31 to 47 percent more than average on this item. Single parents spend 28 percent more. Householders aged 35 to 54, most with children at home, spend 14 to 28 percent above average on frozen fish and shellfish. Asian households spend more than twice the average on frozen fish.

Average household spending on frozen fish rose a healthy 25 percent between 2000 and 2007, after adjusting for inflation. Behind the increase were nutritional claims regarding the benefits of fish consumption. Another factor in the increase was the shift away from canned and fresh fish to the greater convenience of frozen fish. Average household spending on frozen fish may stabilize as more boomers become empty-nesters and household size shrinks.

Table 9.33 Fish and shellfish, frozen

| Total household spending | $5,019,542,670.00 |
| Average household spends | 41.77 |

	AVERAGE HOUSEHOLD SPENDING	BEST CUSTOMERS (index)	BIGGEST CUSTOMERS (market share)
AGE OF HOUSEHOLDER			
Average household	**$41.77**	**100**	**100.0%**
Under age 25	26.77	64	4.3
Aged 25 to 34	34.07	82	13.9
Aged 35 to 44	53.62	128	25.0
Aged 45 to 54	47.82	114	24.1
Aged 55 to 64	42.48	102	16.5
Aged 65 to 74	40.39	97	9.7
Aged 75 or older	29.49	71	6.7

	AVERAGE HOUSEHOLD SPENDING	BEST CUSTOMERS (index)	BIGGEST CUSTOMERS (market share)
HOUSEHOLD INCOME			
Average household	**$41.77**	**100**	**100.0%**
Under $20,000	25.12	60	12.4
$20,000 to $39,999	32.76	78	18.2
$40,000 to $49,999	40.21	96	9.5
$50,000 to $69,999	41.19	99	15.1
$70,000 to $79,999	40.44	97	5.6
$80,000 to $99,999	56.02	134	10.9
$100,000 or more	68.88	165	28.3
HOUSEHOLD TYPE			
Average household	**41.77**	**100**	**100.0**
Married couples	51.66	124	62.5
Married couples, no children	45.84	110	23.7
Married couples, with children	54.67	131	32.7
Oldest child under age 6	44.72	107	5.2
Oldest child aged 6 to 17	54.89	131	16.7
Oldest child aged 18 or older	61.53	147	10.9
Single parent with child under age 18	53.63	128	7.6
Single person	22.46	54	16.0
RACE AND HISPANIC ORIGIN			
Average household	**41.77**	**100**	**100.0**
Asian	86.72	208	7.3
Black	45.65	109	13.1
Hispanic	38.91	93	11.0
Non-Hispanic white and other	41.54	99	75.9
REGION			
Average household	**41.77**	**100**	**100.0**
Northeast	44.34	106	19.8
Midwest	42.04	101	23.0
South	37.21	89	32.0
West	46.68	112	25.3
EDUCATION			
Average household	**41.77**	**100**	**100.0**
Less than high school graduate	37.02	89	13.4
High school graduate	36.05	86	21.8
Some college	42.90	103	22.4
Associate's degree	39.06	94	8.3
College graduate	48.92	117	33.9
Bachelor's degree	45.63	109	20.5
Master's, professional, doctoral degree	54.64	131	13.3

Note: Market shares may not sum to 100.0 because of rounding and missing categories by household type. "Asian" and "black" include Hispanics and non-Hispanics who identify themselves as being of the respective race alone. "Hispanic" includes people of any race who identify themselves as Hispanic. "Other" includes people who identify themselves as non-Hispanic and as Alaska Native, American Indian, Asian (who are also included in the "Asian" row), Native Hawaiian or other Pacific Islander, as well as non-Hispanics reporting more than one race.
Source: Calculations by New Strategist based on the Bureau of Labor Statistics' 2007 Consumer Expenditure Survey.

Flour

Best customers: Householders aged 35 to 44 and 65 to 74
Married couples with school-aged or older children at home
Asians and Hispanics

Customer trends: Average household spending on flour will continue to decline as cooking from scratch becomes less common and the small generation X fills the best-customer age group.

The biggest spenders on flour are the households most likely to cook from scratch—typically married couples with children at home. Couples with school-aged children spend 90 percent more than average on flour, while those with adult children at home spend 45 percent more than average. Asians spend almost three times the average on this item, while Hispanics spend 39 percent more than average on flour. Householders aged 35 to 44 spend 36 percent more than average on this item, while those aged 65 to 74 outspend the average by 24 percent.

Average household spending on flour fell by an enormous 47 percent between 2000 and 2007, after adjusting for inflation. This was the largest percentage drop among grocery items except for frozen fruit juice. Behind the decline is the rise of eating out as busy families find less time to cook from scratch. Average household spending on flour will continue to decline as eating out claims an ever-growing share of the food dollar and as the small generation X fills the best-customer age group.

Table 9.34 Flour

Total household spending $617,678,940.00
Average household spends   5.14

	AVERAGE HOUSEHOLD SPENDING	BEST CUSTOMERS (index)	BIGGEST CUSTOMERS (market share)
AGE OF HOUSEHOLDER			
Average household	$5.14	100	100.0%
Under age 25	3.24	63	4.3
Aged 25 to 34	4.47	87	14.8
Aged 35 to 44	6.98	136	26.5
Aged 45 to 54	4.90	95	20.0
Aged 55 to 64	4.49	87	14.1
Aged 65 to 74	6.38	124	12.4
Aged 75 or older	4.22	82	7.8

	AVERAGE HOUSEHOLD SPENDING	BEST CUSTOMERS (index)	BIGGEST CUSTOMERS (market share)
HOUSEHOLD INCOME			
Average household	**$5.14**	**100**	**100.0%**
Under $20,000	2.91	57	11.6
$20,000 to $39,999	4.72	92	21.3
$40,000 to $49,999	4.84	94	9.3
$50,000 to $69,999	5.78	112	17.2
$70,000 to $79,999	5.22	102	5.9
$80,000 to $99,999	6.16	120	9.8
$100,000 or more	7.37	143	24.6
HOUSEHOLD TYPE			
Average household	**5.14**	**100**	**100.0**
Married couples	7.33	143	72.1
Married couples, no children	5.77	112	24.2
Married couples, with children	8.26	161	40.1
Oldest child under age 6	5.21	101	4.9
Oldest child aged 6 to 17	9.79	190	24.2
Oldest child aged 18 or older	7.46	145	10.7
Single parent with child under age 18	4.53	88	5.2
Single person	1.64	32	9.5
RACE AND HISPANIC ORIGIN			
Average household	**5.14**	**100**	**100.0**
Asian	13.97	272	9.6
Black	3.99	78	9.3
Hispanic	7.14	139	16.4
Non-Hispanic white and other	5.03	98	74.7
REGION			
Average household	**5.14**	**100**	**100.0**
Northeast	4.67	91	16.9
Midwest	5.76	112	25.6
South	5.02	98	35.1
West	5.08	99	22.4
EDUCATION			
Average household	**5.14**	**100**	**100.0**
Less than high school graduate	7.11	138	21.0
High school graduate	3.80	74	18.6
Some college	4.27	83	18.1
Associate's degree	5.74	112	9.9
College graduate	5.84	114	32.9
Bachelor's degree	4.78	93	17.4
Master's, professional, doctoral degree	7.68	149	15.2

Note: Market shares may not sum to 100.0 because of rounding and missing categories by household type. "Asian" and "black" include Hispanics and non-Hispanics who identify themselves as being of the respective race alone. "Hispanic" includes people of any race who identify themselves as Hispanic. "Other" includes people who identify themselves as non-Hispanic and as Alaska Native, American Indian, Asian (who are also included in the "Asian" row), Native Hawaiian or other Pacific Islander, as well as non-Hispanics reporting more than one race.
Source: Calculations by New Strategist based on the Bureau of Labor Statistics' 2007 Consumer Expenditure Survey.

Flour, Prepared Mixes

Best customers: Householders aged 35 to 54
Married couples with school-aged or older children at home

Customer trends: Average household spending on flour mixes will continue to decline as home cooking becomes less common and more boomers become empty-nesters.

The biggest spenders on prepared flour mixes—such as cake and biscuit mixes—are middle-aged married couples. Married couples with school-aged or older children at home spend 69 to 93 percent more than average on prepared flour mixes. Householders aged 35 to 54, most with children, spend 12 to 44 percent more than average on prepared flour mixes and account for 52 percent of the market.

Average household spending on prepared flour mixes fell 28 percent between 2000 and 2007, after adjusting for inflation. Behind the spending cut was the decline in home cooking. Average household spending on prepared flour mixes will continue to decline as home cooking becomes less common and more boomers become empty-nesters.

Table 9.35 Flour, prepared mixes

Total household spending $1,393,983,600.00
Average household spends   11.60

AGE OF HOUSEHOLDER	AVERAGE HOUSEHOLD SPENDING	BEST CUSTOMERS (index)	BIGGEST CUSTOMERS (market share)
Average household	$11.60	100	100.0%
Under age 25	5.38	46	3.1
Aged 25 to 34	9.42	81	13.9
Aged 35 to 44	16.70	144	28.1
Aged 45 to 54	12.97	112	23.5
Aged 55 to 64	11.80	102	16.5
Aged 65 to 74	9.19	79	7.9
Aged 75 or older	8.97	77	7.3

	AVERAGE HOUSEHOLD SPENDING	BEST CUSTOMERS (index)	BIGGEST CUSTOMERS (market share)
HOUSEHOLD INCOME			
Average household	**$11.60**	**100**	**100.0%**
Under $20,000	6.90	59	12.2
$20,000 to $39,999	8.75	75	17.5
$40,000 to $49,999	10.91	94	9.3
$50,000 to $69,999	12.41	107	16.4
$70,000 to $79,999	12.93	111	6.5
$80,000 to $99,999	15.77	136	11.1
$100,000 or more	18.22	157	26.9
HOUSEHOLD TYPE			
Average household	**11.60**	**100**	**100.0**
Married couples	15.54	134	67.7
Married couples, no children	11.46	99	21.3
Married couples, with children	19.52	168	42.0
Oldest child under age 6	11.63	100	4.9
Oldest child aged 6 to 17	22.41	193	24.5
Oldest child aged 18 or older	19.59	169	12.4
Single parent with child under age 18	10.11	87	5.2
Single person	5.52	48	14.2
RACE AND HISPANIC ORIGIN			
Average household	**11.60**	**100**	**100.0**
Asian	5.21	45	1.6
Black	8.82	76	9.1
Hispanic	9.32	80	9.5
Non-Hispanic white and other	12.35	106	81.3
REGION			
Average household	**11.60**	**100**	**100.0**
Northeast	13.13	113	21.1
Midwest	12.08	104	23.8
South	11.07	95	34.3
West	10.67	92	20.8
EDUCATION			
Average household	**11.60**	**100**	**100.0**
Less than high school graduate	8.69	75	11.4
High school graduate	10.60	91	23.1
Some college	10.59	91	19.9
Associate's degree	16.42	142	12.6
College graduate	13.17	114	32.9
Bachelor's degree	12.02	104	19.4
Master's, professional, doctoral degree	15.17	131	13.3

Note: Market shares may not sum to 100.0 because of rounding and missing categories by household type. "Asian" and "black" include Hispanics and non-Hispanics who identify themselves as being of the respective race alone. "Hispanic" includes people of any race who identify themselves as Hispanic. "Other" includes people who identify themselves as non-Hispanic and as Alaska Native, American Indian, Asian (who are also included in the "Asian" row), Native Hawaiian or other Pacific Islander, as well as non-Hispanics reporting more than one race.
Source: Calculations by New Strategist based on the Bureau of Labor Statistics' 2007 Consumer Expenditure Survey.

Frankfurters

Best customers:	**Householders aged 35 to 54** **Married couples with school-aged or older children at home** **Single parents** **Blacks and Hispanics**
Customer trends:	**Average household spending on hot dogs may continue to decline as more boomers become empty-nesters and the small generation X enters the best-customer age group.**

Households with children are the biggest spenders on frankfurters. Married couples with school-aged or older children at home spend, respectively, 43 and 39 percent more than average on this item. Single parents spend 13 percent more. Householders aged 35 to 54, most with children, spend 19 percent more than average on hot dogs. Black households spend 18 percent more than average on this item, and Hispanics spend 13 percent more.

Average household spending on frankfurters fell 25 percent between 2000 and 2007, after adjusting for inflation. Average household spending on hot dogs may continue to decline in the years ahead as more boomers become empty-nesters and the small generation X fills the best-customer age group.

Table 9.36 Frankfurters

Total household spending	$2,250,802,830.00
Average household spends	18.73

	AVERAGE HOUSEHOLD SPENDING	BEST CUSTOMERS (index)	BIGGEST CUSTOMERS (market share)
AGE OF HOUSEHOLDER			
Average household	**$18.73**	**100**	**100.0%**
Under age 25	12.47	67	4.5
Aged 25 to 34	16.81	90	15.3
Aged 35 to 44	22.26	119	23.2
Aged 45 to 54	22.25	119	25.0
Aged 55 to 64	19.84	106	17.2
Aged 65 to 74	18.67	100	10.0
Aged 75 or older	10.00	53	5.1

	AVERAGE HOUSEHOLD SPENDING	BEST CUSTOMERS (index)	BIGGEST CUSTOMERS (market share)
HOUSEHOLD INCOME			
Average household	**$18.73**	**100**	**100.0%**
Under $20,000	13.15	70	14.4
$20,000 to $39,999	18.13	97	22.5
$40,000 to $49,999	16.53	88	8.7
$50,000 to $69,999	20.12	107	16.4
$70,000 to $79,999	21.64	116	6.7
$80,000 to $99,999	17.72	95	7.7
$100,000 or more	25.88	138	23.7
HOUSEHOLD TYPE			
Average household	**18.73**	**100**	**100.0**
Married couples	22.30	119	60.2
Married couples, no children	16.65	89	19.2
Married couples, with children	25.16	134	33.5
Oldest child under age 6	19.74	105	5.1
Oldest child aged 6 to 17	26.72	143	18.1
Oldest child aged 18 or older	26.03	139	10.2
Single parent with child under age 18	21.24	113	6.7
Single person	9.52	51	15.1
RACE AND HISPANIC ORIGIN			
Average household	**18.73**	**100**	**100.0**
Asian	18.61	99	3.5
Black	22.09	118	14.2
Hispanic	21.09	113	13.3
Non-Hispanic white and other	17.87	95	72.8
REGION			
Average household	**18.73**	**100**	**100.0**
Northeast	20.57	110	20.5
Midwest	16.23	87	19.8
South	20.48	109	39.3
West	16.92	90	20.4
EDUCATION			
Average household	**18.73**	**100**	**100.0**
Less than high school graduate	19.80	106	16.0
High school graduate	20.98	112	28.3
Some college	16.34	87	19.0
Associate's degree	21.79	116	10.3
College graduate	17.10	91	26.4
Bachelor's degree	16.54	88	16.6
Master's, professional, doctoral degree	18.08	97	9.8

Note: Market shares may not sum to 100.0 because of rounding and missing categories by household type. "Asian" and "black" include Hispanics and non-Hispanics who identify themselves as being of the respective race alone. "Hispanic" includes people of any race who identify themselves as Hispanic. "Other" includes people who identify themselves as non-Hispanic and as Alaska Native, American Indian, Asian (who are also included in the "Asian" row), Native Hawaiian or other Pacific Islander, as well as non-Hispanics reporting more than one race.
Source: Calculations by New Strategist based on the Bureau of Labor Statistics' 2007 Consumer Expenditure Survey.

Fruit, Canned

Best customers:	**Householders aged 55 to 64 and 75 or older**
	Married couples with children at home
	Single parents
	Households in the Northeast
Customer trends:	**Average household spending on canned fruit may decline as sliced and conveniently packaged fresh fruit becomes more widely available.**

The biggest spenders on canned fruit are older householders and the largest households. Married couples with children at home spend 39 percent more than average on canned fruit, the figure peaking at 47 percent among those with school-aged children. Even single parents outspend the average on this item. Householders aged 75 or older spend 27 percent more than average on canned fruit, while those aged 55 to 64 spend 17 percent more than average. Households in the Northeast spend 25 percent above average on canned fruit.

Average household spending on canned fruit rose 4 percent between 2000 and 2007, after adjusting for inflation. Behind the small increase was the aging of the population and the attempt by consumers to add more fruit to their diet. Average household spending on canned fruit may decline as sliced and conveniently packaged fresh fruit becomes more widely available.

Table 9.37 Fruit, canned

Total household spending	$2,339,729,370.00
Average household spends	19.47

	AVERAGE HOUSEHOLD SPENDING	BEST CUSTOMERS (index)	BIGGEST CUSTOMERS (market share)
AGE OF HOUSEHOLDER			
Average household	**$19.47**	**100**	**100.0%**
Under age 25	10.55	54	3.7
Aged 25 to 34	17.24	89	15.1
Aged 35 to 44	18.06	93	18.1
Aged 45 to 54	21.08	108	22.7
Aged 55 to 64	22.80	117	19.0
Aged 65 to 74	18.99	98	9.7
Aged 75 or older	24.74	127	12.0

	AVERAGE HOUSEHOLD SPENDING	BEST CUSTOMERS (index)	BIGGEST CUSTOMERS (market share)
HOUSEHOLD INCOME			
Average household	**$19.47**	**100**	**100.0%**
Under $20,000	12.15	62	12.8
$20,000 to $39,999	17.73	91	21.2
$40,000 to $49,999	18.86	97	9.5
$50,000 to $69,999	19.57	101	15.4
$70,000 to $79,999	18.84	97	5.6
$80,000 to $99,999	25.09	129	10.5
$100,000 or more	28.18	145	24.8
HOUSEHOLD TYPE			
Average household	**19.47**	**100**	**100.0**
Married couples	24.62	126	63.9
Married couples, no children	20.66	106	22.9
Married couples, with children	27.10	139	34.7
Oldest child under age 6	23.17	119	5.8
Oldest child aged 6 to 17	28.61	147	18.7
Oldest child aged 18 or older	27.00	139	10.2
Single parent with child under age 18	20.49	105	6.3
Single person	11.98	62	18.3
RACE AND HISPANIC ORIGIN			
Average household	**19.47**	**100**	**100.0**
Asian	9.62	49	1.7
Black	16.48	85	10.2
Hispanic	13.44	69	8.1
Non-Hispanic white and other	20.79	107	81.5
REGION			
Average household	**19.47**	**100**	**100.0**
Northeast	24.25	125	23.2
Midwest	19.80	102	23.2
South	16.91	87	31.2
West	19.22	99	22.3
EDUCATION			
Average household	**19.47**	**100**	**100.0**
Less than high school graduate	17.44	90	13.6
High school graduate	18.84	97	24.4
Some college	17.83	92	19.9
Associate's degree	18.88	97	8.6
College graduate	22.32	115	33.2
Bachelor's degree	22.66	116	21.8
Master's, professional, doctoral degree	21.73	112	11.4

Note: Market shares may not sum to 100.0 because of rounding and missing categories by household type. "Asian" and "black" include Hispanics and non-Hispanics who identify themselves as being of the respective race alone. "Hispanic" includes people of any race who identify themselves as Hispanic. "Other" includes people who identify themselves as non-Hispanic and as Alaska Native, American Indian, Asian (who are also included in the "Asian" row), Native Hawaiian or other Pacific Islander, as well as non-Hispanics reporting more than one race.
Source: Calculations by New Strategist based on the Bureau of Labor Statistics' 2007 Consumer Expenditure Survey.

Fruit, Dried

Best customers:	Householders aged 45 or older
	Married couples
	Asians
	Households in the Northeast
Customer trends:	Average household spending on dried fruit could continue to increase as the population ages.

The biggest spenders on dried fruit are older householders and the largest households. Married couples with children at home spend 25 percent more than average on dried fruit, the figure peaking at 30 percent among those with school-aged children. Householders aged 45 or older spend 13 to 30 percent more than average on dried fruit. Married couples without children at home (most of them older) spend 21 percent more than average on this item. Asians spend 51 percent more on dried fruit than average, and households in the Northeast, 25 percent.

Average household spending on dried fruit rose 22 percent between 2000 and 2007, after adjusting for inflation. Spending on dried fruit could continue to increase as the population ages.

Table 9.38 Fruit, dried

| Total household spending | $970,981,680.00 |
| Average household spends | 8.08 |

	AVERAGE HOUSEHOLD SPENDING	BEST CUSTOMERS (index)	BIGGEST CUSTOMERS (market share)
AGE OF HOUSEHOLDER			
Average household	$8.08	100	100.0%
Under age 25	3.44	43	2.9
Aged 25 to 34	6.66	82	14.1
Aged 35 to 44	7.14	88	17.2
Aged 45 to 54	9.22	114	24.0
Aged 55 to 64	9.21	114	18.5
Aged 65 to 74	10.47	130	13.0
Aged 75 or older	9.12	113	10.7

	AVERAGE HOUSEHOLD SPENDING	BEST CUSTOMERS (index)	BIGGEST CUSTOMERS (market share)
HOUSEHOLD INCOME			
Average household	**$8.08**	**100**	**100.0%**
Under $20,000	4.91	61	12.5
$20,000 to $39,999	5.79	72	16.7
$40,000 to $49,999	7.30	90	8.9
$50,000 to $69,999	8.49	105	16.1
$70,000 to $79,999	9.99	124	7.2
$80,000 to $99,999	9.88	122	9.9
$100,000 or more	13.48	167	28.6
HOUSEHOLD TYPE			
Average household	**8.08**	**100**	**100.0**
Married couples	10.38	128	64.9
Married couples, no children	9.81	121	26.2
Married couples, with children	10.10	125	31.2
Oldest child under age 6	10.31	128	6.2
Oldest child aged 6 to 17	10.48	130	16.5
Oldest child aged 18 or older	9.20	114	8.4
Single parent with child under age 18	5.39	67	4.0
Single person	5.08	63	18.7
RACE AND HISPANIC ORIGIN			
Average household	**8.08**	**100**	**100.0**
Asian	12.19	151	5.3
Black	4.17	52	6.2
Hispanic	5.57	69	8.1
Non-Hispanic white and other	9.03	112	85.3
REGION			
Average household	**8.08**	**100**	**100.0**
Northeast	10.06	125	23.2
Midwest	8.18	101	23.1
South	6.26	77	27.8
West	9.21	114	25.8
EDUCATION			
Average household	**8.08**	**100**	**100.0**
Less than high school graduate	4.79	59	9.0
High school graduate	5.32	66	16.6
Some college	8.08	100	21.8
Associate's degree	7.27	90	8.0
College graduate	12.21	151	43.7
Bachelor's degree	10.40	129	24.1
Master's, professional, doctoral degree	15.36	190	19.4

Note: Market shares may not sum to 100.0 because of rounding and missing categories by household type. "Asian" and "black" include Hispanics and non-Hispanics who identify themselves as being of the respective race alone. "Hispanic" includes people of any race who identify themselves as Hispanic. "Other" includes people who identify themselves as non-Hispanic and as Alaska Native, American Indian, Asian (who are also included in the "Asian" row), Native Hawaiian or other Pacific Islander, as well as non-Hispanics reporting more than one race.
Source: Calculations by New Strategist based on the Bureau of Labor Statistics' 2007 Consumer Expenditure Survey.

Fruit-Flavored Drinks, Noncarbonated

Best customers:

Householders aged 35 to 44
Married couples with school-aged or older children at home
Single parents
Blacks and Hispanics

Customer trends:

Average household spending on fruit-flavored drinks may decline in the years ahead as more boomers become empty-nesters, but the decline will be limited by growing numbers of blacks and Hispanics.

The best customers of fruit-flavored drinks are parents with children. Married couples with children at home spend 72 percent more than the average household on this item, while single parents spend 63 percent more. Householders aged 35 to 44, most with children at home, spend 41 percent more than average on this item. Blacks spend 32 percent more than average on fruit-flavored drinks, while Hispanics spend 40 percent more. Together, blacks and Hispanics account for nearly one-third of the market for fruit-flavored drinks.

Average household spending on noncarbonated fruit-flavored drinks purchased at grocery or convenience stores climbed by a small 2.5 percent between 2000 and 2007, after adjusting for inflation. Behind the spending increase were growing black and Hispanic populations, which counteracted the aging of the baby-boom generation out of the best-customer lifestage.

Table 9.39 **Fruit-flavored drinks, noncarbonated**

Total household spending $2,879,297,160.00
Average household spends 23.96

	AVERAGE HOUSEHOLD SPENDING	BEST CUSTOMERS (index)	BIGGEST CUSTOMERS (market share)
AGE OF HOUSEHOLDER			
Average household	**$23.96**	**100**	**100.0%**
Under age 25	24.34	102	6.9
Aged 25 to 34	24.01	100	17.1
Aged 35 to 44	33.78	141	27.5
Aged 45 to 54	28.38	118	24.9
Aged 55 to 64	17.43	73	11.8
Aged 65 to 74	20.31	85	8.5
Aged 75 or older	8.27	35	3.3

	AVERAGE HOUSEHOLD SPENDING	BEST CUSTOMERS (index)	BIGGEST CUSTOMERS (market share)
HOUSEHOLD INCOME			
Average household	**$23.96**	**100**	**100.0%**
Under $20,000	14.86	62	12.8
$20,000 to $39,999	20.51	86	19.9
$40,000 to $49,999	25.92	108	10.6
$50,000 to $69,999	25.78	108	16.5
$70,000 to $79,999	28.93	121	7.0
$80,000 to $99,999	26.62	111	9.0
$100,000 or more	33.65	140	24.1
HOUSEHOLD TYPE			
Average household	**23.96**	**100**	**100.0**
Married couples	30.36	127	64.1
Married couples, no children	14.51	61	13.1
Married couples, with children	41.22	172	42.9
Oldest child under age 6	25.38	106	5.2
Oldest child aged 6 to 17	44.80	187	23.8
Oldest child aged 18 or older	45.75	191	14.1
Single parent with child under age 18	39.02	163	9.7
Single person	9.32	39	11.6
RACE AND HISPANIC ORIGIN			
Average household	**23.96**	**100**	**100.0**
Asian	15.07	63	2.2
Black	31.74	132	15.9
Hispanic	33.61	140	16.6
Non-Hispanic white and other	21.39	89	68.1
REGION			
Average household	**23.96**	**100**	**100.0**
Northeast	22.94	96	17.8
Midwest	19.72	82	18.8
South	25.51	106	38.2
West	26.70	111	25.2
EDUCATION			
Average household	**23.96**	**100**	**100.0**
Less than high school graduate	27.27	114	17.3
High school graduate	22.10	92	23.3
Some college	24.46	102	22.2
Associate's degree	26.67	111	9.9
College graduate	22.91	96	27.7
Bachelor's degree	21.65	90	16.9
Master's, professional, doctoral degree	25.09	105	10.7

Note: Market shares may not sum to 100.0 because of rounding and missing categories by household type. "Asian" and "black" include Hispanics and non-Hispanics who identify themselves as being of the respective race alone. "Hispanic" includes people of any race who identify themselves as Hispanic. "Other" includes people who identify themselves as non-Hispanic and as Alaska Native, American Indian, Asian (who are also included in the "Asian" row), Native Hawaiian or other Pacific Islander, as well as non-Hispanics reporting more than one race.
Source: Calculations by New Strategist based on the Bureau of Labor Statistics' 2007 Consumer Expenditure Survey.

Fruit, Fresh, Other than Apples, Bananas, and Citrus

Best customers:	**Householders aged 35 to 74** **Married couples** **Asians** **Households in the West**
Customer trends:	**Average household spending on fresh fruit should continue to rise along with the aging of the population.**

The biggest spenders on fresh fruit other than apples, bananas, and citrus are middle-aged to older householders and the largest households. Married couples spend 34 percent more than average on other fresh fruit, the figure peaking at 47 percent among couples with preschoolers. Householders ranging in age from 35 to 74 spend 11 to 16 percent more than average on other fresh fruit. Asians spend 41 percent more than average on this item. Households in the West, where many Asians live, spend 20 percent above average on fruit other than apples, bananas, and citrus.

Spending on fresh fruit other than apples, bananas, and citrus ranks sixth among grocery items on which the average household spends the most. Average household spending on other fresh fruit climbed 19 percent between 2000 and 2007, after adjusting for inflation. Behind the increase was the growing variety of sliced and packaged fresh fruit available in grocery stores, boosting sales. Average household spending on other fresh fruit should continue to rise along with the aging of the population.

Table 9.40 **Fruit, fresh, other than apples, bananas, and citrus**

Total household spending	$11,838,045,210.00
Average household spends	98.51

	AVERAGE HOUSEHOLD SPENDING	BEST CUSTOMERS (index)	BIGGEST CUSTOMERS (market share)
AGE OF HOUSEHOLDER			
Average household	**$98.51**	**100**	**100.0%**
Under age 25	55.15	56	3.8
Aged 25 to 34	77.85	79	13.5
Aged 35 to 44	108.95	111	21.6
Aged 45 to 54	114.11	116	24.3
Aged 55 to 64	109.54	111	18.0
Aged 65 to 74	111.00	113	11.3
Aged 75 or older	80.90	82	7.8

	AVERAGE HOUSEHOLD SPENDING	BEST CUSTOMERS (index)	BIGGEST CUSTOMERS (market share)
HOUSEHOLD INCOME			
Average household	**$98.51**	**100**	**100.0%**
Under $20,000	51.26	52	10.7
$20,000 to $39,999	70.87	72	16.7
$40,000 to $49,999	99.35	101	9.9
$50,000 to $69,999	91.93	93	14.3
$70,000 to $79,999	121.13	123	7.1
$80,000 to $99,999	110.95	113	9.2
$100,000 or more	186.44	189	32.4
HOUSEHOLD TYPE			
Average household	**98.51**	**100**	**100.0**
Married couples	131.85	134	67.7
Married couples, no children	119.28	121	26.1
Married couples, with children	138.35	140	35.0
Oldest child under age 6	144.55	147	7.2
Oldest child aged 6 to 17	135.87	138	17.5
Oldest child aged 18 or older	138.70	141	10.4
Single parent with child under age 18	61.85	63	3.7
Single person	52.55	53	15.9
RACE AND HISPANIC ORIGIN			
Average household	**98.51**	**100**	**100.0**
Asian	139.36	141	5.0
Black	57.70	59	7.0
Hispanic	95.71	97	11.5
Non-Hispanic white and other	105.13	107	81.5
REGION			
Average household	**98.51**	**100**	**100.0**
Northeast	104.13	106	19.7
Midwest	94.20	96	21.9
South	86.25	88	31.4
West	117.95	120	27.1
EDUCATION			
Average household	**98.51**	**100**	**100.0**
Less than high school graduate	73.20	74	11.3
High school graduate	73.08	74	18.7
Some college	81.00	82	17.9
Associate's degree	94.38	96	8.5
College graduate	146.14	148	42.9
Bachelor's degree	127.74	130	24.3
Master's, professional, doctoral degree	178.10	181	18.4

Note: Market shares may not sum to 100.0 because of rounding and missing categories by household type. "Asian" and "black" include Hispanics and non-Hispanics who identify themselves as being of the respective race alone. "Hispanic" includes people of any race who identify themselves as Hispanic. "Other" includes people who identify themselves as non-Hispanic and as Alaska Native, American Indian, Asian (who are also included in the "Asian" row), Native Hawaiian or other Pacific Islander, as well as non-Hispanics reporting more than one race.
Source: Calculations by New Strategist based on the Bureau of Labor Statistics' 2007 Consumer Expenditure Survey.

Fruit, Frozen

Best customers:

Householders aged 25 to 44
Married couples
Non-Hispanic whites
Households in the Midwest

Customer trends:

Average household spending on frozen fruit could fall in the years ahead as the small generation X fills the best customer lifestage and fresh fruit competes with the frozen variety.

The largest households are the best customers of frozen fruit. Householders aged 25 to 44 spend 30 to 32 percent more than the average household on this item. Married couples with children at home spend 60 percent more than average on frozen fruit. Non-Hispanic white householders outspend minorities on this item. Households in the Midwest spend 29 percent more than average on frozen fruit.

Average household spending on frozen fruit grew 14 percent between 2000 and 2007, after adjusting for inflation. One factor behind the rise was growing health consciousness among consumers, who were adding more fruit to their diet. Average household spending on frozen fruit could fall in the years ahead as the small generation X fills the best customer lifestage and fresh fruit competes with the frozen variety.

Table 9.41 Fruit, frozen

Total household spending $597,249,870.00
Average household spends 4.97

	AVERAGE HOUSEHOLD SPENDING	BEST CUSTOMERS (index)	BIGGEST CUSTOMERS (market share)
AGE OF HOUSEHOLDER			
Average household	**$4.97**	**100**	**100.0%**
Under age 25	1.73	35	2.4
Aged 25 to 34	6.48	130	22.2
Aged 35 to 44	6.55	132	25.7
Aged 45 to 54	5.61	113	23.7
Aged 55 to 64	4.91	99	16.0
Aged 65 to 74	3.87	78	7.8
Aged 75 or older	1.18	24	2.3

	AVERAGE HOUSEHOLD SPENDING	BEST CUSTOMERS (index)	BIGGEST CUSTOMERS (market share)
HOUSEHOLD INCOME			
Average household	**$4.97**	**100**	**100.0%**
Under $20,000	1.32	27	5.5
$20,000 to $39,999	3.00	60	14.0
$40,000 to $49,999	5.22	105	10.3
$50,000 to $69,999	4.95	100	15.2
$70,000 to $79,999	9.23	186	10.8
$80,000 to $99,999	5.23	105	8.6
$100,000 or more	10.42	210	35.9
HOUSEHOLD TYPE			
Average household	**4.97**	**100**	**100.0**
Married couples	7.11	143	72.3
Married couples, no children	6.55	132	28.4
Married couples, with children	7.96	160	40.0
Oldest child under age 6	8.74	176	8.6
Oldest child aged 6 to 17	7.53	152	19.2
Oldest child aged 18 or older	8.25	166	12.2
Single parent with child under age 18	4.12	83	4.9
Single person	2.11	42	12.6
RACE AND HISPANIC ORIGIN			
Average household	**4.97**	**100**	**100.0**
Asian	2.00	40	1.4
Black	2.77	56	6.7
Hispanic	1.97	40	4.7
Non-Hispanic white and other	5.73	115	88.0
REGION			
Average household	**4.97**	**100**	**100.0**
Northeast	5.51	111	20.6
Midwest	6.42	129	29.5
South	4.04	81	29.2
West	4.51	91	20.5
EDUCATION			
Average household	**4.97**	**100**	**100.0**
Less than high school graduate	3.12	63	9.5
High school graduate	3.40	68	17.3
Some college	3.40	68	14.9
Associate's degree	8.25	166	14.8
College graduate	7.37	148	42.9
Bachelor's degree	6.25	126	23.6
Master's, professional, doctoral degree	9.32	188	19.1

Note: Market shares may not sum to 100.0 because of rounding and missing categories by household type. "Asian" and "black" include Hispanics and non-Hispanics who identify themselves as being of the respective race alone. "Hispanic" includes people of any race who identify themselves as Hispanic. "Other" includes people who identify themselves as non-Hispanic and as Alaska Native, American Indian, Asian (who are also included in the "Asian" row), Native Hawaiian or other Pacific Islander, as well as non-Hispanics reporting more than one race.
Source: Calculations by New Strategist based on the Bureau of Labor Statistics' 2007 Consumer Expenditure Survey.

Fruit Juice, Canned and Bottled

Best customers:

    Householders aged 35 to 44
    Married couples with children at home
    Single parents
    Asians, Blacks, and Hispanics

Customer trends:

    Average household spending on canned and bottled fruit juice may continue to decline as the small generation X fills the best-customer lifestage, but the decline may be limited by the growth of the Asian, black, and Hispanic populations.

Canned and bottled juice dominates fruit juice spending. Households with children are the biggest spenders on canned and bottled fruit juice. Married couples with children at home spend 38 percent more than average on this item. Single parents spend 7 percent more despite their low incomes. Householders aged 35 to 44, most with children, spend 17 percent more than average on this item. Asians spend 18 percent more than average on canned and bottled fruit juice, blacks 10 percent, and Hispanics 9 percent.

Average household spending on canned and bottled fruit juice purchased at grocery or convenience stores fell 17 percent between 2000 and 2007, after adjusting for inflation. Behind the decline is demographic change, with the small generation X filling the best-customer lifestage. This decline is likely to continue, but may be limited by growing Asian, black, and Hispanic populations.

Table 9.42 Fruit juice, canned and bottled

Total household spending $6,784,854,660.00
Average household spends   56.46

	AVERAGE HOUSEHOLD SPENDING	BEST CUSTOMERS (index)	BIGGEST CUSTOMERS (market share)
AGE OF HOUSEHOLDER			
Average household	**$56.46**	**100**	**100.0%**
Under age 25	36.54	65	4.4
Aged 25 to 34	59.39	105	17.9
Aged 35 to 44	65.92	117	22.8
Aged 45 to 54	60.96	108	22.7
Aged 55 to 64	51.69	92	14.8
Aged 65 to 74	56.53	100	10.0
Aged 75 or older	44.57	79	7.5

	AVERAGE HOUSEHOLD SPENDING	BEST CUSTOMERS (index)	BIGGEST CUSTOMERS (market share)
HOUSEHOLD INCOME			
Average household	**$56.46**	**100**	**100.0%**
Under $20,000	32.83	58	12.0
$20,000 to $39,999	48.24	85	19.9
$40,000 to $49,999	50.24	89	8.8
$50,000 to $69,999	58.65	104	15.9
$70,000 to $79,999	64.39	114	6.6
$80,000 to $99,999	67.24	119	9.7
$100,000 or more	89.71	159	27.2
HOUSEHOLD TYPE			
Average household	**56.46**	**100**	**100.0**
Married couples	68.93	122	61.7
Married couples, no children	56.04	99	21.4
Married couples, with children	77.75	138	34.4
Oldest child under age 6	76.03	135	6.6
Oldest child aged 6 to 17	74.70	132	16.8
Oldest child aged 18 or older	85.06	151	11.1
Single parent with child under age 18	60.35	107	6.4
Single person	30.83	55	16.2
RACE AND HISPANIC ORIGIN			
Average household	**56.46**	**100**	**100.0**
Asian	66.50	118	4.2
Black	61.94	110	13.2
Hispanic	61.67	109	12.9
Non-Hispanic white and other	54.96	97	74.3
REGION			
Average household	**56.46**	**100**	**100.0**
Northeast	67.60	120	22.3
Midwest	50.96	90	20.6
South	53.31	94	33.9
West	57.77	102	23.1
EDUCATION			
Average household	**56.46**	**100**	**100.0**
Less than high school graduate	49.65	88	13.3
High school graduate	50.60	90	22.6
Some college	46.30	82	17.9
Associate's degree	63.34	112	10.0
College graduate	70.05	124	35.9
Bachelor's degree	62.59	111	20.8
Master's, professional, doctoral degree	83.00	147	15.0

Note: Market shares may not sum to 100.0 because of rounding and missing categories by household type. "Asian" and "black" include Hispanics and non-Hispanics who identify themselves as being of the respective race alone. "Hispanic" includes people of any race who identify themselves as Hispanic. "Other" includes people who identify themselves as non-Hispanic and as Alaska Native, American Indian, Asian (who are also included in the "Asian" row), Native Hawaiian or other Pacific Islander, as well as non-Hispanics reporting more than one race.
Source: Calculations by New Strategist based on the Bureau of Labor Statistics' 2007 Consumer Expenditure Survey.

Fruit Juice, Fresh

Best customers:

Householders aged 35 to 54
Married couples with school-aged or older children at home
Asians

Customer trends:

Average household spending on fresh fruit juice could continue to fall as more boomers become empty-nesters and household size shrinks.

Middle-aged married couples are the biggest spenders on fresh fruit juice. Householders aged 35 to 54 spend 11 to 19 percent more than average on this item. Married couples with school-aged children at home spend 43 percent more than average on fresh fruit juice, while those with adult children at home spend well more than double the average. Asians spend 32 percent more than average on this item.

Average household spending on fresh fruit juice purchased at grocery or convenience stores fell by a substantial 39 percent between 2000 and 2007, after adjusting for inflation. Behind the decline was the baby-boom generation's exit from the best-customer lifestage, as well as the growing propensity of consumers to eat fast-food breakfasts or no breakfast at all. Average household spending on fresh fruit juice could continue to fall as more boomers become empty-nesters and household size shrinks.

Table 9.43 Fruit juice, fresh

Total household spending $2,068,142,910.00
Average household spends   17.21

	AVERAGE HOUSEHOLD SPENDING	BEST CUSTOMERS (index)	BIGGEST CUSTOMERS (market share)
AGE OF HOUSEHOLDER			
Average household	**$17.21**	**100**	**100.0%**
Under age 25	9.15	53	3.6
Aged 25 to 34	15.68	91	15.5
Aged 35 to 44	20.53	119	23.2
Aged 45 to 54	19.04	111	23.2
Aged 55 to 64	18.03	105	17.0
Aged 65 to 74	18.21	106	10.6
Aged 75 or older	12.74	74	7.0

	AVERAGE HOUSEHOLD SPENDING	BEST CUSTOMERS (index)	BIGGEST CUSTOMERS (market share)
HOUSEHOLD INCOME			
Average household	**$17.21**	**100**	**100.0%**
Under $20,000	8.70	51	10.4
$20,000 to $39,999	13.78	80	18.6
$40,000 to $49,999	16.63	97	9.5
$50,000 to $69,999	16.94	98	15.1
$70,000 to $79,999	20.88	121	7.0
$80,000 to $99,999	24.32	141	11.5
$100,000 or more	27.78	161	27.7
HOUSEHOLD TYPE			
Average household	**17.21**	**100**	**100.0**
Married couples	22.77	132	66.9
Married couples, no children	18.24	106	22.9
Married couples, with children	26.60	155	38.6
Oldest child under age 6	17.33	101	4.9
Oldest child aged 6 to 17	24.64	143	18.2
Oldest child aged 18 or older	37.28	217	16.0
Single parent with child under age 18	12.56	73	4.3
Single person	9.06	53	15.7
RACE AND HISPANIC ORIGIN			
Average household	**17.21**	**100**	**100.0**
Asian	22.69	132	4.7
Black	16.94	98	11.8
Hispanic	17.94	104	12.3
Non-Hispanic white and other	17.13	100	76.0
REGION			
Average household	**17.21**	**100**	**100.0**
Northeast	20.99	122	22.7
Midwest	12.76	74	16.9
South	16.64	97	34.7
West	19.54	114	25.7
EDUCATION			
Average household	**17.21**	**100**	**100.0**
Less than high school graduate	11.89	69	10.5
High school graduate	15.56	90	22.8
Some college	15.21	88	19.2
Associate's degree	17.16	100	8.9
College graduate	22.58	131	38.0
Bachelor's degree	20.90	121	22.8
Master's, professional, doctoral degree	25.50	148	15.1

Note: Market shares may not sum to 100.0 because of rounding and missing categories by household type. "Asian" and "black" include Hispanics and non-Hispanics who identify themselves as being of the respective race alone. "Hispanic" includes people of any race who identify themselves as Hispanic. "Other" includes people who identify themselves as non-Hispanic and as Alaska Native, American Indian, Asian (who are also included in the "Asian" row), Native Hawaiian or other Pacific Islander, as well as non-Hispanics reporting more than one race.
Source: Calculations by New Strategist based on the Bureau of Labor Statistics' 2007 Consumer Expenditure Survey.

Fruit Juice, Frozen

Best customers: **Married couples with school-aged or older children at home**
Single parents
Households in the West

Customer trends: **Average household spending on frozen fruit juice will continue to decline as growing**
numbers of customers choose fruit juice that requires no preparation.

Households with children are the best customers of frozen fruit juice. Married couples with school-aged or older children at home spend 67 to 74 percent more than average on frozen fruit juice. Single parents spend 12 percent more despite their low incomes. Households in the West spend 48 percent more than average on frozen fruit juice.

Average household spending on frozen fruit juice fell by an enormous 53 percent between 2000 and 2007 after adjusting for inflation. This decline occurred because consumers are looking for more convenience from fruit juice, and they are increasingly eating breakfast away from home or skipping the meal entirely. Average household spending on frozen fruit juice is likely to continue to decline as more customers choose fruit juice that does not require preparation.

Table 9.44 Fruit juice, frozen

| Total household spending | $736,648,230.00 |
| Average household spends | 6.13 |

	AVERAGE HOUSEHOLD SPENDING	BEST CUSTOMERS (index)	BIGGEST CUSTOMERS (market share)
AGE OF HOUSEHOLDER			
Average household	**$6.13**	**100**	**100.0%**
Under age 25	5.09	83	5.6
Aged 25 to 34	6.03	98	16.8
Aged 35 to 44	6.64	108	21.1
Aged 45 to 54	6.59	108	22.6
Aged 55 to 64	6.01	98	15.9
Aged 65 to 74	5.11	83	8.3
Aged 75 or older	6.32	103	9.8

	AVERAGE HOUSEHOLD SPENDING	BEST CUSTOMERS (index)	BIGGEST CUSTOMERS (market share)
HOUSEHOLD INCOME			
Average household	**$6.13**	**100**	**100.0%**
Under $20,000	3.77	61	12.6
$20,000 to $39,999	5.74	94	21.7
$40,000 to $49,999	5.14	84	8.3
$50,000 to $69,999	8.45	138	21.1
$70,000 to $79,999	7.77	127	7.3
$80,000 to $99,999	5.80	95	7.7
$100,000 or more	7.41	121	20.7
HOUSEHOLD TYPE			
Average household	**6.13**	**100**	**100.0**
Married couples	7.87	128	64.9
Married couples, no children	6.39	104	22.5
Married couples, with children	9.50	155	38.7
Oldest child under age 6	5.33	87	4.2
Oldest child aged 6 to 17	10.66	174	22.1
Oldest child aged 18 or older	10.26	167	12.3
Single parent with child under age 18	6.87	112	6.7
Single person	3.35	55	16.3
RACE AND HISPANIC ORIGIN			
Average household	**6.13**	**100**	**100.0**
Asian	3.16	52	1.8
Black	4.90	80	9.6
Hispanic	5.43	89	10.5
Non-Hispanic white and other	6.43	105	80.1
REGION			
Average household	**6.13**	**100**	**100.0**
Northeast	4.72	77	14.3
Midwest	6.80	111	25.4
South	4.61	75	27.0
West	9.07	148	33.5
EDUCATION			
Average household	**6.13**	**100**	**100.0**
Less than high school graduate	4.63	76	11.5
High school graduate	4.66	76	19.2
Some college	6.12	100	21.7
Associate's degree	8.21	134	11.9
College graduate	7.50	122	35.4
Bachelor's degree	7.67	125	23.5
Master's, professional, doctoral degree	7.20	117	12.0

Note: Market shares may not sum to 100.0 because of rounding and missing categories by household type. "Asian" and "black" include Hispanics and non-Hispanics who identify themselves as being of the respective race alone. "Hispanic" includes people of any race who identify themselves as Hispanic. "Other" includes people who identify themselves as non-Hispanic and as Alaska Native, American Indian, Asian (who are also included in the "Asian" row), Native Hawaiian or other Pacific Islander, as well as non-Hispanics reporting more than one race.
Source: Calculations by New Strategist based on the Bureau of Labor Statistics' 2007 Consumer Expenditure Survey.

Ground Beef

Best customers:
    Householders aged 35 to 54
    Married couples with school-aged or older children at home
    Single parents
    Hispanics

Customer trends:
    Average household spending on ground beef may decline as more boomers become empty-nesters and eating out claims an ever-growing share of the food dollar.

Ground beef ranks eighth among grocery items on which households spend the most. Households with children are the biggest spenders on ground beef. Married couples with school-aged or older children at home spend 52 to 64 percent more than average on this item. Householders aged 35 to 54, most with children, spend 11 to 27 percent more than average on ground beef and control 48 percent of the market. Single parents spend 12 percent more than average on this item, as do Hispanics.

Average household spending on ground beef declined by 16 percent between 2000 and 2007, after adjusting for inflation. Behind the decline is the growing popularity of fast food as a substitute for home-cooked meals. Average household spending on ground beef may continue to decline as more boomers become empty-nesters and eating out claims an ever-growing share of the food dollar.

Table 9.45 Ground beef

Total household spending $10,708,437,810.00
Average household spends   89.11

	AVERAGE HOUSEHOLD SPENDING	BEST CUSTOMERS (index)	BIGGEST CUSTOMERS (market share)
AGE OF HOUSEHOLDER			
Average household	**$89.11**	**100**	**100.0%**
Under age 25	74.24	83	5.7
Aged 25 to 34	90.08	101	17.2
Aged 35 to 44	112.96	127	24.7
Aged 45 to 54	98.84	111	23.3
Aged 55 to 64	86.94	98	15.8
Aged 65 to 74	70.69	79	7.9
Aged 75 or older	50.82	57	5.4

	AVERAGE HOUSEHOLD SPENDING	BEST CUSTOMERS (index)	BIGGEST CUSTOMERS (market share)
HOUSEHOLD INCOME			
Average household	**$89.11**	**100**	**100.0%**
Under $20,000	56.72	64	13.1
$20,000 to $39,999	79.61	89	20.8
$40,000 to $49,999	101.26	114	11.2
$50,000 to $69,999	97.75	110	16.8
$70,000 to $79,999	108.25	121	7.0
$80,000 to $99,999	104.52	117	9.5
$100,000 or more	109.90	123	21.1
HOUSEHOLD TYPE			
Average household	**89.11**	**100**	**100.0**
Married couples	110.69	124	62.8
Married couples, no children	83.51	94	20.2
Married couples, with children	132.03	148	37.0
Oldest child under age 6	103.56	116	5.7
Oldest child aged 6 to 17	135.26	152	19.3
Oldest child aged 18 or older	146.53	164	12.1
Single parent with child under age 18	99.85	112	6.7
Single person	40.88	46	13.6
RACE AND HISPANIC ORIGIN			
Average household	**89.11**	**100**	**100.0**
Asian	59.81	67	2.4
Black	91.49	103	12.3
Hispanic	99.85	112	13.2
Non-Hispanic white and other	87.15	98	74.7
REGION			
Average household	**89.11**	**100**	**100.0**
Northeast	83.42	94	17.4
Midwest	87.58	98	22.5
South	94.48	106	38.1
West	86.83	97	22.0
EDUCATION			
Average household	**89.11**	**100**	**100.0**
Less than high school graduate	88.39	99	15.0
High school graduate	103.12	116	29.2
Some college	91.02	102	22.2
Associate's degree	84.77	95	8.5
College graduate	77.10	87	25.0
Bachelor's degree	79.46	89	16.7
Master's, professional, doctoral degree	73.01	82	8.4

Note: Market shares may not sum to 100.0 because of rounding and missing categories by household type. "Asian" and "black" include Hispanics and non-Hispanics who identify themselves as being of the respective race alone. "Hispanic" includes people of any race who identify themselves as Hispanic. "Other" includes people who identify themselves as non-Hispanic and as Alaska Native, American Indian, Asian (who are also included in the "Asian" row), Native Hawaiian or other Pacific Islander, as well as non-Hispanics reporting more than one race.
Source: Calculations by New Strategist based on the Bureau of Labor Statistics' 2007 Consumer Expenditure Survey.

Ham

Best customers:

Householders aged 35 to 54
Married couples with school-aged or older children at home
Hispanics

Customer trends:

Average household spending on ham may continue to decline as more boomers become empty-nesters and eating out claims a growing share of the food dollar.

Households with children are the biggest spenders on ham. Married couples with school-aged or older children at home spend 53 percent more than average on this item. Householders aged 35 to 54, most with children, spend 16 to 18 percent more than average on ham. Hispanics outspend the average by 29 percent.

Average household spending on ham declined 27 percent between 2000 and 2007, after adjusting for inflation. Ham is suffering the same fate as many other grocery categories as Americans substitute fast food for home-cooked meals. Average household spending on ham may continue to decline as more boomers become empty-nesters and eating out claims a growing share of the food dollar.

Table 9.46 Ham

Total household spending		$3,827,446,350.00	
Average household spends		31.85	
	AVERAGE HOUSEHOLD SPENDING	BEST CUSTOMERS (index)	BIGGEST CUSTOMERS (market share)
AGE OF HOUSEHOLDER			
Average household	**$31.85**	**100**	**100.0%**
Under age 25	14.71	46	3.1
Aged 25 to 34	25.36	80	13.6
Aged 35 to 44	36.88	116	22.6
Aged 45 to 54	37.50	118	24.7
Aged 55 to 64	32.07	101	16.3
Aged 65 to 74	35.80	112	11.2
Aged 75 or older	29.23	92	8.7

	AVERAGE HOUSEHOLD SPENDING	BEST CUSTOMERS (index)	BIGGEST CUSTOMERS (market share)
HOUSEHOLD INCOME			
Average household	**$31.85**	**100**	**100.0%**
Under $20,000	16.93	53	10.9
$20,000 to $39,999	30.33	95	22.1
$40,000 to $49,999	34.77	109	10.7
$50,000 to $69,999	34.51	108	16.6
$70,000 to $79,999	37.28	117	6.8
$80,000 to $99,999	31.44	99	8.0
$100,000 or more	45.73	144	24.6
HOUSEHOLD TYPE			
Average household	**31.85**	**100**	**100.0**
Married couples	40.08	126	63.6
Married couples, no children	34.28	108	23.2
Married couples, with children	44.47	140	34.8
Oldest child under age 6	27.08	85	4.1
Oldest child aged 6 to 17	48.82	153	19.5
Oldest child aged 18 or older	48.62	153	11.2
Single parent with child under age 18	31.21	98	5.8
Single person	17.12	54	16.0
RACE AND HISPANIC ORIGIN			
Average household	**31.85**	**100**	**100.0**
Asian	26.45	83	2.9
Black	31.56	99	11.9
Hispanic	41.18	129	15.3
Non-Hispanic white and other	30.64	96	73.4
REGION			
Average household	**31.85**	**100**	**100.0**
Northeast	31.91	100	18.7
Midwest	29.94	94	21.5
South	33.66	106	37.9
West	30.87	97	21.9
EDUCATION			
Average household	**31.85**	**100**	**100.0**
Less than high school graduate	32.27	101	15.4
High school graduate	35.52	112	28.1
Some college	29.03	91	19.8
Associate's degree	36.34	114	10.1
College graduate	29.21	92	26.5
Bachelor's degree	29.95	94	17.6
Master's, professional, doctoral degree	27.92	88	8.9

Note: Market shares may not sum to 100.0 because of rounding and missing categories by household type. "Asian" and "black" include Hispanics and non-Hispanics who identify themselves as being of the respective race alone. "Hispanic" includes people of any race who identify themselves as Hispanic. "Other" includes people who identify themselves as non-Hispanic and as Alaska Native, American Indian, Asian (who are also included in the "Asian" row), Native Hawaiian or other Pacific Islander, as well as non-Hispanics reporting more than one race.
Source: Calculations by New Strategist based on the Bureau of Labor Statistics' 2007 Consumer Expenditure Survey.

Ice Cream and Related Products

Best customers:
Householders aged 35 to 44
Married couples with school-aged or older children at home

Customer trends:
Average household spending on ice cream may continue to fall as boomers exit the best-customer lifestage.

Households with children spend the most on ice cream and related products. Married couples with school-aged or older children at home spend 46 to 58 percent more than the average household on this item. Householders aged 35 to 44, most with children at home, spend 22 percent more than average on ice cream.

Average household spending on ice cream and related products fell 16 percent between 2000 and 2007, after adjusting for inflation. Behind the decline was price discounting as private-label brands competed with premium brands in the grocery store. Average household spending on ice cream may continue to fall as boomers exit the best-customer lifestage.

Table 9.47 Ice cream and related products

Total household spending		$6,894,210,270.00	
Average household spends		57.37	

	AVERAGE HOUSEHOLD SPENDING	BEST CUSTOMERS (index)	BIGGEST CUSTOMERS (market share)
AGE OF HOUSEHOLDER			
Average household	**$57.37**	**100**	**100.0%**
Under age 25	32.13	56	3.8
Aged 25 to 34	49.56	86	14.7
Aged 35 to 44	69.88	122	23.7
Aged 45 to 54	61.30	107	22.4
Aged 55 to 64	56.65	99	16.0
Aged 65 to 74	64.59	113	11.3
Aged 75 or older	49.47	86	8.2

	AVERAGE HOUSEHOLD SPENDING	BEST CUSTOMERS (index)	BIGGEST CUSTOMERS (market share)
HOUSEHOLD INCOME			
Average household	**$57.37**	**100**	**100.0%**
Under $20,000	31.80	55	11.4
$20,000 to $39,999	45.93	80	18.6
$40,000 to $49,999	46.02	80	7.9
$50,000 to $69,999	67.45	118	18.0
$70,000 to $79,999	75.39	131	7.6
$80,000 to $99,999	75.67	132	10.7
$100,000 or more	85.19	148	25.4
HOUSEHOLD TYPE			
Average household	**57.37**	**100**	**100.0**
Married couples	75.14	131	66.2
Married couples, no children	66.61	116	25.0
Married couples, with children	82.13	143	35.7
Oldest child under age 6	66.44	116	5.7
Oldest child aged 6 to 17	83.66	146	18.5
Oldest child aged 18 or older	90.62	158	11.6
Single parent with child under age 18	55.62	97	5.8
Single person	30.44	53	15.8
RACE AND HISPANIC ORIGIN			
Average household	**57.37**	**100**	**100.0**
Asian	68.84	120	4.2
Black	38.47	67	8.0
Hispanic	43.17	75	8.9
Non-Hispanic white and other	62.29	109	82.9
REGION			
Average household	**57.37**	**100**	**100.0**
Northeast	64.94	113	21.1
Midwest	52.41	91	20.9
South	53.59	93	33.5
West	62.19	108	24.5
EDUCATION			
Average household	**57.37**	**100**	**100.0**
Less than high school graduate	42.19	74	11.2
High school graduate	53.78	94	23.6
Some college	52.24	91	19.8
Associate's degree	65.09	113	10.1
College graduate	68.99	120	34.8
Bachelor's degree	64.33	112	21.0
Master's, professional, doctoral degree	77.08	134	13.7

Note: Market shares may not sum to 100.0 because of rounding and missing categories by household type. "Asian" and "black" include Hispanics and non-Hispanics who identify themselves as being of the respective race alone. "Hispanic" includes people of any race who identify themselves as Hispanic. "Other" includes people who identify themselves as non-Hispanic and as Alaska Native, American Indian, Asian (who are also included in the "Asian" row), Native Hawaiian or other Pacific Islander, as well as non-Hispanics reporting more than one race.
Source: Calculations by New Strategist based on the Bureau of Labor Statistics' 2007 Consumer Expenditure Survey.

Jams, Preserves, and Other Sweets

Best customers: Householders aged 35 to 54
Married couples with children at home

Customer trends: Average household spending on jams, preserves, and other sweets is likely to
decline as more boomers become empty-nesters and household size shrinks.

Married couples with school-aged children spend the most on jams, preserves, and other sweets—72 percent more than the average household. Householders aged 35 to 54, most with children at home, spend 15 to 26 percent more than average on jams and control 49 percent of the market.

Average household spending on jams, preserves, and other sweets declined 9 percent between 2000 and 2007, after adjusting for inflation. Average household spending on jams will continue to fall in the years ahead as more boomers become empty-nesters and household size shrinks.

Table 9.48 Jams, preserves, and other sweets

Total household spending $2,620,929,510.00
Average household spends   21.81

	AVERAGE HOUSEHOLD SPENDING	BEST CUSTOMERS (index)	BIGGEST CUSTOMERS (market share)
AGE OF HOUSEHOLDER			
Average household	**$21.81**	**100**	**100.0%**
Under age 25	12.47	57	3.9
Aged 25 to 34	18.29	84	14.3
Aged 35 to 44	27.47	126	24.5
Aged 45 to 54	25.01	115	24.1
Aged 55 to 64	20.94	96	15.5
Aged 65 to 74	23.65	108	10.8
Aged 75 or older	16.01	73	7.0

	AVERAGE HOUSEHOLD SPENDING	BEST CUSTOMERS (index)	BIGGEST CUSTOMERS (market share)
HOUSEHOLD INCOME			
Average household	**$21.81**	**100**	**100.0%**
Under $20,000	11.47	53	10.8
$20,000 to $39,999	16.15	74	17.2
$40,000 to $49,999	20.55	94	9.3
$50,000 to $69,999	23.92	110	16.8
$70,000 to $79,999	24.26	111	6.4
$80,000 to $99,999	28.79	132	10.7
$100,000 or more	36.61	168	28.8
HOUSEHOLD TYPE			
Average household	**21.81**	**100**	**100.0**
Married couples	29.46	135	68.3
Married couples, no children	23.79	109	23.5
Married couples, with children	34.26	157	39.2
Oldest child under age 6	28.15	129	6.3
Oldest child aged 6 to 17	37.43	172	21.8
Oldest child aged 18 or older	32.49	149	11.0
Single parent with child under age 18	20.28	93	5.5
Single person	10.62	49	14.5
RACE AND HISPANIC ORIGIN			
Average household	**21.81**	**100**	**100.0**
Asian	19.23	88	3.1
Black	14.32	66	7.9
Hispanic	16.61	76	9.0
Non-Hispanic white and other	23.71	109	83.0
REGION			
Average household	**21.81**	**100**	**100.0**
Northeast	21.95	101	18.7
Midwest	21.68	99	22.7
South	19.78	91	32.6
West	25.11	115	26.0
EDUCATION			
Average household	**21.81**	**100**	**100.0**
Less than high school graduate	15.09	69	10.5
High school graduate	19.10	88	22.1
Some college	19.38	89	19.4
Associate's degree	23.71	109	9.7
College graduate	28.49	131	37.8
Bachelor's degree	25.78	118	22.2
Master's, professional, doctoral degree	33.19	152	15.5

Note: Market shares may not sum to 100.0 because of rounding and missing categories by household type. "Asian" and "black" include Hispanics and non-Hispanics who identify themselves as being of the respective race alone. "Hispanic" includes people of any race who identify themselves as Hispanic. "Other" includes people who identify themselves as non-Hispanic and as Alaska Native, American Indian, Asian (who are also included in the "Asian" row), Native Hawaiian or other Pacific Islander, as well as non-Hispanics reporting more than one race.
Source: Calculations by New Strategist based on the Bureau of Labor Statistics' 2007 Consumer Expenditure Survey.

Lettuce

Best customers:
    Householders aged 35 to 64
Married couples with school-aged or older children at home
Asians

Customer trends:
    Average household spending on lettuce could rise over the next few years as aging boomers try to improve their diets, but competition from restaurants will limit the gains.

The best customers of lettuce are middle-aged married couples, many with children at home. Married couples with school-aged or older children at home spend 37 to 80 percent more than the average household on lettuce, while those without children at home (most of them older) spend 16 percent more. Householders ranging in age from 35 to 64, many with children at home, spend 13 to 18 percent more than the average household on this item. Asians spend 66 percent more than average on lettuce.

Average household spending on lettuce fell 5 percent between 2000 and 2007, after adjusting for inflation. One factor behind the decline is the substitution of fast food for home-cooked meals. Average household spending on lettuce could rise over the next few years as aging boomers try to improve their diets, but competition from restaurants will limit the gains.

Table 9.49 Lettuce

Total household spending $2,858,868,090.00
Average household spends   23.79

	AVERAGE HOUSEHOLD SPENDING	BEST CUSTOMERS (index)	BIGGEST CUSTOMERS (market share)
AGE OF HOUSEHOLDER			
Average household	**$23.79**	**100**	**100.0%**
Under age 25	12.40	52	3.5
Aged 25 to 34	19.27	81	13.8
Aged 35 to 44	27.32	115	22.4
Aged 45 to 54	28.01	118	24.7
Aged 55 to 64	26.95	113	18.3
Aged 65 to 74	23.28	98	9.8
Aged 75 or older	19.26	81	7.7

	AVERAGE HOUSEHOLD SPENDING	BEST CUSTOMERS (index)	BIGGEST CUSTOMERS (market share)
HOUSEHOLD INCOME			
Average household	**$23.79**	**100**	**100.0%**
Under $20,000	13.10	55	11.3
$20,000 to $39,999	18.17	76	17.7
$40,000 to $49,999	22.34	94	9.2
$50,000 to $69,999	23.27	98	15.0
$70,000 to $79,999	27.52	116	6.7
$80,000 to $99,999	31.13	131	10.6
$100,000 or more	40.71	171	29.3
HOUSEHOLD TYPE			
Average household	**23.79**	**100**	**100.0**
Married couples	31.48	132	66.9
Married couples, no children	27.55	116	25.0
Married couples, with children	34.19	144	35.9
Oldest child under age 6	26.76	112	5.5
Oldest child aged 6 to 17	32.56	137	17.4
Oldest child aged 18 or older	42.85	180	13.3
Single parent with child under age 18	17.02	72	4.3
Single person	12.76	54	16.0
RACE AND HISPANIC ORIGIN			
Average household	**23.79**	**100**	**100.0**
Asian	39.38	166	5.8
Black	17.36	73	8.8
Hispanic	25.56	107	12.7
Non-Hispanic white and other	24.52	103	78.7
REGION			
Average household	**23.79**	**100**	**100.0**
Northeast	28.33	119	22.2
Midwest	21.79	92	20.9
South	20.43	86	30.8
West	27.41	115	26.1
EDUCATION			
Average household	**23.79**	**100**	**100.0**
Less than high school graduate	18.60	78	11.9
High school graduate	20.99	88	22.3
Some college	20.93	88	19.2
Associate's degree	26.23	110	9.8
College graduate	29.98	126	36.5
Bachelor's degree	26.07	110	20.5
Master's, professional, doctoral degree	36.76	155	15.8

Note: Market shares may not sum to 100.0 because of rounding and missing categories by household type. "Asian" and "black" include Hispanics and non-Hispanics who identify themselves as being of the respective race alone. "Hispanic" includes people of any race who identify themselves as Hispanic. "Other" includes people who identify themselves as non-Hispanic and as Alaska Native, American Indian, Asian (who are also included in the "Asian" row), Native Hawaiian or other Pacific Islander, as well as non-Hispanics reporting more than one race.
Source: Calculations by New Strategist based on the Bureau of Labor Statistics' 2007 Consumer Expenditure Survey.

Lunch Meats (Cold Cuts)

Best customers: **Householders aged 35 to 54**
Married couples with school-aged or older children at home

Customer trends: **Average household spending on lunch meats will continue to decline as more boomers become empty-nesters.**

Lunch meats rank 13th among the grocery items on which households spend the most. The best customers of lunch meats are the largest households. Married couples with school-aged or adult children at home spend 42 to 100 percent more than the average household on this item. Householders aged 35 to 54, most with children, spend 19 to 24 percent more than average on lunch meats and control 49 percent of the market.

Average household spending on lunch meats fell 7 percent between 2000 and 2009, after adjusting for inflation. Behind the decline is the substitution of fast food for brown bag lunches. Average household spending on lunch meats should continue to decline as more boomers become empty-nesters and eating out claims a growing share of the food dollar.

Table 9.50 Lunch meats (cold cuts)

Total household spending $9,149,819,940.00
Average household spends   76.14

	AVERAGE HOUSEHOLD SPENDING	BEST CUSTOMERS (index)	BIGGEST CUSTOMERS (market share)
AGE OF HOUSEHOLDER			
Average household	**$76.14**	**100**	**100.0%**
Under age 25	54.18	71	4.8
Aged 25 to 34	61.33	81	13.7
Aged 35 to 44	90.80	119	23.2
Aged 45 to 54	94.39	124	26.0
Aged 55 to 64	79.49	104	16.9
Aged 65 to 74	65.45	86	8.6
Aged 75 or older	55.13	72	6.9

	AVERAGE HOUSEHOLD SPENDING	BEST CUSTOMERS (index)	BIGGEST CUSTOMERS (market share)
HOUSEHOLD INCOME			
Average household	**$76.14**	**100**	**100.0%**
Under $20,000	45.88	60	12.4
$20,000 to $39,999	59.08	78	18.0
$40,000 to $49,999	73.67	97	9.5
$50,000 to $69,999	84.22	111	16.9
$70,000 to $79,999	89.17	117	6.8
$80,000 to $99,999	91.57	120	9.8
$100,000 or more	117.63	154	26.5
HOUSEHOLD TYPE			
Average household	**76.14**	**100**	**100.0**
Married couples	96.35	127	64.0
Married couples, no children	75.11	99	21.3
Married couples, with children	113.22	149	37.1
Oldest child under age 6	74.96	98	4.8
Oldest child aged 6 to 17	107.84	142	18.0
Oldest child aged 18 or older	151.96	200	14.7
Single parent with child under age 18	80.29	105	6.3
Single person	40.82	54	15.9
RACE AND HISPANIC ORIGIN			
Average household	**76.14**	**100**	**100.0**
Asian	54.20	71	2.5
Black	62.76	82	9.9
Hispanic	63.47	83	9.8
Non-Hispanic white and other	79.99	105	80.2
REGION			
Average household	**76.14**	**100**	**100.0**
Northeast	89.09	117	21.8
Midwest	81.72	107	24.5
South	70.06	92	33.0
West	69.23	91	20.6
EDUCATION			
Average household	**76.14**	**100**	**100.0**
Less than high school graduate	61.07	80	12.2
High school graduate	78.39	103	26.0
Some college	74.58	98	21.3
Associate's degree	82.70	109	9.7
College graduate	80.40	106	30.6
Bachelor's degree	78.22	103	19.3
Master's, professional, doctoral degree	84.18	111	11.3

Note: Market shares may not sum to 100.0 because of rounding and missing categories by household type. "Asian" and "black" include Hispanics and non-Hispanics who identify themselves as being of the respective race alone. "Hispanic" includes people of any race who identify themselves as Hispanic. "Other" includes people who identify themselves as non-Hispanic and as Alaska Native, American Indian, Asian (who are also included in the "Asian" row), Native Hawaiian or other Pacific Islander, as well as non-Hispanics reporting more than one race.
Source: Calculations by New Strategist based on the Bureau of Labor Statistics' 2007 Consumer Expenditure Survey.

Margarine

Best customers:
Householders aged 55 or older
Married couples without children at home
Married couples with school-aged or older children at home
Single parents
Households in the Midwest

Customer trends:
Average household spending on margarine will continue to decline as the reputation of butter improves.

Margarine's fortunes are waning as the reputation of butter improves. In 2000, the average household spent 68 percent as much on margarine as it did on butter. By 2007, the figure had fallen to 35 percent. The best customers of margarine are older householders, many of them following advice that margarine is healthier than butter. Householders aged 55 or older spend 14 to 54 percent more than average on margarine and control 46 percent of the market. Married couples without children at home (most of them empty-nesters) spend 31 percent more than the average household on this item. Couples with adult children at home spend 53 percent more than average on margarine. Even single parents spend 8 percent more than average. Households in the Midwest spend 25 percent more than average on margarine.

Average household spending on margarine fell 50 percent between 2000 and 2007, after adjusting for inflation. Behind the downward slide are health warnings about trans-fats in margarine and the improving reputation of butter. Average household spending on margarine will continue to decline as more boomers, many of whom prefer butter, age into the best-customer age groups.

Table 9.51 Margarine

Total household spending		$846,003,840.00	
Average household spends		7.04	
	AVERAGE HOUSEHOLD SPENDING	BEST CUSTOMERS (index)	BIGGEST CUSTOMERS (market share)
AGE OF HOUSEHOLDER			
Average household	**$7.04**	**100**	**100.0%**
Under age 25	2.23	32	2.1
Aged 25 to 34	4.56	65	11.0
Aged 35 to 44	6.58	93	18.2
Aged 45 to 54	7.63	108	22.8
Aged 55 to 64	8.02	114	18.4
Aged 65 to 74	10.85	154	15.4
Aged 75 or older	9.10	129	12.3

	AVERAGE HOUSEHOLD SPENDING	BEST CUSTOMERS (index)	BIGGEST CUSTOMERS (market share)
HOUSEHOLD INCOME			
Average household	**$7.04**	**100**	**100.0%**
Under $20,000	3.68	52	10.7
$20,000 to $39,999	7.11	101	23.5
$40,000 to $49,999	6.32	90	8.8
$50,000 to $69,999	7.44	106	16.2
$70,000 to $79,999	8.61	122	7.1
$80,000 to $99,999	8.77	125	10.1
$100,000 or more	9.37	133	22.8
HOUSEHOLD TYPE			
Average household	**7.04**	**100**	**100.0**
Married couples	8.99	128	64.6
Married couples, no children	9.20	131	28.2
Married couples, with children	8.79	125	31.2
Oldest child under age 6	5.60	80	3.9
Oldest child aged 6 to 17	8.95	127	16.1
Oldest child aged 18 or older	10.80	153	11.3
Single parent with child under age 18	7.59	108	6.4
Single person	4.11	58	17.4
RACE AND HISPANIC ORIGIN			
Average household	**7.04**	**100**	**100.0**
Asian	3.41	48	1.7
Black	5.06	72	8.6
Hispanic	4.57	65	7.7
Non-Hispanic white and other	7.72	110	83.7
REGION			
Average household	**7.04**	**100**	**100.0**
Northeast	6.62	94	17.5
Midwest	8.78	125	28.5
South	6.57	93	33.5
West	6.35	90	20.4
EDUCATION			
Average household	**7.04**	**100**	**100.0**
Less than high school graduate	6.85	97	14.8
High school graduate	6.29	89	22.5
Some college	7.12	101	22.0
Associate's degree	7.03	100	8.9
College graduate	7.71	110	31.7
Bachelor's degree	7.21	102	19.2
Master's, professional, doctoral degree	8.59	122	12.4

Note: Market shares may not sum to 100.0 because of rounding and missing categories by household type. "Asian" and "black" include Hispanics and non-Hispanics who identify themselves as being of the respective race alone. "Hispanic" includes people of any race who identify themselves as Hispanic. "Other" includes people who identify themselves as non-Hispanic and as Alaska Native, American Indian, Asian (who are also included in the "Asian" row), Native Hawaiian or other Pacific Islander, as well as non-Hispanics reporting more than one race.
Source: Calculations by New Strategist based on the Bureau of Labor Statistics' 2007 Consumer Expenditure Survey.

Milk, Fresh

Best customers:

Householders aged 35 to 44
Married couples with children at home
Hispanics

Customer trends:

Average household spending on milk will continue to decline as the small generation X fills the best-customer lifestage.

Americans spend more on milk than any other nonalcoholic beverage. The best customers of milk are the largest households. Married couples with children at home spend 57 percent more than the average household on this item. Householders aged 35 to 44, most with children, spend 23 percent more than average on milk. Hispanics, who have relatively large households, spend 12 percent more than average on this item.

Average household spending on milk purchased at grocery or convenience stores fell 4 percent between 2000 and 2007, after adjusting for inflation. Behind the decline is the baby-boom generation's exit from the best-customer lifestage. Another factor is the substitution of sodas, juices, and other drinks for milk. Average household spending on milk will continue to decline as the small generation X fills the best-customer lifestage.

Table 9.52 Milk, fresh

| Total household spending | $16,601,623,650.00 |
| Average household spends | 138.15 |

	AVERAGE HOUSEHOLD SPENDING	BEST CUSTOMERS (index)	BIGGEST CUSTOMERS (market share)
AGE OF HOUSEHOLDER			
Average household	**$138.15**	**100**	**100.0%**
Under age 25	94.64	69	4.6
Aged 25 to 34	143.69	104	17.7
Aged 35 to 44	170.18	123	24.0
Aged 45 to 54	153.15	111	23.3
Aged 55 to 64	125.97	91	14.8
Aged 65 to 74	120.65	87	8.7
Aged 75 or older	100.70	73	6.9

	AVERAGE HOUSEHOLD SPENDING	BEST CUSTOMERS (index)	BIGGEST CUSTOMERS (market share)
HOUSEHOLD INCOME			
Average household	**$138.15**	**100**	**100.0%**
Under $20,000	90.01	65	13.4
$20,000 to $39,999	119.43	86	20.1
$40,000 to $49,999	135.85	98	9.7
$50,000 to $69,999	142.15	103	15.7
$70,000 to $79,999	168.97	122	7.1
$80,000 to $99,999	174.87	127	10.3
$100,000 or more	188.46	136	23.4
HOUSEHOLD TYPE			
Average household	**138.15**	**100**	**100.0**
Married couples	177.36	128	64.9
Married couples, no children	129.43	94	20.2
Married couples, with children	216.76	157	39.1
Oldest child under age 6	213.26	154	7.5
Oldest child aged 6 to 17	229.33	166	21.1
Oldest child aged 18 or older	194.42	141	10.4
Single parent with child under age 18	140.25	102	6.0
Single person	73.04	53	15.7
RACE AND HISPANIC ORIGIN			
Average household	**138.15**	**100**	**100.0**
Asian	145.16	105	3.7
Black	104.51	76	9.1
Hispanic	155.29	112	13.3
Non-Hispanic white and other	140.85	102	77.8
REGION			
Average household	**138.15**	**100**	**100.0**
Northeast	135.34	98	18.2
Midwest	129.09	93	21.4
South	142.83	103	37.1
West	142.33	103	23.3
EDUCATION			
Average household	**138.15**	**100**	**100.0**
Less than high school graduate	135.18	98	14.8
High school graduate	133.22	96	24.3
Some college	134.19	97	21.2
Associate's degree	141.44	102	9.1
College graduate	145.72	105	30.5
Bachelor's degree	140.54	102	19.1
Master's, professional, doctoral degree	154.71	112	11.4

Note: Market shares may not sum to 100.0 because of rounding and missing categories by household type. "Asian" and "black" include Hispanics and non-Hispanics who identify themselves as being of the respective race alone. "Hispanic" includes people of any race who identify themselves as Hispanic. "Other" includes people who identify themselves as non-Hispanic and as Alaska Native, American Indian, Asian (who are also included in the "Asian" row), Native Hawaiian or other Pacific Islander, as well as non-Hispanics reporting more than one race.
Source: Calculations by New Strategist based on the Bureau of Labor Statistics' 2007 Consumer Expenditure Survey.

Nondairy Cream and Imitation Milk

Best customers: Householders aged 35 to 54
Married couples with school-aged or older children at home

Customer trends: Average household spending on nondairy cream and imitation milk may fall in the
years ahead as generation X fills the best-customer lifestage.

Middle-aged married couples and the largest households are the biggest spenders on nondairy cream. Householders aged 35 to 54 spend 26 to 27 percent more than average on this item. Married couples with school-aged or older children at home spend 51 to 70 percent more than average on this item.

Average household spending on nondairy cream and imitation milk grew 23 percent between 2000 and 2007, after adjusting for inflation. Average household spending on nondairy cream and imitation milk may fall in the years ahead as generation X fills the best-customer lifestage.

Table 9.53 **Nondairy cream and imitation milk**

Total household spending $1,629,518,760.00
Average household spends   13.56

	AVERAGE HOUSEHOLD SPENDING	BEST CUSTOMERS (index)	BIGGEST CUSTOMERS (market share)
AGE OF HOUSEHOLDER			
Average household	**$13.56**	**100**	**100.0%**
Under age 25	6.68	49	3.3
Aged 25 to 34	10.60	78	13.3
Aged 35 to 44	17.12	126	24.6
Aged 45 to 54	17.17	127	26.6
Aged 55 to 64	13.46	99	16.1
Aged 65 to 74	12.45	92	9.2
Aged 75 or older	10.23	75	7.2

	AVERAGE HOUSEHOLD SPENDING	BEST CUSTOMERS (index)	BIGGEST CUSTOMERS (market share)
HOUSEHOLD INCOME			
Average household	**$13.56**	**100**	**100.0%**
Under $20,000	6.65	49	10.1
$20,000 to $39,999	12.08	89	20.7
$40,000 to $49,999	12.14	90	8.8
$50,000 to $69,999	15.00	111	16.9
$70,000 to $79,999	18.16	134	7.8
$80,000 to $99,999	19.45	143	11.7
$100,000 or more	18.53	137	23.4
HOUSEHOLD TYPE			
Average household	**13.56**	**100**	**100.0**
Married couples	18.24	135	68.0
Married couples, no children	16.04	118	25.5
Married couples, with children	19.78	146	36.4
Oldest child under age 6	13.37	99	4.8
Oldest child aged 6 to 17	20.50	151	19.2
Oldest child aged 18 or older	23.07	170	12.5
Single parent with child under age 18	8.55	63	3.7
Single person	7.11	52	15.6
RACE AND HISPANIC ORIGIN			
Average household	**13.56**	**100**	**100.0**
Asian	9.87	73	2.6
Black	6.41	47	5.7
Hispanic	11.85	87	10.3
Non-Hispanic white and other	14.91	110	83.9
REGION			
Average household	**13.56**	**100**	**100.0**
Northeast	12.98	96	17.8
Midwest	13.13	97	22.1
South	13.08	96	34.6
West	15.26	113	25.4
EDUCATION			
Average household	**13.56**	**100**	**100.0**
Less than high school graduate	11.86	87	13.3
High school graduate	12.30	91	22.9
Some college	15.94	118	25.6
Associate's degree	16.73	123	11.0
College graduate	12.83	95	27.4
Bachelor's degree	13.28	98	18.4
Master's, professional, doctoral degree	12.03	89	9.1

Note: Market shares may not sum to 100.0 because of rounding and missing categories by household type. "Asian" and "black" include Hispanics and non-Hispanics who identify themselves as being of the respective race alone. "Hispanic" includes people of any race who identify themselves as Hispanic. "Other" includes people who identify themselves as non-Hispanic and as Alaska Native, American Indian, Asian (who are also included in the "Asian" row), Native Hawaiian or other Pacific Islander, as well as non-Hispanics reporting more than one race.
Source: Calculations by New Strategist based on the Bureau of Labor Statistics' 2007 Consumer Expenditure Survey.

Nuts

Best customers:
Householders aged 55 to 74
Married couples without children at home
Married couples with school-aged or older children at home

Customer trends:
Average household spending on nuts will continue to rise because of their health benefits and the entry of millions of boomers into the best-customer age groups.

Older Americans are the biggest spenders on nuts. Householders aged 55 to 74 spend 28 to 42 percent more than the average household on nuts and control over one-third of the market. Married couples without children at home (most of them older) spend 39 percent more than average on nuts, while those with school-aged or older children at home (the largest households) spend 34 to 66 percent more.

Average household spending on nuts increased by a substantial 28 percent between 2000 and 2007, after adjusting for inflation. Behind the increase was the aging of the baby-boom generation into the best-customer age groups, as well as the increased attention to the health benefits of nut consumption. Average household spending on nuts will continue to climb as boomers age.

Table 9.54 Nuts

Total household spending $3,859,892,520.00
Average household spends   32.12

AGE OF HOUSEHOLDER	AVERAGE HOUSEHOLD SPENDING	BEST CUSTOMERS (index)	BIGGEST CUSTOMERS (market share)
Average household	$32.12	100	100.0%
Under age 25	10.36	32	2.2
Aged 25 to 34	20.99	65	11.1
Aged 35 to 44	30.47	95	18.5
Aged 45 to 54	36.78	115	24.1
Aged 55 to 64	45.50	142	22.9
Aged 65 to 74	41.18	128	12.8
Aged 75 or older	29.72	93	8.8

	AVERAGE HOUSEHOLD SPENDING	BEST CUSTOMERS (index)	BIGGEST CUSTOMERS (market share)
HOUSEHOLD INCOME			
Average household	**$32.12**	**100**	**100.0%**
Under $20,000	18.41	57	11.8
$20,000 to $39,999	19.66	61	14.2
$40,000 to $49,999	25.69	80	7.9
$50,000 to $69,999	33.40	104	15.9
$70,000 to $79,999	37.15	116	6.7
$80,000 to $99,999	47.01	146	11.9
$100,000 or more	59.56	185	31.8
HOUSEHOLD TYPE			
Average household	**32.12**	**100**	**100.0**
Married couples	44.20	138	69.6
Married couples, no children	44.54	139	29.9
Married couples, with children	42.87	133	33.3
Oldest child under age 6	28.23	88	4.3
Oldest child aged 6 to 17	43.01	134	17.0
Oldest child aged 18 or older	53.35	166	12.2
Single parent with child under age 18	21.60	67	4.0
Single person	16.50	51	15.3
RACE AND HISPANIC ORIGIN			
Average household	**32.12**	**100**	**100.0**
Asian	25.90	81	2.8
Black	18.13	56	6.8
Hispanic	19.51	61	7.2
Non-Hispanic white and other	36.07	112	85.7
REGION			
Average household	**32.12**	**100**	**100.0**
Northeast	33.15	103	19.2
Midwest	35.35	110	25.2
South	28.78	90	32.2
West	33.29	104	23.4
EDUCATION			
Average household	**32.12**	**100**	**100.0**
Less than high school graduate	21.06	66	9.9
High school graduate	24.03	75	18.9
Some college	30.41	95	20.6
Associate's degree	28.81	90	8.0
College graduate	46.45	145	41.9
Bachelor's degree	42.94	134	25.1
Master's, professional, doctoral degree	52.54	164	16.7

Note: Market shares may not sum to 100.0 because of rounding and missing categories by household type. "Asian" and "black" include Hispanics and non-Hispanics who identify themselves as being of the respective race alone. "Hispanic" includes people of any race who identify themselves as Hispanic. "Other" includes people who identify themselves as non-Hispanic and as Alaska Native, American Indian, Asian (who are also included in the "Asian" row), Native Hawaiian or other Pacific Islander, as well as non-Hispanics reporting more than one race.
Source: Calculations by New Strategist based on the Bureau of Labor Statistics' 2007 Consumer Expenditure Survey.

Olives, Pickles, and Relishes

Best customers: Householders aged 35 to 74
                                     Married couples

Customer trends: Average household spending on olives, pickles, and relishes could continue to grow as boomers age.

The best customers of olives, pickles, and relishes are older married couples with children at home. Couples with children aged 18 or older at home spend 52 percent more than the average household on this item. Householders ranging in age from 35 to 74 spend more than average on olives, pickles, and relishes, with the figure peaking at 31 percent among householders aged 65 to 74.

Average household spending on olives, pickles, and relishes increased 9 percent between 2000 and 2007, after adjusting for inflation. Behind the spending rise is the aging of the baby-boom generation into the best-customer age groups. Also behind the increase is the greater availability of fresh olives and relishes in grocery stores. Average household spending on olives, pickles, and relishes could continue to grow as boomers age.

Table 9.55 Olives, pickles, and relishes

Total household spending	$1,538,188,800.00
Average household spends	12.80

AGE OF HOUSEHOLDER	AVERAGE HOUSEHOLD SPENDING	BEST CUSTOMERS (index)	BIGGEST CUSTOMERS (market share)
Average household	$12.80	100	100.0%
Under age 25	8.04	63	4.3
Aged 25 to 34	11.56	90	15.4
Aged 35 to 44	13.71	107	20.9
Aged 45 to 54	13.50	105	22.2
Aged 55 to 64	14.20	111	18.0
Aged 65 to 74	16.75	131	13.1
Aged 75 or older	8.58	67	6.4

	AVERAGE HOUSEHOLD SPENDING	BEST CUSTOMERS (index)	BIGGEST CUSTOMERS (market share)
HOUSEHOLD INCOME			
Average household	**$12.80**	**100**	**100.0%**
Under $20,000	6.75	53	10.8
$20,000 to $39,999	9.61	75	17.5
$40,000 to $49,999	11.91	93	9.2
$50,000 to $69,999	14.72	115	17.6
$70,000 to $79,999	18.36	143	8.3
$80,000 to $99,999	12.27	96	7.8
$100,000 or more	21.78	170	29.2
HOUSEHOLD TYPE			
Average household	**12.80**	**100**	**100.0**
Married couples	16.33	128	64.5
Married couples, no children	15.07	118	25.4
Married couples, with children	17.69	138	34.5
Oldest child under age 6	16.57	129	6.3
Oldest child aged 6 to 17	17.19	134	17.1
Oldest child aged 18 or older	19.49	152	11.2
Single parent with child under age 18	11.92	93	5.5
Single person	7.48	58	17.4
RACE AND HISPANIC ORIGIN			
Average household	**12.80**	**100**	**100.0**
Asian	7.05	55	1.9
Black	7.80	61	7.3
Hispanic	8.08	63	7.5
Non-Hispanic white and other	14.25	111	85.0
REGION			
Average household	**12.80**	**100**	**100.0**
Northeast	12.46	97	18.1
Midwest	13.06	102	23.3
South	12.26	96	34.4
West	13.70	107	24.2
EDUCATION			
Average household	**12.80**	**100**	**100.0**
Less than high school graduate	7.63	60	9.0
High school graduate	11.50	90	22.7
Some college	12.97	101	22.1
Associate's degree	14.71	115	10.2
College graduate	15.65	122	35.4
Bachelor's degree	14.47	113	21.2
Master's, professional, doctoral degree	17.70	138	14.1

Note: Market shares may not sum to 100.0 because of rounding and missing categories by household type. "Asian" and "black" include Hispanics and non-Hispanics who identify themselves as being of the respective race alone. "Hispanic" includes people of any race who identify themselves as Hispanic. "Other" includes people who identify themselves as non-Hispanic and as Alaska Native, American Indian, Asian (who are also included in the "Asian" row), Native Hawaiian or other Pacific Islander, as well as non-Hispanics reporting more than one race.
Source: Calculations by New Strategist based on the Bureau of Labor Statistics' 2007 Consumer Expenditure Survey.

Oranges

Best customers:
    Householders ages 35 to 44
Married couples with school-aged or older children at home
Asians and Hispanics
Households in the West

Customer trends:
    Average household spending on oranges may continue to drift downward because the small generation X is in the best-customer lifestage, but the decline will be limited by the growth of the Asian and Hispanic populations.

The biggest spenders on oranges are the largest households. Married couples with school-aged or older children at home spend 58 percent more than average on oranges. Householders aged 35 to 44, most with children, spend 22 percent more than average on this item. Asians spend twice the average, and Hispanics, who have the largest families, spend 44 percent more than the average household on oranges.

Average household spending on oranges declined 3 percent between 2000 and 2007, after adjusting for inflation, as growth of the Asian and Hispanic populations limited spending losses in the category. Average household spending on oranges may continue to drift downward because the small generation X is in the best-customer lifestage, but the decline will be limited by the growth of the Asian and Hispanic populations.

Table 9.56 Oranges

Total household spending $2,666,594,490.00
Average household spends   22.19

	AVERAGE HOUSEHOLD SPENDING	BEST CUSTOMERS (index)	BIGGEST CUSTOMERS (market share)
AGE OF HOUSEHOLDER			
Average household	**$22.19**	**100**	**100.0%**
Under age 25	13.00	59	4.0
Aged 25 to 34	18.65	84	14.3
Aged 35 to 44	27.13	122	23.8
Aged 45 to 54	23.84	107	22.6
Aged 55 to 64	23.29	105	17.0
Aged 65 to 74	21.48	97	9.7
Aged 75 or older	20.66	93	8.8

	AVERAGE HOUSEHOLD SPENDING	BEST CUSTOMERS (index)	BIGGEST CUSTOMERS (market share)
HOUSEHOLD INCOME			
Average household	**$22.19**	**100**	**100.0%**
Under $20,000	15.95	72	14.8
$20,000 to $39,999	17.19	77	18.0
$40,000 to $49,999	22.39	101	9.9
$50,000 to $69,999	21.05	95	14.5
$70,000 to $79,999	23.06	104	6.0
$80,000 to $99,999	27.33	123	10.0
$100,000 or more	34.72	156	26.8
HOUSEHOLD TYPE			
Average household	**22.19**	**100**	**100.0**
Married couples	28.70	129	65.4
Married couples, no children	24.52	111	23.8
Married couples, with children	32.05	144	36.0
Oldest child under age 6	19.96	90	4.4
Oldest child aged 6 to 17	34.96	158	20.0
Oldest child aged 18 or older	35.15	158	11.7
Single parent with child under age 18	18.48	83	4.9
Single person	12.86	58	17.2
RACE AND HISPANIC ORIGIN			
Average household	**22.19**	**100**	**100.0**
Asian	44.21	199	7.0
Black	16.67	75	9.0
Hispanic	31.92	144	17.0
Non-Hispanic white and other	21.65	98	74.5
REGION			
Average household	**22.19**	**100**	**100.0**
Northeast	25.40	114	21.3
Midwest	22.49	101	23.2
South	16.98	77	27.5
West	27.58	124	28.1
EDUCATION			
Average household	**22.19**	**100**	**100.0**
Less than high school graduate	24.79	112	16.9
High school graduate	19.56	88	22.2
Some college	14.88	67	14.6
Associate's degree	21.54	97	8.6
College graduate	28.74	130	37.5
Bachelor's degree	24.80	112	20.9
Master's, professional, doctoral degree	35.57	160	16.4

Note: Market shares may not sum to 100.0 because of rounding and missing categories by household type. "Asian" and "black" include Hispanics and non-Hispanics who identify themselves as being of the respective race alone. "Hispanic" includes people of any race who identify themselves as Hispanic. "Other" includes people who identify themselves as non-Hispanic and as Alaska Native, American Indian, Asian (who are also included in the "Asian" row), Native Hawaiian or other Pacific Islander, as well as non-Hispanics reporting more than one race.
Source: Calculations by New Strategist based on the Bureau of Labor Statistics' 2007 Consumer Expenditure Survey.

Pasta, Cornmeal, and Other Cereal Products

Best customers:

Householders aged 35 to 54
Married couples with school-aged or older children at home
Asians

Customer trends:

Average household spending on pasta will continue to decline as more boomers become empty-nesters and household size shrinks.

The biggest spenders on pasta, cornmeal, and other cereal products are households with children. Married couples with school-aged or older children at home spend 46 to 65 percent more than the average household on this item. Householders aged 35 to 54, most with children at home, spend 15 to 21 percent more than average on pasta and account for 48 percent of the market. Asians spend 40 percent more than average on this item.

Average household spending on pasta, cornmeal, and other cereal products fell 28 percent between 2000 and 2007, after adjusting for inflation. Behind the decline was the growing propensity of consumers to eat out rather than cook a meal at home. Average household spending on pasta will continue to decline as more boomers become empty-nesters and household size shrinks.

Table 9.57 Pasta, cornmeal, and other cereal products

Total household spending $2,976,635,670.00
Average household spends 24.77

AGE OF HOUSEHOLDER	AVERAGE HOUSEHOLD SPENDING	BEST CUSTOMERS (index)	BIGGEST CUSTOMERS (market share)
Average household	$24.77	100	100.0%
Under age 25	13.62	55	3.7
Aged 25 to 34	24.71	100	17.0
Aged 35 to 44	28.47	115	22.4
Aged 45 to 54	29.97	121	25.4
Aged 55 to 64	22.28	90	14.6
Aged 65 to 74	29.40	119	11.9
Aged 75 or older	13.38	54	5.1

	AVERAGE HOUSEHOLD SPENDING	BEST CUSTOMERS (index)	BIGGEST CUSTOMERS (market share)
HOUSEHOLD INCOME			
Average household	**$24.77**	**100**	**100.0%**
Under $20,000	14.63	59	12.1
$20,000 to $39,999	20.80	84	19.5
$40,000 to $49,999	21.65	87	8.6
$50,000 to $69,999	25.97	105	16.0
$70,000 to $79,999	25.18	102	5.9
$80,000 to $99,999	31.96	129	10.5
$100,000 or more	39.25	158	27.1
HOUSEHOLD TYPE			
Average household	**24.77**	**100**	**100.0**
Married couples	32.52	131	66.4
Married couples, no children	23.61	95	20.6
Married couples, with children	36.41	147	36.7
Oldest child under age 6	25.02	101	4.9
Oldest child aged 6 to 17	40.79	165	20.9
Oldest child aged 18 or older	36.09	146	10.7
Single parent with child under age 18	22.40	90	5.4
Single person	11.98	48	14.4
RACE AND HISPANIC ORIGIN			
Average household	**24.77**	**100**	**100.0**
Asian	34.57	140	4.9
Black	18.83	76	9.1
Hispanic	24.79	100	11.8
Non-Hispanic white and other	25.71	104	79.2
REGION			
Average household	**24.77**	**100**	**100.0**
Northeast	28.16	114	21.2
Midwest	20.11	81	18.6
South	22.87	92	33.2
West	29.77	120	27.2
EDUCATION			
Average household	**24.77**	**100**	**100.0**
Less than high school graduate	26.73	108	16.4
High school graduate	22.27	90	22.7
Some college	21.72	88	19.1
Associate's degree	22.65	91	8.1
College graduate	28.85	116	33.7
Bachelor's degree	26.69	108	20.2
Master's, professional, doctoral degree	32.60	132	13.4

Note: Market shares may not sum to 100.0 because of rounding and missing categories by household type. "Asian" and "black" include Hispanics and non-Hispanics who identify themselves as being of the respective race alone. "Hispanic" includes people of any race who identify themselves as Hispanic. "Other" includes people who identify themselves as non-Hispanic and as Alaska Native, American Indian, Asian (who are also included in the "Asian" row), Native Hawaiian or other Pacific Islander, as well as non-Hispanics reporting more than one race.
Source: Calculations by New Strategist based on the Bureau of Labor Statistics' 2007 Consumer Expenditure Survey.

Peanut Butter

Best customers:

    Householders aged 35 to 54
    Married couples with children at home
    Households in the Midwest

Customer trends:

    Average household spending on peanut butter may continue to decline as boomers exit the best-customer lifestage.

The largest households spend the most on peanut butter. Married couples with children at home spend 55 percent more than the average household on peanut butter. Householders aged 35 to 54, most with children, spend 23 to 24 percent more and control half the market. Households in the Midwest spend 17 percent more than average on peanut butter.

Average household spending on peanut butter fell 9 percent between 2000 and 2007, after adjusting for inflation. Behind the decline in spending was the baby-boom generation's exit from the best-customer lifestage. Average household spending on peanut butter may continue to decline as more boomers become empty-nesters.

Table 9.58 Peanut butter

Total household spending $1,546,600,770.00
Average household spends   12.87

	AVERAGE HOUSEHOLD SPENDING	BEST CUSTOMERS (index)	BIGGEST CUSTOMERS (market share)
AGE OF HOUSEHOLDER			
Average household	**$12.87**	**100**	**100.0%**
Under age 25	6.73	52	3.5
Aged 25 to 34	11.25	87	14.9
Aged 35 to 44	16.02	124	24.3
Aged 45 to 54	15.77	123	25.7
Aged 55 to 64	13.22	103	16.6
Aged 65 to 74	11.42	89	8.9
Aged 75 or older	8.51	66	6.3

	AVERAGE HOUSEHOLD SPENDING	BEST CUSTOMERS (index)	BIGGEST CUSTOMERS (market share)
HOUSEHOLD INCOME			
Average household	**$12.87**	**100**	**100.0%**
Under $20,000	6.32	49	10.1
$20,000 to $39,999	11.73	91	21.2
$40,000 to $49,999	13.25	103	10.1
$50,000 to $69,999	12.90	100	15.3
$70,000 to $79,999	10.71	83	4.8
$80,000 to $99,999	15.97	124	10.1
$100,000 or more	21.17	164	28.2
HOUSEHOLD TYPE			
Average household	**12.87**	**100**	**100.0**
Married couples	16.79	130	65.9
Married couples, no children	13.08	102	21.9
Married couples, with children	19.90	155	38.6
Oldest child under age 6	15.74	122	6.0
Oldest child aged 6 to 17	19.80	154	19.5
Oldest child aged 18 or older	23.17	180	13.3
Single parent with child under age 18	12.33	96	5.7
Single person	6.94	54	16.0
RACE AND HISPANIC ORIGIN			
Average household	**12.87**	**100**	**100.0**
Asian	9.43	73	2.6
Black	9.62	75	9.0
Hispanic	6.57	51	6.0
Non-Hispanic white and other	14.30	111	84.8
REGION			
Average household	**12.87**	**100**	**100.0**
Northeast	10.76	84	15.6
Midwest	15.09	117	26.8
South	12.38	96	34.5
West	13.16	102	23.1
EDUCATION			
Average household	**12.87**	**100**	**100.0**
Less than high school graduate	7.87	61	9.3
High school graduate	12.92	100	25.3
Some college	13.63	106	23.1
Associate's degree	9.98	78	6.9
College graduate	15.43	120	34.7
Bachelor's degree	14.66	114	21.3
Master's, professional, doctoral degree	16.76	130	13.3

Note: Market shares may not sum to 100.0 because of rounding and missing categories by household type. "Asian" and "black" include Hispanics and non-Hispanics who identify themselves as being of the respective race alone. "Hispanic" includes people of any race who identify themselves as Hispanic. "Other" includes people who identify themselves as non-Hispanic and as Alaska Native, American Indian, Asian (who are also included in the "Asian" row), Native Hawaiian or other Pacific Islander, as well as non-Hispanics reporting more than one race.
Source: Calculations by New Strategist based on the Bureau of Labor Statistics' 2007 Consumer Expenditure Survey.

Pies, Tarts, and Turnovers

Best customers:
Householders aged 35 to 54
Married couples with school-aged or older children at home
Single parents

Customer trends:
Average household spending on pies, tarts, and turnovers may continue to decline as more boomers become empty-nesters.

The best customers of pies, tarts, and turnovers are the largest households. Married couples with school-aged or older children at home spend 57 to 79 percent more than average on pies because they have the largest households. Householders ranging in age from 35 to 54, many with children, spend 19 to 38 percent more than average on this item and control 52 percent of the market.

Average household spending on pies, tarts, and turnovers fell 6 percent between 2000 and 2007, after adjusting for inflation. Average household spending on pies, tarts, and turnovers may continue to decline as more boomers become empty-nesters.

Table 9.59 **Pies, tarts, and turnovers**

Total household spending $1,797,758,160.00
Average household spends   14.96

	AVERAGE HOUSEHOLD SPENDING	BEST CUSTOMERS (index)	BIGGEST CUSTOMERS (market share)
AGE OF HOUSEHOLDER			
Average household	**$14.96**	**100**	**100.0%**
Under age 25	7.90	53	3.6
Aged 25 to 34	12.15	81	13.9
Aged 35 to 44	20.61	138	26.8
Aged 45 to 54	17.77	119	25.0
Aged 55 to 64	15.06	101	16.3
Aged 65 to 74	12.85	86	8.6
Aged 75 or older	9.54	64	6.0

	AVERAGE HOUSEHOLD SPENDING	BEST CUSTOMERS (index)	BIGGEST CUSTOMERS (market share)
HOUSEHOLD INCOME			
Average household	**$14.96**	**100**	**100.0%**
Under $20,000	8.74	58	12.0
$20,000 to $39,999	9.29	62	14.4
$40,000 to $49,999	15.35	103	10.1
$50,000 to $69,999	15.21	102	15.6
$70,000 to $79,999	18.22	122	7.1
$80,000 to $99,999	19.48	130	10.6
$100,000 or more	26.12	175	29.9
HOUSEHOLD TYPE			
Average household	**14.96**	**100**	**100.0**
Married couples	20.00	134	67.6
Married couples, no children	14.23	95	20.5
Married couples, with children	24.39	163	40.7
Oldest child under age 6	19.14	128	6.2
Oldest child aged 6 to 17	26.81	179	22.8
Oldest child aged 18 or older	23.46	157	11.6
Single parent with child under age 18	15.77	105	6.3
Single person	7.49	50	14.9
RACE AND HISPANIC ORIGIN			
Average household	**14.96**	**100**	**100.0**
Asian	8.41	56	2.0
Black	11.31	76	9.1
Hispanic	9.44	63	7.4
Non-Hispanic white and other	16.28	109	83.1
REGION			
Average household	**14.96**	**100**	**100.0**
Northeast	16.23	108	20.2
Midwest	14.93	100	22.8
South	14.68	98	35.2
West	14.34	96	21.7
EDUCATION			
Average household	**14.96**	**100**	**100.0**
Less than high school graduate	13.56	91	13.7
High school graduate	15.58	104	26.3
Some college	14.32	96	20.8
Associate's degree	14.92	100	8.9
College graduate	15.52	104	30.0
Bachelor's degree	15.31	102	19.2
Master's, professional, doctoral degree	15.89	106	10.8

Note: Market shares may not sum to 100.0 because of rounding and missing categories by household type. "Asian" and "black" include Hispanics and non-Hispanics who identify themselves as being of the respective race alone. "Hispanic" includes people of any race who identify themselves as Hispanic. "Other" includes people who identify themselves as non-Hispanic and as Alaska Native, American Indian, Asian (who are also included in the "Asian" row), Native Hawaiian or other Pacific Islander, as well as non-Hispanics reporting more than one race.
Source: Calculations by New Strategist based on the Bureau of Labor Statistics' 2007 Consumer Expenditure Survey.

Pork Chops

Best customers:

Householders aged 35 to 44
Married couples with school-aged or older children at home
Single parents
Blacks

Customer trends:

Average household spending on pork chops will continue to decline as more boomers become empty-nesters and eating out claims a growing share of the food dollar.

Households with children are the biggest spenders on pork chops. Married couples with school-aged or older children at home spend 43 to 74 percent more than average on this item. Householders aged 35 to 44, most with children, spend 41 percent more. Single parents spend 45 percent more than average on pork chops. Black households spend 74 percent more than the average household on this item.

Average household spending on pork chops fell by a substantial 41 percent between 2000 and 2007, after adjusting for inflation. Pork chops are suffering the same fate as many other grocery categories as Americans substitute fast food for home-cooked meals. Average household spending on pork chops is likely to continue to decline as more boomers become empty-nesters and eating out claims a growing share of the food dollar.

Table 9.60 Pork chops

Total household spending $3,469,336,770.00
Average household spends   28.87

	AVERAGE HOUSEHOLD SPENDING	BEST CUSTOMERS (index)	BIGGEST CUSTOMERS (market share)
AGE OF HOUSEHOLDER			
Average household	**$28.87**	**100**	**100.0%**
Under age 25	16.30	56	3.8
Aged 25 to 34	25.03	87	14.8
Aged 35 to 44	40.83	141	27.6
Aged 45 to 54	32.15	111	23.4
Aged 55 to 64	24.33	84	13.6
Aged 65 to 74	31.56	109	10.9
Aged 75 or older	17.90	62	5.9

	AVERAGE HOUSEHOLD SPENDING	BEST CUSTOMERS (index)	BIGGEST CUSTOMERS (market share)
HOUSEHOLD INCOME			
Average household	**$28.87**	**100**	**100.0%**
Under $20,000	20.27	70	14.4
$20,000 to $39,999	28.45	99	22.9
$40,000 to $49,999	30.30	105	10.3
$50,000 to $69,999	35.91	124	19.0
$70,000 to $79,999	27.45	95	5.5
$80,000 to $99,999	29.60	103	8.3
$100,000 or more	32.19	111	19.1
HOUSEHOLD TYPE			
Average household	**28.87**	**100**	**100.0**
Married couples	35.40	123	62.0
Married couples, no children	28.33	98	21.2
Married couples, with children	40.98	142	35.4
Oldest child under age 6	28.08	97	4.7
Oldest child aged 6 to 17	41.15	143	18.1
Oldest child aged 18 or older	50.10	174	12.8
Single parent with child under age 18	41.90	145	8.6
Single person	12.31	43	12.7
RACE AND HISPANIC ORIGIN			
Average household	**28.87**	**100**	**100.0**
Asian	15.92	55	1.9
Black	50.11	174	20.8
Hispanic	29.90	104	12.2
Non-Hispanic white and other	25.41	88	67.2
REGION			
Average household	**28.87**	**100**	**100.0**
Northeast	32.32	112	20.9
Midwest	26.72	93	21.2
South	31.68	110	39.4
West	23.62	82	18.5
EDUCATION			
Average household	**28.87**	**100**	**100.0**
Less than high school graduate	33.12	115	17.4
High school graduate	34.86	121	30.5
Some college	28.05	97	21.2
Associate's degree	31.01	107	9.5
College graduate	21.66	75	21.7
Bachelor's degree	22.02	76	14.3
Master's, professional, doctoral degree	21.03	73	7.4

Note: Market shares may not sum to 100.0 because of rounding and missing categories by household type. "Asian" and "black" include Hispanics and non-Hispanics who identify themselves as being of the respective race alone. "Hispanic" includes people of any race who identify themselves as Hispanic. "Other" includes people who identify themselves as non-Hispanic and as Alaska Native, American Indian, Asian (who are also included in the "Asian" row), Native Hawaiian or other Pacific Islander, as well as non-Hispanics reporting more than one race.
Source: Calculations by New Strategist based on the Bureau of Labor Statistics' 2007 Consumer Expenditure Survey.

Pork Other than Bacon, Chops, Frankfurters, Ham, and Sausage

Best customers:	Householders aged 35 to 54
	Married couples with school-aged or older children at home
	Single parents
	Asians, blacks, and Hispanics

| Customer trends: | Average household spending on other pork may fall as more boomers become empty-nesters, but the decline may be limited by the growth of minority populations. |

Householdswith children spend the most on pork other than bacon, chops, frankfurters, ham, and sausage. Married couples with school-aged or older children at home spend 31 to 54 percent more than average on this item. Single parents spend 7 percent more despite their low incomes. Asian households spend 79 percent more than average on other pork, while Hispanics spend 29 percent more and blacks 9 percent more. Together, Asians, blacks and Hispanics account for 35 percent of the market.

Average household spending on pork other than bacon, chops, frankfurters, ham, and sausage fell 24 percent between 2000 and 2007, after adjusting for inflation. Pork is suffering the same fate as many other grocery categories as Americans substitute fast food for home-cooked meals. Spending on other pork may continue to fall as more boomers become empty-nesters, but the decline may be limited by the growth of minority populations.

Table 9.61 Pork other than bacon, chops, frankfurters, ham, and sausage

| Total household spending | $4,266,070,500.00 |
| Average household spends | 35.50 |

	AVERAGE HOUSEHOLD SPENDING	BEST CUSTOMERS (index)	BIGGEST CUSTOMERS (market share)
AGE OF HOUSEHOLDER			
Average household	**$35.50**	**100**	**100.0%**
Under age 25	23.50	66	4.5
Aged 25 to 34	28.02	79	13.5
Aged 35 to 44	44.59	126	24.5
Aged 45 to 54	44.88	126	26.6
Aged 55 to 64	31.87	90	14.5
Aged 65 to 74	37.66	106	10.6
Aged 75 or older	22.51	63	6.0

	AVERAGE HOUSEHOLD SPENDING	BEST CUSTOMERS (index)	BIGGEST CUSTOMERS (market share)
HOUSEHOLD INCOME			
Average household	**$35.50**	**100**	**100.0%**
Under $20,000	23.63	67	13.7
$20,000 to $39,999	32.46	91	21.3
$40,000 to $49,999	35.40	100	9.8
$50,000 to $69,999	38.40	108	16.6
$70,000 to $79,999	39.76	112	6.5
$80,000 to $99,999	37.37	105	8.6
$100,000 or more	48.93	138	23.6
HOUSEHOLD TYPE			
Average household	**35.50**	**100**	**100.0**
Married couples	44.98	127	64.0
Married couples, no children	40.29	113	24.5
Married couples, with children	46.26	130	32.5
Oldest child under age 6	34.38	97	4.7
Oldest child aged 6 to 17	46.36	131	16.6
Oldest child aged 18 or older	54.79	154	11.4
Single parent with child under age 18	37.94	107	6.3
Single person	14.87	42	12.5
RACE AND HISPANIC ORIGIN			
Average household	**35.50**	**100**	**100.0**
Asian	63.66	179	6.3
Black	38.64	109	13.1
Hispanic	45.66	129	15.2
Non-Hispanic white and other	33.60	95	72.3
REGION			
Average household	**35.50**	**100**	**100.0**
Northeast	35.18	99	18.5
Midwest	32.57	92	21.0
South	36.75	104	37.2
West	36.79	104	23.4
EDUCATION			
Average household	**35.50**	**100**	**100.0**
Less than high school graduate	40.21	113	17.2
High school graduate	42.46	120	30.2
Some college	27.23	77	16.7
Associate's degree	39.60	112	9.9
College graduate	32.05	90	26.1
Bachelor's degree	33.42	94	17.6
Master's, professional, doctoral degree	29.68	84	8.5

Note: Market shares may not sum to 100.0 because of rounding and missing categories by household type. "Asian" and "black" include Hispanics and non-Hispanics who identify themselves as being of the respective race alone. "Hispanic" includes people of any race who identify themselves as Hispanic. "Other" includes people who identify themselves as non-Hispanic and as Alaska Native, American Indian, Asian (who are also included in the "Asian" row), Native Hawaiian or other Pacific Islander, as well as non-Hispanics reporting more than one race.
Source: Calculations by New Strategist based on the Bureau of Labor Statistics' 2007 Consumer Expenditure Survey.

Potato Chips and Other Snacks

Best customers: **Householders aged 35 to 54**
Married couples with children at home
Single parents

Customer trends: **Average household spending on potato chips and other snacks may decline as more boomers become empty-nesters.**

Potato chips and other snacks ranks seventh among grocery items on which the average household spends the most. The best customers of potato chips and other snacks are households with children. Married couples with children at home spend 64 percent more than the average household on this item. Even single parents spend 14 percent more than average. Householders aged 35 to 54, most with children at home, spend 23 to 32 percent more than average on potato chips and other snacks and control 52 percent of the market.

Average household spending on potato chips and other snacks climbed 11 percent between 2000 and 2007, after adjusting for inflation. Americans' penchant for snack food was behind the increase, as was the growing variety of snacks on grocery store shelves. Average household spending on potato chips and other snacks may decline in the years ahead as more boomers become empty-nesters.

Table 9.62 Potato chips and other snacks

Total household spending $11,513,583,510.00
Average household spends   95.81

	AVERAGE HOUSEHOLD SPENDING	BEST CUSTOMERS (index)	BIGGEST CUSTOMERS (market share)
AGE OF HOUSEHOLDER			
Average household	$95.81	100	100.0%
Under age 25	69.89	73	4.9
Aged 25 to 34	90.43	94	16.1
Aged 35 to 44	126.79	132	25.8
Aged 45 to 54	118.27	123	25.9
Aged 55 to 64	85.02	89	14.4
Aged 65 to 74	79.47	83	8.3
Aged 75 or older	47.08	49	4.7

	AVERAGE HOUSEHOLD SPENDING	BEST CUSTOMERS (index)	BIGGEST CUSTOMERS (market share)
HOUSEHOLD INCOME			
Average household	**$95.81**	**100**	**100.0%**
Under $20,000	52.51	55	11.3
$20,000 to $39,999	71.54	75	17.4
$40,000 to $49,999	86.70	90	8.9
$50,000 to $69,999	102.01	106	16.3
$70,000 to $79,999	120.66	126	7.3
$80,000 to $99,999	133.11	139	11.3
$100,000 or more	152.72	159	27.3
HOUSEHOLD TYPE			
Average household	**95.81**	**100**	**100.0**
Married couples	125.55	131	66.2
Married couples, no children	89.83	94	20.2
Married couples, with children	156.75	164	40.8
Oldest child under age 6	131.89	138	6.7
Oldest child aged 6 to 17	167.38	175	22.2
Oldest child aged 18 or older	153.94	161	11.8
Single parent with child under age 18	109.29	114	6.8
Single person	46.39	48	14.4
RACE AND HISPANIC ORIGIN			
Average household	**95.81**	**100**	**100.0**
Asian	72.27	75	2.7
Black	66.36	69	8.3
Hispanic	76.16	79	9.4
Non-Hispanic white and other	103.07	108	82.1
REGION			
Average household	**95.81**	**100**	**100.0**
Northeast	85.91	90	16.7
Midwest	103.92	108	24.8
South	96.40	101	36.1
West	94.88	99	22.4
EDUCATION			
Average household	**95.81**	**100**	**100.0**
Less than high school graduate	71.70	75	11.4
High school graduate	89.34	93	23.5
Some college	88.85	93	20.2
Associate's degree	112.79	118	10.5
College graduate	112.71	118	34.1
Bachelor's degree	111.93	117	21.9
Master's, professional, doctoral degree	114.08	119	12.1

Note: Market shares may not sum to 100.0 because of rounding and missing categories by household type. "Asian" and "black" include Hispanics and non-Hispanics who identify themselves as being of the respective race alone. "Hispanic" includes people of any race who identify themselves as Hispanic. "Other" includes people who identify themselves as non-Hispanic and as Alaska Native, American Indian, Asian (who are also included in the "Asian" row), Native Hawaiian or other Pacific Islander, as well as non-Hispanics reporting more than one race.
Source: Calculations by New Strategist based on the Bureau of Labor Statistics' 2007 Consumer Expenditure Survey.

Potatoes, Fresh

Best customers:	**Householders aged 35 to 74**
	Married couples without children at home
	Married couples with school-aged or older children at home
	Asians
Customer trends:	**Average household spending on potatoes will continue to decline as home cooking becomes less common.**

Families that cook meals from scratch are the best customers of fresh potatoes. Married couples with school-aged or older children at home spend 43 to 55 percent more than average on potatoes. Couples without children at home (most of them empty-nesters) spend 15 percent more. Householders ranging in age from 35 to 74, the age groups most likely to cook, spend 8 to 15 percent more than average on this item.

Average household spending on potatoes fell 8 percent between 2000 and 2007, after adjusting for inflation. Behind the decline was Americans' growing propensity to substitute fast food for home-cooked meals. Average household spending on potatoes will continue to decline as home cooking becomes less common.

Table 9.63 Potatoes, fresh

Total household spending $3,748,133,490.00
Average household spends   31.19

	AVERAGE HOUSEHOLD SPENDING	BEST CUSTOMERS (index)	BIGGEST CUSTOMERS (market share)
AGE OF HOUSEHOLDER			
Average household	**$31.19**	**100**	**100.0%**
Under age 25	14.83	48	3.2
Aged 25 to 34	25.65	82	14.0
Aged 35 to 44	33.70	108	21.1
Aged 45 to 54	36.01	115	24.3
Aged 55 to 64	34.66	111	18.0
Aged 65 to 74	35.59	114	11.4
Aged 75 or older	27.31	88	8.3

	AVERAGE HOUSEHOLD SPENDING	BEST CUSTOMERS (index)	BIGGEST CUSTOMERS (market share)
HOUSEHOLD INCOME			
Average household	**$31.19**	**100**	**100.0%**
Under $20,000	19.93	64	13.1
$20,000 to $39,999	28.08	90	20.9
$40,000 to $49,999	28.38	91	9.0
$50,000 to $69,999	32.29	104	15.8
$70,000 to $79,999	34.38	110	6.4
$80,000 to $99,999	34.95	112	9.1
$100,000 or more	46.62	149	25.6
HOUSEHOLD TYPE			
Average household	**31.19**	**100**	**100.0**
Married couples	40.44	130	65.5
Married couples, no children	35.90	115	24.8
Married couples, with children	42.68	137	34.1
Oldest child under age 6	29.71	95	4.6
Oldest child aged 6 to 17	44.66	143	18.2
Oldest child aged 18 or older	48.30	155	11.4
Single parent with child under age 18	23.61	76	4.5
Single person	16.69	54	15.9
RACE AND HISPANIC ORIGIN			
Average household	**31.19**	**100**	**100.0**
Asian	45.03	144	5.1
Black	25.01	80	9.6
Hispanic	31.58	101	12.0
Non-Hispanic white and other	32.07	103	78.5
REGION			
Average household	**31.19**	**100**	**100.0**
Northeast	34.77	111	20.8
Midwest	26.41	85	19.4
South	31.21	100	35.9
West	33.06	106	24.0
EDUCATION			
Average household	**31.19**	**100**	**100.0**
Less than high school graduate	33.96	109	16.5
High school graduate	29.13	93	23.6
Some college	29.67	95	20.7
Associate's degree	26.33	84	7.5
College graduate	34.20	110	31.7
Bachelor's degree	31.76	102	19.1
Master's, professional, doctoral degree	38.42	123	12.6

Note: Market shares may not sum to 100.0 because of rounding and missing categories by household type. "Asian" and "black" include Hispanics and non-Hispanics who identify themselves as being of the respective race alone. "Hispanic" includes people of any race who identify themselves as Hispanic. "Other" includes people who identify themselves as non-Hispanic and as Alaska Native, American Indian, Asian (who are also included in the "Asian" row), Native Hawaiian or other Pacific Islander, as well as non-Hispanics reporting more than one race.
Source: Calculations by New Strategist based on the Bureau of Labor Statistics' 2007 Consumer Expenditure Survey.

Poultry Other than Chicken

Best customers:
Householders aged 35 to 64
Married couples without children at home
Married couples with school-aged or older children at home
Blacks
Households in the South

Customer trends:
Average household spending on poultry other than chicken will continue to fall as boomers exit one of the best-customer lifestages and home cooking becomes less common.

Families with children and older householders likely to cook meals from scratch spend the most on poultry other than chicken (primarily turkey). Married couples with school-aged or older children at home spend 39 to 96 percent more than the average household on this item. Couples without children at home (most of them empty-nesters) spend 28 percent more. Householders ranging in age from 35 to 64, many with children at home, spend 13 to 28 percent more than average on this item and control 69 percent of the market. Blacks spend 37 percent more than the average household on poultry other than chicken. Households in the South, where many blacks live, spend 14 percent more than average on poultry other than chicken.

Average household spending on other poultry fell 23 percent between 2000 and 2007, after adjusting for inflation. Behind the decline was Americans' growing propensity to eat out rather than cook from scratch. Average household spending on other poultry will continue to decline as boomers exit one of the best-customer lifestages and home cooking becomes less common.

Table 9.64 Poultry other than chicken

Total household spending $3,406,847,850.00
Average household spends   28.35

	AVERAGE HOUSEHOLD SPENDING	BEST CUSTOMERS (index)	BIGGEST CUSTOMERS (market share)
AGE OF HOUSEHOLDER			
Average household	**$28.35**	**100**	**100.0%**
Under age 25	13.60	48	3.3
Aged 25 to 34	21.19	75	12.8
Aged 35 to 44	32.01	113	22.0
Aged 45 to 54	35.43	125	26.3
Aged 55 to 64	36.23	128	20.7
Aged 65 to 74	27.31	96	9.6
Aged 75 or older	17.20	61	5.8

	AVERAGE HOUSEHOLD SPENDING	BEST CUSTOMERS (index)	BIGGEST CUSTOMERS (market share)
HOUSEHOLD INCOME			
Average household	**$28.35**	**100**	**100.0%**
Under $20,000	13.91	49	10.1
$20,000 to $39,999	23.87	84	19.6
$40,000 to $49,999	21.07	74	7.3
$50,000 to $69,999	24.84	88	13.4
$70,000 to $79,999	30.27	107	6.2
$80,000 to $99,999	30.77	109	8.8
$100,000 or more	58.53	206	35.4
HOUSEHOLD TYPE			
Average household	**28.35**	**100**	**100.0**
Married couples	38.56	136	68.8
Married couples, no children	36.26	128	27.6
Married couples, with children	40.20	142	35.4
Oldest child under age 6	21.70	77	3.7
Oldest child aged 6 to 17	39.31	139	17.6
Oldest child aged 18 or older	55.54	196	14.4
Single parent with child under age 18	22.42	79	4.7
Single person	14.08	50	14.8
RACE AND HISPANIC ORIGIN			
Average household	**28.35**	**100**	**100.0**
Asian	27.35	96	3.4
Black	38.71	137	16.4
Hispanic	17.74	63	7.4
Non-Hispanic white and other	28.23	100	76.0
REGION			
Average household	**28.35**	**100**	**100.0**
Northeast	28.06	99	18.4
Midwest	24.61	87	19.8
South	32.42	114	41.1
West	25.89	91	20.7
EDUCATION			
Average household	**28.35**	**100**	**100.0**
Less than high school graduate	21.40	75	11.4
High school graduate	25.69	91	22.9
Some college	23.51	83	18.1
Associate's degree	35.95	127	11.3
College graduate	35.18	124	35.9
Bachelor's degree	34.17	121	22.6
Master's, professional, doctoral degree	36.92	130	13.3

Note: Market shares may not sum to 100.0 because of rounding and missing categories by household type. "Asian" and "black" include Hispanics and non-Hispanics who identify themselves as being of the respective race alone. "Hispanic" includes people of any race who identify themselves as Hispanic. "Other" includes people who identify themselves as non-Hispanic and as Alaska Native, American Indian, Asian (who are also included in the "Asian" row), Native Hawaiian or other Pacific Islander, as well as non-Hispanics reporting more than one race.
Source: Calculations by New Strategist based on the Bureau of Labor Statistics' 2007 Consumer Expenditure Survey.

Prepared Food (Except Desserts, Frozen Meals, and Salads)

Best customers: **Householders aged 35 to 54**
Married couples with children at home
Hispanics
Households in the West

Customer trends: **Average household spending on prepared foods should continue to grow as grocery stores compete with restaurants for customers.**

Grocery stores increasingly offer fresh prepared foods as they compete with fast-food restaurants for customers. Americans have responded, spending an average of $148 on prepared foods in 2007 (not including desserts, frozen meals, or salads). Prepared foods rank first among grocery items on which the average household spends the most. The biggest spenders on prepared foods are the busiest households—married couples with children. Couples with children at home spend 55 percent more than average on this item. Householders aged 35 to 54, most with children, spend 21 to 23 percent more than average on prepared foods and control 49 percent of the market. Hispanic households, which tend to be larger than average, spend 13 percent more than average on prepared food. Households in the West, where many Hispanics live, spend 29 percent more.

Average household spending on prepared foods from grocery stores rose by a substantial 66 percent between 2000 and 2007, after adjusting for inflation. Behind the increase were consumers looking for eat-and-run convenience and the growing variety of prepared food offered by grocery store delis. Average household spending on prepared foods should continue to grow as grocery stores compete with restaurants for customers.

Table 9.65 Prepared food (except desserts, frozen meals, and salads)

Total household spending $17,793,719,970.00
Average household spends 148.07

	AVERAGE HOUSEHOLD SPENDING	BEST CUSTOMERS (index)	BIGGEST CUSTOMERS (market share)
AGE OF HOUSEHOLDER			
Average household	**$148.07**	**100**	**100.0%**
Under age 25	113.65	77	5.2
Aged 25 to 34	145.22	98	16.7
Aged 35 to 44	181.54	123	23.9
Aged 45 to 54	179.48	121	25.5
Aged 55 to 64	131.19	89	14.3
Aged 65 to 74	120.73	82	8.1
Aged 75 or older	98.71	67	6.3

	AVERAGE HOUSEHOLD SPENDING	BEST CUSTOMERS (index)	BIGGEST CUSTOMERS (market share)
HOUSEHOLD INCOME			
Average household	**$148.07**	**100**	**100.0%**
Under $20,000	79.55	54	11.0
$20,000 to $39,999	109.15	74	17.1
$40,000 to $49,999	150.21	101	10.0
$50,000 to $69,999	145.44	98	15.0
$70,000 to $79,999	220.55	149	8.6
$80,000 to $99,999	185.12	125	10.2
$100,000 or more	240.60	162	27.8
HOUSEHOLD TYPE			
Average household	**148.07**	**100**	**100.0**
Married couples	183.06	124	62.5
Married couples, no children	124.00	84	18.1
Married couples, with children	228.77	155	38.5
Oldest child under age 6	190.75	129	6.3
Oldest child aged 6 to 17	218.97	148	18.8
Oldest child aged 18 or older	276.08	186	13.7
Single parent with child under age 18	135.84	92	5.5
Single person	86.78	59	17.4
RACE AND HISPANIC ORIGIN			
Average household	**148.07**	**100**	**100.0**
Asian	127.91	86	3.0
Black	98.57	67	8.0
Hispanic	167.10	113	13.3
Non-Hispanic white and other	153.02	103	78.9
REGION			
Average household	**148.07**	**100**	**100.0**
Northeast	136.64	92	17.2
Midwest	127.75	86	19.7
South	140.30	95	34.0
West	191.25	129	29.2
EDUCATION			
Average household	**148.07**	**100**	**100.0**
Less than high school graduate	143.33	97	14.7
High school graduate	121.27	82	20.7
Some college	131.06	89	19.3
Associate's degree	155.78	105	9.4
College graduate	183.64	124	35.9
Bachelor's degree	172.20	116	21.8
Master's, professional, doctoral degree	203.50	137	14.0

Note: Market shares may not sum to 100.0 because of rounding and missing categories by household type. "Asian" and "black" include Hispanics and non-Hispanics who identify themselves as being of the respective race alone. "Hispanic" includes people of any race who identify themselves as Hispanic. "Other" includes people who identify themselves as non-Hispanic and as Alaska Native, American Indian, Asian (who are also included in the "Asian" row), Native Hawaiian or other Pacific Islander, as well as non-Hispanics reporting more than one race.
Source: Calculations by New Strategist based on the Bureau of Labor Statistics' 2007 Consumer Expenditure Survey.

Prepared Food, Frozen (Other than Meals)

Best customers:
Householders aged 35 to 44
Married couples with children at home
Single parents

Customer trends:
Average household spending on frozen prepared food will continue to fall because of the growing preference for fresh food.

The average household spends less on frozen prepared food (other than meals) than on the fresh variety, but this category still ranks a lofty 15th among grocery items on which the average household spends the most. The biggest spenders on frozen prepared food are the busiest households—parents with children. Married couples with children at home spend 58 percent more than average on this item. Single parents spend 26 percent more. Householders aged 35 to 44, most with children at home, spend 33 percent more than average on frozen prepared food.

Average household spending on frozen prepared food declined by a substantial 40 percent between 2000 and 2007, after adjusting for inflation. One factor behind the decline is the growing availability of fresh rather than frozen prepared food. Average household spending on frozen prepared food will continue to fall because of the preference for fresh food.

Table 9.66 Prepared food, frozen (other than meals)

Total household spending $7,856,779,980.00
Average household spends 65.38

AGE OF HOUSEHOLDER	AVERAGE HOUSEHOLD SPENDING	BEST CUSTOMERS (index)	BIGGEST CUSTOMERS (market share)
Average household	$65.38	100	100.0%
Under age 25	51.93	79	5.4
Aged 25 to 34	74.88	115	19.5
Aged 35 to 44	86.88	133	25.9
Aged 45 to 54	74.37	114	23.9
Aged 55 to 64	51.98	80	12.9
Aged 65 to 74	53.44	82	8.2
Aged 75 or older	29.06	44	4.2

	AVERAGE HOUSEHOLD SPENDING	BEST CUSTOMERS (index)	BIGGEST CUSTOMERS (market share)
HOUSEHOLD INCOME			
Average household	**$65.38**	**100**	**100.0%**
Under $20,000	38.76	59	12.2
$20,000 to $39,999	51.95	79	18.5
$40,000 to $49,999	66.28	101	10.0
$50,000 to $69,999	71.86	110	16.8
$70,000 to $79,999	71.07	109	6.3
$80,000 to $99,999	87.16	133	10.8
$100,000 or more	94.85	145	24.9
HOUSEHOLD TYPE			
Average household	**65.38**	**100**	**100.0**
Married couples	80.50	123	62.2
Married couples, no children	53.45	82	17.6
Married couples, with children	103.37	158	39.4
Oldest child under age 6	90.72	139	6.8
Oldest child aged 6 to 17	99.05	151	19.2
Oldest child aged 18 or older	121.23	185	13.7
Single parent with child under age 18	82.13	126	7.5
Single person	33.29	51	15.1
RACE AND HISPANIC ORIGIN			
Average household	**65.38**	**100**	**100.0**
Asian	48.56	74	2.6
Black	41.96	64	7.7
Hispanic	45.12	69	8.1
Non-Hispanic white and other	71.87	110	83.9
REGION			
Average household	**65.38**	**100**	**100.0**
Northeast	57.81	88	16.5
Midwest	72.67	111	25.4
South	62.49	96	34.3
West	68.94	105	23.8
EDUCATION			
Average household	**65.38**	**100**	**100.0**
Less than high school graduate	52.07	80	12.1
High school graduate	68.95	105	26.6
Some college	63.43	97	21.1
Associate's degree	68.51	105	9.3
College graduate	68.94	105	30.5
Bachelor's degree	65.27	100	18.7
Master's, professional, doctoral degree	75.31	115	11.8

Note: Market shares may not sum to 100.0 because of rounding and missing categories by household type. "Asian" and "black" include Hispanics and non-Hispanics who identify themselves as being of the respective race alone. "Hispanic" includes people of any race who identify themselves as Hispanic. "Other" includes people who identify themselves as non-Hispanic and as Alaska Native, American Indian, Asian (who are also included in the "Asian" row), Native Hawaiian or other Pacific Islander, as well as non-Hispanics reporting more than one race.
Source: Calculations by New Strategist based on the Bureau of Labor Statistics' 2007 Consumer Expenditure Survey.

Prepared Meals, Frozen

Best customers: Householders aged 35 to 54
                             Married couples with children at home

Customer trends: Average household spending on frozen meals may stabilize as grocery stores offer
                             more of the fresh variety.

The biggest spenders on frozen meals are householders who want the least bother. Some are buying low-fat or low-carb frozen meals as part of a dietary regimen. Others are on the go and do not want to take the time to cook or stop at a restaurant. Married couples with preschoolers at home spend the most on frozen meals, 64 percent more than the average household. Couples with school-aged or older children at home spend 22 to 26 percent more. Spending on frozen prepared meals is 13 to 22 percent above average among householders aged 35 to 54.

Average household spending on frozen meals more than doubled between 2000 and 2007, after adjusting for inflation. This increase occurred as consumers demanded greater convenience in meal preparation and as the variety of frozen meals expanded. Average household spending on frozen meals may stabilize as grocery stores offer more of the fresh variety.

Table 9.67 Prepared meals, frozen

Total household spending $8,575,402,560.00
Average household spends   71.36

AGE OF HOUSEHOLDER	AVERAGE HOUSEHOLD SPENDING	BEST CUSTOMERS (index)	BIGGEST CUSTOMERS (market share)
Average household	**$71.36**	**100**	**100.0%**
Under age 25	60.70	85	5.8
Aged 25 to 34	70.04	98	16.7
Aged 35 to 44	86.74	122	23.7
Aged 45 to 54	80.85	113	23.8
Aged 55 to 64	62.01	87	14.1
Aged 65 to 74	61.62	86	8.6
Aged 75 or older	55.24	77	7.3

	AVERAGE HOUSEHOLD SPENDING	BEST CUSTOMERS (index)	BIGGEST CUSTOMERS (market share)
HOUSEHOLD INCOME			
Average household	**$71.36**	**100**	**100.0%**
Under $20,000	45.46	64	13.1
$20,000 to $39,999	55.73	78	18.2
$40,000 to $49,999	70.48	99	9.7
$50,000 to $69,999	73.98	104	15.9
$70,000 to $79,999	92.41	129	7.5
$80,000 to $99,999	88.99	125	10.1
$100,000 or more	105.44	148	25.3
HOUSEHOLD TYPE			
Average household	**71.36**	**100**	**100.0**
Married couples	80.97	113	57.4
Married couples, no children	65.89	92	19.9
Married couples, with children	93.73	131	32.8
Oldest child under age 6	117.07	164	8.0
Oldest child aged 6 to 17	87.03	122	15.5
Oldest child aged 18 or older	89.87	126	9.3
Single parent with child under age 18	70.59	99	5.9
Single person	52.73	74	22.0
RACE AND HISPANIC ORIGIN			
Average household	**71.36**	**100**	**100.0**
Asian	66.22	93	3.3
Black	54.57	76	9.2
Hispanic	39.84	56	6.6
Non-Hispanic white and other	78.37	110	83.8
REGION			
Average household	**71.36**	**100**	**100.0**
Northeast	69.09	97	18.0
Midwest	65.10	91	20.8
South	71.07	100	35.8
West	80.20	112	25.4
EDUCATION			
Average household	**71.36**	**100**	**100.0**
Less than high school graduate	54.68	77	11.6
High school graduate	65.07	91	23.0
Some college	67.31	94	20.5
Associate's degree	92.52	130	11.5
College graduate	81.38	114	33.0
Bachelor's degree	80.30	113	21.1
Master's, professional, doctoral degree	83.25	117	11.9

Note: Market shares may not sum to 100.0 because of rounding and missing categories by household type. "Asian" and "black" include Hispanics and non-Hispanics who identify themselves as being of the respective race alone. "Hispanic" includes people of any race who identify themselves as Hispanic. "Other" includes people who identify themselves as non-Hispanic and as Alaska Native, American Indian, Asian (who are also included in the "Asian" row), Native Hawaiian or other Pacific Islander, as well as non-Hispanics reporting more than one race.
Source: Calculations by New Strategist based on the Bureau of Labor Statistics' 2007 Consumer Expenditure Survey.

Rice

Best customers:

Householders aged 25 to 44
Married couples with school-aged or older children at home
Single parents
Asians and Hispanics

Customer trends:

Average household spending on rice will continue to decline as eating out claims a growing share of the food dollar and more boomers become empty-nesters.

The biggest spenders on rice are households with children. Married couples with school-aged children spend 50 percent more than the average household on this item, while those with adult children at home spend a still substantial 40 percent more than average on rice. Single parents spend 30 percent more than the average household on this item. Householders aged 25 to 54, most with children, spend 11 to 20 percent more than average on rice. Asians spend more than four times the average. Hispanics, who tend to have large families, spend 79 percent more. Together, Asians, blacks, and Hispanics account for 48 percent of the market for rice.

Average household spending on rice fell 29 percent between 2000 and 2007, after adjusting for inflation. Behind the decline is consumer demand for convenience, with more food dollars being devoted to prepared foods and eating out rather than cooking from scratch. Average household spending on rice will continue to decline as eating out grows in popularity and more boomers become empty-nesters.

Table 9.68 Rice

Total household spending: $1,994,838,600.00
Average household spends: 16.60

	AVERAGE HOUSEHOLD SPENDING	BEST CUSTOMERS (index)	BIGGEST CUSTOMERS (market share)
AGE OF HOUSEHOLDER			
Average household	**$16.60**	**100**	**100.0%**
Under age 25	14.22	86	5.8
Aged 25 to 34	19.93	120	20.5
Aged 35 to 44	19.82	119	23.3
Aged 45 to 54	18.42	111	23.3
Aged 55 to 64	13.28	80	13.0
Aged 65 to 74	15.40	93	9.3
Aged 75 or older	8.47	51	4.8

	AVERAGE HOUSEHOLD SPENDING	BEST CUSTOMERS (index)	BIGGEST CUSTOMERS (market share)
HOUSEHOLD INCOME			
Average household	**$16.60**	**100**	**100.0%**
Under $20,000	9.73	59	12.0
$20,000 to $39,999	17.10	103	23.9
$40,000 to $49,999	17.18	103	10.2
$50,000 to $69,999	15.43	93	14.2
$70,000 to $79,999	20.89	126	7.3
$80,000 to $99,999	16.99	102	8.3
$100,000 or more	23.24	140	24.0
HOUSEHOLD TYPE			
Average household	**16.60**	**100**	**100.0**
Married couples	20.08	121	61.1
Married couples, no children	14.37	87	18.7
Married couples, with children	23.59	142	35.5
Oldest child under age 6	20.59	124	6.1
Oldest child aged 6 to 17	24.90	150	19.1
Oldest child aged 18 or older	23.18	140	10.3
Single parent with child under age 18	21.51	130	7.7
Single person	7.77	47	13.9
RACE AND HISPANIC ORIGIN			
Average household	**16.60**	**100**	**100.0**
Asian	69.79	420	14.8
Black	16.89	102	12.2
Hispanic	29.79	179	21.2
Non-Hispanic white and other	14.68	88	67.5
REGION			
Average household	**16.60**	**100**	**100.0**
Northeast	22.89	138	25.7
Midwest	10.51	63	14.5
South	15.01	90	32.5
West	20.12	121	27.4
EDUCATION			
Average household	**16.60**	**100**	**100.0**
Less than high school graduate	21.96	132	20.1
High school graduate	14.44	87	21.9
Some college	12.99	78	17.0
Associate's degree	20.64	124	11.1
College graduate	17.45	105	30.4
Bachelor's degree	16.46	99	18.6
Master's, professional, doctoral degree	19.18	116	11.8

Note: Market shares may not sum to 100.0 because of rounding and missing categories by household type. "Asian" and "black" include Hispanics and non-Hispanics who identify themselves as being of the respective race alone. "Hispanic" includes people of any race who identify themselves as Hispanic. "Other" includes people who identify themselves as non-Hispanic and as Alaska Native, American Indian, Asian (who are also included in the "Asian" row), Native Hawaiian or other Pacific Islander, as well as non-Hispanics reporting more than one race.
Source: Calculations by New Strategist based on the Bureau of Labor Statistics' 2007 Consumer Expenditure Survey.

Roast Beef

Best customers:

Married couples with school-aged or older children at home
Single parents
Asians

Customer trends:

Average household spending on roast beef may continue to decline as more boomers become empty-nesters and eating out claims a growing share of the food dollar.

Households with children are the biggest spenders on roast beef. Married couples with school-aged or older children at home spend 55 to 56 percent more than average on this item. Single parents spend 5 percent more despite their low incomes. Householders aged 35 to 54, many with children, spend 18 to 36 percent more than average on this item. Asians spend 63 percent more than the average household on roast beef.

Average household spending on roast beef fell 28 percent between 2000 and 2007, after adjusting for inflation. Behind the decline is the growing consumer preference for prepared foods and eating out. Average household spending on roast beef may continue to decline in the years ahead as more boomers become empty-nesters and eating out claims a growing share of the food dollar.

Table 9.69 Roast beef

Total household spending $4,131,478,980.00
Average household spends 34.38

AGE OF HOUSEHOLDER	AVERAGE HOUSEHOLD SPENDING	BEST CUSTOMERS (index)	BIGGEST CUSTOMERS (market share)
Average household	$34.38	100	100.0%
Under age 25	16.69	49	3.3
Aged 25 to 34	21.99	64	10.9
Aged 35 to 44	46.60	136	26.4
Aged 45 to 54	40.57	118	24.8
Aged 55 to 64	29.08	85	13.7
Aged 65 to 74	36.77	107	10.7
Aged 75 or older	37.85	110	10.4

	AVERAGE HOUSEHOLD SPENDING	BEST CUSTOMERS (index)	BIGGEST CUSTOMERS (market share)
HOUSEHOLD INCOME			
Average household	**$34.38**	**100**	**100.0%**
Under $20,000	24.08	70	14.4
$20,000 to $39,999	28.72	84	19.4
$40,000 to $49,999	28.84	84	8.3
$50,000 to $69,999	39.72	116	17.7
$70,000 to $79,999	34.02	99	5.7
$80,000 to $99,999	57.27	167	13.6
$100,000 or more	39.66	115	19.8
HOUSEHOLD TYPE			
Average household	**34.38**	**100**	**100.0**
Married couples	42.48	124	62.5
Married couples, no children	33.65	98	21.1
Married couples, with children	48.03	140	34.9
Oldest child under age 6	25.22	73	3.6
Oldest child aged 6 to 17	53.79	156	19.9
Oldest child aged 18 or older	53.37	155	11.4
Single parent with child under age 18	36.27	105	6.3
Single person	18.55	54	16.0
RACE AND HISPANIC ORIGIN			
Average household	**34.38**	**100**	**100.0**
Asian	56.09	163	5.8
Black	27.89	81	9.7
Hispanic	32.55	95	11.2
Non-Hispanic white and other	35.60	104	79.0
REGION			
Average household	**34.38**	**100**	**100.0**
Northeast	29.37	85	15.9
Midwest	36.83	107	24.5
South	32.05	93	33.5
West	39.87	116	26.2
EDUCATION			
Average household	**34.38**	**100**	**100.0**
Less than high school graduate	39.61	115	17.5
High school graduate	32.57	95	23.9
Some college	30.06	87	19.0
Associate's degree	32.03	93	8.3
College graduate	37.33	109	31.4
Bachelor's degree	32.25	94	17.6
Master's, professional, doctoral degree	46.16	134	13.7

Note: Market shares may not sum to 100.0 because of rounding and missing categories by household type. "Asian" and "black" include Hispanics and non-Hispanics who identify themselves as being of the respective race alone. "Hispanic" includes people of any race who identify themselves as Hispanic. "Other" includes people who identify themselves as non-Hispanic and as Alaska Native, American Indian, Asian (who are also included in the "Asian" row), Native Hawaiian or other Pacific Islander, as well as non-Hispanics reporting more than one race.
Source: Calculations by New Strategist based on the Bureau of Labor Statistics' 2007 Consumer Expenditure Survey.

Salad Dressing

Best customers:

Householders aged 45 to 54
Married couples with school-aged or older children at home

Customer trends:

Average household spending on salad dressing may continue to fall as more boomers become empty-nesters and household size shrinks.

Middle-aged married couples with children spend the most on salad dressing. Couples with school-aged or older children at home spend 42 to 74 percent more than the average household on this item. Householders aged 45 to 54, many with children at home, spend 18 percent more than average on salad dressing.

Average household spending on salad dressing fell 17 percent between 2000 and 2007, after adjusting for inflation. The growing popularity of prepared and fast food cut spending on this item. Average household spending on salad dressing may continue to decline as more boomers become empty-nesters and household size shrinks.

Table 9.70 Salad dressings

Total household spending $3,262,642,650.00
Average household spends   27.15

	AVERAGE HOUSEHOLD SPENDING	BEST CUSTOMERS (index)	BIGGEST CUSTOMERS (market share)
AGE OF HOUSEHOLDER			
Average household	**$27.15**	**100**	**100.0%**
Under age 25	18.04	66	4.5
Aged 25 to 34	23.71	87	14.9
Aged 35 to 44	29.69	109	21.3
Aged 45 to 54	32.04	118	24.8
Aged 55 to 64	29.26	108	17.5
Aged 65 to 74	28.63	105	10.5
Aged 75 or older	19.14	70	6.7

	AVERAGE HOUSEHOLD SPENDING	BEST CUSTOMERS (index)	BIGGEST CUSTOMERS (market share)
HOUSEHOLD INCOME			
Average household	**$27.15**	**100**	**100.0%**
Under $20,000	14.89	55	11.3
$20,000 to $39,999	21.80	80	18.7
$40,000 to $49,999	29.54	109	10.7
$50,000 to $69,999	28.77	106	16.2
$70,000 to $79,999	29.18	107	6.2
$80,000 to $99,999	29.53	109	8.8
$100,000 or more	44.61	164	28.1
HOUSEHOLD TYPE			
Average household	**27.15**	**100**	**100.0**
Married couples	35.70	131	66.5
Married couples, no children	31.15	115	24.7
Married couples, with children	39.87	147	36.6
Oldest child under age 6	33.26	123	6.0
Oldest child aged 6 to 17	38.64	142	18.1
Oldest child aged 18 or older	47.16	174	12.8
Single parent with child under age 18	22.14	82	4.8
Single person	14.34	53	15.7
RACE AND HISPANIC ORIGIN			
Average household	**27.15**	**100**	**100.0**
Asian	17.84	66	2.3
Black	23.15	85	10.2
Hispanic	19.52	72	8.5
Non-Hispanic white and other	28.86	106	81.1
REGION			
Average household	**27.15**	**100**	**100.0**
Northeast	25.84	95	17.7
Midwest	25.64	94	21.6
South	26.94	99	35.6
West	30.17	111	25.1
EDUCATION			
Average household	**27.15**	**100**	**100.0**
Less than high school graduate	20.17	74	11.3
High school graduate	26.30	97	24.4
Some college	27.58	102	22.1
Associate's degree	29.52	109	9.7
College graduate	30.14	111	32.1
Bachelor's degree	28.13	104	19.4
Master's, professional, doctoral degree	33.62	124	12.6

Note: Market shares may not sum to 100.0 because of rounding and missing categories by household type. "Asian" and "black" include Hispanics and non-Hispanics who identify themselves as being of the respective race alone. "Hispanic" includes people of any race who identify themselves as Hispanic. "Other" includes people who identify themselves as non-Hispanic and as Alaska Native, American Indian, Asian (who are also included in the "Asian" row), Native Hawaiian or other Pacific Islander, as well as non-Hispanics reporting more than one race.
Source: Calculations by New Strategist based on the Bureau of Labor Statistics' 2007 Consumer Expenditure Survey.

Salads, Prepared

Best customers: Householders aged 45 to 64
Married couples without children at home
Married couples with school-aged or older children at home

Customer trends: Average household spending on prepared salads should continue to
rise as consumers look for healthy, easy lunch options.

The best customers of prepared salads are older married couples. Householders ranging in age from 45 to 64 spend 20 to 22 percent more than the average household on this item and control 45 percent of the market. Married couples with school-aged or older children at home spend 26 to 50 percent more than average on prepared salads. Couples without children at home (most of them empty-nesters) spend 27 percent more.

Average household spending on prepared salads rose by a substantial 46 percent between 2000 and 2007, after adjusting for inflation. Behind the gain is Americans' growing demand for the convenience and quality of fresh prepared food. Average household spending on prepared salads could continue to rise in the years ahead as consumers look for healthy, easy lunch options.

Table 9.71 Salads, prepared

| Total household spending | $3,921,179,730.00 |
| Average household spends | 32.63 |

	AVERAGE HOUSEHOLD SPENDING	BEST CUSTOMERS (index)	BIGGEST CUSTOMERS (market share)
AGE OF HOUSEHOLDER			
Average household	**$32.63**	**100**	**100.0%**
Under age 25	18.54	57	3.9
Aged 25 to 34	27.92	86	14.6
Aged 35 to 44	32.47	100	19.4
Aged 45 to 54	39.05	120	25.1
Aged 55 to 64	39.94	122	19.8
Aged 65 to 74	34.45	106	10.6
Aged 75 or older	23.81	73	6.9

	AVERAGE HOUSEHOLD SPENDING	BEST CUSTOMERS (index)	BIGGEST CUSTOMERS (market share)
HOUSEHOLD INCOME			
Average household	**$32.63**	**100**	**100.0%**
Under $20,000	14.28	44	9.0
$20,000 to $39,999	21.46	66	15.3
$40,000 to $49,999	27.39	84	8.3
$50,000 to $69,999	35.24	108	16.5
$70,000 to $79,999	47.77	146	8.5
$80,000 to $99,999	44.10	135	11.0
$100,000 or more	59.78	183	31.4
HOUSEHOLD TYPE			
Average household	**32.63**	**100**	**100.0**
Married couples	41.84	128	64.8
Married couples, no children	41.40	127	27.4
Married couples, with children	41.89	128	32.0
Oldest child under age 6	34.79	107	5.2
Oldest child aged 6 to 17	41.04	126	16.0
Oldest child aged 18 or older	48.80	150	11.0
Single parent with child under age 18	27.69	85	5.0
Single person	19.03	58	17.3
RACE AND HISPANIC ORIGIN			
Average household	**32.63**	**100**	**100.0**
Asian	19.99	61	2.2
Black	19.98	61	7.3
Hispanic	17.01	52	6.2
Non-Hispanic white and other	36.78	113	86.0
REGION			
Average household	**32.63**	**100**	**100.0**
Northeast	32.37	99	18.5
Midwest	31.04	95	21.7
South	31.17	96	34.3
West	36.84	113	25.5
EDUCATION			
Average household	**32.63**	**100**	**100.0**
Less than high school graduate	16.23	50	7.5
High school graduate	28.10	86	21.7
Some college	29.55	91	19.7
Associate's degree	37.05	114	10.1
College graduate	45.10	138	40.0
Bachelor's degree	41.41	127	23.8
Master's, professional, doctoral degree	51.51	158	16.1

Note: Market shares may not sum to 100.0 because of rounding and missing categories by household type. "Asian" and "black" include Hispanics and non-Hispanics who identify themselves as being of the respective race alone. "Hispanic" includes people of any race who identify themselves as Hispanic. "Other" includes people who identify themselves as non-Hispanic and as Alaska Native, American Indian, Asian (who are also included in the "Asian" row), Native Hawaiian or other Pacific Islander, as well as non-Hispanics reporting more than one race.
Source: Calculations by New Strategist based on the Bureau of Labor Statistics' 2007 Consumer Expenditure Survey.

Salt, Spices, and Other Seasonings

Best customers:
Householders aged 25 to 44
Married couples with school-aged or older children at home
Asians

Customer trends:
Average household spending on salt, spices, and other seasonings may continue to decline as household size shrinks with the aging of the population.

The biggest spenders on salt, spices, and other seasonings are households most likely to cook from scratch—married couples with children. Married couples with school-aged children spend 26 percent more than average on this item, and those with adult children at home spend 52 percent more. Householders aged 25 to 44 spend 12 to 22 percent more than average on salt and spices. Asians spend 35 percent more.

Average household spending on salt, spices, and other seasonings fell 3 percent between 2000 and 2007, after adjusting for inflation. Behind the decline was the growing propensity of Americans to substitute fast food for home-cooked meals. Average household spending on salt, spices, and other seasonings may continue to decline in the years ahead as household size shrinks along with the aging of the population.

Table 9.72 **Salt, spices, and other seasonings**

Total household spending $2,892,515,970.00
Average household spends   24.07

	AVERAGE HOUSEHOLD SPENDING	BEST CUSTOMERS (index)	BIGGEST CUSTOMERS (market share)
AGE OF HOUSEHOLDER			
Average household	$24.07	100	100.0%
Under age 25	13.29	55	3.7
Aged 25 to 34	26.85	112	19.0
Aged 35 to 44	29.37	122	23.8
Aged 45 to 54	25.01	104	21.8
Aged 55 to 64	22.86	95	15.4
Aged 65 to 74	24.81	103	10.3
Aged 75 or older	15.20	63	6.0

	AVERAGE HOUSEHOLD SPENDING	BEST CUSTOMERS (index)	BIGGEST CUSTOMERS (market share)
HOUSEHOLD INCOME			
Average household	**$24.07**	**100**	**100.0%**
Under $20,000	13.49	56	11.5
$20,000 to $39,999	19.09	79	18.4
$40,000 to $49,999	26.50	110	10.8
$50,000 to $69,999	24.95	104	15.9
$70,000 to $79,999	26.41	110	6.4
$80,000 to $99,999	27.06	112	9.1
$100,000 or more	39.25	163	27.9
HOUSEHOLD TYPE			
Average household	**24.07**	**100**	**100.0**
Married couples	31.64	131	66.4
Married couples, no children	28.11	117	25.2
Married couples, with children	30.82	128	31.9
Oldest child under age 6	24.65	102	5.0
Oldest child aged 6 to 17	30.24	126	16.0
Oldest child aged 18 or older	36.48	152	11.2
Single parent with child under age 18	21.52	89	5.3
Single person	12.04	50	14.9
RACE AND HISPANIC ORIGIN			
Average household	**24.07**	**100**	**100.0**
Asian	32.50	135	4.8
Black	20.49	85	10.2
Hispanic	24.02	100	11.8
Non-Hispanic white and other	24.60	102	78.0
REGION			
Average household	**24.07**	**100**	**100.0**
Northeast	25.11	104	19.4
Midwest	22.60	94	21.5
South	22.67	94	33.8
West	26.95	112	25.3
EDUCATION			
Average household	**24.07**	**100**	**100.0**
Less than high school graduate	23.17	96	14.6
High school graduate	20.98	87	22.0
Some college	18.90	79	17.1
Associate's degree	23.27	97	8.6
College graduate	31.12	129	37.4
Bachelor's degree	29.21	121	22.7
Master's, professional, doctoral degree	34.45	143	14.6

Note: Market shares may not sum to 100.0 because of rounding and missing categories by household type. "Asian" and "black" include Hispanics and non-Hispanics who identify themselves as being of the respective race alone. "Hispanic" includes people of any race who identify themselves as Hispanic. "Other" includes people who identify themselves as non-Hispanic and as Alaska Native, American Indian, Asian (who are also included in the "Asian" row), Native Hawaiian or other Pacific Islander, as well as non-Hispanics reporting more than one race.
Source: Calculations by New Strategist based on the Bureau of Labor Statistics' 2007 Consumer Expenditure Survey.

Sauces and Gravies

Best customers:

Householders aged 35 to 54
Married couples with children at home
Households in the West

Customer trends:

Average household spending on sauces and gravies is likely to decline as boomers become empty-nesters and eating out claims a growing share of the food dollar.

Married couples with children at home, who are most likely to cook from scratch, are the best customers of convenience products like sauces and gravies. They spend 54 percent more than average on this item. Householders aged 35 to 54, most with children, spend 19 to 25 percent more than average on sauces and gravies. Households in the West spend 21 percent more than average on this item.

Average household spending on sauces and gravies increased 4 percent between 2000 and 2007, after adjusting for inflation. Average household spending on this item is likely to decline in the years ahead as more boomers become empty-nesters and eating out claims a growing share of the food dollar.

Table 9.73 Sauces and gravies

Total household spending $5,592,758,340.00
Average household spends 46.54

	AVERAGE HOUSEHOLD SPENDING	BEST CUSTOMERS (index)	BIGGEST CUSTOMERS (market share)
AGE OF HOUSEHOLDER			
Average household	**$46.54**	**100**	**100.0%**
Under age 25	35.37	76	5.2
Aged 25 to 34	46.68	100	17.1
Aged 35 to 44	58.15	125	24.3
Aged 45 to 54	55.27	119	24.9
Aged 55 to 64	44.39	95	15.4
Aged 65 to 74	40.05	86	8.6
Aged 75 or older	21.96	47	4.5

	AVERAGE HOUSEHOLD SPENDING	BEST CUSTOMERS (index)	BIGGEST CUSTOMERS (market share)
HOUSEHOLD INCOME			
Average household	**$46.54**	**100**	**100.0%**
Under $20,000	22.89	49	10.1
$20,000 to $39,999	33.93	73	16.9
$40,000 to $49,999	45.09	97	9.5
$50,000 to $69,999	53.34	115	17.5
$70,000 to $79,999	55.41	119	6.9
$80,000 to $99,999	63.43	136	11.1
$100,000 or more	75.06	161	27.6
HOUSEHOLD TYPE			
Average household	**46.54**	**100**	**100.0**
Married couples	62.17	134	67.5
Married couples, no children	49.72	107	23.0
Married couples, with children	71.80	154	38.5
Oldest child under age 6	62.87	135	6.6
Oldest child aged 6 to 17	68.32	147	18.6
Oldest child aged 18 or older	85.26	183	13.5
Single parent with child under age 18	43.38	93	5.5
Single person	21.39	46	13.7
RACE AND HISPANIC ORIGIN			
Average household	**46.54**	**100**	**100.0**
Asian	45.55	98	3.5
Black	36.54	79	9.4
Hispanic	39.43	85	10.0
Non-Hispanic white and other	49.13	106	80.6
REGION			
Average household	**46.54**	**100**	**100.0**
Northeast	45.65	98	18.3
Midwest	44.80	96	22.0
South	41.98	90	32.4
West	56.46	121	27.4
EDUCATION			
Average household	**46.54**	**100**	**100.0**
Less than high school graduate	34.27	74	11.2
High school graduate	41.31	89	22.4
Some college	44.62	96	20.9
Associate's degree	51.31	110	9.8
College graduate	56.79	122	35.3
Bachelor's degree	53.23	114	21.4
Master's, professional, doctoral degree	62.98	135	13.8

Note: Market shares may not sum to 100.0 because of rounding and missing categories by household type. "Asian" and "black" include Hispanics and non-Hispanics who identify themselves as being of the respective race alone. "Hispanic" includes people of any race who identify themselves as Hispanic. "Other" includes people who identify themselves as non-Hispanic and as Alaska Native, American Indian, Asian (who are also included in the "Asian" row), Native Hawaiian or other Pacific Islander, as well as non-Hispanics reporting more than one race.
Source: Calculations by New Strategist based on the Bureau of Labor Statistics' 2007 Consumer Expenditure Survey.

Sausage

Best customers:
Householders aged 35 to 44
Married couples with children at home
Single parents
Blacks

Customer trends:
Average household spending on sausage may continue to decline as more boomers become empty-nesters and the small generation X fills the best-customer lifestage.

Households with children are the biggest spenders on sausage. Married couples with children at home spend 45 percent more than average on this item, the figure peaking at 60 percent more among couples with adult children at home. Single parents spend 7 percent more than average despite their low incomes. Householders aged 35 to 44, most with children at home, spend 23 percent more than average on sausage. Blacks spend 37 percent more than average on this item.

Average household spending on sausage declined 16 percent between 2000 and 2007, after adjusting for inflation. The growing popularity of fast-food breakfasts rather than home-cooked meals is one factor behind the decline. Average household spending on sausage may continue to decline in the years ahead as more boomers become empty-nesters and the small generation X fills the best-customer lifestage.

Table 9.74 Sausage

Total household spending $3,073,974,180.00
Average household spends 25.58

AGE OF HOUSEHOLDER	AVERAGE HOUSEHOLD SPENDING	BEST CUSTOMERS (index)	BIGGEST CUSTOMERS (market share)
Average household	$25.58	100	100.0%
Under age 25	12.12	47	3.2
Aged 25 to 34	24.22	95	16.2
Aged 35 to 44	31.54	123	24.0
Aged 45 to 54	26.98	105	22.2
Aged 55 to 64	28.54	112	18.1
Aged 65 to 74	28.60	112	11.2
Aged 75 or older	14.46	57	5.4

	AVERAGE HOUSEHOLD SPENDING	BEST CUSTOMERS (index)	BIGGEST CUSTOMERS (market share)
HOUSEHOLD INCOME			
Average household	**$25.58**	**100**	**100.0%**
Under $20,000	14.94	58	12.0
$20,000 to $39,999	18.66	73	17.0
$40,000 to $49,999	30.36	119	11.7
$50,000 to $69,999	32.12	126	19.2
$70,000 to $79,999	26.76	105	6.1
$80,000 to $99,999	28.68	112	9.1
$100,000 or more	36.85	144	24.7
HOUSEHOLD TYPE			
Average household	**25.58**	**100**	**100.0**
Married couples	34.38	134	67.9
Married couples, no children	29.95	117	25.3
Married couples, with children	37.15	145	36.2
Oldest child under age 6	35.33	138	6.7
Oldest child aged 6 to 17	35.98	141	17.9
Oldest child aged 18 or older	40.82	160	11.8
Single parent with child under age 18	27.37	107	6.4
Single person	9.92	39	11.5
RACE AND HISPANIC ORIGIN			
Average household	**25.58**	**100**	**100.0**
Asian	29.08	114	4.0
Black	35.14	137	16.5
Hispanic	22.45	88	10.4
Non-Hispanic white and other	24.53	96	73.2
REGION			
Average household	**25.58**	**100**	**100.0**
Northeast	22.37	87	16.3
Midwest	25.27	99	22.6
South	28.25	110	39.7
West	24.34	95	21.5
EDUCATION			
Average household	**25.58**	**100**	**100.0**
Less than high school graduate	27.43	107	16.3
High school graduate	24.58	96	24.2
Some college	23.66	92	20.1
Associate's degree	23.86	93	8.3
College graduate	27.49	107	31.1
Bachelor's degree	24.61	96	18.0
Master's, professional, doctoral degree	32.49	127	13.0

Note: Market shares may not sum to 100.0 because of rounding and missing categories by household type. "Asian" and "black" include Hispanics and non-Hispanics who identify themselves as being of the respective race alone. "Hispanic" includes people of any race who identify themselves as Hispanic. "Other" includes people who identify themselves as non-Hispanic and as Alaska Native, American Indian, Asian (who are also included in the "Asian" row), Native Hawaiian or other Pacific Islander, as well as non-Hispanics reporting more than one race.
Source: Calculations by New Strategist based on the Bureau of Labor Statistics' 2007 Consumer Expenditure Survey.

Soups, Canned and Packaged

Best customers: Householders aged 35 to 74
Married couples with school-aged or older children at home

Customer trends: Average household spending on soup should remain stable if the product can reinvent itself as a convenience food.

Older householders and families with children are the best customers of soup. Householders aged 55 to 74 spend 11 to 13 percent more than average on soup. Couples with school-aged or older children at home spend 34 to 66 percent more than average on soup, while those without children at home (most of them empty-nesters) spend 14 percent more.

Average household spending on soup fell 6 percent between 2000 and 2007, after adjusting for inflation. Average household spending on soup could rise in the years ahead if the product can reinvent itself as a convenience food.

Table 9.75 Soups, canned and packaged

Total household spending	$4,812,848,550.00
Average household spends	40.05

	AVERAGE HOUSEHOLD SPENDING	BEST CUSTOMERS (index)	BIGGEST CUSTOMERS (market share)
AGE OF HOUSEHOLDER			
Average household	**$40.05**	**100**	**100.0%**
Under age 25	21.75	54	3.7
Aged 25 to 34	35.37	88	15.1
Aged 35 to 44	45.27	113	22.0
Aged 45 to 54	41.48	104	21.8
Aged 55 to 64	44.51	111	18.0
Aged 65 to 74	45.23	113	11.3
Aged 75 or older	35.30	88	8.4

	AVERAGE HOUSEHOLD SPENDING	BEST CUSTOMERS (index)	BIGGEST CUSTOMERS (market share)
HOUSEHOLD INCOME			
Average household	**$40.05**	**100**	**100.0%**
Under $20,000	24.36	61	12.5
$20,000 to $39,999	31.61	79	18.3
$40,000 to $49,999	41.13	103	10.1
$50,000 to $69,999	43.71	109	16.7
$70,000 to $79,999	41.29	103	6.0
$80,000 to $99,999	47.48	119	9.6
$100,000 or more	62.16	155	26.6
HOUSEHOLD TYPE			
Average household	**40.05**	**100**	**100.0**
Married couples	50.78	127	64.1
Married couples, no children	45.70	114	24.6
Married couples, with children	55.15	138	34.4
Oldest child under age 6	44.15	110	5.4
Oldest child aged 6 to 17	53.48	134	17.0
Oldest child aged 18 or older	66.53	166	12.2
Single parent with child under age 18	29.71	74	4.4
Single person	25.98	65	19.3
RACE AND HISPANIC ORIGIN			
Average household	**40.05**	**100**	**100.0**
Asian	40.52	101	3.6
Black	28.81	72	8.6
Hispanic	27.91	70	8.2
Non-Hispanic white and other	43.48	109	82.9
REGION			
Average household	**40.05**	**100**	**100.0**
Northeast	45.29	113	21.1
Midwest	38.35	96	21.9
South	36.73	92	32.9
West	42.73	107	24.1
EDUCATION			
Average household	**40.05**	**100**	**100.0**
Less than high school graduate	31.14	78	11.8
High school graduate	36.47	91	23.0
Some college	36.45	91	19.8
Associate's degree	44.70	112	9.9
College graduate	48.54	121	35.1
Bachelor's degree	45.93	115	21.5
Master's, professional, doctoral degree	53.08	133	13.5

Note: Market shares may not sum to 100.0 because of rounding and missing categories by household type. "Asian" and "black" include Hispanics and non-Hispanics who identify themselves as being of the respective race alone. "Hispanic" includes people of any race who identify themselves as Hispanic. "Other" includes people who identify themselves as non-Hispanic and as Alaska Native, American Indian, Asian (who are also included in the "Asian" row), Native Hawaiian or other Pacific Islander, as well as non-Hispanics reporting more than one race.
Source: Calculations by New Strategist based on the Bureau of Labor Statistics' 2007 Consumer Expenditure Survey.

Steak

Best customers:
      Householders aged 35 to 54
      Married couples with children at home
      Hispanics

Customer trends:
      Average household spending on steak should continue to decline as more boomers become empty-nesters and eating out claims a growing share of the food dollar.

The best customers of steak are the largest households. Married couples with children at home spend 51 percent more than average on this item. Householders aged 35 to 54, most with children, spend 10 to 31 percent more than average on steak and account for 49 percent of the market. Hispanics spend 23 percent more than average on steak.

Average household spending on steak dropped 33 percent between 2000 and 2007, after adjusting for inflation. Behind the decline was competition from restaurants, as well as the baby-boom generation's exit from the best-customer lifestage. Average household spending on steak may continue to decline in the years ahead as more boomers become empty-nesters and eating out claims a growing share of the food dollar.

Table 9.76 Steak

Total household spending		$9,170,249,010.00	
Average household spends		76.31	
	AVERAGE HOUSEHOLD SPENDING	BEST CUSTOMERS (index)	BIGGEST CUSTOMERS (market share)
AGE OF HOUSEHOLDER			
Average household	**$76.31**	**100**	**100.0%**
Under age 25	54.08	71	4.8
Aged 25 to 34	69.50	91	15.5
Aged 35 to 44	99.69	131	25.5
Aged 45 to 54	84.02	110	23.1
Aged 55 to 64	71.16	93	15.1
Aged 65 to 74	64.91	85	8.5
Aged 75 or older	60.97	80	7.6

	AVERAGE HOUSEHOLD SPENDING	BEST CUSTOMERS (index)	BIGGEST CUSTOMERS (market share)
HOUSEHOLD INCOME			
Average household	**$76.31**	**100**	**100.0%**
Under $20,000	39.32	52	10.6
$20,000 to $39,999	62.16	81	18.9
$40,000 to $49,999	75.44	99	9.7
$50,000 to $69,999	78.73	103	15.8
$70,000 to $79,999	89.21	117	6.8
$80,000 to $99,999	96.21	126	10.3
$100,000 or more	123.26	162	27.7
HOUSEHOLD TYPE			
Average household	**76.31**	**100**	**100.0**
Married couples	102.45	134	67.9
Married couples, no children	81.35	107	23.0
Married couples, with children	115.05	151	37.6
Oldest child under age 6	109.05	143	7.0
Oldest child aged 6 to 17	111.68	146	18.6
Oldest child aged 18 or older	126.15	165	12.2
Single parent with child under age 18	39.84	52	3.1
Single person	38.48	50	15.0
RACE AND HISPANIC ORIGIN			
Average household	**76.31**	**100**	**100.0**
Asian	69.99	92	3.2
Black	51.15	67	8.0
Hispanic	94.10	123	14.6
Non-Hispanic white and other	77.64	102	77.7
REGION			
Average household	**76.31**	**100**	**100.0**
Northeast	76.25	100	18.6
Midwest	61.93	81	18.5
South	77.67	102	36.5
West	89.03	117	26.4
EDUCATION			
Average household	**76.31**	**100**	**100.0**
Less than high school graduate	77.91	102	15.5
High school graduate	74.36	97	24.6
Some college	70.30	92	20.1
Associate's degree	74.87	98	8.7
College graduate	82.01	107	31.1
Bachelor's degree	81.56	107	20.0
Master's, professional, doctoral degree	82.78	108	11.1

Note: Market shares may not sum to 100.0 because of rounding and missing categories by household type. "Asian" and "black" include Hispanics and non-Hispanics who identify themselves as being of the respective race alone. "Hispanic" includes people of any race who identify themselves as Hispanic. "Other" includes people who identify themselves as non-Hispanic and as Alaska Native, American Indian, Asian (who are also included in the "Asian" row), Native Hawaiian or other Pacific Islander, as well as non-Hispanics reporting more than one race.
Source: Calculations by New Strategist based on the Bureau of Labor Statistics' 2007 Consumer Expenditure Survey.

Sugar

Best customers:
Householders aged 35 to 44
Married couples with school-aged or older children at home
Single parents
Asians, Blacks, and Hispanics

Customer trends:
Average household spending on sugar will continue to decline as cooking from scratch becomes less common and more boomers become empty-nesters.

The biggest spenders on sugar are households that do the most cooking from scratch, typically families with children. Couples with school-aged or older children at home spend 49 to 64 percent more than average on sugar. Single parents spend 14 percent more. Householders aged 35 to 44, most with children, spend 24 percent more than average on this item and control one-quarter the market. Hispanics and blacks, who tend to have large families, spend, respectively, 44 and 25 percent more than average on sugar.

Average household spending on sugar fell 18 percent between 2000 and 2007, after adjusting for inflation. Behind the decline is the rise of eating out as busy families find less time to cook from scratch. Average household spending on sugar will continue to decline as eating out claims a growing share of the food dollar and more boomers become empty-nesters.

Table 9.77 Sugar

| Total household spending | $1,981,619,790.00 |
| Average household spends | 16.49 |

	AVERAGE HOUSEHOLD SPENDING	BEST CUSTOMERS (index)	BIGGEST CUSTOMERS (market share)
AGE OF HOUSEHOLDER			
Average household	**$16.49**	**100**	**100.0%**
Under age 25	9.54	58	3.9
Aged 25 to 34	16.94	103	17.5
Aged 35 to 44	20.50	124	24.2
Aged 45 to 54	17.68	107	22.5
Aged 55 to 64	15.21	92	14.9
Aged 65 to 74	15.89	96	9.6
Aged 75 or older	12.80	78	7.4

	AVERAGE HOUSEHOLD SPENDING	BEST CUSTOMERS (index)	BIGGEST CUSTOMERS (market share)
HOUSEHOLD INCOME			
Average household	**$16.49**	**100**	**100.0%**
Under $20,000	12.11	73	15.1
$20,000 to $39,999	14.93	91	21.0
$40,000 to $49,999	18.15	110	10.8
$50,000 to $69,999	19.25	117	17.9
$70,000 to $79,999	16.20	98	5.7
$80,000 to $99,999	18.86	114	9.3
$100,000 or more	18.89	115	19.6
HOUSEHOLD TYPE			
Average household	**16.49**	**100**	**100.0**
Married couples	21.58	131	66.2
Married couples, no children	17.02	103	22.3
Married couples, with children	23.96	145	36.3
Oldest child under age 6	14.87	90	4.4
Oldest child aged 6 to 17	27.06	164	20.8
Oldest child aged 18 or older	24.50	149	10.9
Single parent with child under age 18	18.75	114	6.8
Single person	6.97	42	12.6
RACE AND HISPANIC ORIGIN			
Average household	**16.49**	**100**	**100.0**
Asian	19.57	119	4.2
Black	20.65	125	15.0
Hispanic	23.80	144	17.0
Non-Hispanic white and other	14.79	90	68.5
REGION			
Average household	**16.49**	**100**	**100.0**
Northeast	17.13	104	19.3
Midwest	14.50	88	20.1
South	18.17	110	39.6
West	15.32	93	21.0
EDUCATION			
Average household	**16.49**	**100**	**100.0**
Less than high school graduate	20.09	122	18.5
High school graduate	17.42	106	26.6
Some college	14.79	90	19.5
Associate's degree	15.82	96	8.5
College graduate	15.45	94	27.1
Bachelor's degree	16.11	98	18.3
Master's, professional, doctoral degree	14.32	87	8.9

Note: Market shares may not sum to 100.0 because of rounding and missing categories by household type. "Asian" and "black" include Hispanics and non-Hispanics who identify themselves as being of the respective race alone. "Hispanic" includes people of any race who identify themselves as Hispanic. "Other" includes people who identify themselves as non-Hispanic and as Alaska Native, American Indian, Asian (who are also included in the "Asian" row), Native Hawaiian or other Pacific Islander, as well as non-Hispanics reporting more than one race.
Source: Calculations by New Strategist based on the Bureau of Labor Statistics' 2007 Consumer Expenditure Survey.

Sweetrolls, Coffee Cakes, and Doughnuts

Best customers:
Householders aged 35 to 44 and 75 or older
Married couples without children at home
Married couples with school-aged or older children at home
Single parents

Customer trends:
Average household spending on sweetrolls, coffee cakes, and doughnuts may continue to decline in the years ahead as eating out claims a growing share of the food dollar.

The biggest spenders on sweetrolls, coffee cakes, and doughnuts are households with children and older householders. Married couples with children at home spend 41 percent more than average on this item. Single parents spend 5 percent more despite their low incomes. Householders aged 35 to 44, most with children, spend 19 percent more than average on sweetrolls, coffee cakes, and doughnuts. Married couples without children at home (most of them older) spend 14 percent more than average. Householders aged 75 or older spend 24 percent more than the average household on the category.

Average household spending on sweetrolls, coffee cakes, and doughnuts fell 22 percent between 2000 and 2007, after adjusting for inflation. Behind the spending decline is the growing propensity of Americans to grab snacks from restaurants rather than grocery stores. Average household spending on sweetrolls, coffee cakes, and doughnuts may continue to decline in the years ahead as eating out claims a growing share of the food dollar.

Table 9.78 Sweetrolls, coffee cakes, and doughnuts

Total household spending $2,545,221,780.00
Average household spends 21.18

	AVERAGE HOUSEHOLD SPENDING	BEST CUSTOMERS (index)	BIGGEST CUSTOMERS (market share)
AGE OF HOUSEHOLDER			
Average household	**$21.18**	**100**	**100.0%**
Under age 25	10.51	50	3.4
Aged 25 to 34	18.54	88	14.9
Aged 35 to 44	25.28	119	23.3
Aged 45 to 54	21.61	102	21.4
Aged 55 to 64	19.47	92	14.9
Aged 65 to 74	22.29	105	10.5
Aged 75 or older	26.35	124	11.8

	AVERAGE HOUSEHOLD SPENDING	BEST CUSTOMERS (index)	BIGGEST CUSTOMERS (market share)
HOUSEHOLD INCOME			
Average household	$21.18	100	100.0%
Under $20,000	11.70	55	11.4
$20,000 to $39,999	19.30	91	21.2
$40,000 to $49,999	20.55	97	9.5
$50,000 to $69,999	22.62	107	16.3
$70,000 to $79,999	21.97	104	6.0
$80,000 to $99,999	28.83	136	11.1
$100,000 or more	29.53	139	23.9
HOUSEHOLD TYPE			
Average household	21.18	100	100.0
Married couples	28.31	134	67.6
Married couples, no children	24.05	114	24.5
Married couples, with children	29.86	141	35.2
Oldest child under age 6	21.07	99	4.9
Oldest child aged 6 to 17	33.01	156	19.8
Oldest child aged 18 or older	30.09	142	10.5
Single parent with child under age 18	22.16	105	6.2
Single person	9.82	46	13.8
RACE AND HISPANIC ORIGIN			
Average household	21.18	100	100.0
Asian	22.23	105	3.7
Black	12.82	61	7.3
Hispanic	23.93	113	13.3
Non-Hispanic white and other	22.07	104	79.5
REGION			
Average household	21.18	100	100.0
Northeast	22.63	107	19.9
Midwest	21.42	101	23.1
South	17.92	85	30.4
West	24.95	118	26.6
EDUCATION			
Average household	21.18	100	100.0
Less than high school graduate	19.75	93	14.1
High school graduate	21.12	100	25.2
Some college	21.64	102	22.2
Associate's degree	21.16	100	8.9
College graduate	21.56	102	29.5
Bachelor's degree	21.12	100	18.7
Master's, professional, doctoral degree	22.33	105	10.8

Note: Market shares may not sum to 100.0 because of rounding and missing categories by household type. "Asian" and "black" include Hispanics and non-Hispanics who identify themselves as being of the respective race alone. "Hispanic" includes people of any race who identify themselves as Hispanic. "Other" includes people who identify themselves as non-Hispanic and as Alaska Native, American Indian, Asian (who are also included in the "Asian" row), Native Hawaiian or other Pacific Islander, as well as non-Hispanics reporting more than one race.
Source: Calculations by New Strategist based on the Bureau of Labor Statistics' 2007 Consumer Expenditure Survey.

Tea

Best customers:
Householders aged 45 to 54
Married couples with school-aged or older children at home
Asians
Households in the Northeast

Customer trends:
Average household spending on tea may continue to rise because of the introduction
of new products and tea's touted health benefits.

Although the media frequently tout the nutritional benefits of tea, Americans still spend far less on tea than on coffee. But tea is closing in. In 2007, the average household spent 56 percent as much on tea ($28.63) as on roasted and instant coffee ($51.07), up from 37 percent in 2000. Middle-aged householders are the best customers of tea, with those aged 45 to 54 spending 33 percent more than average on this item. Married couples with school-aged children spend 28 percent more than average tea, while those with adult children at home spend 75 percent more than average on this item. Asians spend 75 percent more than the average on tea, and households in the Northeast spend 22 percent more.

Average household spending on tea purchased at grocery or convenience stores rose by a substantial 52 percent between 2000 and 2007, after adjusting for inflation. Behind the rise in spending on tea are the health and nutritional claims for green and black tea, as well as the greater variety of tea available in grocery stores. Average household spending on tea may continue to rise because of the introduction of new products and tea's touted health benefits.

Table 9.79 Tea

Total household spending $3,440,495,730.00
Average household spends   28.63

	AVERAGE HOUSEHOLD SPENDING	BEST CUSTOMERS (index)	BIGGEST CUSTOMERS (market share)
AGE OF HOUSEHOLDER			
Average household	**$28.63**	**100**	**100.0%**
Under age 25	12.08	42	2.9
Aged 25 to 34	25.51	89	15.2
Aged 35 to 44	30.03	105	20.4
Aged 45 to 54	38.12	133	28.0
Aged 55 to 64	33.21	116	18.8
Aged 65 to 74	27.28	95	9.5
Aged 75 or older	16.79	59	5.6

	AVERAGE HOUSEHOLD SPENDING	BEST CUSTOMERS (index)	BIGGEST CUSTOMERS (market share)
HOUSEHOLD INCOME			
Average household	**$28.63**	**100**	**100.0%**
Under $20,000	13.69	48	9.8
$20,000 to $39,999	21.55	75	17.5
$40,000 to $49,999	27.56	96	9.5
$50,000 to $69,999	26.71	93	14.3
$70,000 to $79,999	34.32	120	6.9
$80,000 to $99,999	35.20	123	10.0
$100,000 or more	53.74	188	32.2
HOUSEHOLD TYPE			
Average household	**28.63**	**100**	**100.0**
Married couples	36.97	129	65.3
Married couples, no children	32.98	115	24.8
Married couples, with children	39.12	137	34.1
Oldest child under age 6	30.68	107	5.2
Oldest child aged 6 to 17	36.75	128	16.3
Oldest child aged 18 or older	49.99	175	12.9
Single parent with child under age 18	22.92	80	4.8
Single person	16.08	56	16.7
RACE AND HISPANIC ORIGIN			
Average household	**28.63**	**100**	**100.0**
Asian	50.03	175	6.2
Black	24.98	87	10.5
Hispanic	22.47	78	9.3
Non-Hispanic white and other	30.03	105	80.1
REGION			
Average household	**28.63**	**100**	**100.0**
Northeast	34.96	122	22.7
Midwest	24.23	85	19.3
South	26.48	92	33.2
West	31.26	109	24.7
EDUCATION			
Average household	**28.63**	**100**	**100.0**
Less than high school graduate	19.79	69	10.5
High school graduate	27.74	97	24.4
Some college	26.18	91	19.9
Associate's degree	27.29	95	8.5
College graduate	35.63	124	36.0
Bachelor's degree	29.89	104	19.6
Master's, professional, doctoral degree	45.61	159	16.3

Note: Market shares may not sum to 100.0 because of rounding and missing categories by household type. "Asian" and "black" include Hispanics and non-Hispanics who identify themselves as being of the respective race alone. "Hispanic" includes people of any race who identify themselves as Hispanic. "Other" includes people who identify themselves as non-Hispanic and as Alaska Native, American Indian, Asian (who are also included in the "Asian" row), Native Hawaiian or other Pacific Islander, as well as non-Hispanics reporting more than one race.
Source: Calculations by New Strategist based on the Bureau of Labor Statistics' 2007 Consumer Expenditure Survey.

Tomatoes

Best customers:

Householders aged 35 to 44
Married couples with children at home
Asians and Hispanics
Households in the West

Customer trends:

Average household spending on tomatoes may continue to fall as prepared foods
and eating out claim a growing share of the food dollar.

The best customers of fresh tomatoes are the largest households. Married couples with children at home spend 45 percent more than average on tomatoes, and the figure peaks at 61 percent among couples with adult children at home. Householders aged 35 to 44, many with children, spend 24 percent more than average on tomatoes. Asians spend 42 percent more than the average on tomatoes, and Hispanics—who have the largest families—spend 56 percent more than average on this item. Households in the West, where many Asians and Hispanics live, spend 24 percent more than average on tomatoes.

Average household spending on fresh tomatoes fell 1 percent between 2000 and 2007, after adjusting for inflation. Growth of the Asian and Hispanic populations limited spending losses on this item. Average household spending on tomatoes may continue to fall as prepared foods and eating out claim a growing share of the food dollar.

Table 9.80 Tomatoes

Total household spending $4,211,993,550.00
Average household spends 35.05

AGE OF HOUSEHOLDER	AVERAGE HOUSEHOLD SPENDING	BEST CUSTOMERS (index)	BIGGEST CUSTOMERS (market share)
Average household	$35.05	100	100.0%
Under age 25	20.58	59	4.0
Aged 25 to 34	30.70	88	14.9
Aged 35 to 44	43.44	124	24.1
Aged 45 to 54	35.77	102	21.4
Aged 55 to 64	37.68	108	17.4
Aged 65 to 74	37.68	108	10.7
Aged 75 or older	27.50	78	7.4

	AVERAGE HOUSEHOLD SPENDING	BEST CUSTOMERS (index)	BIGGEST CUSTOMERS (market share)
HOUSEHOLD INCOME			
Average household	**$35.05**	**100**	**100.0%**
Under $20,000	21.56	62	12.6
$20,000 to $39,999	27.40	78	18.2
$40,000 to $49,999	35.28	101	9.9
$50,000 to $69,999	39.71	113	17.3
$70,000 to $79,999	39.49	113	6.5
$80,000 to $99,999	36.07	103	8.4
$100,000 or more	55.46	158	27.1
HOUSEHOLD TYPE			
Average household	**35.05**	**100**	**100.0**
Married couples	46.78	133	67.5
Married couples, no children	40.58	116	25.0
Married couples, with children	50.68	145	36.1
Oldest child under age 6	46.14	132	6.4
Oldest child aged 6 to 17	49.43	141	17.9
Oldest child aged 18 or older	56.49	161	11.9
Single parent with child under age 18	23.72	68	4.0
Single person	17.59	50	14.9
RACE AND HISPANIC ORIGIN			
Average household	**35.05**	**100**	**100.0**
Asian	49.74	142	5.0
Black	27.16	77	9.3
Hispanic	54.69	156	18.4
Non-Hispanic white and other	33.45	95	72.9
REGION			
Average household	**35.05**	**100**	**100.0**
Northeast	35.64	102	18.9
Midwest	27.53	79	17.9
South	34.40	98	35.2
West	43.34	124	28.0
EDUCATION			
Average household	**35.05**	**100**	**100.0**
Less than high school graduate	34.49	98	14.9
High school graduate	30.46	87	21.9
Some college	29.91	85	18.6
Associate's degree	34.72	99	8.8
College graduate	43.09	123	35.6
Bachelor's degree	38.17	109	20.4
Master's, professional, doctoral degree	51.64	147	15.0

Note: Market shares may not sum to 100.0 because of rounding and missing categories by household type. "Asian" and "black" include Hispanics and non-Hispanics who identify themselves as being of the respective race alone. "Hispanic" includes people of any race who identify themselves as Hispanic. "Other" includes people who identify themselves as non-Hispanic and as Alaska Native, American Indian, Asian (who are also included in the "Asian" row), Native Hawaiian or other Pacific Islander, as well as non-Hispanics reporting more than one race.
Source: Calculations by New Strategist based on the Bureau of Labor Statistics' 2007 Consumer Expenditure Survey.

Vegetable Juice, Fresh and Canned

Best customers: **Householders aged 35 to 54**
Married couples with school-aged or older children at home
Single parents
Hispanics
Households in the West

Customer trends: **Average household spending on vegetable juice should stabilize in the years ahead as the small generation X fills the best-customer lifestage.**

The biggest spenders on vegetable juice are households with children. Married couples with children at home spend 43 percent more than average on this item. Single parents spend 14 percent more despite their low incomes. Householders aged 35 to 54, most of them parents, spend 10 to 21 percent more than average on vegetable juices. Hispanics spend 20 percent more than average on vegetable juices, and households in the West spend 29 percent more.

Average household spending on vegetable juice purchased at grocery or convenience stores rose 39 percent between 2000 and 2007, after adjusting for inflation. One factor behind the substantial increase is the growing Hispanic population. Average household spending on vegetable juice should stabilize in the years ahead as the small generation X fills the best-customer lifestage.

Table 9.81 Vegetable juice, fresh and canned

| Total household spending | $1,869,860,760.00 |
| Average household spends | 15.56 |

	AVERAGE HOUSEHOLD SPENDING	BEST CUSTOMERS (index)	BIGGEST CUSTOMERS (market share)
AGE OF HOUSEHOLDER			
Average household	**$15.56**	**100**	**100.0%**
Under age 25	12.29	79	5.4
Aged 25 to 34	14.33	92	15.7
Aged 35 to 44	17.10	110	21.4
Aged 45 to 54	18.85	121	25.4
Aged 55 to 64	15.80	102	16.4
Aged 65 to 74	15.58	100	10.0
Aged 75 or older	9.35	60	5.7

	AVERAGE HOUSEHOLD SPENDING	BEST CUSTOMERS (index)	BIGGEST CUSTOMERS (market share)
HOUSEHOLD INCOME			
Average household	**$15.56**	**100**	**100.0%**
Under $20,000	9.08	58	12.0
$20,000 to $39,999	13.25	85	19.8
$40,000 to $49,999	13.09	84	8.3
$50,000 to $69,999	16.16	104	15.9
$70,000 to $79,999	18.51	119	6.9
$80,000 to $99,999	19.87	128	10.4
$100,000 or more	24.19	155	26.6
HOUSEHOLD TYPE			
Average household	**15.56**	**100**	**100.0**
Married couples	19.13	123	62.1
Married couples, no children	15.14	97	21.0
Married couples, with children	22.22	143	35.6
Oldest child under age 6	15.07	97	4.7
Oldest child aged 6 to 17	24.93	160	20.4
Oldest child aged 18 or older	22.12	142	10.5
Single parent with child under age 18	17.75	114	6.8
Single person	9.13	59	17.5
RACE AND HISPANIC ORIGIN			
Average household	**15.56**	**100**	**100.0**
Asian	12.15	78	2.8
Black	11.05	71	8.5
Hispanic	18.67	120	14.2
Non-Hispanic white and other	15.84	102	77.7
REGION			
Average household	**15.56**	**100**	**100.0**
Northeast	15.90	102	19.0
Midwest	13.55	87	19.9
South	13.83	89	31.9
West	20.12	129	29.2
EDUCATION			
Average household	**15.56**	**100**	**100.0**
Less than high school graduate	12.05	77	11.7
High school graduate	14.53	93	23.6
Some college	14.91	96	20.9
Associate's degree	17.44	112	10.0
College graduate	18.00	116	33.5
Bachelor's degree	15.79	101	19.0
Master's, professional, doctoral degree	21.84	140	14.3

Note: Market shares may not sum to 100.0 because of rounding and missing categories by household type. "Asian" and "black" include Hispanics and non-Hispanics who identify themselves as being of the respective race alone. "Hispanic" includes people of any race who identify themselves as Hispanic. "Other" includes people who identify themselves as non-Hispanic and as Alaska Native, American Indian, Asian (who are also included in the "Asian" row), Native Hawaiian or other Pacific Islander, as well as non-Hispanics reporting more than one race.
Source: Calculations by New Strategist based on the Bureau of Labor Statistics' 2007 Consumer Expenditure Survey.

Vegetables, Canned Beans

Best customers:	**Married couples with school-aged or older children at home**
	Single parents
	Hispanics
Customer trends:	**Average household spending on canned beans will continue to decline as more boomers become empty-nesters and eating out claims a growing share of the food dollar.**

Households with children are the biggest spenders on canned beans. Married couples with school-aged or older children at home spend 30 to 53 percent more than average on this item. Single parents spend 16 percent more despite their low incomes. Hispanic households, which include more children, spend 21 percent more than average on canned beans.

Average household spending on canned beans fell 16 percent between 2000 and 2006, after adjusting for inflation. Canned beans are suffering the same fate as many other grocery items as Americans cook less and eat out more. Average household spending on canned beans is likely to continue to decline as more boomers become empty-nesters and eating out claims a growing share of the food dollar.

Table 9.82 **Vegetables, canned beans**

Total household spending $1,540,592,220.00
Average household spends   12.82

	AVERAGE HOUSEHOLD SPENDING	BEST CUSTOMERS (index)	BIGGEST CUSTOMERS (market share)
AGE OF HOUSEHOLDER			
Average household	**$12.82**	**100**	**100.0%**
Under age 25	8.07	63	4.3
Aged 25 to 34	13.36	104	17.8
Aged 35 to 44	14.79	115	22.5
Aged 45 to 54	13.04	102	21.4
Aged 55 to 64	14.65	114	18.5
Aged 65 to 74	11.87	93	9.3
Aged 75 or older	8.74	68	6.5

	AVERAGE HOUSEHOLD SPENDING	BEST CUSTOMERS (index)	BIGGEST CUSTOMERS (market share)
HOUSEHOLD INCOME			
Average household	$12.82	100	100.0%
Under $20,000	8.04	63	12.9
$20,000 to $39,999	11.73	92	21.3
$40,000 to $49,999	13.52	105	10.4
$50,000 to $69,999	15.40	120	18.4
$70,000 to $79,999	15.52	121	7.0
$80,000 to $99,999	11.60	90	7.4
$100,000 or more	17.05	133	22.8
HOUSEHOLD TYPE			
Average household	12.82	100	100.0
Married couples	15.84	124	62.5
Married couples, no children	12.74	99	21.4
Married couples, with children	17.55	137	34.2
Oldest child under age 6	13.26	103	5.0
Oldest child aged 6 to 17	19.59	153	19.4
Oldest child aged 18 or older	16.66	130	9.6
Single parent with child under age 18	14.86	116	6.9
Single person	6.22	49	14.4
RACE AND HISPANIC ORIGIN			
Average household	12.82	100	100.0
Asian	9.40	73	2.6
Black	12.99	101	12.2
Hispanic	15.46	121	14.2
Non-Hispanic white and other	12.41	97	73.9
REGION			
Average household	12.82	100	100.0
Northeast	12.57	98	18.3
Midwest	11.80	92	21.0
South	13.98	109	39.2
West	12.22	95	21.6
EDUCATION			
Average household	12.82	100	100.0
Less than high school graduate	16.53	129	19.6
High school graduate	12.15	95	23.9
Some college	10.90	85	18.5
Associate's degree	12.65	99	8.8
College graduate	13.12	102	29.6
Bachelor's degree	12.16	95	17.8
Master's, professional, doctoral degree	14.79	115	11.8

Note: Market shares may not sum to 100.0 because of rounding and missing categories by household type. "Asian" and "black" include Hispanics and non-Hispanics who identify themselves as being of the respective race alone. "Hispanic" includes people of any race who identify themselves as Hispanic. "Other" includes people who identify themselves as non-Hispanic and as Alaska Native, American Indian, Asian (who are also included in the "Asian" row), Native Hawaiian or other Pacific Islander, as well as non-Hispanics reporting more than one race.
Source: Calculations by New Strategist based on the Bureau of Labor Statistics' 2007 Consumer Expenditure Survey.

Vegetables, Canned Corn

Best customers:

Householders aged 35 to 54
Married couples with school-aged or older children at home
Single parents
Hispanics and blacks

Customer trends:

Average household spending on canned corn will continue to decline as more boom
ers become empty-nesters and eating out claims a growing share of the food dollar.

The pattern of spending on canned corn is similar to that for canned beans. Households with children are the biggest spenders on canned corn. Married couples with school-aged or older children at home spend 40 to 49 percent more than average on this item. Single parents spend 34 percent more than average on canned corn, while householders aged 35 to 54, many with children, spend 17 to 27 percent more. Hispanics and blacks spend, respectively, 19 and 16 percent more than average on this item.

Average household spending on canned corn fell 34 percent between 2000 and 2007, after adjusting for inflation. Canned corn is suffering the same fate as many other grocery items as Americans cook less and eat out more. Average household spending on canned corn is likely to continue to decline as more boomers become empty-nesters and eating out claims a growing share of the food dollar.

Table 9.83 Vegetables, canned corn

Total household spending $645,318,270.00
Average household spends 5.37

	AVERAGE HOUSEHOLD SPENDING	BEST CUSTOMERS (index)	BIGGEST CUSTOMERS (market share)
AGE OF HOUSEHOLDER			
Average household	**$5.37**	**100**	**100.0%**
Under age 25	4.42	82	5.6
Aged 25 to 34	5.18	96	16.5
Aged 35 to 44	6.84	127	24.8
Aged 45 to 54	6.30	117	24.6
Aged 55 to 64	4.98	93	15.0
Aged 65 to 74	4.24	79	7.9
Aged 75 or older	3.23	60	5.7

	AVERAGE HOUSEHOLD SPENDING	BEST CUSTOMERS (index)	BIGGEST CUSTOMERS (market share)
HOUSEHOLD INCOME			
Average household	**$5.37**	**100**	**100.0%**
Under $20,000	3.82	71	14.6
$20,000 to $39,999	5.46	102	23.6
$40,000 to $49,999	5.86	109	10.7
$50,000 to $69,999	4.85	90	13.8
$70,000 to $79,999	7.67	143	8.3
$80,000 to $99,999	6.36	118	9.6
$100,000 or more	5.94	111	19.0
HOUSEHOLD TYPE			
Average household	**5.37**	**100**	**100.0**
Married couples	6.32	118	59.5
Married couples, no children	4.72	88	19.0
Married couples, with children	7.32	136	34.0
Oldest child under age 6	5.23	97	4.8
Oldest child aged 6 to 17	7.98	149	18.9
Oldest child aged 18 or older	7.54	140	10.3
Single parent with child under age 18	7.22	134	8.0
Single person	2.85	53	15.8
RACE AND HISPANIC ORIGIN			
Average household	**5.37**	**100**	**100.0**
Asian	3.15	59	2.1
Black	6.22	116	13.9
Hispanic	6.37	119	14.0
Non-Hispanic white and other	5.09	95	72.4
REGION			
Average household	**5.37**	**100**	**100.0**
Northeast	4.74	88	16.4
Midwest	4.56	85	19.4
South	5.81	108	38.9
West	6.04	112	25.4
EDUCATION			
Average household	**5.37**	**100**	**100.0**
Less than high school graduate	5.67	106	16.0
High school graduate	6.20	115	29.1
Some college	5.40	101	21.9
Associate's degree	5.63	105	9.3
College graduate	4.41	82	23.8
Bachelor's degree	4.42	82	15.4
Master's, professional, doctoral degree	4.40	82	8.4

Note: Market shares may not sum to 100.0 because of rounding and missing categories by household type. "Asian" and "black" include Hispanics and non-Hispanics who identify themselves as being of the respective race alone. "Hispanic" includes people of any race who identify themselves as Hispanic. "Other" includes people who identify themselves as non-Hispanic and as Alaska Native, American Indian, Asian (who are also included in the "Asian" row), Native Hawaiian or other Pacific Islander, as well as non-Hispanics reporting more than one race.
Source: Calculations by New Strategist based on the Bureau of Labor Statistics' 2007 Consumer Expenditure Survey.

Vegetables, Canned, Other than Beans and Corn

Best customers:	**Householders aged 45 to 74** **Married couples**
Customer trends:	**Average household spending on canned vegetables will continue to decline as younger generations opt for the fresh variety and eating out claims a growing share of the food dollar.**

Spending on canned vegetables is on the decline as more households opt for the fresh variety or simply eat out instead of cooking a meal at home. Older householders and the largest households spend the most on canned vegetables other than beans and corn. Married couples without children at home (most of them older) spend 25 percent more than average on this item. Couples with school-aged or older children at home spend 22 to 38 percent more than average on canned vegetables other than beans and corn. Householders ranging in age from 45 to 74 spend 15 to 20 percent more than average on other canned vegetables.

Average household spending on canned vegetables other than beans and corn fell 14 percent between 2000 and 2007, after adjusting for inflation. Canned vegetables are suffering the same fate as many other grocery items as Americans cook less and eat out more. Average household spending on other canned vegetables will continue to decline as these trends continue.

Table 9.84 **Vegetables, canned, other than beans and corn**

Total household spending $2,226,768,630.00
Average household spends 18.53

	AVERAGE HOUSEHOLD SPENDING	BEST CUSTOMERS (index)	BIGGEST CUSTOMERS (market share)
AGE OF HOUSEHOLDER			
Average household	**$18.53**	**100**	**100.0%**
Under age 25	8.56	46	3.1
Aged 25 to 34	16.09	87	14.8
Aged 35 to 44	17.78	96	18.7
Aged 45 to 54	21.47	116	24.3
Aged 55 to 64	21.30	115	18.6
Aged 65 to 74	22.20	120	12.0
Aged 75 or older	17.00	92	8.7

	AVERAGE HOUSEHOLD SPENDING	BEST CUSTOMERS (index)	BIGGEST CUSTOMERS (market share)
HOUSEHOLD INCOME			
Average household	**$18.53**	**100**	**100.0%**
Under $20,000	11.24	61	12.5
$20,000 to $39,999	15.20	82	19.1
$40,000 to $49,999	19.07	103	10.1
$50,000 to $69,999	17.64	95	14.6
$70,000 to $79,999	22.19	120	6.9
$80,000 to $99,999	22.02	119	9.7
$100,000 or more	29.42	159	27.2
HOUSEHOLD TYPE			
Average household	**18.53**	**100**	**100.0**
Married couples	23.79	128	64.9
Married couples, no children	23.10	125	26.9
Married couples, with children	23.94	129	32.2
Oldest child under age 6	21.45	116	5.6
Oldest child aged 6 to 17	25.56	138	17.5
Oldest child aged 18 or older	22.55	122	9.0
Single parent with child under age 18	18.03	97	5.8
Single person	9.81	53	15.7
RACE AND HISPANIC ORIGIN			
Average household	**18.53**	**100**	**100.0**
Asian	11.97	65	2.3
Black	14.46	78	9.4
Hispanic	14.13	76	9.0
Non-Hispanic white and other	19.77	107	81.4
REGION			
Average household	**18.53**	**100**	**100.0**
Northeast	17.69	95	17.8
Midwest	18.44	100	22.7
South	19.24	104	37.3
West	18.19	98	22.2
EDUCATION			
Average household	**18.53**	**100**	**100.0**
Less than high school graduate	15.23	82	12.5
High school graduate	17.07	92	23.2
Some college	17.03	92	20.0
Associate's degree	19.85	107	9.5
College graduate	22.03	119	34.4
Bachelor's degree	21.00	113	21.2
Master's, professional, doctoral degree	23.83	129	13.1

Note: Market shares may not sum to 100.0 because of rounding and missing categories by household type. "Asian" and "black" include Hispanics and non-Hispanics who identify themselves as being of the respective race alone. "Hispanic" includes people of any race who identify themselves as Hispanic. "Other" includes people who identify themselves as non-Hispanic and as Alaska Native, American Indian, Asian (who are also included in the "Asian" row), Native Hawaiian or other Pacific Islander, as well as non-Hispanics reporting more than one race.
Source: Calculations by New Strategist based on the Bureau of Labor Statistics' 2007 Consumer Expenditure Survey.

Vegetables, Dried Beans

Best customers:	**Married couples with school-aged or older children at home** **Single parents** **Hispanics and Asians** **Households in the West**
Customer trends:	**Average household spending on dried beans is likely to continue to decline as more boomers become empty-nesters and household size shrinks.**

Hispanics spend the most by far on dried beans, nearly three times the average. Hispanics, in fact, account for more than one-third of household spending on this item. Asians spend 53 percent more than average on dried beans, and households in the West, where many Hispanics and Asians live, spend 29 percent more. Married couples with school-aged children spend 59 percent more than the average on dried beans, and those with adult children at home, 84 percent. Single parents spend 8 percent more than the average despite their low incomes.

Average household spending on dried beans fell 10 percent between 2000 and 2007, after adjusting for inflation, despite the growth of the Hispanic population. Average household spending on dried beans may continue to decline in the years ahead as more boomers become empty-nesters and household size shrinks.

Table 9.85 Vegetables, dried beans

Total household spending	$328,066,830.00
Average household spends	2.73

	AVERAGE HOUSEHOLD SPENDING	BEST CUSTOMERS (index)	BIGGEST CUSTOMERS (market share)
AGE OF HOUSEHOLDER			
Average household	**$2.73**	**100**	**100.0%**
Under age 25	2.72	100	6.8
Aged 25 to 34	2.37	87	14.8
Aged 35 to 44	3.30	121	23.6
Aged 45 to 54	2.95	108	22.7
Aged 55 to 64	2.72	100	16.1
Aged 65 to 74	3.15	115	11.5
Aged 75 or older	1.27	47	4.4

	AVERAGE HOUSEHOLD SPENDING	BEST CUSTOMERS (index)	BIGGEST CUSTOMERS (market share)
HOUSEHOLD INCOME			
Average household	**$2.73**	**100**	**100.0%**
Under $20,000	2.10	77	15.8
$20,000 to $39,999	2.58	94	21.9
$40,000 to $49,999	2.76	101	9.9
$50,000 to $69,999	3.59	132	20.1
$70,000 to $79,999	2.36	86	5.0
$80,000 to $99,999	1.94	71	5.8
$100,000 or more	3.38	124	21.2
HOUSEHOLD TYPE			
Average household	**2.73**	**100**	**100.0**
Married couples	3.47	127	64.3
Married couples, no children	2.49	91	19.7
Married couples, with children	4.05	148	37.0
Oldest child under age 6	2.00	73	3.6
Oldest child aged 6 to 17	4.34	159	20.2
Oldest child aged 18 or older	5.01	184	13.5
Single parent with child under age 18	2.94	108	6.4
Single person	1.09	40	11.9
RACE AND HISPANIC ORIGIN			
Average household	**2.73**	**100**	**100.0**
Asian	4.19	153	5.4
Black	2.58	95	11.3
Hispanic	8.14	298	35.2
Non-Hispanic white and other	1.98	73	55.4
REGION			
Average household	**2.73**	**100**	**100.0**
Northeast	1.92	70	13.1
Midwest	2.21	81	18.5
South	3.00	110	39.5
West	3.52	129	29.2
EDUCATION			
Average household	**2.73**	**100**	**100.0**
Less than high school graduate	4.24	155	23.6
High school graduate	2.79	102	25.8
Some college	1.90	70	15.2
Associate's degree	2.57	94	8.4
College graduate	2.62	96	27.8
Bachelor's degree	2.13	78	14.6
Master's, professional, doctoral degree	3.47	127	13.0

Note: Market shares may not sum to 100.0 because of rounding and missing categories by household type. "Asian" and "black" include Hispanics and non-Hispanics who identify themselves as being of the respective race alone. "Hispanic" includes people of any race who identify themselves as Hispanic. "Other" includes people who identify themselves as non-Hispanic and as Alaska Native, American Indian, Asian (who are also included in the "Asian" row), Native Hawaiian or other Pacific Islander, as well as non-Hispanics reporting more than one race.
Source: Calculations by New Strategist based on the Bureau of Labor Statistics' 2007 Consumer Expenditure Survey.

Vegetables, Dried, Other than Beans

Best customers:
    Householders aged 35 to 54
    Married couples with school-aged or older children at home
    Hispanics

Customer trends:
    Average household spending on dried vegetables other than beans is likely to decline as more boomers become empty-nesters and household size shrinks.

The largest households spend the most on dried vegetables other than beans. Householders aged 35 to 54, most with children at home, spend 21 to 22 percent more than average on this item. Married couples with school-aged children spend 35 percent more than the average on dried vegetables other than beans, and those with adult children at home spend over twice the average. Hispanics spend 15 percent more than average on this item.

Average household spending on dried vegetables other than beans fell 6 percent between 2000 and 2007, after adjusting for inflation. Average household spending on this item may continue to decline in the years ahead as more boomers become empty-nesters and household size shrinks.

Table 9.86 Vegetables, dried, other than beans

Total household spending $986,603,910.00
Average household spends   8.21

	AVERAGE HOUSEHOLD SPENDING	BEST CUSTOMERS (index)	BIGGEST CUSTOMERS (market share)
AGE OF HOUSEHOLDER			
Average household	**$8.21**	**100**	**100.0%**
Under age 25	5.99	73	4.9
Aged 25 to 34	6.29	77	13.1
Aged 35 to 44	9.96	121	23.6
Aged 45 to 54	10.02	122	25.6
Aged 55 to 64	9.32	114	18.4
Aged 65 to 74	7.81	95	9.5
Aged 75 or older	4.31	52	5.0

	AVERAGE HOUSEHOLD SPENDING	BEST CUSTOMERS (index)	BIGGEST CUSTOMERS (market share)
HOUSEHOLD INCOME			
Average household	**$8.21**	**100**	**100.0%**
Under $20,000	5.53	67	13.9
$20,000 to $39,999	6.47	79	18.3
$40,000 to $49,999	8.48	103	10.2
$50,000 to $69,999	9.47	115	17.7
$70,000 to $79,999	6.27	76	4.4
$80,000 to $99,999	9.59	117	9.5
$100,000 or more	12.38	151	25.8
HOUSEHOLD TYPE			
Average household	**8.21**	**100**	**100.0**
Married couples	10.49	128	64.6
Married couples, no children	7.62	93	20.0
Married couples, with children	12.25	149	37.2
Oldest child under age 6	8.26	101	4.9
Oldest child aged 6 to 17	11.07	135	17.1
Oldest child aged 18 or older	17.52	213	15.7
Single parent with child under age 18	7.64	93	5.5
Single person	4.38	53	15.9
RACE AND HISPANIC ORIGIN			
Average household	**8.21**	**100**	**100.0**
Asian	8.12	99	3.5
Black	8.18	100	12.0
Hispanic	9.41	115	13.5
Non-Hispanic white and other	8.04	98	74.8
REGION			
Average household	**8.21**	**100**	**100.0**
Northeast	7.22	88	16.4
Midwest	7.65	93	21.3
South	8.98	109	39.3
West	8.37	102	23.1
EDUCATION			
Average household	**8.21**	**100**	**100.0**
Less than high school graduate	8.41	102	15.5
High school graduate	7.53	92	23.1
Some college	7.74	94	20.5
Associate's degree	8.63	105	9.3
College graduate	8.93	109	31.5
Bachelor's degree	9.09	111	20.8
Master's, professional, doctoral degree	8.65	105	10.7

Note: Market shares may not sum to 100.0 because of rounding and missing categories by household type. "Asian" and "black" include Hispanics and non-Hispanics who identify themselves as being of the respective race alone. "Hispanic" includes people of any race who identify themselves as Hispanic. "Other" includes people who identify themselves as non-Hispanic and as Alaska Native, American Indian, Asian (who are also included in the "Asian" row), Native Hawaiian or other Pacific Islander, as well as non-Hispanics reporting more than one race.
Source: Calculations by New Strategist based on the Bureau of Labor Statistics' 2007 Consumer Expenditure Survey.

Vegetables, Fresh, Other than Lettuce, Potatoes, and Tomatoes

Best customers:

> Householders aged 35 to 54
> Married couples
> Asians and Hispanics
> Households in the West

Customer trends:

> Average household spending on fresh vegetables other than lettuce, potatoes, and tomatoes may continue to rise as consumers opt for fresh vegetables over frozen and canned, but restaurant meals may limit the increase.

Fresh vegetables are one of the grocery items on which households spend the most. The best customers of fresh vegetables other than lettuce, potatoes, and tomatoes are middle-aged married couples. Householders ranging in age from 35 to 54 spend 15 to 17 percent more than the average household on this item. Married couples without children at home (most of them older) spend 20 percent more than average on this item. Those with school-aged or adult children at home spend 44 to 51 percent more. Asians spend well more than twice the average on fresh vegetables other than lettuce, potatoes, and tomatoes, and Hispanics spend 17 percent more. Households in the West spend 29 percent more than average on this item.

Average household spending on fresh vegetables other than lettuce, potatoes, and tomatoes—already the fifth largest spending category among groceries—rose 4 percent between 2000 and 2007, after adjusting for inflation. Average household spending on fresh vegetables may continue to rise as consumers opt for fresh vegetables over frozen and canned, but restaurant meals may limit the increase.

Table 9.87 Vegetables, fresh, other than lettuce, potatoes, and tomatoes

Total household spending $12,048,344,460.00
Average household spends   100.26

AGE OF HOUSEHOLDER	AVERAGE HOUSEHOLD SPENDING	BEST CUSTOMERS (index)	BIGGEST CUSTOMERS (market share)
Average household	$100.26	100	100.0%
Under age 25	55.53	55	3.8
Aged 25 to 34	87.15	87	14.8
Aged 35 to 44	115.68	115	22.5
Aged 45 to 54	117.42	117	24.6
Aged 55 to 64	107.34	107	17.3
Aged 65 to 74	107.99	108	10.8
Aged 75 or older	67.85	68	6.4

	AVERAGE HOUSEHOLD SPENDING	BEST CUSTOMERS (index)	BIGGEST CUSTOMERS (market share)
HOUSEHOLD INCOME			
Average household	**$100.26**	**100**	**100.0%**
Under $20,000	55.29	55	11.3
$20,000 to $39,999	76.18	76	17.7
$40,000 to $49,999	94.15	94	9.2
$50,000 to $69,999	103.05	103	15.7
$70,000 to $79,999	105.66	105	6.1
$80,000 to $99,999	124.96	125	10.1
$100,000 or more	174.94	174	29.9
HOUSEHOLD TYPE			
Average household	**100.26**	**100**	**100.0**
Married couples	134.14	134	67.6
Married couples, no children	119.98	120	25.8
Married couples, with children	141.23	141	35.1
Oldest child under age 6	119.56	119	5.8
Oldest child aged 6 to 17	144.19	144	18.3
Oldest child aged 18 or older	151.26	151	11.1
Single parent with child under age 18	66.27	66	3.9
Single person	52.78	53	15.7
RACE AND HISPANIC ORIGIN			
Average household	**100.26**	**100**	**100.0**
Asian	234.55	234	8.3
Black	63.21	63	7.6
Hispanic	116.97	117	13.8
Non-Hispanic white and other	103.54	103	78.8
REGION			
Average household	**100.26**	**100**	**100.0**
Northeast	106.21	106	19.7
Midwest	85.15	85	19.4
South	89.00	89	31.9
West	128.97	129	29.1
EDUCATION			
Average household	**100.26**	**100**	**100.0**
Less than high school graduate	82.54	82	12.5
High school graduate	77.37	77	19.5
Some college	82.80	83	18.0
Associate's degree	93.42	93	8.3
College graduate	142.92	143	41.3
Bachelor's degree	125.28	125	23.4
Master's, professional, doctoral degree	173.56	173	17.7

Note: Market shares may not sum to 100.0 because of rounding and missing categories by household type. "Asian" and "black" include Hispanics and non-Hispanics who identify themselves as being of the respective race alone. "Hispanic" includes people of any race who identify themselves as Hispanic. "Other" includes people who identify themselves as non-Hispanic and as Alaska Native, American Indian, Asian (who are also included in the "Asian" row), Native Hawaiian or other Pacific Islander, as well as non-Hispanics reporting more than one race.
Source: Calculations by New Strategist based on the Bureau of Labor Statistics' 2007 Consumer Expenditure Survey.

Vegetables, Frozen

Best customers: Householders aged 35 to 54
Married couples with school-aged or older children at home
Single parents

Customer trends: Average household spending on frozen vegetables will decline as Americans opt for the fresh variety and eating out claims a growing share of the food dollar.

Spending on frozen vegetables is falling as fewer households cook meals at home and many of those that do cook turn to fresh ingredients. The largest households are the best customers of frozen vegetables. Married couples with school-aged or older children at home spend 41 to 58 percent more than average on this item. Single parents spend 11 percent more despite their low incomes. Householders aged 35 to 54, most with children, spend 11 to 25 percent more than average on frozen vegetables.

Average household spending on frozen vegetables fell 1 percent between 2000 and 2007, after adjusting for inflation. Behind the decline is the growing preference for fresh vegetables and for eating out over home cooking. Average household spending on frozen vegetables is likely to decline further as these trends continue.

Table 9.88 Vegetables, frozen

Total household spending $3,766,159,140.00
Average household spends 31.34

AGE OF HOUSEHOLDER	AVERAGE HOUSEHOLD SPENDING	BEST CUSTOMERS (index)	BIGGEST CUSTOMERS (market share)
Average household	$31.34	100	100.0%
Under age 25	15.77	50	3.4
Aged 25 to 34	26.96	86	14.7
Aged 35 to 44	34.76	111	21.6
Aged 45 to 54	39.15	125	26.2
Aged 55 to 64	33.05	105	17.1
Aged 65 to 74	32.87	105	10.5
Aged 75 or older	22.35	71	6.8

	AVERAGE HOUSEHOLD SPENDING	BEST CUSTOMERS (index)	BIGGEST CUSTOMERS (market share)
HOUSEHOLD INCOME			
Average household	$31.34	100	100.0%
Under $20,000	16.34	52	10.7
$20,000 to $39,999	28.09	90	20.8
$40,000 to $49,999	29.22	93	9.2
$50,000 to $69,999	33.86	108	16.5
$70,000 to $79,999	36.74	117	6.8
$80,000 to $99,999	41.20	131	10.7
$100,000 or more	45.49	145	24.9
HOUSEHOLD TYPE			
Average household	31.34	100	100.0
Married couples	39.74	127	64.1
Married couples, no children	34.70	111	23.9
Married couples, with children	43.59	139	34.7
Oldest child under age 6	33.60	107	5.2
Oldest child aged 6 to 17	44.25	141	17.9
Oldest child aged 18 or older	49.61	158	11.7
Single parent with child under age 18	34.75	111	6.6
Single person	14.98	48	14.2
RACE AND HISPANIC ORIGIN			
Average household	31.34	100	100.0
Asian	31.50	101	3.5
Black	27.61	88	10.6
Hispanic	17.91	57	6.7
Non-Hispanic white and other	33.80	108	82.3
REGION			
Average household	31.34	100	100.0
Northeast	32.02	102	19.0
Midwest	29.96	96	21.8
South	32.97	105	37.8
West	29.57	94	21.3
EDUCATION			
Average household	31.34	100	100.0
Less than high school graduate	22.47	72	10.9
High school graduate	28.37	91	22.8
Some college	34.23	109	23.8
Associate's degree	31.87	102	9.0
College graduate	35.79	114	33.1
Bachelor's degree	33.11	106	19.8
Master's, professional, doctoral degree	40.46	129	13.2

Note: Market shares may not sum to 100.0 because of rounding and missing categories by household type. "Asian" and "black" include Hispanics and non-Hispanics who identify themselves as being of the respective race alone. "Hispanic" includes people of any race who identify themselves as Hispanic. "Other" includes people who identify themselves as non-Hispanic and as Alaska Native, American Indian, Asian (who are also included in the "Asian" row), Native Hawaiian or other Pacific Islander, as well as non-Hispanics reporting more than one race.
Source: Calculations by New Strategist based on the Bureau of Labor Statistics' 2007 Consumer Expenditure Survey.

Water, Bottled

Best customers:
Householders aged 35 to 54
Married couples with children at home
Asians

Customer trends:
Average household spending on bottled water should climb in the years ahead as Americans question the quality of tap water and search for alternatives to calorie-laden colas and fruit drinks.

The biggest spenders on bottled water are the largest households. Married couples with children at home spend 44 percent more than average on this item. Couples with adult children at home spend almost twice the average. Householders aged 35 to 54, most of them parents, spend 21 to 22 percent more than average on bottled water.

Bottled water is a new category in the Consumer Expenditure Survey, with no comparative spending data for 2000. Interestingly, the average household spends more on bottled water than it does on coffee. Average household spending on bottled water should climb in the years ahead as Americans question the quality of tap water and search for alternatives to calorie-laden colas and fruit drinks.

Table 9.89 Water, bottled

Total household spending $7,296,783,120.00
Average household spends   60.72

	AVERAGE HOUSEHOLD SPENDING	BEST CUSTOMERS (index)	BIGGEST CUSTOMERS (market share)
AGE OF HOUSEHOLDER			
Average household	**$60.72**	**100**	**100.0%**
Under age 25	33.08	54	3.7
Aged 25 to 34	62.96	104	17.7
Aged 35 to 44	73.24	121	23.5
Aged 45 to 54	74.35	122	25.7
Aged 55 to 64	63.31	104	16.9
Aged 65 to 74	48.84	80	8.0
Aged 75 or older	29.92	49	4.7

	AVERAGE HOUSEHOLD SPENDING	BEST CUSTOMERS (index)	BIGGEST CUSTOMERS (market share)
HOUSEHOLD INCOME			
Average household	**$60.72**	**100**	**100.0%**
Under $20,000	31.91	53	10.8
$20,000 to $39,999	43.13	71	16.5
$40,000 to $49,999	60.92	100	9.9
$50,000 to $69,999	62.90	104	15.9
$70,000 to $79,999	69.23	114	6.6
$80,000 to $99,999	86.92	143	11.6
$100,000 or more	100.74	166	28.4
HOUSEHOLD TYPE			
Average household	**60.72**	**100**	**100.0**
Married couples	75.65	125	63.0
Married couples, no children	60.20	99	21.4
Married couples, with children	87.41	144	35.9
Oldest child under age 6	66.49	110	5.3
Oldest child aged 6 to 17	80.38	132	16.8
Oldest child aged 18 or older	116.70	192	14.2
Single parent with child under age 18	60.72	100	5.9
Single person	35.61	59	17.4
RACE AND HISPANIC ORIGIN			
Average household	**60.72**	**100**	**100.0**
Asian	77.21	127	4.5
Black	59.43	98	11.7
Hispanic	61.60	101	12.0
Non-Hispanic white and other	60.73	100	76.3
REGION			
Average household	**60.72**	**100**	**100.0**
Northeast	70.77	117	21.7
Midwest	52.42	86	19.7
South	55.66	92	32.9
West	68.94	114	25.7
EDUCATION			
Average household	**60.72**	**100**	**100.0**
Less than high school graduate	50.40	83	12.6
High school graduate	55.53	91	23.1
Some college	58.56	96	21.0
Associate's degree	71.82	118	10.5
College graduate	68.38	113	32.6
Bachelor's degree	66.93	110	20.7
Master's, professional, doctoral degree	70.91	117	11.9

Note: Market shares may not sum to 100.0 because of rounding and missing categories by household type. "Asian" and "black" include Hispanics and non-Hispanics who identify themselves as being of the respective race alone. "Hispanic" includes people of any race who identify themselves as Hispanic. "Other" includes people who identify themselves as non-Hispanic and as Alaska Native, American Indian, Asian (who are also included in the "Asian" row), Native Hawaiian or other Pacific Islander, as well as non-Hispanics reporting more than one race.
Source: Calculations by New Strategist based on the Bureau of Labor Statistics' 2007 Consumer Expenditure Survey.

Chapter 10.

Health Care

Household Spending on Health Care, 2007

Out-of-pocket spending by the average household on health care has grown over the past few years as health care costs climbed and employers shifted more costs onto employees. Between 2000 and 2007, average household out-of-pocket spending on health care rose 15 percent, after adjusting for inflation. Out-of-pocket spending on health insurance ranks among the 10 biggest household expenses, averaging $1,545 in 2007, up 31 percent since 2000.

Prescription drugs are the second-biggest health care expense for the average household. Out-of-pocket spending on prescription drugs fell 2 percent between 2000 and 2007. Spending on nonprescription drugs declined by 4 percent, while spending on vitamins fell by an even larger 17 percent during those years.

Spending on a few other health care categories also fell between 2000 and 2007. Households spent 13 percent less on eyeglasses and contact lenses, average spending on dental services fell 8 percent, and spending on eye care services dropped 10 percent—categories one can do without when tightening the household budget.

Older Americans are the biggest out-of-pocket spenders on health care. As the large baby-boom generation enters the older age groups, out-of-pocket spending on health care will soar.

Spending on health insurance

(average out-of-pocket spending by households on health insurance, 2000 to 2007; in 2007 dollars)

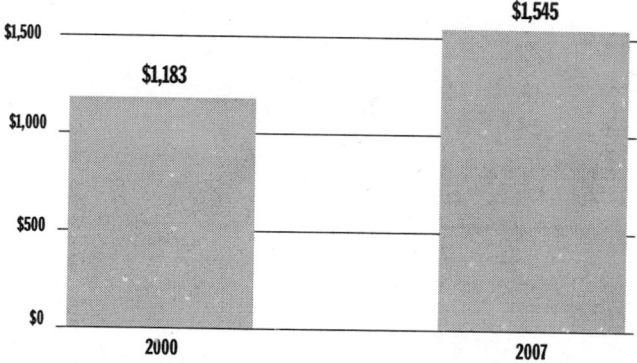

Table 10.1 Out-of-Pocket Health Care Spending, 2000 to 2007

(average annual household spending on out-of-pocket health care expenses, and percent distribution of spending by type, 2000 and 2007; percent change in spending, 2000–07; in 2007 dollars; ranked by amount spent)

	2007		2000		
	average household spending	percent distribution	average household spending (in 2007$)	percent distribution	percent change 2000–07
Average household out-of-pocket spending on health care	**$2,852.77**	**100.0%**	**$2,487.23**	**100.0%**	**14.7%**
Health insurance, incl. Medicare	1,544.83	54.2	1,183.19	47.6	30.6
Drugs, prescription	359.32	12.6	367.45	14.8	–2.2
Medicare premiums	323.35	11.3	197.52	7.9	63.7
Dental services	244.67	8.6	265.85	10.7	–8.0
Physician services	171.10	6.0	161.84	6.5	5.7
Hospital room and services	113.93	4.0	92.81	3.7	22.8
Medicare supplements, commercial	90.44	3.2	106.22	4.3	–14.9
Drugs, nonprescription	75.40	2.6	78.37	3.2	–3.8
Nonphysician health care professional services	72.44	2.5	44.39	1.8	63.2
Long-term care insurance	67.49	2.4			–
Eyeglasses and contact lenses	61.01	2.1	70.35	2.8	–13.3
Medicare prescription drug premiums	48.36	1.7	–	–	–
Vitamins, nonprescription	46.18	1.6	55.62	2.2	–17.0
Lab tests and X-rays	39.08	1.4	24.23	1.0	61.3
Eye care services	37.88	1.3	42.20	1.7	–10.2

Note: Numbers do not add to total because some subcategories are also shown. "–" means data are unavailable.
Source: Bureau of Labor Statistics, 2000 and 2007 Consumer Expenditure Surveys; calculations by New Strategist

Dental Services (Out-of-Pocket Expenses)

Best customers: Householders aged 55 or older
                               Married couples without children at home
                               Married couples with school-aged or older children at home
                               Households in the West

Customer trends: Average household spending on dental services will increase as more boomers enter
                               the age groups that spend the most.

The biggest out-of-pocket spenders on dental services are older Americans. Householders aged 55 or older spend 22 to 53 percent more than the average household on this item, in part because older Americans are less likely to have insurance coverage for dental care. Married couples without children at home (many of them older) spend 45 percent more than average on dental services. Couples with school-aged or older children at home spend 28 to 39 percent more than average on dental services because their households are larger than average, with more teeth that need fixing. Households in the West spend 29 percent more than average on this item.

Average out-of-pocket spending on dental services declined between 2000 and 2007, decreasing by 8 percent after adjusting for inflation. One reason for the decline in spending on dental services is belt tightening as health care costs soar. It is likely that many Americans delayed dental visits as they were forced to pay more for health insurance. Out-of-pocket spending on dental services is likely to climb in the years ahead, as boomers continue to age into the big-spending age groups.

Table 10.2 **Dental services (out-of-pocket expenses)**

Total household spending $29,402,238,570.00
Average household spends   244.67

	AVERAGE HOUSEHOLD SPENDING	BEST CUSTOMERS (index)	BIGGEST CUSTOMERS (market share)
AGE OF HOUSEHOLDER			
Average household	**$244.67**	**100**	**100.0%**
Under age 25	60.43	25	1.7
Aged 25 to 34	149.66	61	10.4
Aged 35 to 44	225.90	92	18.0
Aged 45 to 54	263.35	108	22.6
Aged 55 to 64	298.33	122	19.7
Aged 65 to 74	373.81	153	15.3
Aged 75 or older	316.81	129	12.3

	AVERAGE HOUSEHOLD SPENDING	BEST CUSTOMERS (index)	BIGGEST CUSTOMERS (market share)
HOUSEHOLD INCOME			
Average household	**$244.67**	**100**	**100.0%**
Under $20,000	85.30	35	7.2
$20,000 to $39,999	170.74	70	16.2
$40,000 to $49,999	191.36	78	7.7
$50,000 to $69,999	288.86	118	18.1
$70,000 to $79,999	264.37	108	6.3
$80,000 to $99,999	294.05	120	9.8
$100,000 or more	497.24	203	34.8
HOUSEHOLD TYPE			
Average household	**244.67**	**100**	**100.0**
Married couples	321.46	131	66.4
Married couples, no children	355.09	145	31.3
Married couples, with children	297.98	122	30.4
Oldest child under age 6	166.58	68	3.3
Oldest child aged 6 to 17	339.64	139	17.6
Oldest child aged 18 or older	313.20	128	9.4
Single parent with child under age 18	124.14	51	3.0
Single person	157.40	64	19.1
RACE AND HISPANIC ORIGIN			
Average household	**244.67**	**100**	**100.0**
Asian	228.46	93	3.3
Black	105.67	43	5.2
Hispanic	171.66	70	8.3
Non-Hispanic white and other	277.61	113	86.6
REGION			
Average household	**244.67**	**100**	**100.0**
Northeast	257.97	105	19.6
Midwest	234.72	96	21.9
South	199.36	81	29.3
West	315.71	129	29.2
EDUCATION			
Average household	**244.67**	**100**	**100.0**
Less than high school graduate	93.38	38	5.8
High school graduate	192.23	79	19.8
Some college	263.66	108	23.5
Associate's degree	261.50	107	9.5
College graduate	350.20	143	41.4
Bachelor's degree	321.13	131	24.6
Master's, professional, doctoral degree	403.59	165	16.8

Note: Market shares may not sum to 100.0 because of rounding and missing categories by household type. "Asian" and "black" include Hispanics and non-Hispanics who identify themselves as being of the respective race alone. "Hispanic" includes people of any race who identify themselves as Hispanic. "Other" includes people who identify themselves as non-Hispanic and as Alaska Native, American Indian, Asian (who are also included in the "Asian" row), Native Hawaiian or other Pacific Islander, as well as non-Hispanics reporting more than one race.
Source: Calculations by New Strategist based on the Bureau of Labor Statistics' 2007 Consumer Expenditure Survey.

Drugs, Nonprescription

Best customers:	**Householders aged 55 to 74** **Married couples without children at home** **Married couples with adult children at home**
Customer trends:	**Average household spending on nonprescription drugs should grow as boomers age,** **but only when the economy recovers.**

The biggest spenders on nonprescription drugs are older Americans and the largest households. Householders aged 55 to 74 spend 40 to 55 percent more than the average household on over-the-counter drugs. Married couples without children at home (most of them older) spend 47 percent more than average on this item. Couples with adult children at home spend 40 percent more because their households are larger than average.

Average household spending on nonprescription drugs fell a surprising 4 percent between 2000 and 2007, after adjusting for inflation. Behind the decline is belt tightening. As households are forced to spend more for health insurance, they are cutting their spending on other, more discretionary items. Average household spending on nonprescription drugs should climb as the economy recovers and the large baby-boom generation enters the 65-or-older age group.

Table 10.3 Drugs, nonprescription

Total household spending	$9,060,893,400.00
Average household spends	75.40

	AVERAGE HOUSEHOLD SPENDING	BEST CUSTOMERS (index)	BIGGEST CUSTOMERS (market share)
AGE OF HOUSEHOLDER			
Average household	**$75.40**	**100**	**100.0%**
Under age 25	17.81	24	1.6
Aged 25 to 34	49.29	65	11.2
Aged 35 to 44	64.27	85	16.6
Aged 45 to 54	77.84	103	21.7
Aged 55 to 64	105.57	140	22.7
Aged 65 to 74	117.01	155	15.5
Aged 75 or older	88.68	118	11.1

	AVERAGE HOUSEHOLD SPENDING	BEST CUSTOMERS (index)	BIGGEST CUSTOMERS (market share)
HOUSEHOLD INCOME			
Average household	**$75.40**	**100**	**100.0%**
Under $20,000	46.90	62	12.8
$20,000 to $39,999	63.53	84	19.6
$40,000 to $49,999	75.34	100	9.8
$50,000 to $69,999	69.98	93	14.2
$70,000 to $79,999	71.17	94	5.5
$80,000 to $99,999	87.11	116	9.4
$100,000 or more	126.93	168	28.8
HOUSEHOLD TYPE			
Average household	**75.40**	**100**	**100.0**
Married couples	98.24	130	65.9
Married couples, no children	110.70	147	31.7
Married couples, with children	87.59	116	29.0
Oldest child under age 6	83.77	111	5.4
Oldest child aged 6 to 17	79.89	106	13.5
Oldest child aged 18 or older	105.66	140	10.3
Single parent with child under age 18	49.70	66	3.9
Single person	44.86	59	17.7
RACE AND HISPANIC ORIGIN			
Average household	**75.40**	**100**	**100.0**
Asian	61.80	82	2.9
Black	47.33	63	7.5
Hispanic	48.88	65	7.7
Non-Hispanic white and other	83.41	111	84.4
REGION			
Average household	**75.40**	**100**	**100.0**
Northeast	59.24	79	14.6
Midwest	72.23	96	21.9
South	87.75	116	41.8
West	72.46	96	21.7
EDUCATION			
Average household	**75.40**	**100**	**100.0**
Less than high school graduate	59.53	79	12.0
High school graduate	62.18	82	20.8
Some college	63.81	85	18.4
Associate's degree	80.30	106	9.5
College graduate	101.18	134	38.8
Bachelor's degree	88.38	117	22.0
Master's, professional, doctoral degree	123.40	164	16.7

Note: Market shares may not sum to 100.0 because of rounding and missing categories by household type. "Asian" and "black" include Hispanics and non-Hispanics who identify themselves as being of the respective race alone. "Hispanic" includes people of any race who identify themselves as Hispanic. "Other" includes people who identify themselves as non-Hispanic and as Alaska Native, American Indian, Asian (who are also included in the "Asian" row), Native Hawaiian or other Pacific Islander, as well as non-Hispanics reporting more than one race.
Source: Calculations by New Strategist based on the Bureau of Labor Statistics' 2007 Consumer Expenditure Survey.

Drugs, Prescription (Out-of-Pocket Expenses)

Best customers: Householders aged 55 or older
Married couples without children at home
Married couples with adult children at home

Customer trends: Average household spending on prescription drugs should climb as boomers enter the best-customer age group.

After health insurance, prescription drugs are the largest health care expense for the average household. The biggest out-of-pocket spenders on prescription drugs are older Americans. Householders aged 55 or older spend 40 to 101 percent more than the average householder on this item and control 59 percent of out-of-pocket spending in this market. Married couples without children at home (most of them older) spend 78 percent more than average on prescription drugs. Householders with adult children at home, whose households are larger than average, spend 34 percent more than average on prescription drugs out-of-pocket.

Average household spending on prescription drugs fell by 2 percent between 2000 and 2007, after adjusting for inflation. Behind the decline was the introduction of the Medicare prescription drug program, which began in 2006. The decline is temporary. As the pharmaceutical industry introduces new and improved drugs at a frenzied pace and the baby-boom generation ages, average household spending on prescription drugs will resume its rise.

Table 10.4 Drugs, prescription (out-of-pocket expenses)

| Total household spending | $43,179,843,720.00 |
| Average household spends | 359.32 |

AGE OF HOUSEHOLDER	AVERAGE HOUSEHOLD SPENDING	BEST CUSTOMERS (index)	BIGGEST CUSTOMERS (market share)
Average household	$359.32	100	100.0%
Under age 25	65.34	18	1.2
Aged 25 to 34	139.78	39	6.6
Aged 35 to 44	212.07	59	11.5
Aged 45 to 54	367.34	102	21.5
Aged 55 to 64	503.88	140	22.7
Aged 65 to 74	723.01	201	20.1
Aged 75 or older	619.22	172	16.3

	AVERAGE HOUSEHOLD SPENDING	BEST CUSTOMERS (index)	BIGGEST CUSTOMERS (market share)
HOUSEHOLD INCOME			
Average household	**$359.32**	**100**	**100.0%**
Under $20,000	235.77	66	13.5
$20,000 to $39,999	344.33	96	22.3
$40,000 to $49,999	403.24	112	11.0
$50,000 to $69,999	373.02	104	15.9
$70,000 to $79,999	377.92	105	6.1
$80,000 to $99,999	419.83	117	9.5
$100,000 or more	455.44	127	21.7
HOUSEHOLD TYPE			
Average household	**359.32**	**100**	**100.0**
Married couples	479.45	133	67.5
Married couples, no children	638.57	178	38.3
Married couples, with children	339.77	95	23.6
Oldest child under age 6	196.31	55	2.7
Oldest child aged 6 to 17	312.08	87	11.0
Oldest child aged 18 or older	482.55	134	9.9
Single parent with child under age 18	139.35	39	2.3
Single person	245.66	68	20.3
RACE AND HISPANIC ORIGIN			
Average household	**359.32**	**100**	**100.0**
Asian	129.95	36	1.3
Black	203.07	57	6.8
Hispanic	148.94	41	4.9
Non-Hispanic white and other	416.25	116	88.4
REGION			
Average household	**359.32**	**100**	**100.0**
Northeast	316.92	88	16.4
Midwest	396.56	110	25.2
South	390.42	109	39.0
West	307.23	86	19.3
EDUCATION			
Average household	**359.32**	**100**	**100.0**
Less than high school graduate	325.72	91	13.7
High school graduate	377.80	105	26.5
Some college	326.14	91	19.8
Associate's degree	389.13	108	9.6
College graduate	376.63	105	30.3
Bachelor's degree	365.52	102	19.1
Master's, professional, doctoral degree	397.06	111	11.3

Note: Market shares may not sum to 100.0 because of rounding and missing categories by household type. "Asian" and "black" include Hispanics and non-Hispanics who identify themselves as being of the respective race alone. "Hispanic" includes people of any race who identify themselves as Hispanic. "Other" includes people who identify themselves as non-Hispanic and as Alaska Native, American Indian, Asian (who are also included in the "Asian" row), Native Hawaiian or other Pacific Islander, as well as non-Hispanics reporting more than one race.
Source: Calculations by New Strategist based on the Bureau of Labor Statistics' 2007 Consumer Expenditure Survey.

Eye Care Services (Out-of-Pocket Expenses)

Best customers: Householders aged 45 to 54
Married couples with school-aged or older children at home

Customer trends: Average household spending on eye care services could continue to fall as the small generation X fills the best-customer lifestage.

The biggest out-of-pocket spenders on eye care services are families with children and those who need reading glasses as they enter the second half of their life. Householders aged 45 to 54 spend 29 percent more than average on this item. Married couples with school-aged children at home spend 61 percent more than average on this item as they visit eye care specialists to outfit their children with glasses and contact lenses. Married couples with adult children at home spend 34 percent more than average, partly because their households are larger than average.

Average household spending on eye care services declined 10 percent between 2000 and 2007, after adjusting for inflation. Behind the spending decline is belt tightening as other health care costs increased. Average household spending on eye care services could continue to decline as the small generation X fills the best-customer lifestage.

Table 10.5 Eye care services (out-of-pocket expenses)

Total household spending $4,552,077,480.00
Average household spends   37.88

AGE OF HOUSEHOLDER	AVERAGE HOUSEHOLD SPENDING	BEST CUSTOMERS (index)	BIGGEST CUSTOMERS (market share)
Average household	**$37.88**	**100**	**100.0%**
Under age 25	7.22	19	1.3
Aged 25 to 34	35.64	94	16.0
Aged 35 to 44	37.48	99	19.3
Aged 45 to 54	48.75	129	27.0
Aged 55 to 64	41.11	109	17.6
Aged 65 to 74	41.98	111	11.1
Aged 75 or older	30.68	81	7.7

	AVERAGE HOUSEHOLD SPENDING	BEST CUSTOMERS (index)	BIGGEST CUSTOMERS (market share)
HOUSEHOLD INCOME			
Average household	**$37.88**	**100**	**100.0%**
Under $20,000	14.96	39	8.1
$20,000 to $39,999	23.76	63	14.6
$40,000 to $49,999	33.58	89	8.7
$50,000 to $69,999	29.04	77	11.7
$70,000 to $79,999	56.28	149	8.6
$80,000 to $99,999	78.53	207	16.9
$100,000 or more	69.36	183	31.4
HOUSEHOLD TYPE			
Average household	**37.88**	**100**	**100.0**
Married couples	47.73	126	63.7
Married couples, no children	43.43	115	24.7
Married couples, with children	54.66	144	36.0
Oldest child under age 6	43.86	116	5.7
Oldest child aged 6 to 17	61.09	161	20.5
Oldest child aged 18 or older	50.71	134	9.9
Single parent with child under age 18	26.49	70	4.2
Single person	28.01	74	22.0
RACE AND HISPANIC ORIGIN			
Average household	**37.88**	**100**	**100.0**
Asian	18.90	50	1.8
Black	15.00	40	4.8
Hispanic	24.71	65	7.7
Non-Hispanic white and other	43.48	115	87.6
REGION			
Average household	**37.88**	**100**	**100.0**
Northeast	29.39	78	14.5
Midwest	43.12	114	26.0
South	33.92	90	32.2
West	45.85	121	27.4
EDUCATION			
Average household	**37.88**	**100**	**100.0**
Less than high school graduate	19.97	53	8.0
High school graduate	21.72	57	14.5
Some college	39.75	105	22.9
Associate's degree	34.21	90	8.0
College graduate	61.05	161	46.6
Bachelor's degree	63.51	168	31.4
Master's, professional, doctoral degree	56.54	149	15.2

Note: Market shares may not sum to 100.0 because of rounding and missing categories by household type. "Asian" and "black" include Hispanics and non-Hispanics who identify themselves as being of the respective race alone. "Hispanic" includes people of any race who identify themselves as Hispanic. "Other" includes people who identify themselves as non-Hispanic and as Alaska Native, American Indian, Asian (who are also included in the "Asian" row), Native Hawaiian or other Pacific Islander, as well as non-Hispanics reporting more than one race.
Source: Calculations by New Strategist based on the Bureau of Labor Statistics' 2007 Consumer Expenditure Survey.

Eyeglasses and Contact Lenses (Out-of-Pocket Expenses)

Best customers: Householders aged 45 to 74
Married couples without children at home
Married couples with school-aged or older children at home

Customer trends: Average household spending on eyeglasses and contact lenses should stabilize because the large baby-boom generation will be in the prime-spending age groups.

The biggest out-of-pocket spenders on eyeglasses and contact lenses are middle-aged and older Americans (who need bifocals) and the households with children. Householders ranging in age from 45 to 74 spend 25 to 38 percent more than average on this item. Married couples with school-aged or older children at home spend 41 to 89 percent more than average because their households are relatively large. Couples without children at home (most of them older) spend 41 percent more than average out-of-pocket on eyeglasses and contact lenses.

Average household spending on eyeglasses and contact lenses fell 13 percent between 2000 and 2007, after adjusting for inflation. Behind the decline is competition from discounters in the industry, as well as household belt tightening as other health care costs increased. Spending on eyeglasses and contact lenses should stabilize in the years ahead because the baby-boom generation will be in the prime-spending age groups.

Table 10.6 Eyeglasses and contact lenses (out-of-pocket expenses)

Total household spending $7,331,632,710.00
Average household spends   61.01

AGE OF HOUSEHOLDER	AVERAGE HOUSEHOLD SPENDING	BEST CUSTOMERS (index)	BIGGEST CUSTOMERS (market share)
Average household	$61.01	100	100.0%
Under age 25	17.94	29	2.0
Aged 25 to 34	38.67	63	10.8
Aged 35 to 44	54.09	89	17.3
Aged 45 to 54	82.61	135	28.4
Aged 55 to 64	84.12	138	22.3
Aged 65 to 74	76.55	125	12.5
Aged 75 or older	42.48	70	6.6

	AVERAGE HOUSEHOLD SPENDING	BEST CUSTOMERS (index)	BIGGEST CUSTOMERS (market share)
HOUSEHOLD INCOME			
Average household	**$61.01**	**100**	**100.0%**
Under $20,000	18.79	31	6.3
$20,000 to $39,999	39.80	65	15.2
$40,000 to $49,999	57.82	95	9.3
$50,000 to $69,999	66.09	108	16.6
$70,000 to $79,999	70.52	116	6.7
$80,000 to $99,999	92.53	152	12.3
$100,000 or more	119.52	196	33.6
HOUSEHOLD TYPE			
Average household	**61.01**	**100**	**100.0**
Married couples	84.83	139	70.3
Married couples, no children	85.73	141	30.3
Married couples, with children	86.61	142	35.4
Oldest child under age 6	45.69	75	3.7
Oldest child aged 6 to 17	85.76	141	17.9
Oldest child aged 18 or older	115.18	189	13.9
Single parent with child under age 18	37.89	62	3.7
Single person	32.94	54	16.1
RACE AND HISPANIC ORIGIN			
Average household	**61.01**	**100**	**100.0**
Asian	51.68	85	3.0
Black	40.10	66	7.9
Hispanic	37.10	61	7.2
Non-Hispanic white and other	68.24	112	85.4
REGION			
Average household	**61.01**	**100**	**100.0**
Northeast	55.96	92	17.1
Midwest	74.94	123	28.1
South	49.63	81	29.2
West	69.13	113	25.6
EDUCATION			
Average household	**61.01**	**100**	**100.0**
Less than high school graduate	27.68	45	6.9
High school graduate	45.70	75	18.9
Some college	55.30	91	19.7
Associate's degree	68.71	113	10.0
College graduate	93.73	154	44.5
Bachelor's degree	85.77	141	26.3
Master's, professional, doctoral degree	108.36	178	18.1

Note: Market shares may not sum to 100.0 because of rounding and missing categories by household type. "Asian" and "black" include Hispanics and non-Hispanics who identify themselves as being of the respective race alone. "Hispanic" includes people of any race who identify themselves as Hispanic. "Other" includes people who identify themselves as non-Hispanic and as Alaska Native, American Indian, Asian (who are also included in the "Asian" row), Native Hawaiian or other Pacific Islander, as well as non-Hispanics reporting more than one race.
Source: Calculations by New Strategist based on the Bureau of Labor Statistics' 2007 Consumer Expenditure Survey.

Health Insurance, including Medicare and Supplements (Out-of-Pocket Payments)

Best customers: Householders aged 65 or older
Married couples without children at home
Married couples with adult children at home

Customer trends: Average household spending on health insurance will continue to climb steeply as health care costs rise faster than inflation and the population ages.

Surprisingly, the only age group with universal health insurance coverage is the biggest out-of-pocket spender on health insurance. Americans aged 65 or older, covered by the federal government's Medicare program, spend 76 to 83 percent more than the average household out-of-pocket on health insurance. Married couples without children at home (most of them older) spend 59 percent more than average on this item. Those with adult children at home spend 29 percent more. Behind the higher average spending of older Americans is their Medicare enrollment, the monthly fee being deducted from their Social Security checks. Also, many older Americans purchase commercial Medicare supplements for additional coverage.

The average household spent $1,545 out-of-pocket on health insurance in 2007, making it the ninth largest household expense. Average household spending on health insurance rose 31 percent between 2000 and 2007, after adjusting for inflation. Spending on health insurance will continue to grow rapidly as health care costs rise faster than inflation and the population ages.

Table 10.7 Health insurance, including Medicare and supplements (out-of-pocket payments)

Total household spending $185,643,765,930.00
Average household spends   1,544.83

	AVERAGE HOUSEHOLD SPENDING	BEST CUSTOMERS (index)	BIGGEST CUSTOMERS (market share)
AGE OF HOUSEHOLDER			
Average household	**$1,544.83**	**100**	**100.0%**
Under age 25	397.29	26	1.7
Aged 25 to 34	917.58	59	10.1
Aged 35 to 44	1,268.79	82	16.0
Aged 45 to 54	1,386.40	90	18.9
Aged 55 to 64	1,751.04	113	18.4
Aged 65 to 74	2,820.73	183	18.2
Aged 75 or older	2,715.77	176	16.7

	AVERAGE HOUSEHOLD SPENDING	BEST CUSTOMERS (index)	BIGGEST CUSTOMERS (market share)
HOUSEHOLD INCOME			
Average household	**$1,544.83**	**100**	**100.0%**
Under $20,000	911.91	59	12.1
$20,000 to $39,999	1,427.84	92	21.5
$40,000 to $49,999	1,501.72	97	9.6
$50,000 to $69,999	1,642.82	106	16.3
$70,000 to $79,999	1,719.78	111	6.4
$80,000 to $99,999	1,970.55	128	10.4
$100,000 or more	2,139.00	138	23.7
HOUSEHOLD TYPE			
Average household	**1,544.83**	**100**	**100.0**
Married couples	2,073.86	134	67.9
Married couples, no children	2,459.15	159	34.3
Married couples, with children	1,765.10	114	28.5
Oldest child under age 6	1,479.52	96	4.7
Oldest child aged 6 to 17	1,742.39	113	14.3
Oldest child aged 18 or older	1,993.44	129	9.5
Single parent with child under age 18	640.05	41	2.5
Single person	993.56	64	19.1
RACE AND HISPANIC ORIGIN			
Average household	**1,544.83**	**100**	**100.0**
Asian	1,377.90	89	3.1
Black	1,000.99	65	7.8
Hispanic	743.57	48	5.7
Non-Hispanic white and other	1,752.45	113	86.6
REGION			
Average household	**1,544.83**	**100**	**100.0**
Northeast	1,534.61	99	18.5
Midwest	1,631.53	106	24.1
South	1,538.83	100	35.8
West	1,475.18	95	21.6
EDUCATION			
Average household	**1,544.83**	**100**	**100.0**
Less than high school graduate	1,136.26	74	11.2
High school graduate	1,501.91	97	24.5
Some college	1,381.11	89	19.5
Associate's degree	1,643.02	106	9.5
College graduate	1,889.38	122	35.4
Bachelor's degree	1,776.77	115	21.6
Master's, professional, doctoral degree	2,096.25	136	13.8

Note: Market shares may not sum to 100.0 because of rounding and missing categories by household type. "Asian" and "black" include Hispanics and non-Hispanics who identify themselves as being of the respective race alone. "Hispanic" includes people of any race who identify themselves as Hispanic. "Other" includes people who identify themselves as non-Hispanic and as Alaska Native, American Indian, Asian (who are also included in the "Asian" row), Native Hawaiian or other Pacific Islander, as well as non-Hispanics reporting more than one race.
Source: Calculations by New Strategist based on the Bureau of Labor Statistics' 2007 Consumer Expenditure Survey.

Hospital Room and Services (Out-of-Pocket Expenses)

Best customers: Householders aged 65 to 74
Married couples without children at home
Married couples with preschoolers

Customer trends: Average household spending on hospital rooms and services should continue to rise
as hospitals offer a greater variety of services and the population ages.

The biggest out-of-pocket spenders on hospital rooms and services are Americans aged 65 to 74, many of whom use outpatient facilities to monitor and manage their health. These householders spend 89 percent more than the average household on hospital rooms and services. Married couples without children at home (most of them older) spend 57 percent more than average. Couples with preschoolers at home spend well more than double the average because many are having babies.

Average household spending on hospital rooms and services rose 23 percent between 2000 and 2007, after adjusting for inflation. Spending on this item rose because hospitals increased their offerings to include more services such as diagnostic imaging, physical therapy, and wellness clinics. As the population ages, out-of-pocket spending on hospital services should continue to rise.

Table 10.8 Hospital room and services (out-of-pocket expenses)

Total household spending $13,691,082,030.00
Average household spends 113.93

AGE OF HOUSEHOLDER	AVERAGE HOUSEHOLD SPENDING	BEST CUSTOMERS (index)	BIGGEST CUSTOMERS (market share)
Average household	$113.93	100	100.0%
Under age 25	59.48	52	3.5
Aged 25 to 34	123.26	108	18.5
Aged 35 to 44	88.92	78	15.2
Aged 45 to 54	117.95	104	21.7
Aged 55 to 64	126.24	111	17.9
Aged 65 to 74	215.73	189	18.9
Aged 75 or older	50.19	44	4.2

	AVERAGE HOUSEHOLD SPENDING	BEST CUSTOMERS (index)	BIGGEST CUSTOMERS (market share)
HOUSEHOLD INCOME			
Average household	**$113.93**	**100**	**100.0%**
Under $20,000	33.94	30	6.1
$20,000 to $39,999	110.90	97	22.6
$40,000 to $49,999	109.59	96	9.5
$50,000 to $69,999	124.24	109	16.7
$70,000 to $79,999	88.77	78	4.5
$80,000 to $99,999	166.25	146	11.9
$100,000 or more	190.93	168	28.7
HOUSEHOLD TYPE			
Average household	**113.93**	**100**	**100.0**
Married couples	172.33	151	76.5
Married couples, no children	179.43	157	34.0
Married couples, with children	155.71	137	34.1
Oldest child under age 6	266.52	234	11.4
Oldest child aged 6 to 17	129.72	114	14.5
Oldest child aged 18 or older	127.10	112	8.2
Single parent with child under age 18	76.44	67	4.0
Single person	50.09	44	13.1
RACE AND HISPANIC ORIGIN			
Average household	**113.93**	**100**	**100.0**
Asian	38.25	34	1.2
Black	150.66	132	15.9
Hispanic	70.15	62	7.3
Non-Hispanic white and other	114.85	101	77.0
REGION			
Average household	**113.93**	**100**	**100.0**
Northeast	50.28	44	8.2
Midwest	144.58	127	29.0
South	132.16	116	41.7
West	106.42	93	21.1
EDUCATION			
Average household	**113.93**	**100**	**100.0**
Less than high school graduate	89.40	78	11.9
High school graduate	99.72	88	22.1
Some college	104.53	92	20.0
Associate's degree	123.92	109	9.7
College graduate	143.16	126	36.4
Bachelor's degree	119.93	105	19.7
Master's, professional, doctoral degree	185.85	163	16.6

Note: Market shares may not sum to 100.0 because of rounding and missing categories by household type. "Asian" and "black" include Hispanics and non-Hispanics who identify themselves as being of the respective race alone. "Hispanic" includes people of any race who identify themselves as Hispanic. "Other" includes people who identify themselves as non-Hispanic and as Alaska Native, American Indian, Asian (who are also included in the "Asian" row), Native Hawaiian or other Pacific Islander, as well as non-Hispanics reporting more than one race.
Source: Calculations by New Strategist based on the Bureau of Labor Statistics' 2007 Consumer Expenditure Survey.

Lab Tests and X-Rays (Out-of-Pocket Expenses)

Best customers:	**Householders aged 55 to 64** **Married couples without children at home** **Married couples with school-aged or older children at home**
Customer trends:	**Average household spending on lab tests and X-rays will rise as boomers age.**

Householders aged 55 to 64 spend 73 percent more than the average on lab tests and X-rays. Married couples without children at home (most of them older) spend 43 percent more than average out-of-pocket on this item, and those with school-aged or older children at home spend 30 to 35 percent more.

Average household spending on lab tests and X-rays soared 61 percent between 2000 and 2007, after adjusting for inflation, as medical centers and physicians groups nationwide installed new kinds of imaging and testing equipment. Spending in this category will continue to increase in the next few years as boomers age.

Table 10.9 Lab tests and X-rays (out-of-pocket expenses)

Total household spending		$4,696,282,680.00	
Average household spends		39.08	

	AVERAGE HOUSEHOLD SPENDING	BEST CUSTOMERS (index)	BIGGEST CUSTOMERS (market share)
AGE OF HOUSEHOLDER			
Average household	**$39.08**	**100**	**100.0%**
Under age 25	17.30	44	3.0
Aged 25 to 34	27.85	71	12.2
Aged 35 to 44	39.61	101	19.7
Aged 45 to 54	45.47	116	24.4
Aged 55 to 64	67.56	173	28.0
Aged 65 to 74	30.85	79	7.9
Aged 75 or older	19.63	50	4.8

	AVERAGE HOUSEHOLD SPENDING	BEST CUSTOMERS (index)	BIGGEST CUSTOMERS (market share)
HOUSEHOLD INCOME			
Average household	**$39.08**	**100**	**100.0%**
Under $20,000	15.61	40	8.2
$20,000 to $39,999	28.50	73	17.0
$40,000 to $49,999	40.05	102	10.1
$50,000 to $69,999	50.84	130	19.9
$70,000 to $79,999	46.03	118	6.8
$80,000 to $99,999	56.28	144	11.7
$100,000 or more	60.01	154	26.3
HOUSEHOLD TYPE			
Average household	**39.08**	**100**	**100.0**
Married couples	51.59	132	66.7
Married couples, no children	56.03	143	30.9
Married couples, with children	50.24	129	32.1
Oldest child under age 6	42.77	109	5.3
Oldest child aged 6 to 17	52.80	135	17.2
Oldest child aged 18 or older	50.78	130	9.6
Single parent with child under age 18	18.55	47	2.8
Single person	28.16	72	21.4
RACE AND HISPANIC ORIGIN			
Average household	**39.08**	**100**	**100.0**
Asian	17.46	45	1.6
Black	13.01	33	4.0
Hispanic	23.83	61	7.2
Non-Hispanic white and other	45.47	116	88.8
REGION			
Average household	**39.08**	**100**	**100.0**
Northeast	26.99	69	12.9
Midwest	50.16	128	29.3
South	36.38	93	33.4
West	42.13	108	24.4
EDUCATION			
Average household	**39.08**	**100**	**100.0**
Less than high school graduate	20.24	52	7.9
High school graduate	34.39	88	22.2
Some college	44.50	114	24.8
Associate's degree	34.37	88	7.8
College graduate	50.41	129	37.3
Bachelor's degree	47.33	121	22.7
Master's, professional, doctoral degree	56.08	144	14.6

Note: Market shares may not sum to 100.0 because of rounding and missing categories by household type. "Asian" and "black" include Hispanics and non-Hispanics who identify themselves as being of the respective race alone. "Hispanic" includes people of any race who identify themselves as Hispanic. "Other" includes people who identify themselves as non-Hispanic and as Alaska Native, American Indian, Asian (who are also included in the "Asian" row), Native Hawaiian or other Pacific Islander, as well as non-Hispanics reporting more than one race.
Source: Calculations by New Strategist based on the Bureau of Labor Statistics' 2007 Consumer Expenditure Survey.

Long-Term Care Insurance (Out-of-Pocket Expenses)

Best customers:	Householders aged 55 and older Married couples without children at home Asians
Customer trends:	Average household spending on long-term care insurance will rise as boomers fill the prime-spending age groups.

The best customers of long-term care insurance are older householders worried that they or a family member might require long-term care in a nursing facility. Householders aged 65 to 74 spend more than three times the average on long-term care insurance, and those 75 or older two-and-one-half times. Married couples without children at home (most of them older) spend well more than twice the average on this item.

Because long-term care insurance is a relatively new category in the Consumer Expenditure Survey, there are no comparison data from 2000. Average household spending on long-term care insurance is certain to rise as boomers fill the prime-spending age groups.

Table 10.10 Long-term care insurance (out-of-pocket expenses)

Total household spending $8,110,340,790.00
Average household spends   67.49

	AVERAGE HOUSEHOLD SPENDING	BEST CUSTOMERS (index)	BIGGEST CUSTOMERS (market share)
AGE OF HOUSEHOLDER			
Average household	**$67.49**	**100**	**100.0%**
Under age 25	0.65	1	0.1
Aged 25 to 34	7.52	11	1.9
Aged 35 to 44	22.79	34	6.6
Aged 45 to 54	36.47	54	11.4
Aged 55 to 64	100.98	150	24.2
Aged 65 to 74	214.49	318	31.8
Aged 75 or older	171.68	254	24.1

	AVERAGE HOUSEHOLD SPENDING	BEST CUSTOMERS (index)	BIGGEST CUSTOMERS (market share)
HOUSEHOLD INCOME			
Average household	$67.49	100	100.0%
Under $20,000	13.91	21	4.2
$20,000 to $39,999	58.27	86	20.1
$40,000 to $49,999	49.43	73	7.2
$50,000 to $69,999	69.05	102	15.7
$70,000 to $79,999	43.23	64	3.7
$80,000 to $99,999	100.75	149	12.1
$100,000 or more	145.66	216	37.0
HOUSEHOLD TYPE			
Average household	67.49	100	100.0
Married couples	93.24	138	69.8
Married couples, no children	166.99	247	53.4
Married couples, with children	39.87	59	14.7
Oldest child under age 6	15.88	24	1.1
Oldest child aged 6 to 17	31.48	47	5.9
Oldest child aged 18 or older	70.20	104	7.7
Single parent with child under age 18	6.13	9	0.5
Single person	45.80	68	20.2
RACE AND HISPANIC ORIGIN			
Average household	67.49	100	100.0
Asian	92.08	136	4.8
Black	14.92	22	2.7
Hispanic	9.80	15	1.7
Non-Hispanic white and other	84.56	125	95.6
REGION			
Average household	67.49	100	100.0
Northeast	50.85	75	14.0
Midwest	64.15	95	21.7
South	63.99	95	34.0
West	90.12	134	30.2
EDUCATION			
Average household	67.49	100	100.0
Less than high school graduate	15.80	23	3.6
High school graduate	47.65	71	17.8
Some college	28.65	42	9.2
Associate's degree	96.86	144	12.8
College graduate	132.07	196	56.6
Bachelor's degree	105.21	156	29.2
Master's, professional, doctoral degree	181.42	269	27.4

Note: Market shares may not sum to 100.0 because of rounding and missing categories by household type. "Asian" and "black" include Hispanics and non-Hispanics who identify themselves as being of the respective race alone. "Hispanic" includes people of any race who identify themselves as Hispanic. "Other" includes people who identify themselves as non-Hispanic and as Alaska Native, American Indian, Asian (who are also included in the "Asian" row), Native Hawaiian or other Pacific Islander, as well as non-Hispanics reporting more than one race.
Source: Calculations by New Strategist based on the Bureau of Labor Statistics' 2007 Consumer Expenditure Survey.

Medicare Premiums

Best customers: **Householders aged 65 or older**
Married couples without children at home

Customer trends: **Average household spending on Medicare premiums will rise steadily along with the aging of the population.**

Naturally, the biggest spenders on Medicare premiums are people covered by Medicare—householders aged 65 or older. On average, householders aged 65 to 74 spend $1,284 per year on Medicare premiums, and those aged 75 or older spend $1,307. Married couples without children at home (most of them older) account for 44 percent of spending on this item. Householders without a high school diploma are also above average spenders on Medicare premiums because older Americans make up a large percentage of this group.

Average household spending on Medicare premiums rose 64 percent between 2000 and 2007, after adjusting for inflation. Behind the increase was the aging of the population and the rise in premiums. Average household spending on Medicare premiums will grow even faster in the future as boomers enter the eligible age group.

Table 10.11 Medicare premiums

Total household spending $38,857,292,850.00
Average household spends   323.35

	AVERAGE HOUSEHOLD SPENDING	BEST CUSTOMERS (index)	BIGGEST CUSTOMERS (market share)
AGE OF HOUSEHOLDER			
Average household	**$323.35**	**100**	**100.0%**
Under age 25	27.52	9	0.6
Aged 25 to 34	26.45	8	1.4
Aged 35 to 44	54.27	17	3.3
Aged 45 to 54	94.78	29	6.2
Aged 55 to 64	211.20	65	10.6
Aged 65 to 74	1,284.35	397	39.7
Aged 75 or older	1,307.49	404	38.3

	AVERAGE HOUSEHOLD SPENDING	BEST CUSTOMERS (index)	BIGGEST CUSTOMERS (market share)
HOUSEHOLD INCOME			
Average household	**$323.35**	**100**	**100.0%**
Under $20,000	416.63	129	26.5
$20,000 to $39,999	480.38	149	34.5
$40,000 to $49,999	321.93	100	9.8
$50,000 to $69,999	267.58	83	12.7
$70,000 to $79,999	189.23	59	3.4
$80,000 to $99,999	209.39	65	5.3
$100,000 or more	148.46	46	7.9
HOUSEHOLD TYPE			
Average household	**323.35**	**100**	**100.0**
Married couples	368.30	114	57.6
Married couples, no children	664.34	205	44.3
Married couples, with children	92.17	29	7.1
Oldest child under age 6	26.57	8	0.4
Oldest child aged 6 to 17	33.22	10	1.3
Oldest child aged 18 or older	237.25	73	5.4
Single parent with child under age 18	46.06	14	0.8
Single person	304.34	94	28.0
RACE AND HISPANIC ORIGIN			
Average household	**323.35**	**100**	**100.0**
Asian	204.79	63	2.2
Black	240.59	74	8.9
Hispanic	175.20	54	6.4
Non-Hispanic white and other	359.02	111	84.8
REGION			
Average household	**323.35**	**100**	**100.0**
Northeast	337.19	104	19.4
Midwest	319.48	99	22.6
South	333.04	103	37.0
West	300.49	93	21.0
EDUCATION			
Average household	**323.35**	**100**	**100.0**
Less than high school graduate	463.36	143	21.7
High school graduate	426.93	132	33.3
Some college	240.32	74	16.2
Associate's degree	251.10	78	6.9
College graduate	244.38	76	21.9
Bachelor's degree	223.62	69	13.0
Master's, professional, doctoral degree	282.51	87	8.9

Note: Market shares may not sum to 100.0 because of rounding and missing categories by household type. "Asian" and "black" include Hispanics and non-Hispanics who identify themselves as being of the respective race alone. "Hispanic" includes people of any race who identify themselves as Hispanic. "Other" includes people who identify themselves as non-Hispanic and as Alaska Native, American Indian, Asian (who are also included in the "Asian" row), Native Hawaiian or other Pacific Islander, as well as non-Hispanics reporting more than one race.
Source: Calculations by New Strategist based on the Bureau of Labor Statistics' 2007 Consumer Expenditure Survey.

Medicare Prescription Drug Premiums

Best customers: Householders aged 65 or older
Married couples without children at home

Customer trends: Average household spending on Medicare prescription drug premiums will rise
steadily along with the aging of the population.

Naturally, the biggest spenders on Medicare prescription drug premiums are people covered by Medicare—householders aged 65 or older. On average householders aged 65 to 74 spend $202 per year on Medicare prescription drug premiums, and those aged 75 or older spend a slightly lower $193. Married couples without children at home (most of them older) account for 43 percent of spending on this item. Householders without a high school diploma are also above average spenders on Medicare prescription drug premiums because older Americans make up a large percentage of this group.

Because Medicare prescription drug premiums are a relatively new category in the Consumer Expenditure Survey, there are no comparison data from 2000. Average household spending on Medicare prescription drug premiums is certain to rise as boomers fill the prime-spending age groups.

Table 10.12 Medicare prescription drug premiums

Total household spending $5,811,469,560.00
Average household spends 48.36

	AVERAGE HOUSEHOLD SPENDING	BEST CUSTOMERS (index)	BIGGEST CUSTOMERS (market share)
AGE OF HOUSEHOLDER			
Average household	**$48.36**	**100**	**100.0%**
Under age 25	0.72	1	0.1
Aged 25 to 34	3.67	8	1.3
Aged 35 to 44	10.30	21	4.2
Aged 45 to 54	16.62	34	7.2
Aged 55 to 64	22.81	47	7.6
Aged 65 to 74	202.25	418	41.8
Aged 75 or older	192.84	399	37.8

	AVERAGE HOUSEHOLD SPENDING	BEST CUSTOMERS (index)	BIGGEST CUSTOMERS (market share)
HOUSEHOLD INCOME			
Average household	**$48.36**	**100**	**100.0%**
Under $20,000	72.58	150	30.9
$20,000 to $39,999	72.17	149	34.7
$40,000 to $49,999	41.04	85	8.3
$50,000 to $69,999	30.86	64	9.8
$70,000 to $79,999	26.21	54	3.1
$80,000 to $99,999	25.87	53	4.4
$100,000 or more	24.98	52	8.8
HOUSEHOLD TYPE			
Average household	**48.36**	**100**	**100.0**
Married couples	53.41	110	55.8
Married couples, no children	97.13	201	43.3
Married couples, with children	10.11	21	5.2
Oldest child under age 6	0.64	1	0.1
Oldest child aged 6 to 17	1.70	4	0.4
Oldest child aged 18 or older	30.86	64	4.7
Single parent with child under age 18	8.18	17	1.0
Single person	52.50	109	32.3
RACE AND HISPANIC ORIGIN			
Average household	**48.36**	**100**	**100.0**
Asian	27.67	57	2.0
Black	41.71	86	10.4
Hispanic	25.91	54	6.3
Non-Hispanic white and other	52.94	109	83.6
REGION			
Average household	**48.36**	**100**	**100.0**
Northeast	49.95	103	19.2
Midwest	51.48	106	24.3
South	46.39	96	34.4
West	47.03	97	22.0
EDUCATION			
Average household	**48.36**	**100**	**100.0**
Less than high school graduate	76.72	159	24.1
High school graduate	59.38	123	31.0
Some college	32.82	68	14.8
Associate's degree	29.45	61	5.4
College graduate	41.39	86	24.8
Bachelor's degree	35.35	73	13.7
Master's, professional, doctoral degree	52.48	109	11.1

Note: Market shares may not sum to 100.0 because of rounding and missing categories by household type. "Asian" and "black" include Hispanics and non-Hispanics who identify themselves as being of the respective race alone. "Hispanic" includes people of any race who identify themselves as Hispanic. "Other" includes people who identify themselves as non-Hispanic and as Alaska Native, American Indian, Asian (who are also included in the "Asian" row), Native Hawaiian or other Pacific Islander, as well as non-Hispanics reporting more than one race.
Source: Calculations by New Strategist based on the Bureau of Labor Statistics' 2007 Consumer Expenditure Survey.

Medicare Supplements, Commercial

Best customers: Householders aged 65 or older
                       Married couples without children at home

Customer trends: Average household spending on commercial Medicare supplements could continue to
                       decline in the years ahead if health insurance reform fills some of the gaps in the
                       Medicare program.

As with Medicare premiums, the biggest spenders on commercial Medicare supplements are people covered by Medicare—householders aged 65 or older. On average, householders aged 65 to 74 spend $596 per year on Medicare supplements, which cover services not included in Medicare. Householders aged 75 or older spend $715 per year on this item. Married couples without children at home (most of them older) spend 79 percent more than the average on Medicare supplements and account for 39 percent of spending on this item.

Average household spending on commercial Medicare supplements declined 15 percent between 2000 and 2007, after adjusting for inflation. Behind the decline was the introduction of the Medicare prescription drug program in 2006, which reduced the need for commercial supplements that covered prescription drugs. Average household spending on this item could continue to decline in the years ahead if health insurance reform fills some of the gaps in the Medicare program.

Table 10.13 **Medicare supplements, commercial**

Total household spending $26,121,570,270.00
Average household spends   217.37

	AVERAGE HOUSEHOLD SPENDING	BEST CUSTOMERS (index)	BIGGEST CUSTOMERS (market share)
AGE OF HOUSEHOLDER			
Average household	**$217.37**	**100**	**100.0%**
Under age 25	53.44	25	1.7
Aged 25 to 34	108.56	50	8.5
Aged 35 to 44	101.72	47	9.1
Aged 45 to 54	105.88	49	10.2
Aged 55 to 64	159.41	73	11.9
Aged 65 to 74	596.35	274	27.4
Aged 75 or older	714.78	329	31.2

	AVERAGE HOUSEHOLD SPENDING	BEST CUSTOMERS (index)	BIGGEST CUSTOMERS (market share)
HOUSEHOLD INCOME			
Average household	**$217.37**	**100**	**100.0%**
Under $20,000	172.52	79	16.3
$20,000 to $39,999	294.40	135	31.5
$40,000 to $49,999	236.30	109	10.7
$50,000 to $69,999	186.69	86	13.1
$70,000 to $79,999	153.58	71	4.1
$80,000 to $99,999	280.13	129	10.5
$100,000 or more	174.97	80	13.8
HOUSEHOLD TYPE			
Average household	**217.37**	**100**	**100.0**
Married couples	253.71	117	59.0
Married couples, no children	388.46	179	38.6
Married couples, with children	138.33	64	15.9
Oldest child under age 6	117.67	54	2.6
Oldest child aged 6 to 17	141.34	65	8.3
Oldest child aged 18 or older	146.80	68	5.0
Single parent with child under age 18	77.16	35	2.1
Single person	197.89	91	27.1
RACE AND HISPANIC ORIGIN			
Average household	**217.37**	**100**	**100.0**
Asian	100.96	46	1.6
Black	71.26	33	3.9
Hispanic	63.29	29	3.4
Non-Hispanic white and other	263.77	121	92.6
REGION			
Average household	**217.37**	**100**	**100.0**
Northeast	177.70	82	15.2
Midwest	281.83	130	29.6
South	212.75	98	35.1
West	192.23	88	20.0
EDUCATION			
Average household	**217.37**	**100**	**100.0**
Less than high school graduate	223.54	103	15.6
High school graduate	261.73	120	30.4
Some college	187.04	86	18.7
Associate's degree	204.10	94	8.3
College graduate	202.37	93	26.9
Bachelor's degree	168.84	78	14.6
Master's, professional, doctoral degree	263.98	121	12.4

Note: Market shares may not sum to 100.0 because of rounding and missing categories by household type. "Asian" and "black" include Hispanics and non-Hispanics who identify themselves as being of the respective race alone. "Hispanic" includes people of any race who identify themselves as Hispanic. "Other" includes people who identify themselves as non-Hispanic and as Alaska Native, American Indian, Asian (who are also included in the "Asian" row), Native Hawaiian or other Pacific Islander, as well as non-Hispanics reporting more than one race.
Source: Calculations by New Strategist based on the Bureau of Labor Statistics' 2007 Consumer Expenditure Survey.

Nonphysician Health Care Professional Services
(Out-of-Pocket Expenses)

Best customers: Householders aged 55 to 74
Married couples
Households in the Midwest

Customer trends: Average household spending on nonphysician health care professional services will rise as nonphysicians provide more health care services.

Alternative health care has become popular over the past few decades, and millions of Americans seek the medical advice of nonphysicians such as chiropractors, acupuncturists, and nurse practitioners. The best customers of these services are householders aged 55 to 74, who spend 33 to 87 percent more than average on this item. Married couples without children at home (most of them older) spend 82 percent more than average on nonphysician services, while those with children at home spend 42 percent more, in part because their households are relatively large. Households in the Midwest spend 58 percent more than average on this item.

Average household spending on nonphysician health care professional services rose 63 percent between 2000 and 2007, after adjusting for inflation. Behind the increase are the greater variety of services provided by these professionals, as well as the growing number of uninsured Americans seeking care outside established medical circles. Spending in this category is likely to increase as nonphysicians provide more health care services.

Table 10.14 **Nonphysician health care professional services (out-of-pocket expenses)**
(acupuncturists, chiropractors, nurse practitioners, etc.)

Total household spending $8,705,187,240.00
Average household spends 72.44

AGE OF HOUSEHOLDER	AVERAGE HOUSEHOLD SPENDING	BEST CUSTOMERS (index)	BIGGEST CUSTOMERS (market share)
Average household	$72.44	100	100.0%
Under age 25	18.22	25	1.7
Aged 25 to 34	52.30	72	12.3
Aged 35 to 44	46.86	65	12.6
Aged 45 to 54	76.67	106	22.2
Aged 55 to 64	96.62	133	21.6
Aged 65 to 74	135.32	187	18.7
Aged 75 or older	83.07	115	10.9

	AVERAGE HOUSEHOLD SPENDING	BEST CUSTOMERS (index)	BIGGEST CUSTOMERS (market share)
HOUSEHOLD INCOME			
Average household	$72.44	100	100.0%
Under $20,000	16.75	23	4.8
$20,000 to $39,999	29.22	40	9.4
$40,000 to $49,999	55.86	77	7.6
$50,000 to $69,999	58.08	80	12.3
$70,000 to $79,999	95.35	132	7.6
$80,000 to $99,999	150.89	208	16.9
$100,000 or more	175.25	242	41.4
HOUSEHOLD TYPE			
Average household	72.44	100	100.0
Married couples	113.65	157	79.3
Married couples, no children	132.04	182	39.3
Married couples, with children	102.81	142	35.4
Oldest child under age 6	102.58	142	6.9
Oldest child aged 6 to 17	106.44	147	18.7
Oldest child aged 18 or older	96.70	133	9.8
Single parent with child under age 18	19.20	27	1.6
Single person	33.97	47	13.9
RACE AND HISPANIC ORIGIN			
Average household	72.44	100	100.0
Asian	14.51	20	0.7
Black	15.77	22	2.6
Hispanic	43.79	60	7.1
Non-Hispanic white and other	85.64	118	90.2
REGION			
Average household	72.44	100	100.0
Northeast	39.10	54	10.1
Midwest	114.71	158	36.2
South	61.17	84	30.3
West	75.07	104	23.4
EDUCATION			
Average household	72.44	100	100.0
Less than high school graduate	35.44	49	7.4
High school graduate	31.10	43	10.8
Some college	84.15	116	25.3
Associate's degree	51.72	71	6.3
College graduate	125.41	173	50.1
Bachelor's degree	104.72	145	27.1
Master's, professional, doctoral degree	163.41	226	23.0

Note: Market shares may not sum to 100.0 because of rounding and missing categories by household type. "Asian" and "black" include Hispanics and non-Hispanics who identify themselves as being of the respective race alone. "Hispanic" includes people of any race who identify themselves as Hispanic. "Other" includes people who identify themselves as non-Hispanic and as Alaska Native, American Indian, Asian (who are also included in the "Asian" row), Native Hawaiian or other Pacific Islander, as well as non-Hispanics reporting more than one race.
Source: Calculations by New Strategist based on the Bureau of Labor Statistics' 2007 Consumer Expenditure Survey.

Physician Services (Out-of-Pocket Expenses)

Best customers:	**Householders aged 45 to 64** **Married couples**
Customer trends:	**Average household out-of-pocket spending on physician services is unlikely to grow much in the years ahead because boomers will be joining Medicare, which largely covers these costs.**

The biggest out-of-pocket spenders on physician services are householders nearing retirement and married couples. Householders aged 45 to 64 spend 15 to 23 percent more than average out-of-pocket on this item. Married couples without children at home spend 38 percent more than average on physician services because most are older. Couples with children at home spend 45 percent more than average because they have the largest households.

Average household spending on physician services increased 6 percent between 2000 and 2007, after adjusting for inflation. Behind the increase were rising copayments. Spending in this category is unlikely to grow much in the future because boomers will soon be eligible for Medicare, which covers most physician expenses.

Table 10.15 **Physician services (out-of-pocket expenses)**

Total household spending	$20,561,258,100.00
Average household spends	171.10

	AVERAGE HOUSEHOLD SPENDING	BEST CUSTOMERS (index)	BIGGEST CUSTOMERS (market share)
AGE OF HOUSEHOLDER			
Average household	**$171.10**	**100**	**100.0%**
Under age 25	96.88	57	3.8
Aged 25 to 34	155.26	91	15.5
Aged 35 to 44	179.07	105	20.4
Aged 45 to 54	197.06	115	24.2
Aged 55 to 64	210.42	123	19.9
Aged 65 to 74	179.07	105	10.5
Aged 75 or older	103.25	60	5.7

	AVERAGE HOUSEHOLD SPENDING	BEST CUSTOMERS (index)	BIGGEST CUSTOMERS (market share)
HOUSEHOLD INCOME			
Average household	**$171.10**	**100**	**100.0%**
Under $20,000	65.69	38	7.9
$20,000 to $39,999	139.48	82	18.9
$40,000 to $49,999	196.16	115	11.3
$50,000 to $69,999	184.60	108	16.5
$70,000 to $79,999	206.56	121	7.0
$80,000 to $99,999	234.04	137	11.1
$100,000 or more	272.19	159	27.3
HOUSEHOLD TYPE			
Average household	**171.10**	**100**	**100.0**
Married couples	238.84	140	70.6
Married couples, no children	236.90	138	29.9
Married couples, with children	247.57	145	36.1
Oldest child under age 6	296.33	173	8.5
Oldest child aged 6 to 17	237.66	139	17.6
Oldest child aged 18 or older	232.35	136	10.0
Single parent with child under age 18	103.20	60	3.6
Single person	88.22	52	15.3
RACE AND HISPANIC ORIGIN			
Average household	**171.10**	**100**	**100.0**
Asian	103.99	61	2.1
Black	75.52	44	5.3
Hispanic	103.45	60	7.1
Non-Hispanic white and other	196.65	115	87.7
REGION			
Average household	**171.10**	**100**	**100.0**
Northeast	135.49	79	14.7
Midwest	196.84	115	26.3
South	166.12	97	34.9
West	182.34	107	24.1
EDUCATION			
Average household	**171.10**	**100**	**100.0**
Less than high school graduate	126.79	74	11.2
High school graduate	137.93	81	20.3
Some college	149.60	87	19.0
Associate's degree	166.34	97	8.6
College graduate	240.88	141	40.7
Bachelor's degree	218.49	128	23.9
Master's, professional, doctoral degree	282.01	165	16.8

Note: Market shares may not sum to 100.0 because of rounding and missing categories by household type. "Asian" and "black" include Hispanics and non-Hispanics who identify themselves as being of the respective race alone. "Hispanic" includes people of any race who identify themselves as Hispanic. "Other" includes people who identify themselves as non-Hispanic and as Alaska Native, American Indian, Asian (who are also included in the "Asian" row), Native Hawaiian or other Pacific Islander, as well as non-Hispanics reporting more than one race.
Source: Calculations by New Strategist based on the Bureau of Labor Statistics' 2007 Consumer Expenditure Survey.

Vitamins, Nonprescription

Best customers: **Householders aged 55 or older**
                                      Married couples without children at home
                                      Married couples with preschoolers

Customer trends: **Average household spending on vitamins will increase substantially as boomers age.**

As people age they become more health conscious. Consequently, older people are the best customers of vitamins. Householders aged 55 or older spend 40 to 207 percent more than average on this item and control 57 percent of the market. Married couples without children at home (most of them older) spend 74 percent more than average on vitamins, while those with preschoolers spend 30 percent more.

Average household spending on vitamins fell 17 percent between 2000 and 2007, after adjusting for inflation. Behind the decline was price competition from discounters, as well as belt tightening as other health care costs increased. Average household spending on vitamins should climb as boomers age and seek to prevent ailments through better nutrition.

Table 10.16 Vitamins, nonprescription

Total household spending $5,549,496,780.00
Average household spends   46.18

	AVERAGE HOUSEHOLD SPENDING	BEST CUSTOMERS (index)	BIGGEST CUSTOMERS (market share)
AGE OF HOUSEHOLDER			
Average household	**$46.18**	**100**	**100.0%**
Under age 25	19.79	43	2.9
Aged 25 to 34	13.64	30	5.0
Aged 35 to 44	26.21	57	11.1
Aged 45 to 54	52.57	114	23.9
Aged 55 to 64	64.80	140	22.7
Aged 65 to 74	95.41	207	20.6
Aged 75 or older	68.66	149	14.1

	AVERAGE HOUSEHOLD SPENDING	BEST CUSTOMERS (index)	BIGGEST CUSTOMERS (market share)
HOUSEHOLD INCOME			
Average household	$46.18	100	100.0%
Under $20,000	23.48	51	10.5
$20,000 to $39,999	40.30	87	20.3
$40,000 to $49,999	36.84	80	7.8
$50,000 to $69,999	45.38	98	15.0
$70,000 to $79,999	50.85	110	6.4
$80,000 to $99,999	50.97	110	9.0
$100,000 or more	84.34	183	31.3
HOUSEHOLD TYPE			
Average household	46.18	100	100.0
Married couples	61.57	133	67.4
Married couples, no children	80.14	174	37.4
Married couples, with children	44.92	97	24.3
Oldest child under age 6	60.12	130	6.4
Oldest child aged 6 to 17	41.88	91	11.5
Oldest child aged 18 or older	39.77	86	6.3
Single parent with child under age 18	13.12	28	1.7
Single person	34.38	74	22.1
RACE AND HISPANIC ORIGIN			
Average household	46.18	100	100.0
Asian	27.75	60	2.1
Black	11.20	24	2.9
Hispanic	15.05	33	3.8
Non-Hispanic white and other	55.98	121	92.5
REGION			
Average household	46.18	100	100.0
Northeast	44.59	97	18.0
Midwest	45.42	98	22.5
South	48.04	104	37.4
West	45.32	98	22.2
EDUCATION			
Average household	46.18	100	100.0
Less than high school graduate	25.91	56	8.5
High school graduate	25.94	56	14.2
Some college	41.44	90	19.5
Associate's degree	62.58	136	12.0
College graduate	71.87	156	45.0
Bachelor's degree	62.18	135	25.2
Master's, professional, doctoral degree	88.69	192	19.6

Note: Market shares may not sum to 100.0 because of rounding and missing categories by household type. "Asian" and "black" include Hispanics and non-Hispanics who identify themselves as being of the respective race alone. "Hispanic" includes people of any race who identify themselves as Hispanic. "Other" includes people who identify themselves as non-Hispanic and as Alaska Native, American Indian, Asian (who are also included in the "Asian" row), Native Hawaiian or other Pacific Islander, as well as non-Hispanics reporting more than one race.
Source: Calculations by New Strategist based on the Bureau of Labor Statistics' 2007 Consumer Expenditure Survey.

Chapter 11.

Household Services

Household Spending on Household Services, 2007

Spending on household services is dominated by day care needs. Spending on day care centers and babysitting accounted for 47 percent of the $755 the average household spent on household services in 2007. While the $268 the average household spent on day care centers seems low, this—like all spending figures here—is an average that includes both purchasers and nonpurchasers. The 5 percent of households that paid for day care services during the average quarter of 2007 spent an average of $1,241 (see Appendix B), for an estimated annual expense of $4,966—a much more realistic figure.

The average household spent 11 percent more on household services in 2007 than in 2000, after adjusting for inflation. Spending on day care centers increased 7 percent. Spending on most other household service categories also grew during those years, including a 29 percent rise in spending on moving, storage, and freight express; a 32 percent rise in spending on appliance repair, including at a service center; a 53 percent rise in spending on termite and pest control products and services; and a more than doubling in spending on repair of computer systems for nonbusiness use. Spending fell in only two household services categories: spending on care for the elderly, invalids, and handicapped was down 5 percent; security system service fee spending declined 12 percent.

Average household spending on household services should continue to grow as the millennial generation enters the lifestage at which day care needs are greatest.

Spending on household services

(average spending by households on household services, 2000 to 2007; in 2007 dollars)

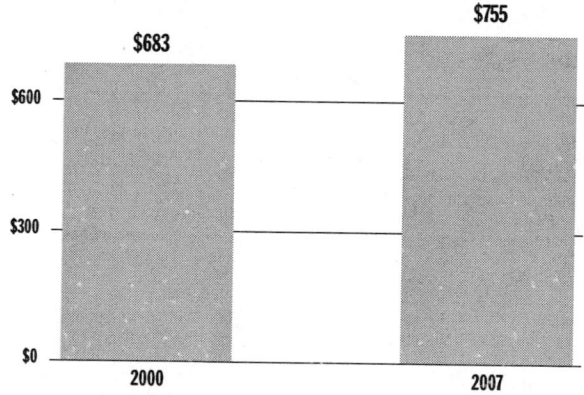

Table 11.1 Household Services Spending, 2000 TO 2007

(average annual household spending on household services, and percent distribution of spending by type, 2000 and 2007; percent change, 2000–07; in 2007 dollars)

	2007		2000		
	average household spending	percent distribution	average household spending (in 2007$)	percent distribution	percent change 2000–07
Average household spending on household services	**$754.85**	**100.0%**	**$682.82**	**100.0%**	**10.5%**
Day care centers, nursery schools, and preschools	267.66	35.6	250.95	36.8	6.7
Housekeeping services	118.26	15.7	106.14	15.5	11.4
Gardening and lawn care services	106.94	14.2	94.23	13.8	13.5
Babysitting and childcare in own or other home	85.91	11.4	78.02	11.4	10.1
Care for the elderly, invalids, handicapped	57.52	7.6	60.66	8.9	-5.2
Moving, storage, and freight express	50.22	6.7	39.05	5.7	28.6
Security system service fee	19.89	2.6	22.48	3.3	-11.5
Termite and pest control products and services	18.49	2.5	12.11	1.8	52.6
Appliance repair, including at service center	15.93	2.1	12.11	1.8	31.5
Repair of computer systems for nonbusiness use	6.99	0.9	3.31	0.5	111.1
Water softening service	4.49	0.6	3.74	0.5	19.9

Source: Bureau of Labor Statistics, 2000 and 2007 Consumer Expenditure Surveys; calculations by New Strategist

Appliance Repair, including at Service Center

Best customers: **Householders aged 55 to 74**
                            Married couples

Customer trends: **Average household spending on appliance repair may continue to increase as**
                            financially strapped boomers enter the older age groups.

The best customers of appliance repair are older householders and married couples. Not only do older householders have older appliances, but their appliances are often of higher quality, which makes it costlier to replace than to repair. Householders aged 55 to 74 spend 36 to 67 percent more than the average household on appliance repair and control 39 percent of spending in this market. Married couples spend 30 percent more than average on this item.

Average household spending on appliance repair rose by a substantial 32 percent between 2000 and 2007, after adjusting for inflation. Behind the trend is the aging of the large baby-boom generation. Average household spending on appliance repair may continue to increase as financially strapped boomers enter the older age groups.

Table 11.2 Appliance repair, including at service center

Total household spending $1,914,324,030.00
Average household spends   15.93

	AVERAGE HOUSEHOLD SPENDING	BEST CUSTOMERS (index)	BIGGEST CUSTOMERS (market share)
AGE OF HOUSEHOLDER			
Average household	**$15.93**	**100**	**100.0%**
Under age 25	3.03	19	1.3
Aged 25 to 34	9.92	62	10.6
Aged 35 to 44	14.05	88	17.2
Aged 45 to 54	16.96	106	22.4
Aged 55 to 64	21.67	136	22.0
Aged 65 to 74	26.59	167	16.7
Aged 75 or older	16.48	103	9.8

	AVERAGE HOUSEHOLD SPENDING	BEST CUSTOMERS (index)	BIGGEST CUSTOMERS (market share)
HOUSEHOLD INCOME			
Average household	**$15.93**	**100**	**100.0%**
Under $20,000	5.95	37	7.7
$20,000 to $39,999	12.51	79	18.3
$40,000 to $49,999	11.03	69	6.8
$50,000 to $69,999	13.77	86	13.2
$70,000 to $79,999	23.13	145	8.4
$80,000 to $99,999	27.19	171	13.9
$100,000 or more	29.49	185	31.7
HOUSEHOLD TYPE			
Average household	**15.93**	**100**	**100.0**
Married couples	20.73	130	65.8
Married couples, no children	20.93	131	28.3
Married couples, with children	19.51	122	30.6
Oldest child under age 6	19.59	123	6.0
Oldest child aged 6 to 17	18.40	116	14.7
Oldest child aged 18 or older	21.36	134	9.9
Single parent with child under age 18	6.98	44	2.6
Single person	10.65	67	19.9
RACE AND HISPANIC ORIGIN			
Average household	**15.93**	**100**	**100.0**
Asian	13.11	82	2.9
Black	7.24	45	5.5
Hispanic	10.83	68	8.0
Non-Hispanic white and other	18.05	113	86.5
REGION			
Average household	**15.93**	**100**	**100.0**
Northeast	16.28	102	19.0
Midwest	18.53	116	26.6
South	13.88	87	31.3
West	16.24	102	23.1
EDUCATION			
Average household	**15.93**	**100**	**100.0**
Less than high school graduate	6.13	38	5.8
High school graduate	12.65	79	20.0
Some college	14.63	92	20.0
Associate's degree	21.02	132	11.7
College graduate	23.32	146	42.4
Bachelor's degree	23.62	148	27.8
Master's, professional, doctoral degree	22.77	143	14.6

Note: Market shares may not sum to 100.0 because of rounding and missing categories by household type. "Asian" and "black" include Hispanics and non-Hispanics who identify themselves as being of the respective race alone. "Hispanic" includes people of any race who identify themselves as Hispanic. "Other" includes people who identify themselves as non-Hispanic and as Alaska Native, American Indian, Asian (who are also included in the "Asian" row), Native Hawaiian or other Pacific Islander, as well as non-Hispanics reporting more than one race.
Source: Calculations by New Strategist based on the Bureau of Labor Statistics' 2007 Consumer Expenditure Survey.

Babysitting and Child Care in Own or Other Home

Best customers:
    Householders aged 25 to 44
    High-income households
    Married couples with children under age 18
    Single parents
    Hispanics

Customer trends:
    Average household spending on babysitting should continue to rise as the large millennial generation has children.

Child care is one of the largest expenses parents face. Those who spend the most on babysitting (which includes arrangements from hiring a teen to be with the kids on a Saturday night to a live-in nanny) are married couples with preschoolers. This household type spends over six times the average on babysitting. Couples with school-aged children spend two-and-one-half times the average on this item, and single parents spend twice the average. Householders aged 25 to 44, most with children, spend over twice the average on babysitting. Hispanics, who have relatively large families, spend 27 percent more than average on babysitting.

Average household spending on babysitting rose 10 percent between 2000 and 2007, after adjusting for inflation. Behind the increase was the entry of the large millennial generation into the childbearing lifestage. In the years ahead, spending on babysitting should continue to rise as the large millennial generation has children.

Table 11.3 Babysitting and child care in own or other home

Total household spending $10,323,890,610.00
Average household spends   85.91

	AVERAGE HOUSEHOLD SPENDING	BEST CUSTOMERS (index)	BIGGEST CUSTOMERS (market share)
AGE OF HOUSEHOLDER			
Average household	**$85.91**	**100**	**100.0%**
Under age 25	42.08	49	3.3
Aged 25 to 34	189.79	221	37.7
Aged 35 to 44	197.43	230	44.8
Aged 45 to 54	51.21	60	12.5
Aged 55 to 64	5.13	6	1.0
Aged 65 to 74	5.80	7	0.7
Aged 75 or older	0.41	0	0.0

	AVERAGE HOUSEHOLD SPENDING	BEST CUSTOMERS (index)	BIGGEST CUSTOMERS (market share)
HOUSEHOLD INCOME			
Average household	**$85.91**	**100**	**100.0%**
Under $20,000	21.83	25	5.2
$20,000 to $39,999	33.99	40	9.2
$40,000 to $49,999	33.04	38	3.8
$50,000 to $69,999	77.76	91	13.9
$70,000 to $79,999	74.15	86	5.0
$80,000 to $99,999	101.59	118	9.6
$100,000 or more	267.40	311	53.3
HOUSEHOLD TYPE			
Average household	**85.91**	**100**	**100.0**
Married couples	130.68	152	76.9
Married couples, no children	0.44	1	0.1
Married couples, with children	228.84	266	66.5
Oldest child under age 6	546.79	636	31.1
Oldest child aged 6 to 17	222.60	259	32.9
Oldest child aged 18 or older	28.97	34	2.5
Single parent with child under age 18	185.23	216	12.8
Single person	5.21	6	1.8
RACE AND HISPANIC ORIGIN			
Average household	**85.91**	**100**	**100.0**
Asian	75.83	88	3.1
Black	53.59	62	7.5
Hispanic	108.91	127	15.0
Non-Hispanic white and other	87.37	102	77.6
REGION			
Average household	**85.91**	**100**	**100.0**
Northeast	112.11	130	24.3
Midwest	57.52	67	15.3
South	78.98	92	33.0
West	104.00	121	27.4
EDUCATION			
Average household	**85.91**	**100**	**100.0**
Less than high school graduate	36.66	43	6.5
High school graduate	45.87	53	13.5
Some college	62.06	72	15.7
Associate's degree	88.23	103	9.1
College graduate	163.83	191	55.2
Bachelor's degree	138.89	162	30.3
Master's, professional, doctoral degree	209.62	244	24.9

Note: Market shares may not sum to 100.0 because of rounding and missing categories by household type. "Asian" and "black" include Hispanics and non-Hispanics who identify themselves as being of the respective race alone. "Hispanic" includes people of any race who identify themselves as Hispanic. "Other" includes people who identify themselves as non-Hispanic and as Alaska Native, American Indian, Asian (who are also included in the "Asian" row), Native Hawaiian or other Pacific Islander, as well as non-Hispanics reporting more than one race.
Source: Calculations by New Strategist based on the Bureau of Labor Statistics' 2007 Consumer Expenditure Survey.

Care for the Elderly, Invalids, Handicapped, Etc.

Best customers: Householders aged 55 to 64 and aged 75 or older
Married couples without children at home
Married couples with adult children at home

Customer trends: Average household spending on care for the elderly, invalids, and handicapped should rise as boomers age.

The best customers of care for the elderly, invalids, handicapped, etc. are middle-aged and older householders. Householders aged 55 to 64 spend more than twice the average on this items, many of them caring for aging parents. Householders aged 75 or older spend more than five times the average on this item, many of them caring for ailing spouses. Married couples without children at home, most of them empty-nesters, spend 23 percent more than average on this item, while those with adult children at home spend almost three times the average.

Average household spending on care for the elderly, invalids, and handicapped fell 5 percent between 2000 and 2007, after adjusting for inflation, despite the aging of the population. Average household spending on this item should rise as boomers age.

Table 11.4 **Care for the elderly, invalids, handicapped, etc.**

	AVERAGE HOUSEHOLD SPENDING	BEST CUSTOMERS (index)	BIGGEST CUSTOMERS (market share)
Total household spending	$6,912,235,920.00		
Average household spends	57.52		
AGE OF HOUSEHOLDER			
Average household	**$57.52**	**100**	**100.0%**
Under age 25	–	–	–
Aged 25 to 34	2.77	5	0.8
Aged 35 to 44	0.17	0	0.1
Aged 45 to 54	17.66	31	6.4
Aged 55 to 64	124.84	217	35.1
Aged 65 to 74	42.74	74	7.4
Aged 75 or older	304.06	529	50.1

	AVERAGE HOUSEHOLD SPENDING	BEST CUSTOMERS (index)	BIGGEST CUSTOMERS (market share)
HOUSEHOLD INCOME			
Average household	**$57.52**	**100**	**100.0%**
Under $20,000	35.96	63	12.9
$20,000 to $39,999	25.59	44	10.3
$40,000 to $49,999	45.62	79	7.8
$50,000 to $69,999	58.33	101	15.5
$70,000 to $79,999	68.89	120	6.9
$80,000 to $99,999	77.65	135	11.0
$100,000 or more	119.46	208	35.6
HOUSEHOLD TYPE			
Average household	**57.52**	**100**	**100.0**
Married couples	60.07	104	52.8
Married couples, no children	69.91	122	26.2
Married couples, with children	47.58	83	20.6
Oldest child under age 6	–	–	–
Oldest child aged 6 to 17	1.59	3	0.4
Oldest child aged 18 or older	158.38	275	20.3
Single parent with child under age 18	–	–	–
Single person	69.33	121	35.8
RACE AND HISPANIC ORIGIN			
Average household	**57.52**	**100**	**100.0**
Asian	23.79	41	1.5
Black	17.63	31	3.7
Hispanic	12.55	22	2.6
Non-Hispanic white and other	70.75	123	93.9
REGION			
Average household	**57.52**	**100**	**100.0**
Northeast	34.10	59	11.0
Midwest	121.77	212	48.4
South	46.35	81	28.9
West	29.64	52	11.7
EDUCATION			
Average household	**57.52**	**100**	**100.0**
Less than high school graduate	29.77	52	7.9
High school graduate	42.92	75	18.8
Some college	46.20	80	17.5
Associate's degree	137.02	238	21.2
College graduate	68.91	120	34.7
Bachelor's degree	82.04	143	26.7
Master's, professional, doctoral degree	44.78	78	7.9

Note: Market shares may not sum to 100.0 because of rounding and missing categories by household type. "Asian" and "black" include Hispanics and non-Hispanics who identify themselves as being of the respective race alone. "Hispanic" includes people of any race who identify themselves as Hispanic. "Other" includes people who identify themselves as non-Hispanic and as Alaska Native, American Indian, Asian (who are also included in the "Asian" row), Native Hawaiian or other Pacific Islander, as well as non-Hispanics reporting more than one race.
Source: Calculations by New Strategist based on the Bureau of Labor Statistics' 2007 Consumer Expenditure Survey.

Day Care Centers, Nursery Schools, and Preschools

Best customers:
Householders aged 25 to 44
Married couples with children under age 18
Single parents
Asians

Customer trends:
Average household spending on day care centers should continue to rise as the large millennial generation has children.

The best customers of day care centers are married couples with preschoolers. This household type spends over eight times the average on day care centers. Married couples with school-aged children spend two-and-one-half times the average on this item, while single parents spend 78 percent more than average. Householders aged 25 to 44, most of them parents, spend more than twice the average on day care centers and control 84 percent of the market. Asians spend 60 percent more than average on day care.

Average household spending on day care centers rose 7 percent between 2000 and 2007, after adjusting for inflation. Average household spending on day care centers should continue to rise in the years ahead as the large millennial generation has children.

Table 11.5 **Day care centers, nursery schools, and preschools**

Total household spending $32,164,969,860.00
Average household spends   267.66

	AVERAGE HOUSEHOLD SPENDING	BEST CUSTOMERS (index)	BIGGEST CUSTOMERS (market share)
AGE OF HOUSEHOLDER			
Average household	$267.66	100	100.0%
Under age 25	131.85	49	3.3
Aged 25 to 34	587.59	220	37.4
Aged 35 to 44	645.86	241	47.0
Aged 45 to 54	116.74	44	9.2
Aged 55 to 64	21.86	8	1.3
Aged 65 to 74	33.76	13	1.3
Aged 75 or older	12.64	5	0.4

	AVERAGE HOUSEHOLD SPENDING	BEST CUSTOMERS (index)	BIGGEST CUSTOMERS (market share)
HOUSEHOLD INCOME			
Average household	$267.66	100	100.0%
Under $20,000	36.55	14	2.8
$20,000 to $39,999	94.46	35	8.2
$40,000 to $49,999	134.39	50	4.9
$50,000 to $69,999	263.87	99	15.1
$70,000 to $79,999	372.79	139	8.1
$80,000 to $99,999	501.73	187	15.3
$100,000 or more	713.19	266	45.6
HOUSEHOLD TYPE			
Average household	267.66	100	100.0
Married couples	420.38	157	79.4
Married couples, no children	13.46	5	1.1
Married couples, with children	797.41	298	74.3
Oldest child under age 6	2,264.12	846	41.3
Oldest child aged 6 to 17	661.40	247	31.4
Oldest child aged 18 or older	60.28	23	1.7
Single parent with child under age 18	476.36	178	10.6
Single person	16.63	6	1.8
RACE AND HISPANIC ORIGIN			
Average household	267.66	100	100.0
Asian	427.91	160	5.6
Black	225.54	84	10.1
Hispanic	213.67	80	9.4
Non-Hispanic white and other	282.44	106	80.6
REGION			
Average household	267.66	100	100.0
Northeast	273.41	102	19.0
Midwest	213.60	80	18.2
South	274.60	103	36.8
West	306.53	115	25.9
EDUCATION			
Average household	267.66	100	100.0
Less than high school graduate	69.89	26	4.0
High school graduate	128.95	48	12.2
Some college	240.45	90	19.6
Associate's degree	263.46	98	8.7
College graduate	513.94	192	55.6
Bachelor's degree	469.16	175	32.9
Master's, professional, doctoral degree	596.20	223	22.7

Note: Market shares may not sum to 100.0 because of rounding and missing categories by household type. "Asian" and "black" include Hispanics and non-Hispanics who identify themselves as being of the respective race alone. "Hispanic" includes people of any race who identify themselves as Hispanic. "Other" includes people who identify themselves as non-Hispanic and as Alaska Native, American Indian, Asian (who are also included in the "Asian" row), Native Hawaiian or other Pacific Islander, as well as non-Hispanics reporting more than one race.
Source: Calculations by New Strategist based on the Bureau of Labor Statistics' 2007 Consumer Expenditure Survey.

Gardening and Lawn Care Services

Best customers:

Householders aged 55 or older
Married couples without children at home
Married couples with adult children at home
Asians

Customer trends:

Average household spending on gardening and lawn care services will rise as the population ages.

Older householders are most likely to spend on gardening and lawn care services. Householders aged 55 or older, many of whom need help maintaining their lawns, spend 45 to 62 percent more than average on this item and control 54 percent of the market. Married couples without children at home (most of them older) spend 63 percent more than average on gardening and lawn care services. Asians, who have above-average incomes, spend 59 percent more than average on this item.

Average household spending on gardening and lawn care services climbed 13 percent between 2000 and 2007, after adjusting for inflation. This category should continue to grow with the aging of the baby-boom generation into the best-customer age groups.

Table 11.6 Gardening and lawn care services

Total household spending $12,851,086,740.00
Average household spends   106.94

	AVERAGE HOUSEHOLD SPENDING	BEST CUSTOMERS (index)	BIGGEST CUSTOMERS (market share)
AGE OF HOUSEHOLDER			
Average household	**$106.94**	**100**	**100.0%**
Under age 25	13.73	13	0.9
Aged 25 to 34	36.83	34	5.9
Aged 35 to 44	84.30	79	15.4
Aged 45 to 54	121.84	114	23.9
Aged 55 to 64	159.41	149	24.1
Aged 65 to 74	155.09	145	14.5
Aged 75 or older	172.91	162	15.3

	AVERAGE HOUSEHOLD SPENDING	BEST CUSTOMERS (index)	BIGGEST CUSTOMERS (market share)
HOUSEHOLD INCOME			
Average household	**$106.94**	**100**	**100.0%**
Under $20,000	38.13	36	7.3
$20,000 to $39,999	55.09	52	12.0
$40,000 to $49,999	64.03	60	5.9
$50,000 to $69,999	75.72	71	10.8
$70,000 to $79,999	106.48	100	5.8
$80,000 to $99,999	123.68	116	9.4
$100,000 or more	304.59	285	48.8
HOUSEHOLD TYPE			
Average household	**106.94**	**100**	**100.0**
Married couples	140.72	132	66.5
Married couples, no children	174.83	163	35.3
Married couples, with children	115.55	108	27.0
Oldest child under age 6	91.65	86	4.2
Oldest child aged 6 to 17	110.99	104	13.2
Oldest child aged 18 or older	139.23	130	9.6
Single parent with child under age 18	58.58	55	3.3
Single person	81.64	76	22.7
RACE AND HISPANIC ORIGIN			
Average household	**106.94**	**100**	**100.0**
Asian	169.95	159	5.6
Black	62.81	59	7.0
Hispanic	57.84	54	6.4
Non-Hispanic white and other	121.42	114	86.7
REGION			
Average household	**106.94**	**100**	**100.0**
Northeast	118.31	111	20.6
Midwest	77.81	73	16.6
South	106.40	99	35.7
West	127.87	120	27.0
EDUCATION			
Average household	**106.94**	**100**	**100.0**
Less than high school graduate	37.89	35	5.4
High school graduate	59.41	56	14.0
Some college	69.03	65	14.1
Associate's degree	109.30	102	9.1
College graduate	212.34	199	57.5
Bachelor's degree	162.70	152	28.5
Master's, professional, doctoral degree	303.56	284	29.0

Note: Market shares may not sum to 100.0 because of rounding and missing categories by household type. "Asian" and "black" include Hispanics and non-Hispanics who identify themselves as being of the respective race alone. "Hispanic" includes people of any race who identify themselves as Hispanic. "Other" includes people who identify themselves as non-Hispanic and as Alaska Native, American Indian, Asian (who are also included in the "Asian" row), Native Hawaiian or other Pacific Islander, as well as non-Hispanics reporting more than one race.
Source: Calculations by New Strategist based on the Bureau of Labor Statistics' 2007 Consumer Expenditure Survey.

Housekeeping Services

Best customers: **Householders aged 45 or older**
High-income households
Married couples without children at home
Married couples with school-aged children
Households in the West
College graduates

Customer trends: **Average household spending on housekeeping services should rise as the population ages.**

The best customers of housekeeping services are middle-aged and older householders and the affluent—the first group often needs such services, while the second group can afford them. Householders aged 45 or older spend more than average on housekeeping services. Households with incomes of $100,000 or more spend three-and-one-half times the average on this item. Married couples without children at home, most of them older, spend 41 percent more than average on housekeeping services, while those with school-aged children (the busiest households) spend 57 percent more. Western householders spend 41 percent more than average on housekeeping services. College graduates, who dominate the nation's affluent, spend more than twice the average.

Average household spending on housekeeping services rose 11 percent between 2000 and 2007, after adjusting for inflation. Behind the increase was the aging of the baby-boom generation into the best-customer age groups. Spending on housekeeping services should continue to rise in the years ahead along with the aging of the population.

Table 11.7 Housekeeping services

Total household spending $14,211,422,460.00
Average household spends   118.26

	AVERAGE HOUSEHOLD SPENDING	BEST CUSTOMERS (index)	BIGGEST CUSTOMERS (market share)
AGE OF HOUSEHOLDER			
Average household	**$118.26**	**100**	**100.0%**
Under age 25	6.50	5	0.4
Aged 25 to 34	52.95	45	7.6
Aged 35 to 44	116.44	98	19.2
Aged 45 to 54	137.59	116	24.4
Aged 55 to 64	144.50	122	19.8
Aged 65 to 74	129.13	109	10.9
Aged 75 or older	220.33	186	17.7

	AVERAGE HOUSEHOLD SPENDING	BEST CUSTOMERS (index)	BIGGEST CUSTOMERS (market share)
HOUSEHOLD INCOME			
Average household	$118.26	100	100.0%
Under $20,000	55.69	47	9.7
$20,000 to $39,999	37.61	32	7.4
$40,000 to $49,999	41.61	35	3.5
$50,000 to $69,999	65.43	55	8.5
$70,000 to $79,999	68.18	58	3.3
$80,000 to $99,999	118.76	100	8.2
$100,000 or more	410.64	347	59.5
HOUSEHOLD TYPE			
Average household	118.26	100	100.0
Married couples	156.74	133	67.0
Married couples, no children	166.44	141	30.4
Married couples, with children	157.48	133	33.2
Oldest child under age 6	140.17	119	5.8
Oldest child aged 6 to 17	185.42	157	19.9
Oldest child aged 18 or older	120.78	102	7.5
Single parent with child under age 18	71.11	60	3.6
Single person	93.95	79	23.6
RACE AND HISPANIC ORIGIN			
Average household	118.26	100	100.0
Asian	137.19	116	4.1
Black	26.96	23	2.7
Hispanic	57.78	49	5.8
Non-Hispanic white and other	141.74	120	91.5
REGION			
Average household	118.26	100	100.0
Northeast	135.78	115	21.4
Midwest	82.37	70	15.9
South	101.13	86	30.7
West	167.27	141	32.0
EDUCATION			
Average household	118.26	100	100.0
Less than high school graduate	30.17	26	3.9
High school graduate	49.00	41	10.5
Some college	75.55	64	13.9
Associate's degree	90.90	77	6.8
College graduate	265.30	224	64.9
Bachelor's degree	213.17	180	33.8
Master's, professional, doctoral degree	361.07	305	31.1

Note: Market shares may not sum to 100.0 because of rounding and missing categories by household type. "Asian" and "black" include Hispanics and non-Hispanics who identify themselves as being of the respective race alone. "Hispanic" includes people of any race who identify themselves as Hispanic. "Other" includes people who identify themselves as non-Hispanic and as Alaska Native, American Indian, Asian (who are also included in the "Asian" row), Native Hawaiian or other Pacific Islander, as well as non-Hispanics reporting more than one race.
Source: Calculations by New Strategist based on the Bureau of Labor Statistics' 2007 Consumer Expenditure Survey.

Moving, Storage, and Freight Express

Best customers: Householders aged 45 to 54 and 65 to 74
Married couples without children at home
Non-Hispanic whites
Households in the West

Customer trends: Average household spending on moving, storage, and freight is likely to fall in the
next few years because of the collapse of the housing market.

The biggest spenders on moving, storage, and freight express are households that can afford to pay for moving services or that need storage space. Householders aged 65 to 74 do not move much, but when they do many can afford to hire moving services. In addition, older householders have accumulated belongings over the years that may require additional storage space. These factors explain why householders aged 65 to 74 spend 36 percent more than average on moving and storage services. Householders aged 45 to 54 spend 43 percent more than average on this item. Married couples without children at home, most of them empty-nesters, spend 90 percent more than average on this item. Non-Hispanic whites outspend the minorities by a 3:1 margin and control 91 percent of the market. Households in the West spend more than twice the average on moving, storage, and freight express.

Average household spending on moving, storage and freight express grew 29 percent between 2000 and 2007, after adjusting for inflation. Average household spending on this item is likely to fall during the next few years because of the collapse of the housing market.

Table 11.8 Moving, storage, and freight express

Total household spending $6,034,987,620.00
Average household spends   50.22

	AVERAGE HOUSEHOLD SPENDING	BEST CUSTOMERS (index)	BIGGEST CUSTOMERS (market share)
AGE OF HOUSEHOLDER			
Average household	**$50.22**	**100**	**100.0%**
Under age 25	23.61	47	3.2
Aged 25 to 34	41.87	83	14.2
Aged 35 to 44	49.69	99	19.3
Aged 45 to 54	71.61	143	30.0
Aged 55 to 64	43.67	87	14.1
Aged 65 to 74	68.16	136	13.6
Aged 75 or older	30.20	60	5.7

	AVERAGE HOUSEHOLD SPENDING	BEST CUSTOMERS (index)	BIGGEST CUSTOMERS (market share)
HOUSEHOLD INCOME			
Average household	**$50.22**	**100**	**100.0%**
Under $20,000	19.47	39	8.0
$20,000 to $39,999	31.65	63	14.6
$40,000 to $49,999	38.63	77	7.6
$50,000 to $69,999	35.46	71	10.8
$70,000 to $79,999	38.74	77	4.5
$80,000 to $99,999	57.40	114	9.3
$100,000 or more	132.61	264	45.2
HOUSEHOLD TYPE			
Average household	**50.22**	**100**	**100.0**
Married couples	67.08	134	67.5
Married couples, no children	95.66	190	41.1
Married couples, with children	45.33	90	22.5
Oldest child under age 6	24.33	48	2.4
Oldest child aged 6 to 17	57.93	115	14.7
Oldest child aged 18 or older	37.52	75	5.5
Single parent with child under age 18	41.12	82	4.9
Single person	30.67	61	18.2
RACE AND HISPANIC ORIGIN			
Average household	**50.22**	**100**	**100.0**
Asian	13.61	27	1.0
Black	16.89	34	4.0
Hispanic	20.87	42	4.9
Non-Hispanic white and other	59.90	119	91.1
REGION			
Average household	**50.22**	**100**	**100.0**
Northeast	27.53	55	10.2
Midwest	34.83	69	15.8
South	38.11	76	27.2
West	103.67	206	46.7
EDUCATION			
Average household	**50.22**	**100**	**100.0**
Less than high school graduate	13.28	26	4.0
High school graduate	22.10	44	11.1
Some college	60.69	121	26.3
Associate's degree	41.55	83	7.4
College graduate	88.86	177	51.2
Bachelor's degree	98.23	196	36.7
Master's, professional, doctoral degree	71.64	143	14.6

Note: Market shares may not sum to 100.0 because of rounding and missing categories by household type. "Asian" and "black" include Hispanics and non-Hispanics who identify themselves as being of the respective race alone. "Hispanic" includes people of any race who identify themselves as Hispanic. "Other" includes people who identify themselves as non-Hispanic and as Alaska Native, American Indian, Asian (who are also included in the "Asian" row), Native Hawaiian or other Pacific Islander, as well as non-Hispanics reporting more than one race.
Source: Calculations by New Strategist based on the Bureau of Labor Statistics' 2007 Consumer Expenditure Survey.

Repair of Computer Systems for Nonbusiness Use

Best customers:	**Householders aged 45 to 54 and 65 to 74** **Married couples with adult children at home** **People living alone**
Customer trends:	**Average household spending on repair of computer systems for nonbusiness use will continue to increase in the years ahead as aging boomers turn to professionals for help.**

The best customers of repair of computer systems for nonbusiness use are older householders. This explains why householders aged 65 to 74 spend 29 percent more than average on computer repair. Married couples with adult children at home, who have the largest families with the most computers, spend two-thirds more than average on this item. People living alone spend 26 percent more than average on repair of computer systems for nonbusiness use and account for a sizeable 38 percent of the market.

Average household spending on repair of computer systems for nonbusiness use more than doubled between 2000 and 2007, after adjusting for inflation. One reason for the growth was the near universal adoption of computers by Americans of all ages during those years. Average household spending on computer repair will continue to increase in the years ahead as aging boomers turn to professionals for help.

Table 11.9 Repair of computer systems for nonbusiness use

Total household spending	$839,995,290.00
Average household spends	6.99

	AVERAGE HOUSEHOLD SPENDING	BEST CUSTOMERS (index)	BIGGEST CUSTOMERS (market share)
AGE OF HOUSEHOLDER			
Average household	**$6.99**	**100**	**100.0%**
Under age 25	7.92	113	7.7
Aged 25 to 34	4.27	61	10.4
Aged 35 to 44	7.64	109	21.3
Aged 45 to 54	9.59	137	28.8
Aged 55 to 64	4.23	61	9.8
Aged 65 to 74	9.00	129	12.9
Aged 75 or older	6.73	96	9.1

	AVERAGE HOUSEHOLD SPENDING	BEST CUSTOMERS (index)	BIGGEST CUSTOMERS (market share)
HOUSEHOLD INCOME			
Average household	**$6.99**	**100**	**100.0%**
Under $20,000	6.35	91	18.7
$20,000 to $39,999	4.86	70	16.2
$40,000 to $49,999	10.67	153	15.0
$50,000 to $69,999	5.32	76	11.6
$70,000 to $79,999	8.28	118	6.9
$80,000 to $99,999	4.89	70	5.7
$100,000 or more	12.25	175	30.0
HOUSEHOLD TYPE			
Average household	**6.99**	**100**	**100.0**
Married couples	7.33	105	53.0
Married couples, no children	6.24	89	19.3
Married couples, with children	8.89	127	31.7
Oldest child under age 6	6.98	100	4.9
Oldest child aged 6 to 17	8.14	116	14.8
Oldest child aged 18 or older	11.44	164	12.1
Single parent with child under age 18	2.22	32	1.9
Single person	8.84	126	37.6
RACE AND HISPANIC ORIGIN			
Average household	**6.99**	**100**	**100.0**
Asian	2.83	40	1.4
Black	3.19	46	5.5
Hispanic	4.22	60	7.1
Non-Hispanic white and other	8.00	114	87.4
REGION			
Average household	**6.99**	**100**	**100.0**
Northeast	6.26	90	16.7
Midwest	6.09	87	19.9
South	6.98	100	35.9
West	8.52	122	27.6
EDUCATION			
Average household	**6.99**	**100**	**100.0**
Less than high school graduate	1.28	18	2.8
High school graduate	3.05	44	11.0
Some college	7.08	101	22.1
Associate's degree	9.33	133	11.9
College graduate	12.63	181	52.3
Bachelor's degree	11.30	162	30.3
Master's, professional, doctoral degree	15.07	216	22.0

Note: Market shares may not sum to 100.0 because of rounding and missing categories by household type. "Asian" and "black" include Hispanics and non-Hispanics who identify themselves as being of the respective race alone. "Hispanic" includes people of any race who identify themselves as Hispanic. "Other" includes people who identify themselves as non-Hispanic and as Alaska Native, American Indian, Asian (who are also included in the "Asian" row), Native Hawaiian or other Pacific Islander, as well as non-Hispanics reporting more than one race.
Source: Calculations by New Strategist based on the Bureau of Labor Statistics' 2007 Consumer Expenditure Survey.

Security System Service Fee

Best customers:
Householders aged 35 or older
Married couples without children at home
Married couples with children under age 18
Asians and blacks
Households in the South

Customer trends:
Average household spending on home security system service fees should rise along with the aging of the population.

The best customers of home security system service fees are middle-aged or older married couples. Householders aged 35 or older spend 8 to 34 percent more than average on this item, with a lone dip in the 65-to-74 age group. Married couples without children at home, most of them empty-nesters, spend 41 percent more than average on security system service fees, while those with children under age 18 spend 33 to 56 percent. Black householders spend 17 percent more than average on this item, while Asians spend 39 percent more. Households in the South spend 27 percent more than average on security system service fees.

Average household spending on home security system service fees fell 12 percent between 2000 and 2007, after adjusting for inflation. Average household spending on home security system service fees should rise along with the aging of the population.

Table 11.10 Security system service fee

	Total household spending	$2,390,201,190.00
	Average household spends	19.89

AGE OF HOUSEHOLDER	AVERAGE HOUSEHOLD SPENDING	BEST CUSTOMERS (index)	BIGGEST CUSTOMERS (market share)
Average household	**$19.89**	**100**	**100.0%**
Under age 25	2.35	12	0.8
Aged 25 to 34	12.95	65	11.1
Aged 35 to 44	23.97	121	23.5
Aged 45 to 54	21.45	108	22.7
Aged 55 to 64	26.65	134	21.7
Aged 65 to 74	19.38	97	9.7
Aged 75 or older	22.02	111	10.5

	AVERAGE HOUSEHOLD SPENDING	BEST CUSTOMERS (index)	BIGGEST CUSTOMERS (market share)
HOUSEHOLD INCOME			
Average household	$19.89	100	100.0%
Under $20,000	5.69	29	5.9
$20,000 to $39,999	8.87	45	10.4
$40,000 to $49,999	15.64	79	7.7
$50,000 to $69,999	15.48	78	11.9
$70,000 to $79,999	21.46	108	6.2
$80,000 to $99,999	29.24	147	12.0
$100,000 or more	53.26	268	45.9
HOUSEHOLD TYPE			
Average household	19.89	100	100.0
Married couples	25.80	130	65.6
Married couples, no children	28.09	141	30.5
Married couples, with children	23.87	120	29.9
Oldest child under age 6	31.00	156	7.6
Oldest child aged 6 to 17	26.42	133	16.9
Oldest child aged 18 or older	14.73	74	5.5
Single parent with child under age 18	12.23	61	3.7
Single person	13.04	66	19.5
RACE AND HISPANIC ORIGIN			
Average household	19.89	100	100.0
Asian	27.60	139	4.9
Black	23.30	117	14.1
Hispanic	12.89	65	7.6
Non-Hispanic white and other	20.45	103	78.5
REGION			
Average household	19.89	100	100.0
Northeast	17.84	90	16.7
Midwest	12.28	62	14.1
South	25.19	127	45.5
West	20.84	105	23.7
EDUCATION			
Average household	19.89	100	100.0
Less than high school graduate	5.73	29	4.4
High school graduate	11.96	60	15.2
Some college	15.68	79	17.2
Associate's degree	20.45	103	9.1
College graduate	37.20	187	54.1
Bachelor's degree	35.63	179	33.6
Master's, professional, doctoral degree	40.09	202	20.6

Note: Market shares may not sum to 100.0 because of rounding and missing categories by household type. "Asian" and "black" include Hispanics and non-Hispanics who identify themselves as being of the respective race alone. "Hispanic" includes people of any race who identify themselves as Hispanic. "Other" includes people who identify themselves as non-Hispanic and as Alaska Native, American Indian, Asian (who are also included in the "Asian" row), Native Hawaiian or other Pacific Islander, as well as non-Hispanics reporting more than one race.
Source: Calculations by New Strategist based on the Bureau of Labor Statistics' 2007 Consumer Expenditure Survey.

Termite and Pest Control Products and Services

Best customers: **Householders aged 55 or older**
                               Married couples
                               Households in the South

Customer trends: **Average household spending on termite and pest control should continue to increase along with the Sunbelt population.**

The best customers of termite and pest control products and services are older married couples in the South, where insect problems are abundant because of the warm climate. Southern households spend 51 percent more than average on this item and control 54 percent of the market. Householders aged 55 or older spend 21 to 53 percent more than average on termite and pest control products and services. Married couples spend 50 percent more than average on this item.

Average household spending on termite and pest control rose by a substantial 53 percent between 2000 and 2007, after adjusting for inflation. Behind the increase was the growing population of the South, where these services are often necessary. Spending on termite and pest control should continue to rise along with the Sunbelt population.

Table 11.11 Termite and pest control products and services

Total household spending		$2,221,961,790.00	
Average household spends		18.49	

	AVERAGE HOUSEHOLD SPENDING	BEST CUSTOMERS (index)	BIGGEST CUSTOMERS (market share)
AGE OF HOUSEHOLDER			
Average household	**$18.49**	**100**	**100.0%**
Under age 25	0.96	5	0.4
Aged 25 to 34	11.92	64	11.0
Aged 35 to 44	16.25	88	17.1
Aged 45 to 54	20.04	108	22.8
Aged 55 to 64	22.29	121	19.5
Aged 65 to 74	27.29	148	14.8
Aged 75 or older	28.24	153	14.5

	AVERAGE HOUSEHOLD SPENDING	BEST CUSTOMERS (index)	BIGGEST CUSTOMERS (market share)
HOUSEHOLD INCOME			
Average household	**$18.49**	**100**	**100.0%**
Under $20,000	5.79	31	6.4
$20,000 to $39,999	8.99	49	11.3
$40,000 to $49,999	12.53	68	6.7
$50,000 to $69,999	15.44	84	12.8
$70,000 to $79,999	28.08	152	8.8
$80,000 to $99,999	29.09	157	12.8
$100,000 or more	44.50	241	41.2
HOUSEHOLD TYPE			
Average household	**18.49**	**100**	**100.0**
Married couples	27.71	150	75.8
Married couples, no children	34.48	186	40.2
Married couples, with children	23.90	129	32.3
Oldest child under age 6	22.95	124	6.1
Oldest child aged 6 to 17	25.11	136	17.3
Oldest child aged 18 or older	22.47	122	9.0
Single parent with child under age 18	9.04	49	2.9
Single person	9.23	50	14.8
RACE AND HISPANIC ORIGIN			
Average household	**18.49**	**100**	**100.0**
Asian	14.06	76	2.7
Black	7.46	40	4.8
Hispanic	8.84	48	5.6
Non-Hispanic white and other	21.68	117	89.5
REGION			
Average household	**18.49**	**100**	**100.0**
Northeast	12.64	68	12.7
Midwest	6.82	37	8.4
South	27.83	151	54.0
West	20.26	110	24.8
EDUCATION			
Average household	**18.49**	**100**	**100.0**
Less than high school graduate	5.70	31	4.7
High school graduate	12.18	66	16.6
Some college	16.85	91	19.8
Associate's degree	22.36	121	10.7
College graduate	30.73	166	48.1
Bachelor's degree	24.13	131	24.5
Master's, professional, doctoral degree	42.88	232	23.7

Note: Market shares may not sum to 100.0 because of rounding and missing categories by household type. "Asian" and "black" include Hispanics and non-Hispanics who identify themselves as being of the respective race alone. "Hispanic" includes people of any race who identify themselves as Hispanic. "Other" includes people who identify themselves as non-Hispanic and as Alaska Native, American Indian, Asian (who are also included in the "Asian" row), Native Hawaiian or other Pacific Islander, as well as non-Hispanics reporting more than one race.
Source: Calculations by New Strategist based on the Bureau of Labor Statistics' 2007 Consumer Expenditure Survey.

Water Softening Services

Best customers:	Householders aged 45 to 74
	Married couples without children at home
	Blacks
	Households in the Midwest

Customer trends: Average household spending on water softening services should continue to increase as the large baby-boom generation fills the best-customer age groups, but the economic downturn may limit the gain.

The biggest spenders on water softening services are older married couples. Householders ranging in age from 45 to 74 spend 22 to 28 percent more than the average household on this item. Married couples without children at home, most of them older empty-nesters, spend 29 percent more. Black households spend 36 percent more than average on water softening services, while households in the Midwest spend 63 percent above average.

Average household spending on water softening services rose 20 percent between 2000 and 2007, after adjusting for inflation. Behind the gain was the aging of the baby-boom generation into the best-customer age groups. Average household spending on water softening services should continue to increase as boomers continue to fill the best-customer age groups, but the economic downturn may limit the gain.

Table 11.12 Water softening service

Total household spending $539,567,790.00
Average household spends 4.49

	AVERAGE HOUSEHOLD SPENDING	BEST CUSTOMERS (index)	BIGGEST CUSTOMERS (market share)
AGE OF HOUSEHOLDER			
Average household	**$4.49**	**100**	**100.0%**
Under age 25	3.26	73	4.9
Aged 25 to 34	2.49	55	9.5
Aged 35 to 44	4.29	96	18.6
Aged 45 to 54	5.50	122	25.7
Aged 55 to 64	5.80	129	20.9
Aged 65 to 74	5.75	128	12.8
Aged 75 or older	3.53	79	7.5

	AVERAGE HOUSEHOLD SPENDING	BEST CUSTOMERS (index)	BIGGEST CUSTOMERS (market share)
HOUSEHOLD INCOME			
Average household	$4.49	100	100.0%
Under $20,000	2.91	65	13.3
$20,000 to $39,999	3.42	76	17.7
$40,000 to $49,999	3.74	83	8.2
$50,000 to $69,999	5.87	131	20.0
$70,000 to $79,999	4.92	110	6.3
$80,000 to $99,999	4.84	108	8.8
$100,000 or more	6.70	149	25.6
HOUSEHOLD TYPE			
Average household	4.49	100	100.0
Married couples	5.11	114	57.5
Married couples, no children	5.79	129	27.8
Married couples, with children	4.29	96	23.8
Oldest child under age 6	1.92	43	2.1
Oldest child aged 6 to 17	4.91	109	13.9
Oldest child aged 18 or older	4.80	107	7.9
Single parent with child under age 18	4.40	98	5.8
Single person	2.72	61	18.0
RACE AND HISPANIC ORIGIN			
Average household	4.49	100	100.0
Asian	3.68	82	2.9
Black	6.10	136	16.3
Hispanic	3.06	68	8.0
Non-Hispanic white and other	4.44	99	75.5
REGION			
Average household	4.49	100	100.0
Northeast	3.02	67	12.5
Midwest	7.34	163	37.4
South	3.66	82	29.3
West	4.12	92	20.8
EDUCATION			
Average household	4.49	100	100.0
Less than high school graduate	3.89	87	13.1
High school graduate	5.59	124	31.4
Some college	4.46	99	21.6
Associate's degree	3.62	81	7.2
College graduate	4.11	92	26.5
Bachelor's degree	3.71	83	15.5
Master's, professional, doctoral degree	4.86	108	11.0

Note: Market shares may not sum to 100.0 because of rounding and missing categories by household type. "Asian" and "black" include Hispanics and non-Hispanics who identify themselves as being of the respective race alone. "Hispanic" includes people of any race who identify themselves as Hispanic. "Other" includes people who identify themselves as non-Hispanic and as Alaska Native, American Indian, Asian (who are also included in the "Asian" row), Native Hawaiian or other Pacific Islander, as well as non-Hispanics reporting more than one race.
Source: Calculations by New Strategist based on the Bureau of Labor Statistics' 2007 Consumer Expenditure Survey.

Chapter 12.

Housekeeping Supplies

Household Spending on Housekeeping Supplies, 2007

Housekeeping supplies is a catchall category that includes a variety of products such as laundry detergent, toilet paper, paper towels, vegetable seeds, insecticides, postage, stationery, and giftwrap. In 2007, the average household spent $639 on these items, 10 percent more than in 2000 after adjusting for inflation.

The largest category within housekeeping supplies, laundry and cleaning supplies, accounts for 22 percent of spending in the category. Between 2000 and 2007, average household spending on laundry and cleaning supplies fell 11 percent, after adjusting for inflation. Lawn and garden supplies saw the largest growth in average household spending during these years, a whopping 43 percent increase. Lawn and garden supplies now account for 18 percent of spending on housekeeping supplies. Because the primary customers of lawn and garden supplies are older householders, continued growth in the lawn and garden category is likely. Spending on cleansing and toilet tissue, paper towels, and napkins rose 20 percent between 2000 and 2007, after adjusting for inflation.

Spending on housekeeping supplies

(average spending by households on housekeeping supplies, 2000 to 2007; in 2007 dollars)

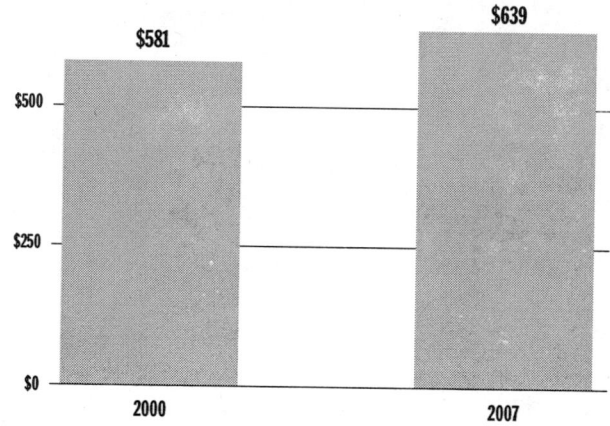

Table 12.1 Housekeeping Supplies Spending, 2000 to 2007

(average annual household spending on housekeeping supplies, and percent distribution of spending by type, 2000 and 2007; percent change, 2000–07; in 2007 dollars)

	2007		2000		
	average household spending	percent distribution	average household spending (in 2007$)	percent distribution	percent change 2000–07
Average household spending on housekeeping supplies	**$638.78**	**100.0%**	**$580.75**	**100.0%**	**10.0%**
Laundry and cleaning supplies	139.99	21.9	$157.45	27.1	−11.1
Lawn and garden supplies	115.03	18.0	$80.64	13.9	42.7
Cleansing and toilet tissue, paper towels, and napkins	98.65	15.4	$82.42	14.2	19.7
Stationery, stationery supplies, giftwrap	75.19	11.8	$76.64	13.2	−1.9
Postage	74.12	11.6	$72.97	12.6	1.6

Note: Numbers do not add to total because not all categories are shown.
Source: Bureau of Labor Statistics, 2000 and 2007 Consumer Expenditure Surveys; calculations by New Strategist

Cleansing and Toilet Tissue, Paper Towels, and Napkins

Best customers: **Householders aged 45 to 74**
Married couples with children at home

Customer trends: **Average household spending on cleansing and toilet tissue, paper towels, and napkins is likely to fall as household size declines with the aging of the baby-boom generation.**

Because everyone buys cleansing and toilet tissue, paper towels, and napkins, there are few differences in spending on this item by demographic characteristic. Householders ranging in age from 45 to 74 spend 8 to 21 percent more than average on this item. Married couples with children at home spend 35 percent more the figure peaking at 66 percent more than average among couples with adult children at home, who have the largest households. Hispanics, who have the largest families, spend 10 percent more than average on cleansing and toilet tissue, paper towels, and napkins.

Average household spending on cleansing and toilet tissue, paper towels, and napkins rose 20 percent between 2000 and 2007, after adjusting for inflation. One factor behind the increase is the rapidly growing Hispanic population. Average household spending on this item may fall in the years ahead as boomers age and average household size resumes its long-term decline.

Table 12.2 Cleansing and toilet tissue, paper towels, and napkins

Total household spending $11,854,869,150.00
Average household spends   98.65

	AVERAGE HOUSEHOLD SPENDING	BEST CUSTOMERS (index)	BIGGEST CUSTOMERS (market share)
AGE OF HOUSEHOLDER			
Average household	**$98.65**	**100**	**100.0%**
Under age 25	55.29	56	3.8
Aged 25 to 34	84.99	86	14.7
Aged 35 to 44	102.75	104	20.3
Aged 45 to 54	118.97	121	25.3
Aged 55 to 64	106.57	108	17.5
Aged 65 to 74	110.18	112	11.2
Aged 75 or older	77.43	78	7.4

	AVERAGE HOUSEHOLD SPENDING	BEST CUSTOMERS (index)	BIGGEST CUSTOMERS (market share)
HOUSEHOLD INCOME			
Average household	$98.65	100	100.0%
Under $20,000	61.81	63	12.9
$20,000 to $39,999	82.97	84	19.5
$40,000 to $49,999	90.87	92	9.1
$50,000 to $69,999	97.47	99	15.1
$70,000 to $79,999	103.46	105	6.1
$80,000 to $99,999	131.62	133	10.9
$100,000 or more	150.62	153	26.2
HOUSEHOLD TYPE			
Average household	98.65	100	100.0
Married couples	124.89	127	64.0
Married couples, no children	113.77	115	24.9
Married couples, with children	132.98	135	33.6
Oldest child under age 6	123.09	125	6.1
Oldest child aged 6 to 17	120.95	123	15.6
Oldest child aged 18 or older	164.05	166	12.3
Single parent with child under age 18	100.29	102	6.0
Single person	55.50	56	16.7
RACE AND HISPANIC ORIGIN			
Average household	98.65	100	100.0
Asian	82.68	84	3.0
Black	91.05	92	11.1
Hispanic	108.99	110	13.0
Non-Hispanic white and other	98.40	100	76.1
REGION			
Average household	98.65	100	100.0
Northeast	98.55	100	18.6
Midwest	91.40	93	21.2
South	104.66	106	38.1
West	96.51	98	22.1
EDUCATION			
Average household	98.65	100	100.0
Less than high school graduate	90.78	92	14.0
High school graduate	93.84	95	24.0
Some college	84.96	86	18.8
Associate's degree	110.29	112	9.9
College graduate	112.97	115	33.1
Bachelor's degree	108.30	110	20.6
Master's, professional, doctoral degree	121.07	123	12.5

Note: Market shares may not sum to 100.0 because of rounding and missing categories by household type. "Asian" and "black" include Hispanics and non-Hispanics who identify themselves as being of the respective race alone. "Hispanic" includes people of any race who identify themselves as Hispanic. "Other" includes people who identify themselves as non-Hispanic and as Alaska Native, American Indian, Asian (who are also included in the "Asian" row), Native Hawaiian or other Pacific Islander, as well as non-Hispanics reporting more than one race.
Source: Calculations by New Strategist based on the Bureau of Labor Statistics' 2007 Consumer Expenditure Survey.

Laundry and Cleaning Supplies

Best customers:
Householders aged 35 to 54
Married couples with school-aged or older children at home
Single parents
Hispanics

Customer trends:
Average household spending on laundry and cleaning supplies could continue to fall as the small generation X enters the best-customer lifestage.

Households with children spend the most on laundry and cleaning supplies. Householders aged 35 to 54, most with children at home, spend 15 to 27 percent more than average on this item. Married couples with school-aged or older children at home spend 41 to 48 percent more than average on laundry and cleaning supplies. Single parents spend 24 percent more. Hispanics, who have the largest families, spend 21 percent more than average on laundry and cleaning supplies.

Average household spending on laundry and cleaning supplies fell by 11 percent between 2000 and 2007, after adjusting for inflation. Behind the decline was the baby-boom generation's exit from the crowded nest lifestage. Average household spending on this item could continue to fall as boomers age and the much smaller generation X enters the best-customer lifestage.

Table 12.3 **Laundry and cleaning supplies**

Total household spending $16,822,738,290.00
Average household spends 139.99

AGE OF HOUSEHOLDER	AVERAGE HOUSEHOLD SPENDING	BEST CUSTOMERS (index)	BIGGEST CUSTOMERS (market share)
Average household	**$139.99**	**100**	**100.0%**
Under age 25	84.08	60	4.1
Aged 25 to 34	129.06	92	15.7
Aged 35 to 44	177.55	127	24.7
Aged 45 to 54	161.00	115	24.2
Aged 55 to 64	133.58	95	15.5
Aged 65 to 74	138.33	99	9.9
Aged 75 or older	90.28	64	6.1

	AVERAGE HOUSEHOLD SPENDING	BEST CUSTOMERS (index)	BIGGEST CUSTOMERS (market share)
HOUSEHOLD INCOME			
Average household	$139.99	100	100.0%
Under $20,000	81.21	58	11.9
$20,000 to $39,999	118.88	85	19.7
$40,000 to $49,999	149.79	107	10.5
$50,000 to $69,999	149.50	107	16.3
$70,000 to $79,999	151.81	108	6.3
$80,000 to $99,999	167.44	120	9.7
$100,000 or more	205.01	146	25.1
HOUSEHOLD TYPE			
Average household	139.99	100	100.0
Married couples	176.59	126	63.8
Married couples, no children	148.75	106	22.9
Married couples, with children	191.47	137	34.1
Oldest child under age 6	153.87	110	5.4
Oldest child aged 6 to 17	197.32	141	17.9
Oldest child aged 18 or older	207.47	148	10.9
Single parent with child under age 18	173.58	124	7.4
Single person	68.87	49	14.6
RACE AND HISPANIC ORIGIN			
Average household	139.99	100	100.0
Asian	103.17	74	2.6
Black	141.54	101	12.1
Hispanic	169.79	121	14.3
Non-Hispanic white and other	135.53	97	73.9
REGION			
Average household	139.99	100	100.0
Northeast	120.75	86	16.1
Midwest	144.78	103	23.6
South	151.87	108	39.0
West	132.20	94	21.4
EDUCATION			
Average household	139.99	100	100.0
Less than high school graduate	127.99	91	13.9
High school graduate	128.21	92	23.1
Some college	148.96	106	23.2
Associate's degree	142.08	101	9.0
College graduate	148.73	106	30.8
Bachelor's degree	145.26	104	19.4
Master's, professional, doctoral degree	154.74	111	11.3

Note: Market shares may not sum to 100.0 because of rounding and missing categories by household type. "Asian" and "black" include Hispanics and non-Hispanics who identify themselves as being of the respective race alone. "Hispanic" includes people of any race who identify themselves as Hispanic. "Other" includes people who identify themselves as non-Hispanic and as Alaska Native, American Indian, Asian (who are also included in the "Asian" row), Native Hawaiian or other Pacific Islander, as well as non-Hispanics reporting more than one race.
Source: Calculations by New Strategist based on the Bureau of Labor Statistics' 2007 Consumer Expenditure Survey.

Lawn and Garden Supplies

Best customers: **Householders aged 55 to 64**
                                                  High-income households
                                                  Married couples without children at home
                                                  Non-Hispanic whites
                                                  Households in the West
                                                  College graduates

Customer trends: **Average household spending on lawn and garden supplies should continue to rise as more boomers enter the empty-nest lifestage.**

The best customers of lawn and garden supplies are older, affluent married couples, most of whom are homeowners with lawns and gardens to tend. Householders aged 55 to 64 spend almost three times the average on lawn and garden supplies, while those with incomes of $100,000 or more spend over three times the average. College graduates, an affluent demographic, spend over twice the average on this item. Married couples without children at home (most of them older) spend over two-and-one-half times the average on lawn and garden supplies. Non-Hispanic whites account for 94 percent of the market for lawn and garden supplies. Households in the West spend more than twice the average on lawn and garden supplies.

Average household spending on lawn and garden supplies increased by 43 percent between 2000 and 2007, after adjusting for inflation. Behind the rise was the entry of the baby-boom generation into the empty-nest lifestage. As more boomers become empty-nesters over the next few years, spending on lawn and garden supplies should continue to rise.

Table 12.4 Lawn and garden supplies

Total household spending $13,823,270,130.00
Average household spends   115.03

	AVERAGE HOUSEHOLD SPENDING	BEST CUSTOMERS (index)	BIGGEST CUSTOMERS (market share)
AGE OF HOUSEHOLDER			
Average household	**$115.03**	**100**	**100.0%**
Under age 25	18.66	16	1.1
Aged 25 to 34	61.79	54	9.2
Aged 35 to 44	70.73	61	12.0
Aged 45 to 54	98.56	86	18.0
Aged 55 to 64	323.36	281	45.5
Aged 65 to 74	99.62	87	8.7
Aged 75 or older	77.69	68	6.4

	AVERAGE HOUSEHOLD SPENDING	BEST CUSTOMERS (index)	BIGGEST CUSTOMERS (market share)
HOUSEHOLD INCOME			
Average household	$115.03	100	100.0%
Under $20,000	14.90	13	2.7
$20,000 to $39,999	44.81	39	9.1
$40,000 to $49,999	101.34	88	8.7
$50,000 to $69,999	90.76	79	12.1
$70,000 to $79,999	120.98	105	6.1
$80,000 to $99,999	96.11	84	6.8
$100,000 or more	379.60	330	56.5
HOUSEHOLD TYPE			
Average household	115.03	100	100.0
Married couples	186.99	163	82.2
Married couples, no children	304.80	265	57.2
Married couples, with children	93.79	82	20.3
Oldest child under age 6	58.94	51	2.5
Oldest child aged 6 to 17	84.39	73	9.3
Oldest child aged 18 or older	137.96	120	8.8
Single parent with child under age 18	27.56	24	1.4
Single person	40.49	35	10.5
RACE AND HISPANIC ORIGIN			
Average household	115.03	100	100.0
Asian	58.64	51	1.8
Black	17.51	15	1.8
Hispanic	33.62	29	3.4
Non-Hispanic white and other	141.72	123	94.0
REGION			
Average household	115.03	100	100.0
Northeast	77.96	68	12.6
Midwest	77.90	68	15.5
South	74.48	65	23.3
West	250.08	217	49.2
EDUCATION			
Average household	115.03	100	100.0
Less than high school graduate	22.11	19	2.9
High school graduate	61.32	53	13.4
Some college	67.33	59	12.7
Associate's degree	69.05	60	5.3
College graduate	252.27	219	63.5
Bachelor's degree	141.74	123	23.1
Master's, professional, doctoral degree	444.20	386	39.4

Note: Market shares may not sum to 100.0 because of rounding and missing categories by household type. "Asian" and "black" include Hispanics and non-Hispanics who identify themselves as being of the respective race alone. "Hispanic" includes people of any race who identify themselves as Hispanic. "Other" includes people who identify themselves as non-Hispanic and as Alaska Native, American Indian, Asian (who are also included in the "Asian" row), Native Hawaiian or other Pacific Islander, as well as non-Hispanics reporting more than one race.
Source: Calculations by New Strategist based on the Bureau of Labor Statistics' 2007 Consumer Expenditure Survey.

Postage

Best customers:

Householders aged 45 to 74
Married couples without children at home
Married couples with adult children at home
Hispanics
Households in the West

Customer trends:

Average household spending on postage will decline as younger, wired Americans replace older, off-line generations.

Older Americans are the biggest spenders on postage. Householders ranging in age from 45 to 74 spend 19 to 44 percent more than average on this item. Married couples without children at home (most of them older) spend 44 percent more than average on postage. Those with adult children at home spend 17 percent more than average. Hispanics spend 53 percent more than average on postage, and households in the West, where many Hispanics reside, spend 38 percent above average on this item.

Average household spending on postage rose 2 percent between 2000 and 2007, after adjusting for inflation. Postage spending would have fallen, but was stabilized by repeated hikes in the cost of postage as well as the popularity of the U.S. Postal Service's priority mail options. Average household spending on postage is likely to decline sharply in the years ahead as wired generations move into the older age groups.

Table 12.5 Postage

Total household spending $8,907,074,520.00
Average household spends   74.12

	AVERAGE HOUSEHOLD SPENDING	BEST CUSTOMERS (index)	BIGGEST CUSTOMERS (market share)
AGE OF HOUSEHOLDER			
Average household	**$74.12**	**100**	**100.0%**
Under age 25	26.52	36	2.4
Aged 25 to 34	53.28	72	12.3
Aged 35 to 44	39.07	53	10.3
Aged 45 to 54	106.31	143	30.1
Aged 55 to 64	106.58	144	23.3
Aged 65 to 74	88.49	119	11.9
Aged 75 or older	80.70	109	10.3

	AVERAGE HOUSEHOLD SPENDING	BEST CUSTOMERS (index)	BIGGEST CUSTOMERS (market share)
HOUSEHOLD INCOME			
Average household	**$74.12**	**100**	**100.0%**
Under $20,000	41.18	56	11.4
$20,000 to $39,999	76.50	103	24.0
$40,000 to $49,999	51.45	69	6.8
$50,000 to $69,999	64.97	88	13.4
$70,000 to $79,999	68.52	92	5.4
$80,000 to $99,999	94.51	128	10.4
$100,000 or more	124.78	168	28.8
HOUSEHOLD TYPE			
Average household	**74.12**	**100**	**100.0**
Married couples	84.67	114	57.7
Married couples, no children	106.68	144	31.0
Married couples, with children	68.01	92	22.9
Oldest child under age 6	52.90	71	3.5
Oldest child aged 6 to 17	64.14	87	11.0
Oldest child aged 18 or older	86.78	117	8.6
Single parent with child under age 18	34.93	47	2.8
Single person	48.52	65	19.5
RACE AND HISPANIC ORIGIN			
Average household	**74.12**	**100**	**100.0**
Asian	86.66	117	4.1
Black	32.90	44	5.3
Hispanic	113.56	153	18.1
Non-Hispanic white and other	74.80	101	77.0
REGION			
Average household	**74.12**	**100**	**100.0**
Northeast	76.79	104	19.3
Midwest	64.22	87	19.8
South	61.50	83	29.8
West	102.40	138	31.2
EDUCATION			
Average household	**74.12**	**100**	**100.0**
Less than high school graduate	81.93	111	16.8
High school graduate	50.98	69	17.3
Some college	56.25	76	16.5
Associate's degree	64.63	87	7.7
College graduate	106.24	143	41.5
Bachelor's degree	99.14	134	25.1
Master's, professional, doctoral degree	118.58	160	16.3

Note: Market shares may not sum to 100.0 because of rounding and missing categories by household type. "Asian" and "black" include Hispanics and non-Hispanics who identify themselves as being of the respective race alone. "Hispanic" includes people of any race who identify themselves as Hispanic. "Other" includes people who identify themselves as non-Hispanic and as Alaska Native, American Indian, Asian (who are also included in the "Asian" row), Native Hawaiian or other Pacific Islander, as well as non-Hispanics reporting more than one race.
Source: Calculations by New Strategist based on the Bureau of Labor Statistics' 2007 Consumer Expenditure Survey.

Stationery, Stationery Supplies, and Giftwrap

Best customers: **Householders aged 35 to 74**
Married couples

Customer trends: **Average household spending on stationery and giftwrap will continue to decline**
in the years ahead as the small generation X fills one of the best-customer lifestages
and the economic downturn slashes discretionary spending.

The biggest spenders on the discretionary category of stationery, stationery supplies, and giftwrap are middle-aged and older married couples. These households are the best customers of giftwrap because of their extended families and large network of friends. Householders aged 35 to 74 spend 7 to 20 percent more than average on this item and control three-quarters of the market. Married couples spend 36 percent more than average on this item, the figure peaking at 65 percent above average among couples with school-aged children.

Average household spending on stationery, stationery supplies, and giftwrap fell 2 percent between 2000 and 2007, after adjusting for inflation. Average household spending on stationery and giftwrap will continue to decline in the years ahead as the small generation X fills one of the best-customer lifestages and the economic downturn slashes discretionary spending.

Table 12.6 Stationery, stationery supplies, giftwrap

Total household spending $9,035,657,490.00
Average household spends   75.19

	AVERAGE HOUSEHOLD SPENDING	BEST CUSTOMERS (index)	BIGGEST CUSTOMERS (market share)
AGE OF HOUSEHOLDER			
Average household	**$75.19**	**100**	**100.0%**
Under age 25	33.46	45	3.0
Aged 25 to 34	73.28	97	16.6
Aged 35 to 44	82.65	110	21.4
Aged 45 to 54	90.01	120	25.1
Aged 55 to 64	80.81	107	17.4
Aged 65 to 74	84.92	113	11.3
Aged 75 or older	41.99	56	5.3

	AVERAGE HOUSEHOLD SPENDING	BEST CUSTOMERS (index)	BIGGEST CUSTOMERS (market share)
HOUSEHOLD INCOME			
Average household	$75.19	100	100.0%
Under $20,000	28.18	37	7.7
$20,000 to $39,999	48.99	65	15.1
$40,000 to $49,999	50.26	67	6.6
$50,000 to $69,999	74.22	99	15.1
$70,000 to $79,999	122.73	163	9.4
$80,000 to $99,999	125.48	167	13.6
$100,000 or more	140.92	187	32.1
HOUSEHOLD TYPE			
Average household	75.19	100	100.0
Married couples	102.40	136	68.8
Married couples, no children	100.10	133	28.7
Married couples, with children	108.93	145	36.1
Oldest child under age 6	92.99	124	6.0
Oldest child aged 6 to 17	124.29	165	21.0
Oldest child aged 18 or older	90.22	120	8.8
Single parent with child under age 18	54.23	72	4.3
Single person	40.52	54	16.0
RACE AND HISPANIC ORIGIN			
Average household	75.19	100	100.0
Asian	65.98	88	3.1
Black	24.59	33	3.9
Hispanic	42.51	57	6.7
Non-Hispanic white and other	87.57	116	88.9
REGION			
Average household	75.19	100	100.0
Northeast	72.60	97	18.0
Midwest	89.27	119	27.1
South	68.45	91	32.7
West	73.70	98	22.2
EDUCATION			
Average household	75.19	100	100.0
Less than high school graduate	27.21	36	5.5
High school graduate	52.25	69	17.5
Some college	77.46	103	22.4
Associate's degree	83.67	111	9.9
College graduate	113.26	151	43.6
Bachelor's degree	104.69	139	26.1
Master's, professional, doctoral degree	128.14	170	17.4

Note: Market shares may not sum to 100.0 because of rounding and missing categories by household type. "Asian" and "black" include Hispanics and non-Hispanics who identify themselves as being of the respective race alone. "Hispanic" includes people of any race who identify themselves as Hispanic. "Other" includes people who identify themselves as non-Hispanic and as Alaska Native, American Indian, Asian (who are also included in the "Asian" row), Native Hawaiian or other Pacific Islander, as well as non-Hispanics reporting more than one race.
Source: Calculations by New Strategist based on the Bureau of Labor Statistics' 2007 Consumer Expenditure Survey.

Chapter 13.

Personal Care

Household Spending on Personal Care Products and Services, 2007

The average household spent $588 in 2007 on personal care products and services. This category includes everything from haircuts, facials, and manicures to cosmetics, shampoo, and toothpaste. Spending on personal care products and services fell 13 percent between 2000 and 2007, after adjusting for inflation.

Personal care services (haircuts, manicures, etc.) account for the largest share of spending in the personal care category. Forty-eight percent of personal care spending was devoted to services in 2007. But spending on services fell by a substantial 24 percent between 2000 and 2007, after adjusting for inflation. Other personal care items that experienced spending decreases during those years were deodorants, feminine hygiene, and miscellaneous products (down 15 percent), oral hygiene products (down 11 percent), and shaving products (down 6 percent). The only personal care category to see a spending increase was cosmetics, perfume, and bath products, average household spending on which grew by a modest 5 percent between 2000 and 2007, after adjusting for inflation.

Behind the decline in spending on personal care services was price discounting, with consumers able to buy more for less. Because older householders are among the biggest spenders on personal care products and services, average household spending on these items should rise along with the aging of the population.

Spending on personal care products and services

(average spending by households on personal care products and services, 2000 and 2007; in 2007 dollars)

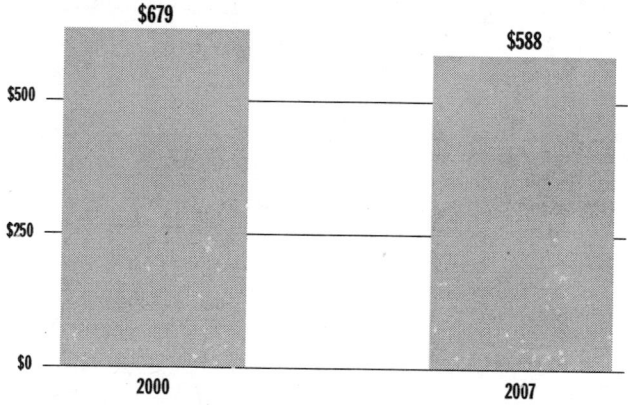

Table 13.1 Personal Care Spending, 2000 to 2007

(average annual household spending on personal care products and services, and percent distribution of spending by type, 2000 and 2007; percent change in spending, 2000–07; in 2007 dollars; ranked by amount spent)

	2007		2000		
	average household spending	percent distribution	average household spending (in 2007$)	percent distribution	percent change 2000–07
Average household spending on personal care products, services	**$587.68**	**100.0%**	**$678.64**	**100.0%**	**–13.4%**
Personal care services	282.91	48.1	370.02	54.5	–23.5
Cosmetics, perfume, bath products	152.03	25.9	144.38	21.3	5.3
Hair care products	56.10	9.5	61.96	9.1	–9.5
Deodorants, feminine hygiene, miscellaneous products	30.00	5.1	35.17	5.2	–14.7
Oral hygiene products	27.64	4.7	31.04	4.6	–11.0
Shaving products	14.94	2.5	15.88	2.3	–5.9

Note: Numbers do not add to total because not all categories are shown.
Source: Bureau of Labor Statistics, 2000 and 2007 Consumer Expenditure Surveys; calculations by New Strategist

Cosmetics, Perfume, and Bath Products

Best customers:

Householders aged 35 to 74
Married couples without children at home
Married couples with adult children at home
Asians

Customer trends:

Average household spending on cosmetics, perfume, and bath products should remain steady now that boomers are solidly in the best-customer age groups.

The best customers of cosmetics, perfume, and bath products are households with the most women. Householders aged 35 to 74—many of the younger ones with teenage or older children at home—spend 7 to 14 percent more than average on this item and control three-quarters of the market. Married couples without children at home spend 31 percent more than average on cosmetics, perfume, and bath products. Those with adult children at home spend 44 percent more than average on this item. Asian households spend 45 percent more than average.

Average household spending on cosmetics, perfume, and bath products rose 5 percent between 2000 and 2007, after adjusting for inflation. One factor behind the increase was the expansion of the teenage population thanks to the large millennial generation. Average household spending on cosmetics, perfume, and bath products should remain steady as aging boomers seek to look their best.

Table 13.2 Cosmetics, perfume, and bath products

Total household spending $18,269,597,130.00
Average household spends 152.03

AGE OF HOUSEHOLDER	AVERAGE HOUSEHOLD SPENDING	BEST CUSTOMERS (index)	BIGGEST CUSTOMERS (market share)
Average household	**$152.03**	**100**	**100.0%**
Under age 25	86.05	57	3.8
Aged 25 to 34	142.14	93	15.9
Aged 35 to 44	163.01	107	20.9
Aged 45 to 54	172.99	114	23.9
Aged 55 to 64	172.84	114	18.4
Aged 65 to 74	168.17	111	11.1
Aged 75 or older	98.23	65	6.1

	AVERAGE HOUSEHOLD SPENDING	BEST CUSTOMERS (index)	BIGGEST CUSTOMERS (market share)
HOUSEHOLD INCOME			
Average household	$152.03	100	100.0%
Under $20,000	55.20	36	7.5
$20,000 to $39,999	96.33	63	14.7
$40,000 to $49,999	134.99	89	8.7
$50,000 to $69,999	142.16	94	14.3
$70,000 to $79,999	200.00	132	7.6
$80,000 to $99,999	237.35	156	12.7
$100,000 or more	303.42	200	34.2
HOUSEHOLD TYPE			
Average household	152.03	100	100.0
Married couples	190.18	125	63.2
Married couples, no children	199.71	131	28.3
Married couples, with children	186.72	123	30.6
Oldest child under age 6	165.57	109	5.3
Oldest child aged 6 to 17	178.47	117	14.9
Oldest child aged 18 or older	218.56	144	10.6
Single parent with child under age 18	127.54	84	5.0
Single person	87.38	57	17.1
RACE AND HISPANIC ORIGIN			
Average household	152.03	100	100.0
Asian	221.19	145	5.1
Black	94.79	62	7.5
Hispanic	140.28	92	10.9
Non-Hispanic white and other	163.04	107	81.9
REGION			
Average household	152.03	100	100.0
Northeast	152.59	100	18.7
Midwest	144.68	95	21.7
South	143.51	94	33.9
West	172.86	114	25.7
EDUCATION			
Average household	152.03	100	100.0
Less than high school graduate	68.27	45	6.8
High school graduate	115.26	76	19.1
Some college	155.30	102	22.2
Associate's degree	166.87	110	9.8
College graduate	216.13	142	41.1
Bachelor's degree	189.88	125	23.4
Master's, professional, doctoral degree	261.73	172	17.6

Note: Market shares may not sum to 100.0 because of rounding and missing categories by household type. "Asian" and "black" include Hispanics and non-Hispanics who identify themselves as being of the respective race alone. "Hispanic" includes people of any race who identify themselves as Hispanic. "Other" includes people who identify themselves as non-Hispanic and as Alaska Native, American Indian, Asian (who are also included in the "Asian" row), Native Hawaiian or other Pacific Islander, as well as non-Hispanics reporting more than one race.
Source: Calculations by New Strategist based on the Bureau of Labor Statistics' 2007 Consumer Expenditure Survey.

Deodorants, Feminine Hygiene, and Miscellaneous Personal Care Products

Best customers:

Householders aged 35 to 54
Married couples with children at home
Single parents

Customer trends:

Average household spending on deodorants, feminine hygiene, and miscellaneous personal care products may decline as the small generation X enters the best-customer age group.

The best customers of deodorants, feminine hygiene, and miscellaneous personal care products are households with the most women of childbearing age. Married couples with children at home spend 40 percent more than average on this item, the figure peaking among those with adult children at home at 71 percent above average. Householders aged 35 to 54, many with teenage girls at home, spend 14 to 21 percent more than average on deodorants, feminine hygiene, and miscellaneous products. Single parents, most of them women, spend 7 percent more than average on this item.

Average household spending on deodorants, feminine hygiene, and miscellaneous personal care products declined 15 percent between 2000 and 2007, after adjusting for inflation. Behind the decline was price discounting, allowing consumers to buy more for less. Average household spending on this item may continue to fall as boomers age and the much smaller generation X enters the best-customer age group.

Table 13.3 **Deodorants, feminine hygiene, and miscellaneous personal care products**

Total household spending $3,605,130,000.00
Average household spends 30.00

AGE OF HOUSEHOLDER	AVERAGE HOUSEHOLD SPENDING	BEST CUSTOMERS (index)	BIGGEST CUSTOMERS (market share)
Average household	$30.00	100	100.0%
Under age 25	18.47	62	4.2
Aged 25 to 34	25.52	85	14.5
Aged 35 to 44	36.20	121	23.5
Aged 45 to 54	34.32	114	24.0
Aged 55 to 64	28.93	96	15.6
Aged 65 to 74	24.29	81	8.1
Aged 75 or older	32.56	109	10.3

	AVERAGE HOUSEHOLD SPENDING	BEST CUSTOMERS (index)	BIGGEST CUSTOMERS (market share)
HOUSEHOLD INCOME			
Average household	$30.00	100	100.0%
Under $20,000	17.30	58	11.9
$20,000 to $39,999	21.35	71	16.5
$40,000 to $49,999	28.59	95	9.4
$50,000 to $69,999	29.95	100	15.3
$70,000 to $79,999	31.76	106	6.1
$80,000 to $99,999	41.45	138	11.2
$100,000 or more	51.28	171	29.3
HOUSEHOLD TYPE			
Average household	30.00	100	100.0
Married couples	39.03	130	65.8
Married couples, no children	32.59	109	23.4
Married couples, with children	42.05	140	35.0
Oldest child under age 6	36.96	123	6.0
Oldest child aged 6 to 17	39.33	131	16.7
Oldest child aged 18 or older	51.16	171	12.6
Single parent with child under age 18	32.10	107	6.4
Single person	15.46	52	15.3
RACE AND HISPANIC ORIGIN			
Average household	30.00	100	100.0
Asian	23.56	79	2.8
Black	24.62	82	9.8
Hispanic	29.68	99	11.7
Non-Hispanic white and other	30.85	103	78.5
REGION			
Average household	30.00	100	100.0
Northeast	24.12	80	15.0
Midwest	26.04	87	19.8
South	34.31	114	41.1
West	32.11	107	24.2
EDUCATION			
Average household	30.00	100	100.0
Less than high school graduate	21.99	73	11.1
High school graduate	27.33	91	23.0
Some college	24.85	83	18.0
Associate's degree	36.97	123	11.0
College graduate	37.72	126	36.4
Bachelor's degree	38.08	127	23.8
Master's, professional, doctoral degree	37.10	124	12.6

Note: Market shares may not sum to 100.0 because of rounding and missing categories by household type. "Asian" and "black" include Hispanics and non-Hispanics who identify themselves as being of the respective race alone. "Hispanic" includes people of any race who identify themselves as Hispanic. "Other" includes people who identify themselves as non-Hispanic and as Alaska Native, American Indian, Asian (who are also included in the "Asian" row), Native Hawaiian or other Pacific Islander, as well as non-Hispanics reporting more than one race.
Source: Calculations by New Strategist based on the Bureau of Labor Statistics' 2007 Consumer Expenditure Survey.

Hair Care Products

Best customers:

    Householders aged 35 to 54
    Married couples with children at home
    Single parents
    Hispanics
    Households in the West

Customer trends:

    Average household spending on hair care products may decline as boomers exit the best-customer age groups.

The best customers of hair care products are the largest households and households with the most women. Married couples with children at home spend 45 percent more than average on this item, while single parents (most of whom are women) spend 35 percent more than average. Householders aged 35 to 54, many with children at home, spend 23 to 31 percent more than average on hair care products and control 52 percent of the market. Hispanics, who have the largest households, spend 48 percent more than average on this item. Households in the West spend 23 percent more than average on hair care products.

Average household spending on hair care products declined 9 percent between 2000 and 2007, after adjusting for inflation. Average household spending on hair care products may continue to decline in the years ahead as boomers age out of the best-customer lifestage.

Table 13.4 Hair care products

Total household spending	$6,741,593,100.00
Average household spends	56.10

AGE OF HOUSEHOLDER	AVERAGE HOUSEHOLD SPENDING	BEST CUSTOMERS (index)	BIGGEST CUSTOMERS (market share)
Average household	$56.10	100	100.0%
Under age 25	39.42	70	4.8
Aged 25 to 34	55.71	99	16.9
Aged 35 to 44	69.23	123	24.0
Aged 45 to 54	73.75	131	27.6
Aged 55 to 64	54.37	97	15.7
Aged 65 to 74	38.14	68	6.8
Aged 75 or older	25.62	46	4.3

	AVERAGE HOUSEHOLD SPENDING	BEST CUSTOMERS (index)	BIGGEST CUSTOMERS (market share)
HOUSEHOLD INCOME			
Average household	**$56.10**	**100**	**100.0%**
Under $20,000	25.19	45	9.2
$20,000 to $39,999	37.73	67	15.6
$40,000 to $49,999	52.91	94	9.3
$50,000 to $69,999	56.31	100	15.4
$70,000 to $79,999	80.42	143	8.3
$80,000 to $99,999	71.95	128	10.4
$100,000 or more	104.18	186	31.8
HOUSEHOLD TYPE			
Average household	**56.10**	**100**	**100.0**
Married couples	71.41	127	64.3
Married couples, no children	56.81	101	21.8
Married couples, with children	81.07	145	36.1
Oldest child under age 6	70.33	125	6.1
Oldest child aged 6 to 17	72.89	130	16.5
Oldest child aged 18 or older	105.15	187	13.8
Single parent with child under age 18	75.99	135	8.0
Single person	28.91	52	15.3
RACE AND HISPANIC ORIGIN			
Average household	**56.10**	**100**	**100.0**
Asian	44.26	79	2.8
Black	31.84	57	6.8
Hispanic	82.97	148	17.5
Non-Hispanic white and other	56.04	100	76.3
REGION			
Average household	**56.10**	**100**	**100.0**
Northeast	54.84	98	18.2
Midwest	51.80	92	21.1
South	51.62	92	33.0
West	68.82	123	27.7
EDUCATION			
Average household	**56.10**	**100**	**100.0**
Less than high school graduate	41.91	75	11.3
High school graduate	43.50	78	19.6
Some college	47.20	84	18.3
Associate's degree	66.21	118	10.5
College graduate	77.14	138	39.8
Bachelor's degree	75.98	135	25.4
Master's, professional, doctoral degree	79.16	141	14.4

Note: Market shares may not sum to 100.0 because of rounding and missing categories by household type. "Asian" and "black" include Hispanics and non-Hispanics who identify themselves as being of the respective race alone. "Hispanic" includes people of any race who identify themselves as Hispanic. "Other" includes people who identify themselves as non-Hispanic and as Alaska Native, American Indian, Asian (who are also included in the "Asian" row), Native Hawaiian or other Pacific Islander, as well as non-Hispanics reporting more than one race.
Source: Calculations by New Strategist based on the Bureau of Labor Statistics' 2007 Consumer Expenditure Survey.

Oral Hygiene Products

Best customers:
    Householders aged 45 to 74
    Married couples
    Hispanics

Customer trends:
    Average household spending on oral hygiene products should rise as aging boomers try to maintain their teeth.

Older married couples are the best customers of oral hygiene products because they are trying to look their best. Householders aged 45 to 74 spend 9 to 22 percent more than average on oral hygiene products. Overall, married couples spend 32 percent more than average on this item. Those with adult children at home (who are older) spend 67 percent more than average on oral hygiene products. Hispanics, whose households are larger than average, spend 21 percent more than the average household on this item.

Average household spending on oral hygiene products declined 11 percent between 2000 and 2007, after adjusting for inflation. One factor behind the decline was price discounting, allowing consumers to buy more for less. Average household spending on oral hygiene products should grow as boomers age and try to maintain the health of their teeth.

Table 13.5 Oral hygiene products

Total household spending	$3,321,526,440.00
Average household spends	27.64

	AVERAGE HOUSEHOLD SPENDING	BEST CUSTOMERS (index)	BIGGEST CUSTOMERS (market share)
AGE OF HOUSEHOLDER			
Average household	**$27.64**	**100**	**100.0%**
Under age 25	13.66	49	3.4
Aged 25 to 34	23.86	86	14.7
Aged 35 to 44	27.35	99	19.3
Aged 45 to 54	33.17	120	25.2
Aged 55 to 64	30.07	109	17.6
Aged 65 to 74	33.85	122	12.2
Aged 75 or older	22.76	82	7.8

	AVERAGE HOUSEHOLD SPENDING	BEST CUSTOMERS (index)	BIGGEST CUSTOMERS (market share)
HOUSEHOLD INCOME			
Average household	**$27.64**	**100**	**100.0%**
Under $20,000	14.46	52	10.8
$20,000 to $39,999	18.70	68	15.7
$40,000 to $49,999	26.03	94	9.3
$50,000 to $69,999	29.87	108	16.5
$70,000 to $79,999	31.87	115	6.7
$80,000 to $99,999	35.64	129	10.5
$100,000 or more	49.21	178	30.5
HOUSEHOLD TYPE			
Average household	**27.64**	**100**	**100.0**
Married couples	36.45	132	66.7
Married couples, no children	34.68	125	27.1
Married couples, with children	37.68	136	34.0
Oldest child under age 6	33.57	121	5.9
Oldest child aged 6 to 17	34.89	126	16.0
Oldest child aged 18 or older	46.22	167	12.3
Single parent with child under age 18	19.34	70	4.2
Single person	16.49	60	17.7
RACE AND HISPANIC ORIGIN			
Average household	**27.64**	**100**	**100.0**
Asian	22.21	80	2.8
Black	19.12	69	8.3
Hispanic	33.35	121	14.2
Non-Hispanic white and other	28.16	102	77.8
REGION			
Average household	**27.64**	**100**	**100.0**
Northeast	24.18	87	16.3
Midwest	24.08	87	19.9
South	31.13	113	40.4
West	28.62	104	23.4
EDUCATION			
Average household	**27.64**	**100**	**100.0**
Less than high school graduate	18.94	69	10.4
High school graduate	25.40	92	23.2
Some college	19.54	71	15.4
Associate's degree	27.32	99	8.8
College graduate	39.53	143	41.4
Bachelor's degree	38.73	140	26.3
Master's, professional, doctoral degree	40.92	148	15.1

Note: Market shares may not sum to 100.0 because of rounding and missing categories by household type. "Asian" and "black" include Hispanics and non-Hispanics who identify themselves as being of the respective race alone. "Hispanic" includes people of any race who identify themselves as Hispanic. "Other" includes people who identify themselves as non-Hispanic and as Alaska Native, American Indian, Asian (who are also included in the "Asian" row), Native Hawaiian or other Pacific Islander, as well as non-Hispanics reporting more than one race.
Source: Calculations by New Strategist based on the Bureau of Labor Statistics' 2007 Consumer Expenditure Survey.

Personal Care Services

Best customers:

Householders aged 35 to 74
Married couples without children at home
Married couples with school-aged or older children at home

Customer trends:

Average household spending on personal care services grow in the years ahead as aging boomers attempt to look their best, but only if discretionary income rebounds.

The largest households and older householders are the best customers of personal care services such as haircuts, massages, manicures, facials, and so on. Householders aged 35 to 64 spend 8 to 16 percent more than average on this item. Married couples without children at home (most of them empty-nesters) spend 23 percent more than average on personal care services, while those with school-aged or older children at home (the largest households) spend 36 to 38 percent more than average.

Average household spending on personal care services fell by a substantial 24 percent between 2000 and 2007, after adjusting for inflation. Price discounting was one factor behind the decline, and another factor was household belt tightening. Average household spending on personal care services may grow in the years ahead as aging boomers attempt to look their best, but only if discretionary income rebounds.

Table 13.6 Personal care services

Total household spending $33,997,577,610.00
Average household spends   282.91

	AVERAGE HOUSEHOLD SPENDING	BEST CUSTOMERS (index)	BIGGEST CUSTOMERS (market share)
AGE OF HOUSEHOLDER			
Average household	**$282.91**	**100**	**100.0%**
Under age 25	156.04	55	3.7
Aged 25 to 34	227.76	81	13.7
Aged 35 to 44	315.20	111	21.7
Aged 45 to 54	327.25	116	24.3
Aged 55 to 64	305.96	108	17.5
Aged 65 to 74	295.37	104	10.4
Aged 75 or older	255.73	90	8.6

	AVERAGE HOUSEHOLD SPENDING	BEST CUSTOMERS (index)	BIGGEST CUSTOMERS (market share)
HOUSEHOLD INCOME			
Average household	$282.91	100	100.0%
Under $20,000	113.69	40	8.3
$20,000 to $39,999	183.54	65	15.1
$40,000 to $49,999	230.88	82	8.0
$50,000 to $69,999	278.53	98	15.1
$70,000 to $79,999	307.74	109	6.3
$80,000 to $99,999	397.86	141	11.4
$100,000 or more	591.58	209	35.8
HOUSEHOLD TYPE			
Average household	282.91	100	100.0
Married couples	354.23	125	63.3
Married couples, no children	349.06	123	26.6
Married couples, with children	365.65	129	32.2
Oldest child under age 6	277.78	98	4.8
Oldest child aged 6 to 17	384.56	136	17.3
Oldest child aged 18 or older	391.27	138	10.2
Single parent with child under age 18	232.74	82	4.9
Single person	188.72	67	19.8
RACE AND HISPANIC ORIGIN			
Average household	282.91	100	100.0
Asian	221.01	78	2.8
Black	286.24	101	12.1
Hispanic	207.14	73	8.6
Non-Hispanic white and other	294.17	104	79.4
REGION			
Average household	282.91	100	100.0
Northeast	314.67	111	20.7
Midwest	266.48	94	21.5
South	267.36	95	33.9
West	298.03	105	23.8
EDUCATION			
Average household	282.91	100	100.0
Less than high school graduate	136.30	48	7.3
High school graduate	214.95	76	19.2
Some college	258.22	91	19.9
Associate's degree	305.26	108	9.6
College graduate	430.66	152	44.1
Bachelor's degree	405.84	143	26.9
Master's, professional, doctoral degree	476.27	168	17.2

Note: Market shares may not sum to 100.0 because of rounding and missing categories by household type. "Asian" and "black" include Hispanics and non-Hispanics who identify themselves as being of the respective race alone. "Hispanic" includes people of any race who identify themselves as Hispanic. "Other" includes people who identify themselves as non-Hispanic and as Alaska Native, American Indian, Asian (who are also included in the "Asian" row), Native Hawaiian or other Pacific Islander, as well as non-Hispanics reporting more than one race.
Source: Calculations by New Strategist based on the Bureau of Labor Statistics' 2007 Consumer Expenditure Survey.

Shaving Products

Best customers: Householders aged 35 to 44
Married couples with children at home

Customer trends: Average household spending on shaving products should continue to decline because the small generation X is in the best-customer age group.

The best customers of shaving products are households with the most men. Householders aged 35 to 44 spend 27 percent more than average on this item. Married couples with children at home (who have the largest households) spend 68 percent more than average on shaving products.

Average household spending on shaving products fell by 6 percent between 2000 and 2007, after adjusting for inflation. Behind the decline was the exit of baby boomers from the best-customer age group. Average household spending on shaving products should continue to decline because the small generation X is in the best-customer age group.

Table 13.7 Shaving products

Total household spending $1,795,354,740.00
Average household spends   14.94

	AVERAGE HOUSEHOLD SPENDING	BEST CUSTOMERS (index)	BIGGEST CUSTOMERS (market share)
AGE OF HOUSEHOLDER			
Average household	**$14.94**	**100**	**100.0%**
Under age 25	8.45	57	3.8
Aged 25 to 34	15.82	106	18.1
Aged 35 to 44	21.02	141	27.4
Aged 45 to 54	14.77	99	20.8
Aged 55 to 64	16.64	111	18.0
Aged 65 to 74	11.01	74	7.4
Aged 75 or older	7.22	48	4.6

	AVERAGE HOUSEHOLD SPENDING	BEST CUSTOMERS (index)	BIGGEST CUSTOMERS (market share)
HOUSEHOLD INCOME			
Average household	**$14.94**	**100**	**100.0%**
Under $20,000	2.56	17	3.5
$20,000 to $39,999	9.49	63	14.8
$40,000 to $49,999	10.98	73	7.2
$50,000 to $69,999	14.15	95	14.5
$70,000 to $79,999	16.96	114	6.6
$80,000 to $99,999	30.17	202	16.4
$100,000 or more	31.61	212	36.2
HOUSEHOLD TYPE			
Average household	**14.94**	**100**	**100.0**
Married couples	19.57	131	66.2
Married couples, no children	15.88	106	22.9
Married couples, with children	25.08	168	41.9
Oldest child under age 6	28.72	192	9.4
Oldest child aged 6 to 17	22.52	151	19.1
Oldest child aged 18 or older	27.46	184	13.5
Single parent with child under age 18	8.93	60	3.6
Single person	8.14	54	16.2
RACE AND HISPANIC ORIGIN			
Average household	**14.94**	**100**	**100.0**
Asian	9.92	66	2.3
Black	7.95	53	6.4
Hispanic	13.02	87	10.3
Non-Hispanic white and other	16.27	109	83.1
REGION			
Average household	**14.94**	**100**	**100.0**
Northeast	11.64	78	14.5
Midwest	12.66	85	19.4
South	15.87	106	38.1
West	18.57	124	28.1
EDUCATION			
Average household	**14.94**	**100**	**100.0**
Less than high school graduate	10.08	67	10.2
High school graduate	9.93	66	16.8
Some college	10.54	71	15.4
Associate's degree	13.65	91	8.1
College graduate	25.07	168	48.6
Bachelor's degree	25.67	172	32.2
Master's, professional, doctoral degree	24.02	161	16.4

Note: Market shares may not sum to 100.0 because of rounding and missing categories by household type. "Asian" and "black" include Hispanics and non-Hispanics who identify themselves as being of the respective race alone. "Hispanic" includes people of any race who identify themselves as Hispanic. "Other" includes people who identify themselves as non-Hispanic and as Alaska Native, American Indian, Asian (who are also included in the "Asian" row), Native Hawaiian or other Pacific Islander, as well as non-Hispanics reporting more than one race.
Source: Calculations by New Strategist based on the Bureau of Labor Statistics' 2007 Consumer Expenditure Survey.

Chapter 14.

Reading Material

Household Spending on Reading Material, 2007

The average American household spent just $118 on books, newspapers, and magazines in 2007. Spending on reading material fell by a precipitous 33 percent between 2000 and 2007, after adjusting for inflation. Behind the decline is the rise of the Internet, with online news and features substituting for print magazines and newspapers among boomers and younger generations.

The best customers of periodicals are older Americans. Householders aged 55 or older are the biggest spenders on newspaper and magazine subscriptions. Books, however, skew a bit younger. Householders aged 45 to 64 spend the most on books—22 percent more than average—and control 45 percent of the market. Average household spending on books fell by a smaller amount than spending on newspapers and magazines, which suggests that printed books have a more stable future than printed newspapers and magazines. Print versions of newspapers and magazines face uncertainty in the years ahead as computer-savvy younger generations—who get their news and information online—replace older customers. These trends suggest that average household spending on reading material will continue to decline.

Spending on reading material

(average spending by households on reading material, 2000 to 2007; in 2007 dollars)

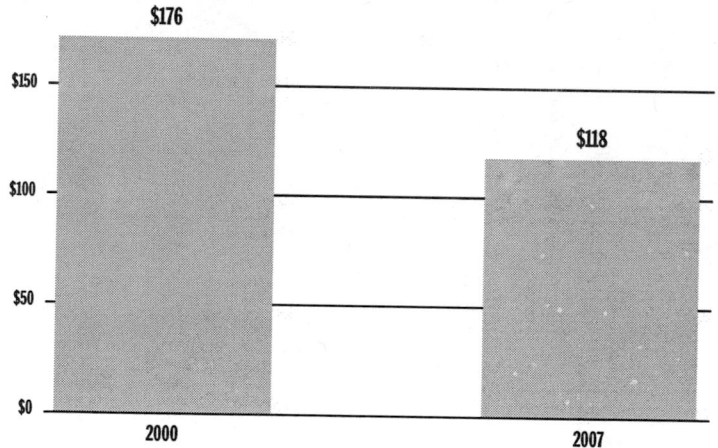

Table 14.1 Reading Material Spending, 2000 to 2007

(average annual household spending on information products and services, and percent distribution of spending by type, 2000 and 2007; percent change in spending, 2000–07; in 2007 dollars)

	2007		2000		
	average household spending	percent distribution	average household spending (in 2007$)	percent distribution	percent change 2000–07
Average household spending on reading material	**$117.69**	**100.0%**	**$176.36**	**100.0%**	**–33.3%**
Books	55.93	47.5	69.91	39.6	–20.0
Newspaper and magazine subscriptions	47.29	40.2	80.11	45.4	–41.0
Newspapers and magazines, nonsubscription	14.46	12.3	26.20	14.9	–44.8

Note: Numbers do not add to total because not all categories are shown.
Source: Bureau of Labor Statistics, 2000 and 2007 Consumer Expenditure Surveys; calculations by New Strategist

Books

Best customers:
Householders aged 45 to 64
Married couples without children at home
Married couples with school-aged children
Non-Hispanic whites
Households in the West
College graduates

Customer trends:
Average household spending on books may rise as boomers become empty-nesters with more free time.

Book buying is the province of college graduates. Householders with a college degree spend more than twice the average on books and account for 59 percent of the market. Householders aged 45 to 64 spend 22 percent more than average on books. Many of them are empty-nesters with time to read. Married couples without children at home spend 27 percent more than average on books, while couples with school-aged children spend 43 percent more than average on this item—buying books not only for themselves but also for their children.

Average household spending on books fell 19 percent between 2000 and 2007, after adjusting for inflation. The decline was smaller than that for newspapers and magazines, which may be good news for the book industry. Books are likely to weather the Internet revolution better than other print media because there are no freely available electronic alternatives. Some of the decline in spending on books may be due to price competition from discounters and used book sales. Average household spending on books could rise as boomers become empty-nesters with more time to read.

Table 14.2 Books

Total household spending $6,721,164,030.00
Average household spends   55.93

	AVERAGE HOUSEHOLD SPENDING	BEST CUSTOMERS (index)	BIGGEST CUSTOMERS (market share)
AGE OF HOUSEHOLDER			
Average household	**$55.93**	**100**	**100.0%**
Under age 25	34.27	61	4.2
Aged 25 to 34	44.69	80	13.6
Aged 35 to 44	61.71	110	21.5
Aged 45 to 54	68.35	122	25.7
Aged 55 to 64	68.31	122	19.8
Aged 65 to 74	53.58	96	9.6
Aged 75 or older	33.59	60	5.7

	AVERAGE HOUSEHOLD SPENDING	BEST CUSTOMERS (index)	BIGGEST CUSTOMERS (market share)
HOUSEHOLD INCOME			
Average household	**$55.93**	**100**	**100.0%**
Under $20,000	22.13	40	8.1
$20,000 to $39,999	26.95	48	11.2
$40,000 to $49,999	41.29	74	7.3
$50,000 to $69,999	49.58	89	13.6
$70,000 to $79,999	70.05	125	7.3
$80,000 to $99,999	83.11	149	12.1
$100,000 or more	132.21	236	40.5
HOUSEHOLD TYPE			
Average household	**55.93**	**100**	**100.0**
Married couples	69.49	124	62.8
Married couples, no children	70.90	127	27.3
Married couples, with children	71.37	128	31.8
Oldest child under age 6	59.64	107	5.2
Oldest child aged 6 to 17	79.88	143	18.1
Oldest child aged 18 or older	64.47	115	8.5
Single parent with child under age 18	35.93	64	3.8
Single person	45.41	81	24.1
RACE AND HISPANIC ORIGIN			
Average household	**55.93**	**100**	**100.0**
Asian	53.71	96	3.4
Black	18.84	34	4.0
Hispanic	19.06	34	4.0
Non-Hispanic white and other	67.40	121	92.0
REGION			
Average household	**55.93**	**100**	**100.0**
Northeast	58.38	104	19.4
Midwest	54.13	97	22.1
South	41.29	74	26.5
West	78.99	141	31.9
EDUCATION			
Average household	**55.93**	**100**	**100.0**
Less than high school graduate	10.20	18	2.8
High school graduate	27.86	50	12.6
Some college	46.65	83	18.2
Associate's degree	48.24	86	7.7
College graduate	113.71	203	58.8
Bachelor's degree	93.17	167	31.2
Master's, professional, doctoral degree	151.42	271	27.6

Note: Market shares may not sum to 100.0 because of rounding and missing categories by household type. "Asian" and "black" include Hispanics and non-Hispanics who identify themselves as being of the respective race alone. "Hispanic" includes people of any race who identify themselves as Hispanic. "Other" includes people who identify themselves as non-Hispanic and as Alaska Native, American Indian, Asian (who are also included in the "Asian" row), Native Hawaiian or other Pacific Islander, as well as non-Hispanics reporting more than one race.
Source: Calculations by New Strategist based on the Bureau of Labor Statistics' 2007 Consumer Expenditure Survey.

Magazines and Newspapers, Nonsubscription

Best customers: **Householders aged 45 to 74**
                                     Married couples with adult children at home
                                     Households in the Northeast

Customer trends: **Average household spending on nonsubscription newspapers and magazines will continue to decline as the availability of online news dampens impulse purchasing.**

The best customers of nonsubscription magazines and newspapers are the mass-transit-riding residents of the Northeast's commuter-friendly cities. Households in the Northeast spend 50 percent more than average on this item, many buying from newsstands or vending machines. Householders aged 45 to 74 spend 10 to 29 percent more than average on this item. Married couples with adult children at home spend 46 percent more than average on this item.

Average household spending on nonsubscription magazines and newspapers declined prodigiously between 2000 and 2007, down an enormous 45 percent after adjusting for inflation. The downward spiral is due in part to easy (and free) access to newspapers online, which dampens impulse purchasing. This trend is likely to intensify as wireless Internet access becomes more widely available to commuters and long-distance travelers.

Table 14.3 Magazines and newspapers, nonsubscription

Total household spending	$1,737,672,660.00
Average household spends	14.46

	AVERAGE HOUSEHOLD SPENDING	BEST CUSTOMERS (index)	BIGGEST CUSTOMERS (market share)
AGE OF HOUSEHOLDER			
Average household	**$14.46**	**100**	**100.0%**
Under age 25	8.17	57	3.8
Aged 25 to 34	12.28	85	14.5
Aged 35 to 44	14.52	100	19.6
Aged 45 to 54	18.67	129	27.1
Aged 55 to 64	15.75	109	17.6
Aged 65 to 74	15.96	110	11.0
Aged 75 or older	9.69	67	6.4

	AVERAGE HOUSEHOLD SPENDING	BEST CUSTOMERS (index)	BIGGEST CUSTOMERS (market share)
HOUSEHOLD INCOME			
Average household	**$14.46**	**100**	**100.0%**
Under $20,000	7.63	53	10.9
$20,000 to $39,999	10.52	73	16.9
$40,000 to $49,999	15.22	105	10.4
$50,000 to $69,999	14.62	101	15.5
$70,000 to $79,999	19.05	132	7.6
$80,000 to $99,999	18.99	131	10.7
$100,000 or more	23.74	164	28.1
HOUSEHOLD TYPE			
Average household	**14.46**	**100**	**100.0**
Married couples	16.30	113	57.0
Married couples, no children	16.12	111	24.0
Married couples, with children	16.60	115	28.6
Oldest child under age 6	14.63	101	4.9
Oldest child aged 6 to 17	14.73	102	12.9
Oldest child aged 18 or older	21.15	146	10.8
Single parent with child under age 18	11.00	76	4.5
Single person	12.66	88	26.0
RACE AND HISPANIC ORIGIN			
Average household	**14.46**	**100**	**100.0**
Asian	7.26	50	1.8
Black	10.44	72	8.7
Hispanic	7.38	51	6.0
Non-Hispanic white and other	16.17	112	85.4
REGION			
Average household	**14.46**	**100**	**100.0**
Northeast	21.63	150	27.9
Midwest	15.98	111	25.3
South	10.90	75	27.1
West	12.69	88	19.8
EDUCATION			
Average household	**14.46**	**100**	**100.0**
Less than high school graduate	7.97	55	8.4
High school graduate	12.16	84	21.2
Some college	14.20	98	21.4
Associate's degree	16.34	113	10.0
College graduate	19.49	135	39.0
Bachelor's degree	17.97	124	23.3
Master's, professional, doctoral degree	22.29	154	15.7

Note: Market shares may not sum to 100.0 because of rounding and missing categories by household type. "Asian" and "black" include Hispanics and non-Hispanics who identify themselves as being of the respective race alone. "Hispanic" includes people of any race who identify themselves as Hispanic. "Other" includes people who identify themselves as non-Hispanic and as Alaska Native, American Indian, Asian (who are also included in the "Asian" row), Native Hawaiian or other Pacific Islander, as well as non-Hispanics reporting more than one race.
Source: Calculations by New Strategist based on the Bureau of Labor Statistics' 2007 Consumer Expenditure Survey.

Magazines and Newspapers, Subscription

Best customers:
Householders aged 55 or older
Married couples without children at home
Married couples with adult children at home
Non-Hispanic whites

Customer trends:
Average household spending on newspaper and magazine subscriptions will continue to decline as Internet-savvy younger generations flock to electronic alternatives.

Older householders are by far the best customers of newspaper and magazine subscriptions. Householders aged 55 or older spend 41 to 95 percent more than average on this item and control 58 percent of the market. Married couples without children at home (most of them older) spend 68 percent more than average on this item. Couples with adult children at home spend 34 percent above normal on this item. Non-Hispanic white households spend 22 percent more than average on subscriptions.

Average household spending on subscriptions fell by a substantial 41 percent between 2000 and 2007, after adjusting for inflation. The downward trend is likely to continue as Internet-savvy younger generations flock to electronic alternatives. This trend will make magazine and newspaper publishers increasingly dependent on advertisers, rather than subscribers, for revenues.

Table 14.4 Magazines and newspapers, subscription

Total household spending — $5,682,886,590.00
Average household spends — 47.29

AGE OF HOUSEHOLDER	AVERAGE HOUSEHOLD SPENDING	BEST CUSTOMERS (index)	BIGGEST CUSTOMERS (market share)
Average household	$47.29	100	100.0%
Under age 25	8.76	19	1.3
Aged 25 to 34	14.76	31	5.3
Aged 35 to 44	30.92	65	12.7
Aged 45 to 54	50.21	106	22.3
Aged 55 to 64	66.50	141	22.8
Aged 65 to 74	81.05	171	17.1
Aged 75 or older	92.22	195	18.5

	AVERAGE HOUSEHOLD SPENDING	BEST CUSTOMERS (index)	BIGGEST CUSTOMERS (market share)
HOUSEHOLD INCOME			
Average household	**$47.29**	**100**	**100.0%**
Under $20,000	25.65	54	11.2
$20,000 to $39,999	32.96	70	16.2
$40,000 to $49,999	39.68	84	8.3
$50,000 to $69,999	46.01	97	14.9
$70,000 to $79,999	52.30	111	6.4
$80,000 to $99,999	65.82	139	11.3
$100,000 or more	87.73	186	31.8
HOUSEHOLD TYPE			
Average household	**47.29**	**100**	**100.0**
Married couples	61.54	130	65.8
Married couples, no children	79.44	168	36.2
Married couples, with children	49.11	104	25.9
Oldest child under age 6	30.99	66	3.2
Oldest child aged 6 to 17	47.88	101	12.9
Oldest child aged 18 or older	63.22	134	9.8
Single parent with child under age 18	14.05	30	1.8
Single person	38.58	82	24.3
RACE AND HISPANIC ORIGIN			
Average household	**47.29**	**100**	**100.0**
Asian	37.30	79	2.8
Black	16.99	36	4.3
Hispanic	11.50	24	2.9
Non-Hispanic white and other	57.56	122	92.9
REGION			
Average household	**47.29**	**100**	**100.0**
Northeast	55.39	117	21.8
Midwest	55.93	118	27.0
South	37.01	78	28.1
West	48.22	102	23.1
EDUCATION			
Average household	**47.29**	**100**	**100.0**
Less than high school graduate	21.86	46	7.0
High school graduate	39.76	84	21.2
Some college	39.28	83	18.1
Associate's degree	45.66	97	8.6
College graduate	73.71	156	45.1
Bachelor's degree	64.63	137	25.6
Master's, professional, doctoral degree	90.40	191	19.5

Note: Market shares may not sum to 100.0 because of rounding and missing categories by household type. "Asian" and "black" include Hispanics and non-Hispanics who identify themselves as being of the respective race alone. "Hispanic" includes people of any race who identify themselves as Hispanic. "Other" includes people who identify themselves as non-Hispanic and as Alaska Native, American Indian, Asian (who are also included in the "Asian" row), Native Hawaiian or other Pacific Islander, as well as non-Hispanics reporting more than one race.
Source: Calculations by New Strategist based on the Bureau of Labor Statistics' 2007 Consumer Expenditure Survey.

Chapter 15.

Restaurants and Carry-Outs

Household Spending at Restaurants and Carry-Outs, 2007

In 2007, the average household spent a considerable $2,467 at restaurants and carry-outs—a figure that does not include alcoholic beverage spending (see the Alcohol chapter for those figures). What once was a special occasion—eating out—has become a necessity as busy two-earner families try to save time. The Bureau of Labor Statistics reports that during the average week of 2007, fully 73 percent of households purchased food from restaurants, spending an average of $58. Recently, however, households have begun to cut back on their restaurant spending. Between 2006 and 2007, average household spending at restaurants and carry-outs fell by 4 percent, after adjusting for inflation. (Comparisons with 2000 are not valid because of changes in methodology.) Behind the decline is price discounting, as well as belt tightening as the economic downturn began to take hold.

Households devote more of their restaurant dollars to dinners (43 percent) than to lunches (31 percent). Breakfasts account for another 9 percent of restaurant spending, snacks for 7 percent, and restaurant meals on trips (which are not broken down by type of restaurant) account for the remaining 10 percent.

The average household devotes less of the eating-out dollar to fast food than to full-service restaurants. Of the $2,467 the average household spent on eating out in 2007, fast-food restaurants captured a 37 percent share, and full-service restaurants took a larger 47 percent. The remainder is spent at employer and school cafeterias, vending machines, mobile vendors, and on trips.

Older Americans, particularly empty-nesters, are far more likely to choose full-service over fast-food restaurants. Consequently, as the population ages, expect to see faster growth in spending on the full-service category—but only if discretionary income grows.

Restaurant Spending

(average annual spending by households on fast-food and full-service restaurants, 2000 to 2007; in 2007 dollars)

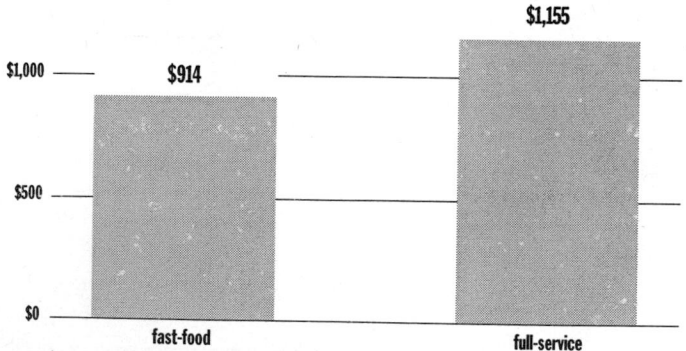

Table 15.1 Restaurant and carry-out spending, 2006 and 2007

(average annual household spending at restaurants and carry-outs, and percent distribution of spending by type of meal and restaurant, 2006 and 2007; percent change in spending, 2006–07; in 2007 dollars; ranked by amount spent)

	2007		2006		
	average household spending	percent distribution	average household spending (in 2007$)	percent distribution	percent change 2006–07
AVERAGE HOUSEHOLD SPENDING AT RESTAURANTS BY TYPE OF MEAL					
Total restaurant spending	**$2,467.37**	**100.0%**	**$2,563.29**	**100.0%**	**–3.7%**
Dinner	1,073.51	43.5	1,103.25	43.0	–2.7
Lunch	761.38	30.9	790.51	30.8	–3.7
Restaurant meals on trips	245.53	10.0	249.85	9.7	–1.7
Breakfast and brunch	215.13	8.7	240.08	9.4	–10.4
Snacks and nonalcoholic beverages	171.82	7.0	179.60	7.0	–4.3
AVERAGE HOUSEHOLD SPENDING BY TYPE OF MEAL AND RESTAURANT					
Total restaurant spending	**$2,467.37**	**100.0%**	**$2,563.29**	**100.0%**	**–3.7%**
Dinner	1,073.51	43.5	1,103.25	43.0	–2.7
At full-service restaurants	730.76	29.6	745.21	29.1	–1.9
At fast-food restaurants*	334.88	13.6	347.52	13.6	–3.6
Lunch	761.38	30.9	790.51	30.8	–3.7
At fast-food restaurants*	358.00	14.5	380.60	14.8	–5.9
At full-service restaurants	307.84	12.5	309.67	12.1	–0.6
At employer and school cafeterias	85.68	3.5	88.60	3.5	–3.3
Breakfast and brunch	215.13	8.7	240.08	9.4	–10.4
At fast-food restaurants*	112.13	4.5	111.27	4.3	0.8
At full-service restaurants	88.22	3.6	113.10	4.4	–22.0
Snacks and nonalcoholic beverages	171.82	7.0	179.60	7.0	–4.3
At fast-food restaurants*	109.46	4.4	110.51	4.3	–1.0
At vending machines, mobile vendors	27.72	1.1	31.43	1.2	–11.8
At full-service restaurants	28.39	1.2	30.65	1.2	–7.4
At employer and school cafeterias	6.25	0.3	7.01	0.3	–10.9
Restaurant meals on trips	245.53	10.0	249.85	9.7	–1.7

* The category "fast-food restaurants" also includes take-out, delivery, concession stands, buffets, and cafeterias other than employer and school.
Note: Subcategories do not add to total because not all types of restaurants or meals are shown.
Source: Bureau of Labor Statistics, 2006 and 2007 Consumer Expenditure Surveys; calculations by New Strategist

Breakfast and Brunch at Fast-Food Restaurants
Including Take-Outs, Deliveries, Concession Stands, Buffets, and Cafeterias (except Employer and School)

Best customers:	**Householders aged 25 to 54** **Married couples with school-aged or older children at home** **Hispanics** **Households in the Northeast**
Customer trends:	**Average household spending on breakfast at fast-food restaurants may decline as baby boomers become empty-nesters with more free time.**

The busiest people are the biggest spenders on breakfast at fast-food restaurants—workers and parents. Householders of prime working age, 25 to 54, spend 16 to 27 percent more than average on this item and account for 69 percent of the market. Married couples with school-aged or older children at home spend 39 to 42 percent more than average on breakfast at fast-food restaurants as they try to fit meals into their busy schedules. Hispanics spend 31 percent more than average on breakfast at fast-food restaurants, while households in the Northeast spend 30 percent more than average.

Average household spending on breakfast at fast-food restaurants barely changed between 2006 and 2007, rising 0.8 percent after adjusting for inflation. Spending on this item may decline in the years ahead as baby boomers shift their breakfast spending from fast-food to full-service restaurants—but only if discretionary income rises.

Table 15.2 Breakfast and brunch at fast-food restaurants, including take-outs, deliveries, concession stands, buffets, and cafeterias (except employer and school)

Total household spending $13,474,774,230.00
Average household spends   112.13

	AVERAGE HOUSEHOLD SPENDING	BEST CUSTOMERS (index)	BIGGEST CUSTOMERS (market share)
AGE OF HOUSEHOLDER			
Average household	**$112.13**	**100**	**100.0%**
Under age 25	74.52	66	4.5
Aged 25 to 34	132.25	118	20.1
Aged 35 to 44	142.94	127	24.8
Aged 45 to 54	130.01	116	24.4
Aged 55 to 64	122.67	109	17.7
Aged 65 to 74	58.46	52	5.2
Aged 75 or older	40.30	36	3.4

	AVERAGE HOUSEHOLD SPENDING	BEST CUSTOMERS (index)	BIGGEST CUSTOMERS (market share)
HOUSEHOLD INCOME			
Average household	$112.13	100	100.0%
Under $20,000	54.28	48	10.0
$20,000 to $39,999	79.39	71	16.5
$40,000 to $49,999	106.46	95	9.3
$50,000 to $69,999	127.20	113	17.4
$70,000 to $79,999	150.11	134	7.8
$80,000 to $99,999	156.02	139	11.3
$100,000 or more	179.98	161	27.5
HOUSEHOLD TYPE			
Average household	112.13	100	100.0
Married couples	128.33	114	57.9
Married couples, no children	106.14	95	20.4
Married couples, with children	146.58	131	32.6
Oldest child under age 6	105.22	94	4.6
Oldest child aged 6 to 17	155.43	139	17.6
Oldest child aged 18 or older	159.44	142	10.5
Single parent with child under age 18	97.34	87	5.2
Single person	79.03	70	21.0
RACE AND HISPANIC ORIGIN			
Average household	112.13	100	100.0
Asian	133.65	119	4.2
Black	110.78	99	11.9
Hispanic	147.30	131	15.5
Non-Hispanic white and other	107.40	96	73.1
REGION			
Average household	112.13	100	100.0
Northeast	145.35	130	24.1
Midwest	88.81	79	18.1
South	101.89	91	32.6
West	124.57	111	25.1
EDUCATION			
Average household	112.13	100	100.0
Less than high school graduate	100.35	89	13.6
High school graduate	108.25	97	24.4
Some college	104.67	93	20.3
Associate's degree	110.97	99	8.8
College graduate	126.66	113	32.7
Bachelor's degree	129.03	115	21.6
Master's, professional, doctoral degree	122.55	109	11.1

Note: Market shares may not sum to 100.0 because of rounding and missing categories by household type. "Asian" and "black" include Hispanics and non-Hispanics who identify themselves as being of the respective race alone. "Hispanic" includes people of any race who identify themselves as Hispanic. "Other" includes people who identify themselves as non-Hispanic and as Alaska Native, American Indian, Asian (who are also included in the "Asian" row), Native Hawaiian or other Pacific Islander, as well as non-Hispanics reporting more than one race.
Source: Calculations by New Strategist based on the Bureau of Labor Statistics' 2007 Consumer Expenditure Survey.

Breakfast and Brunch at Full-Service Restaurants

Best customers:

Householders aged 55 to 64
Married couples without children at home
Married couples with adult children at home
Households in the Northeast and West

Customer trends:

Average household spending on breakfast at full-service restaurants could rise as growing numbers of baby boomers age and gain more free time—but only if discretionary income grows.

The biggest spenders on breakfast and brunch at full-service restaurants are older married couples enjoying a leisurely meal. Householders aged 55 to 64 spend 39 percent more than average on this item. Married couples without children at home (many of them empty-nesters) spend 43 percent more than average on breakfast and brunch at full-service restaurants. Couples with adult children at home spend 60 percent more than average on full-service breakfast, in part because their households are larger. Households in the Northeast and West spend 20 percent more than average on this item.

Average household spending on breakfast at full-service restaurants fell by a substantial 22 percent between 2006 and 2007 as households tightened their belts in the midst of the economic downturn. In the years ahead, spending on full-service breakfasts could rise as growing numbers of baby boomers age and gain more free time—but only if discretionary income grows.

Table 15.3 Breakfast and brunch at full-service restaurants

Total household spending $10,601,485,620.00
Average household spends 88.22

	AVERAGE HOUSEHOLD SPENDING	BEST CUSTOMERS (index)	BIGGEST CUSTOMERS (market share)
AGE OF HOUSEHOLDER			
Average household	$88.22	100	100.0%
Under age 25	33.22	38	2.6
Aged 25 to 34	70.19	80	13.6
Aged 35 to 44	90.55	103	20.0
Aged 45 to 54	102.64	116	24.4
Aged 55 to 64	122.26	139	22.4
Aged 65 to 74	94.26	107	10.7
Aged 75 or older	62.20	71	6.7

	AVERAGE HOUSEHOLD SPENDING	BEST CUSTOMERS (index)	BIGGEST CUSTOMERS (market share)
HOUSEHOLD INCOME			
Average household	$88.22	100	100.0%
Under $20,000	43.22	49	10.1
$20,000 to $39,999	55.16	63	14.5
$40,000 to $49,999	81.14	92	9.0
$50,000 to $69,999	99.37	113	17.2
$70,000 to $79,999	103.65	117	6.8
$80,000 to $99,999	141.09	160	13.0
$100,000 or more	148.14	168	28.8
HOUSEHOLD TYPE			
Average household	88.22	100	100.0
Married couples	112.48	127	64.5
Married couples, no children	126.00	143	30.8
Married couples, with children	101.63	115	28.7
Oldest child under age 6	57.69	65	3.2
Oldest child aged 6 to 17	98.13	111	14.1
Oldest child aged 18 or older	140.82	160	11.8
Single parent with child under age 18	74.77	85	5.0
Single person	51.21	58	17.3
RACE AND HISPANIC ORIGIN			
Average household	88.22	100	100.0
Asian	98.46	112	3.9
Black	48.48	55	6.6
Hispanic	88.56	100	11.8
Non-Hispanic white and other	94.26	107	81.6
REGION			
Average household	88.22	100	100.0
Northeast	105.48	120	22.3
Midwest	89.08	101	23.1
South	67.43	76	27.4
West	106.21	120	27.2
EDUCATION			
Average household	88.22	100	100.0
Less than high school graduate	59.86	68	10.3
High school graduate	83.38	95	23.8
Some college	81.50	92	20.1
Associate's degree	122.43	139	12.3
College graduate	100.57	114	33.0
Bachelor's degree	99.53	113	21.1
Master's, professional, doctoral degree	102.37	116	11.8

Note: Market shares may not sum to 100.0 because of rounding and missing categories by household type. "Asian" and "black" include Hispanics and non-Hispanics who identify themselves as being of the respective race alone. "Hispanic" includes people of any race who identify themselves as Hispanic. "Other" includes people who identify themselves as non-Hispanic and as Alaska Native, American Indian, Asian (who are also included in the "Asian" row), Native Hawaiian or other Pacific Islander, as well as non-Hispanics reporting more than one race.
Source: Calculations by New Strategist based on the Bureau of Labor Statistics' 2007 Consumer Expenditure Survey.

Dinner at Fast-Food Restaurants
Including Take-Outs, Deliveries, Concession Stands, Buffets, and Cafeterias (except Employer and School)

Best customers:	Householders aged 25 to 54 Married couples with children at home Single parents
Customer trends:	Average household spending on dinner at fast-food restaurants could continue to decline because the small generation X is in the best-customer lifestage.

Families with children are the biggest spenders on dinners at fast-food restaurants. Householders aged 25 to 54 spend 20 to 34 percent more than average on this item and account for 73 percent of the market. Married couples with children at home spend 58 percent more than average on dinner at fast-food restaurants as they try to fit meals into their busy schedules. Single parents spend 19 percent more than average on this item.

Average household spending on dinner at fast-food restaurants fell 4 percent between 2006 and 2007 as households cut their spending in the economic downturn. Because the small generation X is in the best-customer lifestage, average household spending on fast-food restaurant dinners could continue to decline.

Table 15.4 **Dinner at fast-food restaurants, including take-outs, deliveries, concession stands, buffets, and cafeterias (except employer and school)**

Total household spending $40,242,864,480.00
Average household spends 334.88

	AVERAGE HOUSEHOLD SPENDING	BEST CUSTOMERS (index)	BIGGEST CUSTOMERS (market share)
AGE OF HOUSEHOLDER			
Average household	**$334.88**	**100**	**100.0%**
Under age 25	327.19	98	6.6
Aged 25 to 34	428.82	128	21.8
Aged 35 to 44	447.43	134	26.0
Aged 45 to 54	401.57	120	25.2
Aged 55 to 64	267.39	80	12.9
Aged 65 to 74	169.02	50	5.0
Aged 75 or older	80.11	24	2.3

	AVERAGE HOUSEHOLD SPENDING	BEST CUSTOMERS (index)	BIGGEST CUSTOMERS (market share)
HOUSEHOLD INCOME			
Average household	$334.88	100	100.0%
Under $20,000	162.90	49	10.0
$20,000 to $39,999	224.02	67	15.5
$40,000 to $49,999	335.17	100	9.8
$50,000 to $69,999	387.06	116	17.7
$70,000 to $79,999	473.85	141	8.2
$80,000 to $99,999	457.60	137	11.1
$100,000 or more	534.33	160	27.3
HOUSEHOLD TYPE			
Average household	334.88	100	100.0
Married couples	404.01	121	61.0
Married couples, no children	259.11	77	16.7
Married couples, with children	530.24	158	39.5
Oldest child under age 6	437.70	131	6.4
Oldest child aged 6 to 17	553.86	165	21.0
Oldest child aged 18 or older	551.40	165	12.1
Single parent with child under age 18	397.15	119	7.0
Single person	181.82	54	16.1
RACE AND HISPANIC ORIGIN			
Average household	334.88	100	100.0
Asian	340.53	102	3.6
Black	337.36	101	12.1
Hispanic	383.79	115	13.5
Non-Hispanic white and other	327.35	98	74.6
REGION			
Average household	334.88	100	100.0
Northeast	315.65	94	17.6
Midwest	333.02	99	22.7
South	328.09	98	35.2
West	364.01	109	24.6
EDUCATION			
Average household	334.88	100	100.0
Less than high school graduate	235.18	70	10.7
High school graduate	305.63	91	23.0
Some college	354.28	106	23.0
Associate's degree	379.08	113	10.1
College graduate	379.76	113	32.8
Bachelor's degree	390.68	117	21.9
Master's, professional, doctoral degree	360.79	108	11.0

Note: Market shares may not sum to 100.0 because of rounding and missing categories by household type. "Asian" and "black" include Hispanics and non-Hispanics who identify themselves as being of the respective race alone. "Hispanic" includes people of any race who identify themselves as Hispanic. "Other" includes people who identify themselves as non-Hispanic and as Alaska Native, American Indian, Asian (who are also included in the "Asian" row), Native Hawaiian or other Pacific Islander, as well as non-Hispanics reporting more than one race.
Source: Calculations by New Strategist based on the Bureau of Labor Statistics' 2007 Consumer Expenditure Survey.

Dinner at Full-Service Restaurants

Best customers:	Householders aged 35 to 64
	Married couples without children at home
	Married couples with school-aged or older children at home

Customer trends:	Average household spending on dinner at full-service restaurants should rise in the years ahead as growing numbers of baby boomers retire and gain more free time—but only if discretionary income grows.

The biggest spenders on dinners at full-service restaurants are middle-aged married couples enjoying a leisurely meal. Householders ranging in age from 35 to 64 spend 13 to 19 percent more than average on this item. Married couples without children at home (many of them empty-nesters) spend 37 percent more than average on full-service restaurant dinners. Those with school-aged or adult children at home spend 28 to 46 percent more than average on this item.

Average household spending on dinners in full-service restaurants fell by 2 percent between 2006 and 2007, after adjusting for inflation, as households cut their budgets in the midst of the economic downturn. Spending in the category should rise in the years ahead as baby boomers retire and gain more free time—but only if discretionary income grows.

Table 15.5 Dinner at full-service restaurants

Total household spending $87,816,159,960.00
Average household spends   730.76

	AVERAGE HOUSEHOLD SPENDING	BEST CUSTOMERS (index)	BIGGEST CUSTOMERS (market share)
AGE OF HOUSEHOLDER			
Average household	**$730.76**	**100**	**100.0%**
Under age 25	373.93	51	3.5
Aged 25 to 34	720.38	99	16.8
Aged 35 to 44	827.44	113	22.1
Aged 45 to 54	826.05	113	23.7
Aged 55 to 64	867.16	119	19.2
Aged 65 to 74	633.38	87	8.7
Aged 75 or older	483.35	66	6.3

	AVERAGE HOUSEHOLD SPENDING	BEST CUSTOMERS (index)	BIGGEST CUSTOMERS (market share)
HOUSEHOLD INCOME			
Average household	**$730.76**	**100**	**100.0%**
Under $20,000	240.25	33	6.8
$20,000 to $39,999	389.15	53	12.4
$40,000 to $49,999	591.98	81	8.0
$50,000 to $69,999	706.93	97	14.8
$70,000 to $79,999	985.16	135	7.8
$80,000 to $99,999	976.85	134	10.9
$100,000 or more	1,700.80	233	39.9
HOUSEHOLD TYPE			
Average household	**730.76**	**100**	**100.0**
Married couples	962.92	132	66.6
Married couples, no children	1,000.05	137	29.5
Married couples, with children	946.58	130	32.3
Oldest child under age 6	810.45	111	5.4
Oldest child aged 6 to 17	937.79	128	16.3
Oldest child aged 18 or older	1,063.87	146	10.7
Single parent with child under age 18	498.73	68	4.1
Single person	427.03	58	17.4
RACE AND HISPANIC ORIGIN			
Average household	**730.76**	**100**	**100.0**
Asian	808.76	111	3.9
Black	381.30	52	6.3
Hispanic	538.88	74	8.7
Non-Hispanic white and other	811.20	111	84.7
REGION			
Average household	**730.76**	**100**	**100.0**
Northeast	822.95	113	21.0
Midwest	650.31	89	20.3
South	695.84	95	34.2
West	791.95	108	24.5
EDUCATION			
Average household	**730.76**	**100**	**100.0**
Less than high school graduate	285.05	39	5.9
High school graduate	505.79	69	17.5
Some college	643.23	88	19.2
Associate's degree	733.92	100	8.9
College graduate	1,194.71	163	47.3
Bachelor's degree	1,079.11	148	27.7
Master's, professional, doctoral degree	1,395.45	191	19.5

Note: Market shares may not sum to 100.0 because of rounding and missing categories by household type. "Asian" and "black" include Hispanics and non-Hispanics who identify themselves as being of the respective race alone. "Hispanic" includes people of any race who identify themselves as Hispanic. "Other" includes people who identify themselves as non-Hispanic and as Alaska Native, American Indian, Asian (who are also included in the "Asian" row), Native Hawaiian or other Pacific Islander, as well as non-Hispanics reporting more than one race.
Source: Calculations by New Strategist based on the Bureau of Labor Statistics' 2007 Consumer Expenditure Survey.

Lunch at Employer and School Cafeterias

Best customers:
Householders aged 35 to 54
Married couples with school-aged or older children at home
Single parents
Asians

Customer trends:
Average household spending on lunch at employer and school cafeterias could continue to decline as more children qualify for subsidized lunches and fewer employers offer cafeteria meals in an attempt to cut costs.

Not surprisingly, parents and workers are the biggest spenders on lunch at employer and school cafeterias. Householders aged 35 to 54, most of them in the workforce, spend 42 to 104 percent more than average on this item and account for 70 percent of the market. Married couples with school-aged children, many of them dual-income couples, spend triple the average on this item. Couples with adult children at home spend 91 percent more than average on employer and school cafeteria lunches, while single parents spend 92 more. Asians spend 46 percent more than the average on this item.

Average household spending on lunch at employer and school cafeterias fell 3 percent between 2006 and 2007, after adjusting for inflation. Behind the decline was household budget cutting in the midst of the economic downturn. This category could continue to decline as a growing percentage of children qualify for subsidized lunches and fewer employers offer cafeteria meals in an attempt to cut costs.

Table 15.6 Lunch at employer and school cafeterias

Total household spending $10,296,251,280.00
Average household spends   85.68

	AVERAGE HOUSEHOLD SPENDING	BEST CUSTOMERS (index)	BIGGEST CUSTOMERS (market share)
AGE OF HOUSEHOLDER			
Average household	**$85.68**	**100**	**100.0%**
Under age 25	52.55	61	4.2
Aged 25 to 34	70.12	82	14.0
Aged 35 to 44	174.72	204	39.7
Aged 45 to 54	121.83	142	29.9
Aged 55 to 64	42.93	50	8.1
Aged 65 to 74	28.48	33	3.3
Aged 75 or older	8.11	9	0.9

	AVERAGE HOUSEHOLD SPENDING	BEST CUSTOMERS (index)	BIGGEST CUSTOMERS (market share)
HOUSEHOLD INCOME			
Average household	$85.68	100	100.0%
Under $20,000	27.41	32	6.6
$20,000 to $39,999	49.36	58	13.4
$40,000 to $49,999	72.80	85	8.4
$50,000 to $69,999	92.20	108	16.5
$70,000 to $79,999	122.57	143	8.3
$80,000 to $99,999	129.21	151	12.3
$100,000 or more	174.28	203	34.8
HOUSEHOLD TYPE			
Average household	85.68	100	100.0
Married couples	112.46	131	66.4
Married couples, no children	25.58	30	6.4
Married couples, with children	191.09	223	55.6
Oldest child under age 6	48.58	57	2.8
Oldest child aged 6 to 17	257.87	301	38.2
Oldest child aged 18 or older	163.43	191	14.1
Single parent with child under age 18	164.85	192	11.4
Single person	32.46	38	11.3
RACE AND HISPANIC ORIGIN			
Average household	85.68	100	100.0
Asian	125.02	146	5.1
Black	84.92	99	11.9
Hispanic	85.85	100	11.8
Non-Hispanic white and other	85.67	100	76.3
REGION			
Average household	85.68	100	100.0
Northeast	95.40	111	20.7
Midwest	105.61	123	28.2
South	83.25	97	34.9
West	60.81	71	16.1
EDUCATION			
Average household	85.68	100	100.0
Less than high school graduate	43.96	51	7.8
High school graduate	63.89	75	18.8
Some college	85.16	99	21.6
Associate's degree	97.09	113	10.1
College graduate	121.04	141	40.9
Bachelor's degree	126.02	147	27.6
Master's, professional, doctoral degree	112.41	131	13.4

Note: Market shares may not sum to 100.0 because of rounding and missing categories by household type. "Asian" and "black" include Hispanics and non-Hispanics who identify themselves as being of the respective race alone. "Hispanic" includes people of any race who identify themselves as Hispanic. "Other" includes people who identify themselves as non-Hispanic and as Alaska Native, American Indian, Asian (who are also included in the "Asian" row), Native Hawaiian or other Pacific Islander, as well as non-Hispanics reporting more than one race.
Source: Calculations by New Strategist based on the Bureau of Labor Statistics' 2007 Consumer Expenditure Survey.

Lunch at Fast-Food Restaurants
Including Take-Outs, Deliveries, Concession Stands, Buffets, and Cafeterias (except Employer and School)

Best customers: Householders aged 25 to 54
Married couples with children at home
Asians and Hispanics

Customer trends: Average household spending on lunches at fast-food restaurants may continue to decline as boomers begin to retire and have time for more leisurely lunches at full-service restaurants.

Workers and parents are the best customers of fast-food lunches. Householders of prime working age, 25 to 54, spend 16 to 29 percent more than average on this item and account for 70 percent of the market. Married couples with children at home spend 45 percent more than average on lunches at fast-food restaurants as they try to fit meals into their busy schedules. Asians and Hispanics, respectively, spend 32 and 23 percent more than average on this item.

Average household spending on fast-food lunches fell by 6 percent between 2006 and 2007, after adjusting for inflation. Behind the decline was household budget cutting in the midst of the economic downturn. Spending on this item could continue to decline in the years ahead as boomers begin to retire and have time for more leisurely lunches at full-service restaurants.

Table 15.7 **Lunch at fast-food restaurants, including take-outs, deliveries, concession stands, buffets, and cafeterias (except employer and school)**

Total household spending $43,021,218,000.00
Average household spends 358.00

AGE OF HOUSEHOLDER	AVERAGE HOUSEHOLD SPENDING	BEST CUSTOMERS (index)	BIGGEST CUSTOMERS (market share)
Average household	$358.00	100	100.0%
Under age 25	354.90	99	6.7
Aged 25 to 34	463.16	129	22.1
Aged 35 to 44	431.05	120	23.5
Aged 45 to 54	416.47	116	24.4
Aged 55 to 64	306.22	86	13.9
Aged 65 to 74	207.73	58	5.8
Aged 75 or older	136.58	38	3.6

	AVERAGE HOUSEHOLD SPENDING	BEST CUSTOMERS (index)	BIGGEST CUSTOMERS (market share)
HOUSEHOLD INCOME			
Average household	$358.00	100	100.0%
Under $20,000	173.06	48	9.9
$20,000 to $39,999	246.43	69	16.0
$40,000 to $49,999	339.83	95	9.3
$50,000 to $69,999	404.58	113	17.3
$70,000 to $79,999	429.11	120	6.9
$80,000 to $99,999	494.22	138	11.2
$100,000 or more	604.93	169	28.9
HOUSEHOLD TYPE			
Average household	358.00	100	100.0
Married couples	446.67	125	63.1
Married couples, no children	354.88	99	21.4
Married couples, with children	520.82	145	36.3
Oldest child under age 6	527.38	147	7.2
Oldest child aged 6 to 17	517.56	145	18.4
Oldest child aged 18 or older	522.45	146	10.8
Single parent with child under age 18	328.07	92	5.4
Single person	210.86	59	17.5
RACE AND HISPANIC ORIGIN			
Average household	358.00	100	100.0
Asian	473.29	132	4.7
Black	299.94	84	10.1
Hispanic	439.81	123	14.5
Non-Hispanic white and other	355.43	99	75.8
REGION			
Average household	358.00	100	100.0
Northeast	338.96	95	17.6
Midwest	304.32	85	19.4
South	360.75	101	36.2
West	425.11	119	26.9
EDUCATION			
Average household	358.00	100	100.0
Less than high school graduate	275.68	77	11.7
High school graduate	321.07	90	22.6
Some college	358.56	100	21.8
Associate's degree	359.36	100	8.9
College graduate	427.42	119	34.6
Bachelor's degree	424.70	119	22.2
Master's, professional, doctoral degree	432.13	121	12.3

Note: Market shares may not sum to 100.0 because of rounding and missing categories by household type. "Asian" and "black" include Hispanics and non-Hispanics who identify themselves as being of the respective race alone. "Hispanic" includes people of any race who identify themselves as Hispanic. "Other" includes people who identify themselves as non-Hispanic and as Alaska Native, American Indian, Asian (who are also included in the "Asian" row), Native Hawaiian or other Pacific Islander, as well as non-Hispanics reporting more than one race.
Source: Calculations by New Strategist based on the Bureau of Labor Statistics' 2007 Consumer Expenditure Survey.

Lunch at Full-Service Restaurants

Best customers:

Householders aged 55 to 64
Married couples without children at home
Married couples with adult children at home
Asians

Customer trends:

Average household spending on lunch at full-service restaurants will rise as growing numbers of baby boomers become empty-nesters with more free time—but only if discretionary income grows.

The biggest spenders on lunch at full-service restaurants are the same customers who spend big on full-service dinners—older married couples enjoying a leisurely meal. Householders aged 55 to 64 spend 15 percent more than average on this item. Married couples without children at home (many of them empty-nesters) spend 37 percent more than average on lunch at full-service restaurants. Couples with adult children at home spend 49 percent more, in part because their households are larger than average. Asians spend 26 percent more than the average household on full-service lunches.

Average household spending on full-service lunches was stable between 2006 and 2007, falling by just 0.6 percent after adjusting for inflation. Behind the relative stability in spending on this item is the aging of the baby-boom generation into the best-customer age group. Spending on full-service lunches could increase in the years ahead as boomers become empty-nesters with more free time to enjoy a leisurely meal—but only if discretionary income grows.

Table 15.8 Lunch at full-service restaurants

Total household spending $36,993,440,640.00
Average household spends 307.84

	AVERAGE HOUSEHOLD SPENDING	BEST CUSTOMERS (index)	BIGGEST CUSTOMERS (market share)
AGE OF HOUSEHOLDER			
Average household	**$307.84**	**100**	**100.0%**
Under age 25	154.19	50	3.4
Aged 25 to 34	301.35	98	16.7
Aged 35 to 44	327.14	106	20.7
Aged 45 to 54	330.56	107	22.6
Aged 55 to 64	355.05	115	18.7
Aged 65 to 74	278.63	91	9.0
Aged 75 or older	298.34	97	9.2

	AVERAGE HOUSEHOLD SPENDING	BEST CUSTOMERS (index)	BIGGEST CUSTOMERS (market share)
HOUSEHOLD INCOME			
Average household	**$307.84**	**100**	**100.0%**
Under $20,000	121.83	40	8.1
$20,000 to $39,999	199.00	65	15.0
$40,000 to $49,999	284.33	92	9.1
$50,000 to $69,999	295.75	96	14.7
$70,000 to $79,999	404.04	131	7.6
$80,000 to $99,999	454.00	147	12.0
$100,000 or more	598.11	194	33.3
HOUSEHOLD TYPE			
Average household	**307.84**	**100**	**100.0**
Married couples	398.06	129	65.4
Married couples, no children	422.68	137	29.6
Married couples, with children	381.56	124	30.9
Oldest child under age 6	321.89	105	5.1
Oldest child aged 6 to 17	364.54	118	15.0
Oldest child aged 18 or older	459.05	149	11.0
Single parent with child under age 18	182.49	59	3.5
Single person	200.07	65	19.3
RACE AND HISPANIC ORIGIN			
Average household	**307.84**	**100**	**100.0**
Asian	388.33	126	4.5
Black	158.82	52	6.2
Hispanic	293.43	95	11.3
Non-Hispanic white and other	332.63	108	82.5
REGION			
Average household	**307.84**	**100**	**100.0**
Northeast	288.19	94	17.4
Midwest	274.59	89	20.4
South	307.88	100	35.9
West	358.74	117	26.4
EDUCATION			
Average household	**307.84**	**100**	**100.0**
Less than high school graduate	167.74	54	8.3
High school graduate	218.43	71	17.9
Some college	285.60	93	20.2
Associate's degree	359.09	117	10.4
College graduate	451.73	147	42.5
Bachelor's degree	432.29	140	26.3
Master's, professional, doctoral degree	485.50	158	16.1

Note: Market shares may not sum to 100.0 because of rounding and missing categories by household type. "Asian" and "black" include Hispanics and non-Hispanics who identify themselves as being of the respective race alone. "Hispanic" includes people of any race who identify themselves as Hispanic. "Other" includes people who identify themselves as non-Hispanic and as Alaska Native, American Indian, Asian (who are also included in the "Asian" row), Native Hawaiian or other Pacific Islander, as well as non-Hispanics reporting more than one race.
Source: Calculations by New Strategist based on the Bureau of Labor Statistics' 2007 Consumer Expenditure Survey.

Restaurant and Carry-Out Food on Trips

Best customers:
Householders aged 45 to 64
Married couples without children at home
Married couples with school-aged or older children at home
Asians

Customer trends:
Average household spending on restaurant and carry-out food on trips should grow as boomers fill the best-customer lifestage, but only if discretionary income rises.

The biggest spenders on restaurant and carry-out meals on trips are the most avid travelers—older married couples. Householders aged 45 to 64 spend 24 to 39 percent more than average on this item. Married couples without children at home (most of them empty-nesters) spend 66 percent more than average on restaurant and carry-out meals on trips and control 36 percent of the market. Those with school-aged or older children at home spend 31 to 59 percent more. Asians, the most-affluent racial and ethnic group, spend 32 percent more than average on eating out while traveling.

Average household spending on restaurant and carry-out meals on trips fell by 2 percent between 2006 and 2007, after adjusting for inflation. Behind the decline was household budget cutting in the midst of the economic downturn. Spending on this item should grow in the years ahead as boomers fill the best-customer lifestage, but only if discretionary income grows.

Table 15.9 Restaurant and carry-out food on trips

Total household spending $29,505,585,630.00
Average household spends 245.53

AGE OF HOUSEHOLDER	AVERAGE HOUSEHOLD SPENDING	BEST CUSTOMERS (index)	BIGGEST CUSTOMERS (market share)
Average household	$245.53	100	100.0%
Under age 25	105.56	43	2.9
Aged 25 to 34	178.53	73	12.4
Aged 35 to 44	265.50	108	21.1
Aged 45 to 54	304.79	124	26.1
Aged 55 to 64	341.36	139	22.5
Aged 65 to 74	261.98	107	10.7
Aged 75 or older	112.72	46	4.4

	AVERAGE HOUSEHOLD SPENDING	BEST CUSTOMERS (index)	BIGGEST CUSTOMERS (market share)
HOUSEHOLD INCOME			
Average household	**$245.53**	**100**	**100.0%**
Under $20,000	58.01	24	4.9
$20,000 to $39,999	108.97	44	10.3
$40,000 to $49,999	146.31	60	5.9
$50,000 to $69,999	234.72	96	14.6
$70,000 to $79,999	263.23	107	6.2
$80,000 to $99,999	355.84	145	11.8
$100,000 or more	664.06	270	46.3
HOUSEHOLD TYPE			
Average household	**245.53**	**100**	**100.0**
Married couples	358.77	146	73.9
Married couples, no children	406.40	166	35.7
Married couples, with children	337.77	138	34.3
Oldest child under age 6	228.13	93	4.5
Oldest child aged 6 to 17	389.70	159	20.2
Oldest child aged 18 or older	320.85	131	9.6
Single parent with child under age 18	102.25	42	2.5
Single person	131.54	54	15.9
RACE AND HISPANIC ORIGIN			
Average household	**245.53**	**100**	**100.0**
Asian	323.70	132	4.7
Black	89.22	36	4.4
Hispanic	142.25	58	6.8
Non-Hispanic white and other	286.08	117	88.9
REGION			
Average household	**245.53**	**100**	**100.0**
Northeast	261.53	107	19.8
Midwest	244.63	100	22.8
South	195.31	80	28.6
West	312.99	127	28.8
EDUCATION			
Average household	**245.53**	**100**	**100.0**
Less than high school graduate	69.40	28	4.3
High school graduate	136.98	56	14.1
Some college	204.57	83	18.1
Associate's degree	231.97	94	8.4
College graduate	467.39	190	55.1
Bachelor's degree	385.88	157	29.5
Master's, professional, doctoral degree	617.15	251	25.6

Note: Market shares may not sum to 100.0 because of rounding and missing categories by household type. "Asian" and "black" include Hispanics and non-Hispanics who identify themselves as being of the respective race alone. "Hispanic" includes people of any race who identify themselves as Hispanic. "Other" includes people who identify themselves as non-Hispanic and as Alaska Native, American Indian, Asian (who are also included in the "Asian" row), Native Hawaiian or other Pacific Islander, as well as non-Hispanics reporting more than one race.
Source: Calculations by New Strategist based on the Bureau of Labor Statistics' 2007 Consumer Expenditure Survey.

Snacks at Employer and School Cafeterias

Best customers:
Householders aged 35 to 54
Married couples with school-aged children
Asians
Households in the Northeast

Customer trends:
Average household spending on snacks at employer and school cafeterias may continue to decline as fewer employers provide cafeterias in an attempt to cut costs.

Not surprisingly, parents and workers are the biggest spenders on snacks at employer and school cafeterias. Householders aged 35 to 54, most of them in the workforce, spend 37 to 57 percent more than average on this item and account for 60 percent of the market. Married couples with school-aged children at home, many of them dual-income couples, spend 60 percent more than the average household on this item. Asians spend 40 percent more than average on snacks at employer and school cafeterias. Northeastern householders spend two-thirds more than average on cafeteria snacks.

Average household spending on snacks at employer and school cafeterias fell by a substantial 11 percent between 2006 and 2007, after adjusting for inflation. Behind the decline was household budget cutting, with discretionary expenses such as snacks experiencing especially deep declines. In the years ahead, average household spending on snacks at employer and school cafeterias could continue to decline as employers attempt to cut costs by eliminating cafeterias.

Table 15.10 Snacks at employer and school cafeterias

Total household spending $751,068,750.00
Average household spends   6.25

	AVERAGE HOUSEHOLD SPENDING	BEST CUSTOMERS (index)	BIGGEST CUSTOMERS (market share)
AGE OF HOUSEHOLDER			
Average household	**$6.25**	**100**	**100.0%**
Under age 25	5.99	96	6.5
Aged 25 to 34	6.57	105	17.9
Aged 35 to 44	9.84	157	30.7
Aged 45 to 54	8.58	137	28.8
Aged 55 to 64	3.54	57	9.2
Aged 65 to 74	3.06	49	4.9
Aged 75 or older	1.33	21	2.0

	AVERAGE HOUSEHOLD SPENDING	BEST CUSTOMERS (index)	BIGGEST CUSTOMERS (market share)
HOUSEHOLD INCOME			
Average household	**$6.25**	**100**	**100.0%**
Under $20,000	2.30	37	7.6
$20,000 to $39,999	4.59	73	17.1
$40,000 to $49,999	5.56	89	8.8
$50,000 to $69,999	7.00	112	17.1
$70,000 to $79,999	9.06	145	8.4
$80,000 to $99,999	8.40	134	10.9
$100,000 or more	10.94	175	30.0
HOUSEHOLD TYPE			
Average household	**6.25**	**100**	**100.0**
Married couples	6.67	107	53.9
Married couples, no children	3.51	56	12.1
Married couples, with children	8.59	137	34.3
Oldest child under age 6	6.93	111	5.4
Oldest child aged 6 to 17	10.01	160	20.3
Oldest child aged 18 or older	7.01	112	8.3
Single parent with child under age 18	6.71	107	6.4
Single person	4.35	70	20.7
RACE AND HISPANIC ORIGIN			
Average household	**6.25**	**100**	**100.0**
Asian	8.75	140	4.9
Black	5.40	86	10.4
Hispanic	5.03	80	9.5
Non-Hispanic white and other	6.58	105	80.4
REGION			
Average household	**6.25**	**100**	**100.0**
Northeast	10.46	167	31.2
Midwest	6.17	99	22.6
South	4.95	79	28.4
West	4.87	78	17.6
EDUCATION			
Average household	**6.25**	**100**	**100.0**
Less than high school graduate	5.04	81	12.2
High school graduate	5.55	89	22.4
Some college	4.97	80	17.3
Associate's degree	6.37	102	9.1
College graduate	8.32	133	38.5
Bachelor's degree	6.85	110	20.5
Master's, professional, doctoral degree	10.88	174	17.8

Note: Market shares may not sum to 100.0 because of rounding and missing categories by household type. "Asian" and "black" include Hispanics and non-Hispanics who identify themselves as being of the respective race alone. "Hispanic" includes people of any race who identify themselves as Hispanic. "Other" includes people who identify themselves as non-Hispanic and as Alaska Native, American Indian, Asian (who are also included in the "Asian" row), Native Hawaiian or other Pacific Islander, as well as non-Hispanics reporting more than one race.
Source: Calculations by New Strategist based on the Bureau of Labor Statistics' 2007 Consumer Expenditure Survey.

Snacks at Fast-Food Restaurants
Including Take-Outs, Deliveries, Concession Stands, Buffets, and Cafeterias (except Employer and School)

Best customers:	**Householders aged 35 to 54** **Married couples with children at home** **Single parents** **Asians** **Households in the West**
Customer trends:	**Average household spending on snacks from fast-food restaurants should continue to decline as the small generation X fills the best-customer lifestage.**

Parents are the best customers of snacks from fast-food restaurants. Householders aged 35 to 54, many with children at home, spend 21 to 41 percent more than the average household on fast-food snacks. Married couples with children at home spend 59 percent more than average on this item, the figure peaking at 74 percent more than average among parents with school-aged children. Single parents spend 9 percent more. Asians spend one-third more than average on this item, and households in the West, where many Asians reside, spend 43 percent more than average.

Average household spending on snacks from fast-food restaurants fell by 1 percent between 2006 and 2007, after adjusting for inflation. Spending on this item should continue to fall in the years ahead as the small generation X enters the best-customer lifestage.

Table 15.11 Snacks at fast-food restaurants, including take-outs, deliveries, concession stands, buffets, and cafeterias (except employer and school)

Total household spending $13,153,917,660.00
Average household spends 109.46

	AVERAGE HOUSEHOLD SPENDING	BEST CUSTOMERS (index)	BIGGEST CUSTOMERS (market share)
AGE OF HOUSEHOLDER			
Average household	**$109.46**	**100**	**100.0%**
Under age 25	98.45	90	6.1
Aged 25 to 34	120.92	110	18.8
Aged 35 to 44	154.06	141	27.4
Aged 45 to 54	132.37	121	25.4
Aged 55 to 64	98.63	90	14.6
Aged 65 to 74	53.21	49	4.9
Aged 75 or older	32.32	30	2.8

	AVERAGE HOUSEHOLD SPENDING	BEST CUSTOMERS (index)	BIGGEST CUSTOMERS (market share)
HOUSEHOLD INCOME			
Average household	**$109.46**	**100**	**100.0%**
Under $20,000	44.57	41	8.4
$20,000 to $39,999	66.18	60	14.1
$40,000 to $49,999	100.61	92	9.0
$50,000 to $69,999	101.47	93	14.2
$70,000 to $79,999	156.66	143	8.3
$80,000 to $99,999	171.47	157	12.7
$100,000 or more	211.98	194	33.2
HOUSEHOLD TYPE			
Average household	**109.46**	**100**	**100.0**
Married couples	136.95	125	63.2
Married couples, no children	95.38	87	18.8
Married couples, with children	173.95	159	39.7
Oldest child under age 6	135.14	123	6.0
Oldest child aged 6 to 17	190.43	174	22.1
Oldest child aged 18 or older	169.81	155	11.4
Single parent with child under age 18	119.65	109	6.5
Single person	57.35	52	15.6
RACE AND HISPANIC ORIGIN			
Average household	**109.46**	**100**	**100.0**
Asian	144.32	132	4.7
Black	60.12	55	6.6
Hispanic	109.05	100	11.8
Non-Hispanic white and other	117.24	107	81.8
REGION			
Average household	**109.46**	**100**	**100.0**
Northeast	114.24	104	19.4
Midwest	98.97	90	20.7
South	84.48	77	27.7
West	156.48	143	32.3
EDUCATION			
Average household	**109.46**	**100**	**100.0**
Less than high school graduate	59.15	54	8.2
High school graduate	74.79	68	17.2
Some college	112.52	103	22.4
Associate's degree	134.87	123	11.0
College graduate	153.39	140	40.6
Bachelor's degree	155.52	142	26.6
Master's, professional, doctoral degree	149.70	137	14.0

Note: Market shares may not sum to 100.0 because of rounding and missing categories by household type. "Asian" and "black" include Hispanics and non-Hispanics who identify themselves as being of the respective race alone. "Hispanic" includes people of any race who identify themselves as Hispanic. "Other" includes people who identify themselves as non-Hispanic and as Alaska Native, American Indian, Asian (who are also included in the "Asian" row), Native Hawaiian or other Pacific Islander, as well as non-Hispanics reporting more than one race.
Source: Calculations by New Strategist based on the Bureau of Labor Statistics' 2007 Consumer Expenditure Survey.

Snacks at Full-Service Restaurants

Best customers:

Householders aged 55 to 64
Married couples with adult children at home
Asians
Households in the Northeast

Customer trends:

Average household spending on snacks at full-service restaurants could rise in the years ahead as casual sit-down restaurants compete with fast-food establishments for the dollars of snackers, but only if discretionary income grows.

The biggest spenders on snacks at full-service restaurants are older adults and married couples with adult children at home. Householders aged 55 to 64 spend 34 percent more than average on snacks at full-service restaurants and account for 22 percent of the market. Married couples with adult children at home spend 71 percent more than average on this item in part because their households include young adults—who are known for their big appetites. Asian householders spend more than double the average on full-service restaurant snacks. Householders in the Northeast spend one-third more than average on the item.

Average household spending on snacks at full-service restaurants fell by 7 percent between 2006 and 2007, after adjusting for inflation. Behind the decline was household budget cutting, with discretionary expenses such as snacks experiencing especially deep declines. Spending on this item could grow in the years ahead as casual sit-down restaurants compete with fast-food establishments for the dollars of snackers—but only if discretionary income grows.

Table 15.12 Snacks at full-service restaurants

Total household spending — $3,411,654,690.00
Average household spends — 28.39

AGE OF HOUSEHOLDER	AVERAGE HOUSEHOLD SPENDING	BEST CUSTOMERS (index)	BIGGEST CUSTOMERS (market share)
Average household	$28.39	100	100.0%
Under age 25	21.25	75	5.1
Aged 25 to 34	32.88	116	19.8
Aged 35 to 44	29.65	104	20.4
Aged 45 to 54	30.43	107	22.5
Aged 55 to 64	38.07	134	21.7
Aged 65 to 74	15.66	55	5.5
Aged 75 or older	15.85	56	5.3

	AVERAGE HOUSEHOLD SPENDING	BEST CUSTOMERS (index)	BIGGEST CUSTOMERS (market share)
HOUSEHOLD INCOME			
Average household	**$28.39**	**100**	**100.0%**
Under $20,000	12.12	43	8.8
$20,000 to $39,999	19.12	67	15.7
$40,000 to $49,999	30.23	106	10.5
$50,000 to $69,999	29.80	105	16.1
$70,000 to $79,999	35.94	127	7.3
$80,000 to $99,999	55.31	195	15.9
$100,000 or more	40.71	143	24.6
HOUSEHOLD TYPE			
Average household	**28.39**	**100**	**100.0**
Married couples	32.83	116	58.5
Married couples, no children	30.99	109	23.5
Married couples, with children	32.47	114	28.5
Oldest child under age 6	24.78	87	4.3
Oldest child aged 6 to 17	27.24	96	12.2
Oldest child aged 18 or older	48.46	171	12.6
Single parent with child under age 18	24.68	87	5.2
Single person	23.22	82	24.3
RACE AND HISPANIC ORIGIN			
Average household	**28.39**	**100**	**100.0**
Asian	66.80	235	8.3
Black	14.01	49	5.9
Hispanic	26.69	94	11.1
Non-Hispanic white and other	30.85	109	83.0
REGION			
Average household	**28.39**	**100**	**100.0**
Northeast	38.47	136	25.2
Midwest	33.86	119	27.3
South	19.34	68	24.5
West	28.79	101	22.9
EDUCATION			
Average household	**28.39**	**100**	**100.0**
Less than high school graduate	26.70	94	14.3
High school graduate	19.57	69	17.4
Some college	27.57	97	21.1
Associate's degree	26.49	93	8.3
College graduate	37.99	134	38.7
Bachelor's degree	34.50	122	22.8
Master's, professional, doctoral degree	44.06	155	15.8

Note: Market shares may not sum to 100.0 because of rounding and missing categories by household type. "Asian" and "black" include Hispanics and non-Hispanics who identify themselves as being of the respective race alone. "Hispanic" includes people of any race who identify themselves as Hispanic. "Other" includes people who identify themselves as non-Hispanic and as Alaska Native, American Indian, Asian (who are also included in the "Asian" row), Native Hawaiian or other Pacific Islander, as well as non-Hispanics reporting more than one race.
Source: Calculations by New Strategist based on the Bureau of Labor Statistics' 2007 Consumer Expenditure Survey.

Snacks at Vending Machines and Mobile Vendors

Best customers: **Householders under age 45**
     Married couples with children at home
     Hispanics

Customer trends: **Average household spending on snacks from vending machines and mobile vendors could continue to decline as restaurants compete for snack dollars.**

The biggest spenders on snacks from vending machines and mobile vendors are young adults and parents with children. Householders under age 45, most of them parents, spend 21 to 48 percent more than average on this item. Married couples with children at home spend 58 percent more than average on vending machine snacks, the figure peaking at 62 percent more than average among those with preschoolers. Hispanics, who tend to have large families, spend 30 percent more than average on this item.

Average household spending on snacks from vending machines and mobile vendors fell by a substantial 12 percent between 2006 and 2007, after adjusting for inflation. Behind the decline was household budget cutting, with discretionary expenses such as snacks experiencing especially deep declines. Spending on this category could continue to decline in the years ahead as fast-food and full-service restaurants compete for the snack dollar.

Table 15.13 Snacks at vending machines and mobile vendors

Total household spending	$3,331,140,120.00		
Average household spends	27.72		

	AVERAGE HOUSEHOLD SPENDING	BEST CUSTOMERS (index)	BIGGEST CUSTOMERS (market share)
AGE OF HOUSEHOLDER			
Average household	**$27.72**	**100**	**100.0%**
Under age 25	40.20	145	9.8
Aged 25 to 34	33.65	121	20.7
Aged 35 to 44	40.90	148	28.8
Aged 45 to 54	31.43	113	23.8
Aged 55 to 64	19.49	70	11.4
Aged 65 to 74	8.33	30	3.0
Aged 75 or older	6.50	23	2.2

	AVERAGE HOUSEHOLD SPENDING	BEST CUSTOMERS (index)	BIGGEST CUSTOMERS (market share)
HOUSEHOLD INCOME			
Average household	$27.72	100	100.0%
Under $20,000	11.53	42	8.6
$20,000 to $39,999	21.07	76	17.7
$40,000 to $49,999	32.94	119	11.7
$50,000 to $69,999	34.05	123	18.8
$70,000 to $79,999	42.13	152	8.8
$80,000 to $99,999	44.47	160	13.1
$100,000 or more	32.92	119	20.3
HOUSEHOLD TYPE			
Average household	27.72	100	100.0
Married couples	32.89	119	60.0
Married couples, no children	21.16	76	16.5
Married couples, with children	43.79	158	39.4
Oldest child under age 6	45.02	162	7.9
Oldest child aged 6 to 17	43.21	156	19.8
Oldest child aged 18 or older	44.05	159	11.7
Single parent with child under age 18	26.85	97	5.8
Single person	14.29	52	15.3
RACE AND HISPANIC ORIGIN			
Average household	27.72	100	100.0
Asian	24.81	90	3.2
Black	26.80	97	11.6
Hispanic	36.12	130	15.4
Non-Hispanic white and other	26.65	96	73.4
REGION			
Average household	27.72	100	100.0
Northeast	23.50	85	15.8
Midwest	32.84	118	27.1
South	28.21	102	36.5
West	25.20	91	20.6
EDUCATION			
Average household	27.72	100	100.0
Less than high school graduate	24.55	89	13.4
High school graduate	27.03	98	24.6
Some college	32.39	117	25.4
Associate's degree	39.72	143	12.7
College graduate	22.97	83	24.0
Bachelor's degree	24.32	88	16.4
Master's, professional, doctoral degree	20.62	74	7.6

Note: Market shares may not sum to 100.0 because of rounding and missing categories by household type. "Asian" and "black" include Hispanics and non-Hispanics who identify themselves as being of the respective race alone. "Hispanic" includes people of any race who identify themselves as Hispanic. "Other" includes people who identify themselves as non-Hispanic and as Alaska Native, American Indian, Asian (who are also included in the "Asian" row), Native Hawaiian or other Pacific Islander, as well as non-Hispanics reporting more than one race.
Source: Calculations by New Strategist based on the Bureau of Labor Statistics' 2007 Consumer Expenditure Survey.

Chapter 16.

Shelter

Household Spending on Shelter, 2007

Americans spend more on shelter than on any other major category, a total of $10,023 per household in 2007. More than one-third of this total goes toward mortgage interest, while 17 percent is devoted to property taxes. The average household spent 17 percent more on shelter in 2007 than in 2000, after adjusting for inflation. Spending on mortgage interest rose 21 percent, while spending on property taxes increased 25 percent.

The biggest spenders on shelter are the most-affluent householders, who tend to buy the most expensive homes. But the biggest spenders on many items, such as homeowner's insurance and property taxes, are older householders because they have the highest homeownership rate. Older homeowners are also the biggest spenders on maintenance and repair services since they are more likely than younger homeowners to hire others to do the work rather than do it themselves. Average household spending on shelter will continue to rise as the population ages.

Spending on mortgage interest

(average spending by households on mortgage interest, 2000 and 2007; in 2007 dollars)

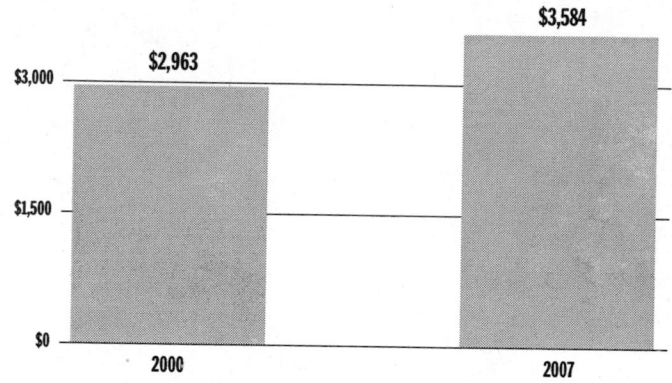

Table 16.1 Shelter Spending, 2000 to 2007

(average annual household spending on shelter, and percent distribution of spending by type, 2000 and 2007; percent change in spending, 2000–07; in 2007 dollars; ranked by amount spent)

	2007		2000		
	average household spending	percent distribution	average household spending (in 2007$)	percent distribution	percent change 2000–07
Average household spending on shelter	**$10,022.69**	**100.0%**	**$8,566.11**	**100.0%**	**17.0%**
Mortgage interest	3,583.53	35.8	$2,962.61	34.6	21.0
Rent	2,491.52	24.9	$2,380.86	27.8	4.6
Property taxes	1,708.86	17.0	$1,370.90	16.0	24.7
Maintenance and repair services, owned home	574.87	5.7	$528.49	6.2	8.8
Insurance, homeowner's	340.31	3.4	$282.77	3.3	20.4
Home equity loan/line of credit interest	306.49	3.1	$214.30	2.5	43.0
Vacation homes, owned	286.81	2.9	$178.09	2.1	61.0
Maintenance and repair materials, owned home	90.20	0.9	$94.01	1.1	–4.1
Maintenance and repair services and materials, rented home	30.41	0.3	$22.49	0.3	35.2
Property management and security, owned home	54.65	0.5	$37.31	0.4	46.5
Insurance, tenant's	10.30	0.1	$10.67	0.1	–3.5

Note: The average household also spent $1,429 on mortgage principal payments and $1,213 on capital improvements to owned homes. These figures are not included in the shelter spending total because the Consumer Expenditure Survey considers them assets rather than expenditures. Numbers do not add to total because not all categories are shown.
Source: Bureau of Labor Statistics, 2000 and 2007 Consumer Expenditure Surveys; calculations by New Strategist

Home Equity Loan and Line of Credit Interest

Best customers:
        Householders aged 35 to 64
        Married couples without children at home
        Married couples with school-aged or older children at home

Customer trends:
        Average household spending on home equity loan and line of credit interest is likely
        to stabilize or even decline as lending standards tighten and home values fall.

Householders aged 35 to 64 spend 22 to 56 percent more than the average household on interest for home equity loans and lines of credit. Married couples without children at home (most of them older empty-nesters) spend 32 percent more than average, while couples with school-aged children spend 70 percent more. Spending on this item peaks among couples with adult children at home, who spend more than twice the average on home equity loan interest payments. Many of these householders have children in college, and they are borrowing to pay the bills.

Average household spending on interest for home equity loans and lines of credit grew by a substantial 43 percent between 2000 and 2007, after adjusting for inflation. Behind the increase were rising home values and relaxed lending standards during the housing bubble, encouraging more people to borrow against their home. Spending on home equity interest is likely to stabilize or even decline in the coming years as lending standards tighten and home values fall.

Table 16.2 Home equity loan and line of credit interest

Total household spending $36,831,209,790.00
Average household spends   306.49

	AVERAGE HOUSEHOLD SPENDING	BEST CUSTOMERS (index)	BIGGEST CUSTOMERS (market share)
AGE OF HOUSEHOLDER			
Average household	**$306.49**	**100**	**100.0%**
Under age 25	11.62	4	0.3
Aged 25 to 34	178.53	58	9.9
Aged 35 to 44	373.16	122	23.7
Aged 45 to 54	477.21	156	32.7
Aged 55 to 64	422.11	138	22.3
Aged 65 to 74	268.24	88	8.7
Aged 75 or older	75.12	25	2.3

	AVERAGE HOUSEHOLD SPENDING	BEST CUSTOMERS (index)	BIGGEST CUSTOMERS (market share)
HOUSEHOLD INCOME			
Average household	**$306.49**	**100**	**100.0%**
Under $20,000	46.55	15	3.1
$20,000 to $39,999	91.04	30	6.9
$40,000 to $49,999	150.29	49	4.8
$50,000 to $69,999	267.72	87	13.4
$70,000 to $79,999	427.35	139	8.1
$80,000 to $99,999	479.07	156	12.7
$100,000 or more	912.27	298	51.0
HOUSEHOLD TYPE			
Average household	**306.49**	**100**	**100.0**
Married couples	464.31	151	76.6
Married couples, no children	403.59	132	28.4
Married couples, with children	530.94	173	43.2
Oldest child under age 6	329.70	108	5.3
Oldest child aged 6 to 17	522.53	170	21.7
Oldest child aged 18 or older	678.75	221	16.3
Single parent with child under age 18	148.97	49	2.9
Single person	141.64	46	13.7
RACE AND HISPANIC ORIGIN			
Average household	**306.49**	**100**	**100.0**
Asian	324.30	106	3.7
Black	98.28	32	3.8
Hispanic	137.42	45	5.3
Non-Hispanic white and other	364.81	119	90.9
REGION			
Average household	**306.49**	**100**	**100.0**
Northeast	377.20	123	22.9
Midwest	362.50	118	27.0
South	197.32	64	23.1
West	365.01	119	26.9
EDUCATION			
Average household	**306.49**	**100**	**100.0**
Less than high school graduate	95.10	31	4.7
High school graduate	195.21	64	16.1
Some college	286.38	93	20.3
Associate's degree	311.48	102	9.0
College graduate	527.85	172	49.8
Bachelor's degree	464.77	152	28.4
Master's, professional, doctoral degree	643.75	210	21.4

Note: Market shares may not sum to 100.0 because of rounding and missing categories by household type. "Asian" and "black" include Hispanics and non-Hispanics who identify themselves as being of the respective race alone. "Hispanic" includes people of any race who identify themselves as Hispanic. "Other" includes people who identify themselves as non-Hispanic and as Alaska Native, American Indian, Asian (who are also included in the "Asian" row), Native Hawaiian or other Pacific Islander, as well as non-Hispanics reporting more than one race.
Source: Calculations by New Strategist based on the Bureau of Labor Statistics' 2007 Consumer Expenditure Survey.

Insurance, Homeowner's

Best customers:	**Householders aged 55 to 74** **Married couples without children at home** **Married couples with school-aged or older children at home**
Customer trends:	**Average household spending on homeowner's insurance will rise along with disaster-related insurance claims.**

Homeownership rises with age. This explains why householders aged 55 to 74 spend the most on homeowner's insurance—25 to 29 percent more than the average household. Married couples without children at home (most of them empty-nesters) and those with school-aged or older children at home spend 34 to 41 percent more than average on this item.

Average household spending on homeowner's insurance rose 20 percent between 2000 and 2007, after adjusting for inflation. This increase is likely to continue as boomers age and disaster-related insurance claims boost rates.

Table 16.3 **Insurance, homeowner's**

Total household spending	$40,895,393,010.00
Average household spends	340.31

	AVERAGE HOUSEHOLD SPENDING	BEST CUSTOMERS (index)	BIGGEST CUSTOMERS (market share)
AGE OF HOUSEHOLDER			
Average household	**$340.31**	**100**	**100.0%**
Under age 25	59.09	17	1.2
Aged 25 to 34	215.47	63	10.8
Aged 35 to 44	366.83	108	21.0
Aged 45 to 54	386.43	114	23.9
Aged 55 to 64	425.53	125	20.3
Aged 65 to 74	437.51	129	12.8
Aged 75 or older	361.39	106	10.1

	AVERAGE HOUSEHOLD SPENDING	BEST CUSTOMERS (index)	BIGGEST CUSTOMERS (market share)
HOUSEHOLD INCOME			
Average household	$340.31	100	100.0%
Under $20,000	116.66	34	7.0
$20,000 to $39,999	234.15	69	16.0
$40,000 to $49,999	292.02	86	8.4
$50,000 to $69,999	348.20	102	15.7
$70,000 to $79,999	425.36	125	7.2
$80,000 to $99,999	514.90	151	12.3
$100,000 or more	661.75	194	33.3
HOUSEHOLD TYPE			
Average household	340.31	100	100.0
Married couples	463.70	136	68.9
Married couples, no children	479.72	141	30.4
Married couples, with children	447.01	131	32.8
Oldest child under age 6	356.71	105	5.1
Oldest child aged 6 to 17	476.77	140	17.8
Oldest child aged 18 or older	455.53	134	9.9
Single parent with child under age 18	179.20	53	3.1
Single person	208.81	61	18.2
RACE AND HISPANIC ORIGIN			
Average household	340.31	100	100.0
Asian	310.69	91	3.2
Black	217.00	64	7.7
Hispanic	195.24	57	6.8
Non-Hispanic white and other	381.95	112	85.7
REGION			
Average household	340.31	100	100.0
Northeast	312.98	92	17.1
Midwest	327.11	96	22.0
South	389.52	114	41.1
West	298.04	88	19.8
EDUCATION			
Average household	340.31	100	100.0
Less than high school graduate	184.57	54	8.2
High school graduate	304.36	89	22.6
Some college	307.07	90	19.6
Associate's degree	386.62	114	10.1
College graduate	464.05	136	39.5
Bachelor's degree	434.70	128	23.9
Master's, professional, doctoral degree	517.99	152	15.5

Note: Market shares may not sum to 100.0 because of rounding and missing categories by household type. "Asian" and "black" include Hispanics and non-Hispanics who identify themselves as being of the respective race alone. "Hispanic" includes people of any race who identify themselves as Hispanic. "Other" includes people who identify themselves as non-Hispanic and as Alaska Native, American Indian, Asian (who are also included in the "Asian" row), Native Hawaiian or other Pacific Islander, as well as non-Hispanics reporting more than one race.
Source: Calculations by New Strategist based on the Bureau of Labor Statistics' 2007 Consumer Expenditure Survey.

Insurance, Tenant's

Best customers:
:   **Householders aged 25 to 34**
    Single parents
    People living alone
    Households in the West

Customer trends:
:   **Average household spending on tenant's insurance may rise as millennials fill the best-customer age group.**

Young adults, single parents, and people who live alone are the best customers of tenant's insurance because they are most likely to be renters. Householders aged 25 to 34 spend 61 percent more than the average household on renter's insurance. Single parents spend 76 percent more than average on tenant's insurance, and people who live alone spend 24 percent more than average on this item. Households in the West spend 40 percent more than average on tenant's insurance.

Average household spending on tenant's insurance fell 3 percent between 2000 and 2007, after adjusting for inflation. One factor behind the decline was the presence of the small generation X in the best-customer age group. Spending on this item may rise as the large millennial generation fills the 25-to-34 age group.

Table 16.4 Insurance, tenant's

Total household spending $1,237,761,300.00
Average household spends 10.30

AGE OF HOUSEHOLDER	AVERAGE HOUSEHOLD SPENDING	BEST CUSTOMERS (index)	BIGGEST CUSTOMERS (market share)
Average household	$10.30	100	100.0%
Under age 25	10.33	100	6.8
Aged 25 to 34	16.56	161	27.4
Aged 35 to 44	8.51	83	16.1
Aged 45 to 54	5.30	51	10.8
Aged 55 to 64	12.05	117	18.9
Aged 65 to 74	10.52	102	10.2
Aged 75 or older	10.54	102	9.7

	AVERAGE HOUSEHOLD SPENDING	BEST CUSTOMERS (index)	BIGGEST CUSTOMERS (market share)
HOUSEHOLD INCOME			
Average household	$10.30	100	100.0%
Under $20,000	6.61	64	13.2
$20,000 to $39,999	14.33	139	32.3
$40,000 to $49,999	13.05	127	12.5
$50,000 to $69,999	12.26	119	18.2
$70,000 to $79,999	9.40	91	5.3
$80,000 to $99,999	8.37	81	6.6
$100,000 or more	7.12	69	11.8
HOUSEHOLD TYPE			
Average household	10.30	100	100.0
Married couples	6.61	64	32.4
Married couples, no children	8.49	82	17.8
Married couples, with children	5.43	53	13.2
Oldest child under age 6	10.16	99	4.8
Oldest child aged 6 to 17	4.50	44	5.5
Oldest child aged 18 or older	3.88	38	2.8
Single parent with child under age 18	18.12	176	10.5
Single person	12.81	124	37.0
RACE AND HISPANIC ORIGIN			
Average household	10.30	100	100.0
Asian	6.43	62	2.2
Black	9.13	89	10.6
Hispanic	4.30	42	4.9
Non-Hispanic white and other	11.39	111	84.4
REGION			
Average household	10.30	100	100.0
Northeast	7.54	73	13.6
Midwest	11.48	111	25.5
South	8.38	81	29.2
West	14.40	140	31.6
EDUCATION			
Average household	10.30	100	100.0
Less than high school graduate	4.94	48	7.3
High school graduate	6.69	65	16.4
Some college	11.67	113	24.7
Associate's degree	14.17	138	12.2
College graduate	14.01	136	39.4
Bachelor's degree	16.25	158	29.6
Master's, professional, doctoral degree	9.91	96	9.8

Note: Market shares may not sum to 100.0 because of rounding and missing categories by household type. "Asian" and "black" include Hispanics and non-Hispanics who identify themselves as being of the respective race alone. "Hispanic" includes people of any race who identify themselves as Hispanic. "Other" includes people who identify themselves as non-Hispanic and as Alaska Native, American Indian, Asian (who are also included in the "Asian" row), Native Hawaiian or other Pacific Islander, as well as non-Hispanics reporting more than one race.
Source: Calculations by New Strategist based on the Bureau of Labor Statistics' 2007 Consumer Expenditure Survey.

Maintenance and Repair Materials, Owned Home

Best customers:
> Householders aged 45 to 54
> Married couples with school-aged or older children at home
> Non-Hispanic whites
> Households in the Northeast

Customer trends:
> Average household spending on maintenance and repair materials for owned homes may continue to decline as boomers move out of the best-customer lifestage.

Middle-age married couples are the best customers of maintenance and repair materials for owned home. These householders are likely to be homeowners, and they are still youthful enough to tackle home improvement tasks themselves. Householders aged 45 to 54 spend 44 percent more than average on this item. Married couples with school-aged or adult children at home spend 45 to 86 percent more than average on maintenance and repair materials for owned homes. Non-Hispanic whites far outspend minority householders on this item, in part because they are more likely to be homeowners. Households in the Northeast spend 42 percent more than average on maintenance and repair materials for owned homes.

Average household spending on maintenance and repair materials for owned homes fell 4 percent between 2000 and 2007, after adjusting for inflation. Average household spending on maintenance and repair materials may continue to decline as boomers age out of the best-customer lifestage, especially if discretionary income is squeezed by the nation's economic problems.

Table 16.5 Maintenance and repair materials, owned home

Total household spending	$10,839,424,200.00
Average household spends	90.20

	AVERAGE HOUSEHOLD SPENDING	BEST CUSTOMERS (index)	BIGGEST CUSTOMERS (market share)
AGE OF HOUSEHOLDER			
Average household	**$90.20**	**100**	**100.0%**
Under age 25	19.36	21	1.5
Aged 25 to 34	97.95	109	18.5
Aged 35 to 44	99.32	110	21.5
Aged 45 to 54	129.52	144	30.2
Aged 55 to 64	98.00	109	17.6
Aged 65 to 74	68.17	76	7.6
Aged 75 or older	30.94	34	3.3

	AVERAGE HOUSEHOLD SPENDING	BEST CUSTOMERS (index)	BIGGEST CUSTOMERS (market share)
HOUSEHOLD INCOME			
Average household	**$90.20**	**100**	**100.0%**
Under $20,000	19.89	22	4.5
$20,000 to $39,999	35.70	40	9.2
$40,000 to $49,999	85.98	95	9.4
$50,000 to $69,999	112.57	125	19.1
$70,000 to $79,999	163.72	182	10.5
$80,000 to $99,999	137.20	152	12.4
$100,000 or more	183.79	204	34.9
HOUSEHOLD TYPE			
Average household	**90.20**	**100**	**100.0**
Married couples	131.46	146	73.7
Married couples, no children	103.24	114	24.7
Married couples, with children	144.08	160	39.9
Oldest child under age 6	103.37	115	5.6
Oldest child aged 6 to 17	167.46	186	23.6
Oldest child aged 18 or older	130.74	145	10.7
Single parent with child under age 18	26.15	29	1.7
Single person	43.15	48	14.2
RACE AND HISPANIC ORIGIN			
Average household	**90.20**	**100**	**100.0**
Asian	30.20	33	1.2
Black	24.40	27	3.2
Hispanic	55.22	61	7.2
Non-Hispanic white and other	105.79	117	89.5
REGION			
Average household	**90.20**	**100**	**100.0**
Northeast	128.11	142	26.5
Midwest	80.74	90	20.5
South	70.33	78	28.0
West	100.09	111	25.1
EDUCATION			
Average household	**90.20**	**100**	**100.0**
Less than high school graduate	44.88	50	7.5
High school graduate	99.71	111	27.9
Some college	84.67	94	20.4
Associate's degree	139.74	155	13.8
College graduate	94.61	105	30.4
Bachelor's degree	110.74	123	23.0
Master's, professional, doctoral degree	64.98	72	7.3

Note: Market shares may not sum to 100.0 because of rounding and missing categories by household type. "Asian" and "black" include Hispanics and non-Hispanics who identify themselves as being of the respective race alone. "Hispanic" includes people of any race who identify themselves as Hispanic. "Other" includes people who identify themselves as non-Hispanic and as Alaska Native, American Indian, Asian (who are also included in the "Asian" row), Native Hawaiian or other Pacific Islander, as well as non-Hispanics reporting more than one race.
Source: Calculations by New Strategist based on the Bureau of Labor Statistics' 2007 Consumer Expenditure Survey.

Maintenance and Repair Services, Owned Home

Best customers:
Householders aged 45 or older
Married couples without children at home
Married couples with adult children at home
Non-Hispanic whites

Customer trends:
Average household spending on maintenance and repair services for owned homes will continue to rise as aging boomers hire others to maintain and improve their homes.

The best customers of maintenance and repair services for owned homes are householders aged 45 or older. Some are physically unable to do the work themselves, while others can better afford to hire help after the expenses of childrearing are over. Householders aged 45 or older spend 17 to 49 percent more than average on this item and control three-fourths of the market. Married couples without children at home (most of them empty-nesters) and those with adult children at home spend 56 to 57 percent more than average on maintenance and repair services for their homes. Non-Hispanic whites, because they are most likely to be homeowners, spend 19 percent more than average on this item and represent 91 percent of the market.

Average household spending on maintenance and repair services for owned homes rose 9 percent between 2000 and 2007, after adjusting for inflation. Behind the increase is the aging of the baby-boom generation into the best-customer lifestage, a trend that will continue to drive growth in this market.

Table 16.6 Maintenance and repair services, owned home

Total household spending	$69,082,702,770.00
Average household spends	574.87

AGE OF HOUSEHOLDER	AVERAGE HOUSEHOLD SPENDING	BEST CUSTOMERS (index)	BIGGEST CUSTOMERS (market share)
Average household	$574.87	100	100.0%
Under age 25	51.98	9	0.6
Aged 25 to 34	248.13	43	7.4
Aged 35 to 44	494.31	86	16.8
Aged 45 to 54	747.67	130	27.3
Aged 55 to 64	856.98	149	24.1
Aged 65 to 74	733.82	128	12.8
Aged 75 or older	669.98	117	11.0

	AVERAGE HOUSEHOLD SPENDING	BEST CUSTOMERS (index)	BIGGEST CUSTOMERS (market share)
HOUSEHOLD INCOME			
Average household	**$574.87**	**100**	**100.0%**
Under $20,000	194.20	34	6.9
$20,000 to $39,999	338.01	59	13.7
$40,000 to $49,999	423.97	74	7.3
$50,000 to $69,999	608.03	106	16.2
$70,000 to $79,999	687.04	120	6.9
$80,000 to $99,999	669.71	116	9.5
$100,000 or more	1,327.09	231	39.5
HOUSEHOLD TYPE			
Average household	**574.87**	**100**	**100.0**
Married couples	791.95	138	69.6
Married couples, no children	903.19	157	33.9
Married couples, with children	729.04	127	31.6
Oldest child under age 6	625.06	109	5.3
Oldest child aged 6 to 17	671.05	117	14.8
Oldest child aged 18 or older	897.90	156	11.5
Single parent with child under age 18	169.73	30	1.8
Single person	378.19	66	19.6
RACE AND HISPANIC ORIGIN			
Average household	**574.87**	**100**	**100.0**
Asian	408.04	71	2.5
Black	205.36	36	4.3
Hispanic	258.26	45	5.3
Non-Hispanic white and other	683.75	119	90.8
REGION			
Average household	**574.87**	**100**	**100.0**
Northeast	638.42	111	20.7
Midwest	632.37	110	25.1
South	493.86	86	30.8
West	593.06	103	23.3
EDUCATION			
Average household	**574.87**	**100**	**100.0**
Less than high school graduate	243.47	42	6.4
High school graduate	377.55	66	16.6
Some college	420.36	73	15.9
Associate's degree	645.90	112	10.0
College graduate	1,014.93	177	51.1
Bachelor's degree	926.48	161	30.2
Master's, professional, doctoral degree	1,177.43	205	20.9

Note: Market shares may not sum to 100.0 because of rounding and missing categories by household type. "Asian" and "black" include Hispanics and non-Hispanics who identify themselves as being of the respective race alone. "Hispanic" includes people of any race who identify themselves as Hispanic. "Other" includes people who identify themselves as non-Hispanic and as Alaska Native, American Indian, Asian (who are also included in the "Asian" row), Native Hawaiian or other Pacific Islander, as well as non-Hispanics reporting more than one race.
Source: Calculations by New Strategist based on the Bureau of Labor Statistics' 2007 Consumer Expenditure Survey.

Mortgage Interest

Best customers:
    Householders aged 35 to 54
    Married couples with children at home
    Asians
    Households in the West

Customer trends:
    Average household spending on mortgage interest is likely to stabilize during the next few years as housing prices fall and the homeownership rate dips.

The longer people have owned their home, the less they spend on mortgage interest. This explains why older householders spend less than younger ones, and why empty-nesters spend less than couples with children. Householders aged 35 to 44 spend the most on mortgage interest—64 percent more than the average household. Householders aged 45 to 54 rank second, spending 29 percent more than average on mortgage interest. Married couples with children under age 18 spend about twice the average on mortgage interest, while those with adult children at home spend 32 percent more than average. High-priced homes explain the 40 percent higher-than-average spending of households in the West on mortgage interest. Because many Asians live in the West, their spending on mortgage interest is 69 percent above average.

Average household spending on mortgage interest rose by 21 percent between 2000 and 2007, after adjusting for inflation. This increase occurred despite the decline in mortgage interest rates during those years. Behind the increase was the rise in housing prices and homeownership. Average household spending on mortgage interest may stabilize in the years ahead as housing prices fall and the homeownership rate dips.

Table 16.7 Mortgage interest

Total household spending $430,636,383,630.00
Average household spends   3,583.53

AGE OF HOUSEHOLDER	AVERAGE HOUSEHOLD SPENDING	BEST CUSTOMERS (index)	BIGGEST CUSTOMERS (market share)
Average household	$3,583.53	100	100.0%
Under age 25	907.31	25	1.7
Aged 25 to 34	4,107.63	115	19.6
Aged 35 to 44	5,866.33	164	31.9
Aged 45 to 54	4,615.33	129	27.1
Aged 55 to 64	2,998.71	84	13.6
Aged 65 to 74	1,781.21	50	5.0
Aged 75 or older	474.88	13	1.3

	AVERAGE HOUSEHOLD SPENDING	BEST CUSTOMERS (index)	BIGGEST CUSTOMERS (market share)
HOUSEHOLD INCOME			
Average household	**$3,583.53**	**100**	**100.0%**
Under $20,000	632.99	18	3.6
$20,000 to $39,999	1,495.20	42	9.7
$40,000 to $49,999	2,404.39	67	6.6
$50,000 to $69,999	3,736.77	104	16.0
$70,000 to $79,999	4,947.24	138	8.0
$80,000 to $99,999	6,077.51	170	13.8
$100,000 or more	8,852.37	247	42.3
HOUSEHOLD TYPE			
Average household	**3,583.53**	**100**	**100.0**
Married couples	5,026.41	140	70.9
Married couples, no children	3,353.50	94	20.2
Married couples, with children	6,430.38	179	44.8
Oldest child under age 6	7,237.97	202	9.9
Oldest child aged 6 to 17	7,098.53	198	25.2
Oldest child aged 18 or older	4,743.42	132	9.8
Single parent with child under age 18	2,434.77	68	4.0
Single person	1,676.19	47	13.9
RACE AND HISPANIC ORIGIN			
Average household	**3,583.53**	**100**	**100.0**
Asian	6,058.81	169	6.0
Black	2,625.16	73	8.8
Hispanic	3,471.63	97	11.4
Non-Hispanic white and other	3,752.75	105	79.9
REGION			
Average household	**3,583.53**	**100**	**100.0**
Northeast	3,337.96	93	17.3
Midwest	2,947.98	82	18.8
South	3,222.83	90	32.3
West	5,000.76	140	31.6
EDUCATION			
Average household	**3,583.53**	**100**	**100.0**
Less than high school graduate	1,732.05	48	7.3
High school graduate	2,426.07	68	17.1
Some college	3,148.84	88	19.1
Associate's degree	3,999.69	112	9.9
College graduate	5,761.73	161	46.5
Bachelor's degree	5,504.96	154	28.8
Master's, professional, doctoral degree	6,233.50	174	17.7

Note: Market shares may not sum to 100.0 because of rounding and missing categories by household type. "Asian" and "black" include Hispanics and non-Hispanics who identify themselves as being of the respective race alone. "Hispanic" includes people of any race who identify themselves as Hispanic. "Other" includes people who identify themselves as non-Hispanic and as Alaska Native, American Indian, Asian (who are also included in the "Asian" row), Native Hawaiian or other Pacific Islander, as well as non-Hispanics reporting more than one race.
Source: Calculations by New Strategist based on the Bureau of Labor Statistics' 2007 Consumer Expenditure Survey.

Property Management and Security, Owned Home

Best customers:	**Householders aged 55 or older** **Married couples without children at home** **People living alone** **Asians** **Households in the Northeast** **College graduates**
Customer trends:	**Average household spending on property management and security will rise along with the aging of the population.**

Older householders are the best customers of property management and security for owned homes. Householders aged 55 to 74 spend 21 to 28 percent more than average on this item, while householders aged 75 or older spend more than twice the average. Married couples without children at home (most of them empty-nesters) spend 28 percent more than average on property management and security. Single-person households (many of them older) spend 42 percent more. Asians spend 85 percent more than the average household on these property services. Northeastern householders spend well more than twice the average on home upkeep and security. College graduates spend twice the average amount on this item.

Average household spending on property management and security for owned homes increased by 46 percent between 2000 and 2007, after adjusting for inflation. Average household spending on this item will continue to rise along with the aging of the population.

Table 16.8 Property management and security, owned home

Total household spending $6,567,345,150.00
Average household spends 54.65

	AVERAGE HOUSEHOLD SPENDING	BEST CUSTOMERS (index)	BIGGEST CUSTOMERS (market share)
AGE OF HOUSEHOLDER			
Average household	**$54.65**	**100**	**100.0%**
Under age 25	5.28	10	0.7
Aged 25 to 34	28.13	51	8.8
Aged 35 to 44	33.78	62	12.0
Aged 45 to 54	51.62	94	19.8
Aged 55 to 64	69.83	128	20.7
Aged 65 to 74	66.07	121	12.1
Aged 75 or older	149.33	273	25.9

	AVERAGE HOUSEHOLD SPENDING	BEST CUSTOMERS (index)	BIGGEST CUSTOMERS (market share)
HOUSEHOLD INCOME			
Average household	**$54.65**	**100**	**100.0%**
Under $20,000	22.32	41	8.4
$20,000 to $39,999	38.59	71	16.4
$40,000 to $49,999	32.15	59	5.8
$50,000 to $69,999	44.51	81	12.5
$70,000 to $79,999	56.96	104	6.0
$80,000 to $99,999	73.89	135	11.0
$100,000 or more	127.26	233	39.9
HOUSEHOLD TYPE			
Average household	**54.65**	**100**	**100.0**
Married couples	52.30	96	48.4
Married couples, no children	69.80	128	27.6
Married couples, with children	34.86	64	15.9
Oldest child under age 6	37.99	70	3.4
Oldest child aged 6 to 17	32.43	59	7.5
Oldest child aged 18 or older	36.96	68	5.0
Single parent with child under age 18	19.71	36	2.1
Single person	77.48	142	42.2
RACE AND HISPANIC ORIGIN			
Average household	**54.65**	**100**	**100.0**
Asian	100.84	185	6.5
Black	17.79	33	3.9
Hispanic	28.00	51	6.0
Non-Hispanic white and other	64.73	118	90.4
REGION			
Average household	**54.65**	**100**	**100.0**
Northeast	127.29	233	43.4
Midwest	24.67	45	10.3
South	33.28	61	21.9
West	59.03	108	24.4
EDUCATION			
Average household	**54.65**	**100**	**100.0**
Less than high school graduate	21.43	39	5.9
High school graduate	26.66	49	12.3
Some college	34.50	63	13.7
Associate's degree	52.28	96	8.5
College graduate	112.33	206	59.5
Bachelor's degree	105.75	194	36.3
Master's, professional, doctoral degree	124.42	228	23.2

Note: Market shares may not sum to 100.0 because of rounding and missing categories by household type. "Asian" and "black" include Hispanics and non-Hispanics who identify themselves as being of the respective race alone. "Hispanic" includes people of any race who identify themselves as Hispanic. "Other" includes people who identify themselves as non-Hispanic and as Alaska Native, American Indian, Asian (who are also included in the "Asian" row), Native Hawaiian or other Pacific Islander, as well as non-Hispanics reporting more than one race.
Source: Calculations by New Strategist based on the Bureau of Labor Statistics' 2007 Consumer Expenditure Survey.

Property Taxes

Best customers:	Householders aged 35 to 64
	Married couples
	Asians
	Households in the Northeast

| Customer trends: | Average household spending on property taxes is likely to continue to rise as local governments raise taxes to pay for services. |

Households in the Northeast spend 55 percent more than average on property taxes, while households in the South spend 26 percent less than average. Variations in state property tax law and rates are behind these regional differences. Married couples spend 37 percent more than average on property taxes because they are likely to be homeowners. This also explains the 14 to 27 percent greater spending of householders aged 35 to 64. Asian householders, a relatively well-off demographic, spend 61 percent more on property taxes than the average household.

Average household spending on property taxes rose by 25 percent between 2000 and 2007, after adjusting for inflation. Behind the increase was the rise in homeownership and tax hikes. Spending on property taxes is likely to continue to rise as local governments raise taxes to pay for services.

Table 16.9 Property taxes

Total household spending $205,355,415,060.00
Average household spends 1,708.86

	AVERAGE HOUSEHOLD SPENDING	BEST CUSTOMERS (index)	BIGGEST CUSTOMERS (market share)
AGE OF HOUSEHOLDER			
Average household	**$1,708.86**	**100**	**100.0%**
Under age 25	325.02	19	1.3
Aged 25 to 34	1,075.55	63	10.7
Aged 35 to 44	1,949.55	114	22.2
Aged 45 to 54	2,178.16	127	26.8
Aged 55 to 64	2,126.71	124	20.2
Aged 65 to 74	1,766.60	103	10.3
Aged 75 or older	1,528.98	89	8.5

	AVERAGE HOUSEHOLD SPENDING	BEST CUSTOMERS (index)	BIGGEST CUSTOMERS (market share)
HOUSEHOLD INCOME			
Average household	$1,708.86	100	100.0%
Under $20,000	609.11	36	7.3
$20,000 to $39,999	969.98	57	13.2
$40,000 to $49,999	1,209.29	71	7.0
$50,000 to $69,999	1,546.62	91	13.9
$70,000 to $79,999	2,052.31	120	7.0
$80,000 to $99,999	2,326.87	136	11.1
$100,000 or more	4,053.24	237	40.6
HOUSEHOLD TYPE			
Average household	1,708.86	100	100.0
Married couples	2,347.95	137	69.5
Married couples, no children	2,273.31	133	28.7
Married couples, with children	2,470.38	145	36.1
Oldest child under age 6	2,037.25	119	5.8
Oldest child aged 6 to 17	2,619.36	153	19.5
Oldest child aged 18 or older	2,500.46	146	10.8
Single parent with child under age 18	901.66	53	3.1
Single person	1,029.75	60	17.9
RACE AND HISPANIC ORIGIN			
Average household	1,708.86	100	100.0
Asian	2,754.41	161	5.7
Black	892.66	52	6.3
Hispanic	1,217.78	71	8.4
Non-Hispanic white and other	1,912.05	112	85.4
REGION			
Average household	1,708.86	100	100.0
Northeast	2,648.91	155	28.9
Midwest	1,801.36	105	24.1
South	1,259.14	74	26.5
West	1,555.27	91	20.6
EDUCATION			
Average household	1,708.86	100	100.0
Less than high school graduate	782.60	46	6.9
High school graduate	1,246.43	73	18.4
Some college	1,393.65	82	17.8
Associate's degree	1,794.41	105	9.3
College graduate	2,808.14	164	47.6
Bachelor's degree	2,555.03	150	28.0
Master's, professional, doctoral degree	3,273.16	192	19.5

Note: Market shares may not sum to 100.0 because of rounding and missing categories by household type. "Asian" and "black" include Hispanics and non-Hispanics who identify themselves as being of the respective race alone. "Hispanic" includes people of any race who identify themselves as Hispanic. "Other" includes people who identify themselves as non-Hispanic and as Alaska Native, American Indian, Asian (who are also included in the "Asian" row), Native Hawaiian or other Pacific Islander, as well as non-Hispanics reporting more than one race.
Source: Calculations by New Strategist based on the Bureau of Labor Statistics' 2007 Consumer Expenditure Survey.

Rent

Best customers:

Householders under age 35
Single parents
People living alone
Asians, blacks, and Hispanics

Customer trends:

Average household spending on rent should rise as the large millennial generation
fills the best-customer age groups.

Young adults are the best customers of rental housing. Householders under age 35 spend 66 to 83 percent more than average on this item. Single parents spend 66 percent more than average on rent, and single-person households (many of them young adults) spend 23 percent more. Asians, blacks and Hispanics spend 42 to 60 percent more than average on this item.

Average household spending on rent climbed by 5 percent between 2000 and 2007, after adjusting for inflation. As the large millennial generation fills the best-customer age groups in the next few years, average household spending on rent should continue to rise.

Table 16.10 Rent

| Total household spending | $299,408,449,920.00 |
| Average household spends | 2,491.52 |

AGE OF HOUSEHOLDER	AVERAGE HOUSEHOLD SPENDING	BEST CUSTOMERS (index)	BIGGEST CUSTOMERS (market share)
Average household	$2,491.52	100	100.0%
Under age 25	4,554.25	183	12.4
Aged 25 to 34	4,138.77	166	28.3
Aged 35 to 44	2,695.75	108	21.1
Aged 45 to 54	1,962.42	79	16.5
Aged 55 to 64	1,467.68	59	9.5
Aged 65 to 74	1,161.68	47	4.7
Aged 75 or older	1,955.57	78	7.4

	AVERAGE HOUSEHOLD SPENDING	BEST CUSTOMERS (index)	BIGGEST CUSTOMERS (market share)
HOUSEHOLD INCOME			
Average household	**$2,491.52**	**100**	**100.0%**
Under $20,000	2,926.70	117	24.1
$20,000 to $39,999	3,192.39	128	29.8
$40,000 to $49,999	3,127.24	126	12.3
$50,000 to $69,999	2,524.56	101	15.5
$70,000 to $79,999	1,914.46	77	4.4
$80,000 to $99,999	1,716.49	69	5.6
$100,000 or more	1,186.93	48	8.2
HOUSEHOLD TYPE			
Average household	**2,491.52**	**100**	**100.0**
Married couples	1,592.48	64	32.3
Married couples, no children	1,308.77	53	11.3
Married couples, with children	1,704.60	68	17.1
Oldest child under age 6	2,512.67	101	4.9
Oldest child aged 6 to 17	1,717.45	69	8.8
Oldest child aged 18 or older	1,147.12	46	3.4
Single parent with child under age 18	4,132.69	166	9.9
Single person	3,075.09	123	36.7
RACE AND HISPANIC ORIGIN			
Average household	**2,491.52**	**100**	**100.0**
Asian	3,955.16	159	5.6
Black	3,544.21	142	17.1
Hispanic	3,978.69	160	18.8
Non-Hispanic white and other	2,099.62	84	64.3
REGION			
Average household	**2,491.52**	**100**	**100.0**
Northeast	2,901.72	116	21.7
Midwest	1,795.44	72	16.5
South	1,991.64	80	28.7
West	3,650.82	147	33.1
EDUCATION			
Average household	**2,491.52**	**100**	**100.0**
Less than high school graduate	2,836.79	114	17.3
High school graduate	2,359.87	95	23.9
Some college	2,749.85	110	24.0
Associate's degree	2,214.48	89	7.9
College graduate	2,316.03	93	26.9
Bachelor's degree	2,503.66	100	18.8
Master's, professional, doctoral degree	1,971.32	79	8.1

Note: Market shares may not sum to 100.0 because of rounding and missing categories by household type. "Asian" and "black" include Hispanics and non-Hispanics who identify themselves as being of the respective race alone. "Hispanic" includes people of any race who identify themselves as Hispanic. "Other" includes people who identify themselves as non-Hispanic and as Alaska Native, American Indian, Asian (who are also included in the "Asian" row), Native Hawaiian or other Pacific Islander, as well as non-Hispanics reporting more than one race.
Source: Calculations by New Strategist based on the Bureau of Labor Statistics' 2007 Consumer Expenditure Survey.

Vacation Homes, Owned

Best customers:

Householders aged 45 to 64
High-income households
Married couples without children at home
Married couples with school-aged or older children at home
Households in the Northeast
College graduates

Customer trends:

Average household spending on owned vacation homes may stabilize because aging boomers have almost completely filled the best-customer lifestage and discretionary income is dwindling.

Not surprisingly, the affluent are the best customers of owned vacation homes. Households with incomes of $100,000 or more spend nearly four times the average on this item and control 66 percent of the market. Householders aged 45 to 64 spend 27 to 78 percent more than average on owned vacation homes. Married couples without children at home (most of them empty-nesters) spend 84 percent more than the average on this item. Couples with school-aged or adult children at home spend 30 to 36 percent more. Northeastern householders spend nearly twice the average amount on owned vacation homes. College graduates, who dominate the affluent, spend over twice the average.

Average household spending on owned vacation homes rose 61 percent between 2000 and 2007, after adjusting for inflation. Behind the increase was the entry of the baby-boom into the best-customer age groups and the boom in the housing market. Average household spending on owned vacation homes is likely to fall now that aging boomers have almost completely filled the best-customer lifestage and the financial crisis diminishes discretionary income.

Table 16.11 Vacation homes, owned

Total household spending $34,466,244,510.00
Average household spends   286.81

	AVERAGE HOUSEHOLD SPENDING	BEST CUSTOMERS (index)	BIGGEST CUSTOMERS (market share)
AGE OF HOUSEHOLDER			
Average household	**$286.81**	**100**	**100.0%**
Under age 25	15.64	5	0.4
Aged 25 to 34	41.22	14	2.5
Aged 35 to 44	319.35	111	21.7
Aged 45 to 54	362.89	127	26.6
Aged 55 to 64	510.39	178	28.8
Aged 65 to 74	249.17	87	8.7
Aged 75 or older	345.01	120	11.4

	AVERAGE HOUSEHOLD SPENDING	BEST CUSTOMERS (index)	BIGGEST CUSTOMERS (market share)
HOUSEHOLD INCOME			
Average household	**$286.81**	**100**	**100.0%**
Under $20,000	25.70	9	1.8
$20,000 to $39,999	84.70	30	6.9
$40,000 to $49,999	120.79	42	4.1
$50,000 to $69,999	201.32	70	10.7
$70,000 to $79,999	227.26	79	4.6
$80,000 to $99,999	214.50	75	6.1
$100,000 or more	1,100.52	384	65.7
HOUSEHOLD TYPE			
Average household	**286.81**	**100**	**100.0**
Married couples	422.44	147	74.5
Married couples, no children	528.73	184	39.8
Married couples, with children	329.25	115	28.6
Oldest child under age 6	109.35	38	1.9
Oldest child aged 6 to 17	388.70	136	17.2
Oldest child aged 18 or older	372.44	130	9.6
Single parent with child under age 18	85.33	30	1.8
Single person	149.23	52	15.5
RACE AND HISPANIC ORIGIN			
Average household	**286.81**	**100**	**100.0**
Asian	346.60	121	4.3
Black	161.33	56	6.8
Hispanic	89.77	31	3.7
Non-Hispanic white and other	336.50	117	89.6
REGION			
Average household	**286.81**	**100**	**100.0**
Northeast	524.09	183	34.0
Midwest	267.73	93	21.3
South	138.93	48	17.4
West	345.49	120	27.2
EDUCATION			
Average household	**286.81**	**100**	**100.0**
Less than high school graduate	33.81	12	1.8
High school graduate	145.73	51	12.8
Some college	178.76	62	13.6
Associate's degree	173.11	60	5.4
College graduate	658.56	230	66.5
Bachelor's degree	586.42	204	38.3
Master's, professional, doctoral degree	791.09	276	28.1

Note: Market shares may not sum to 100.0 because of rounding and missing categories by household type. "Asian" and "black" include Hispanics and non-Hispanics who identify themselves as being of the respective race alone. "Hispanic" includes people of any race who identify themselves as Hispanic. "Other" includes people who identify themselves as non-Hispanic and as Alaska Native, American Indian, Asian (who are also included in the "Asian" row), Native Hawaiian or other Pacific Islander, as well as non-Hispanics reporting more than one race.
Source: Calculations by New Strategist based on the Bureau of Labor Statistics' 2007 Consumer Expenditure Survey.

Chapter 17.

Telephone

Household Spending on Telephones, 2007

Americans spent $1,135 on telephone service, equipment, and accessories in 2007, making the category one of the larger household expenses. Spending on this category rose by 4 percent between 2000 and 2007, after adjusting for inflation.

Spending on residential phone service (a category that includes the miniscule amount of money households spend on pay phones) fell 47 percent between 2000 and 2007 as prices for long-distance service plummeted and a growing number of households abandoned landline service altogether. Spending on telephone equipment also fell, by 17 percent, as cell phone companies gave away phones to attract customers. Not surprisingly, spending on cell phone service surged, rising 322 percent between 2000 and 2007 as cell phones became the norm. The average household now spends well more on cell phone service than on landline service.

Spending on cell versus landline phone service

(average spending by households on cell and landline phone service, 2000 and 2007; in 2007 dollars)

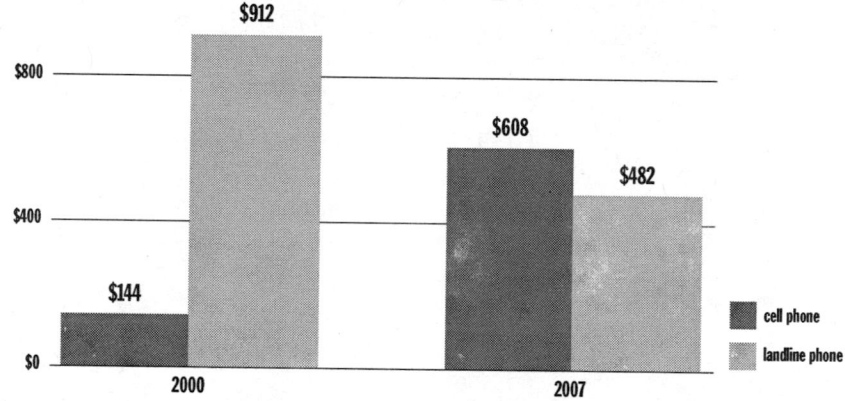

Table 17.1 Telephone Spending, 2000 to 2007

(average annual household spending on telephone service and equipment, and percent distribution of spending by type, 2000 and 2007; percent change in spending, 2000–07; in 2007 dollars)

	2007		2000		
	average household spending	percent distribution	average household spending (in 2007$)	percent distribution	percent change 2000–07
Telephone	**$1,135.55**	**100.0%**	**$1,093.19**	**100.0%**	**3.9%**
Cellular phone service	607.58	53.5	143.88	13.2	322.3
Residential telephone and pay phones	482.12	42.5	911.80	83.4	–47.1
Telephones and answering machines	30.97	2.7	37.52	3.4	–17.5
Phone cards	14.88	1.3	–	–	–

Note: "–" means data are unavailable.
Source: Bureau of Labor Statistics, 2000 and 2007 Consumer Expenditure Surveys; calculations by New Strategist

Cellular Phone Service

Best customers:

Householders aged 25 to 54
Married couples with school-aged or older children at home
Single parents

Customer trends:

Average household spending on cellular phone service should stabilize as cell phones become the norm and prices for cell phone service fall.

Parents are the biggest spenders on cell phone service. Couples with school-aged children spend 36 percent more than average on this item, while those with adult children at home spend 58 percent more. Single parents spend 13 percent more than average on cell phone service. Householders aged 25 to 54, most with children at home, spend 20 to 25 percent more than average on cell phone service and control 71 percent of the market.

Average household spending on cell phone service soared between 2000 and 2007, more than tripling after adjusting for inflation. Behind the increase is the growing share of households that spend on cell service, rising from 21 percent during the average quarter of 2000 to 58 percent in 2007. The enormous growth in spending on cell service may mean slower growth in the future. Not only is cell service becoming the norm, but cutthroat competition is lowering service prices.

Table 17.2 Cellular phone service

Total household spending $73,013,496,180.00
Average household spends 607.58

AGE OF HOUSEHOLDER	AVERAGE HOUSEHOLD SPENDING	BEST CUSTOMERS (index)	BIGGEST CUSTOMERS (market share)
Average household	$607.58	100	100.0%
Under age 25	559.82	92	6.2
Aged 25 to 34	727.58	120	20.4
Aged 35 to 44	756.95	125	24.3
Aged 45 to 54	752.87	124	26.0
Aged 55 to 64	545.82	90	14.5
Aged 65 to 74	374.35	62	6.2
Aged 75 or older	148.13	24	2.3

	AVERAGE HOUSEHOLD SPENDING	BEST CUSTOMERS (index)	BIGGEST CUSTOMERS (market share)
HOUSEHOLD INCOME			
Average household	**$607.58**	**100**	**100.0%**
Under $20,000	280.94	46	9.5
$20,000 to $39,999	472.19	78	18.1
$40,000 to $49,999	580.53	96	9.4
$50,000 to $69,999	702.04	116	17.7
$70,000 to $79,999	797.15	131	7.6
$80,000 to $99,999	833.96	137	11.2
$100,000 or more	942.80	155	26.6
HOUSEHOLD TYPE			
Average household	**607.58**	**100**	**100.0**
Married couples	723.03	119	60.2
Married couples, no children	559.78	92	19.9
Married couples, with children	839.14	138	34.5
Oldest child under age 6	698.61	115	5.6
Oldest child aged 6 to 17	824.80	136	17.2
Oldest child aged 18 or older	956.95	158	11.6
Single parent with child under age 18	687.36	113	6.7
Single person	346.11	57	16.9
RACE AND HISPANIC ORIGIN			
Average household	**607.58**	**100**	**100.0**
Asian	675.44	111	3.9
Black	625.25	103	12.4
Hispanic	678.95	112	13.2
Non-Hispanic white and other	593.99	98	74.6
REGION			
Average household	**607.58**	**100**	**100.0**
Northeast	575.27	95	17.6
Midwest	564.60	93	21.2
South	635.66	105	37.6
West	633.03	104	23.6
EDUCATION			
Average household	**607.58**	**100**	**100.0**
Less than high school graduate	412.22	68	10.3
High school graduate	554.25	91	23.0
Some college	639.24	105	22.9
Associate's degree	688.07	113	10.1
College graduate	707.90	117	33.7
Bachelor's degree	702.65	116	21.7
Master's, professional, doctoral degree	717.53	118	12.0

Note: Market shares may not sum to 100.0 because of rounding and missing categories by household type. "Asian" and "black" include Hispanics and non-Hispanics who identify themselves as being of the respective race alone. "Hispanic" includes people of any race who identify themselves as Hispanic. "Other" includes people who identify themselves as non-Hispanic and as Alaska Native, American Indian, Asian (who are also included in the "Asian" row), Native Hawaiian or other Pacific Islander, as well as non-Hispanics reporting more than one race.
Source: Calculations by New Strategist based on the Bureau of Labor Statistics' 2007 Consumer Expenditure Survey.

Phone Cards

Best customers:

Householders under age 45
Married couples with adult children at home
Hispanics and Asians
Households in the West
Householders without a high school diploma

Customer trends:

Average household spending on phone cards should grow along with the Asian and Hispanic populations.

The biggest spenders on phone cards are households making international calls, many of them immigrants to the United States. Because immigrants tend to be younger adults, householders under age 45 spend more than others on this item—23 to 45 percent more than the average household. Married couples with adult children at home spend 47 percent more than average on phone cards. Hispanics spend more than three-and-one-half times the average on this item, and Asians spend nearly three times the average. Together Hispanic and Asian households, despite representing just 15 percent of consumer units, control 53 percent of the market. Households in the West, where many Hispanics and Asians reside, spend 44 percent more than average on phone cards. Householders without a high school diploma (many of them recent Hispanic immigrants) spend over twice the average on this item.

Phone cards were not included in the Consumer Expenditure Survey until recently, which limits the analysis of spending trends. Average household spending on phone cards is likely to rise in the years ahead along with the Asian and Hispanic populations.

Table 17.3 Phone cards

Total household spending $1,788,144,480.00
Average household spends 14.88

	AVERAGE HOUSEHOLD SPENDING	BEST CUSTOMERS (index)	BIGGEST CUSTOMERS (market share)
AGE OF HOUSEHOLDER			
Average household	**$14.88**	**100**	**100.0%**
Under age 25	18.24	123	8.3
Aged 25 to 34	21.63	145	24.8
Aged 35 to 44	18.59	125	24.3
Aged 45 to 54	16.58	111	23.4
Aged 55 to 64	11.05	74	12.0
Aged 65 to 74	6.82	46	4.6
Aged 75 or older	3.93	26	2.5

	AVERAGE HOUSEHOLD SPENDING	BEST CUSTOMERS (index)	BIGGEST CUSTOMERS (market share)
HOUSEHOLD INCOME			
Average household	**$14.88**	**100**	**100.0%**
Under $20,000	12.51	84	17.3
$20,000 to $39,999	16.16	109	25.2
$40,000 to $49,999	15.40	103	10.2
$50,000 to $69,999	14.79	99	15.2
$70,000 to $79,999	18.35	123	7.1
$80,000 to $99,999	17.31	116	9.5
$100,000 or more	13.40	90	15.4
HOUSEHOLD TYPE			
Average household	**14.88**	**100**	**100.0**
Married couples	14.75	99	50.1
Married couples, no children	9.18	62	13.3
Married couples, with children	16.45	111	27.6
Oldest child under age 6	15.14	102	5.0
Oldest child aged 6 to 17	13.78	93	11.8
Oldest child aged 18 or older	21.92	147	10.9
Single parent with child under age 18	13.77	93	5.5
Single person	9.09	61	18.2
RACE AND HISPANIC ORIGIN			
Average household	**14.88**	**100**	**100.0**
Asian	42.36	285	10.0
Black	12.59	85	10.2
Hispanic	53.84	362	42.7
Non-Hispanic white and other	9.28	62	47.6
REGION			
Average household	**14.88**	**100**	**100.0**
Northeast	17.61	118	22.0
Midwest	8.85	59	13.6
South	13.18	89	31.8
West	21.40	144	32.5
EDUCATION			
Average household	**14.88**	**100**	**100.0**
Less than high school graduate	34.45	232	35.1
High school graduate	11.33	76	19.2
Some college	11.97	80	17.5
Associate's degree	9.69	65	5.8
College graduate	11.49	77	22.4
Bachelor's degree	9.47	64	11.9
Master's, professional, doctoral degree	15.18	102	10.4

Note: Market shares may not sum to 100.0 because of rounding and missing categories by household type. "Asian" and "black" include Hispanics and non-Hispanics who identify themselves as being of the respective race alone. "Hispanic" includes people of any race who identify themselves as Hispanic. "Other" includes people who identify themselves as non-Hispanic and as Alaska Native, American Indian, Asian (who are also included in the "Asian" row), Native Hawaiian or other Pacific Islander, as well as non-Hispanics reporting more than one race.
Source: Calculations by New Strategist based on the Bureau of Labor Statistics' 2007 Consumer Expenditure Survey.

Residential Telephone Service and Pay Phones

Best customers: Householders aged 45 to 74
Married couples with school-aged or older children at home
Blacks

Customer trends: Average household spending on residential telephone service will continue to decline as cell phones replace residential phones, especially among the younger generations.

Because most households buy residential phone service, there is little variation in spending on this item by demographic characteristic—although householders under age 25 spend far less on this item than older householders because many of the youngest householders are cell-phone only users. Householders ranging in age from 45 to 74 spend 15 to 19 percent more than average on residential phone service. Married couples with school-aged or older children at home are the biggest spenders on residential phone service because their households are larger than average. These households spend 24 to 32 percent more than average on this service. Black households spend 15 percent more than average on residential phone service.

Average household spending on residential phone service fell 47 percent between 2000 and 2007, after adjusting for inflation. Substitution of cell phones for residential phones was behind the decline. As a consequence of the spending decline, residential phone service relinquished its position as the number-one expenditure in the information and consumer electronics category in 2007, tumbling to third place behind cellular phone service and cable and satellite television service. Average household spending on residential telephone service will continue to decline as as cell phones replace residential phones, especially among the younger generations.

Table 17.4 Residential telephone service and pay phones

Total household spending $57,936,842,520.00
Average household spends   482.12

AGE OF HOUSEHOLDER	AVERAGE HOUSEHOLD SPENDING	BEST CUSTOMERS (index)	BIGGEST CUSTOMERS (market share)
Average household	**$482.12**	**100**	**100.0%**
Under age 25	163.68	34	2.3
Aged 25 to 34	337.76	70	12.0
Aged 35 to 44	512.98	106	20.7
Aged 45 to 54	555.28	115	24.2
Aged 55 to 64	574.04	119	19.3
Aged 65 to 74	559.31	116	11.6
Aged 75 or older	505.70	105	9.9

	AVERAGE HOUSEHOLD SPENDING	BEST CUSTOMERS (index)	BIGGEST CUSTOMERS (market share)
HOUSEHOLD INCOME			
Average household	**$482.12**	**100**	**100.0%**
Under $20,000	350.19	73	14.9
$20,000 to $39,999	429.81	89	20.7
$40,000 to $49,999	471.77	98	9.6
$50,000 to $69,999	509.16	106	16.2
$70,000 to $79,999	552.42	115	6.6
$80,000 to $99,999	548.60	114	9.3
$100,000 or more	637.86	132	22.7
HOUSEHOLD TYPE			
Average household	**482.12**	**100**	**100.0**
Married couples	573.71	119	60.2
Married couples, no children	551.93	114	24.7
Married couples, with children	586.22	122	30.3
Oldest child under age 6	482.99	100	4.9
Oldest child aged 6 to 17	597.73	124	15.7
Oldest child aged 18 or older	634.77	132	9.7
Single parent with child under age 18	416.41	86	5.1
Single person	348.09	72	21.5
RACE AND HISPANIC ORIGIN			
Average household	**482.12**	**100**	**100.0**
Asian	443.75	92	3.2
Black	554.90	115	13.8
Hispanic	430.35	89	10.5
Non-Hispanic white and other	478.71	99	75.8
REGION			
Average household	**482.12**	**100**	**100.0**
Northeast	515.66	107	19.9
Midwest	446.87	93	21.2
South	515.49	107	38.4
West	437.12	91	20.5
EDUCATION			
Average household	**482.12**	**100**	**100.0**
Less than high school graduate	460.48	96	14.5
High school graduate	473.62	98	24.8
Some college	432.62	90	19.5
Associate's degree	506.22	105	9.3
College graduate	530.70	110	31.9
Bachelor's degree	514.84	107	20.0
Master's, professional, doctoral degree	559.85	116	11.8

Note: Market shares may not sum to 100.0 because of rounding and missing categories by household type. "Asian" and "black" include Hispanics and non-Hispanics who identify themselves as being of the respective race alone. "Hispanic" includes people of any race who identify themselves as Hispanic. "Other" includes people who identify themselves as non-Hispanic and as Alaska Native, American Indian, Asian (who are also included in the "Asian" row), Native Hawaiian or other Pacific Islander, as well as non-Hispanics reporting more than one race.
Source: Calculations by New Strategist based on the Bureau of Labor Statistics' 2007 Consumer Expenditure Survey.

Telephones, Answering Machines, and Accessories

Best customers:
Householders aged 25 to 44
Married couples with children under age 18
Single parents
Households in the Northeast

Customer trends:
Average household spending on telephones could rise as smart cell phones (such as Blackberries and iPhones) become must-have items.

The best customers of telephones and answering machines are families with children. Married couples with school-aged or younger children spend over twice the average on this item. Single parents spend 13 percent above average on telephones. Householders aged 25 to 44, most with children at home, spend 49 to 57 percent more than average on telephones. Households in the Northeast spend 46 percent more than average on telephones, answering machines, and accessories.

Average household spending on telephones, answering machines, and accessories fell 17 percent between 2000 and 2007, after adjusting for inflation. One factor behind the decline is cell phone promotions, whereby cell phone service providers give away phones to lure customers. Average household spending on telephones could rise as smart cell phones (such as Blackberries and iPhones) become must-have items.

Table 17.5 Telephones, answering machines, and accessories

Total household spending $3,721,695,870.00
Average household spends   30.97

	AVERAGE HOUSEHOLD SPENDING	BEST CUSTOMERS (index)	BIGGEST CUSTOMERS (market share)
AGE OF HOUSEHOLDER			
Average household	**$30.97**	**100**	**100.0%**
Under age 25	10.22	33	2.2
Aged 25 to 34	48.73	157	26.8
Aged 35 to 44	46.08	149	29.0
Aged 45 to 54	28.27	91	19.2
Aged 55 to 64	28.70	93	15.0
Aged 65 to 74	14.64	47	4.7
Aged 75 or older	9.98	32	3.1

	AVERAGE HOUSEHOLD SPENDING	BEST CUSTOMERS (index)	BIGGEST CUSTOMERS (market share)
HOUSEHOLD INCOME			
Average household	$30.97	100	100.0%
Under $20,000	7.16	23	4.8
$20,000 to $39,999	21.74	70	16.3
$40,000 to $49,999	15.13	49	4.8
$50,000 to $69,999	30.16	97	14.9
$70,000 to $79,999	20.51	66	3.8
$80,000 to $99,999	53.58	173	14.1
$100,000 or more	74.98	242	41.5
HOUSEHOLD TYPE			
Average household	30.97	100	100.0
Married couples	46.06	149	75.2
Married couples, no children	33.89	109	23.6
Married couples, with children	60.43	195	48.7
Oldest child under age 6	84.19	272	13.3
Oldest child aged 6 to 17	65.32	211	26.8
Oldest child aged 18 or older	33.41	108	7.9
Single parent with child under age 18	35.14	113	6.7
Single person	14.11	46	13.6
RACE AND HISPANIC ORIGIN			
Average household	30.97	100	100.0
Asian	8.34	27	1.0
Black	14.49	47	5.6
Hispanic	32.93	106	12.6
Non-Hispanic white and other	33.21	107	81.9
REGION			
Average household	30.97	100	100.0
Northeast	45.12	146	27.1
Midwest	20.74	67	15.3
South	31.19	101	36.2
West	29.17	94	21.3
EDUCATION			
Average household	30.97	100	100.0
Less than high school graduate	16.05	52	7.9
High school graduate	24.42	79	19.9
Some college	21.19	68	14.9
Associate's degree	63.86	206	18.3
College graduate	41.17	133	38.5
Bachelor's degree	42.21	136	25.5
Master's, professional, doctoral degree	39.36	127	13.0

Note: Market shares may not sum to 100.0 because of rounding and missing categories by household type. "Asian" and "black" include Hispanics and non-Hispanics who identify themselves as being of the respective race alone. "Hispanic" includes people of any race who identify themselves as Hispanic. "Other" includes people who identify themselves as non-Hispanic and as Alaska Native, American Indian, Asian (who are also included in the "Asian" row), Native Hawaiian or other Pacific Islander, as well as non-Hispanics reporting more than one race.
Source: Calculations by New Strategist based on the Bureau of Labor Statistics' 2007 Consumer Expenditure Survey.

Chapter 18.

Tobacco Products

Household Spending on Tobacco Products, 2007

The average American household spent $323 on cigarettes, other tobacco products, and smoking accessories in 2007. Spending on this category declined 16 percent between 2000 and 2007 as consumers cut back on their tobacco purchases.

Average household spending on cigarettes fell 17 percent between 2000 and 2007, after adjusting for inflation, despite rising prices. Behind the decline is the shrinking percentage of people who smoke cigarettes. Spending on other tobacco products (such as cigars and chewing tobacco) held essentially level during those years, while spending on smoking accessories fell by one-half.

Spending on tobacco products

(average spending by households on tobacco products, 2000 and 2007; in 2007 dollars)

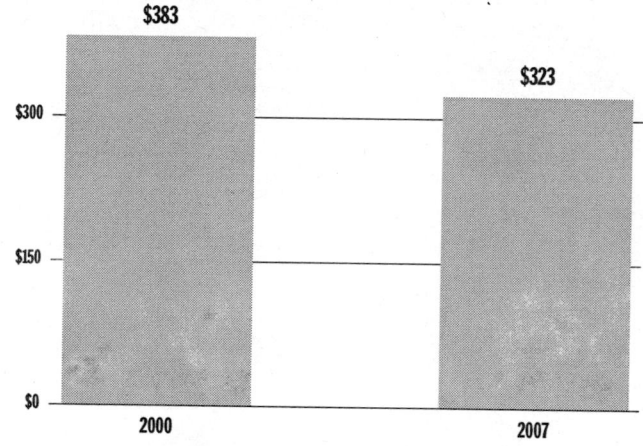

Table 18.1 Tobacco Products Spending, 2000 to 2007

(average annual household spending on tobacco products, and percent distribution of spending by type, 2000 to 2007; percent change in spending, 2000–07; in 2007 dollars; ranked by amount spent)

	2007		2000		
	average household spending	percent distribution	average household spending (in 2007$)	percent distribution	percent change 2000–07
Average household spending on tobacco products	**$322.89**	**100.0%**	**$383.44**	**100.0%**	**–15.8%**
Cigarettes	294.95	91.3	$353.88	92.3	–16.7
Tobacco products other than cigarettes	26.73	8.3	$27.12	7.1	–1.4
Smoking accessories	1.21	0.4	$2.44	0.6	–50.5

Source: Bureau of Labor Statistics, 2000 and 2007 Consumer Expenditure Surveys; calculations by New Strategist

Cigarettes

Best customers:
Householders aged 35 to 64
Married couples with adult children at home
Non-Hispanic whites
Some college or less education

Customer trends:
Average household spending on cigarettes should decline as smoking becomes less common.

Householders aged 35 to 64 spend 12 to 21 percent more than average on cigarettes and account for two-thirds of the market. Married couples with adult children at home spend 8 percent more than average on this item, in part because their households are the largest. Non-Hispanic whites spend 12 percent more than average. Householders with some college or less education spend 14 to 46 percent more than average on cigarettes.

Average household spending on cigarettes fell 17 percent between 2000 and 2007, after adjusting for inflation. Behind the decline is the smaller proportion of smokers in the population as health warnings and higher prices drive consumers away. Spending on cigarettes is likely to continue to decline as smoking continues to become less common.

Table 18.2 Cigarettes

Total household spending $35,444,436,450.00
Average household spends 294.95

	AVERAGE HOUSEHOLD SPENDING	BEST CUSTOMERS (index)	BIGGEST CUSTOMERS (market share)
AGE OF HOUSEHOLDER			
Average household	**$294.95**	**100**	**100.0%**
Under age 25	263.62	89	6.1
Aged 25 to 34	303.70	103	17.6
Aged 35 to 44	346.35	117	22.9
Aged 45 to 54	356.87	121	25.4
Aged 55 to 64	329.36	112	18.1
Aged 65 to 74	216.23	73	7.3
Aged 75 or older	82.89	28	2.7

	AVERAGE HOUSEHOLD SPENDING	BEST CUSTOMERS (index)	BIGGEST CUSTOMERS (market share)
HOUSEHOLD INCOME			
Average household	**$294.95**	**100**	**100.0%**
Under $20,000	240.89	82	16.8
$20,000 to $39,999	325.23	110	25.6
$40,000 to $49,999	328.39	111	11.0
$50,000 to $69,999	375.59	127	19.5
$70,000 to $79,999	323.37	110	6.3
$80,000 to $99,999	311.10	105	8.6
$100,000 or more	210.23	71	12.2
HOUSEHOLD TYPE			
Average household	**294.95**	**100**	**100.0**
Married couples	290.06	98	49.7
Married couples, no children	255.61	87	18.7
Married couples, with children	285.88	97	24.2
Oldest child under age 6	233.47	79	3.9
Oldest child aged 6 to 17	286.66	97	12.3
Oldest child aged 18 or older	319.27	108	8.0
Single parent with child under age 18	241.82	82	4.9
Single person	201.59	68	20.3
RACE AND HISPANIC ORIGIN			
Average household	**294.95**	**100**	**100.0**
Asian	131.96	45	1.6
Black	201.03	68	8.2
Hispanic	156.78	53	6.3
Non-Hispanic white and other	330.75	112	85.6
REGION			
Average household	**294.95**	**100**	**100.0**
Northeast	333.72	113	21.1
Midwest	331.92	113	25.7
South	304.24	103	37.0
West	210.91	72	16.2
EDUCATION			
Average household	**294.95**	**100**	**100.0**
Less than high school graduate	341.31	116	17.6
High school graduate	430.44	146	36.8
Some college	335.29	114	24.8
Associate's degree	267.83	91	8.1
College graduate	130.55	44	12.8
Bachelor's degree	152.02	52	9.7
Master's, professional, doctoral degree	91.11	31	3.2

Note: Market shares may not sum to 100.0 because of rounding and missing categories by household type. "Asian" and "black" include Hispanics and non-Hispanics who identify themselves as being of the respective race alone. "Hispanic" includes people of any race who identify themselves as Hispanic. "Other" includes people who identify themselves as non-Hispanic and as Alaska Native, American Indian, Asian (who are also included in the "Asian" row), Native Hawaiian or other Pacific Islander, as well as non-Hispanics reporting more than one race.
Source: Calculations by New Strategist based on the Bureau of Labor Statistics' 2007 Consumer Expenditure Survey.

Smoking Accessories

Best customers:
Householders under age 25 and aged 45 to 54
Married couples without children at home
Married couples with adult children at home
Non-Hispanic whites

Customer trends:
Average household spending on smoking accessories should decline as smoking becomes less common.

Smoking accessories include cigarette papers, pipes, lighters, and so on. Householders under age 25 spend almost twice the average on those items, while those aged 45 to 54 spend 31 percent more than average. Married couples without children at home, most of them older empty-nesters, spend 48 percent more than average on smoking accessories. Couples with adult children at home spend 17 percent more. Non-Hispanic white householders spend 15 percent more than average on this item.

Average household spending on smoking accessories fell by half between 2000 and 2007, after adjusting for inflation. Behind the decline is the shrinking percentage of smokers in the population. Spending on this item should continue to decline as smoking becomes less common.

Table 18.3 Smoking accessories

Total household spending $145,406,910.00
Average household spends   1.21

	AVERAGE HOUSEHOLD SPENDING	BEST CUSTOMERS (index)	BIGGEST CUSTOMERS (market share)
AGE OF HOUSEHOLDER			
Average household	**$1.21**	**100**	**100.0%**
Under age 25	2.32	192	13.0
Aged 25 to 34	1.36	112	19.2
Aged 35 to 44	0.81	67	13.0
Aged 45 to 54	1.59	131	27.6
Aged 55 to 64	1.31	108	17.5
Aged 65 to 74	0.91	75	7.5
Aged 75 or older	0.30	25	2.3

	AVERAGE HOUSEHOLD SPENDING	BEST CUSTOMERS (index)	BIGGEST CUSTOMERS (market share)
HOUSEHOLD INCOME			
Average household	**$1.21**	**100**	**100.0%**
Under $20,000	0.84	69	14.2
$20,000 to $39,999	1.02	84	19.6
$40,000 to $49,999	1.05	87	8.5
$50,000 to $69,999	1.82	150	23.0
$70,000 to $79,999	0.64	53	3.1
$80,000 to $99,999	1.76	145	11.8
$100,000 or more	1.38	114	19.5
HOUSEHOLD TYPE			
Average household	**1.21**	**100**	**100.0**
Married couples	1.32	109	55.1
Married couples, no children	1.79	148	31.9
Married couples, with children	0.99	82	20.4
Oldest child under age 6	0.84	69	3.4
Oldest child aged 6 to 17	0.83	69	8.7
Oldest child aged 18 or older	1.42	117	8.6
Single parent with child under age 18	0.61	50	3.0
Single person	0.62	51	15.2
RACE AND HISPANIC ORIGIN			
Average household	**1.21**	**100**	**100.0**
Asian	0.09	7	0.3
Black	0.42	35	4.2
Hispanic	0.82	68	8.0
Non-Hispanic white and other	1.39	115	87.7
REGION			
Average household	**1.21**	**100**	**100.0**
Northeast	0.96	79	14.8
Midwest	1.44	119	27.2
South	1.36	112	40.4
West	0.96	79	17.9
EDUCATION			
Average household	**1.21**	**100**	**100.0**
Less than high school graduate	1.53	126	19.2
High school graduate	0.81	67	16.9
Some college	1.31	108	23.6
Associate's degree	2.21	183	16.2
College graduate	1.07	88	25.6
Bachelor's degree	0.88	73	13.6
Master's, professional, doctoral degree	1.40	116	11.8

Note: Market shares may not sum to 100.0 because of rounding and missing categories by household type. "Asian" and "black" include Hispanics and non-Hispanics who identify themselves as being of the respective race alone. "Hispanic" includes people of any race who identify themselves as Hispanic. "Other" includes people who identify themselves as non-Hispanic and as Alaska Native, American Indian, Asian (who are also included in the "Asian" row), Native Hawaiian or other Pacific Islander, as well as non-Hispanics reporting more than one race.
Source: Calculations by New Strategist based on the Bureau of Labor Statistics' 2007 Consumer Expenditure Survey.

Tobacco Products Other than Cigarettes

Best customers: Householders aged 35 to 54
Married couples without children at home
Married couples with school-aged children
Non-Hispanic whites
Households in the Midwest

Customer trends: Average household spending on tobacco products other than cigarettes
should decline as smoking becomes less common.

Cigars, chewing tobacco, and pipe tobacco are some of the products included in this category. Householders aged 35 to 54 spend 11 to 18 percent more than average on noncigarette tobacco products and account for 46 percent of the market. Married couples without children at home, most of them older empty-nesters, spend 31 percent more than average on this item, while married couples with school-aged children at home spend 25 percent more than average. Non-Hispanic whites spend 17 percent more than average on tobacco products other than cigarettes. Midwestern householders spend one-fifth more than average on this item.

Average household spending on noncigarette tobacco products fell 1 percent between 2000 and 2007, after adjusting for inflation. Spending on this item is likely to decline as tobacco use becomes less common.

Table 18.4 Tobacco products other than cigarettes

Total household spending $3,212,170,830.00
Average household spends   26.73

	AVERAGE HOUSEHOLD SPENDING	BEST CUSTOMERS (index)	BIGGEST CUSTOMERS (market share)
AGE OF HOUSEHOLDER			
Average household	**$26.73**	**100**	**100.0%**
Under age 25	23.27	87	5.9
Aged 25 to 34	26.20	98	16.7
Aged 35 to 44	31.48	118	22.9
Aged 45 to 54	29.61	111	23.3
Aged 55 to 64	22.36	84	13.5
Aged 65 to 74	25.50	95	9.5
Aged 75 or older	22.82	85	8.1

	AVERAGE HOUSEHOLD SPENDING	BEST CUSTOMERS (index)	BIGGEST CUSTOMERS (market share)
HOUSEHOLD INCOME			
Average household	**$26.73**	**100**	**100.0%**
Under $20,000	19.19	72	14.8
$20,000 to $39,999	21.25	80	18.5
$40,000 to $49,999	31.53	118	11.6
$50,000 to $69,999	27.13	101	15.5
$70,000 to $79,999	31.65	118	6.9
$80,000 to $99,999	37.39	140	11.4
$100,000 or more	33.39	125	21.4
HOUSEHOLD TYPE			
Average household	**26.73**	**100**	**100.0**
Married couples	32.30	121	61.1
Married couples, no children	35.13	131	28.4
Married couples, with children	28.97	108	27.0
Oldest child under age 6	22.97	86	4.2
Oldest child aged 6 to 17	33.53	125	15.9
Oldest child aged 18 or older	25.08	94	6.9
Single parent with child under age 18	13.39	50	3.0
Single person	20.45	77	22.8
RACE AND HISPANIC ORIGIN			
Average household	**26.73**	**100**	**100.0**
Asian	3.30	12	0.4
Black	17.07	64	7.7
Hispanic	7.65	29	3.4
Non-Hispanic white and other	31.16	117	89.0
REGION			
Average household	**26.73**	**100**	**100.0**
Northeast	25.92	97	18.1
Midwest	31.95	120	27.3
South	26.66	100	35.8
West	22.25	83	18.8
EDUCATION			
Average household	**26.73**	**100**	**100.0**
Less than high school graduate	31.13	116	17.7
High school graduate	25.93	97	24.5
Some college	30.25	113	24.6
Associate's degree	27.19	102	9.0
College graduate	22.34	84	24.2
Bachelor's degree	24.47	92	17.2
Master's, professional, doctoral degree	18.42	69	7.0

Note: Market shares may not sum to 100.0 because of rounding and missing categories by household type. "Asian" and "black" include Hispanics and non-Hispanics who identify themselves as being of the respective race alone. "Hispanic" includes people of any race who identify themselves as Hispanic. "Other" includes people who identify themselves as non-Hispanic and as Alaska Native, American Indian, Asian (who are also included in the "Asian" row), Native Hawaiian or other Pacific Islander, as well as non-Hispanics reporting more than one race.
Source: Calculations by New Strategist based on the Bureau of Labor Statistics' 2007 Consumer Expenditure Survey.

Chapter 19.

Transportation

Household Spending on Transportation, 2007

Transportation is one of the biggest expenses of American households, behind only spending on shelter. In 2007, the average households spent $8,758 on transportation, 2 percent less than in 2000, after adjusting for inflation. More than one-quarter of transportation spending is devoted to gasoline, making it the largest single transportation expense.

Sharply reduced spending on new and used cars was behind the trend in spending on transportation. Even as car dealers pushed no-interest loans on new vehicles and as the price of used vehicles fell, spending on car purchases slipped substantially, down 35 percent for new cars and 30 percent for used cars between 2000 and 2007. Spending on new trucks increased 4 percent during those years as many households purchased sport utility vehicles, which are considered trucks. At the same time, spending on leased vehicles fell 38 to 45 percent as leasing became less popular. Spending on vehicle maintenance fell as well, by a small 2 percent, as new vehicles required fewer repairs.

Spending on transportation may continue to decline during the next few years as households cut back on vehicle purchases.

Spending on transportation

(average spending by households on transportation, 2000 to 2007; in 2007 dollars)

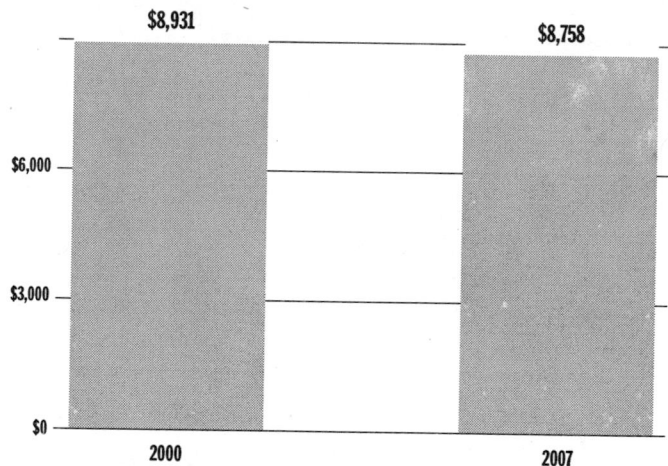

Table 19.1 Transportation Spending, 2000 to 2007

(average annual household spending on transportation, and percent distribution of spending by type, 2000 and 2007; percent change in spending, 2000–07; in 2007 dollars; ranked by amount spent)

	2007		2000		
	average household spending	percent distribution	average household spending (in 2007$)	percent distribution	percent change 2000–07
Average household spending on transportation	**$8,757.65**	**100.0%**	**$8,931.07**	**100.0%**	**−1.9%**
Gasoline and motor oil (incl. on trips)	2,383.67	27.2	1,554.76	17.4	53.3
Vehicle insurance	1,071.37	12.2	936.93	10.5	14.3
Trucks, new	859.60	9.8	828.33	9.3	3.8
Cars, used	852.18	9.7	1,217.62	13.6	−30.0
Vehicle maintenance and repair (including tires, oil changes)	737.62	8.4	751.05	8.4	−1.8
Trucks, used	714.69	8.2	913.41	10.2	−21.8
Cars, new	712.20	8.1	1,104.16	12.4	−35.5
Airline fares	359.71	4.1	329.94	3.7	9.0
Vehicle finance charges	305.21	3.5	395.23	4.4	−22.8
Car lease payments	116.64	1.3	210.52	2.4	−44.6
Tires (purchased, replaced, installed)	115.90	1.3	105.03	1.2	10.3
Truck lease payments	111.39	1.3	178.75	2.0	−37.7
Motorcycles (new and used)	105.33	1.2	43.14	0.5	144.1
Oil change, lube, and oil filters	69.34	0.8	70.74	0.8	−2.0
Mass transit, intracity fares	55.10	0.6	57.09	0.6	−3.5
Ship fares	53.23	0.6	44.05	0.5	20.9
Rented vehicles (incl. rentals on trips)	39.87	0.5	54.12	0.6	−26.3
Parking fees, excluding residence	35.17	0.4	22.17	0.2	58.7
Taxis and local transportation on trips	21.39	0.2	35.00	0.4	−38.9
Train fares, intercity	20.75	0.2	25.43	0.3	−18.4
Automobile service clubs	16.94	0.2	10.05	0.1	68.5
Taxi fares and limousine service in home town	16.12	0.2	14.63	0.2	10.2
Global positioning devices, services	15.31	0.2	–	–	–
Bus fares, intercity	10.49	0.1	19.39	0.2	−45.9
Towing charges	5.97	0.1	5.64	0.1	5.9
Vehicle video equipment	2.48	0.0	–	–	–

Note: Numbers do not add to total because spending on tires and oil changes is also included in vehicle maintenance and repairs and because some subcategories are not shown. "–" means data are unavailable.
Source: Bureau of Labor Statistics, 2000 and 2007 Consumer Expenditure Surveys; calculations by New Strategist

Automobile Service Clubs

Best customers: Householders aged 55 or older
Married couples without children at home
Married couples with adult children at home

Customer trends: Average household spending on automobile service clubs should continue to rise as the population ages.

Older householders are the best customers of automobile service club memberships. Householders aged 55 or older spend 32 to 50 percent more than average on this item and control just over half the market. Married couples without children at home (most of them empty-nesters) spend 49 percent more than average. Those with adult children at home spend 46 percent more. Behind the higher spending of older households is their greater interest in security—both on the road and at home.

Average household spending on automobile service club memberships rose by a substantial 68 percent between 2000 and 2007, after adjusting for inflation. Spending on this item is likely to continue to rise along with the aging of the population.

Table 19.2 **Automobile service clubs**

Total household spending $2,035,696,740.00
Average household spends 16.94

	AVERAGE HOUSEHOLD SPENDING	BEST CUSTOMERS (index)	BIGGEST CUSTOMERS (market share)
AGE OF HOUSEHOLDER			
Average household	**$16.94**	**100**	**100.0%**
Under age 25	3.76	22	1.5
Aged 25 to 34	8.05	48	8.1
Aged 35 to 44	12.91	76	14.8
Aged 45 to 54	20.17	119	25.0
Aged 55 to 64	25.39	150	24.3
Aged 65 to 74	23.36	138	13.8
Aged 75 or older	22.30	132	12.5

	AVERAGE HOUSEHOLD SPENDING	BEST CUSTOMERS (index)	BIGGEST CUSTOMERS (market share)
HOUSEHOLD INCOME			
Average household	**$16.94**	**100**	**100.0%**
Under $20,000	7.95	47	9.7
$20,000 to $39,999	12.27	72	16.8
$40,000 to $49,999	14.22	84	8.3
$50,000 to $69,999	17.27	102	15.6
$70,000 to $79,999	22.35	132	7.6
$80,000 to $99,999	23.66	140	11.4
$100,000 or more	30.30	179	30.6
HOUSEHOLD TYPE			
Average household	**16.94**	**100**	**100.0**
Married couples	20.62	122	61.5
Married couples, no children	25.16	149	32.0
Married couples, with children	17.93	106	26.4
Oldest child under age 6	13.07	77	3.8
Oldest child aged 6 to 17	15.90	94	11.9
Oldest child aged 18 or older	24.65	146	10.7
Single parent with child under age 18	8.04	47	2.8
Single person	14.31	84	25.1
RACE AND HISPANIC ORIGIN			
Average household	**16.94**	**100**	**100.0**
Asian	18.37	108	3.8
Black	8.72	51	6.2
Hispanic	9.54	56	6.6
Non-Hispanic white and other	19.40	115	87.4
REGION			
Average household	**16.94**	**100**	**100.0**
Northeast	21.03	124	23.1
Midwest	16.60	98	22.4
South	11.77	69	24.9
West	22.12	131	29.5
EDUCATION			
Average household	**16.94**	**100**	**100.0**
Less than high school graduate	7.12	42	6.4
High school graduate	13.32	79	19.8
Some college	16.70	99	21.5
Associate's degree	19.76	117	10.4
College graduate	24.55	145	41.9
Bachelor's degree	21.66	128	24.0
Master's, professional, doctoral degree	29.85	176	18.0

Note: Market shares may not sum to 100.0 because of rounding and missing categories by household type. "Asian" and "black" include Hispanics and non-Hispanics who identify themselves as being of the respective race alone. "Hispanic" includes people of any race who identify themselves as Hispanic. "Other" includes people who identify themselves as non-Hispanic and as Alaska Native, American Indian, Asian (who are also included in the "Asian" row), Native Hawaiian or other Pacific Islander, as well as non-Hispanics reporting more than one race.
Source: Calculations by New Strategist based on the Bureau of Labor Statistics' 2007 Consumer Expenditure Survey.

Car Lease Payments

Best customers: Householders aged 25 to 64
High-income households
Married couples with children at home
Households in the Northeast

Customer trends: Average household spending on car lease payments will fluctuate depending on vehicle financing incentives.

The best customers of car leasing are married couples with children at home. Married couples with children at home spend 57 percent more than average on car lease payments, the figure peaking at 85 percent above average for those with preschoolers. Householders ranging in age from 25 to 64, many with children at home, spend 12 to 27 percent more than average on car lease payments. Households in the Northeast spend 57 percent more than average on car leases. High-income households spend three times the average on this item.

Average household spending on car lease payments fell 45 percent between 2000 and 2007, after adjusting for inflation, one of the steepest declines in the transportation category. Behind the spending drop was the shift to buying rather than leasing as car dealers offered no-interest loans and other purchasing incentives. Spending on leasing will continue to fluctuate, depending on dealer incentives.

Table 19.3 Car lease payments

Total household spending $14,016,745,440.00
Average household spends   116.64

	AVERAGE HOUSEHOLD SPENDING	BEST CUSTOMERS (index)	BIGGEST CUSTOMERS (market share)
AGE OF HOUSEHOLDER			
Average household	**$116.64**	**100**	**100.0%**
Under age 25	51.15	44	3.0
Aged 25 to 34	135.57	116	19.8
Aged 35 to 44	135.97	117	22.7
Aged 45 to 54	130.90	112	23.6
Aged 55 to 64	147.58	127	20.5
Aged 65 to 74	53.88	46	4.6
Aged 75 or older	71.36	61	5.8

	AVERAGE HOUSEHOLD SPENDING	BEST CUSTOMERS (index)	BIGGEST CUSTOMERS (market share)
HOUSEHOLD INCOME			
Average household	**$116.64**	**100**	**100.0%**
Under $20,000	22.84	20	4.0
$20,000 to $39,999	39.23	34	7.8
$40,000 to $49,999	88.41	76	7.5
$50,000 to $69,999	83.14	71	10.9
$70,000 to $79,999	127.71	109	6.3
$80,000 to $99,999	153.83	132	10.7
$100,000 or more	358.93	308	52.7
HOUSEHOLD TYPE			
Average household	**116.64**	**100**	**100.0**
Married couples	153.35	131	66.5
Married couples, no children	127.60	109	23.6
Married couples, with children	182.93	157	39.1
Oldest child under age 6	215.59	185	9.0
Oldest child aged 6 to 17	173.26	149	18.9
Oldest child aged 18 or older	177.96	153	11.2
Single parent with child under age 18	68.42	59	3.5
Single person	66.11	57	16.9
RACE AND HISPANIC ORIGIN			
Average household	**116.64**	**100**	**100.0**
Asian	67.68	58	2.0
Black	124.53	107	12.8
Hispanic	98.30	84	9.9
Non-Hispanic white and other	118.43	102	77.5
REGION			
Average household	**116.64**	**100**	**100.0**
Northeast	183.12	157	29.2
Midwest	125.01	107	24.5
South	63.71	55	19.6
West	137.46	118	26.7
EDUCATION			
Average household	**116.64**	**100**	**100.0**
Less than high school graduate	46.75	40	6.1
High school graduate	73.87	63	16.0
Some college	90.58	78	16.9
Associate's degree	85.71	73	6.5
College graduate	219.62	188	54.5
Bachelor's degree	210.64	181	33.8
Master's, professional, doctoral degree	236.12	202	20.7

Note: Market shares may not sum to 100.0 because of rounding and missing categories by household type. "Asian" and "black" include Hispanics and non-Hispanics who identify themselves as being of the respective race alone. "Hispanic" includes people of any race who identify themselves as Hispanic. "Other" includes people who identify themselves as non-Hispanic and as Alaska Native, American Indian, Asian (who are also included in the "Asian" row), Native Hawaiian or other Pacific Islander, as well as non-Hispanics reporting more than one race.
Source: Calculations by New Strategist based on the Bureau of Labor Statistics' 2007 Consumer Expenditure Survey.

Cars, New

Best customers:	**Householders aged 45 to 54** **Married couples without children at home** **Married couples with adult children at home** **Asians**
Customer trends:	**Average household spending on new cars is likely to rise as downsizing boomers replace sport utility vehicles and minivans with cars—but only if discretionary income grows.**

The best customers of new cars are middle-aged adults. Householders aged 45 to 54 spend 21 percent more than average on new cars. Married couples without children at home, most of them empty-nesters, spend 52 percent more than average. Couples with adult children at home, a demographic with more earners and drivers than average, spend 77 percent more than the average household on new cars. Asians, who have the highest incomes, spend over twice the average on new cars.

Average household spending on new cars fell 35 percent between 2000 and 2007, after adjusting for inflation. Behind the decline in spending on new cars was the growing popularity of sport utility vehicles (considered trucks) during the time period. Rising gasoline prices are likely to turn this trend around, as is the downsizing of transportation needs as boomers become empty-nesters—but only if discretionary income grows.

Table 19.4 Cars, new

Total household spending $85,585,786,200.00
Average household spends   712.20

	AVERAGE HOUSEHOLD SPENDING	BEST CUSTOMERS (index)	BIGGEST CUSTOMERS (market share)
AGE OF HOUSEHOLDER			
Average household	**$712.20**	**100**	**100.0%**
Under age 25	638.74	90	6.1
Aged 25 to 34	826.65	116	19.8
Aged 35 to 44	669.56	94	18.3
Aged 45 to 54	858.23	121	25.3
Aged 55 to 64	717.78	101	16.3
Aged 65 to 74	661.68	93	9.3
Aged 75 or older	366.53	51	4.9

	AVERAGE HOUSEHOLD SPENDING	BEST CUSTOMERS (index)	BIGGEST CUSTOMERS (market share)
HOUSEHOLD INCOME			
Average household	**$712.20**	**100**	**100.0%**
Under $20,000	249.30	35	7.2
$20,000 to $39,999	363.53	51	11.9
$40,000 to $49,999	500.22	70	6.9
$50,000 to $69,999	799.55	112	17.2
$70,000 to $79,999	614.65	86	5.0
$80,000 to $99,999	1,253.73	176	14.3
$100,000 or more	1,560.24	219	37.5
HOUSEHOLD TYPE			
Average household	**712.20**	**100**	**100.0**
Married couples	955.10	134	67.8
Married couples, no children	1,080.88	152	32.7
Married couples, with children	865.27	121	30.3
Oldest child under age 6	588.26	83	4.0
Oldest child aged 6 to 17	742.70	104	13.2
Oldest child aged 18 or older	1,260.11	177	13.0
Single parent with child under age 18	307.90	43	2.6
Single person	472.74	66	19.7
RACE AND HISPANIC ORIGIN			
Average household	**712.20**	**100**	**100.0**
Asian	1,646.08	231	8.2
Black	336.18	47	5.7
Hispanic	706.40	99	11.7
Non-Hispanic white and other	775.11	109	83.1
REGION			
Average household	**712.20**	**100**	**100.0**
Northeast	702.27	99	18.4
Midwest	635.86	89	20.4
South	590.71	83	29.8
West	990.46	139	31.5
EDUCATION			
Average household	**712.20**	**100**	**100.0**
Less than high school graduate	435.81	61	9.3
High school graduate	488.35	69	17.3
Some college	538.26	76	16.5
Associate's degree	971.75	136	12.1
College graduate	1,103.30	155	44.8
Bachelor's degree	1,006.78	141	26.5
Master's, professional, doctoral degree	1,280.64	180	18.3

Note: Market shares may not sum to 100.0 because of rounding and missing categories by household type. "Asian" and "black" include Hispanics and non-Hispanics who identify themselves as being of the respective race alone. "Hispanic" includes people of any race who identify themselves as Hispanic. "Other" includes people who identify themselves as non-Hispanic and as Alaska Native, American Indian, Asian (who are also included in the "Asian" row), Native Hawaiian or other Pacific Islander, as well as non-Hispanics reporting more than one race.
Source: Calculations by New Strategist based on the Bureau of Labor Statistics' 2007 Consumer Expenditure Survey.

Cars, Used

Best customers:
Householders aged 25 to 44
Married couples with adult children at home
Single parents

Customer trends:
Average household spending on used cars may climb because of the economic downturn and the entry of the millennial generation into the best-customer age groups.

The best customers of used cars are young adults and married couples with adult children at home. Householders aged 25 to 44 spend 21 to 36 percent more than average on used cars. Married couples with adult children at home spend 72 percent more than average on this item. Single parents, a demographic that can rarely afford above-average spending, lays out a surprising 13 percent more than the average household on used cars.

Average household spending on used cars fell 30 percent between 2000 and 2007, after adjusting for inflation. Behind the decline was the growing popularity of sport utility vehicles (considered trucks), as well as dealer incentives to buy new rather than used vehicles. Average household spending on used cars may climb because of the economic downturn and the entry of the millennial generation into the best-customer age groups.

Table 19.5 Cars, used

| Total household spending | $102,407,322,780.00 |
| Average household spends | 852.18 |

AGE OF HOUSEHOLDER	AVERAGE HOUSEHOLD SPENDING	BEST CUSTOMERS (index)	BIGGEST CUSTOMERS (market share)
Average household	$852.18	100	100.0%
Under age 25	802.01	94	6.4
Aged 25 to 34	1,161.48	136	23.2
Aged 35 to 44	1,028.29	121	23.5
Aged 45 to 54	703.22	83	17.3
Aged 55 to 64	937.91	110	17.8
Aged 65 to 74	664.79	78	7.8
Aged 75 or older	350.61	41	3.9

	AVERAGE HOUSEHOLD SPENDING	BEST CUSTOMERS (index)	BIGGEST CUSTOMERS (market share)
HOUSEHOLD INCOME			
Average household	$852.18	100	100.0%
Under $20,000	467.05	55	11.3
$20,000 to $39,999	742.70	87	20.3
$40,000 to $49,999	451.96	53	5.2
$50,000 to $69,999	1,239.50	145	22.3
$70,000 to $79,999	891.30	105	6.1
$80,000 to $99,999	868.82	102	8.3
$100,000 or more	1,325.62	156	26.7
HOUSEHOLD TYPE			
Average household	852.18	100	100.0
Married couples	965.84	113	57.3
Married couples, no children	711.26	83	18.0
Married couples, with children	1,113.64	131	32.6
Oldest child under age 6	956.40	112	5.5
Oldest child aged 6 to 17	968.65	114	14.4
Oldest child aged 18 or older	1,467.77	172	12.7
Single parent with child under age 18	958.73	113	6.7
Single person	491.15	58	17.1
RACE AND HISPANIC ORIGIN			
Average household	852.18	100	100.0
Asian	641.45	75	2.7
Black	958.24	112	13.5
Hispanic	681.25	80	9.4
Non-Hispanic white and other	863.11	101	77.3
REGION			
Average household	852.18	100	100.0
Northeast	660.40	77	14.4
Midwest	980.72	115	26.3
South	763.98	90	32.2
West	1,020.29	120	27.1
EDUCATION			
Average household	852.18	100	100.0
Less than high school graduate	700.77	82	12.5
High school graduate	829.19	97	24.5
Some college	860.15	101	22.0
Associate's degree	832.73	98	8.7
College graduate	951.53	112	32.3
Bachelor's degree	1,054.14	124	23.2
Master's, professional, doctoral degree	763.00	90	9.1

Note: Market shares may not sum to 100.0 because of rounding and missing categories by household type. "Asian" and "black" include Hispanics and non-Hispanics who identify themselves as being of the respective race alone. "Hispanic" includes people of any race who identify themselves as Hispanic. "Other" includes people who identify themselves as non-Hispanic and as Alaska Native, American Indian, Asian (who are also included in the "Asian" row), Native Hawaiian or other Pacific Islander, as well as non-Hispanics reporting more than one race.
Source: Calculations by New Strategist based on the Bureau of Labor Statistics' 2007 Consumer Expenditure Survey.

Gasoline and Motor Oil (Including on Trips)

Best customers:	**Householders aged 35 to 54** **Married couples with school-aged or older children at home**
Customer trends:	**Average household spending on gasoline will rise and fall along with the price of gas.**

Gasoline is the biggest transportation expense for the average household, accounting for 27 percent of transportation spending. The biggest spenders on gasoline are middle-aged married couples because they have the largest households and the most vehicles. Householders aged 35 to 54 spend 19 to 20 percent more than average on gasoline and account for 49 percent of the market. Married couples with school-aged children at home spend 46 percent more than average on this item, while those with adult children at home spend 59 percent more than average on gasoline.

Average household spending on gasoline rose by a substantial 53 percent between 2000 and 2007, after adjusting for inflation. Behind the increase was the rise in gasoline prices. Average household spending on gasoline will fluctuate with gasoline prices.

Table 19.6 **Gasoline and motor oil (including on trips)**

Total household spending	$286,448,007,570.00
Average household spends	2,383.67

	AVERAGE HOUSEHOLD SPENDING	BEST CUSTOMERS (index)	BIGGEST CUSTOMERS (market share)
AGE OF HOUSEHOLDER			
Average household	**$2,383.67**	**100**	**100.0%**
Under age 25	1,760.00	74	5.0
Aged 25 to 34	2,445.99	103	17.5
Aged 35 to 44	2,869.55	120	23.5
Aged 45 to 54	2,846.03	119	25.1
Aged 55 to 64	2,503.87	105	17.0
Aged 65 to 74	1,861.64	78	7.8
Aged 75 or older	1,039.04	44	4.1

	AVERAGE HOUSEHOLD SPENDING	BEST CUSTOMERS (index)	BIGGEST CUSTOMERS (market share)
HOUSEHOLD INCOME			
Average household	$2,383.67	100	100.0%
Under $20,000	1,056.62	44	9.1
$20,000 to $39,999	1,839.02	77	17.9
$40,000 to $49,999	2,335.15	98	9.6
$50,000 to $69,999	2,788.20	117	17.9
$70,000 to $79,999	3,041.21	128	7.4
$80,000 to $99,999	3,243.19	136	11.1
$100,000 or more	3,751.09	157	27.0
HOUSEHOLD TYPE			
Average household	2,383.67	100	100.0
Married couples	3,108.51	130	65.9
Married couples, no children	2,649.23	111	24.0
Married couples, with children	3,421.28	144	35.8
Oldest child under age 6	2,717.36	114	5.6
Oldest child aged 6 to 17	3,474.04	146	18.5
Oldest child aged 18 or older	3,796.63	159	11.7
Single parent with child under age 18	1,771.41	74	4.4
Single person	1,275.54	54	15.9
RACE AND HISPANIC ORIGIN			
Average household	2,383.67	100	100.0
Asian	2,391.22	100	3.5
Black	1,934.71	81	9.7
Hispanic	2,304.38	97	11.4
Non-Hispanic white and other	2,465.55	103	79.0
REGION			
Average household	2,383.67	100	100.0
Northeast	2,080.02	87	16.3
Midwest	2,407.54	101	23.1
South	2,522.39	106	38.0
West	2,389.35	100	22.7
EDUCATION			
Average household	2,383.67	100	100.0
Less than high school graduate	1,784.67	75	11.4
High school graduate	2,269.27	95	24.0
Some college	2,428.89	102	22.2
Associate's degree	2,740.03	115	10.2
College graduate	2,653.80	111	32.2
Bachelor's degree	2,653.93	111	20.9
Master's, professional, doctoral degree	2,653.58	111	11.4

Note: Market shares may not sum to 100.0 because of rounding and missing categories by household type. "Asian" and "black" include Hispanics and non-Hispanics who identify themselves as being of the respective race alone. "Hispanic" includes people of any race who identify themselves as Hispanic. "Other" includes people who identify themselves as non-Hispanic and as Alaska Native, American Indian, Asian (who are also included in the "Asian" row), Native Hawaiian or other Pacific Islander, as well as non-Hispanics reporting more than one race.
Source: Calculations by New Strategist based on the Bureau of Labor Statistics' 2007 Consumer Expenditure Survey.

Mass Transit Fares, Intracity

Best customers:
Householders under age 55
Married couples with adult children at home
Single parents
Asians, blacks, and Hispanics
Households in the Northeast

Customer trends:
Average household spending on mass transit could increase as higher gas prices and the economic downturn encourage more workers to use mass transit for their daily commute.

Workers in the central cities of the Northeast are the best customers of mass transit. Households in the Northeast spend three times the average on intracity mass transit fares and account for 56 percent of the market. Householders under age 55, most in the workforce, spend 10 to 31 percent more than average on intracity mass transit fares. Blacks and Hispanics spend, respectively, 64 and 52 percent more than average on this item because many live in central cities, and Asians spend two-and-one-half times the average on mass transit. Married couples with adult children at home spend 42 percent more than average on this item because they have the most workers in their households. Least likely to own a car, single parents spend one-third more than average on mass transit fares.

Average household spending on intracity mass transit fares fell 3 percent between 2000 and 2007, after adjusting for inflation. Behind the decline was the continuing shift of jobs from central cities to suburbs, reducing the use of mass transit. Average household spending on mass transit could increase as higher gas prices and the economic downturn encourage more workers to use mass transit for their daily commute.

Table 19.7 Mass transit fares, intracity

Total household spending $6,621,422,100.00
Average household spends   55.10

	AVERAGE HOUSEHOLD SPENDING	BEST CUSTOMERS (index)	BIGGEST CUSTOMERS (market share)
AGE OF HOUSEHOLDER			
Average household	**$55.10**	**100**	**100.0%**
Under age 25	70.68	128	8.7
Aged 25 to 34	67.44	122	20.9
Aged 35 to 44	60.42	110	21.4
Aged 45 to 54	71.98	131	27.4
Aged 55 to 64	49.66	90	14.6
Aged 65 to 74	21.04	38	3.8
Aged 75 or older	18.62	34	3.2

	AVERAGE HOUSEHOLD SPENDING	BEST CUSTOMERS (index)	BIGGEST CUSTOMERS (market share)
HOUSEHOLD INCOME			
Average household	**$55.10**	**100**	**100.0%**
Under $20,000	44.14	80	16.5
$20,000 to $39,999	44.18	80	18.6
$40,000 to $49,999	50.07	91	8.9
$50,000 to $69,999	43.57	79	12.1
$70,000 to $79,999	39.52	72	4.2
$80,000 to $99,999	49.69	90	7.3
$100,000 or more	104.09	189	32.4
HOUSEHOLD TYPE			
Average household	**55.10**	**100**	**100.0**
Married couples	50.76	92	46.6
Married couples, no children	39.32	71	15.4
Married couples, with children	56.02	102	25.4
Oldest child under age 6	64.43	117	5.7
Oldest child aged 6 to 17	39.83	72	9.2
Oldest child aged 18 or older	78.36	142	10.5
Single parent with child under age 18	73.04	133	7.9
Single person	43.51	79	23.5
RACE AND HISPANIC ORIGIN			
Average household	**55.10**	**100**	**100.0**
Asian	138.53	251	8.9
Black	90.50	164	19.7
Hispanic	83.64	152	17.9
Non-Hispanic white and other	45.39	82	62.9
REGION			
Average household	**55.10**	**100**	**100.0**
Northeast	166.55	302	56.3
Midwest	28.00	51	11.6
South	20.31	37	13.2
West	45.94	83	18.9
EDUCATION			
Average household	**55.10**	**100**	**100.0**
Less than high school graduate	57.62	105	15.9
High school graduate	31.19	57	14.3
Some college	41.47	75	16.4
Associate's degree	31.69	58	5.1
College graduate	92.07	167	48.4
Bachelor's degree	91.28	166	31.0
Master's, professional, doctoral degree	93.53	170	17.3

Note: Market shares may not sum to 100.0 because of rounding and missing categories by household type. "Asian" and "black" include Hispanics and non-Hispanics who identify themselves as being of the respective race alone. "Hispanic" includes people of any race who identify themselves as Hispanic. "Other" includes people who identify themselves as non-Hispanic and as Alaska Native, American Indian, Asian (who are also included in the "Asian" row), Native Hawaiian or other Pacific Islander, as well as non-Hispanics reporting more than one race.
Source: Calculations by New Strategist based on the Bureau of Labor Statistics' 2007 Consumer Expenditure Survey.

Motorcycles, New and Used

Best customers:	**Householders aged 25 to 54** **Married couples without children at home** **Married couples with school-aged or older children at home** **Households in the Midwest**
Customer trends:	**Average household spending on motorcycles could continue to rise as the economic downturn forces Americans to search for ways to save money.**

The best customers of motorcycles are young and middle-aged adults buying fuel-efficient two-wheelers for daily commuting and weekend cruising. Householders aged 25 to 54 spend 16 to 65 percent more than average on motorcycles and account for 79 percent of the market. Married couples without children at home, most of them empty-nesters, spend 61 percent more than average on motorcycles, while those with school-aged or older children at home spend 36 to 107 percent more than average on this item. Households in the Midwest spend 69 percent more than average on motorcycles.

Average household spending on motorcycles rose by a whopping 144 percent from 2000 to 2007, after adjusting for inflation. The rising price of gasoline was one factor behind the increase, as more turned to motorcycles for fuel efficiency. Average household spending on motorcycles could continue to rise as the economic downturn forces Americans to search for ways to save money.

Table 19.8 Motorcycles, new and used

Total household spending	$12,657,611,430.00
Average household spends	105.33

	AVERAGE HOUSEHOLD SPENDING	BEST CUSTOMERS (index)	BIGGEST CUSTOMERS (market share)
AGE OF HOUSEHOLDER			
Average household	**$105.33**	**100**	**100.0%**
Under age 25	88.93	84	5.7
Aged 25 to 34	132.53	126	21.5
Aged 35 to 44	122.20	116	22.6
Aged 45 to 54	174.31	165	34.8
Aged 55 to 64	65.73	62	10.1
Aged 65 to 74	56.15	53	5.3
Aged 75 or older	0.00	0	0.0

	AVERAGE HOUSEHOLD SPENDING	BEST CUSTOMERS (index)	BIGGEST CUSTOMERS (market share)
HOUSEHOLD INCOME			
Average household	**$105.33**	**100**	**100.0%**
Under $20,000	18.66	18	3.6
$20,000 to $39,999	65.90	63	14.5
$40,000 to $49,999	22.01	21	2.1
$50,000 to $69,999	116.72	111	17.0
$70,000 to $79,999	282.98	269	15.6
$80,000 to $99,999	197.38	187	15.2
$100,000 or more	190.08	180	30.9
HOUSEHOLD TYPE			
Average household	**105.33**	**100**	**100.0**
Married couples	158.36	150	76.0
Married couples, no children	169.36	161	34.7
Married couples, with children	159.32	151	37.7
Oldest child under age 6	29.04	28	1.3
Oldest child aged 6 to 17	218.44	207	26.3
Oldest child aged 18 or older	143.70	136	10.1
Single parent with child under age 18	4.63	4	0.3
Single person	52.70	50	14.9
RACE AND HISPANIC ORIGIN			
Average household	**105.33**	**100**	**100.0**
Asian	0.00	0	0.0
Black	34.31	33	3.9
Hispanic	63.31	60	7.1
Non-Hispanic white and other	122.79	117	89.0
REGION			
Average household	**105.33**	**100**	**100.0**
Northeast	39.92	38	7.1
Midwest	177.97	169	38.6
South	95.54	91	32.6
West	101.32	96	21.8
EDUCATION			
Average household	**105.33**	**100**	**100.0**
Less than high school graduate	18.95	18	2.7
High school graduate	105.02	100	25.2
Some college	194.54	185	40.2
Associate's degree	158.36	150	13.4
College graduate	67.44	64	18.5
Bachelor's degree	73.76	70	13.1
Master's, professional, doctoral degree	55.84	53	5.4

Note: Market shares may not sum to 100.0 because of rounding and missing categories by household type. "Asian" and "black" include Hispanics and non-Hispanics who identify themselves as being of the respective race alone. "Hispanic" includes people of any race who identify themselves as Hispanic. "Other" includes people who identify themselves as non-Hispanic and as Alaska Native, American Indian, Asian (who are also included in the "Asian" row), Native Hawaiian or other Pacific Islander, as well as non-Hispanics reporting more than one race.
Source: Calculations by New Strategist based on the Bureau of Labor Statistics' 2007 Consumer Expenditure Survey.

Oil Change, Lube, and Oil Filters

Best customers: **Householders aged 45 to 64**
                                 Married couples

Customer trends: **Average household spending on oil changes may decline as boomers become empty-nesters and downsize their fleets.**

Older married couples are the biggest spenders on oil changes, lubes, and oil filters. Householders ranging in age from 45 to 64 spend 12 to 16 percent more than average on this item. Married couples, particularly those with children at home, own more cars than average, which boosts spending on this item. Overall, married couples spend 28 percent more than average on oil changes. Couples with adult children at home (many with three cars) spend 42 percent more than average on this item.

Average household spending on oil changes, lubes, and oil filters fell 2 percent between 2000 and 2007, after adjusting for inflation. Behind the decline is increasing competition from discount oil change shops and big-box retailers. Average household spending on this item may continue to decline as boomers become empty-nesters and downsize their fleets.

Table 19.9 Oil change, lube, and oil filters

Total household spending $8,332,657,140.00
Average household spends   69.34

	AVERAGE HOUSEHOLD SPENDING	BEST CUSTOMERS (index)	BIGGEST CUSTOMERS (market share)
AGE OF HOUSEHOLDER			
Average household	**$69.34**	**100**	**100.0%**
Under age 25	48.83	70	4.8
Aged 25 to 34	67.14	97	16.5
Aged 35 to 44	73.76	106	20.7
Aged 45 to 54	77.75	112	23.6
Aged 55 to 64	80.10	116	18.7
Aged 65 to 74	72.70	105	10.5
Aged 75 or older	38.31	55	5.2

	AVERAGE HOUSEHOLD SPENDING	BEST CUSTOMERS (index)	BIGGEST CUSTOMERS (market share)
HOUSEHOLD INCOME			
Average household	$69.34	100	100.0%
Under $20,000	29.49	43	8.7
$20,000 to $39,999	51.83	75	17.4
$40,000 to $49,999	65.03	94	9.2
$50,000 to $69,999	77.66	112	17.1
$70,000 to $79,999	80.71	116	6.7
$80,000 to $99,999	96.63	139	11.3
$100,000 or more	119.15	172	29.4
HOUSEHOLD TYPE			
Average household	69.34	100	100.0
Married couples	88.61	128	64.6
Married couples, no children	86.24	124	26.8
Married couples, with children	91.14	131	32.8
Oldest child under age 6	85.41	123	6.0
Oldest child aged 6 to 17	89.02	128	16.3
Oldest child aged 18 or older	98.61	142	10.5
Single parent with child under age 18	48.21	70	4.1
Single person	44.10	64	18.9
RACE AND HISPANIC ORIGIN			
Average household	69.34	100	100.0
Asian	69.50	100	3.5
Black	50.26	72	8.7
Hispanic	54.86	79	9.3
Non-Hispanic white and other	74.51	107	82.0
REGION			
Average household	69.34	100	100.0
Northeast	61.59	89	16.5
Midwest	76.93	111	25.4
South	68.11	98	35.3
West	69.99	101	22.8
EDUCATION			
Average household	69.34	100	100.0
Less than high school graduate	36.11	52	7.9
High school graduate	59.47	86	21.6
Some college	69.58	100	21.9
Associate's degree	79.93	115	10.2
College graduate	91.91	133	38.4
Bachelor's degree	88.03	127	23.8
Master's, professional, doctoral degree	99.04	143	14.6

Note: Market shares may not sum to 100.0 because of rounding and missing categories by household type. "Asian" and "black" include Hispanics and non-Hispanics who identify themselves as being of the respective race alone. "Hispanic" includes people of any race who identify themselves as Hispanic. "Other" includes people who identify themselves as non-Hispanic and as Alaska Native, American Indian, Asian (who are also included in the "Asian" row), Native Hawaiian or other Pacific Islander, as well as non-Hispanics reporting more than one race.
Source: Calculations by New Strategist based on the Bureau of Labor Statistics' 2007 Consumer Expenditure Survey.

Parking Fees, Excluding Residence

Best customers:
Householders aged 45 to 54
Married couples
Asians
Households in the Northeast
College graduates

Customer trends:
Average household spending on parking should continue to rise as localities recoup infrastructure costs by raising parking fees.

The biggest spenders on parking fees (excluding residential parking) are educated, middle-aged married couples out and about with their children and grandchildren—many of them shopping, visiting museums, going to concerts, and participating in other events. Married couples with preschoolers spend 20 percent more than average on this item. Couples with adult children at home spend 66 percent more. College graduates spend more than twice the average and account for 62 percent of the market. Asians spend 61 percent more on parking than average. Households in the Northeast spend 64 percent more than average on parking fees.

Average household spending on parking fees rose 59 percent between 2000 and 2007, after adjusting for inflation. Spending on parking should continue to rise as localities recover infrastructure costs by raising parking fees.

Table 19.10 Parking fees, excluding residence

Total household spending $4,226,414,070.00
Average household spends 35.17

	AVERAGE HOUSEHOLD SPENDING	BEST CUSTOMERS (index)	BIGGEST CUSTOMERS (market share)
AGE OF HOUSEHOLDER			
Average household	**$35.17**	**100**	**100.0%**
Under age 25	34.25	97	6.6
Aged 25 to 34	32.96	94	16.0
Aged 35 to 44	35.64	101	19.7
Aged 45 to 54	53.10	151	31.7
Aged 55 to 64	33.85	96	15.6
Aged 65 to 74	21.04	60	6.0
Aged 75 or older	16.26	46	4.4

	AVERAGE HOUSEHOLD SPENDING	BEST CUSTOMERS (index)	BIGGEST CUSTOMERS (market share)
HOUSEHOLD INCOME			
Average household	$35.17	100	100.0%
Under $20,000	13.16	37	7.7
$20,000 to $39,999	14.35	41	9.5
$40,000 to $49,999	26.18	74	7.3
$50,000 to $69,999	24.91	71	10.8
$70,000 to $79,999	44.42	126	7.3
$80,000 to $99,999	33.43	95	7.7
$100,000 or more	101.86	290	49.6
HOUSEHOLD TYPE			
Average household	35.17	100	100.0
Married couples	43.07	122	61.9
Married couples, no children	41.82	119	25.7
Married couples, with children	44.23	126	31.4
Oldest child under age 6	42.34	120	5.9
Oldest child aged 6 to 17	36.77	105	13.3
Oldest child aged 18 or older	58.37	166	12.2
Single parent with child under age 18	29.78	85	5.0
Single person	25.21	72	21.3
RACE AND HISPANIC ORIGIN			
Average household	35.17	100	100.0
Asian	56.64	161	5.7
Black	22.79	65	7.8
Hispanic	19.22	55	6.5
Non-Hispanic white and other	39.59	113	85.9
REGION			
Average household	35.17	100	100.0
Northeast	57.71	164	30.6
Midwest	39.83	113	25.9
South	19.05	54	19.5
West	37.50	107	24.1
EDUCATION			
Average household	35.17	100	100.0
Less than high school graduate	6.49	18	2.8
High school graduate	11.94	34	8.6
Some college	29.02	83	18.0
Associate's degree	36.11	103	9.1
College graduate	74.79	213	61.6
Bachelor's degree	67.73	193	36.1
Master's, professional, doctoral degree	87.77	250	25.5

Note: Market shares may not sum to 100.0 because of rounding and missing categories by household type. "Asian" and "black" include Hispanics and non-Hispanics who identify themselves as being of the respective race alone. "Hispanic" includes people of any race who identify themselves as Hispanic. "Other" includes people who identify themselves as non-Hispanic and as Alaska Native, American Indian, Asian (who are also included in the "Asian" row), Native Hawaiian or other Pacific Islander, as well as non-Hispanics reporting more than one race.
Source: Calculations by New Strategist based on the Bureau of Labor Statistics' 2007 Consumer Expenditure Survey.

Taxi Fares and Limousine Service in Home Town

Best customers:

Householders aged 35 to 54
Single parents
Households in the Northeast

Customer trends:

Average household spending on taxi fares and limousine services
is likely to fall because of the economic downturn.

Households in the highly urbanized Northeast are the best customers of taxi and limousine services. They spend well over twice the average on this item and control 44 percent of the market. Much of this spending probably occurs in New York City, where many households do not own cars. The very best customers of taxi and limousine service are single parents, who spend nearly four times the average on this item. Householders aged 35 to 54 spend 26 to 62 percent more than average on this item.

Average household spending on taxi fares and limousine services rose 10 percent between 2000 and 2007, after adjusting for inflation. Average household spending on taxi fares and limousine services is likely to fall because of the economic downturn.

Table 19.11 Taxi fares and limousine service in home town

Total household spending $1,937,156,520.00
Average household spends   16.12

	AVERAGE HOUSEHOLD SPENDING	BEST CUSTOMERS (index)	BIGGEST CUSTOMERS (market share)
AGE OF HOUSEHOLDER			
Average household	**$16.12**	**100**	**100.0%**
Under age 25	8.45	52	3.6
Aged 25 to 34	12.92	80	13.7
Aged 35 to 44	20.33	126	24.6
Aged 45 to 54	26.16	162	34.1
Aged 55 to 64	11.46	71	11.5
Aged 65 to 74	11.02	68	6.8
Aged 75 or older	10.42	65	6.1

	AVERAGE HOUSEHOLD SPENDING	BEST CUSTOMERS (index)	BIGGEST CUSTOMERS (market share)
HOUSEHOLD INCOME			
Average household	$16.12	100	100.0%
Under $20,000	13.54	84	17.3
$20,000 to $39,999	12.63	78	18.2
$40,000 to $49,999	14.68	91	9.0
$50,000 to $69,999	19.15	119	18.2
$70,000 to $79,999	11.46	71	4.1
$80,000 to $99,999	12.46	77	6.3
$100,000 or more	25.75	160	27.4
HOUSEHOLD TYPE			
Average household	16.12	100	100.0
Married couples	10.82	67	33.9
Married couples, no children	6.28	39	8.4
Married couples, with children	14.82	92	22.9
Oldest child under age 6	21.00	130	6.4
Oldest child aged 6 to 17	15.57	97	12.3
Oldest child aged 18 or older	8.83	55	4.0
Single parent with child under age 18	60.68	376	22.4
Single person	15.00	93	27.7
RACE AND HISPANIC ORIGIN			
Average household	16.12	100	100.0
Asian	8.88	55	1.9
Black	15.71	97	11.7
Hispanic	19.03	118	13.9
Non-Hispanic white and other	15.75	98	74.6
REGION			
Average household	16.12	100	100.0
Northeast	37.78	234	43.7
Midwest	11.68	72	16.6
South	8.14	50	18.1
West	15.20	94	21.3
EDUCATION			
Average household	16.12	100	100.0
Less than high school graduate	12.90	80	12.1
High school graduate	9.58	59	15.0
Some college	17.66	110	23.9
Associate's degree	7.88	49	4.3
College graduate	24.56	152	44.1
Bachelor's degree	20.67	128	24.0
Master's, professional, doctoral degree	31.29	194	19.8

Note: Market shares may not sum to 100.0 because of rounding and missing categories by household type. "Asian" and "black" include Hispanics and non-Hispanics who identify themselves as being of the respective race alone. "Hispanic" includes people of any race who identify themselves as Hispanic. "Other" includes people who identify themselves as non-Hispanic and as Alaska Native, American Indian, Asian (who are also included in the "Asian" row), Native Hawaiian or other Pacific Islander, as well as non-Hispanics reporting more than one race.
Source: Calculations by New Strategist based on the Bureau of Labor Statistics' 2007 Consumer Expenditure Survey.

Tires (Purchased, Replaced, Installed)

Best customers: **Householders aged 35 to 64**
Married couples with school-aged or older children at home

Customer trends: **Average household spending on tires will decline as more boomers become empty-nesters and downsize their fleets.**

The best customers of tires are households with the most cars—those headed by middle-aged or older married couples, particularly households with teenage or adult children at home. Householders aged 35 to 64, many with teens and young adults at home, spend 14 to 32 percent more than the average household on tires and account for 69 percent of the market. Married couples with school-aged or older children at home spend 54 to 67 percent more than average on tires.

Average household spending on tires rose 10 percent between 2000 and 2007, after adjusting for inflation. Average household spending on tires will decline in the years ahead as more boomers become empty-nesters and downsize their fleets.

Table 19.12 Tires (purchased, replaced, installed)

Total household spending   **$13,927,818,900.00**
Average household spends   **115.90**

	AVERAGE HOUSEHOLD SPENDING	BEST CUSTOMERS (index)	BIGGEST CUSTOMERS (market share)
AGE OF HOUSEHOLDER			
Average household	**$115.90**	**100**	**100.0%**
Under age 25	62.47	54	3.7
Aged 25 to 34	102.15	88	15.0
Aged 35 to 44	136.00	117	22.9
Aged 45 to 54	153.52	132	27.8
Aged 55 to 64	131.56	114	18.4
Aged 65 to 74	99.11	86	8.5
Aged 75 or older	45.08	39	3.7

	AVERAGE HOUSEHOLD SPENDING	BEST CUSTOMERS (index)	BIGGEST CUSTOMERS (market share)
HOUSEHOLD INCOME			
Average household	$115.90	100	100.0%
Under $20,000	37.05	32	6.6
$20,000 to $39,999	82.45	71	16.5
$40,000 to $49,999	115.83	100	9.8
$50,000 to $69,999	146.99	127	19.4
$70,000 to $79,999	129.33	112	6.5
$80,000 to $99,999	143.34	124	10.1
$100,000 or more	210.57	182	31.1
HOUSEHOLD TYPE			
Average household	115.90	100	100.0
Married couples	154.50	133	67.4
Married couples, no children	137.17	118	25.5
Married couples, with children	172.07	148	37.0
Oldest child under age 6	123.09	106	5.2
Oldest child aged 6 to 17	178.67	154	19.6
Oldest child aged 18 or older	193.12	167	12.3
Single parent with child under age 18	83.45	72	4.3
Single person	65.02	56	16.7
RACE AND HISPANIC ORIGIN			
Average household	115.90	100	100.0
Asian	91.35	79	2.8
Black	87.00	75	9.0
Hispanic	80.59	70	8.2
Non-Hispanic white and other	125.83	109	82.9
REGION			
Average household	115.90	100	100.0
Northeast	108.39	94	17.4
Midwest	100.02	86	19.7
South	117.72	102	36.5
West	135.23	117	26.4
EDUCATION			
Average household	115.90	100	100.0
Less than high school graduate	63.86	55	8.4
High school graduate	103.38	89	22.5
Some college	126.42	109	23.8
Associate's degree	110.98	96	8.5
College graduate	147.67	127	36.9
Bachelor's degree	140.83	122	22.8
Master's, professional, doctoral degree	160.23	138	14.1

Note: Market shares may not sum to 100.0 because of rounding and missing categories by household type. "Asian" and "black" include Hispanics and non-Hispanics who identify themselves as being of the respective race alone. "Hispanic" includes people of any race who identify themselves as Hispanic. "Other" includes people who identify themselves as non-Hispanic and as Alaska Native, American Indian, Asian (who are also included in the "Asian" row), Native Hawaiian or other Pacific Islander, as well as non-Hispanics reporting more than one race.
Source: Calculations by New Strategist based on the Bureau of Labor Statistics' 2007 Consumer Expenditure Survey.

Towing Charges

Best customers:

Householders aged 45 to 54
Married couples with adult children at home
Hispanics
Households in the West

Customer trends:

Average household spending on towing charges should fall as boomers age and reduce the number of vehicles they own.

The biggest spenders on towing charges are householders who do not spend on automobile service clubs (which usually cover towing charges). They are also the heads of the largest households and most likely to own multiple and used vehicles, with frequent breakdowns. Householders aged 45 to 54 spend 62 percent more than the average on towing charges. Married couples with adult children at home spend two-and-one-half times the average on towing charges. Hispanics, who tend to have the largest families, spend 34 percent more than average on towing charges, and households in the West, where many Hispanics live, spend 41 percent more than average on towing.

Average household spending on towing charges rose 6 percent between 2000 and 2007, after adjusting for inflation. Average household spending on this item should decline as boomers age and reduce the number of vehicles they own.

Table 19.13 Towing charges

| Total household spending | $717,420,870.00 |
| Average household spends | 5.97 |

AGE OF HOUSEHOLDER	AVERAGE HOUSEHOLD SPENDING	BEST CUSTOMERS (index)	BIGGEST CUSTOMERS (market share)
Average household	**$5.97**	**100**	**100.0%**
Under age 25	7.93	133	9.0
Aged 25 to 34	5.84	98	16.7
Aged 35 to 44	5.97	100	19.5
Aged 45 to 54	9.69	162	34.1
Aged 55 to 64	4.44	74	12.0
Aged 65 to 74	3.18	53	5.3
Aged 75 or older	2.13	36	3.4

	AVERAGE HOUSEHOLD SPENDING	BEST CUSTOMERS (index)	BIGGEST CUSTOMERS (market share)
HOUSEHOLD INCOME			
Average household	$5.97	100	100.0%
Under $20,000	4.64	78	16.0
$20,000 to $39,999	4.64	78	18.1
$40,000 to $49,999	6.32	106	10.4
$50,000 to $69,999	5.73	96	14.7
$70,000 to $79,999	8.49	142	8.2
$80,000 to $99,999	10.72	180	14.6
$100,000 or more	6.29	105	18.1
HOUSEHOLD TYPE			
Average household	5.97	100	100.0
Married couples	6.70	112	56.7
Married couples, no children	4.58	77	16.5
Married couples, with children	9.06	152	37.9
Oldest child under age 6	4.60	77	3.8
Oldest child aged 6 to 17	7.69	129	16.4
Oldest child aged 18 or older	14.38	241	17.7
Single parent with child under age 18	5.27	88	5.2
Single person	4.44	74	22.1
RACE AND HISPANIC ORIGIN			
Average household	5.97	100	100.0
Asian	6.60	111	3.9
Black	3.26	55	6.6
Hispanic	8.02	134	15.9
Non-Hispanic white and other	6.07	102	77.6
REGION			
Average household	5.97	100	100.0
Northeast	6.05	101	18.9
Midwest	5.57	93	21.3
South	4.64	78	27.9
West	8.43	141	31.9
EDUCATION			
Average household	5.97	100	100.0
Less than high school graduate	4.94	83	12.6
High school graduate	4.32	72	18.3
Some college	8.74	146	31.9
Associate's degree	6.54	110	9.7
College graduate	5.69	95	27.6
Bachelor's degree	5.37	90	16.9
Master's, professional, doctoral degree	6.28	105	10.7

Note: Market shares may not sum to 100.0 because of rounding and missing categories by household type. "Asian" and "black" include Hispanics and non-Hispanics who identify themselves as being of the respective race alone. "Hispanic" includes people of any race who identify themselves as Hispanic. "Other" includes people who identify themselves as non-Hispanic and as Alaska Native, American Indian, Asian (who are also included in the "Asian" row), Native Hawaiian or other Pacific Islander, as well as non-Hispanics reporting more than one race.
Source: Calculations by New Strategist based on the Bureau of Labor Statistics' 2007 Consumer Expenditure Survey.

Truck Lease Payments

Best customers:
Householders aged 25 to 44
Married couples with children at home
Households in the Northeast and Midwest

Customer trends:
Average household spending on truck lease payments is likely to continue to decline as the economic downturn drives consumers toward fuel-efficient cars.

The best customers of truck leasing are married couples with children at home, leasing a pickup, minivan, or sport utility vehicle (all are considered trucks). Householders aged 25 to 44 spend 31 to 66 percent more than average on truck lease payments and account for 55 percent of the market for this item. Married couples with children under age 18 at home spend well over twice the average on truck lease payments. Households in the Northeast and Midwest spend, respectively, 52 and 43 percent above average on this item.

Average household spending on truck lease payments fell by a substantial 38 percent between 2000 and 2007, after adjusting for inflation. Behind the spending decline was the shift to buying rather than leasing as automotive dealers offered no-interest loans and other purchasing incentives. Average household spending on truck leases is likely to continue to decline in the years ahead as the economic downturn drives consumers toward fuel-efficient cars.

Table 19.14 Truck lease payments

Total household spending $13,385,847,690.00
Average household spends 111.39

AGE OF HOUSEHOLDER	AVERAGE HOUSEHOLD SPENDING	BEST CUSTOMERS (index)	BIGGEST CUSTOMERS (market share)
Average household	**$111.39**	**100**	**100.0%**
Under age 25	23.34	21	1.4
Aged 25 to 34	145.91	131	22.3
Aged 35 to 44	184.61	166	32.3
Aged 45 to 54	110.24	99	20.8
Aged 55 to 64	117.54	106	17.1
Aged 65 to 74	62.97	57	5.7
Aged 75 or older	4.81	4	0.4

	AVERAGE HOUSEHOLD SPENDING	BEST CUSTOMERS (index)	BIGGEST CUSTOMERS (market share)
HOUSEHOLD INCOME			
Average household	**$111.39**	**100**	**100.0%**
Under $20,000	21.30	19	3.9
$20,000 to $39,999	36.86	33	7.7
$40,000 to $49,999	67.36	60	6.0
$50,000 to $69,999	98.46	88	13.5
$70,000 to $79,999	161.83	145	8.4
$80,000 to $99,999	146.87	132	10.7
$100,000 or more	323.54	290	49.8
HOUSEHOLD TYPE			
Average household	**111.39**	**100**	**100.0**
Married couples	178.67	160	81.1
Married couples, no children	119.36	107	23.1
Married couples, with children	233.54	210	52.3
Oldest child under age 6	293.05	263	12.8
Oldest child aged 6 to 17	245.55	220	28.0
Oldest child aged 18 or older	173.42	156	11.5
Single parent with child under age 18	53.53	48	2.9
Single person	28.33	25	7.6
RACE AND HISPANIC ORIGIN			
Average household	**111.39**	**100**	**100.0**
Asian	88.25	79	2.8
Black	72.28	65	7.8
Hispanic	92.66	83	9.8
Non-Hispanic white and other	120.23	108	82.4
REGION			
Average household	**111.39**	**100**	**100.0**
Northeast	169.02	152	28.3
Midwest	158.81	143	32.6
South	54.75	49	17.6
West	105.93	95	21.5
EDUCATION			
Average household	**111.39**	**100**	**100.0**
Less than high school graduate	41.72	37	5.7
High school graduate	88.34	79	20.0
Some college	89.83	81	17.6
Associate's degree	118.96	107	9.5
College graduate	181.87	163	47.3
Bachelor's degree	161.73	145	27.2
Master's, professional, doctoral degree	218.87	196	20.0

Note: Market shares may not sum to 100.0 because of rounding and missing categories by household type. "Asian" and "black" include Hispanics and non-Hispanics who identify themselves as being of the respective race alone. "Hispanic" includes people of any race who identify themselves as Hispanic. "Other" includes people who identify themselves as non-Hispanic and as Alaska Native, American Indian, Asian (who are also included in the "Asian" row), Native Hawaiian or other Pacific Islander, as well as non-Hispanics reporting more than one race.
Source: Calculations by New Strategist based on the Bureau of Labor Statistics' 2007 Consumer Expenditure Survey.

Trucks, New

Best customers:
Householders aged 35 to 44
Married couples
Asians

Customer trends:
Average household spending on new trucks is likely to decline because of surging gas prices and aging boomers.

The best customers of new trucks (a category that includes minivans, sport utility vehicles, and pickups) are middle-aged married couples, many with children. Householders aged 35 to 44 spend 50 percent more than average on new trucks and control 29 percent of the market. Married couples with children at home spend 54 percent more than average on this item, while couples without children at home spend 48 percent more. Asians spend one-third above average on new trucks.

Average household spending on new trucks rose 4 percent between 2000 and 2007, after adjusting for inflation. Behind the increase was the popularity of sport utility vehicles for families with children. Spending on new trucks is likely to decline in the years ahead because of surging gas prices. Also, as boomers become empty-nesters, they are likely to replace their SUVs and minivans with smaller, more fuel-efficient cars.

Table 19.15 Trucks, new

| Total household spending | $103,298,991,600.00 |
| Average household spends | 859.60 |

	AVERAGE HOUSEHOLD SPENDING	BEST CUSTOMERS (index)	BIGGEST CUSTOMERS (market share)
AGE OF HOUSEHOLDER			
Average household	**$859.60**	**100**	**100.0%**
Under age 25	419.29	49	3.3
Aged 25 to 34	714.55	83	14.2
Aged 35 to 44	1,285.43	150	29.1
Aged 45 to 54	786.40	91	19.2
Aged 55 to 64	982.65	114	18.5
Aged 65 to 74	1,059.07	123	12.3
Aged 75 or older	301.91	35	3.3

	AVERAGE HOUSEHOLD SPENDING	BEST CUSTOMERS (index)	BIGGEST CUSTOMERS (market share)
HOUSEHOLD INCOME			
Average household	**$859.60**	**100**	**100.0%**
Under $20,000	360.31	42	8.6
$20,000 to $39,999	335.65	39	9.1
$40,000 to $49,999	400.67	47	4.6
$50,000 to $69,999	708.00	82	12.6
$70,000 to $79,999	1,241.05	144	8.4
$80,000 to $99,999	1,884.37	219	17.8
$100,000 or more	2,120.83	247	42.3
HOUSEHOLD TYPE			
Average household	**859.60**	**100**	**100.0**
Married couples	1,299.48	151	76.4
Married couples, no children	1,270.73	148	31.9
Married couples, with children	1,319.79	154	38.3
Oldest child under age 6	1,347.10	157	7.6
Oldest child aged 6 to 17	1,475.42	172	21.8
Oldest child aged 18 or older	1,033.35	120	8.9
Single parent with child under age 18	327.55	38	2.3
Single person	269.89	31	9.3
RACE AND HISPANIC ORIGIN			
Average household	**859.60**	**100**	**100.0**
Asian	1,150.99	134	4.7
Black	392.93	46	5.5
Hispanic	564.74	66	7.8
Non-Hispanic white and other	976.98	114	86.8
REGION			
Average household	**859.60**	**100**	**100.0**
Northeast	670.67	78	14.5
Midwest	895.72	104	23.8
South	933.20	109	39.0
West	861.84	100	22.7
EDUCATION			
Average household	**859.60**	**100**	**100.0**
Less than high school graduate	411.31	48	7.3
High school graduate	599.79	70	17.6
Some college	771.75	90	19.6
Associate's degree	1,354.17	158	14.0
College graduate	1,235.18	144	41.6
Bachelor's degree	1,172.45	136	25.6
Master's, professional, doctoral degree	1,350.44	157	16.0

Note: Market shares may not sum to 100.0 because of rounding and missing categories by household type. "Asian" and "black" include Hispanics and non-Hispanics who identify themselves as being of the respective race alone. "Hispanic" includes people of any race who identify themselves as Hispanic. "Other" includes people who identify themselves as non-Hispanic and as Alaska Native, American Indian, Asian (who are also included in the "Asian" row), Native Hawaiian or other Pacific Islander, as well as non-Hispanics reporting more than one race.
Source: Calculations by New Strategist based on the Bureau of Labor Statistics' 2007 Consumer Expenditure Survey.

Trucks, Used

Best customers: Householders aged 25 to 44
Married couples with children at home
Hispanics

Customer trends: Average household spending on used trucks is likely to fall as high gas prices and the economic downturn drive consumer toward fuel-efficient cars.

The best customers of used trucks (a category that includes minivans, sport utility vehicles, and pickups) are married couples with children, a group that spends twice the average on used trucks. Householders aged 25 to 44, most with children, spend 51 to 53 percent more than average on used trucks and control 55 percent of the market. Hispanics spend 20 percent more than average on used trucks.

Average household spending on used trucks fell 22 percent between 2000 and 2007, after adjusting for inflation. Behind the decline were the generous incentives car dealers offered on new trucks. Average household spending on used trucks is likely to fall as high gas prices and the economic downturn drive consumer toward fuel-efficient cars.

Table 19.16 Trucks, used

Total household spending $85,885,011,990.00
Average household spends 714.69

	AVERAGE HOUSEHOLD SPENDING	BEST CUSTOMERS (index)	BIGGEST CUSTOMERS (market share)
AGE OF HOUSEHOLDER			
Average household	**$714.69**	**100**	**100.0%**
Under age 25	323.85	45	3.1
Aged 25 to 34	1,094.92	153	26.1
Aged 35 to 44	1,077.43	151	29.4
Aged 45 to 54	701.28	98	20.6
Aged 55 to 64	644.27	90	14.6
Aged 65 to 74	259.72	36	3.6
Aged 75 or older	194.11	27	2.6

	AVERAGE HOUSEHOLD SPENDING	BEST CUSTOMERS (index)	BIGGEST CUSTOMERS (market share)
HOUSEHOLD INCOME			
Average household	$714.69	100	100.0%
Under $20,000	160.84	23	4.6
$20,000 to $39,999	543.06	76	17.7
$40,000 to $49,999	774.47	108	10.7
$50,000 to $69,999	976.51	137	20.9
$70,000 to $79,999	1,015.95	142	8.2
$80,000 to $99,999	1,182.06	165	13.5
$100,000 or more	1,020.17	143	24.5
HOUSEHOLD TYPE			
Average household	714.69	100	100.0
Married couples	1,056.06	148	74.7
Married couples, no children	595.46	83	18.0
Married couples, with children	1,461.10	204	51.0
Oldest child under age 6	1,608.57	225	11.0
Oldest child aged 6 to 17	1,506.60	211	26.8
Oldest child aged 18 or older	1,284.95	180	13.2
Single parent with child under age 18	539.76	76	4.5
Single person	191.87	27	8.0
RACE AND HISPANIC ORIGIN			
Average household	714.69	100	100.0
Asian	568.17	79	2.8
Black	501.40	70	8.4
Hispanic	859.88	120	14.2
Non-Hispanic white and other	724.69	101	77.4
REGION			
Average household	714.69	100	100.0
Northeast	434.44	61	11.3
Midwest	717.07	100	22.9
South	832.84	117	41.8
West	755.49	106	23.9
EDUCATION			
Average household	714.69	100	100.0
Less than high school graduate	544.78	76	11.6
High school graduate	738.52	103	26.1
Some college	865.94	121	26.4
Associate's degree	606.60	85	7.5
College graduate	702.36	98	28.4
Bachelor's degree	814.26	114	21.4
Master's, professional, doctoral degree	496.79	70	7.1

Note: Market shares may not sum to 100.0 because of rounding and missing categories by household type. "Asian" and "black" include Hispanics and non-Hispanics who identify themselves as being of the respective race alone. "Hispanic" includes people of any race who identify themselves as Hispanic. "Other" includes people who identify themselves as non-Hispanic and as Alaska Native, American Indian, Asian (who are also included in the "Asian" row), Native Hawaiian or other Pacific Islander, as well as non-Hispanics reporting more than one race.
Source: Calculations by New Strategist based on the Bureau of Labor Statistics' 2007 Consumer Expenditure Survey.

Vehicle Finance Charges

Best customers:
Householders aged 25 to 44
Married couples with children at home

Customer trends:
Average household spending on vehicle finance charges could continue to decline as boomers become empty-nesters and downsize their fleets.

The biggest spenders on vehicle finance charges are households with little savings and lots of vehicles—primarily young adults and couples with kids. Householders aged 25 to 44 spend 26 to 31 percent more than average on vehicle finance charges and account for 47 percent of household spending on this item. Married couples with children at home spend 56 percent more than average on vehicle finance charges.

Average household spending on vehicle finance charges fell 23 percent between 2000 and 2007, after adjusting for inflation. Behind the decline were low-interest and no-interest loans on vehicles during the time period. Average household spending on vehicle finance charges could continue to decline as boomers become empty-nesters and downsize their fleets.

Table 19.17 Vehicle finance charges

Total household spending $36,677,390,910.00
Average household spends 305.21

AGE OF HOUSEHOLDER	AVERAGE HOUSEHOLD SPENDING	BEST CUSTOMERS (index)	BIGGEST CUSTOMERS (market share)
Average household	$305.21	100	100.0%
Under age 25	221.10	72	4.9
Aged 25 to 34	383.67	126	21.4
Aged 35 to 44	400.11	131	25.5
Aged 45 to 54	335.36	110	23.1
Aged 55 to 64	324.80	106	17.2
Aged 65 to 74	197.36	65	6.5
Aged 75 or older	42.52	14	1.3

	AVERAGE HOUSEHOLD SPENDING	BEST CUSTOMERS (index)	BIGGEST CUSTOMERS (market share)
HOUSEHOLD INCOME			
Average household	**$305.21**	**100**	**100.0%**
Under $20,000	71.67	23	4.8
$20,000 to $39,999	175.88	58	13.4
$40,000 to $49,999	266.79	87	8.6
$50,000 to $69,999	400.33	131	20.1
$70,000 to $79,999	457.44	150	8.7
$80,000 to $99,999	503.24	165	13.4
$100,000 or more	552.52	181	31.0
HOUSEHOLD TYPE			
Average household	**305.21**	**100**	**100.0**
Married couples	424.33	139	70.3
Married couples, no children	349.08	114	24.7
Married couples, with children	476.12	156	38.9
Oldest child under age 6	476.27	156	7.6
Oldest child aged 6 to 17	478.17	157	19.9
Oldest child aged 18 or older	472.49	155	11.4
Single parent with child under age 18	216.93	71	4.2
Single person	122.04	40	11.9
RACE AND HISPANIC ORIGIN			
Average household	**305.21**	**100**	**100.0**
Asian	236.02	77	2.7
Black	252.01	83	9.9
Hispanic	313.50	103	12.1
Non-Hispanic white and other	311.98	102	78.0
REGION			
Average household	**305.21**	**100**	**100.0**
Northeast	249.53	82	15.2
Midwest	280.63	92	21.0
South	341.53	112	40.2
West	318.24	104	23.6
EDUCATION			
Average household	**305.21**	**100**	**100.0**
Less than high school graduate	154.12	50	7.7
High school graduate	288.99	95	23.9
Some college	358.41	117	25.6
Associate's degree	395.04	129	11.5
College graduate	330.91	108	31.4
Bachelor's degree	339.85	111	20.9
Master's, professional, doctoral degree	314.50	103	10.5

Note: Market shares may not sum to 100.0 because of rounding and missing categories by household type. "Asian" and "black" include Hispanics and non-Hispanics who identify themselves as being of the respective race alone. "Hispanic" includes people of any race who identify themselves as Hispanic. "Other" includes people who identify themselves as non-Hispanic and as Alaska Native, American Indian, Asian (who are also included in the "Asian" row), Native Hawaiian or other Pacific Islander, as well as non-Hispanics reporting more than one race.
Source: Calculations by New Strategist based on the Bureau of Labor Statistics' 2007 Consumer Expenditure Survey.

Vehicle Insurance

Best customers: **Householders aged 45 to 74**
Married couples with school-aged or older children at home
Asians

Customer trends: **Average household spending on vehicle insurance should fall as boomers become empty-nesters and downsize their fleets.**

The biggest spenders on vehicle insurance are households with multiple cars and drivers—particularly teens and young adults. Householders aged 45 to 54 (the age group most likely to have teen or young-adult children in the home) spend 29 percent more than average on vehicle insurance, while those aged 55 to 74 spend 13 to 23 percent more. Married couples with school-aged or adult children at home spend 30 to 51 percent more than average on this item. Asians outspend the average by 45 percent.

Average household spending on vehicle insurance grew 14 percent between 2000 and 2007, after adjusting for inflation. Behind the growth was the entry of the baby-boom generation into the best-customer age groups. Average household spending on this item may fall in the years ahead as boomers become empty-nesters and downsize their fleets.

Table 19.18 Vehicle insurance

Total household spending $128,747,604,270.00
Average household spends   1,071.37

	AVERAGE HOUSEHOLD SPENDING	BEST CUSTOMERS (index)	BIGGEST CUSTOMERS (market share)
AGE OF HOUSEHOLDER			
Average household	**$1,071.37**	**100**	**100.0%**
Under age 25	491.90	46	3.1
Aged 25 to 34	802.15	75	12.8
Aged 35 to 44	1,172.89	109	21.3
Aged 45 to 54	1,381.53	129	27.1
Aged 55 to 64	1,214.18	113	18.4
Aged 65 to 74	1,320.51	123	12.3
Aged 75 or older	596.76	56	5.3

	AVERAGE HOUSEHOLD SPENDING	BEST CUSTOMERS (index)	BIGGEST CUSTOMERS (market share)
HOUSEHOLD INCOME			
Average household	**$1,071.37**	**100**	**100.0%**
Under $20,000	488.00	46	9.4
$20,000 to $39,999	885.32	83	19.2
$40,000 to $49,999	1,213.06	113	11.1
$50,000 to $69,999	1,179.47	110	16.8
$70,000 to $79,999	1,234.48	115	6.7
$80,000 to $99,999	1,515.41	141	11.5
$100,000 or more	1,547.89	144	24.8
HOUSEHOLD TYPE			
Average household	**1,071.37**	**100**	**100.0**
Married couples	1,310.83	122	61.8
Married couples, no children	1,213.82	113	24.4
Married couples, with children	1,391.24	130	32.4
Oldest child under age 6	1,074.89	100	4.9
Oldest child aged 6 to 17	1,393.01	130	16.5
Oldest child aged 18 or older	1,619.90	151	11.1
Single parent with child under age 18	1,069.35	100	5.9
Single person	620.69	58	17.2
RACE AND HISPANIC ORIGIN			
Average household	**1,071.37**	**100**	**100.0**
Asian	1,549.55	145	5.1
Black	872.41	81	9.8
Hispanic	1,280.03	119	14.1
Non-Hispanic white and other	1,072.51	100	76.4
REGION			
Average household	**1,071.37**	**100**	**100.0**
Northeast	1,069.37	100	18.6
Midwest	908.04	85	19.4
South	1,041.29	97	34.9
West	1,290.10	120	27.2
EDUCATION			
Average household	**1,071.37**	**100**	**100.0**
Less than high school graduate	766.44	72	10.9
High school graduate	1,123.47	105	26.5
Some college	1,091.45	102	22.2
Associate's degree	1,386.49	129	11.5
College graduate	1,062.04	99	28.7
Bachelor's degree	1,070.32	100	18.7
Master's, professional, doctoral degree	1,047.67	98	10.0

Note: Market shares may not sum to 100.0 because of rounding and missing categories by household type. "Asian" and "black" include Hispanics and non-Hispanics who identify themselves as being of the respective race alone. "Hispanic" includes people of any race who identify themselves as Hispanic. "Other" includes people who identify themselves as non-Hispanic and as Alaska Native, American Indian, Asian (who are also included in the "Asian" row), Native Hawaiian or other Pacific Islander, as well as non-Hispanics reporting more than one race.
Source: Calculations by New Strategist based on the Bureau of Labor Statistics' 2007 Consumer Expenditure Survey.

Vehicle Maintenance and Repair (Includes Oil Changes and Tires)

Best customers: Householders aged 45 to 64
Married couples with school-aged or older children at home

Customer trends: Average household spending on vehicle maintenance and repair is likely to rise as the economic downturn forces more Americans to drive aging cars.

The biggest spenders on vehicle maintenance and repair are households with the most vehicles—married couples with teenagers and young adults at home. Householders aged 45 to 64, many living with teens and young adults, spend 20 to 28 percent more than average on vehicle maintenance and repair. Married couples with school-aged or older children at home spend 35 to 63 percent more than average on this item.

Average household spending on vehicle maintenance and repair fell 2 percent between 2000 and 2007, after adjusting for inflation. Behind the decline in spending was the increased ownership of new vehicles as dealers offered low-interest loans and other incentives. Average household spending on vehicle maintenance and repair is likely to rise in the years ahead as the economic downturn forces more Americans to drive aging cars.

Table 19.19 Vehicle maintenance and repair (includes oil changes and tires)

Total household spending $88,640,533,020.00
Average household spends   737.62

	AVERAGE HOUSEHOLD SPENDING	BEST CUSTOMERS (index)	BIGGEST CUSTOMERS (market share)
AGE OF HOUSEHOLDER			
Average household	**$737.62**	**100**	**100.0%**
Under age 25	436.54	59	4.0
Aged 25 to 34	609.25	83	14.1
Aged 35 to 44	808.68	110	21.4
Aged 45 to 54	940.85	128	26.8
Aged 55 to 64	884.95	120	19.4
Aged 65 to 74	692.95	94	9.4
Aged 75 or older	383.83	52	4.9

	AVERAGE HOUSEHOLD SPENDING	BEST CUSTOMERS (index)	BIGGEST CUSTOMERS (market share)
HOUSEHOLD INCOME			
Average household	**$737.62**	**100**	**100.0%**
Under $20,000	275.91	37	7.7
$20,000 to $39,999	511.46	69	16.1
$40,000 to $49,999	688.05	93	9.2
$50,000 to $69,999	768.73	104	15.9
$70,000 to $79,999	1,039.64	141	8.2
$80,000 to $99,999	1,060.68	144	11.7
$100,000 or more	1,337.12	181	31.1
HOUSEHOLD TYPE			
Average household	**737.62**	**100**	**100.0**
Married couples	938.65	127	64.3
Married couples, no children	875.25	119	25.6
Married couples, with children	1,009.98	137	34.2
Oldest child under age 6	759.95	103	5.0
Oldest child aged 6 to 17	998.11	135	17.2
Oldest child aged 18 or older	1,201.85	163	12.0
Single parent with child under age 18	503.94	68	4.1
Single person	471.20	64	19.0
RACE AND HISPANIC ORIGIN			
Average household	**737.62**	**100**	**100.0**
Asian	729.27	99	3.5
Black	504.94	68	8.2
Hispanic	556.57	75	8.9
Non-Hispanic white and other	802.23	109	83.0
REGION			
Average household	**737.62**	**100**	**100.0**
Northeast	716.47	97	18.1
Midwest	693.74	94	21.5
South	689.28	93	33.6
West	876.39	119	26.9
EDUCATION			
Average household	**737.62**	**100**	**100.0**
Less than high school graduate	425.35	58	8.7
High school graduate	615.01	83	21.0
Some college	756.80	103	22.3
Associate's degree	755.12	102	9.1
College graduate	986.62	134	38.7
Bachelor's degree	927.79	126	23.6
Master's, professional, doctoral degree	1,094.29	148	15.1

Note: Market shares may not sum to 100.0 because of rounding and missing categories by household type. "Asian" and "black" include Hispanics and non-Hispanics who identify themselves as being of the respective race alone. "Hispanic" includes people of any race who identify themselves as Hispanic. "Other" includes people who identify themselves as non-Hispanic and as Alaska Native, American Indian, Asian (who are also included in the "Asian" row), Native Hawaiian or other Pacific Islander, as well as non-Hispanics reporting more than one race.
Source: Calculations by New Strategist based on the Bureau of Labor Statistics' 2007 Consumer Expenditure Survey.

Vehicle Rentals (Includes Rentals on Trips)

Best customers:
Householders aged 35 to 64
Married couples without children at home
Married couples with children under age 18

Customer trends:
Average household spending on vehicle rentals should rise as boomers age into the best-customer lifestage for travel, but only if discretionary income increases.

The biggest spenders on rented vehicles are travelers, since three-quarters of spending on rented vehicles occurs on trips. Middle-aged and older married couples are the biggest travelers, which accounts for their above-average spending on rented vehicles. Householders ranging in age from 35 to 64 spend 19 to 42 percent more than average on rented vehicles. Married couples without children at home (most of them empty-nesters) spend 24 percent more than average on this item. Those with school-aged or younger children spend 38 to 58 percent more than average on vehicle rentals.

Average household spending on rented vehicles fell 26 percent between 2000 and 2007, after adjusting for inflation. Average household spending on vehicle rentals should rise as boomers age into the best-customer lifestage for travel, but only if discretionary income increases.

Table 19.20 Vehicle rentals (includes rentals on trips)

Total household spending $4,791,217,770.00
Average household spends 39.87

AGE OF HOUSEHOLDER	AVERAGE HOUSEHOLD SPENDING	BEST CUSTOMERS (index)	BIGGEST CUSTOMERS (market share)
Average household	**$39.87**	**100**	**100.0%**
Under age 25	17.19	43	2.9
Aged 25 to 34	36.99	93	15.8
Aged 35 to 44	47.37	119	23.2
Aged 45 to 54	45.22	113	23.8
Aged 55 to 64	56.46	142	22.9
Aged 65 to 74	31.59	79	7.9
Aged 75 or older	14.33	36	3.4

	AVERAGE HOUSEHOLD SPENDING	BEST CUSTOMERS (index)	BIGGEST CUSTOMERS (market share)
HOUSEHOLD INCOME			
Average household	**$39.87**	**100**	**100.0%**
Under $20,000	12.54	31	6.5
$20,000 to $39,999	17.52	44	10.2
$40,000 to $49,999	19.61	49	4.8
$50,000 to $69,999	37.18	93	14.3
$70,000 to $79,999	52.79	132	7.7
$80,000 to $99,999	57.15	143	11.7
$100,000 or more	104.43	262	44.9
HOUSEHOLD TYPE			
Average household	**39.87**	**100**	**100.0**
Married couples	50.70	127	64.3
Married couples, no children	49.45	124	26.8
Married couples, with children	52.64	132	32.9
Oldest child under age 6	62.82	158	7.7
Oldest child aged 6 to 17	54.98	138	17.5
Oldest child aged 18 or older	41.88	105	7.7
Single parent with child under age 18	28.01	70	4.2
Single person	28.84	72	21.5
RACE AND HISPANIC ORIGIN			
Average household	**39.87**	**100**	**100.0**
Asian	39.47	99	3.5
Black	30.64	77	9.2
Hispanic	16.92	42	5.0
Non-Hispanic white and other	44.83	112	85.8
REGION			
Average household	**39.87**	**100**	**100.0**
Northeast	36.76	92	17.2
Midwest	38.17	96	21.9
South	33.44	84	30.1
West	54.34	136	30.8
EDUCATION			
Average household	**39.87**	**100**	**100.0**
Less than high school graduate	13.12	33	5.0
High school graduate	23.99	60	15.2
Some college	28.95	73	15.8
Associate's degree	39.18	98	8.7
College graduate	76.14	191	55.3
Bachelor's degree	62.62	157	29.4
Master's, professional, doctoral degree	100.99	253	25.8

Note: Market shares may not sum to 100.0 because of rounding and missing categories by household type. "Asian" and "black" include Hispanics and non-Hispanics who identify themselves as being of the respective race alone. "Hispanic" includes people of any race who identify themselves as Hispanic. "Other" includes people who identify themselves as non-Hispanic and as Alaska Native, American Indian, Asian (who are also included in the "Asian" row), Native Hawaiian or other Pacific Islander, as well as non-Hispanics reporting more than one race.
Source: Calculations by New Strategist based on the Bureau of Labor Statistics' 2007 Consumer Expenditure Survey.

Chapter 20.

Travel

Household Spending on Travel, 2007

Travel is one of the most popular leisure-time activities of Americans. In 2007, the average household spent $1,466 on travel, including airfares, gasoline, lodging, luggage, food, and recreational expenses. Airline fares, lodging, and restaurant meals account for nearly two-thirds of travel spending. Ranking fourth are recreational expenses (such as theme park admissions), which account for 10 percent of the total.

Average household spending on travel grew 2 percent between 2000 and 2007, after adjusting for inflation. Behind the growth in spending on travel was the aging of the baby-boom generation into the best customer lifestage. This demographic shift should have boosted household spending on travel even more, but the collapse of the housing market reduced discretionary income and limited travel spending. Some travel items saw larger than average increases. Average household spending on airline fares, for example, increased 9 percent between 2000 and 2007. Spending on ship fares rose 21 percent, spending on gasoline on trips increased 21 percent, and spending on luggage grew 20 percent. Spending on lodging rose 13 percent, and spending on alcoholic beverages purchased on trips increased by 6 percent.

Because the best customers of travel are older Americans, average household spending on travel should rise in the future as the baby-boom generation ages—but only if discretionary income grows.

Spending on travel

(average spending by households on travel, 2000 to 2007; in 2007 dollars)

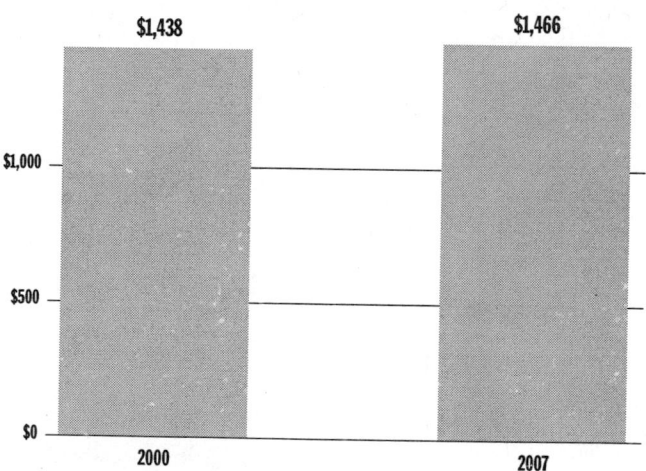

Table 20.1 Travel Spending, 2000 to 2007

(average annual household spending on travel, and percent distribution of spending by type, 2000 and 2007; percent change in spending, 2000–07; in 2007 dollars; ranked by amount spent)

	2007		2000		
	average household spending	percent distribution	average household spending (in 2007$)	percent distribution	percent change 2000–07
Average household spending on travel	**$1,465.92**	**100.0%**	**$1,438.33**	**100.0%**	**1.9%**
Airline fares	359.71	24.5	329.94	22.9	9.0
Lodging on trips	342.57	23.4	302.97	21.1	13.1
Restaurant and carry-out food on trips	245.53	16.7	260.15	18.1	−5.6
Recreational expenses on trips	144.83	9.9	175.73	12.2	−17.6
Gasoline on trips	130.30	8.9	110.52	7.7	17.9
Ship fares	53.23	3.6	44.05	3.1	20.9
Alcoholic beverages on trips	43.62	3.0	41.23	2.9	5.8
Groceries on trips	43.00	2.9	48.09	3.3	−10.6
Vehicle rentals on trips	28.11	1.9	41.34	2.9	−32.0
Taxis and local transportation on trips	21.39	1.5	20.37	1.4	5.0
Train fares, intercity	20.75	1.4	25.43	1.8	−18.4
Luggage	12.06	0.8	10.02	0.7	20.4
Bus fares, intercity	10.49	0.7	19.39	1.3	−45.9
Parking fees and tolls on trips	10.33	0.7	9.10	0.6	13.5

Source: Bureau of Labor Statistics, 2000 and 2007 Consumer Expenditure Surveys; calculations by New Strategist

Airline Fares

Best customers:

Householders aged 45 to 64
High-income households
Married couples without children at home
Married couples with school-aged children
Asians
Households in the West
College graduates

Customer trends:

Average household spending on airline fares is likely to decline because of the economic downturn, despite the presence of baby boomers in the peak-spending age groups.

The biggest spenders on airline fares are affluent, college-educated, middle-aged adults. Householders with incomes of $100,000 or more spend three times the average on this item and account for 52 percent of the market, while college graduates spend over twice the average on airfares and account for 64 percent of the market. Householders aged 45 to 64 spend 24 to 49 percent more than average on this item. Married couples without children at home (most of them empty-nesters) spend 65 percent more than average on airfares, while those with school-aged spend 46 percent more than average on this item. Asians spend well more than three times the average on airfares, while households in the West—where many Asians live—spend 41 percent more.

Average household spending on airline fares grew 9 percent between 2000 and 2007, after adjusting for inflation. Behind the increase was the baby-boom generation's entry into the best-customer lifestage. Average household spending on airline fares is likely to decline because of the economic downturn, despite the presence of baby boomers in the peak-spending age groups.

Table 20.2 Airline fares

Total household spending		$43,226,710,410.00	
Average household spends		359.71	

	AVERAGE HOUSEHOLD SPENDING	BEST CUSTOMERS (index)	BIGGEST CUSTOMERS (market share)
AGE OF HOUSEHOLDER			
Average household	**$359.71**	**100**	**100.0%**
Under age 25	184.12	51	3.5
Aged 25 to 34	256.59	71	12.2
Aged 35 to 44	370.93	103	20.1
Aged 45 to 54	446.57	124	26.1
Aged 55 to 64	535.48	149	24.1
Aged 65 to 74	357.30	99	9.9
Aged 75 or older	157.59	44	4.2

	AVERAGE HOUSEHOLD SPENDING	BEST CUSTOMERS (index)	BIGGEST CUSTOMERS (market share)
HOUSEHOLD INCOME			
Average household	$359.71	100	100.0%
Under $20,000	82.56	23	4.7
$20,000 to $39,999	152.55	42	9.9
$40,000 to $49,999	170.19	47	4.7
$50,000 to $69,999	280.39	78	11.9
$70,000 to $79,999	343.70	96	5.5
$80,000 to $99,999	513.79	143	11.6
$100,000 or more	1,085.28	302	51.7
HOUSEHOLD TYPE			
Average household	359.71	100	100.0
Married couples	507.35	141	71.3
Married couples, no children	594.76	165	35.7
Married couples, with children	454.57	126	31.5
Oldest child under age 6	346.43	96	4.7
Oldest child aged 6 to 17	523.79	146	18.5
Oldest child aged 18 or older	406.86	113	8.3
Single parent with child under age 18	166.63	46	2.8
Single person	206.46	57	17.1
RACE AND HISPANIC ORIGIN			
Average household	359.71	100	100.0
Asian	1,192.86	332	11.7
Black	148.81	41	5.0
Hispanic	184.39	51	6.1
Non-Hispanic white and other	420.11	117	89.2
REGION			
Average household	359.71	100	100.0
Northeast	408.32	114	21.1
Midwest	325.58	91	20.7
South	263.77	73	26.3
West	506.51	141	31.8
EDUCATION			
Average household	359.71	100	100.0
Less than high school graduate	117.85	33	5.0
High school graduate	139.05	39	9.8
Some college	245.52	68	14.9
Associate's degree	277.97	77	6.9
College graduate	789.78	220	63.6
Bachelor's degree	564.80	157	29.4
Master's, professional, doctoral degree	1,203.11	334	34.1

Note: Market shares may not sum to 100.0 because of rounding and missing categories by household type. "Asian" and "black" include Hispanics and non-Hispanics who identify themselves as being of the respective race alone. "Hispanic" includes people of any race who identify themselves as Hispanic. "Other" includes people who identify themselves as non-Hispanic and as Alaska Native, American Indian, Asian (who are also included in the "Asian" row), Native Hawaiian or other Pacific Islander, as well as non-Hispanics reporting more than one race.
Source: Calculations by New Strategist based on the Bureau of Labor Statistics' 2007 Consumer Expenditure Survey.

Alcoholic Beverages Purchased on Trips

Best customers:

Householders aged 45 to 64
Married couples without children at home
Non-Hispanic whites
Households in the Northeast and West
College graduates

Customer trends:

Average household spending on alcoholic beverages while traveling should continue to grow as more boomers become empty-nesters.

The biggest spenders on alcoholic beverages purchased on trips are older, white, married travelers. Householders aged 45 to 64 spend 16 to 36 percent more than average on this item. Married couples without children at home (most of them older) spend 61 percent more than average on alcoholic beverages while on trips. These empty-nesters spend more than other household types on alcoholic beverages while traveling because they no longer need to devote their time and money to children's wants and needs. Non-Hispanic whites spend 21 percent more than average on alcoholic beverages while traveling, while all the other racial and ethnic groups spend considerably less than average.

Average household spending on alcoholic beverages purchased on trips rose 6 percent between 2000 and 2007, after adjusting for inflation. In the years ahead, spending on this item should continue to grow as more boomers become empty-nesters.

Table 20.3 Alcoholic beverages purchased on trips

Total household spending $5,241,859,020.00
Average household spends 43.62

	AVERAGE HOUSEHOLD SPENDING	BEST CUSTOMERS (index)	BIGGEST CUSTOMERS (market share)
AGE OF HOUSEHOLDER			
Average household	**$43.62**	**100**	**100.0%**
Under age 25	32.67	75	5.1
Aged 25 to 34	35.90	82	14.0
Aged 35 to 44	45.69	105	20.4
Aged 45 to 54	50.53	116	24.3
Aged 55 to 64	59.41	136	22.1
Aged 65 to 74	40.60	93	9.3
Aged 75 or older	22.02	50	4.8

	AVERAGE HOUSEHOLD SPENDING	BEST CUSTOMERS (index)	BIGGEST CUSTOMERS (market share)
HOUSEHOLD INCOME			
Average household	**$43.62**	**100**	**100.0%**
Under $20,000	11.94	27	5.6
$20,000 to $39,999	17.93	41	9.6
$40,000 to $49,999	22.09	51	5.0
$50,000 to $69,999	38.11	87	13.4
$70,000 to $79,999	41.37	95	5.5
$80,000 to $99,999	58.08	133	10.8
$100,000 or more	127.67	293	50.1
HOUSEHOLD TYPE			
Average household	**43.62**	**100**	**100.0**
Married couples	57.00	131	66.1
Married couples, no children	70.40	161	34.8
Married couples, with children	49.10	113	28.1
Oldest child under age 6	55.44	127	6.2
Oldest child aged 6 to 17	47.28	108	13.8
Oldest child aged 18 or older	48.05	110	8.1
Single parent with child under age 18	13.46	31	1.8
Single person	35.29	81	24.1
RACE AND HISPANIC ORIGIN			
Average household	**43.62**	**100**	**100.0**
Asian	31.16	71	2.5
Black	8.70	20	2.4
Hispanic	19.24	44	5.2
Non-Hispanic white and other	52.85	121	92.5
REGION			
Average household	**43.62**	**100**	**100.0**
Northeast	55.75	128	23.8
Midwest	43.24	99	22.7
South	30.21	69	24.9
West	55.30	127	28.7
EDUCATION			
Average household	**43.62**	**100**	**100.0**
Less than high school graduate	9.65	22	3.4
High school graduate	16.69	38	9.7
Some college	34.98	80	17.5
Associate's degree	47.17	108	9.6
College graduate	90.30	207	59.9
Bachelor's degree	81.75	187	35.1
Master's, professional, doctoral degree	106.00	243	24.8

Note: Market shares may not sum to 100.0 because of rounding and missing categories by household type. "Asian" and "black" include Hispanics and non-Hispanics who identify themselves as being of the respective race alone. "Hispanic" includes people of any race who identify themselves as Hispanic. "Other" includes people who identify themselves as non-Hispanic and as Alaska Native, American Indian, Asian (who are also included in the "Asian" row), Native Hawaiian or other Pacific Islander, as well as non-Hispanics reporting more than one race.
Source: Calculations by New Strategist based on the Bureau of Labor Statistics' 2007 Consumer Expenditure Survey.

Bus Fares, Intercity

Best customers:

Householders aged 55 to 74
Married couples without children at home
Asians
Households in the West

Customer trends:

Average household spending on intercity bus fares may stabilize as boomers fill the best-customer age groups and the economic downturn reduces discretionary income.

The best customers of intercity bus fares are older travelers. Householders aged 55 to 74 spend 39 to 85 percent more than average on this item and account for 41 percent of the market. Married couples without children at home, most of them empty-nesters, spend 41 percent more than average on this item. Many have children in college who travel back and forth by bus. Asians spend twice the average on intercity bus travel, and households in the West, where many Asians reside, spend 55 percent more than average on bus fares.

Average household spending on intercity bus fares fell by a substantial 46 percent between 2000 and 2007, after adjusting for inflation. Average household spending on intercity bus fares may stabilize as boomers fill the best-customer age groups and the economic downturn reduces discretionary income.

Table 20.4 Bus fares, intercity

| Total household spending | $1,260,593,790.00 |
| Average household spends | 10.49 |

	AVERAGE HOUSEHOLD SPENDING	BEST CUSTOMERS (index)	BIGGEST CUSTOMERS (market share)
AGE OF HOUSEHOLDER			
Average household	**$10.49**	**100**	**100.0%**
Under age 25	6.06	58	3.9
Aged 25 to 34	7.12	68	11.6
Aged 35 to 44	9.66	92	17.9
Aged 45 to 54	9.17	87	18.4
Aged 55 to 64	14.59	139	22.5
Aged 65 to 74	19.36	185	18.4
Aged 75 or older	7.97	76	7.2

	AVERAGE HOUSEHOLD SPENDING	BEST CUSTOMERS (index)	BIGGEST CUSTOMERS (market share)
HOUSEHOLD INCOME			
Average household	**$10.49**	**100**	**100.0%**
Under $20,000	7.79	74	15.3
$20,000 to $39,999	6.23	59	13.8
$40,000 to $49,999	8.70	83	8.2
$50,000 to $69,999	10.04	96	14.6
$70,000 to $79,999	9.79	93	5.4
$80,000 to $99,999	15.74	150	12.2
$100,000 or more	18.66	178	30.5
HOUSEHOLD TYPE			
Average household	**10.49**	**100**	**100.0**
Married couples	12.19	116	58.7
Married couples, no children	14.82	141	30.5
Married couples, with children	9.87	94	23.5
Oldest child under age 6	4.72	45	2.2
Oldest child aged 6 to 17	11.45	109	13.9
Oldest child aged 18 or older	10.55	101	7.4
Single parent with child under age 18	8.81	84	5.0
Single person	9.65	92	27.4
RACE AND HISPANIC ORIGIN			
Average household	**10.49**	**100**	**100.0**
Asian	21.27	203	7.2
Black	6.40	61	7.3
Hispanic	8.92	85	10.0
Non-Hispanic white and other	11.38	108	82.8
REGION			
Average household	**10.49**	**100**	**100.0**
Northeast	9.79	93	17.4
Midwest	9.79	93	21.3
South	7.63	73	26.1
West	16.30	155	35.1
EDUCATION			
Average household	**10.49**	**100**	**100.0**
Less than high school graduate	4.90	47	7.1
High school graduate	5.01	48	12.0
Some college	9.88	94	20.5
Associate's degree	8.69	83	7.4
College graduate	19.20	183	53.0
Bachelor's degree	16.27	155	29.1
Master's, professional, doctoral degree	24.57	234	23.9

Note: Market shares may not sum to 100.0 because of rounding and missing categories by household type. "Asian" and "black" include Hispanics and non-Hispanics who identify themselves as being of the respective race alone. "Hispanic" includes people of any race who identify themselves as Hispanic. "Other" includes people who identify themselves as non-Hispanic and as Alaska Native, American Indian, Asian (who are also included in the "Asian" row), Native Hawaiian or other Pacific Islander, as well as non-Hispanics reporting more than one race.
Source: Calculations by New Strategist based on the Bureau of Labor Statistics' 2007 Consumer Expenditure Survey.

Gasoline on Trips

Best customers: Householders aged 45 to 74
Married couples without children at home
Married couples with school-aged children
Households in the Midwest and West

Customer trends: Average household spending on gasoline while traveling should continue to rise in the next few years as more boomers fill the peak-traveling lifestage.

The biggest spenders on gasoline purchased while traveling are the largest households as well as the most avid travelers—empty-nesters. Householders aged 45 to 74 spend 12 to 23 percent more than average on this item. Married couples without children at home (most of them empty-nesters) spend 50 percent more than average on gasoline while traveling. Couples with school-aged children spend 48 more than average on this item. Households in the Midwest and West spend, respectively, 20 and 27 percent more than average on gasoline while traveling.

Average household spending on gasoline while on trips rose 18 percent between 2000 and 2007, after adjusting for inflation, as gas prices increased. Average household spending on gasoline while traveling should continue to rise in the next few years as more boomers fill the peak-traveling lifestage.

Table 20.5 Gasoline on trips

Total household spending $15,658,281,300.00
Average household spends   130.30

	AVERAGE HOUSEHOLD SPENDING	BEST CUSTOMERS (index)	BIGGEST CUSTOMERS (market share)
AGE OF HOUSEHOLDER			
Average household	**$130.30**	**100**	**100.0%**
Under age 25	97.65	75	5.1
Aged 25 to 34	121.76	93	15.9
Aged 35 to 44	134.74	103	20.1
Aged 45 to 54	145.97	112	23.5
Aged 55 to 64	160.41	123	19.9
Aged 65 to 74	145.68	112	11.2
Aged 75 or older	57.46	44	4.2

	AVERAGE HOUSEHOLD SPENDING	BEST CUSTOMERS (index)	BIGGEST CUSTOMERS (market share)
HOUSEHOLD INCOME			
Average household	$130.30	100	100.0%
Under $20,000	50.32	39	7.9
$20,000 to $39,999	82.30	63	14.7
$40,000 to $49,999	105.06	81	7.9
$50,000 to $69,999	147.64	113	17.3
$70,000 to $79,999	179.80	138	8.0
$80,000 to $99,999	189.32	145	11.8
$100,000 or more	245.62	189	32.3
HOUSEHOLD TYPE			
Average household	130.30	100	100.0
Married couples	178.72	137	69.3
Married couples, no children	195.44	150	32.4
Married couples, with children	173.42	133	33.2
Oldest child under age 6	156.27	120	5.9
Oldest child aged 6 to 17	193.13	148	18.8
Oldest child aged 18 or older	150.80	116	8.5
Single parent with child under age 18	63.22	49	2.9
Single person	81.60	63	18.6
RACE AND HISPANIC ORIGIN			
Average household	130.30	100	100.0
Asian	91.04	70	2.5
Black	55.15	42	5.1
Hispanic	91.61	70	8.3
Non-Hispanic white and other	147.94	114	86.7
REGION			
Average household	130.30	100	100.0
Northeast	83.36	64	11.9
Midwest	156.61	120	27.5
South	115.93	89	31.9
West	165.17	127	28.7
EDUCATION			
Average household	130.30	100	100.0
Less than high school graduate	55.45	43	6.5
High school graduate	98.41	76	19.1
Some college	132.92	102	22.2
Associate's degree	159.39	122	10.9
College graduate	186.40	143	41.4
Bachelor's degree	170.42	131	24.5
Master's, professional, doctoral degree	215.76	166	16.9

Note: Market shares may not sum to 100.0 because of rounding and missing categories by household type. "Asian" and "black" include Hispanics and non-Hispanics who identify themselves as being of the respective race alone. "Hispanic" includes people of any race who identify themselves as Hispanic. "Other" includes people who identify themselves as non-Hispanic and as Alaska Native, American Indian, Asian (who are also included in the "Asian" row), Native Hawaiian or other Pacific Islander, as well as non-Hispanics reporting more than one race.
Source: Calculations by New Strategist based on the Bureau of Labor Statistics' 2007 Consumer Expenditure Survey.

Groceries on Trips

Best customers:

Householders aged 55 to 64
Married couples without children at home
Married couples with school-aged children
Households in the West

Customer trends:

Average household spending on groceries while traveling should rise in the next few years as more boomers become empty-nesters.

The biggest spenders on groceries purchased on trips are older married couples, the most avid travelers. These couples are stocking up on food and drink for their hotel rooms or RVs. Householders aged 55 to 64 spend 46 percent more than average on this item. Married couples without children at home (most of them empty-nesters) spend 56 percent more than average on groceries while traveling. Couples with school-aged children spend 70 percent more. Households in the West spend 47 percent more than average on this item.

Average household spending on groceries while traveling fell 11 percent between 2000 and 2007, after adjusting for inflation. Average household spending on groceries while traveling should rise in the next few years as more boomers become empty-nesters.

Table 20.6 Groceries on trips

Total household spending $5,167,353,000.00
Average household spends   43.00

	AVERAGE HOUSEHOLD SPENDING	BEST CUSTOMERS (index)	BIGGEST CUSTOMERS (market share)
AGE OF HOUSEHOLDER			
Average household	**$43.00**	**100**	**100.0%**
Under age 25	17.06	40	2.7
Aged 25 to 34	29.57	69	11.7
Aged 35 to 44	49.93	116	22.6
Aged 45 to 54	49.88	116	24.4
Aged 55 to 64	62.90	146	23.7
Aged 65 to 74	48.88	114	11.4
Aged 75 or older	15.98	37	3.5

	AVERAGE HOUSEHOLD SPENDING	BEST CUSTOMERS (index)	BIGGEST CUSTOMERS (market share)
HOUSEHOLD INCOME			
Average household	**$43.00**	**100**	**100.0%**
Under $20,000	12.16	28	5.8
$20,000 to $39,999	21.55	50	11.7
$40,000 to $49,999	28.63	67	6.6
$50,000 to $69,999	43.20	100	15.4
$70,000 to $79,999	57.70	134	7.8
$80,000 to $99,999	56.75	132	10.7
$100,000 or more	105.65	246	42.1
HOUSEHOLD TYPE			
Average household	**43.00**	**100**	**100.0**
Married couples	61.98	144	72.9
Married couples, no children	67.21	156	33.7
Married couples, with children	61.07	142	35.4
Oldest child under age 6	44.80	104	5.1
Oldest child aged 6 to 17	73.10	170	21.6
Oldest child aged 18 or older	51.11	119	8.8
Single parent with child under age 18	20.88	49	2.9
Single person	22.70	53	15.7
RACE AND HISPANIC ORIGIN			
Average household	**43.00**	**100**	**100.0**
Asian	39.85	93	3.3
Black	15.19	35	4.2
Hispanic	26.53	62	7.3
Non-Hispanic white and other	49.84	116	88.5
REGION			
Average household	**43.00**	**100**	**100.0**
Northeast	43.88	102	19.0
Midwest	42.05	98	22.3
South	30.53	71	25.5
West	63.02	147	33.1
EDUCATION			
Average household	**43.00**	**100**	**100.0**
Less than high school graduate	15.22	35	5.4
High school graduate	27.76	65	16.3
Some college	38.02	88	19.3
Associate's degree	45.30	105	9.4
College graduate	73.87	172	49.7
Bachelor's degree	64.97	151	28.3
Master's, professional, doctoral degree	90.22	210	21.4

Note: Market shares may not sum to 100.0 because of rounding and missing categories by household type. "Asian" and "black" include Hispanics and non-Hispanics who identify themselves as being of the respective race alone. "Hispanic" includes people of any race who identify themselves as Hispanic. "Other" includes people who identify themselves as non-Hispanic and as Alaska Native, American Indian, Asian (who are also included in the "Asian" row), Native Hawaiian or other Pacific Islander, as well as non-Hispanics reporting more than one race.
Source: Calculations by New Strategist based on the Bureau of Labor Statistics' 2007 Consumer Expenditure Survey.

Lodging on Trips

Best customers:
Householders aged 45 to 74
High-income households
Married couples without children at home
Married couples with school-aged children
Asians
College graduates

Customer trends:
Average household spending on lodging should continue to grow as more boomers become empty-nesters, but only if discretionary income rises.

Lodging is the second biggest travel expense after airline fares. It accounts for $23 of every $100 spent by the average household on travel. The biggest spenders on lodging are the most avid travelers—affluent, older, college-educated empty-nesters. Householders aged 45 to 74 spend 20 to 56 percent more than average on this item and account for 62 percent of the market. Households with incomes of $100,000 or more spend three times the average on lodging. Married couples without children at home (most of them empty-nesters) spend 84 percent more than average on lodging. Couples with school-aged children spend 47 percent more. Asians, a relatively wealthy demographic, spend one-third more than the average household on lodging, while college graduates spend slightly more than double the average on this item

Average household spending on lodging rose 13 percent between 2000 and 2007, after adjusting for inflation. This rise in spending occurred as the baby-boom generation aged into the peak-spending lifestage. Average household spending on lodging should continue to grow as more boomers become empty-nesters, but only if discretionary income rises.

Table 20.7 Lodging on trips

| Total household spending | $41,166,979,470.00 |
| Average household spends | 342.57 |

AGE OF HOUSEHOLDER	AVERAGE HOUSEHOLD SPENDING	BEST CUSTOMERS (index)	BIGGEST CUSTOMERS (market share)
Average household	$342.57	100	100.0%
Under age 25	100.66	29	2.0
Aged 25 to 34	217.46	63	10.8
Aged 35 to 44	341.47	100	19.4
Aged 45 to 54	412.54	120	25.3
Aged 55 to 64	532.96	156	25.2
Aged 65 to 74	410.90	120	12.0
Aged 75 or older	190.68	56	5.3

	AVERAGE HOUSEHOLD SPENDING	BEST CUSTOMERS (index)	BIGGEST CUSTOMERS (market share)
HOUSEHOLD INCOME			
Average household	$342.57	100	100.0%
Under $20,000	67.26	20	4.0
$20,000 to $39,999	114.01	33	7.7
$40,000 to $49,999	165.72	48	4.8
$50,000 to $69,999	328.84	96	14.7
$70,000 to $79,999	352.46	103	6.0
$80,000 to $99,999	477.62	139	11.3
$100,000 or more	1,029.39	300	51.5
HOUSEHOLD TYPE			
Average household	342.57	100	100.0
Married couples	504.52	147	74.4
Married couples, no children	631.40	184	39.8
Married couples, with children	434.62	127	31.7
Oldest child under age 6	304.07	89	4.3
Oldest child aged 6 to 17	504.48	147	18.7
Oldest child aged 18 or older	400.66	117	8.6
Single parent with child under age 18	157.72	46	2.7
Single person	184.14	54	16.0
RACE AND HISPANIC ORIGIN			
Average household	342.57	100	100.0
Asian	455.68	133	4.7
Black	103.15	30	3.6
Hispanic	132.72	39	4.6
Non-Hispanic white and other	412.62	120	91.9
REGION			
Average household	342.57	100	100.0
Northeast	398.61	116	21.7
Midwest	354.80	104	23.7
South	253.80	74	26.6
West	425.03	124	28.1
EDUCATION			
Average household	342.57	100	100.0
Less than high school graduate	78.81	23	3.5
High school graduate	153.68	45	11.3
Some college	249.59	73	15.9
Associate's degree	334.40	98	8.7
College graduate	717.88	210	60.7
Bachelor's degree	570.56	167	31.2
Master's, professional, doctoral degree	988.54	289	29.4

Note: Market shares may not sum to 100.0 because of rounding and missing categories by household type. "Asian" and "black" include Hispanics and non-Hispanics who identify themselves as being of the respective race alone. "Hispanic" includes people of any race who identify themselves as Hispanic. "Other" includes people who identify themselves as non-Hispanic and as Alaska Native, American Indian, Asian (who are also included in the "Asian" row), Native Hawaiian or other Pacific Islander, as well as non-Hispanics reporting more than one race.
Source: Calculations by New Strategist based on the Bureau of Labor Statistics' 2007 Consumer Expenditure Survey.

Luggage

Best customers:

Householders aged 55 to 64
Married couples without children at home
Married couples with adult children at home
Asians

Customer trends:

Average household spending on luggage could continue to grow as more boomers become empty-nesters, but the economic downturn and the loss of discretionary income may hurt this market.

The biggest spenders on luggage are the most avid travelers—older married couples. Householders aged 55 to 64 spend 70 percent more than average on this item and control 28 percent of the market. Married couples without children at home (most of them empty-nesters) spend 71 percent more than average on luggage, while those with adult children at home spend 72 percent more than average on this item. Asians spend twice the average on luggage.

Average household spending on luggage rose 20 percent between 2000 and 2007, after adjusting for inflation. Behind the increase was the baby-boom generation's entry into the best-customer lifestage. Average household spending on luggage could continue to grow as more boomers become empty-nesters, but the economic downturn and the loss of discretionary income may hurt this market.

Table 20.8 Luggage

Total household spending $1,449,262,260.00
Average household spends 12.06

AGE OF HOUSEHOLDER	AVERAGE HOUSEHOLD SPENDING	BEST CUSTOMERS (index)	BIGGEST CUSTOMERS (market share)
Average household	$12.06	100	100.0%
Under age 25	1.68	14	0.9
Aged 25 to 34	11.14	92	15.8
Aged 35 to 44	13.36	111	21.6
Aged 45 to 54	11.46	95	20.0
Aged 55 to 64	20.56	170	27.6
Aged 65 to 74	13.99	116	11.6
Aged 75 or older	3.64	30	2.9

	AVERAGE HOUSEHOLD SPENDING	BEST CUSTOMERS (index)	BIGGEST CUSTOMERS (market share)
HOUSEHOLD INCOME			
Average household	**$12.06**	**100**	**100.0%**
Under $20,000	3.54	29	6.0
$20,000 to $39,999	2.50	21	4.8
$40,000 to $49,999	18.55	154	15.1
$50,000 to $69,999	11.63	96	14.8
$70,000 to $79,999	7.71	64	3.7
$80,000 to $99,999	12.13	101	8.2
$100,000 or more	34.09	283	48.4
HOUSEHOLD TYPE			
Average household	**12.06**	**100**	**100.0**
Married couples	16.73	139	70.1
Married couples, no children	20.58	171	36.8
Married couples, with children	14.18	118	29.3
Oldest child under age 6	7.70	64	3.1
Oldest child aged 6 to 17	13.27	110	14.0
Oldest child aged 18 or older	20.75	172	12.7
Single parent with child under age 18	1.70	14	0.8
Single person	9.87	82	24.3
RACE AND HISPANIC ORIGIN			
Average household	**12.06**	**100**	**100.0**
Asian	24.72	205	7.2
Black	6.21	51	6.2
Hispanic	2.47	20	2.4
Non-Hispanic white and other	14.31	119	90.6
REGION			
Average household	**12.06**	**100**	**100.0**
Northeast	10.61	88	16.4
Midwest	16.21	134	30.7
South	10.02	83	29.8
West	12.29	102	23.0
EDUCATION			
Average household	**12.06**	**100**	**100.0**
Less than high school graduate	4.92	41	6.2
High school graduate	8.75	73	18.3
Some college	8.65	72	15.6
Associate's degree	6.81	56	5.0
College graduate	22.19	184	53.3
Bachelor's degree	21.55	179	33.5
Master's, professional, doctoral degree	23.30	193	19.7

Note: Market shares may not sum to 100.0 because of rounding and missing categories by household type. "Asian" and "black" include Hispanics and non-Hispanics who identify themselves as being of the respective race alone. "Hispanic" includes people of any race who identify themselves as Hispanic. "Other" includes people who identify themselves as non-Hispanic and as Alaska Native, American Indian, Asian (who are also included in the "Asian" row), Native Hawaiian or other Pacific Islander, as well as non-Hispanics reporting more than one race.
Source: Calculations by New Strategist based on the Bureau of Labor Statistics' 2007 Consumer Expenditure Survey.

Parking Fees and Tolls on Trips

Best customers: Householders aged 45 to 64
Married couples
Asians
Households in the Northeast

Customer trends: Average household spending on parking fees and tolls on trips should rise as more boomers become empty-nesters and avid travelers—but only if discretionary income increases.

The most avid travelers spend the most on parking fees and tolls on trips. Householders aged 45 to 64 spend 28 percent more than average on this item. Married couples, with or without children at home, spend 39 percent more than average on parking fees and tolls on trips. Asian spending on this item is 44 percent above average. Households in the Northeast spend 36 percent more than average on parking and tolls on trips because of the many toll roads in the region and the relatively high parking fees in congested Northeastern cities.

Average household spending on parking fees and tolls on trips rose 13 percent between 2000 and 2007, after adjusting for inflation. Average household spending on parking fees and tolls on trips should rise as more boomers become empty-nesters and avid travelers—but only if discretionary income increases.

Table 20.9 Parking fees and tolls on trips

Total household spending $1,241,366,430.00
Average household spends 10.33

	AVERAGE HOUSEHOLD SPENDING	BEST CUSTOMERS (index)	BIGGEST CUSTOMERS (market share)
AGE OF HOUSEHOLDER			
Average household	**$10.33**	**100**	**100.0%**
Under age 25	4.37	42	2.9
Aged 25 to 34	7.80	76	12.9
Aged 35 to 44	11.61	112	21.9
Aged 45 to 54	13.27	128	27.0
Aged 55 to 64	13.23	128	20.7
Aged 65 to 74	11.75	114	11.4
Aged 75 or older	3.61	35	3.3

	AVERAGE HOUSEHOLD SPENDING	BEST CUSTOMERS (index)	BIGGEST CUSTOMERS (market share)
HOUSEHOLD INCOME			
Average household	$10.33	100	100.0%
Under $20,000	2.03	20	4.0
$20,000 to $39,999	5.13	50	11.6
$40,000 to $49,999	8.99	87	8.6
$50,000 to $69,999	7.28	70	10.8
$70,000 to $79,999	13.84	134	7.8
$80,000 to $99,999	12.47	121	9.8
$100,000 or more	28.67	278	47.5
HOUSEHOLD TYPE			
Average household	10.33	100	100.0
Married couples	14.31	139	70.0
Married couples, no children	15.33	148	32.0
Married couples, with children	14.38	139	34.7
Oldest child under age 6	13.24	128	6.3
Oldest child aged 6 to 17	14.36	139	17.7
Oldest child aged 18 or older	15.18	147	10.8
Single parent with child under age 18	4.91	48	2.8
Single person	6.56	64	18.9
RACE AND HISPANIC ORIGIN			
Average household	10.33	100	100.0
Asian	14.86	144	5.1
Black	5.05	49	5.9
Hispanic	6.06	59	6.9
Non-Hispanic white and other	11.83	115	87.4
REGION			
Average household	10.33	100	100.0
Northeast	14.08	136	25.4
Midwest	10.58	102	23.4
South	7.18	70	25.0
West	12.02	116	26.3
EDUCATION			
Average household	10.33	100	100.0
Less than high school graduate	2.96	29	4.3
High school graduate	4.88	47	11.9
Some college	7.41	72	15.6
Associate's degree	12.80	124	11.0
College graduate	20.40	197	57.2
Bachelor's degree	16.99	164	30.8
Master's, professional, doctoral degree	26.67	258	26.3

Note: Market shares may not sum to 100.0 because of rounding and missing categories by household type. "Asian" and "black" include Hispanics and non-Hispanics who identify themselves as being of the respective race alone. "Hispanic" includes people of any race who identify themselves as Hispanic. "Other" includes people who identify themselves as non-Hispanic and as Alaska Native, American Indian, Asian (who are also included in the "Asian" row), Native Hawaiian or other Pacific Islander, as well as non-Hispanics reporting more than one race.
Source: Calculations by New Strategist based on the Bureau of Labor Statistics' 2007 Consumer Expenditure Survey.

Recreational Expenses on Trips

Best customers:
    Householders aged 35 to 74
Married couples without children at home
Married couples with school-aged children
Asians
Households in the West

Customer trends:
    Average household spending on recreational expenses while traveling should grow as more boomers become empty-nesters and avid travelers, but only if discretionary income rises.

Recreational expenses on trips, the fourth largest travel expense, account for 10 percent of the average household's travel budget. These expenses include admissions to theme parks and museums, greens fees, and tickets for sightseeing tours and sporting events. The biggest spenders on recreational expenses on trips are middle-aged and older married couples. Householders ranging in age from 35 to 74 spend 11 to 33 percent more than average on this item. Married couples without children at home (most of them empty-nesters) spend 53 percent more than average on recreational expenses on trips, while those with school-aged children spend 69 percent more than average. Together these two household types control 54 percent of spending on recreational expenses while traveling. Asians, who have the highest incomes among ethnic and racial groups, spend 49 percent more than average on recreational expenses on trips. Households in the West, where many Asians live, spend 31 percent more than average on this item.

Average household spending on recreational expenses on trips fell 18 percent between 2000 and 2007, after adjusting for inflation. Average household spending on recreational expenses while traveling should grow as more boomers become empty-nesters and avid travelers, but only if discretionary income rises.

Table 20.10 Recreational expenses on trips

Total household spending $17,404,365,930.00
Average household spends   144.83

	AVERAGE HOUSEHOLD SPENDING	BEST CUSTOMERS (index)	BIGGEST CUSTOMERS (market share)
AGE OF HOUSEHOLDER			
Average household	**$144.83**	**100**	**100.0%**
Under age 25	65.87	45	3.1
Aged 25 to 34	111.31	77	13.1
Aged 35 to 44	160.69	111	21.6
Aged 45 to 54	172.08	119	25.0
Aged 55 to 64	192.23	133	21.5
Aged 65 to 74	174.83	121	12.1
Aged 75 or older	56.04	39	3.7

	AVERAGE HOUSEHOLD SPENDING	BEST CUSTOMERS (index)	BIGGEST CUSTOMERS (market share)
HOUSEHOLD INCOME			
Average household	**$144.83**	**100**	**100.0%**
Under $20,000	28.75	20	4.1
$20,000 to $39,999	62.58	43	10.0
$40,000 to $49,999	81.67	56	5.5
$50,000 to $69,999	127.44	88	13.5
$70,000 to $79,999	133.05	92	5.3
$80,000 to $99,999	204.91	141	11.5
$100,000 or more	422.95	292	50.0
HOUSEHOLD TYPE			
Average household	**144.83**	**100**	**100.0**
Married couples	206.21	142	72.0
Married couples, no children	221.56	153	33.0
Married couples, with children	196.45	136	33.8
Oldest child under age 6	111.79	77	3.8
Oldest child aged 6 to 17	244.45	169	21.4
Oldest child aged 18 or older	169.77	117	8.6
Single parent with child under age 18	72.78	50	3.0
Single person	84.87	59	17.4
RACE AND HISPANIC ORIGIN			
Average household	**144.83**	**100**	**100.0**
Asian	215.79	149	5.3
Black	49.29	34	4.1
Hispanic	76.26	53	6.2
Non-Hispanic white and other	170.24	118	89.7
REGION			
Average household	**144.83**	**100**	**100.0**
Northeast	170.04	117	21.9
Midwest	129.08	89	20.4
South	113.32	78	28.1
West	190.01	131	29.7
EDUCATION			
Average household	**144.83**	**100**	**100.0**
Less than high school graduate	39.57	27	4.1
High school graduate	77.07	53	13.4
Some college	112.44	78	16.9
Associate's degree	131.93	91	8.1
College graduate	287.37	198	57.4
Bachelor's degree	245.05	169	31.7
Master's, professional, doctoral degree	365.14	252	25.7

Note: Market shares may not sum to 100.0 because of rounding and missing categories by household type. "Asian" and "black" include Hispanics and non-Hispanics who identify themselves as being of the respective race alone. "Hispanic" includes people of any race who identify themselves as Hispanic. "Other" includes people who identify themselves as non-Hispanic and as Alaska Native, American Indian, Asian (who are also included in the "Asian" row), Native Hawaiian or other Pacific Islander, as well as non-Hispanics reporting more than one race.
Source: Calculations by New Strategist based on the Bureau of Labor Statistics' 2007 Consumer Expenditure Survey.

Restaurant and Carry-Out Food on Trips

Best customers:	Householders aged 45 to 64
	Married couples without children at home
	Married couples with school-aged or older children at home
	Asians
	Households in the West

Customer trends:	Average household spending on restaurant and carry-out meals on trips should grow as more boomers become empty-nesters and avid travelers—but only if discretionary income increases.

The biggest spenders on restaurant and carry-out meals on trips are the most avid travelers—older married couples. Householders aged 45 to 64 spend 24 to 39 percent more than average on this item. Married couples without children at home (most of them empty-nesters) spend 66 percent more than average on restaurant and carry-out meals on trips and control over one-third of the market. Those with school-aged or older children at home spend 31 to 59 percent more. Asians, who have the highest incomes among ethnic and racial groups, spend 32 percent more than average on meals while traveling. Households in the West, where many Asians live, spend 27 percent more than average on this item.

Average household spending on restaurant and carry-out meals on trips fell 6 percent between 2000 and 2007, after adjusting for inflation. Average household spending on restaurant and carry-out meals on trips should grow as more boomers become empty-nesters and avid travelers—but only if discretionary income increases.

Table 20.11 Restaurant and carry-out food on trips

Total household spending $29,505,585,630.00
Average household spends 245.53

AGE OF HOUSEHOLDER	AVERAGE HOUSEHOLD SPENDING	BEST CUSTOMERS (index)	BIGGEST CUSTOMERS (market share)
Average household	$245.53	100	100.0%
Under age 25	105.56	43	2.9
Aged 25 to 34	178.53	73	12.4
Aged 35 to 44	265.50	108	21.1
Aged 45 to 54	304.79	124	26.1
Aged 55 to 64	341.36	139	22.5
Aged 65 to 74	261.98	107	10.7
Aged 75 or older	112.72	46	4.4

	AVERAGE HOUSEHOLD SPENDING	BEST CUSTOMERS (index)	BIGGEST CUSTOMERS (market share)
HOUSEHOLD INCOME			
Average household	$245.53	100	100.0%
Under $20,000	58.01	24	4.9
$20,000 to $39,999	108.97	44	10.3
$40,000 to $49,999	146.31	60	5.9
$50,000 to $69,999	234.72	96	14.6
$70,000 to $79,999	263.23	107	6.2
$80,000 to $99,999	355.84	145	11.8
$100,000 or more	664.06	270	46.3
HOUSEHOLD TYPE			
Average household	245.53	100	100.0
Married couples	358.77	146	73.9
Married couples, no children	406.40	166	35.7
Married couples, with children	337.77	138	34.3
Oldest child under age 6	228.13	93	4.5
Oldest child aged 6 to 17	389.70	159	20.2
Oldest child aged 18 or older	320.85	131	9.6
Single parent with child under age 18	102.25	42	2.5
Single person	131.54	54	15.9
RACE AND HISPANIC ORIGIN			
Average household	245.53	100	100.0
Asian	323.70	132	4.7
Black	89.22	36	4.4
Hispanic	142.25	58	6.8
Non-Hispanic white and other	286.08	117	88.9
REGION			
Average household	245.53	100	100.0
Northeast	261.53	107	19.8
Midwest	244.63	100	22.8
South	195.31	80	28.6
West	312.99	127	28.8
EDUCATION			
Average household	245.53	100	100.0
Less than high school graduate	69.40	28	4.3
High school graduate	136.98	56	14.1
Some college	204.57	83	18.1
Associate's degree	231.97	94	8.4
College graduate	467.39	190	55.1
Bachelor's degree	385.88	157	29.5
Master's, professional, doctoral degree	617.15	251	25.6

Note: Market shares may not sum to 100.0 because of rounding and missing categories by household type. "Asian" and "black" include Hispanics and non-Hispanics who identify themselves as being of the respective race alone. "Hispanic" includes people of any race who identify themselves as Hispanic. "Other" includes people who identify themselves as non-Hispanic and as Alaska Native, American Indian, Asian (who are also included in the "Asian" row), Native Hawaiian or other Pacific Islander, as well as non-Hispanics reporting more than one race.
Source: Calculations by New Strategist based on the Bureau of Labor Statistics' 2007 Consumer Expenditure Survey.

Ship Fares

Best customers:
 Householders aged 55 to 74
 High-income households
 Married couples without children at home
 Asians
 Households in the Northeast and West
 College graduates

Customer trends:
 Average household spending on ship fares will continue to increase as boomers fill the peak-spending lifestage—but only if discretionary income grows.

The biggest spenders on ship fares are well-off older Americans. Householders aged 55 to 64 spend 52 percent more than average on this item, and those aged 65 to 74 spend nearly twice the average. Householders with incomes of $100,000 or more spend over three times the average on ship fares. Married couples without children at home (most of them empty-nesters) spend over two-and-one-half times the average on cruises and account for 57 percent of household spending on this item. Asians, a relatively affluent demographic, spend 88 percent more than average on ship fares, while college graduates, another affluent demographic, spend more than twice the average on this item. Households in the Northeast and West spend, respectively, 37 and 46 percent more than average on ship fares.

Average household spending on ship fares rose 21 percent between 2000 and 2007, after adjusting for inflation. Behind the increase was the baby-boom generation's entry into the best-customer age groups. Average household spending on ship fares should continue to increase in the years ahead as boomers fill the peak-spending lifestage—but only if discretionary income grows.

Table 20.12 Ship fares

Total household spending $6,396,702,330.00
Average household spends   53.23

	AVERAGE HOUSEHOLD SPENDING	BEST CUSTOMERS (index)	BIGGEST CUSTOMERS (market share)
AGE OF HOUSEHOLDER			
Average household	**$53.23**	**100**	**100.0%**
Under age 25	18.69	35	2.4
Aged 25 to 34	24.26	46	7.8
Aged 35 to 44	39.08	73	14.3
Aged 45 to 54	59.34	111	23.4
Aged 55 to 64	80.92	152	24.6
Aged 65 to 74	106.06	199	19.9
Aged 75 or older	42.63	80	7.6

	AVERAGE HOUSEHOLD SPENDING	BEST CUSTOMERS (index)	BIGGEST CUSTOMERS (market share)
HOUSEHOLD INCOME			
Average household	**$53.23**	**100**	**100.0%**
Under $20,000	13.35	25	5.2
$20,000 to $39,999	19.49	37	8.5
$40,000 to $49,999	76.85	144	14.2
$50,000 to $69,999	27.72	52	8.0
$70,000 to $79,999	22.19	42	2.4
$80,000 to $99,999	52.61	99	8.0
$100,000 or more	166.87	313	53.7
HOUSEHOLD TYPE			
Average household	**53.23**	**100**	**100.0**
Married couples	84.46	159	80.2
Married couples, no children	141.84	266	57.5
Married couples, with children	47.39	89	22.2
Oldest child under age 6	41.35	78	3.8
Oldest child aged 6 to 17	59.21	111	14.1
Oldest child aged 18 or older	31.01	58	4.3
Single parent with child under age 18	30.15	57	3.4
Single person	20.02	38	11.2
RACE AND HISPANIC ORIGIN			
Average household	**53.23**	**100**	**100.0**
Asian	99.84	188	6.6
Black	13.83	26	3.1
Hispanic	14.35	27	3.2
Non-Hispanic white and other	65.57	123	94.0
REGION			
Average household	**53.23**	**100**	**100.0**
Northeast	72.80	137	25.5
Midwest	38.51	72	16.5
South	37.11	70	25.0
West	77.61	146	33.0
EDUCATION			
Average household	**53.23**	**100**	**100.0**
Less than high school graduate	7.82	15	2.2
High school graduate	16.28	31	7.7
Some college	36.27	68	14.8
Associate's degree	47.45	89	7.9
College graduate	123.78	233	67.3
Bachelor's degree	105.58	198	37.2
Master's, professional, doctoral degree	157.20	295	30.1

Note: Market shares may not sum to 100.0 because of rounding and missing categories by household type. "Asian" and "black" include Hispanics and non-Hispanics who identify themselves as being of the respective race alone. "Hispanic" includes people of any race who identify themselves as Hispanic. "Other" includes people who identify themselves as non-Hispanic and as Alaska Native, American Indian, Asian (who are also included in the "Asian" row), Native Hawaiian or other Pacific Islander, as well as non-Hispanics reporting more than one race.
Source: Calculations by New Strategist based on the Bureau of Labor Statistics' 2007 Consumer Expenditure Survey.

Taxi Fares, Limousine Service, and Local Transportation on Trips

Best customers:

Householders aged 55 to 74
Married couples without children at home
Asians
Households in the Northeast and West
College graduates

Customer trends:

Average household spending on local transportation on trips should rise as more boomers become empty-nesters and avid travelers, but only if discretionary income increases.

The most avid travelers spend the most on taxi fares, limousine services, and local transportation on trips. Householders aged 55 to 74 spend 27 to 71 percent more than average on this item. Married couples without children at home (most of them empty-nesters) spend 89 percent more than average on taxi fares and local transportation on trips. Asians spend almost double the average on local transportation on trips. Households in the Northeast and West spend, respectively, 28 and 45 percent more than average on this item. College graduates spend more than twice the average on these services and control two-thirds of the market.

Average household spending on taxi fares, limousine services, and local transportation on trips climbed 5 percent between 2000 and 2007, after adjusting for inflation. Average household spending on local transportation on trips should rise as more boomers become empty-nesters and avid travelers, but only if discretionary income increases.

Table 20.13 Taxi fares, limousine service, and local transportation on trips

Total household spending $2,570,457,690.00
Average household spends   21.39

	AVERAGE HOUSEHOLD SPENDING	BEST CUSTOMERS (index)	BIGGEST CUSTOMERS (market share)
AGE OF HOUSEHOLDER			
Average household	**$21.39**	**100**	**100.0%**
Under age 25	8.67	41	2.7
Aged 25 to 34	13.59	64	10.8
Aged 35 to 44	18.14	85	16.5
Aged 45 to 54	23.81	111	23.4
Aged 55 to 64	36.48	171	27.6
Aged 65 to 74	27.24	127	12.7
Aged 75 or older	13.92	65	6.2

	AVERAGE HOUSEHOLD SPENDING	BEST CUSTOMERS (index)	BIGGEST CUSTOMERS (market share)
HOUSEHOLD INCOME			
Average household	$21.39	100	100.0%
Under $20,000	4.69	22	4.5
$20,000 to $39,999	8.22	38	8.9
$40,000 to $49,999	14.56	68	6.7
$50,000 to $69,999	18.30	86	13.1
$70,000 to $79,999	19.08	89	5.2
$80,000 to $99,999	31.25	146	11.9
$100,000 or more	62.08	290	49.7
HOUSEHOLD TYPE			
Average household	21.39	100	100.0
Married couples	28.65	134	67.7
Married couples, no children	40.51	189	40.9
Married couples, with children	19.71	92	23.0
Oldest child under age 6	9.35	44	2.1
Oldest child aged 6 to 17	21.65	101	12.9
Oldest child aged 18 or older	23.24	109	8.0
Single parent with child under age 18	9.03	42	2.5
Single person	16.14	75	22.4
RACE AND HISPANIC ORIGIN			
Average household	21.39	100	100.0
Asian	42.06	197	6.9
Black	10.24	48	5.7
Hispanic	10.38	49	5.7
Non-Hispanic white and other	24.89	116	88.8
REGION			
Average household	21.39	100	100.0
Northeast	27.32	128	23.8
Midwest	18.20	85	19.4
South	14.29	67	24.0
West	31.02	145	32.8
EDUCATION			
Average household	21.39	100	100.0
Less than high school graduate	3.71	17	2.6
High school graduate	7.24	34	8.5
Some college	15.70	73	16.0
Associate's degree	13.79	64	5.7
College graduate	49.60	232	67.1
Bachelor's degree	39.59	185	34.7
Master's, professional, doctoral degree	67.98	318	32.4

Note: Market shares may not sum to 100.0 because of rounding and missing categories by household type. "Asian" and "black" include Hispanics and non-Hispanics who identify themselves as being of the respective race alone. "Hispanic" includes people of any race who identify themselves as Hispanic. "Other" includes people who identify themselves as non-Hispanic and as Alaska Native, American Indian, Asian (who are also included in the "Asian" row), Native Hawaiian or other Pacific Islander, as well as non-Hispanics reporting more than one race.
Source: Calculations by New Strategist based on the Bureau of Labor Statistics' 2007 Consumer Expenditure Survey.

Train Fares, Intercity

Best customers:
Householders aged 55 to 74
High-income households
Married couples without children at home
Asians
Households in the Northeast and West
College graduates

Customer trends:
Average household spending on train fares will continue to decline unless train service improves.

Well-off older Americans are the best customers of intercity train fares. Householders aged 55 to 74 spend 30 to 64 percent more than average on intercity train tickets. Householders with incomes of $100,000 or more spend three times the average on train fares. Married couples without children at home (most of them empty-nesters) spend 81 percent more than average on intercity train fares, while those with children at home spend 24 percent more than average. Asians, a relatively wealthy demographic, spend 81 percent more than average on train travel, and households in the West, where many Asians live, spend one-third more than average on the item. Households in the Northeast spend 21 percent more. College graduates, who dominate the affluent, spend over twice the average on train travel.

Average household spending on intercity train fares fell 18 percent between 2000 and 2007, after adjusting for inflation. Behind the decline is the increasingly limited train service in the United States. Unless train service improves, average household spending on this item is likely to continue to decline.

Table 20.14 Train fares, intercity

Total household spending $2,493,548,250.00
Average household spends   20.75

	AVERAGE HOUSEHOLD SPENDING	BEST CUSTOMERS (index)	BIGGEST CUSTOMERS (market share)
AGE OF HOUSEHOLDER			
Average household	**$20.75**	**100**	**100.0%**
Under age 25	13.36	64	4.4
Aged 25 to 34	13.61	66	11.2
Aged 35 to 44	18.65	90	17.5
Aged 45 to 54	22.47	108	22.7
Aged 55 to 64	33.94	164	26.5
Aged 65 to 74	26.91	130	13.0
Aged 75 or older	10.40	50	4.8

	AVERAGE HOUSEHOLD SPENDING	BEST CUSTOMERS (index)	BIGGEST CUSTOMERS (market share)
HOUSEHOLD INCOME			
Average household	$20.75	100	100.0%
Under $20,000	8.06	39	8.0
$20,000 to $39,999	7.34	35	8.2
$40,000 to $49,999	12.56	61	6.0
$50,000 to $69,999	11.81	57	8.7
$70,000 to $79,999	24.03	116	6.7
$80,000 to $99,999	27.57	133	10.8
$100,000 or more	62.54	301	51.6
HOUSEHOLD TYPE			
Average household	20.75	100	100.0
Married couples	29.58	143	72.1
Married couples, no children	37.65	181	39.1
Married couples, with children	25.69	124	30.9
Oldest child under age 6	28.76	139	6.8
Oldest child aged 6 to 17	23.12	111	14.2
Oldest child aged 18 or older	28.10	135	10.0
Single parent with child under age 18	8.02	39	2.3
Single person	13.44	65	19.3
RACE AND HISPANIC ORIGIN			
Average household	20.75	100	100.0
Asian	37.46	181	6.4
Black	13.08	63	7.6
Hispanic	7.42	36	4.2
Non-Hispanic white and other	24.03	116	88.4
REGION			
Average household	20.75	100	100.0
Northeast	25.17	121	22.6
Midwest	18.46	89	20.3
South	15.60	75	27.0
West	27.62	133	30.1
EDUCATION			
Average household	20.75	100	100.0
Less than high school graduate	3.63	17	2.7
High school graduate	7.50	36	9.1
Some college	17.63	85	18.5
Associate's degree	16.89	81	7.2
College graduate	44.81	216	62.5
Bachelor's degree	31.80	153	28.7
Master's, professional, doctoral degree	68.72	331	33.8

Note: Market shares may not sum to 100.0 because of rounding and missing categories by household type. "Asian" and "black" include Hispanics and non-Hispanics who identify themselves as being of the respective race alone. "Hispanic" includes people of any race who identify themselves as Hispanic. "Other" includes people who identify themselves as non-Hispanic and as Alaska Native, American Indian, Asian (who are also included in the "Asian" row), Native Hawaiian or other Pacific Islander, as well as non-Hispanics reporting more than one race.
Source: Calculations by New Strategist based on the Bureau of Labor Statistics' 2007 Consumer Expenditure Survey.

Vehicle Rentals on Trips

Best customers:
Householders aged 35 to 64
Married couples without children at home
Married couples with children under age 18
Households in the West
College graduates

Customer trends:
Average household spending on vehicle rentals on trips should grow in the years ahead as more boomers become empty-nesters and avid travelers, but only if discretionary income increases.

The biggest spenders on rented vehicles while traveling are middle-aged and older married couples. Householders ranging in age from 35 to 64 spend 25 to 53 percent more than average on this item. Married couples without children at home (most of them empty-nesters) spend 38 percent more than average on vehicle rentals while traveling. Couples with children under age 18 spend 32 to 61 percent more than average on this item. Households in the West spend 56 percent more than average on vehicle rentals while traveling. College graduates spend more than twice the average on this item.

Average household spending on vehicle rentals while traveling declined 32 percent between 2000 and 2007, after adjusting for inflation. Price discounting was one factor behind the decline. Average household spending on vehicle rentals while traveling should grow in the years ahead as more boomers become empty-nesters and avid travelers, but only if discretionary income increases.

Table 20.15 Vehicle rentals on trips

Total household spending $3,378,006,810.00
Average household spends   28.11

	AVERAGE HOUSEHOLD SPENDING	BEST CUSTOMERS (index)	BIGGEST CUSTOMERS (market share)
AGE OF HOUSEHOLDER			
Average household	$28.11	100	100.0%
Under age 25	6.73	24	1.6
Aged 25 to 34	19.70	70	12.0
Aged 35 to 44	35.68	127	24.7
Aged 45 to 54	35.24	125	26.3
Aged 55 to 64	43.13	153	24.8
Aged 65 to 74	24.78	88	8.8
Aged 75 or older	5.06	18	1.7

	AVERAGE HOUSEHOLD SPENDING	BEST CUSTOMERS (index)	BIGGEST CUSTOMERS (market share)
HOUSEHOLD INCOME			
Average household	**$28.11**	**100**	**100.0%**
Under $20,000	4.77	17	3.5
$20,000 to $39,999	9.45	34	7.8
$40,000 to $49,999	13.84	49	4.8
$50,000 to $69,999	25.66	91	14.0
$70,000 to $79,999	40.42	144	8.3
$80,000 to $99,999	39.89	142	11.5
$100,000 or more	82.20	292	50.1
HOUSEHOLD TYPE			
Average household	**28.11**	**100**	**100.0**
Married couples	38.19	136	68.7
Married couples, no children	38.81	138	29.8
Married couples, with children	39.45	140	35.0
Oldest child under age 6	36.97	132	6.4
Oldest child aged 6 to 17	45.21	161	20.4
Oldest child aged 18 or older	31.15	111	8.2
Single parent with child under age 18	12.81	46	2.7
Single person	18.85	67	19.9
RACE AND HISPANIC ORIGIN			
Average household	**28.11**	**100**	**100.0**
Asian	31.01	110	3.9
Black	15.43	55	6.6
Hispanic	10.87	39	4.6
Non-Hispanic white and other	32.73	116	88.9
REGION			
Average household	**28.11**	**100**	**100.0**
Northeast	24.00	85	15.9
Midwest	28.44	101	23.1
South	20.08	71	25.7
West	43.95	156	35.4
EDUCATION			
Average household	**28.11**	**100**	**100.0**
Less than high school graduate	5.82	21	3.1
High school graduate	14.42	51	12.9
Some college	19.11	68	14.8
Associate's degree	27.37	97	8.7
College graduate	58.75	209	60.5
Bachelor's degree	43.16	154	28.8
Master's, professional, doctoral degree	87.37	311	31.7

Note: Market shares may not sum to 100.0 because of rounding and missing categories by household type. "Asian" and "black" include Hispanics and non-Hispanics who identify themselves as being of the respective race alone. "Hispanic" includes people of any race who identify themselves as Hispanic. "Other" includes people who identify themselves as non-Hispanic and as Alaska Native, American Indian, Asian (who are also included in the "Asian" row), Native Hawaiian or other Pacific Islander, as well as non-Hispanics reporting more than one race.
Source: Calculations by New Strategist based on the Bureau of Labor Statistics' 2007 Consumer Expenditure Survey.

Chapter 21.

Utilities

Household Spending on Utilities, 2007

Utilities—such as electricity and water—are one of the larger expenditure categories for American households. Electricity, in fact, ranks 10th among household expenditures. Overall, the average household spent $2,364 on utilities in 2007, 22 percent more than the $1,939 spent in 2000, after adjusting for inflation.

Average household spending on utilities increased between 2000 and 2007 because energy prices climbed during the time period. Average household spending on fuel oil rose 33 percent. Spending on natural gas and bottled gas was up 30 percent. Average household spending on electricity increased by 19 percent during those years. Spending on water and sewer services rose 24 percent, and trash collection climbed 15 percent as local communities raised their rates for those services. The only utility category that experienced a spending decrease was coal, wood, and other fuels as they declined in popularity.

With oil prices volatile, it is likely that average household spending on utilities will increase substantially in the years ahead. Only if consumers switch to more energy efficient appliances and attempt to conserve resources will spending remain stable or decline.

Spending on utilities

(average spending by households on utilities, 2000 and 2007; in 2007 dollars)

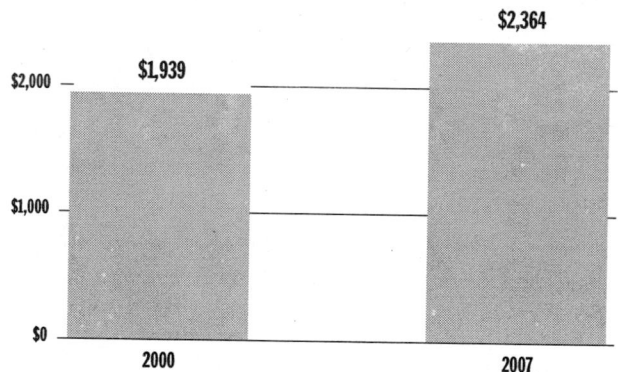

Table 21.1 Utilities Spending, 2000 to 2007

(average annual household spending on utilities, and percent distribution of spending by type, 2000 to 2007; percent change in spending, 2000–07; in 2007 dollars; ranked by amount spent)

	2007		2000		
	average household spending	percent distribution	average household spending (in 2007$)	percent distribution	percent change 2000–07
Average household spending on utilities	**$2,364.43**	**100.0%**	**$1,938.79**	**100.0%**	**22.0%**
Electricity	1,302.85	55.1	$1,097.44	56.6	18.7
Natural gas	480.39	20.3	$370.07	19.1	29.8
Water and sewer	317.25	13.4	$256.13	13.2	23.9
Trash collection	113.33	4.8	$98.42	5.1	15.1
Fuel oil	88.18	3.7	$66.32	3.4	33.0
Bottled gas	55.25	2.3	$42.46	2.2	30.1
Coal, wood, and other fuels	7.18	0.3	$7.95	0.4	–9.7

Source: Bureau of Labor Statistics, 2000 and 2007 Consumer Expenditure Surveys; calculations by New Strategist

Bottled Gas

Best customers:

Householders aged 45 or older
Married couples
Non-Hispanic whites
Households in the Midwest

Customer trends:

Average household spending on bottled gas should decline as rural areas lose population.

Householders aged 45 or older spend 22 to 32 percent more than average on bottled gas. Married couples spend 30 percent more than average on bottled gas. The average household in the Midwest, where bottled gas is most popular, spends 58 percent more than the national average on this item. Non-Hispanic white householders spend 23 percent more than average on bottled gas and control 94 percent of the market.

Average household spending on bottled gas rose 30 percent between 2000 and 2007, after adjusting for inflation, despite the shift from bottled gas to other fuels during the time period. Average household spending on bottled gas should decline as rural areas lose population.

Table 21.2 Bottled gas

Total household spending		$6,639,447,750.00	
Average household spends		55.25	

	AVERAGE HOUSEHOLD SPENDING	BEST CUSTOMERS (index)	BIGGEST CUSTOMERS (market share)
AGE OF HOUSEHOLDER			
Average household	**$55.25**	**100**	**100.0%**
Under age 25	16.75	30	2.1
Aged 25 to 34	35.25	64	10.9
Aged 35 to 44	43.59	79	15.4
Aged 45 to 54	70.28	127	26.7
Aged 55 to 64	67.45	122	19.8
Aged 65 to 74	70.04	127	12.7
Aged 75 or older	73.05	132	12.5

	AVERAGE HOUSEHOLD SPENDING	BEST CUSTOMERS (index)	BIGGEST CUSTOMERS (market share)
HOUSEHOLD INCOME			
Average household	**$55.25**	**100**	**100.0%**
Under $20,000	30.63	55	11.4
$20,000 to $39,999	48.35	88	20.3
$40,000 to $49,999	50.56	92	9.0
$50,000 to $69,999	71.01	129	19.7
$70,000 to $79,999	78.66	142	8.2
$80,000 to $99,999	56.68	103	8.3
$100,000 or more	74.22	134	23.0
HOUSEHOLD TYPE			
Average household	**55.25**	**100**	**100.0**
Married couples	71.68	130	65.6
Married couples, no children	73.80	134	28.8
Married couples, with children	67.04	121	30.3
Oldest child under age 6	66.87	121	5.9
Oldest child aged 6 to 17	75.16	136	17.3
Oldest child aged 18 or older	53.15	96	7.1
Single parent with child under age 18	20.11	36	2.2
Single person	39.58	72	21.3
RACE AND HISPANIC ORIGIN			
Average household	**55.25**	**100**	**100.0**
Asian	19.25	35	1.2
Black	11.59	21	2.5
Hispanic	15.21	28	3.2
Non-Hispanic white and other	68.21	123	94.2
REGION			
Average household	**55.25**	**100**	**100.0**
Northeast	62.02	112	20.9
Midwest	87.52	158	36.2
South	36.85	67	24.0
West	46.30	84	19.0
EDUCATION			
Average household	**55.25**	**100**	**100.0**
Less than high school graduate	44.98	81	12.3
High school graduate	59.82	108	27.3
Some college	47.36	86	18.7
Associate's degree	83.40	151	13.4
College graduate	53.96	98	28.3
Bachelor's degree	45.77	83	15.5
Master's, professional, doctoral degree	69.00	125	12.7

Note: Market shares may not sum to 100.0 because of rounding and missing categories by household type. "Asian" and "black" include Hispanics and non-Hispanics who identify themselves as being of the respective race alone. "Hispanic" includes people of any race who identify themselves as Hispanic. "Other" includes people who identify themselves as non-Hispanic and as Alaska Native, American Indian, Asian (who are also included in the "Asian" row), Native Hawaiian or other Pacific Islander, as well as non-Hispanics reporting more than one race.
Source: Calculations by New Strategist based on the Bureau of Labor Statistics' 2007 Consumer Expenditure Survey.

Electricity

Best customers:	**Householders aged 35 to 64** **Married couples with school-aged or older children at home** **Households in the South**
Customer trends:	**Average household spending on electricity will increase as energy prices rise.**

Electricity is one of the biggest expenses for the average household, ranking 10th in 2007. Because almost every household buys electricity, there are few differences in spending by demographic characteristic. Household and dwelling sizes are the biggest factors in determining electricity consumption. Consequently, middle-aged married couples with children spend the most on this item. Householders aged 35 to 64 spend 8 to 15 percent more than average on electricity. Married couples with school-aged or older children at home spend 32 to 38 percent more than average. Households in the South spend 20 percent more than average on electricity because most homes in the region are cooled (and heated) by electricity.

Average household spending on electricity rose by 19 percent between 2000 and 2007, after adjusting for inflation. Average household spending on electricity is certain to rise in the years ahead as energy prices climb.

Table 21.3 **Electricity**

Total household spending	$156,564,787,350.00
Average household spends	1,302.85

	AVERAGE HOUSEHOLD SPENDING	BEST CUSTOMERS (index)	BIGGEST CUSTOMERS (market share)
AGE OF HOUSEHOLDER			
Average household	**$1,302.85**	**100**	**100.0%**
Under age 25	705.58	54	3.7
Aged 25 to 34	1,148.38	88	15.0
Aged 35 to 44	1,479.32	114	22.1
Aged 45 to 54	1,498.61	115	24.2
Aged 55 to 64	1,403.31	108	17.4
Aged 65 to 74	1,288.61	99	9.9
Aged 75 or older	1,054.92	81	7.7

	AVERAGE HOUSEHOLD SPENDING	BEST CUSTOMERS (index)	BIGGEST CUSTOMERS (market share)
HOUSEHOLD INCOME			
Average household	$1,302.85	100	100.0%
Under $20,000	854.49	66	13.5
$20,000 to $39,999	1,132.85	87	20.2
$40,000 to $49,999	1,255.51	96	9.5
$50,000 to $69,999	1,362.69	105	16.0
$70,000 to $79,999	1,468.47	113	6.5
$80,000 to $99,999	1,523.23	117	9.5
$100,000 or more	1,884.63	145	24.8
HOUSEHOLD TYPE			
Average household	1,302.85	100	100.0
Married couples	1,596.88	123	62.0
Married couples, no children	1,431.33	110	23.7
Married couples, with children	1,687.95	130	32.3
Oldest child under age 6	1,430.69	110	5.4
Oldest child aged 6 to 17	1,721.60	132	16.8
Oldest child aged 18 or older	1,800.36	138	10.2
Single parent with child under age 18	1,264.81	97	5.8
Single person	803.95	62	18.4
RACE AND HISPANIC ORIGIN			
Average household	1,302.85	100	100.0
Asian	1,168.75	90	3.2
Black	1,354.93	104	12.5
Hispanic	1,258.10	97	11.4
Non-Hispanic white and other	1,300.96	100	76.2
REGION			
Average household	1,302.85	100	100.0
Northeast	1,275.77	98	18.2
Midwest	1,115.91	86	19.6
South	1,567.76	120	43.2
West	1,093.44	84	19.0
EDUCATION			
Average household	1,302.85	100	100.0
Less than high school graduate	1,184.24	91	13.8
High school graduate	1,285.34	99	24.9
Some college	1,250.07	96	20.9
Associate's degree	1,352.69	104	9.2
College graduate	1,404.68	108	31.2
Bachelor's degree	1,359.23	104	19.6
Master's, professional, doctoral degree	1,488.19	114	11.7

Note: Market shares may not sum to 100.0 because of rounding and missing categories by household type. "Asian" and "black" include Hispanics and non-Hispanics who identify themselves as being of the respective race alone. "Hispanic" includes people of any race who identify themselves as Hispanic. "Other" includes people who identify themselves as non-Hispanic and as Alaska Native, American Indian, Asian (who are also included in the "Asian" row), Native Hawaiian or other Pacific Islander, as well as non-Hispanics reporting more than one race.
Source: Calculations by New Strategist based on the Bureau of Labor Statistics' 2007 Consumer Expenditure Survey.

Fuel Oil

Best customers:
Householders aged 45 or older
Married couples
Non-Hispanic whites
Households in the Northeast

Customer trends:
Average household spending on fuel oil may decline as a growing proportion of households heat with natural gas or electricity.

Older householders living in the Northeast are the biggest spenders on fuel oil. Households in the Northeast, where fuel oil heating systems are most common, spend more than four times the average on fuel oil and account for 80 percent of the market. Householders aged 45 or older spend 6 to 71 percent more than average on this item, in large part because they are most likely to live in older homes with fuel oil heating systems. Married couples without children at home (most of them empty-nesters) spend 23 percent more than average on this item. Those with school-aged or older children at home spend 14 to 15 percent more. Non-Hispanic white householders spend 16 percent more than average on fuel oil.

Average household spending on fuel oil rose 33 percent between 2000 and 2007, after adjusting for inflation—the largest increase in the utility category. Average household spending on fuel oil may decline as it is replaced by other energy sources.

Table 21.4 **Fuel oil**

Total household spending	$10,596,678,780.00
Average household spends	88.18

	AVERAGE HOUSEHOLD SPENDING	BEST CUSTOMERS (index)	BIGGEST CUSTOMERS (market share)
AGE OF HOUSEHOLDER			
Average household	**$88.18**	**100**	**100.0%**
Under age 25	7.35	8	0.6
Aged 25 to 34	45.36	51	8.8
Aged 35 to 44	81.28	92	18.0
Aged 45 to 54	113.36	129	27.0
Aged 55 to 64	93.63	106	17.2
Aged 65 to 74	108.40	123	12.3
Aged 75 or older	150.86	171	16.2

	AVERAGE HOUSEHOLD SPENDING	BEST CUSTOMERS (index)	BIGGEST CUSTOMERS (market share)
HOUSEHOLD INCOME			
Average household	$88.18	100	100.0%
Under $20,000	47.78	54	11.1
$20,000 to $39,999	73.69	84	19.4
$40,000 to $49,999	60.83	69	6.8
$50,000 to $69,999	78.26	89	13.6
$70,000 to $79,999	91.95	104	6.0
$80,000 to $99,999	93.30	106	8.6
$100,000 or more	177.20	201	34.4
HOUSEHOLD TYPE			
Average household	88.18	100	100.0
Married couples	103.38	117	59.3
Married couples, no children	108.71	123	26.6
Married couples, with children	99.78	113	28.2
Oldest child under age 6	94.57	107	5.2
Oldest child aged 6 to 17	101.30	115	14.6
Oldest child aged 18 or older	100.61	114	8.4
Single parent with child under age 18	57.98	66	3.9
Single person	62.69	71	21.1
RACE AND HISPANIC ORIGIN			
Average household	88.18	100	100.0
Asian	24.86	28	1.0
Black	42.39	48	5.8
Hispanic	44.70	51	6.0
Non-Hispanic white and other	102.39	116	88.6
REGION			
Average household	88.18	100	100.0
Northeast	378.59	429	80.0
Midwest	22.90	26	5.9
South	29.78	34	12.1
West	7.71	9	2.0
EDUCATION			
Average household	88.18	100	100.0
Less than high school graduate	69.50	79	12.0
High school graduate	89.47	101	25.6
Some college	61.08	69	15.1
Associate's degree	115.13	131	11.6
College graduate	108.96	124	35.8
Bachelor's degree	102.15	116	21.7
Master's, professional, doctoral degree	121.48	138	14.1

Note: Market shares may not sum to 100.0 because of rounding and missing categories by household type. "Asian" and "black" include Hispanics and non-Hispanics who identify themselves as being of the respective race alone. "Hispanic" includes people of any race who identify themselves as Hispanic. "Other" includes people who identify themselves as non-Hispanic and as Alaska Native, American Indian, Asian (who are also included in the "Asian" row), Native Hawaiian or other Pacific Islander, as well as non-Hispanics reporting more than one race.
Source: Calculations by New Strategist based on the Bureau of Labor Statistics' 2007 Consumer Expenditure Survey.

Natural Gas

Best customers:	**Householders aged 35 to 74** **Married couples with school-aged or older children at home** **Households in the Northeast and Midwest**
Customer trends:	**Average household spending on natural gas will increase as energy prices rise.**

Because so many households heat with natural gas, there are few differences in spending on this item by demographic characteristic. Household and housing sizes are the biggest factors in determining natural gas consumption. Householders ranging in age from 35 to 74 spend 9 to 16 percent more than average on natural gas. Married couples with school-aged or older children at home spend 32 to 45 percent more than average on natural gas. Households in the Northeast and Midwest, the coldest part of the country, spend 36 to 43 percent more than average on natural gas.

Average household spending on natural gas rose by 30 percent between 2000 and 2007, after adjusting for inflation. Average household spending on natural gas is likely to rise in the years ahead as energy prices increase.

Table 21.5 Natural gas

Total household spending	$57,728,946,690.00
Average household spends	480.39

	AVERAGE HOUSEHOLD SPENDING	BEST CUSTOMERS (index)	BIGGEST CUSTOMERS (market share)
AGE OF HOUSEHOLDER			
Average household	**$480.39**	**100**	**100.0%**
Under age 25	169.06	35	2.4
Aged 25 to 34	379.50	79	13.5
Aged 35 to 44	534.49	111	21.7
Aged 45 to 54	538.85	112	23.6
Aged 55 to 64	556.50	116	18.8
Aged 65 to 74	521.81	109	10.9
Aged 75 or older	470.19	98	9.3

	AVERAGE HOUSEHOLD SPENDING	BEST CUSTOMERS (index)	BIGGEST CUSTOMERS (market share)
HOUSEHOLD INCOME			
Average household	$480.39	100	100.0%
Under $20,000	277.38	58	11.9
$20,000 to $39,999	376.80	78	18.2
$40,000 to $49,999	426.53	89	8.7
$50,000 to $69,999	481.19	100	15.3
$70,000 to $79,999	589.80	123	7.1
$80,000 to $99,999	609.80	127	10.3
$100,000 or more	796.32	166	28.4
HOUSEHOLD TYPE			
Average household	480.39	100	100.0
Married couples	587.81	122	61.9
Married couples, no children	537.22	112	24.1
Married couples, with children	630.65	131	32.8
Oldest child under age 6	526.37	110	5.3
Oldest child aged 6 to 17	632.21	132	16.7
Oldest child aged 18 or older	697.03	145	10.7
Single parent with child under age 18	368.68	77	4.6
Single person	324.68	68	20.1
RACE AND HISPANIC ORIGIN			
Average household	480.39	100	100.0
Asian	576.72	120	4.2
Black	475.20	99	11.9
Hispanic	377.58	79	9.3
Non-Hispanic white and other	497.05	103	79.0
REGION			
Average household	480.39	100	100.0
Northeast	652.72	136	25.3
Midwest	689.08	143	32.8
South	285.29	59	21.3
West	437.37	91	20.6
EDUCATION			
Average household	480.39	100	100.0
Less than high school graduate	374.13	78	11.8
High school graduate	439.43	91	23.1
Some college	407.52	85	18.5
Associate's degree	484.08	101	9.0
College graduate	625.45	130	37.7
Bachelor's degree	592.53	123	23.1
Master's, professional, doctoral degree	685.93	143	14.6

Note: Market shares may not sum to 100.0 because of rounding and missing categories by household type. "Asian" and "black" include Hispanics and non-Hispanics who identify themselves as being of the respective race alone. "Hispanic" includes people of any race who identify themselves as Hispanic. "Other" includes people who identify themselves as non-Hispanic and as Alaska Native, American Indian, Asian (who are also included in the "Asian" row), Native Hawaiian or other Pacific Islander, as well as non-Hispanics reporting more than one race.
Source: Calculations by New Strategist based on the Bureau of Labor Statistics' 2007 Consumer Expenditure Survey.

Trash Collection

Best customers:

Householders aged 55 to 74
Married couples
Households in the West

Customer trends:

Average household spending on trash collection should rise as local communities and private companies charge more for waste disposal.

The biggest spenders on trash collection are homeowners, who are most likely to be older householders and married couples. Householders aged 55 to 74 spend 13 to 19 percent more than average on trash collection. Married couples without children at home spend 22 percent more than average on trash collection, and those with the largest households, married couples with school-aged or older children at home, spend 28 percent more than average. Households in the West spend 47 percent more than average on this category.

Average household spending on trash collection increased 15 percent between 2000 and 2007, after adjusting for inflation. Although governments strengthened recycling laws nationwide over the period, rising disposal fees counteracted the cost savings. Average household spending on trash collection should continue its long-term rise as it to becomes more expensive to dispose of waste.

Table 21.6 Trash collection

Total household spending $13,618,979,430.00
Average household spends 113.33

AGE OF HOUSEHOLDER	AVERAGE HOUSEHOLD SPENDING	BEST CUSTOMERS (index)	BIGGEST CUSTOMERS (market share)
Average household	**$113.33**	**100**	**100.0%**
Under age 25	37.71	33	2.3
Aged 25 to 34	90.23	80	13.6
Aged 35 to 44	123.36	109	21.2
Aged 45 to 54	120.27	106	22.3
Aged 55 to 64	135.11	119	19.3
Aged 65 to 74	128.40	113	11.3
Aged 75 or older	119.94	106	10.0

	AVERAGE HOUSEHOLD SPENDING	BEST CUSTOMERS (index)	BIGGEST CUSTOMERS (market share)
HOUSEHOLD INCOME			
Average household	$113.33	100	100.0%
Under $20,000	59.76	53	10.8
$20,000 to $39,999	94.06	83	19.3
$40,000 to $49,999	102.34	90	8.9
$50,000 to $69,999	119.49	105	16.1
$70,000 to $79,999	130.91	116	6.7
$80,000 to $99,999	140.10	124	10.1
$100,000 or more	185.93	164	28.1
HOUSEHOLD TYPE			
Average household	113.33	100	100.0
Married couples	139.13	123	62.1
Married couples, no children	138.23	122	26.3
Married couples, with children	139.98	124	30.8
Oldest child under age 6	121.12	107	5.2
Oldest child aged 6 to 17	144.53	128	16.2
Oldest child aged 18 or older	144.64	128	9.4
Single parent with child under age 18	93.39	82	4.9
Single person	78.26	69	20.5
RACE AND HISPANIC ORIGIN			
Average household	113.33	100	100.0
Asian	101.20	89	3.2
Black	76.32	67	8.1
Hispanic	101.45	90	10.6
Non-Hispanic white and other	120.87	107	81.4
REGION			
Average household	113.33	100	100.0
Northeast	78.53	69	12.9
Midwest	106.89	94	21.6
South	101.66	90	32.2
West	167.05	147	33.3
EDUCATION			
Average household	113.33	100	100.0
Less than high school graduate	84.45	75	11.3
High school graduate	96.95	86	21.6
Some college	108.27	96	20.8
Associate's degree	112.66	99	8.8
College graduate	146.76	129	37.5
Bachelor's degree	140.32	124	23.2
Master's, professional, doctoral degree	158.60	140	14.3

Note: Market shares may not sum to 100.0 because of rounding and missing categories by household type. "Asian" and "black" include Hispanics and non-Hispanics who identify themselves as being of the respective race alone. "Hispanic" includes people of any race who identify themselves as Hispanic. "Other" includes people who identify themselves as non-Hispanic and as Alaska Native, American Indian, Asian (who are also included in the "Asian" row), Native Hawaiian or other Pacific Islander, as well as non-Hispanics reporting more than one race.
Source: Calculations by New Strategist based on the Bureau of Labor Statistics' 2007 Consumer Expenditure Survey.

Water and Sewer

Best customers:

Householders aged 35 to 54
Married couples
Households in the South and West

Customer trends:

Average household spending on water and sewer will rise as clean water becomes increasingly scarce and expensive.

Every household needs water and sewer service, but the category accounts for only 13 percent of household utility spending. Because most households consume water, there are few differences in spending on this item by demographic characteristic. Household and housing sizes are the biggest factors in determining spending on water and sewer. Householders aged 35 to 54, whose households are likely to include children, spend 14 to 17 percent more than average on this item. Married couples control nearly two-thirds of spending on water and sewer. Married couples with school-aged or older children at home, who have the largest households, spend 38 to 44 percent more than average on this item. Households in the South and West, where water can be scarce, spend 11 to 17 percent more than average on water and sewer.

Average household spending on water and sewer rose 24 percent between 2000 and 2007, after adjusting for inflation. Higher fees charged by local communities were behind the increase. Average household spending on water and sewer is certain to rise in the years ahead as clean water becomes increasingly scarce and expensive.

Table 21.7 Water and sewer

| Total household spending | $38,124,249,750.00 |
| Average household spends | 317.25 |

	AVERAGE HOUSEHOLD SPENDING	BEST CUSTOMERS (index)	BIGGEST CUSTOMERS (market share)
AGE OF HOUSEHOLDER			
Average household	**$317.25**	**100**	**100.0%**
Under age 25	127.59	40	2.7
Aged 25 to 34	265.80	84	14.3
Aged 35 to 44	361.19	114	22.2
Aged 45 to 54	369.70	117	24.5
Aged 55 to 64	348.20	110	17.8
Aged 65 to 74	316.91	100	10.0
Aged 75 or older	286.39	90	8.6

	AVERAGE HOUSEHOLD SPENDING	BEST CUSTOMERS (index)	BIGGEST CUSTOMERS (market share)
HOUSEHOLD INCOME			
Average household	$317.25	100	100.0%
Under $20,000	180.44	57	11.7
$20,000 to $39,999	246.64	78	18.1
$40,000 to $49,999	300.05	95	9.3
$50,000 to $69,999	338.25	107	16.3
$70,000 to $79,999	386.76	122	7.1
$80,000 to $99,999	413.77	130	10.6
$100,000 or more	498.98	157	26.9
HOUSEHOLD TYPE			
Average household	317.25	100	100.0
Married couples	402.90	127	64.2
Married couples, no children	357.48	113	24.3
Married couples, with children	430.84	136	33.9
Oldest child under age 6	375.28	118	5.8
Oldest child aged 6 to 17	436.41	138	17.5
Oldest child aged 18 or older	458.05	144	10.6
Single parent with child under age 18	283.86	89	5.3
Single person	185.00	58	17.3
RACE AND HISPANIC ORIGIN			
Average household	317.25	100	100.0
Asian	373.94	118	4.2
Black	339.44	107	12.8
Hispanic	307.44	97	11.4
Non-Hispanic white and other	315.32	99	75.9
REGION			
Average household	317.25	100	100.0
Northeast	247.67	78	14.5
Midwest	267.76	84	19.3
South	351.85	111	39.8
West	369.61	117	26.3
EDUCATION			
Average household	317.25	100	100.0
Less than high school graduate	251.52	79	12.0
High school graduate	286.71	90	22.8
Some college	299.71	94	20.6
Associate's degree	317.71	100	8.9
College graduate	391.35	123	35.7
Bachelor's degree	375.80	118	22.2
Master's, professional, doctoral degree	419.92	132	13.5

Note: Market shares may not sum to 100.0 because of rounding and missing categories by household type. "Asian" and "black" include Hispanics and non-Hispanics who identify themselves as being of the respective race alone. "Hispanic" includes people of any race who identify themselves as Hispanic. "Other" includes people who identify themselves as non-Hispanic and as Alaska Native, American Indian, Asian (who are also included in the "Asian" row), Native Hawaiian or other Pacific Islander, as well as non-Hispanics reporting more than one race.
Source: Calculations by New Strategist based on the Bureau of Labor Statistics' 2007 Consumer Expenditure Survey.

Appendix A: About the Consumer Expenditure Survey

History

The Consumer Expenditure Survey is an ongoing study of the day-to-day spending of American households. In taking the survey, government interviewers collect spending data on products and services as well as the amount and sources of household income, changes in saving and debt, and demographic and economic characteristics of household members. The Bureau of the Census collects data for the Consumer Expenditure Survey under contract with the Bureau of Labor Statistics, which is responsible for analysis and release of the survey data.

Since the late 19th century, the federal government has conducted expenditure surveys about every 10 years. Although the results have been used for a variety of purposes, their primary application is to track consumer prices. Beginning in 1980, the Consumer Expenditure Survey became a continuous survey with annual release of data (and a lag time of about two years between data collection and release). The survey is used to update prices for the market basket of products and services used in calculating the Consumer Price Index.

Description of the Consumer Expenditure Survey

The Consumer Expenditure Survey consists of two separate surveys: an interview survey and a diary survey. In the interview portion of the survey, respondents are asked each quarter for five consecutive quarters to report their expenditures for the previous three months. The interview survey records purchases of big-ticket items such as houses, cars, and major appliances as well as recurring expenses such as insurance premiums, utility payments, and rent. It covers about 95 percent of all expenditures.

The diary survey records expenditures on small, frequently purchased items during a two-week period. These detailed records include expenses for food and beverages purchased in grocery stores and at restaurants as well as other items such as tobacco, housekeeping supplies, nonprescription drugs, and personal care products and services. The diary survey is intended to capture expenditures respondents are likely to forget or recall incorrectly over longer periods of time.

The average spending figures shown in this report are the integrated data from both the diary and interview components of the survey. Integrated data provide a more complete accounting of consumer expenditures than either component of the survey is designed to do alone.

Data collection and processing

Two separate, nationally representative samples are used for the interview and diary surveys. For the interview survey, about 7,000 consumer units are interviewed on a rotating panel basis each quarter for five consecutive quarters. Another 7,000 consumer units kept weekly diaries of spending for two consecutive weeks. Data collection is carried out in 91 areas of the country.

The Bureau of Labor Statistics reviews, audits, and cleanses the data, then weights them to reflect the number and characteristics of all U.S. consumer units. Like any sample survey, the Consumer Expenditure Survey is subject to two major types of error. Nonsampling error occurs when respondents misinterpret questions or interviewers are inconsistent in the way they ask questions or record answers. Respondents may forget items, recall expenses incorrectly, or deliberately give wrong answers. A respondent may remember how much he or she spent at the grocery store but forget the items picked up at a local convenience store. Most surveys of alcohol consumption or spending on alcohol, for example, suffer from underreporting. Mistakes during the various stages of data processing and refinement can also cause nonsampling error.

Sampling error occurs when a sample does not accurately represent the population it is supposed to represent. This kind of error is present in every sample-based survey and is minimized by using a proper sampling procedure. Standard error tables documenting the extent of sampling error in the Consumer Expenditure Survey are available from the Bureau of Labor Statistics at http://www.bls.gov/cex/csxstnderror.htm.

Although the Consumer Expenditure Survey is the best source of information about the spending behavior of American households, it should be treated with caution because of the above problems. Comparisons with consumption data from other sources show that Consumer Expenditure Survey data tend to underestimate expenditures except for rent, fuel, telephone service, furniture, transportation, and personal care services. Despite these problems, the data reveal important spending patterns by demographic segment that can be used to better understand consumer behavior.

Definition of consumer unit

The Consumer Expenditure Survey uses the consumer unit as the sampling unit rather than the household, which is the sampling unit used by the Census Bureau. The term household is used interchangeably with the term consumer unit in this book for convenience, although they are not exactly the same. Some households contain more than one consumer unit.

The Bureau of Labor Statistics defines consumer unit as (1) members of a household who are related by blood, marriage, adoption, or other legal arrangements; (2) a person living alone or sharing a household with others or living as a roomer in a private home or lodging house or in permanent living quarters in a hotel or motel, but who is financially independent; or (3) two or more persons living together who pool their income to make joint expenditure decisions. The bureau defines financial independence in terms of the three major expenses categories: housing, food, and other living expenses. To be considered financially independent, at least two of the three major expense categories have to be provided by the respondent.

The Census Bureau uses the household as its sampling unit in the decennial census and in the monthly Current Population Survey. The Census Bureau's household consists of all persons who occupy a housing unit. A house, an apartment or other group of rooms, or a single room is regarded as a housing unit when it is occupied or intended for occupancy as separate living quarters; that is, when the occupants do not live and eat with any other persons in the structure and there is direct access from the outside or through a common hall.

The definition goes on to specify that a household includes the related family members and all the unrelated persons, if any, such as lodgers, foster children, wards, or employees who share the housing unit. A person living alone in a housing unit or a group of unrelated persons sharing a housing unit as partners is also counted as a household. The count of households excludes group quarters.

Because there can be more than one consumer unit in a household, consumer units outnumber households by several million. Young adults under age 25 head most of the additional consumer units.

For more information

If you want to know more about the Consumer Expenditure Survey, contact the specialists at the Bureau of Labor Statistics at (202) 691-6900, or visit the Consumer Expenditure Survey home page at http://www.bls.gov/cex/. The web site includes news releases, technical documentation, and current and historical summary-level data.

For a comprehensive look at detailed household spending data for all products and services, see the 14th edition of *Household Spending: Who Spends How Much on What*. New Strategist's books are available in hardcopy or as downloads with links to the Excel version of each table. Find out more by visiting http://www.newstrategist.com or by calling 800-848-0842.

Appendix B: Percent Reporting Expenditure and Amount Spent, Average Quarter 2007

(percent of consumer units reporting expenditure and amount spent by purchasers during the average quarter, 2007)

	percent reporting expenditure during quarter	average amount spent by purchasers per quarter
ALCOHOLIC BEVERAGES	**36.8%**	**$227.01**
At home	31.3	145.20
Away from home	24.2	157.01
Alcoholic beverages at restaurants, taverns	18.4	147.47
Alcoholic beverages purchased on trips	11.6	94.25
APPAREL AND SERVICES	**75.5**	**421.00**
Men's apparel	**30.4**	**184.19**
Suits	1.6	373.73
Sportcoats and tailored jackets	1.3	212.02
Coats and jackets	3.6	133.82
Underwear	5.4	35.10
Hosiery	4.4	21.27
Nightwear	0.9	41.28
Accessories	3.4	56.25
Sweaters and vests	2.5	87.10
Active sportswear	1.8	61.36
Shirts	17.9	83.47
Pants and shorts	18.6	92.52
Uniforms	0.5	150.94
Costumes	0.2	78.13
Boys' (aged 2 to 15) apparel	**11.1**	**154.38**
Coats and jackets	1.6	84.91
Sweaters	0.8	64.94
Shirts	6.8	67.69
Underwear	2.4	35.29
Nightwear	0.8	34.15
Hosiery	1.7	17.75
Accessories	0.7	37.50
Suits, sportcoats, and vests	0.3	102.34
Pants and shorts	7.9	86.74
Uniforms	0.7	133.21
Active sportswear	1.1	40.00
Costumes	0.6	35.66
Women's apparel	**41.5**	**237.88**
Coats and jackets	5.4	121.81
Dresses	7.4	170.05
Sportcoats and tailored jackets	1.4	122.79
Sweaters and vests	6.7	92.93
Shirts, blouses, and tops	25.2	87.90
Skirts	3.8	68.26
Pants and shorts	23.7	95.57
Active sportswear	3.7	77.64
Nightwear	4.3	52.68
Undergarments	9.4	55.61
Hosiery	5.9	23.85

	percent reporting expenditure during quarter	average amount spent by purchasers per quarter
Suits	2.0%	$212.82
Accessories	5.8	87.24
Uniforms	1.2	100.63
Costumes	0.6	102.38
Girls'(aged 2 to 15) apparel	**12.0**	**180.75**
Coats and jackets	1.8	77.41
Dresses and suits	2.4	82.31
Shirts, blouses, and sweaters	7.6	84.63
Skirts, pants, and shorts	7.9	88.96
Active sportswear	1.5	47.19
Underwear and nightwear	3.5	48.41
Hosiery	1.7	18.17
Accessories	1.1	38.66
Uniforms	0.5	149.51
Costumes	0.7	68.57
Children's (under age 2) apparel	**14.1**	**133.71**
Coats, jackets, and snowsuits	1.1	58.10
Outerwear including dresses	7.6	82.98
Underwear	7.6	116.02
Nightwear and loungewear	2.6	42.95
Accessories	3.7	55.88
Footwear	**32.9**	**117.36**
Men's	12.7	99.10
Boys'	6.1	75.45
Women's	19.4	87.69
Girls'	6.4	67.83
Other apparel products and services	**38.9**	**171.89**
Material for making clothes	1.3	63.27
Sewing patterns and notions	1.6	29.50
Watches	3.5	147.84
Jewelry	7.9	397.06
Shoe repair and other shoe services	0.9	38.44
Coin-operated apparel laundry and dry cleaning	13.7	74.20
Apparel alteration, repair, and tailoring services	3.0	52.17
Clothing rental	0.4	137.82
Watch and jewelry repair	1.9	47.77
Professional laundry, dry cleaning	16.6	92.15
Clothing storage	0.1	218.75
COMPUTERS		
Computer information services	51.3	94.67
Computers and computer hardware, nonbusiness use	5.3	694.56
Computer software and accessories, nonbusiness use	4.2	125.77
Repair of computer systems for nonbusiness use	0.8	221.20
EDUCATION	**13.9**	**1,620.27**
College tuition	5.0	2,943.66
Elementary and high school tuition	1.5	2,570.13
Vocational and technical school tuition	0.2	1,676.09
Other school tuition	0.5	949.53
Other school expenses including rentals	3.4	314.00
Books and supplies for college	3.9	398.07
Books and supplies for elementary and high school	3.4	120.24
Books and supplies for vocational and technical schools	0.1	200.00
Books and supplies for day care and nursery	0.1	78.85
Books and suppliesfor other schools	0.3	192.19

	percent reporting expenditure during quarter	average amount spent by purchasers per quarter
ENTERTAINMENT	**90.7%**	**$663.46**
Fees and admissions	**46.9**	**330.66**
Recreation expenses, on trips	7.9	87.81
Social, recreation, civic club membership	12.7	242.31
Fees for participant sports	11.4	174.06
Participant sports on trips	3.6	220.72
Movie, theater, opera, ballet	30.1	96.79
Movie, other admissions on trips	8.4	127.14
Admission to sports events	6.7	189.08
Admission to sports events on trips	8.4	42.37
Fees for recreational lessons	6.5	409.15
Other entertainment services on trips	7.9	87.81
Audio and visual equipment and services	**83.6**	**284.99**
Televisions	4.0	1,026.84
Cable and satellite television services	72.8	190.56
Satellite radio service	2.6	114.16
Online gaming services	0.8	46.13
VCRs and video disc players	2.3	161.90
Video cassettes, tapes, and discs	16.0	59.84
Video game hardware and software	4.9	214.69
Streaming, downloading video	0.5	52.55
Repair of TV, radio, and sound equipment	0.5	226.60
Rental of televisions	0.1	300.00
Radios	0.9	76.97
Tape recorders and players	0.1	94.23
Personal digital audio players	1.9	227.62
Sound components and component systems	0.9	388.53
CDs, records, audio tapes	14.5	47.26
Streamed, downloaded audio	2.6	35.25
Rental of VCR, radio, sound equipment	0.1	155.00
Musical instruments and accessories	1.2	304.67
Rental and repair of musical instruments	0.3	119.44
Rental of video cassettes, tapes, discs, films	21.2	36.33
Rental of computer and video game hardware and software	0.0	62.50
Sound equipment accessories	0.9	181.61
Satellite dishes	0.2	136.11
Pets, toys, hobbies, and playground equipment	**42.2**	**238.33**
Pets	31.1	221.67
Pet purchase, supplies, and medicines	25.8	134.85
Pet services	5.2	151.72
Veterinary services	9.1	287.46
Toys, games, arts and crafts, and tricycles	17.4	167.97
Stamp and coin collecting	0.8	121.08
Playground equipment	0.4	336.25
Other entertainment supplies, equipment, services	**23.9**	**451.25**
Unmotored recreational vehicles	0.2	8,572.62
Boat without motor and boat trailers	0.1	4,888.64
Trailer and other attachable campers	0.1	12,625.00
Motorized recreational vehicles	0.3	14,207.69
Purchase of motorized camper	0.0	48,816.67
Purchase of other vehicle	0.1	7,068.18
Purchase of boat with motor	0.1	13,202.27
Rental of recreational vehicles	0.5	370.37
Outboard motors	0.0	658.33
Docking and landing fees	0.3	334.85

	percent reporting expenditure during quarter	average amount spent by purchasers per quarter
Sports, recreation, exercise equipment	10.2%	$257.26
Athletic gear, game tables, exercise equipment	5.9	210.12
Bicycles	1.4	296.45
Camping equipment	0.9	113.04
Hunting and fishing equipment	1.8	226.23
Winter sports equipment	0.3	375.93
Water sports equipment	0.5	215.87
Other sports equipment	0.9	204.36
Rental and repair of miscellaneous sports equipment	0.3	178.68
Photographic equipment and supplies	15.8	116.84
Film	4.9	23.78
Photo processing	10.2	39.01
Repair and rental of photographic equipment	0.1	143.18
Photographic equipment	2.7	301.87
Photographer fees	2.5	202.41
Live entertainment for catered affairs	0.4	588.46
Rental of party supplies for catered affairs	0.6	365.63
FINANCIAL PRODUCTS AND SERVICES		
Miscellaneous financial products and services	**39.9**	**464.83**
Lotteries and parimutuel losses	12.0	104.90
Legal fees	2.4	1,651.79
Funeral expenses	0.9	1,674.71
Safe deposit box rental	2.2	39.40
Checking accounts, other bank service charges	12.2	42.74
Cemetery lots, vaults, and maintenance fees	0.6	620.56
Accounting fees	5.0	383.86
Finance charges, except mortgage and vehicles	6.2	674.84
Dating services	0.2	66.67
Vacation clubs	0.3	784.62
Expenses for other properties	5.1	618.86
Occupational expenses	5.8	212.09
Credit card memberships	0.6	64.84
Shopping club membership fees	3.2	56.09
Cash contributions	**50.1**	**908.56**
Support for college students	2.9	868.95
Alimony expenditures	0.3	2,695.54
Child support expenditures	3.2	1,556.68
Gifts of stocks, bonds and mutual funds to people in other households	0.3	6,225.00
Cash contributions to charities	17.2	401.31
Cash contributions to religious organizations	28.6	598.36
Cash contributions to educational organizations	2.3	562.78
Cash contributions to political organizations	1.4	185.64
Other cash gifts to people in other households	16.9	607.88
Personal insurance and pensions	**84.5**	**1,578.74**
Life and other personal insurance	28.2	274.26
Life, endowment, annuity, other personal insurance	27.3	273.17
Other nonhealth insurance	2.0	138.92
Pensions and Social Security	**80.6**	**1,558.37**
Deductions for government retirement	2.3	800.11
Deductions for railroad retirement	0.0	1,831.25
Deductions for private pensions	10.7	1,308.79
Nonpayroll deposit to retirement plans	7.8	1,548.97
Deductions for Social Security	80.5	1,214.40

	percent reporting expenditure during quarter	average amount spent by purchasers per quarter
Personal taxes	**57.1%**	**$978.22**
Federal income taxes	50.2	781.44
Federal income tax deducted	24.5	1,880.88
Additional federal income tax paid	9.5	1,465.98
Federal income tax refunds	35.3	−587.08
State and local income taxes	34.8	336.64
State and local income tax deducted	17.4	689.75
Additional state and local income tax paid	7.5	356.25
State and local income tax refunds	22.0	−133.33
Other taxes	16.9	289.84
FURNISHINGS AND EQUIPMENT FOR THE HOME	**53.4**	**628.30**
Household textiles	**19.8**	**120.41**
Bathroom linens	6.6	50.57
Bedroom linens	10.7	106.75
Kitchen and dining room linens	1.9	26.60
Curtains and draperies	2.5	188.29
Slipcovers and decorative pillows	1.4	59.68
Sewing materials for household items	3.2	86.50
Other linens	0.5	56.67
Furniture	**10.8**	**1,032.84**
Mattress and springs	1.7	821.45
Other bedroom furniture	2.3	850.77
Sofas	2.3	1,224.13
Living room chairs	1.9	593.91
Living room tables	1.5	272.07
Kitchen and dining room furniture	1.4	846.22
Infants' furniture	0.7	334.19
Outdoor furniture	1.3	470.96
Wall units, cabinets, and other furniture	2.9	491.26
Floor coverings	**3.1**	**369.98**
Wall-to-wall carpeting, replacement (owner)	0.3	2,012.50
Floor coverings, nonpermanent	2.8	185.82
Major appliances	**8.5**	**667.40**
Dishwashers (built-in), garbage disposals, range hoods (renter)	0.0	575.00
Dishwashers (built-in), garbage disposals, range hoods (owner)	0.9	567.13
Refrigerators and freezers (renter)	0.4	459.03
Refrigerators and freezers (owner)	1.4	975.54
Washing machines (renter)	0.4	390.71
Washing machines (owner)	1.2	691.38
Clothes dryers (renter)	0.3	337.50
Clothes dryers (owner)	1.1	602.59
Cooking stoves, ovens (renter)	0.2	450.00
Cooking stoves, ovens (owner)	0.9	1,027.65
Microwave ovens (renter)	0.7	77.65
Microwave ovens (owner)	1.0	198.18
Portable dishwasher (renter)	0.0	550.00
Portable dishasher (owner)	0.0	291.67
Window air conditioners (renter)	0.2	222.22
Window air conditioners (owner)	0.3	308.93
Electric floor cleaning equipment	2.2	186.83
Sewing machines	0.3	538.79

	percent reporting expenditure during quarter	average amount spent by purchasers per quarter
Small appliances and miscellaneous housewares	**16.6%**	**$85.20**
Housewares	10.5	75.81
Plastic dinnerware	2.8	22.06
China and other dinnerware	2.6	95.58
Flatware	1.5	68.58
Glassware	2.2	34.98
Silver serving pieces	0.1	71.43
Other serving pieces	0.6	57.26
Nonelectric cookware	3.5	76.96
Small appliances	8.1	76.38
Small electric kitchen appliances	7.0	68.27
Portable heating and cooling equipment	1.4	103.26
Miscellaneous household equipment	36.4	325.22
Window coverings	1.6	510.03
Infants' equipment	0.8	147.84
Outdoor equipment	1.0	254.29
Lamps and lighting fixtures	3.7	127.24
Clocks and household decorative items	6.4	164.23
Telephones and accessories	4.5	125.72
Lawn and garden equipment	2.5	431.98
Power tools	2.2	225.00
Office furniture for home use	0.7	361.49
Hand tools	2.0	100.62
Indoor plants and fresh flowers	15.5	94.46
Closet and storage items	1.4	57.81
Rental of furniture	0.3	399.00
Luggage	1.4	111.33
Computers and computer hardware, nonbusiness use	5.3	694.56
Computer software and accessories, nonbusiness use	4.2	125.77
Personal digital assistants	0.3	306.67
Internet services away from home	0.9	71.47
Telephone answering devices	0.3	52.68
Business equipment for home use	0.6	89.68
Smoke alarms (owner)	0.7	71.64
Smoke alarms (renter)	0.1	38.64
Other household appliances (owner)	1.0	135.26
Other household appliances (renter)	0.4	75.68
GIFTS	**28.4**	**786.89**
Food	**1.2**	**842.21**
Housing	**9.9**	**389.64**
Household textiles	2.2	75.34
Appliances and miscellaneous housewares	1.8	194.69
Major appliances	0.3	530.47
Small appliances and miscellaneous housewares	1.5	117.60
Miscellaneous household equipment	4.6	154.15
Other housing	3.1	860.54
Apparel and services	**15.8**	**201.25**
Males aged two or older	3.9	173.85
Females aged two or older	5.0	189.63
Children under age two	9.0	94.50
Other apparel products and services	3.8	184.88
Jewelry and watches	1.8	257.47
All other apparel products and services	2.2	103.84

	percent reporting expenditure during quarter	average amount spent by purchasers per quarter
Transportation	**4.4%**	**$563.06**
Health care	**1.0**	**505.53**
Entertainment	**8.6**	**238.94**
Toys, games, hobbies, and tricycles	5.4	145.61
Other entertainment	4.1	315.62
Education	**2.1**	**3,282.19**
All other gifts	**4.7**	**484.73**
GROCERIES	**98.9**	**1,135.75**
Purchased on trips	10.0	107.50
HEALTH CARE	**77.6**	**869.71**
Health insurance	**62.8**	**615.18**
Commercial health insurance	14.3	512.28
Traditional fee for service health plan (not BCBS)	4.6	482.08
Preferred provider health plan (not BCBS)	9.8	520.13
Blue Cross, Blue Shield	19.9	546.66
Traditional fee for service health plan	3.6	540.34
Preferred provider health plan	8.4	578.96
Health maintenance organization	6.1	516.91
Commercial Medicare supplement	1.7	510.23
Other BCBS health insurance	0.7	152.57
Health maintenance plans (HMOs)	13.3	471.20
Medicare payments	21.8	370.47
Medicare prescription drug premium	7.2	168.38
Commercial Medicare supplements/other health insurance	11.1	285.36
Commercial Medicare supplement (not BCBS)	4.8	467.15
Other health insurance (not BCBS)	6.8	135.15
Long-term care insurance	3.2	528.92
Medical services	**41.3**	**429.14**
Physician's services	26.0	164.27
Dental services	14.2	429.55
Eye care services	6.4	147.74
Service by professionals other than physician	4.8	374.17
Lab tests, X-rays	5.3	183.65
Hospital room and services	4.2	684.68
Care in convalescent or nursing home	0.1	2,789.29
Other medical services	1.7	202.96
Prescription drugs	**41.6**	**215.83**
Medical supplies	**7.5**	**284.95**
Eyeglasses and contact lenses	6.2	245.22
Hearing aids	0.3	1,406.48
Medical equipment for general use	0.5	227.04
Supportive/convalescent medical equipment	0.5	169.15
Rental of medical equipment	0.3	143.00
Rental of supportive, convalescent medical equipment	0.2	73.91
HOUSEHOLD SERVICES	**63.8**	**385.15**
Personal services	**8.0**	**1,303.20**
Babysitting and child care in your own home	1.8	721.67
Babysitting and child care in someone else's home	1.3	652.88
Care for elderly, invalids, handicapped, etc.	0.5	2,995.83
Adult day care centers	0.1	1,560.71
Day care centers, nursery and preschools	5.4	1,241.47

	percent reporting expenditure during quarter	average amount spent by purchasers per quarter
Other household services	62.0%	$229.10
Housekeeping services	6.0	490.30
Gardening, lawn care service	13.3	201.47
Water softening service	1.4	80.18
Nonclothing laundry and dry cleaning, sent out	0.7	39.77
Nonclothing laundry and dry cleaning, coin-operated	3.4	23.69
Termite/pest control services	3.2	124.92
Home security system service fee	4.2	117.28
Other home services	1.9	197.84
Termite/pest control products	2.2	29.38
Moving, storage, and freight express	2.0	627.75
Appliance repair, including service center	2.3	170.19
Reupholstering and furniture repair	0.5	266.67
Repairs/rentals of lawn/garden equipment, hand/power tools, etc.	1.0	165.59
Appliance rental	0.2	144.57
Rental of office equipment for nonbusiness use	0.1	157.14
Repair of computer systems for nonbusiness use	0.8	221.20
Computer information services	51.3	94.67
Installation of computer	0.1	128.13
PERSONAL CARE PRODUCTS AND SERVICES	**62.4**	**116.83**
Wigs and hairpieces	0.7	70.95
Electric personal care appliances	3.4	48.21
Personal care services	61.4	115.25
READING	**42.0**	**70.09**
Newspaper and magazine subscriptions	21.2	55.77
Newspapers and magazines, nonsubscription	15.9	22.69
Books purchased through book clubs	1.6	58.01
Books not purchased through book clubs	19.3	67.08
RESTAURANTS AND CARRY-OUTS	**80.5**	**663.89**
Restaurant food on trips	23.5	261.09
SHELTER	**97.8**	**2,562.82**
Owned dwellings	**66.9**	**2,515.01**
Mortgage interest and charges	44.7	2,174.17
Mortgage interest	42.4	2,112.93
Interest paid, home equity loan	4.0	593.53
Interest paid, home equity line of credit	5.7	933.10
Property taxes	65.8	649.76
Maintenance, repairs, insurance, other expenses	35.1	804.84
Homeowners insurance	23.6	360.04
Ground rent	1.6	996.29
Maintenance and repair services	11.9	1,212.81
Painting and papering	1.2	1,600.62
Plumbing and water heating	3.0	386.91
Heat, air conditioning, electrical work	3.4	650.22
Roofing and gutters	1.1	2,182.52
Other repair and maintenance services	4.4	1,235.05
Repair/replacement of hard surface flooring	0.4	2,457.14
Repair of built-in appliances	1.0	188.46
Maintenance and repair materials	5.3	423.08
Paints, wallpaper and supplies	2.2	174.89
Tools/equipment for painting, wallpapering	2.2	18.75
Plumbing supplies and equipment	0.6	176.72
Electrical supplies, heating/cooling equipment	0.3	262.12

	percent reporting expenditure during quarter	average amount spent by purchasers per quarter
Hard surface flooring, repair and replacement	0.3%	$957.58
Roofing and gutters	0.2	996.67
Plaster, paneling, siding, windows, doors, screens, awnings	0.7	584.62
Patio, walk, fence, driveway, masonry, brick, and stucco work	0.3	111.21
Miscellaneous supplies and equipment	1.8	428.23
Insulation, other maintenance/repair	1.8	428.23
Property management and security	5.6	243.54
Property management	5.3	211.70
Management and upkeep services for security	1.4	164.69
Parking	1.7	142.22
Rented dwellings	**31.8**	**2,047.42**
Rent	30.7	2,028.26
Rent as pay	1.3	1,392.60
Maintenance, insurance, and other expenses	3.8	265.04
Tenant's insurance	2.7	96.08
Maintenance and repair services	0.4	997.16
Maintenance and repair materials	0.9	373.84
Other lodging	**18.5**	**931.30**
Owned vacation homes	4.9	1,475.36
Mortgage interest and charges	1.6	1,852.48
Property taxes	4.7	510.65
Maintenance, insurance and other expenses	1.7	905.35
Housing while attending school	0.8	1,891.05
Lodging on trips	14.5	592.68
TELEPHONE	**93.2**	**297.57**
Residential phone service and pay phones	75.3	160.15
Cellular phone service	58.5	259.87
Telephone answering devices	0.3	52.68
Phone cards	6.0	62.10
TOBACCO PRODUCTS AND SMOKING SUPPLIES	**22.2**	**362.42**
Cigarettes	19.7	373.73
Other tobacco products	3.4	198.29
TRANSPORTATION	**94.4**	**2,253.32**
Vehicle purchases	**5.5**	**14,692.03**
Cars and trucks, new	1.6	24,713.84
New cars	0.8	21,196.43
New trucks	0.8	28,276.32
Cars and trucks, used	3.8	10,445.80
Used cars	2.2	9,596.62
Used trucks	1.6	11,308.39
Other vehicles	0.3	9,403.57
New motorcycles	0.1	12,269.23
Used motorcycles	0.2	6,921.67
Gasoline and motor oil	**90.2**	**660.52**
Gasoline	89.5	614.83
Diesel fuel	2.0	520.96
Gasoline on trips	20.0	162.71
Motor oil	8.0	28.75
Other vehicle expenses	**80.7**	**726.67**
Vehicle finance charges	32.2	237.26
Automobile finance charges	16.3	186.70
Truck finance charges	18.2	224.68
Motorcycle and plane finance charges	1.1	144.72
Other vehicle finance charges	1.2	277.22

	percent reporting expenditure during quarter	average amount spent by purchasers per quarter
Maintenance and repairs	52.6%	$321.92
Coolant, additives, brake, transmission fluids	5.3	16.63
Tires	7.7	374.35
Vehicle products and cleaning services	3.8	41.03
Parts, equipment, and accessories	8.6	127.63
Vechicle audio equipment	0.2	255.21
Vehicle video equipment	0.2	326.32
Body work and painting	1.2	604.09
Clutch, transmission repair	1.3	656.35
Drive shaft and rear-end repair	0.4	447.92
Brake work	4.7	312.85
Repair to steering or front-end	1.2	462.30
Repair to engine cooling system	1.8	300.54
Motor tune-up	4.5	253.74
Lube, oil change, and oil filters	34.1	50.91
Front-end alignment, wheel balance, rotation	2.7	137.50
Shock absorber replacement	0.4	346.05
Repair tires and other repair work	5.6	222.92
Exhaust system repair	0.9	296.51
Electrical system repair	2.1	321.14
Motor repair, replacement	2.8	658.42
Auto repair service policy	0.5	823.47
Vehicle accessories, including labor	0.5	314.58
Vehicle air conditioning repair	1.0	355.10
Vehicle insurance	50.2	437.13
Vehicle rental, leases, licenses, other charges	43.1	280.59
Leased and rented vehicles	7.0	1,019.35
Rented vehicles	3.1	322.57
Auto rental	0.6	325.39
Auto rental, on trips	2.0	309.70
Truck rental	0.3	266.67
Truck rental, on trips	0.2	401.25
Leased vehicles	4.2	1,466.21
Car lease payments	2.3	1,256.90
Truck lease payments	2.1	1,301.29
Vehicle registration, state	16.3	131.86
Vehicle registration, local	1.9	115.18
Driver's license	5.0	37.45
Vehicle inspection	6.2	43.43
Parking fees	11.9	73.70
Parking fees in home city, excluding residence	9.6	75.65
Parking fees, on trips	3.3	46.15
Tolls or electronic toll passes	9.1	57.84
Tolls on trips	6.5	16.78
Towing charges	1.1	138.19
Global positioning services	0.5	116.67
Automobile service clubs	4.9	86.96
Public transportation	**18.5**	**721.18**
Airline fares	10.3	874.78
Intercity bus fares	4.0	65.24
Intracity mass transit fares	6.9	200.80
Local transportation on trips	5.0	67.00
Taxi fares and limousine service on trips	5.0	39.31
Taxi fares and limousine service	3.2	100.31

	percent reporting expenditure during quarter	average amount spent by purchasers per quarter
Intercity train fares	3.9%	$133.70
Ship fares	2.1	646.00
School bus	0.1	315.63
TRAVEL		
Admission to sports events, on trips	8.4	42.37
Airline fares	10.3	874.78
Alcoholic beverages purchased on trips	11.6	94.25
Auto rental on trips	2.0	309.70
Bus fares, intercity	4.0	65.24
Gasoline on trips	20.0	162.71
Groceries purchased on trips	10.0	107.50
Local transportation on trips	5.0	67.00
Lodging on trips	14.5	592.68
Luggage	1.4	111.33
Movie, other admissions on trips	8.4	127.14
Parking fees on trips	3.3	46.15
Participant sports on trips	3.6	220.72
Recreation expenses on trips	7.9	87.81
Restaurant food on trips	23.5	261.09
Ship fares	2.1	646.00
Taxi fares and limousine service	3.2	100.31
Tolls on trips	6.5	16.78
Train fares, intercity	3.9	133.70
Truck rental on trips	0.2	401.25
UTILITIES	**97.6**	**890.31**
Natural gas	49.0	244.90
Electricity	91.9	354.38
Fuel oil and other fuels	8.4	446.68
Fuel oil	3.4	656.10
Coal, Wood and other fuels	0.7	271.97
Bottled gas	4.8	287.16
Water and other public services	62.4	173.66
Water and sewerage maintenance	56.1	141.45
Trash and garbage collection	37.6	75.31
Septic tank cleaning	0.3	240.63

Note: The categories shown here may be different from those analyzed in the book because these are from only the interview portion of the Consumer Expenditure Survey. Some categories shown here are not analyzed in the book because the sample size was too small to make reliable estimates.
Source: Calculations by New Strategist based on the 2007 Consumer Expenditure Survey

Appendix C: Spending by Product and Service, Ranked by Amount Spent, 2007

(average annual spending of consumer units on products and services, ranked by amount spent, 2007)

1.	Deductions for Social Security	$3,907.94
2.	Mortgage interest (or rent, $2,491.52)	3,583.53
3.	Groceries (also shown by individual category)	3,465.01
4.	Vehicle purchases (net outlay)	3,244.00
5.	Restaurants (also shown by meal category)	2,467.37
6.	Gasoline and motor oil	2,383.67
7.	Property taxes	1,708.86
8.	Federal income taxes	1,569.13
9.	Health insurance	1,544.83
10.	Electricity	1,302.85
11.	Dinner at restaurants	1,073.51
12.	Vehicle insurance	1,071.37
13.	Lunch at restaurants	761.38
14.	Women's apparel	748.93
15.	Vehicle maintenance and repairs	737.62
16.	Cash contributions to church, religious organizations	684.76
17.	Cellular phone service	607.58
18.	College tuition	585.20
19.	Maintenance and repair services, owner	574.87
20.	Deductions for private pensions	558.59
21.	Cable and satellite television services	555.13
22.	Nonpayroll deposit to retirement plans	482.66
23.	Residential telephone service and pay phones	482.12
24.	Natural gas	480.39
25.	State and local income taxes	468.06
26.	Cash gifts to members of other households	409.71
27.	Airline fares	359.71
28.	Prescription drugs	359.32
29.	Men's apparel	351.05
30.	Lodging on trips	342.57
31.	Homeowner's insurance	340.31
32.	Water and sewerage maintenance	317.25
33.	Life and other personal insurance	309.47
34.	Interest paid, home equity loan/line of credit	306.49
35.	Vehicle finance charges	305.21
36.	Cigarettes	294.95
37.	Owned vacation homes	286.81
38.	Personal care services	282.91
39.	Cash contributions to charities	275.94
40.	Day care centers, nurseries, and preschools	267.66
41.	Restaurant meals on trips	245.53
42.	Leased vehicles	245.15
43.	Dental services	244.67
44.	Beef	216.25
45.	Breakfast at restaurants	215.13
46.	Fresh fruits	201.74
47.	Child support expenditures	198.01

48.	Other taxes	$196.28
49.	Computer information services	194.11
50.	Fresh vegetables	190.29
51.	Snacks at restaurants	171.82
52.	Physician's services	171.10
53.	Finance charges, except mortgage and vehicles	167.63
54.	Television sets	162.24
55.	Women's footwear	160.33
56.	Movie, theater, amusement park, and other admissions	159.35
57.	Legal fees	156.59
58.	Household decorative items	154.92
59.	Elementary and high school tuition	153.18
60.	Cosmetics, perfume, and bath products	152.03
61.	Pork	149.64
62.	Computers and computer hardware for nonbusiness use	148.08
63.	Prepared foods except frozen, salads, and desserts	148.07
64.	Motorized recreational vehicles	147.76
65.	Pet food	146.88
66.	Poultry	141.85
67.	Laundry and cleaning supplies	139.99
68.	Pet purchase, supplies, and medicines	139.06
69.	Fresh milk, all types	138.15
70.	Miscellaneous household products	132.92
71.	Carbonated drinks	131.75
72.	Expenses for other properties	126.00
73.	Jewelry	125.79
74.	Social, recreation, civic club membership	123.48
75.	Fish and seafood	121.93
76.	Girls' (aged 2 to 15) apparel	121.62
77.	Toys, games, hobbies, and tricycles	119.93
78.	Housekeeping services	118.26
79.	Cheese	117.15
80.	Fees for participant sports	116.94
81.	Lawn and garden supplies	115.03
82.	Beer and ale at home	114.93
83.	Lawn and garden equipment	114.63
84.	Hospital room and services	113.93
85.	Trash and garbage collection	113.33
86.	Veterinarian services	113.18
87.	Sofas	112.62
88.	Gardening, lawn care service	106.94
89.	Fees for recreational lessons	105.56
90.	Meats other than pork or beef	104.49
91.	Men's footwear	102.60
92.	Support for college students	99.06
93.	Cleansing and toilet tissue, paper towels, and napkins	98.65
94.	Wine at home	97.21
95.	Potato chips and other snacks	95.81
96.	Vehicle registration	94.51
97.	Children's (under age 2) apparel	93.36
98.	Maintenance and repair materials, owner	90.20
99.	Fuel oil	88.18
100.	Babysitting and child care	85.91
101.	Ready-to-eat and cooked cereals	84.57
102.	Boys' (aged 2 to 15) apparel	84.32
103.	Candy and chewing gum	80.35

104.	Accounting fees	$77.08
105.	Bedroom furniture except mattresses and springs	76.91
106.	Lunch meats (cold cuts)	76.14
107.	Nonprescription drugs	75.40
108.	Beer and ale at bars, restaurants	75.29
109.	Stationery, stationery supplies, giftwrap	75.19
110.	Deductions for government retirement	74.57
111.	Postage	74.12
112.	Catered affairs	74.07
113.	Lottery and gambling losses	72.53
114.	Service by professionals other than physician	72.44
115.	Unmotored recreational vehicles	72.01
116.	Frozen meals	71.36
117.	School lunches	71.09
118.	Rent as pay	69.63
119.	Bedroom linens	67.07
120.	Athletic gear, game tables, exercise equipment	65.55
121.	Frozen prepared foods, except meals	65.38
122.	Admission to sports events	65.02
123.	Video game hardware and software	63.10
124.	Gifts of stocks, bonds, and mutual funds to members of other households	62.25
125.	Books and supplies for college	61.94
126.	Ground rent	61.77
127.	Professional laundry, dry cleaning	61.30
128.	Housing while attending school	61.27
129.	Refrigerators and freezers	61.24
130.	Other alcoholic beverages at bars, restaurants	61.07
131.	Eyeglasses and contact lenses	61.01
132.	Bottled water	60.72
133.	Funeral expenses	58.28
134.	Care for elderly, invalids, handicapped, etc.	57.52
135.	Ice cream and related products	57.37
136.	Wall units, cabinets, and other furniture	56.79
137.	Indoor plants and fresh flowers	56.78
138.	Canned and bottled fruit juice	56.46
139.	Hair care products	56.10
140.	Books	55.93
141.	Mattresses and springs	55.53
142.	Bread, other than white	55.32
143.	Bottled gas	55.25
144.	Intracity mass transit fares	55.10
145.	Ship fares	53.23
146.	Cash contributions to educational institutions	51.10
147.	Coffee	51.07
148.	Moving, storage, and freight express	50.22
149.	Occupational expenses	48.95
150.	Newspaper and magazine subscriptions	47.29
151.	Kitchen and dining room furniture	47.05
152.	Sauces and gravies	46.54
153.	Nonprescription vitamins	46.18
154.	Living room chairs	45.85
155.	Property management, owner	45.22
156.	Cookies	44.89
157.	Biscuits and rolls	44.32
158.	Alcoholic beverages purchased on trips	43.62
159.	Food prepared by consumer unit on trips	43.00

160.	Eggs	$42.71
161.	Baby food	42.34
162.	Miscellaneous personal services	41.61
163.	Coin-operated apparel laundry and dry cleaning	40.75
164.	Cakes and cupcakes	40.26
165.	Canned and packaged soups	40.05
166.	Rented vehicles	39.87
167.	Outdoor equipment	39.82
168.	Lab tests, X-rays	39.08
169.	Video cassettes, tapes, and discs	38.32
170.	Cooking stoves, ovens	38.00
171.	Eye care services	37.88
172.	Canned vegetables	37.68
173.	Washing machines	37.55
174.	Wine at bars, restaurants	36.91
175.	Lamps and lighting fixtures	36.69
176.	Nonalcoholic beverages (except carbonated, coffee, fruit-flavored drinks, tea, bottled water) and ice	36.47
177.	Parking fees	35.17
178.	Girls' footwear	34.18
179.	White bread	33.86
180.	Prepared salads	32.63
181.	Photographic equipment	32.24
182.	Meals as pay	32.18
183.	Nuts	32.12
184.	Window coverings	32.03
185.	Topicals and dressings	31.81
186.	Crackers	31.70
187.	Pet services	31.68
188.	Frozen vegetables	31.34
189.	Rental of video cassettes, tapes, discs, films	30.87
190.	Fats and oils	30.63
191.	Telephones and accessories	30.38
192.	Alimony expenditures	30.19
193.	Deodorants, feminine hygiene, miscellaneous products	30.00
194.	Boys' footwear	29.95
195.	Hunting and fishing equipment	29.66
196.	Clothes dryers	29.60
197.	Tea	28.63
198.	Recreation expenses on trips	27.89
199.	Oral hygiene products	27.64
200.	Compact discs, records, and audio tapes	27.39
201.	Salad dressings	27.15
202.	Wall-to-wall carpeting	26.87
203.	Tobacco products other than cigarettes	26.73
204.	Frozen and refrigerated bakery products	26.27
205.	Outdoor furniture	26.06
206.	Tableware, nonelectric kitchenware	25.66
207.	Photographer fees	25.13
208.	Bathroom linens	24.80
209.	Pasta, cornmeal, and other cereal products	24.77
210.	Baking needs	24.60
211.	Power tools	24.41
212.	Salt, spices, and other seasonings	24.07
213.	Noncarbonated fruit-flavored drinks	23.96
214.	Board (including at school)	23.69

215.	Jams, preserves, other sweets	$21.81
216.	Local transportation on trips	21.39
217.	Computer software and accessories for nonbusiness use	21.28
218.	Sweetrolls, coffee cakes, doughnuts	21.18
219.	Floor coverings, nonpermanent	20.96
220.	Dishwashers (built-in), garbage disposals, range hoods	20.88
221.	Checking accounts, other bank service charges	20.77
222.	Intercity train fares	20.75
223.	Watches	20.55
224.	Closet and storage items	20.32
225.	School tuition other than college, vocational/technical, elementary, high school	20.13
226.	Butter	20.11
227.	Tolls	19.90
228.	Home security system service fee	19.89
229.	Canned fruits	19.47
230.	Small electric kitchen appliances	19.17
231.	Curtains and draperies	18.98
232.	Other alcoholic beverages at home	18.92
233.	Frankfurters	18.73
234.	Laundry and cleaning equipment	18.62
235.	Maintenance and repair services, renter	17.55
236.	Personal digital audio players	17.39
237.	Fresh fruit juice	17.21
238.	Automobile service clubs	16.94
239.	Hand tools	16.77
240.	Electric floor-cleaning equipment	16.74
241.	Bicycles	16.72
242.	Rice	16.60
243.	Sugar	16.49
244.	Books and supplies for elementary and high school	16.16
245.	Taxi fares and limousine service	16.12
246.	Photo processing	15.98
247.	Termite and pest control services	15.94
248.	Appliance repair, including at service center	15.93
249.	Living room tables	15.78
250.	Care in convalescent or nursing home	15.62
251.	Vegetable juices	15.56
252.	Cream	15.53
253.	Vocational and technical school tuition	15.42
254.	Cemetery lots, vaults, and maintenance fees	15.39
255.	Hearing aids	15.19
256.	Musical instruments and accessories	14.99
257.	Pies, tarts, turnovers	14.96
258.	Shaving products	14.94
259.	Phone cards	14.88
260.	VCRs and video disc players	14.83
261.	Nonelectric cookware	14.47
262.	Newspapers and magazines, nonsubscription	14.46
263.	Infants' equipment	14.07
264.	Glassware	13.80
265.	Sound equipment accessories	13.79
266.	Nondairy cream and imitation milk	13.56
267.	Sound components and component systems	13.21
268.	Global positioning system devices	13.07
269.	Peanut butter	12.87
270.	Maintenance and repair materials, renter	12.86

271.	Olives, pickles, relishes	$12.80
272.	Electric personal care appliances	12.64
273.	Prepared desserts	12.30
274.	Luggage	12.06
275.	Satellite radio service	12.01
276.	Prepared flour mixes	11.60
277.	Portable heating and cooling equipment	11.46
278.	Camping equipment	11.39
279.	Sewing materials for household items	11.21
280.	Dried vegetables	10.94
281.	Office furniture for home use	10.70
282.	Vehicle inspection	10.70
283.	Intercity bus fares	10.49
284.	Cash contributions to political organizations	10.47
285.	Tenant's insurance	10.30
286.	Microwave ovens	9.66
287.	Lamb, organ meats, and others	9.62
288.	Parking at owned home	9.50
289.	Security services, owner	9.42
290.	Rental of party supplies for catered affairs	9.36
291.	Hair accessories	9.33
292.	Live entertainment for catered affairs	9.18
293.	Infants' furniture	9.09
294.	Whiskey at home	8.64
295.	China and other dinnerware	8.56
296.	Vacation clubs	8.16
297.	Dried fruits	8.08
298.	Rental of recreational vehicles	8.00
299.	Driver's license	7.52
300.	Coal, wood, and other fuels	7.18
301.	Shopping club membership fees	7.09
302.	Margarine	7.04
303.	Repair of computer systems for nonbusiness use	6.99
304.	Sewing patterns and notions	6.77
305.	Repairs and rentals of lawn and garden equipment, hand and power tools, etc.	6.69
306.	Material for making clothes	6.65
307.	Kitchen and dining room linens	6.63
308.	Sewing machines	6.25
309.	Apparel alteration, repair, and tailoring services	6.24
310.	Frozen fruit juices	6.12
311.	Towing charges	5.97
312.	Artificial sweeteners	5.83
313.	Playground equipment	5.38
314.	Flour	5.14
315.	Voice over IP	5.12
316.	Window air conditioners	5.06
317.	Frozen fruits	4.97
318.	Reupholstering and furniture repair	4.80
319.	Film	4.69
320.	Water-softening service	4.49
321.	Water sports equipment	4.49
322.	Medical equipment for general use	4.45
323.	Docking and landing fees	4.42
324.	Repair of TV, radio, and sound equipment	4.26
325.	Bread and cracker products	4.10
326.	Flatware	4.06

327.	Winter sports equipment	$4.06
328.	Stamp and coin collecting	4.02
329.	Rental of furniture	3.99
330.	Personal digital assistants	3.68
331.	Streamed and downloaded audio	3.68
332.	Watch and jewelry repair	3.65
333.	Safe deposit box rental	3.42
334.	Slipcovers and decorative pillows	3.39
335.	Tape recorders and players	3.38
336.	Nonclothing laundry and dry cleaning, coin-operated	3.26
337.	Supportive and convalescent medical equipment	3.18
338.	Septic tank cleaning	3.08
339.	Deductions for railroad retirement	2.93
340.	Delivery services	2.88
341.	Radios	2.74
342.	Termite and pest control products	2.55
343.	Miscellaneous sound equipment	2.54
344.	Plastic dinnerware	2.48
345.	Fireworks	2.44
346.	Internet services away from home	2.43
347.	Rental and repair of miscellaneous sports equipment	2.43
348.	Business equipment for home use	2.26
349.	Global positioning services	2.24
350.	Clothing rental	2.15
351.	Wigs and hairpieces	2.10
352.	Smoke alarms	2.09
353.	Credit card memberships	1.66
354.	Online gaming services	1.55
355.	Shoe repair and other shoe services	1.43
356.	Rental of medical equipment	1.43
357.	Other serving pieces	1.42
358.	Appliance rental	1.33
359.	Rental and repair of musical instruments	1.29
360.	Smoking accessories	1.21
361.	Nonclothing laundry and dry cleaning, sent out	1.05
362.	Pinball, electronic video games	1.04
363.	Streamed and downloaded video	1.03
364.	School bus	1.01
365.	Satellite dishes	0.98
366.	Installation of television sets	0.98
367.	Rental of television sets	0.72
368.	Clothing storage	0.70
369.	Rental of supportive and convalescent medical equipment	0.68
370.	Repair and rental of photographic equipment	0.63
371.	Telephone answering devices	0.59
372.	Portable dishwashers	0.57
373.	Books and supplies for vocational and technical schools	0.56
374.	Rental of office equipment for nonbusiness use	0.44
375.	Installation of computer	0.41
376.	Books and supplies for day care and nursery	0.41
377.	Dating services	0.40
378.	Rental of VCR, radio, and sound equipment	0.31
379.	Rental of computer and video game hardware and software	0.05

Source: Calculations by New Strategist based on the 2007 Consumer Expenditure Survey

Appendix D: Average Annual Household Spending, 2000 and 2007

(average annual spending of consumer units, 2000 and 2007; percent change, 2000–07; in 2007 dollars)

	2007	2000	percent change 2000–07
Number of consumer units (in 000s)	120,171	109,367	9.9%
Average before-tax income of consumer units	$63,091	$53,761	17.4
Average annual spending of consumer units	49,638	45,809	8.4
FOOD	6,133	6,211	–1.2
Food at home	3,465	3,638	–4.7
Cereals and bakery products	460	545	–15.7
Cereals and cereal products	143	188	–23.9
Bakery products	317	358	–11.4
Meats, poultry, fish, and eggs	777	957	–18.8
Beef	216	287	–24.6
Pork	150	201	–25.4
Other meats	104	122	–14.5
Poultry	142	175	–18.7
Fish and seafood	122	132	–7.9
Eggs	43	41	5.0
Dairy products	387	391	–1.1
Fresh milk and cream	154	158	–2.4
Other dairy products	234	232	0.7
Fruits and vegetables	600	627	–4.4
Fresh fruits	202	196	2.9
Fresh vegetables	190	191	–0.8
Processed fruits	112	138	–19.1
Processed vegetables	96	101	–5.1
Other food at home	1,241	1,116	11.2
Sugar and other sweets	124	141	–12.0
Fats and oils	91	100	–8.9
Miscellaneous foods	650	526	23.5
Nonalcoholic beverages	333	301	10.6
Food prepared by household on trips	43	48	–10.7
Food away from home	2,668	2,573	3.7
ALCOHOLIC BEVERAGES	457	448	2.0
HOUSING	16,920	14,833	14.1
Shelter	10,023	8,566	17.0
Owned dwellings	6,730	5,541	21.5
Mortgage interest and charges	3,890	3,178	22.4
Property taxes	1,709	1,371	24.6
Maintenance, repairs, insurance, other expenses	1,131	993	13.9
Rented dwellings	2,602	2,449	6.2
Other lodging	691	576	20.1
Utilities, fuels, and public services	3,477	2,997	16.0
Natural gas	480	370	29.9
Electricity	1,303	1,097	18.8

	2007	2000	percent change 2000–07
Fuel oil and other fuels	$151	$117	29.3%
Telephone services	1,110	1,056	5.1
Water and other public services	434	356	21.8
Household services	**984**	**824**	**19.5**
Personal services	415	393	5.7
Other household services	569	431	32.0
Housekeepingn supplies	**639**	**580**	**10.1**
Laundry and cleaning supplies	140	158	–11.2
Other household products	347	272	27.5
Postage and stationery	152	152	0.2
Household furnishings and equipment	**1,797**	**1,865**	**–3.7**
Household textiles	133	128	4.2
Furniture	446	471	–5.3
Floor coverings	46	53	–13.2
Major appliances	231	228	1.5
Small appliances, miscellaneous housewares	101	105	–3.6
Miscellaneous household equipment	840	880	–4.6
APPAREL AND SERVICES	**1,881**	**2,235**	**–15.8**
Men and boys	**435**	**530**	**–17.9**
Men, aged 16 or older	351	414	–15.3
Boys, aged 2 to 15	84	116	–27.3
Women and girls	**749**	**873**	**–14.2**
Women, aged 16 or older	627	731	–14.2
Girls, aged 2 to 15	122	142	–14.1
Children under age 2	**93**	**99**	**–5.8**
Footwear	**327**	**413**	**–20.8**
Other apparel products and services	**276**	**320**	**–13.8**
TRANSPORTATION	**8,758**	**8,931**	**–1.9**
Vehicle purchases	**3,244**	**4,116**	**–21.2**
Cars and trucks, new	1,572	1,933	–18.7
Cars and trucks, used	1,567	2,131	–26.5
Other vehicles	105	52	102.8
Gasoline and motor oil	**2,384**	**1,554**	**53.4**
Other vehicle expenses	**2,592**	**2,746**	**–5.6**
Vehicle finance charges	305	395	–22.8
Maintenance and repairs	738	751	–1.8
Vehicle insurance	1,071	937	14.3
Vehicle rental, leases, licenses, other charges	478	663	–28.0
Public transportation	**538**	**514**	**4.6**
HEALTH CARE	**2,853**	**2,488**	**14.7**
Health insurance	1,545	1,184	30.5
Medical services	709	684	3.7
Drugs	481	501	–4.0
Medical supplies	118	119	–1.0
ENTERTAINMENT	**2,698**	**2,243**	**20.3**
Fees and admissions	658	620	6.1
Audio and visual equipment and services	987	749	31.8
Pets, toys, hobbies, and playground equipment	560	402	39.2
Other entertainment supplies, services	493	473	4.2
PERSONAL CARE PRODUCTS, SERVICES	**588**	**679**	**–13.4**
READING	**118**	**176**	**–32.9**

	2007	2000	percent change 2000–07
EDUCATION	$945	$761	24.2%
TOBACCO PRODUCTS, SMOKING SUPPLIES	323	384	–15.9
MISCELLANEOUS	808	934	–13.5
CASH CONTRIBUTIONS	1,821	1,435	26.9
PERSONAL INSURANCE AND PENSIONS	5,336	4,052	31.7
Life and other personal insurance	309	480	–35.7
Pensions and Social Security	5,027	3,571	*
PERSONAL TAXES	2,233	3,753	–40.5
Federal income taxes	1,569	2,901	–45.9
State and local income taxes	468	677	–30.8
Other taxes	196	176	11.5
GIFTS FOR PEOPLE IN OTHER HOUSEHOLDS	1,198	1,304	–8.1

Spending in 2007 on Social Security and pensions is not comparable with 2000 because of changes in methodology.

Note: Average spending is rounded to the nearest dollar, but the percent change calculation is based on un-rounded figures. Spending by category does not add to total spending because gift spending is also included in the preceding product and service categories and personal taxes are not included in the total. Source: Bureau of Labor Statistics, 2000 and 2007 Consumer Expenditure Surveys, Internet site http://www .bls.gov/cex/; calculations by New Strategist

Glossary

age The age of the reference person.

alcoholic beverages Includes beer and ale, wine, whiskey, gin, vodka, rum, and other alcoholic beverages.

annual spending The annual amount spent per household. The Bureau of Labor Statistics calculates the annual average for all households in a segment, not just for those that purchased an item. The averages are calculated by integrating the results of the diary (weekly) and interview (quarterly) portions of the Consumer Expenditure Survey. For items purchased by most households—such as bread—average annual spending figures are a fairly accurate account of actual spending. For products and services purchased by few households during a year's time—such as cars—the average annual amount spent is much less than what purchasers spend.

apparel, accessories, and related services Includes the following:

• *men's and boys' apparel* Includes coats, jackets, sweaters, vests, sport coats, tailored jackets, slacks, shorts and short sets, sportswear, shirts, underwear, nightwear, hosiery, uniforms, and other accessories.

• *women's and girls' apparel* Includes coats, jackets, furs, sport coats, tailored jackets, sweaters, vests, blouses, shirts, dresses, dungarees, culottes, slacks, shorts, sportswear, underwear, nightwear, uniforms, hosiery, and other accessories.

• *infants' apparel* Includes coats, jackets, snowsuits, underwear, diapers, dresses, crawlers, sleeping garments, hosiery, footwear, and other accessories for children.

• *footwear* Includes articles such as shoes, slippers, boots, and other similar items. It excludes footwear for babies and footwear used for sports such as bowling or golf shoes.

• *other apparel products and services* Includes material for making clothes, shoe repair, alterations and sewing patterns and notions, clothing rental, clothing storage, dry cleaning, sent-out laundry, watches, jewelry, and repairs to watches and jewelry.

baby boom Americans born between 1946 and 1964.

cash contributions Includes cash contributed to persons or organizations outside the consumer unit including court-ordered alimony, child support payments, and support for college students, and contributions to religious, educational, charitable, or political organizations.

consumer unit (1) All members of a household who are related by blood, marriage, adoption, or other legal arrangements; (2) a person living alone or sharing a household with others or living as a roomer in a private home or lodging house or in permanent living quarters in a hotel or motel, but who is financially independent; or (3) two or more persons living together who pool their income to make joint expenditure decisions. Financial independence is determined by the three major expense categories: housing, food, and other living expenses. To be considered financially independent, at least two of the three major expense categories have to be provided by the respondent. For convenience, called household in the text of this report.

consumer unit, composition of The classification of interview households by type according to (1) relationship of other household members to the reference person; (2) age of the children of the reference person; and (3) combination of relationship to the reference person and age of the children. Stepchildren and adopted children are included with the reference person's own children.

earner A consumer unit member aged 14 or older who worked at least one week during the twelve months prior to the interview date.

education Includes tuition, fees, books, supplies, and equipment for public and private nursery schools, elementary and high schools, colleges and universities, and other schools.

entertainment Includes the following:

• *fees and admissions* Includes fees for participant sports; admissions to sporting events, movies, concerts, plays; health, swimming, tennis, and country club memberships, and other social recreational and fraternal organizations; recreational lessons or instructions; and recreational expenses on trips.

• *audio and visual equipment and services* Includes television sets; radios; cable TV; tape recorders and players; video cassettes, tapes, and discs; video cassette recorders and video disc players; video game hardware and software; personal digital audio players; streaming and downloading audio and video; sound components; CDs, records, and tapes; musical instruments; and rental and repair of TV and sound equipment.

• *pets, toys, hobbies, and playground equipment* Includes pet food, pet services, veterinary expenses, toys, games, hobbies, and playground equipment.

• *other entertainment equipment and services* Includes indoor exercise equipment, athletic shoes, bicycles, trailers, campers, camping equipment, rental of cameras and trailers, hunting and fishing equipment, sports equipment, winter sports equipment, water sports equipment, boats, boat motors and boat trailers, rental of boats, landing and docking fees, rental and repair of sports equipment, photographic equipment, film, photo processing, photographer fees, repair and rental of photo equipment, fireworks, pinball and electronic video games.

expenditure The transaction cost including excise and sales taxes of goods and services acquired during the survey period. The full cost of each purchase is recorded even though full payment may not have been made at the date of purchase. Expenditure estimates include gifts. Excluded from expenditures are purchases or portions of purchases directly assignable to business purposes and periodic credit or installment payments on goods and services already acquired.

federal income tax Includes federal income tax withheld in the survey year to pay for income earned in survey year plus additional tax paid in survey year to cover any underpayment or underwithholding of tax in the year prior to the survey.

financial products and services Includes accounting fees, legal fees, union dues, professional dues and fees, other occupational expenses, funerals, cemetery lots, dating services, shopping club memberships, and unclassified fees and personal services.

food Includes the following:

• *food at home* Refers to the total expenditures for food at grocery stores or other food stores during the interview period. It is calculated by multiplying the number of visits to a grocery or other food store by the average amount spent per visit. It excludes the purchase of nonfood items.

• *food away from home* Includes all meals (breakfast, lunch, brunch, and dinner) at restaurants, carry-outs, and vending machines, including tips, plus meals as pay, special catered affairs such as weddings, bar mitzvahs, and confirmations, and meals away from home on trips.

Generation X Americans born between 1965 and 1976, also known as the baby-bust generation.

gifts for people in other households Includes gift expenditures for people living in other consumer units. The amount spent on gifts is also included in individual product and service categories.

health care Includes the following:

• *health insurance* Includes health maintenance plans (HMOs), Blue Cross/Blue Shield, commercial health insurance, Medicare, Medicare supplemental insurance, long-term care insurance, and other health insurance.

• *medical services* Includes hospital room and services, physicians' services, services of a practitioner other than a

physician, eye and dental care, lab tests, X-rays, nursing, therapy services, care in convalescent or nursing home, and other medical care.

• *drugs* Includes prescription and nonprescription drugs, internal and respiratory over-the-counter drugs.

• *medical supplies* Includes eyeglasses and contact lenses, topicals and dressings, antiseptics, bandages, cotton, first aid kits, contraceptives; medical equipment for general use such as syringes, ice bags, thermometers, vaporizers, heating pads; supportive or convalescent medical equipment such as hearing aids, braces, canes, crutches, and walkers.

Hispanic origin The self-identified Hispanic origin of the consumer unit reference person. All consumer units are included in one of two Hispanic origin groups based on the reference person's Hispanic origin: Hispanic or non-Hispanic. Hispanics may be of any race.

household According to the Census Bureau, all the people who occupy a household. A group of unrelated people who share a housing unit as roommates or unmarried partners is also counted as a household. Households do not include group quarters such as college dormitories, prisons, or nursing homes. A household may contain more than one consumer unit. The terms "household" and "consumer unit" are used interchangeably in this report.

household furnishings and equipment Includes the following:

• *household textiles* Includes bathroom, kitchen, dining room, and other linens, curtains and drapes, slipcovers and decorative pillows, and sewing materials.

• *furniture* Includes living room, dining room, kitchen, bedroom, nursery, porch, lawn, and other outdoor furniture.

• *carpet, rugs, and other floor coverings* Includes installation and replacement of wall-to-wall carpets, room-size rugs, and other soft floor coverings.

• *major appliances* Includes refrigerators, freezers, dishwashers, stoves, ovens, garbage disposals, vacuum cleaners, microwave ovens, air-conditioners, sewing machines, washing machines, clothes dryers, and floor-cleaning equipment.

• *small appliances and miscellaneous housewares* Includes small electrical kitchen appliances, portable heating and cooling equipment, china and other dinnerware, flatware, glassware, silver and other serving pieces, nonelectric cookware, and plastic dinnerware. Excludes personal care appliances.

• *miscellaneous household equipment* Includes computer hardware and software, luggage, lamps and other lighting fixtures, window coverings, clocks, lawn mowers and gardening equipment, hand and power tools, telephone answering devices, personal digital assistants, Internet services away from home, office equipment for home use, fresh flowers and house plants, rental of furniture, closet and storage items, household decorative items, infants' equipment, outdoor equipment, smoke alarms, other household appliances, and small miscellaneous furnishing.

household services Includes the following:

• *personal services* Includes baby sitting, day care, and care of elderly and handicapped persons.

• *other household services* Includes computer information services; housekeeping services; gardening and lawn care services; coin-operated laundry and dry-cleaning of household textiles; termite and pest control products; moving, storage, and freight expenses; repair of household appliances and other household equipment; reupholstering and furniture repair; rental and repair of lawn and gardening tools; and rental of other household equipment.

housekeeping supplies Includes soaps, detergents, other laundry cleaning products, cleansing and toilet tissue, paper towels, napkins, and miscellaneous household products; lawn and garden supplies, postage, stationery, stationery supplies, and gift wrap.

housing tenure "Owner" includes households living in their own homes, cooperatives, condominiums, or townhouses. "Renter" includes households paying rent as well as families living rent free in lieu of wages.

income before taxes The total money earnings and selected money receipts accruing to a consumer unit during the 12 months prior to the interview date. Income includes the following components:

• *wages and salaries* Includes total money earnings for all members of the consumer unit aged 14 or older from all jobs, including civilian wages and salaries, Armed Forces pay and allowances, piece-rate payments, commissions, tips, National Guard or Reserve pay (received for training periods), and cash bonuses before deductions for taxes, pensions, union dues, etc.

• *self-employment income* Includes net business and farm income, which consists of net income (gross receipts minus operating expenses) from a profession or unincorporated business or from the operation of a farm by an owner, tenant, or sharecropper. If the business or farm is a partnership, only an appropriate share of net income is recorded. Losses are also recorded.

• *Social Security, private and government retirement* Includes payments by the federal government made under retirement, survivor, and disability insurance programs to retired persons, dependents of deceased insured workers, or to disabled workers; and private pensions or retirement benefits received by retired persons or their survivors, either directly or through an insurance company.

• *interest, dividends, rental income, and other property income* Includes interest income on savings or bonds; payments made by a corporation to its stockholders, periodic receipts from estates or trust funds; net income or loss from the rental of property, real estate, or farms, and net income or loss from roomers or boarders.

• *unemployment and workers' compensation and veterans' benefits* Includes income from unemployment compensation and workers' compensation, and veterans' payments including educational benefits, but excluding military retirement.

• *public assistance, supplemental security income, and food stamps* Includes public assistance or welfare, including money received from job training grants; supplemental security income paid by federal, state, and local welfare agencies to low-income persons who are aged 65 or older, blind, or disabled; and the value of food stamps obtained.

• *regular contributions for support* Includes alimony and child support as well as any regular contributions from persons outside the consumer unit.

• *other income* Includes money income from care of foster children, cash scholarships, fellowships, or stipends not based on working; and meals and rent as pay.

indexed spending Indexed spending figures compare the spending of particular demographic segments with that of the average household. To compute an index, the amount spent on an item by a demographic segment is divided by the amount spent on the item by the average household. That figure is then multiplied by 100. An index of 100 is the average for all households. An index of 132 means average spending by households in a segment is 32 percent above average (100 plus 32). An index of 75 means average spending by households in a segment is 25 percent below average (100 minus 25). Indexed spending figures identify the consumer units that spend the most on a product or service.

life and other personal insurance Includes premiums from whole life and term insurance; endowments; income and other life insurance; mortgage guarantee insurance; mortgage life insurance; premiums for personal life liability, accident and disability; and other non–health insurance other than homes and vehicles.

market share The market share is the percentage of total household spending on an item that is accounted for by a demographic segment. Market shares are calculated by dividing a demographic segment's total spending on an item by the total spending of all households on the item. Total spending on an item for all households is calculated by multiplying average spending by the total number of households. Total spending on an item for each demographic segment is calculated by multiplying the segment's average spending by the number of households in the segment. Market shares reveal the demographic segments that account for the largest share of spending on a product or service.

Millennial generation Americans born between 1977 and 1994.

occupation The occupation in which the reference person received the most earnings during the survey period. The occupational categories follow those of the Census of Population. Categories shown in the tables include the following:

• *self-employed* Includes all occupational categories; the reference person is self-employed in own business, professional practice, or farm.

• *wage and salary earners, managers and professionals* Includes executives, administrators, managers, and professional specialties such as architects, engineers, natural and social scientists, lawyers, teachers, writers, health diagnosis and treatment workers, entertainers, and athletes.

• *wage and salary earners, technical, sales, and clerical workers* Includes technicians and related support workers; sales representatives, sales workers, cashiers, and sales-related occupations; and administrative support, including clerical.

• *retired* People who did not work either full- or part-time during the survey period.

owner See housing tenure.

pensions and Social Security Includes all Social Security contributions paid by employees; employees' contributions to railroad retirement, government retirement and private pensions programs; retirement programs for self-employed.

personal care Includes products for the hair, oral hygiene products, shaving needs, cosmetics, bath products, suntan lotions, hand creams, electric personal care appliances, incontinence products, other personal care products, personal care services such as hair care services (haircuts, bleaching, tinting, coloring, conditioning treatments, permanents, press, and curls), styling and other services for wigs and hairpieces, body massages or slenderizing treatments, facials, manicures, pedicures, shaves, electrolysis.

quarterly spending Quarterly spending data are collected in the interview portion of the Consumer Expenditure Survey. The quarterly spending tables show the percentage of households that purchased an item during an average quarter, and the amount spent during the quarter on the item by purchasers. Not all items are included in the interview portion of the Consumer Expenditure Survey.

reading Includes subscriptions for newspapers, magazines, and books through book clubs; purchase of single-copy newspapers and magazines, books, and encyclopedias and other reference books.

reference person The first member mentioned by the respondent when asked to "Start with the name of the person or one of the persons who owns or rents the home." It is with respect to this person that the relationship of other consumer unit members is determined. Also called the householder or head of household.

region Consumer units are classified according to their address at the time of their participation in the survey. The four major census regions of the United States are the following state groupings:

• *Northeast* Connecticut, Maine, Massachusetts, New Hampshire, New Jersey, New York, Pennsylvania, Rhode Island, and Vermont.

• *Midwest* Illinois, Indiana, Iowa, Kansas, Michigan, Minnesota, Mississippi, Nebraska, North Dakota, Ohio, South Dakota, and Wisconsin.

• *South* Alabama, Arkansas, Delaware, District of Columbia, Florida, Georgia, Kentucky, Louisiana, Maryland, Mississippi, North Carolina, Oklahoma, South Carolina, Tennessee, Texas, Virginia, and West Virginia.

• *West* Alaska, Arizona, California, Colorado, Hawaii, Idaho, Minnesota, Nevada, New Mexico, Oregon, Utah, Washington, and Wyoming.

renter *See* Housing tenure.

shelter Includes the following:

• *owned dwellings* Includes interest on mortgages, property taxes and insurance, refinancing and prepayment charges, ground rent, expenses for property management and security, homeowner's insurance, fire insurance and extended coverage, landscaping expenses for repairs and maintenance contracted out (including periodic maintenance and service contracts), and expenses of materials for owner-performed repairs and maintenance for dwellings used or maintained by the consumer unit, but not dwellings maintained for business or rent.

• *rented dwellings* Includes rent paid for dwellings, rent received as pay, parking fees, maintenance, and other expenses.

• *other lodging* Includes all expenses for vacation homes, school, college, hotels, motels, cottages, trailer camps, and other lodging while out of town.

• *utilities, fuels, and public services* Includes natural gas, electricity, fuel oil, coal, bottled gas, wood, other fuels; residential telephone service, cell phone service, phone cards; water, garbage, trash collection; sewerage maintenance, septic tank cleaning; and other public services.

size of consumer unit The number of people whose usual place of residence at the time of the interview is in the consumer unit.

state and local income taxes Includes state and local income taxes withheld in the survey year to pay for income earned in survey year plus additional taxes paid in the survey year to cover any underpayment or underwithholding of taxes in the year prior to the survey.

tobacco and smoking supplies Includes cigarettes, cigars, snuff, loose smoking tobacco, chewing tobacco, and smoking accessories such as cigarette or cigar holders, pipes, flints, lighters, pipe cleaners, and other smoking products and accessories.

transportation Includes the following:

• *vehicle purchases (net outlay)* Includes the net outlay (purchase price minus trade-in value) on new and used domestic and imported cars and trucks and other vehicles, including motorcycles and private planes.

• *gasoline and motor oil* Includes gasoline, diesel fuel, and motor oil.

• *other vehicle expenses* Includes vehicle finance charges, maintenance and repairs, vehicle insurance, and vehicle rental licenses and other charges.

• *vehicle finance charges* Includes the dollar amount of interest paid for a loan contracted for the purchase of vehicles described above.

• *maintenance and repairs* Includes tires, batteries, tubes, lubrication, filters, coolant, additives, brake and transmission fluids, oil change, brake adjustment and repair, front-end alignment, wheel balancing, steering repair, shock absorber replacement, clutch and transmission repair, electrical system repair, repair to cooling system, drive train repair, drive shaft and rear-end repair, tire repair, vehicle video equipment, other maintenance and services, and auto repair policies.

• *vehicle insurance* Includes the premium paid for insuring cars, trucks, and other vehicles.

• *vehicle rental, licenses, and other charges* Includes leased and rented cars, trucks, motorcycles, and aircraft, inspection fees, state and local registration, drivers' license fees, parking fees, towing charges, tolls on trips, and global positioning services.

• *public transportation* Includes fares for mass transit, buses, trains, airlines, taxis, private school buses, and fares paid on trips for trains, boats, taxis, buses, and trains.

weekly spending Weekly spending data are collected in the diary portion of the Consumer Expenditure Survey. The data show the percentage of households that purchased an item during the average week, and the amount spent per week on the item by purchasers. Not all items are included in the diary portion of the Consumer Expenditure Survey.

Index